the
magazine
from cover to cover

cover to cover

second edition

Sammye Johnson
Trinity University

Patricia Prijatel
Drake University

the magazine
from cover to cover

to cover

New York   Oxford
Oxford University Press
2007

Oxford University Press, Inc., publishes works that further Oxford University's
objective of excellence in research, scholarship, and education.

Oxford   New York
Auckland   Cape Town   Dar es Salaam   Hong Kong   Karachi
Kuala Lumpur   Madrid   Melbourne   Mexico City   Nairobi
New Delhi   Shanghai   Taipei   Toronto

With offices in
Argentina   Austria   Brazil   Chile   Czech Republic   France   Greece
Guatemala   Hungary   Italy   Japan   Poland   Portugal   Singapore
South Korea   Switzerland   Thailand   Turkey   Ukraine   Vietnam

Published by Oxford University Press, Inc.
198 Madison Avenue, New York, New York 10016
http://www.oup.com

Oxford is a registered trademark of Oxford University Press

Library of Congress Cataloging-in-Publication Data

Johnson, Sammye, 1946–
   The magazine from cover to cover / by Sammye Johnson and Patricia Prijatel.—2nd ed.
      p. cm.
   Includes bibliographical references and index.
   ISBN-13: 978-0-19-530417-6 (alk. paper)
   ISBN-10: 0-19-530417-9 (alk. paper)
  1. Periodicals—Publishing—United States. 2. Journalism—United States. 3. American
periodicals. 4. Magazine design.   I. Prijatel, Patricia, 1945– II. Title.

PN4734.J64 2006
070.1′750973—dc22   2006045306

Printing number: 9 8 7 6 5 4 3 2 1

Printed in the United States of America
on acid-free paper

contents

xi   BOXES

xiii   FOREWORD BY WILLIAM T. KERR

xv   PREFACE

xviii   CREDITS

PART ONE
the enduring medium

2   chapter 1
the magazine as a storehouse: the scope of the medium

4   magazines and the media mix

   5   Depth and Timelessness

   5   Specialization of Content and Audience

  10   Opinion, Interpretation, and Advocacy

  13   Permanence

  13   Consistency

  14   Frequency

  14   Definition

14   the scope of the medium

  14   Magazine Types

  19   Number of Magazines

  22   Readership

23   emerging technology

  23   Interactive Media

  24   Online Business Practices

26   chapter 2
the magazine as a marketplace: the role of advertising

28   why advertisers choose magazines

  28   Credibility

  28   Reader Quality

  31   Product

  31   Brands

  31   Ancillary Products

  34   Advertising Rates

36   who advertises in magazines?

36 where they advertise

37 the birth of advertising in magazines

46 advertising-editorial conflicts
46   Clear Ad-Edit Distinction

47   Advertiser Prenotification
48   Complementary Editorial
49   Adjacencies
50   Entire Issue Sponsorship
50   Advertisers on the Cover

51 responsibility to the reader

54 chapter 3
the magazine as a historical document: trends over time

56 the beginning

59 literacy and education
59   18th Century: Educated Elite
64   19th Century: Rising Literacy
66   20th Century: Niche Audiences

67 content
68   18th Century: Assorted Articles
68   19th Century: Material Mania
72   20th Century: Subtle Specialization

76 appearance
77   18th Century: Deficient Design
78   19th Century: Engraved Embellishments

78   20th Century: Popular Photography

80 transportation and delivery
80   18th Century: Limited Restraints
81   19th Century: Postal Improvements
83   20th Century: Complex Costs

83 production and technology
84   18th Century: Intensive Hand Labors
84   19th Century: Mass Production Procedures
84   20th Century: Technological Techniques

88 chapter 4
the magazine as a social barometer: political and cultural interaction

90 the interaction of magazines and society

90 magazines as political influences
91   Agenda Setters

94   Advocacy

95 political influences on magazines
95   Independence
96   Abolition
96   The Cold War

97   **Civil Rights**

99   **Vietnam Era**

100   **Watergate**

100   **Feminism**

101   **September 11, 2001**

104   magazines as cultural influences

107   **Community Builders**

111   **Symbolic Meaning**

117   cultural influences on magazines

118   **Baby Boomers**

121   **Racial and Ethnic Shifts**

125   **Youth**

PART TWO

the magazine's blueprint

132   chapter 5

conceptualizing the magazine: formulas for success

5

134   magazine success and failure

135   editorial philosophy

136   **Title**

137   **Magazine Purpose**

138   **Type of Content**

143   **Voice**

143   editorial formula

144   **Advertising and Editorial Pages**

146   **Departments and Columns**

147   **Features**

148   **Placement of Content**

150   audience

153   anatomy of a failure

156   launches and life cycles

157   **Emergence of the Audience**

158   **Creation of the Magazine**

158   **Growth and Change**

159   **Refocus or Death**

161   living to a ripe old age

164   chapter 6

magazine business plans: determining the bottom line

6

166   the magazine budget

166   **Revenue**

168   **Expenses**

169   the business plan

170   the marketing plan

170   **Advertising Promotion**

170   **Circulation Promotion**

176   **Frequency**

177   **Advertising Rates**

179   **Circulation Rates**

182   **Subscriptions and Memberships**

183   **Distribution**

184 executive summary of
profitability

184   Income
186   Expenses

190   chapter 7
magazine structures: staff organization

192 who's running the show?

193   President and CEO
195   Publisher
195   Editor-in-Chief/Editor
200   Managing Editor
201   Executive Editor
201   Creative Director
201   Art Director
202   Senior Editor/Section Editor
204   Associate Editor/Assistant Editor
204   Copy Editor
204   Online Editor
204   Staff Writer
204   Photographer
205   Contributing Editor
205   Editorial Assistant/Fact Checker
205   Freelance Writer/Designer
205   Circulation Director

206   Marketing Director
207   Public Relations
       Director/Promotion Director
207   Ad Sales Director
207   Ad Sales Representative
207   Production Director
207   Assistant Publisher/Business
       Manager
207   Research Director

208 magazine ownership

208   Consumer and Trade Magazine
       Ownership
210   Organization Magazine
       Ownership

213 mergers and acquisitions

213   Corporate Conflicts of Interest
215   Publishers Owning Advertisers

215 the work environment

PART THREE
the magazine's content

222   chapter 8
molding the magazine's content: editorial style

224 article types

224   Service
232   Profile
237   Investigative Reporting

244   Essay
246   Fiction

249 the editor and the reader

252 chapter 9
creating the magazine's look: designs for readability

254 form follows function

256 the coming of age of magazine design
  256 Design Golden Age
  258 Design Turning Point
  261 Computers and Design
  261 "More Is Better"
  262 Relationship with the Reader

262 design elements
  263 Eye Movement
  263 The Grid

264 Typography
268 Color
269 Design Principles

271 integration of words and pictures
  271 Illustrative Images
  277 Readout Synergy
  280 Special Material

280 covers
  283 Logo
  284 Cover Types
  287 Redesigns

292 chapter 10
manufacturing the magazine: the production process

294 the production process

295 production planning
  295 Break-of-the-Book
  297 Paper Stock
  300 Special Coatings
  300 Color
  303 Art

304 the printing process
  304 Sheet-Fed
  304 Web
  304 Offset

305 Rotogravure
305 Binding
307 Signatures
308 Imposition
308 Image Transfers

312 digital manipulation

314 the quality product

316 chapter 11
magazine legalities: understanding the law

318 access to information
  318 Fair Access

319 Protecting Sources
320 Freedom of Information Act

321   **Sunshine Laws**

322   **Access to Information During Wartime**

322   prior restraints

323   **National Security**

323   **Administration of Justice**

325   **Unequal Taxation**

326   magazine distribution and sales

326   libel

327   **Publication**

327   **Identification**

330   **Defamation**

331   **Falsity**

331   **Fault**

335   **Libel Defenses**

336   invasions of privacy

336   **Embarrassing Private Facts**

338   **Intrusion**

338   **False Light**

339   **Appropriation**

339   intentional infliction of emotional distress

343   third-party liability

343   **Incitement**

343   **Negligence**

345   copyright

345   **Original Works**

346   **Tangible Medium**

348   **Ownership**

348   **Fair Use**

350   obscenity

354   chapter 12
moral frameworks: codes of ethics

356   hodges's essential questions

357   bok's model

358   codes of ethics

360   Appendix 12.1 American Society of Magazine Editors (ASME) Guidelines for Editors and Publishers, Thirteenth Edition

361   Appendix 12.2 American Business Media: Editorial Code of Ethics

365   Appendix 12.3 Society of Professional Journalists Code of Ethics

367   INDEX

Color plate sections follow pages 94 and 254.

boxes

5 Research in Brief: Magazine Uses and Gratifications

9 European Magazines React to September 11 Attacks

10 City Magazines: Catering to Instant Status and Ego Gratification

17 Why a Magazine? The Iowa Natural Heritage Foundation

20 The "I's" Have It: Interactive and Integrated

29 What Do People Read in the Bathroom?

32 Confidence in the *Good Housekeeping* Seal of Approval

35 CPM: The Little Number with the Big Job

38 Magazine Numbers: Who's Counting?

41 Research in Brief: Magazine-Made America

44 *Ms.* Magazine: It Just Feels Like Journalism

58 British Magazines Take Precedence by a Decade

62 Research in Brief: Portrayal of Women in 18th-Century Magazines

69 Roll Call of Famous Authors

71 Urban Humor in 19th-Century Magazines

74 Research in Brief: Magazines and Memory

92 Research in Brief: Agenda Setting

98 Reactions to Race and Rights

103 Magazine Deaths and Terrorist Acts in 2001

105 The Alternative Magazine: Building Community

110 The Reader and *Country Home*

112 Research in Brief: Mixed Messages on Women

114 Sex and the Single Magazine

139 *Mamm* and *Poz*: Helping Readers Survive

142 Ad-Free Magazines

145 The *Entrepreneurial* Spirit: Dissecting a Philosophy and Formula

149 *Harper's* Formula: A Tool of Success

151 Research in Brief: Teens Got *Sassy*, Advertisers Got Nervous

155 *Flair* Meets *Flaunt*: Twins Born 50 Years Apart?

169 Editorial Costs per Page

173 Research in Brief: *Reader's Digest* Keeps Riding the Culture Wave

175 Direct Appeals

178 Public Relations Techniques: Innovation Sells

180 Buying Versus Starting a Magazine: A Dollars and Cents View

181 Finding Fulfillment

187 Magazine Salaries: A Glimpse at the Field

195 Typical Magazine Job Titles

197 Long Live *The New Yorker*: An Editorial Genealogy

201 Out and About: Why Employees Quit

202 Research in Brief: Magazine Careers 1850–1926: Inhospitable Climate for Women

206 From Intern to Editor-in-Chief in Just 6 Years

209 Some Top Magazine Publishing Houses

211 A New Family of Jobs

213 Variations on a Title

216 Research in Brief: Women Wielding Power at the Top

226 Marriages Still Being Saved by *Ladies' Home Journal*

227 A Little Extra on the Side: Sidebars and Tip Boxes

228 How to Improve Editorial Content

231 Awards: A Measurement of How Well Magazines Serve Their Readers

234 The Two-page, 800-word *People* Profile

236 Longevity, Celebrity, and Topicality in Special Issues

238 Research in Brief: Hidden Biases in Editorial Content

241 Contest Categories as a Learning Tool

248 Research in Brief: Readers Don't Care About Bad Journalism

250 *National Geographic*'s Editorial Standards

255 You Say Title and I Say Headline

259 Research in Brief: If It's Ljubljana, It Must Be *Cosmopolitan*

265 Flipping Through Folios

272 Iconic Photos and 1,000 Words

274 Research in Brief: *Life*'s Photojournalism Essay Formula

279 The Pithy Promises of Pull-Quotes

282 Table of Contents: Location, Location, Location

288 Creation of Cultural Images Through Covers

295 Advertisers Know Their Place

297 Adding Pages: How Many Before It Pays Off?

301 Garbage In, Garbage Out

302 Too Hot to Print

304 The $450,000 Word Choice

305 Research in Brief: When Desktop Publishing Was New

307 Signatures and Color Placement

310 Request for Printing Estimate

311 Standard Deviations

312 The UPC Bar: Check It Out

321 Freedom of Information Act After September 11, 2001

324 Government Censorship and *The Masses*

327 Research in Brief: Fact-checking Is More Than a "Fetish of Facticity"

337 One Way to Prevent Libel Suits: Be Polite

340 Poisonous or Precious: Parodies Pay Off

346 The Name Game

foreword

When I wrote the foreword for the first edition of *The Magazine from Cover to Cover* in 1999, I predicted it would have strong appeal for graduate and undergraduate magazine students, as well as for professionals in the field. I am happy to say that my prediction proved accurate. Over 15,000 copies have been sold, both nationally and internationally. Students at Boston University, Temple, the University of Missouri, the University of Kansas, Kent State, Ball State, and the University of Oregon, among others, have benefited from its cogent style and in-depth research. I expect this second edition will find an even wider audience—because the magazine industry is stronger than ever, serving enthusiastic readers hungry for information about their favorite topics.

In fact, the readers of a magazine are the reason for its existence, and the magazines that succeed are those that continuously focus on reader needs and interests. Not only are successful magazines well written, creatively designed, and carefully managed, they are positioned well to compete in an ever-changing and often crowded marketplace.

But those who make a magazine must bring to it more than technical consistency and marketing savvy. They must, quite simply, imbue it with a heart. They must have a passion for their subject matter and the intellectual energy to share their knowledge with readers. If they succeed, a magazine has the ability—like no other medium does—to capture readers, to draw them in as friends and intimates. To do that, those who create the magazine must continually listen to its readers—consciously, attentively, and intuitively.

Every day, I observe magazine editors doing these very things, and it gives me a great deal of confidence in the future of magazines, the industry that produces them, and the contributions they make to our society. The industry continues to change at a rapid pace, and there are always new challenges and opportunities to be met. Here are a few we currently face:

- **The world as our market:** We have realized the needs of the burgeoning Hispanic population within our own country, and we are now producing magazines that meet those needs. While we still have growth potential at home, we are now casting an eye eastward. In China's urban areas, for instance, disposable income has increased fourfold in the last 2 years, and home ownership has doubled in the last 5 years. As is the case with most of Asia, the market potential is enormous.

■ **Building brands, not just selling advertising:** Beautiful ads in beautiful magazines are still the lifeblood of our business. But we must also continue to expand the marketing opportunities made possible by the content we produce. We must keep extending powerful magazine brands across many platforms, such as books, video, special interest publications, online, events, licensing, and promotions.

■ **The Internet as our friend:** Once viewed as a threat, the Internet is a medium that magazine companies are now using as a catalyst for growth. For editors, it allows a more frequent dialogue with readers. For marketers, it provides a source of revenue growth. For circulation professionals, it serves as a low-cost alternative for generating magazine subscriptions. And it is growing at a phenomenal rate.

■ **Profitable circulation:** Given that some in our industry have been remiss in reporting accurate circulation figures, the ability to offer advertisers a reliable and verifiable readership number is essential. In order for a magazine to remain viable, it must possess a profitable, direct-to-publisher rate base.

■ **Committing to integrity:** We must cherish the trust placed in us by readers and advertisers. With so many information and entertainment choices available, we as an industry must stress integrity in everything that we do. This is crucial not only in our home markets, but as we work within partnerships worldwide.

Readers still reach for magazines, even in this high-tech age. Magazines have a place in our future, a leadership role in the ever-expanding communications arena, a world to describe, and generations to educate and entertain. This book will help prepare magazine makers of the future for the challenging world of magazine publishing.

William T. Kerr
Chairman
Meredith Corporation

preface

The relationship Americans enjoy with their magazines is one of the most intimate, yet least understood, aspects of our culture. Since the mid-1700s, the magazine has played a role in shaping what individuals think and how they respond to the world around them. Magazines help us understand ourselves, live more fully, and vicariously enjoy different lifestyles. The result: We are what we read.

We believe this book reflects the spirit and spunk of the American magazine—and the industry that supports it. For three centuries, the magazine has endured as the medium for thoughtful analysis, perspective, context, information, and sheer fun. The magazine was an established national medium before the nation itself was established. In the midst of war, peace, or apathy, the magazine thrived. During depressed, recessed, and inflated economies, the magazine endured. It has adapted to change in mores, morals, and the marketplace. Unlike many national trends, the magazine is not only here today, but it will be here tomorrow.

The first edition of this book was published under two titles, *The Magazine from Cover to Cover* and *Magazine Publishing*. With our move to Oxford University Press, we have selected *The Magazine from Cover to Cover* as the one and only title for this second edition.

A comprehensive overview of the magazine industry, *The Magazine from Cover to Cover* guides readers through the dynamic magazine world from concept to finished product, including the historical context and trends that affect the industry. The book focuses on how magazines use information to build relationships with specific audiences to meet emotional, social, economic, and intellectual needs. It helps readers understand, analyze, and appreciate new dimensions of the magazine, as well as plan and implement managerial and publishing strategies. Emphasizing a pragmatic approach to the theories and principles of magazine publishing, *The Magazine from Cover to Cover* focuses on why we do what we do in the magazine field, rather than simply how to do it. It uses vignettes and case histories of selected magazines and interviews with publishers and editors to demonstrate in detail the extraordinary creativity and energy of the field.

As was the case with the first edition of our book, the industry continued to evolve from the time we wrote the first drafts to the final edit stage, sometimes at a maddening rate. Several of the editors we quoted in the text changed jobs; some of the magazines died. Nevertheless, we felt it important to include real people and real examples so this book not only reflects the vitality of the industry, but it also reads with the energy expected of magazine writing. It is a picture of a moment in time. Even though some of the names on the mastheads may now be different and the mastheads themselves no longer in existence, the message remains valuable and timely. We have, of course, updated the information up to the last possible minute, a tricky task in an industry that changes from second to second.

We used personal interviews when possible to get current and on-the-spot information. In those cases, we did not use endnotes. In other instances, we have used magazines, the Internet, national and local newspapers, industry seminars, and academic conferences as our sources; we have referenced these. Teachers and students alike can gain a great deal by searching through our original sources.

In this book, we define "magazine" to include consumer titles as well as the business press, organization and association publications, public relations magazines, and custom publishing. We've defined the Internet as a valuable resource for magazines, especially in terms of their connection with their audiences, but have not attempted to analyze and explain publications created entirely on the Internet; we consider those a separate medium, worthy of their own book. In all instances, we've tried to explain the unique nature of magazines.

guide to the second edition
. . . .

We maintained the overall organization used in the first edition, with a few changes. We integrated ethical examples and discussions throughout the text, rather than saving all those issues for chapter 12. Chapter 12 is now a short essay that provides a framework for codes of ethics and their interpretation and implementation.

In addition to updating all data, we spent more time walking the reader through issues that do not necessarily come easily to journalists, such as how to compute CPMs. We highlighted social and cul-tural trends that represented themselves in magazines, such as the growth of magazines for Hispanic, Black, and Asian readers as well as for children and teens; technical developments such as the expanding influence of the Internet and other evolving media; changes in production techniques related to digital information and delivery methods; and economic issues such as the influence of advertising income on a magazine's bottom line and the advertising-editorial conflicts this relationship spawns. We have eliminated the Magazine Voices section, but have turned Robin Morgan's and Jay Walljasper's essays into sidebars in chapter 2 and chapter 4, respectively.

Part 1, The Enduring Medium, provides an introduction to the field and gives a historical and social context. It includes chapters 1 through 4. Chapter 1, The Magazine as a Storehouse, defines the medium, explains magazine types, and offers a picture of the size and scope of the industry. Chapter 2, The Magazine as a Marketplace, describes the place of advertising and marketing with a historical as well as contemporary perspective. Chapter 3, The Magazine as a Historical Document, examines trends over time, tracing the development of the magazine through three centuries of American history. Chapter 4, The Magazine as a Social Barometer, asks whether magazines lead or follow social change and focuses on their political and cultural impact.

Part 2, The Magazine's Blueprint, takes a pragmatic approach to planning and organizing a magazine and its staff. It includes chapters 5 through 7. Chapter 5, Conceptualizing the Magazine, explores proven formulas for success as an answer to why some magazines fail and others thrive. Chapter 6, Magazine Business Plans, takes a hands-on approach to how magazines make and lose money; it offers an outline for determining a magazine's budget and bottom line. Chapter 7, Magazine Structures, introduces the business and creative staffs—the people who make the magazine work—and provides job descriptions and organizational charts.

Part 3, The Magazine's Content, explores editorial, design, production, legal, and ethical issues. It includes chapters 8 through 12. Chapter 8, Molding the Magazine's Content, analyzes the variety of magazine articles written today as a way of recognizing quality magazine editorial content. Chapter 9, Creating the Magazine's Look, looks at the package of words, graphics, and illustrations that entice and satisfy readers—turning the casual browser into the committed subscriber. Chapter 10, Manufacturing the Magazine, introduces methods of planning for and managing the manufacture of the printed product. Chapter 11, Magazine Legalities, makes sense of the legal ramifications of creative and business decisions. Chapter 12, Moral Frameworks, offers guidance in evaluating and resolving ethical conflicts.

acknowledgments

We want to thank all those who offered us information, guidance, and support: Karen Chiovaro, Linda Eggerss, Karla Jeffries, Rick Jost, Bill Krier, David Kurns, Sue Miller, Art Slusark, and Joanne William, Meredith Corporation; Marlene Kahan and Andrew Rhodes, American Society of Magazine Editors; Sandy Jimenez and Deborah Martin, Magazine Publishers of America; the editorial and research staffs of *Country Home*; Mary Kay Baumann and Will Hopkins, Hopkins/Baumann; and Louisa McCune, *Oklahoma Today*. Thanks to all the Drake University graduates who helped their former professor with insight into their jobs and the industry, including Michael Mettler, *Sound and Vision*; Elizabeth Muhler, *Walgreens* magazine; Nicholas Fonseca, *Entertainment Weekly*; Wendy Naugle, *Glamour;* Polly Flug, *Family Ties;* and Travis Daub, *Foreign Policy.*

A special long-distance thank you in memory of Michael Perkins, who penned the law chapter in our first edition, which was updated in this edition by Michael's former student, Jennifer Henderson of Trinity University. We offer a huge thanks to the reviewers throughout the United States who gave us advice and direction for both editions and to the magazine professors from around the world who encouraged us to write a second edition. Our colleagues at Drake University and at Trinity University have been supportive and helpful in a variety of ways. Our thanks to the following people from Drake University: Carla McCrea, Angela Renkoski, Kathleen Richardson, Shari Tenney, and David Wright. And thanks to the following people from Trinity University: John R. Brazil, James Bynum, Ronald K. Calgaard, William G. Christ, Michael Fischer, Jennifer Henderson, and Delia Rios.

Finally, our deepest thanks to our family and friends without whom we could not have made this journey: Nancy Jay; Joe, Ellen, and Joshua Kucera; Sam and Poppy Malosky; Katherine West; and last, but never least, Marty West.

Sammye Johnson
Patricia Prijatel

credits

PART

one

PART ONE

the enduring medium

chapter 1

chapter 1

the magazine as a storehouse: the scope of the medium

When you walk down the main street in Colonial Williamsburg, Virginia, you will see a sign that points the way to a "Magazine." Follow the directions on the sign and you will end up at a tall, narrow brick building that once housed ammunition. Today, we would call that building a storehouse. ▇ In the 1800s, almost two centuries after Williamsburg was founded, American children read a magazine named *Merry's Museum.* Started in 1841, the publication was later edited by Louisa May Alcott, author of *Little Women*. Even though it resembles what we would today call a magazine, it—like some other publications of the time—was called a museum. What is one definition of museum? Storehouse. ▇ Magazines in America have taken a variety of shapes and have been given a variety of names. In the 1800s, some were even called caskets, a name now limited to a less pleasant and more permanent form of storage. All the names and all the forms had one thing in common: the concept of storage. The word *magazine*, in fact, comes from the Arabic *makhazin*, which means warehouse or storehouse. Today, magazines no longer house gunshot and cannon balls; instead they house ideas, opinions, and information. ▇ Magazines have been the medium of our country's brightest minds and have provided a forum for some of our most important political, social, and cultural discussions. In recent years, however, magazine professionals as well as critics outside the industry have bemoaned some magazines' tendencies toward advertiser influence on content, tabloidization, celebrity journalism, and an overall appeal to our basest instincts.

Poets, novelists, essayists, and journalists have used magazines to reach the heart and soul of America. Our best American writers have been published in magazines: Annie Dillard, William Faulkner, Ernest Hemingway, Toni Morrison, Edgar Allan Poe, and scores of others who have penned our classics and have won Pulitzer and Nobel Prizes.

Photographers have used magazines to engage and enlarge the American consciousness by showing us images of ourselves that are both raw and wonderful. Mathew Brady photographed the Civil War for *Harper's Weekly*, Margaret Bourke-White captured World War II on film for *Life*, and Annie Leibovitz gave us a lasting Vietnam era icon: Yoko Ono and John Lennon nude on the cover of *Rolling Stone*. During the initial months of the second Gulf War in 2003, *Time* magazine emphasized visual rather than verbal content, presenting photographic portfolios of American forces and Iraqi people.

Artists have used magazines to experiment with techniques and styles and to show us their vision of the world. Winslow Homer created stark black-and-white engravings of life in New York City in the 1870s for *Harper's Weekly;* six decades later, Salvador Dali colorfully illustrated *Vogue* covers of the 1930s. Magazines helped refine cartoons as a medium of expression, with Charles Addams giving birth to his delightfully ghoulish creation, the Addams Family, on the pages of *The New Yorker*. Designers, from the legendary *Harper's Bazaar* art director Alexey Brodovitch to contemporary creators of *Details* and *W,* also have used magazines to blend words and pictures to catch the eye and capture the spirit.

On a less impressive note, magazines have given us *Playboy* Playmates and made Demi Moore a household name for modeling nude and pregnant on the cover of *Vanity Fair* in 1991 and beginning an affair with the much-younger Ashton Kutcher more than a decade later. Magazines have even been sued for matching hit men with husbands who want to kill their wives, as happened in the classified ad section of *Soldier of Fortune*.[1] Some contemporary magazines take a tabloid approach to content, emphasizing sensationalism and catering to the lowest levels of readers' intelligence—Laci Peterson's death and the subsequent trial of her husband Scott kept some magazines panting for months.

Magazines, however, remain a vibrant and healthy medium, serving the rabble, the rebel, and the responsible citizen. Magazines, in a way, are a voice of the country. They are published by huge media conglomerates and tiny publishing houses, by trade and religious groups, by professional associations, and by academics. They are created for thinkers, laborers, activists, and couch potatoes. Some are huge financial machines; others don't make a dime. Some need two city blocks to staff their offices; others need nothing more than a kitchen table. No other medium is as diverse, nor does any other medium have such a rich past and limitless future.

magazines and the media mix

Developing an operational definition of the word *magazine* has kept scholars twitching and arguing, looking for commonality in a medium that's as in-

NOVEMBER 23, 1936. Margaret Bourke-White's photo of the Fort Peck Dam appeared on the first cover of *Life* magazine. Bourke-White later chronicled World War II for *Life*.

dividualistic as the Americans it serves. We can work toward a definition of magazines by comparing them with other media. Magazines exist in both print and broadcast format. The broadcast programs *60 Minutes, 20/20,* and *Dateline* call themselves magazines. There's good reason for this name: These shows follow some basic magazine guidelines. If we look at how these programs differ from their televised news counterparts, we can get an idea why broadcasters have usurped the term *magazine.*

■ DEPTH AND TIMELESSNESS

A magazine has more in-depth coverage than its news counterpart, and it deals with less timely information, often on trends and issues. It takes what we generally call a feature, rather than a hard news, approach. That is, its articles go beyond the news. If an earthquake hits Los Angeles, the news media will give the current information on the size and effect of the quake. The magazine—or the broadcast magazine show—will give background information and analysis on, perhaps, the history of quakes in California, the geological formations that cause them, and architectural developments that might make them less deadly. The *Los Angeles Times* will be on top of the day-to-day story of the quake, while *Los Angeles Magazine* might profile families who live on the fault line.

■ SPECIALIZATION OF CONTENT AND AUDIENCE

Magazines are highly specialized in content and in audience. Want sports information? Try a sports magazine. There are general titles (*Sports Illustrated* and *The Sporting News*), but the field narrows according to types of sport (*Golf Illustrated* and *Practical Horseman*), then narrows further by gender (*Golf for Women*) and region *(Texas Golfer).*

Research in Brief

Magazine Uses and Gratifications

The American media consumer is a savvy individual. She knows what she expects from the various forms of media and she heads for a specific medium to fill a specific need.

Media researchers of the 1920s and 1930s who studied mass media effects saw the media audience as a faceless blob, a huge mass of unnamed and undifferentiated nobodies. Researchers in the 1970s said it was time to stop and look at these people as individuals, to question what motivated them and why. In response, media scholars have studied the way in which Americans use their media, and the gratifications they receive from this use. Called, not surprisingly, uses and gratifications theory, this approach encourages researchers to focus not on the medium, but on the user of that medium. Researchers have suggested that contemporary consumers use media for the following five needs: cognitive, affective, personal, social, and tension release.[1]

Cognitive

Magazines help us acquire information, knowledge, and understanding. They inform us on issues and events that might affect us; they tell us what's going on in our world and what that means to us. *Newsweek*

1. Several researchers were responsible for developing a list of media uses, including Elihu Katz, Jack McLeod, Denis McQuail, Jay G. Blumler, Michael Gurevitch, and H. Haas. The list used was taken from Katz, Gurevitch, and Haas, "On the Use of the Mass Media for Important Things," *American Sociological Review,* 38 (1973): 164–81.

(continued)

Magazine Uses and Gratifications (continued)

and *Time* give us the background on methods of cloning animals and analyze the possibilities and problems of human cloning. *RN* magazine helps nurses assess changes in health care, and *Tricycle* explains how Buddhism is influencing mainstream America.

Affective

We use magazines to seek emotional, pleasurable, or aesthetic experiences. Will we ever be able to afford that house in *Architectural Digest*? Maybe not, but we can dream. Magazines are great dream machines, and readers know that, using magazines for vicarious experiences. We scan fashion magazines for trends we may never adopt, but which are fun to imagine. We read *Print* to see the beauty that graphic designers are creating, and to aspire to that level of creativity ourselves. We look at *Cooking Light* and think that someday we might make that low-calorie kiwi torte on the cover. We read *Travel and Leisure* and lose ourselves in a mythical vacation to the Greek isles.

Personal

Magazines can help us live our lives as sane individuals, strengthening our credibility, confidence, stability, and status. They reinforce our values, provide us with psychological reassurance and self-understanding, and give us a chance to explore reality. *Glamour* tells us it's okay to hate those fashionable shoes; *Self* gives us healthy ways to look and feel better; *GQ* provides us with fashion rules and the courage to break them; *Essence* reminds us we're not alone in our worldview.

Social

We use the media to help us fit in with our society. Researchers call this function the "social utility of information." You, too, can be a brilliant conversationalist, if you read enough. You can use that article on insomnia in *Health* to offer advice to the boss's wife with whom you thought you had nothing in common. That article you read in *The Atlantic Monthly* on the cause of Middle America's cynicism might even help you through that political science test.

Tension Release

Readers often head for magazines for escape and diversion. We read *Entertainment Weekly*, *People*, and *Soap Opera Digest* to get away from our own mundane world and live for a while in the world of the stars, to peek for a moment into the bedrooms and boardrooms of the glamorous and the powerful. Sure, you're up to your ears in student loans and your short-sighted girlfriend just dumped you. But, the cast of *The O.C.* is featured in *People* . That'll take your mind off your problems for a while. ■

By comparison, network television has both a broad audience and broad content. Cable television competes with its network counterpart in much the same way magazines do: It is more specialized, and this specialization helps cable television compete head-on with magazines in many ways. Cable television viewers, like magazine readers, appreciate information that seems aimed directly at their needs and interests.

A newspaper covers topics of general interest for a specific geographic area. Many newspapers have strong features sections, which increasingly contain specialized information on, for example, wedding planning, home remodeling, and parenting. These, however, are a supplement to the newspaper's primary goal of presenting timely information. Readers depend on the newspaper for day-to-day news, not for the specialized information in these sections. If you want to build a house, you'll head to the newsstand for home building magazines; you won't wait for the Friday feature in the newspaper, although you'll enjoy reading it when it comes. In 1982, the Magazine Publishers of America (MPA) offered an expansion of this point:

A magazine is like no other medium for the simple reason that it isn't a daily routine. Depending on its scope and its point of view, it may be published once every week, once every two weeks, or once every three months. Its subject matter may be the world at large, but more often, it's a study in depth of a vital part of someone's world—an art, a science, a sport, or a certain way of looking at the world for a certain man, a certain woman, a certain child.[2]

Audience and content work in tandem: All content must be geared to the magazine's specific audience. Articles or photos that miss the mark in terms of audience are ineffective, no matter how brilliantly composed and technically elegant they might be. An article on menopause has no place in *Elle Girl*, even if the information is groundbreaking. Likewise, articles on great bars to visit during spring break won't cut it in *AARP: The Magazine*.

Magazine editors see their readers as part of a community; readers of a successful publication have a sense of ownership of *their* magazine. Any editor who changes a popular feature has to steel herself for the inevitable letters asking "What have you done to *my* magazine?"

Many editors run ideas by a panel of readers before an article is even written. When *Country Home* began planning a redesign in 2004, the editors went to subscribers as well as nonsubscribers who fit the magazine's profile and asked them specific details about how they live their lives. *Better Homes and Gardens* editors monitor online chat rooms at bhg.com to gauge reader response to content, looking at whether or not story lines and graphic presentations are having their intended effect: Were readers able to negotiate instructions and achieve desired results? Did they respond to the emotional component in a positive way? Editors say that online chat rooms provide fairly instantaneous feedback about various components of the magazine's content, and often provide the seeds for new story proposals. The magazine also holds regular focus groups with readers.

In other cases, the readers are already enthusiastic about the content—they've written it. *A Taste of Home* contains recipes and cooking ideas submitted by readers. The magazine's tagline: "The Magazine Edited by a Thousand Country Cooks."

A magazine's audience is well defined and can be national, international, regional, or local.

well defined

Magazines do not try to be all things to all people. Magazine editors target a precise niche—a narrowly

defined focus—and study the characteristics of the individuals in that niche. They then aim the magazine directly at those individuals. These characteristics concern both demographics—easily quantified elements such as age, income, geographic location—and psychographics—harder-to-measure issues such as values, attitudes, and beliefs. Advertisers look at demographics and psychographics and match them with the characteristics of the target audience for their products.

The readers of *Black Enterprise* illustrate the detail with which magazines define their readers:

Demographics

Median Age: 38 years
Median Household Income:
$74,200
Gender: 51 percent men; 49
percent women
Marital Status: 49 percent
married
Educational Level: 72 percent
college graduates; 33 percent
hold graduate degrees

Psychographics

Readers are professionals, corporate executives, entrepreneurs, and decision-makers seeking advice and information on the black business market to help them build a solid foundation for professional and personal success.[3]

national

Until the advent of television, magazines were America's only national medium. Magazines now combine their national reach with an appeal to specialized audiences, providing a package available with no other medium. If you're a gourmet cook living in a small town in which fried chicken

In 1743, Alexander Pope described magazines as "upstart collections in prose and verse . . . where Dulness assumes all the various shapes of Folly to draw in and cajole the rabble."

SEPTEMBER 1994: *The Economist*, **published in London, England, serves a worldwide audience.**

is considered a delicacy, you can reach for *Gourmet* magazine and immediately be among friends. If you're an advertiser of quality food products with franchises nationally, *Gourmet* will deliver an audience that newspapers, radio, and television can't touch. Why advertise in the local newspaper and reach only a small percentage of your audience when you can advertise in a magazine whose readers are *all* possible customers?

international

Visit a newsstand in London, and there's your faithful *Esquire*. The British edition, however, has John Cleese on the cover, with a subtitle under his name: "Britain's funniest man gets indiscreet." Other cover lines are obviously geared to British readers: "The Ruling Class: The 25 men who really run Britain (and the ones who only think they do)," plus a teaser on a Scottish murder. Ads are for British products and services.

Globalization is a given in the magazine industry. According to the Global Entertainment and Media Outlook, magazines worldwide—in the

United States, Europe, the Middle East, Africa, Asia-Pacific, Latin America, and Canada—will grow in earnings from \$80.7 billion in 2003 to \$93.4 billion in 2008.[4] International magazines can be exported from the United States to other countries, published elsewhere and distributed here, or imported to this country as distinct American editions.

Exports include the newsweeklies, which span the globe, with *Time* and *Newsweek* editions available throughout Europe, South America, Africa, Asia, and Australia. With the fall of the Soviet Union, Russia became a hot market for American magazines; titles such as *Men's Health, Cosmopolitan,* and *Harper's Bazaar* began hitting Russian newsstands in the 1990s. *Cosmo* now has more than 40 international editions, including a 127,000-circulation edition in Indonesia, the world's largest Islamic nation.[5] *Modern Plastics Worldwide* is distributed in 41 countries in Europe, 13 in the Middle East, 22 in Asia and the Pacific, 13 in Africa, and 26 in the Americas. Its readers are primarily managers in the plastics-processing industries.[6]

One of the most esteemed worldwide titles distributed in the United States is *The Economist*, published in London, with a 1 million weekly circulation in more than 200 countries. One boost to the magazine's healthy numbers were the events of September 11, 2001, when people across the globe searched for an objective voice to make sense of the American tragedy.[7]

Successful international magazine imports—those started elsewhere that now have full-fledged American editions—include *Elle* and *Marie Claire* from France and *Maxim* from England.

regional

Conversely, some magazines succeed by aiming at a narrow geographic target. Some have a regional appeal as part of their editorial focus; others have a national reach but offer regional editions. *Midwest Living* was one of the success stories of the 1980s because it spoke enthusiastically about an area of the country too long ignored, and this message resonated with those living in America's heartland. It followed other regional successes, such as *Southern Living, Texas Monthly,* and *Arizona Highways.*

National magazines recognize the importance of targeting regional readers. Initially this was done to give regional advertisers the chance to advertise in a

European Magazines React to September 11 Attacks

For more images and details of coverage of September 11, go to the website of the E.T. Meredith Center for Magazine Studies at Drake University: www.magazinestudies.com.

The terrorist attacks on the United States were a major news event in Europe and were the cover story of news, opinion, and business magazines across the continent in the weeks after September 11, 2001. The coverage demonstrated the outrage and fear with which the European people reacted to the attacks and the empathy they felt for the American people. There was a sense of camaraderie in some of the coverage, with the implication that this was an attack on the entire Western world, rather than just on the United States. Some approaches were highly sensational, invoking references to the Apocalypse and a World War III.

Der Spiegel, a German news magazine, used rough typewriter type for its cover line, "The Terror Attack. War in the 21st century," with a blurry extreme close-up image of the second plane heading directly to the second tower.

The French *L'Express* also ran a blurry image of the second plane heading into the second tower. The cover line: "The Islamics Declare War on the Western World."

Next, an Austrian title, used a cover flap with a photograph of the exploding World Trade Center and the cover line: "The USA at War." The main cover image was a close-up of Osama bin Laden with the cover line: "Osama bin Laden: Murderer. The Hunt for the Terrorists."

The Italian *Panorama* ran a special edition titled "The Third World War." The cover image of a World Trade Center tower exploding included a smaller cutline: "New York, September 11: Death in Manhattan. Fanatical Islamics Sow Terror in America and the Entire Western World."

Stern, from Germany, used the same cover image as the European *Newsweek*: three New York firefighters raising the flag over the ashes of the World Trade Center. The cover line: "After the Inferno. The Victims, The Attackers. The Tightrope."

Gospodarski Vestnik, a Slovene business weekly whose title translates into English as *Economic Herald*, ran a tightly cropped shot of the exploding World Trade Center, with the cryptic and oversized cover line: "Apocalypse Now." Articles inside analyzed the economic effects of the attacks. ∎

---

national magazine, thereby targeting their narrow audience while at the same time enjoying the credibility and reputation of the national publication. That's why you see your local bank's ads in *Time* and *Newsweek*. In recent years, regional editions have also included specialized editorial content. Likewise, publishers have combined geographic characteristics with other demographic traits that have narrowed the audience dramatically.

Technology has made it increasingly easy for magazines to create multiple editions for specific regions. *Successful Farming* has more than 140 regional and demographic editions, which are further narrowed into demographic categories—size of farm, type of production, income—into a whopping 3,700 special editions, some so highly targeted they consist of only six subscribers. The magazine has more than 21,000 different editions of the 12 issues combined.

Field and Stream includes regional inserts that focus on outdoor activities such as hunting and fishing within specific areas of the country. The Midwest Edition has articles on Missouri's wild trout and rabbit season in Ohio, while the South Edition offers pieces on North Carolina wolves and their effects on the state's game population.

local

The success of city magazines has proven that magazines need not have a large geographic reach to be successful. In fact, many of our top magazines in reputation, readership, advertising volume, and circulation income are city magazines. *The New Yorker*, hailed at various times in recent history as America's premier magazine, also has a national audience, although its attitude and emphasis is strictly Big Apple.

Most large cities have at least one city magazine: *Chicago, Atlanta, Baltimore, Phoenix.* City magazine readers look to these publications to supplement their daily newspapers and to improve the experience of living in their communities. Today, like all other magazines, city magazines are finding increasingly narrower niches, as illustrated by such local bridal magazines as *New Hampshire*

Weddings and *Minnesota Bride.* Nevertheless, Northwestern University magazine professor Abe Peck argues that some niches may be too narrow. Peck asks, "How thin can you slice it before it is all baloney? We have to look for authentic niches."[8]

■ OPINION, INTERPRETATION, AND ADVOCACY

Because their communities of readers are so well defined and close-knit, magazines are far more comfortable than any other medium in providing opinion and interpretation, and in advocating for the causes of their audiences. Journals of opinion,

City Magazines: Catering to Instant Status and Ego Gratification

City magazines—published for a local, urban market—have been a significant development in niche magazine publishing since 1968 when *New York* magazine burst on the scene with an exciting new look that was soon emulated in city after city. Designed for upscale, sophisticated, status-conscious readers, city magazines primarily compete against local newspapers for their audience and their advertisers. Because national advertisers also want to reach the desirable demographic package of the affluent urbanite, city magazines often carry the same liquor and cigarette ads found in national publications.

City magazines can trace their history back to 1888,

when *Honolulu* began life as *Paradise of the Pacific.* Boston has had various city titles since 1900, while *Philadelphia* has been published since 1909. However, the period of greatest growth for city magazines was 1962–1974, with the heyday for the genre occurring during the late 1970s and early 1980s, when virtually every large and medium-sized city had its own magazine. By 1980, as many as 250 cities had a magazine of their own.

City magazines have a breezy, sassy style of writing and a definite orientation. Because they publish strictly local stories, they usually do not make interesting reading for people in other cities. In topic and tone, city magazines are less formal and more eclectic

than national magazines, tending to concentrate on three kinds of articles: informational or service features, personality profiles, and investigative pieces. As early as 1976, David Shaw of the *Los Angeles Times* offered an assessment of the city magazine genre: "City magazines have tapped not just an audience but a neurosis—an audience increasingly anxious (if not, indeed, desperate) about the challenges, complexities and frustrations of the contemporary urban environment. . . . Most people, it seems, read city magazines either to learn how to cope with their environment, or to enjoy, vicariously, the success that others more wealthy and fortunate than themselves have had in doing so."[1]

1. David Shaw, "List Grows: Magazines of the Cities, A Success Story," *Los Angeles Times* (April 5, 1976): 3, 16.

City Magazines (continued)

Under publisher Clay Felker and his merry band of writers (Tom Wolfe, Gloria Steinem, Gail Sheehy, and Jimmy Breslin), *New York* offered New Journalism—outrageous, bold, and stylistically innovative writing that allowed readers to vicariously participate in an event. The magazine's powerful and provocative design, by Milton Glaser, complemented the examination of the city's ethos from a variety of fresh perspectives. *New York* set the tone for city magazines with upbeat, consumer-oriented pieces, such as "A Smart-Ass Guide to Designer Jeans" which ran in the July 23, 1979, issue. This approach is still found in successful city magazines.

For many, the quintessential city magazine article appeared in the June 8, 1970, issue of *New York* under Tom Wolfe's byline. With his usual irreverent Wolfean wit, he skewered "limousine liberals" who threw elaborate parties and invited the less fortunate as social pets, in "Radical Chic: That Party at Lenny's." According to Felker, the article "killed radical chic."[2]

City magazines have produced cutting-edge journalism, top-flight graphics, and literary gems. But they've also served as content-weak promotional vehicles for local governments or civic boosters of chambers of commerce. Most have tended to locate themselves in the middle of these extremes,

with lists citing the best the city has to offer running side by side with trenchant features on the uses and abuses of power, designed to rattle the town's movers and shakers. City magazines generally provide an alternative point of view to local newspapers, often taking thoughtful stands on critical issues of the day.

Lately, however, city magazines have accentuated the positive in the urban and suburban landscape, focusing on the accouterments and accessories found in the elegant habitats and lush gardens of their upscale readers. The traditional city name for the logo has been garnished with the words "lifestyle" or "home and garden" as a distinguishing factor. For example, *San Diego Magazine* competes against *San Diego Home/Garden Lifestyles*, and *Atlanta* operates in the same marketplace as *Atlanta Homes and Lifestyles*. Additionally, states and regions have emulated their urban counterparts in magazine development, with *Yankee* being the oldest (established in 1935) and largest (500,000 New Englanders) of the regional publications.

More than 85 magazines belong to the City and Regional Magazine Association (CRMA)—ranging from the windy city of *Chicago* (186,638 circulation) to Connecticut's swanky *Greenwich* (10,500

JUNE 8, 1970: Tom Wolfe's *New York* article, "Radical Chic: That Party at Lenny's," mocked the late-1960s tendency for rich liberals to flaunt their friendships with the less fortunate in elegant—and, some say, inappropriate—parties.

circulation), and from tiny *Delaware Today* (2,443 circulation) to giant *Texas Monthly* (300,000 circulation). A 2001 readership study commissioned by CRMA revealed that the city magazine consumer has a median household income in excess of $273,000, is college educated, and has lived in the community more than 7 years. The CRMA Network offers advertisers a group buy in 88 key markets across the nation, reaching a circulation of 4.3 million "affluent, involved, educated, influential, active consumers who take action based on what they read."[3]

2. Ibid., 18.

3. http://www.citymag.org/index.html.

City Magazines (continued)

One of the authors of this text was a city magazine editor in the late 1970s, and she still can recite by heart her magazine's editorial philosophy:

> *San Antonio Magazine* offers an urban survival manual consisting of entertaining human interest stories and specific service guides in a lively, conversational tone not found in local newspapers. Like all magazines, we offer readers vicarious experiences as well as information that can be used. What distinguishes us is that our readers know they, too, *really* can experience what we write about because they live in this city. The topics we cover—where to dine, where to shop, and what to see—are right here, waiting for the reader to participate along with us.

In retrospect, the former city magazine editor realizes that *San Antonio Magazine*, and every other city magazine, perfectly fulfills all five needs of the uses and gratification theory. But she admits that such fulfillment was intuitive rather than conscious at the time, and, therefore, a lot more fun than fuss.

In a 2004 interview, Clay Felker was asked what made *New York* so successful. "The secret of a magazine is passion," Felker replied. "The original group of people who put together *New York* had a passion for living in New York City."[4] That secret is what fuels all good magazines—city and otherwise. ■

4. Lauren Barack, "Clay Felker on Running New York," *Folio* (January 1, 2004): 19.

such as *The Nation* and *The Atlantic Monthly*, have been magazine standard-bearers throughout American history, and magazines have traditionally provided interpretation and analysis. In recent years, much of the growth in magazines has been related to the growth and influence of special interest groups with an advocacy function.

Historian Arthur Schlesinger Jr. called magazines "the means of expression for the more reflective interpretation so vital to the educational process."[9] Magazine scholar Theodore Peterson called them the "medium of instruction and interpretation for the leisurely, critical reader."[10] The MPA says, "A magazine is a friend, a tangible and enduring companion and an integral part of a reader's personal and professional life."[11]

Magazines, in short, take the time to help us make sense of our world and our lives. They require that we sit down, read, and reflect. To use a magazine, we have to pay close attention to it, and we have to invest a bit of ourselves in that use. In the process, we become more thoughtful and critical.

In 1979, former *Esquire* publisher Sam Ferber penned one of the most eloquent statements on magazines. In it he said, "Magazines must probe, analyze, and offer background material. They must provide a broader perspective, they must synthesize and define complex issues." What's more, Ferber noted, "A magazine today must stand for something or it represents nothing."[12]

According to the MPA, "The art of editing a magazine is to look beneath and beyond the surface of daily events. And whenever a magazine does its job particularly well, it is not only capable of opening the eyes of its readers, the truth is, it can often open the eyes of the very journalists whose job it is to deliver the news day and night."[13]

Many trade and organization magazines were built on advocacy. The growth and decline of certain businesses and industries, in fact, have historically been marked by these magazines. *The American Railroad Journal* was first published in 1832, a year before a railroad was built; *Quill*, the magazine of the Society of Professional Journalists, was founded in 1912, when journalism itself was first recognized as a legitimate profession.[14]

Religion magazines have long been advocates. Many of these are published by religious organizations: *On Course* is a magazine for students in grades 6–12 in the United States and Canada and is published through the National Youth Ministries of Assemblies of God. *Tricycle:The Buddhist Review*, published by The Buddhist Ray, advocates meditation and Zen in the workplace.

Catholic Rural Life magazine, published by the National Catholic Rural Life Conference, is an ecumenical voice and has long been an advocate of the family farm. In 1985, it won top awards from the Catholic Press Association for its November issue on violence in rural America, spotlighting the activities of militias and separatist groups that were recruiting for members among farmers who were losing their land during the farm crisis of the 1980s.

Within the past 40 years, several consumer magazines have been launched to advocate specific causes, including *Ms.*, for feminism; *The American Spectator*, for conservative politics; and *The Advocate*, for gay and lesbian issues. *American Rifleman*, published by the National Rifle Association, is also available on the newsstand. As the association's voice, it has been a solid advocate of the rights of gun owners for more than 120 years.

■ PERMANENCE

The pages of a magazine are stapled, glued, or sewn together—that is, they are bound—to create what often looks like a small book. And because magazines are printed and bound, they are the most permanent of all media. We shut off the television, leave the room, and forget about it. But we keep our magazines, stockpiling old issues of *National Geographic* in the spare room until we're forced to sell them to make room for the baby.

The broadcast media are ephemeral by nature. The sitcom comes and goes within 30 minutes. Broadcast news stories last, at most, 3–5 minutes. More and more, television is aimed at a moving target, geared to a short attention span. Newspapers take more time with the information, but focus on day-to day issues. Magazines, however, are created to last.

This permanence means that we can use and reuse magazines. We pass along the article in *Mother Earth News* on new roofing material to our brother who is building a cabin, or the story on a real-life murder mystery in *Vanity Fair* to our mystery-loving friends.

The average issue of an American magazine typically goes to more than one reader. Publishers track this additional exposure, which they call pass-along readership, and use that number to refer to readership, as opposed to circulation. For example, if a magazine has a pass-along readership of 2.5 and a circulation of 100,000, it has a total readership of 250,000. This count, however, can be controversial, with some publishers saying that it is the only reliable measurement of true reader engagement, and that it is consistent with the way other media, such as television, are measured. Others say there's no way to really determine whether the initial subscriber even reads the magazine, let alone passes it on to others.

Demonstrating the synergy between television and magazines, the *Smithsonian* celebrated its 35th anniversary in 2005 by starring as an entire category on the television game show *Jeopardy*. The $1,000 answer stumped all three contestants: "From hand-hewn hideaways to rustic mansions, these wooden residences were featured in the March 1992 issue." The correct question: "What are log cabins?"

■ CONSISTENCY

When *Wood* magazine was launched in 1985, it profiled one kind of wood—ebony, tiger wood, cherry—in each issue. In the first years of the magazine, these profiles always appeared on the same page. As the magazine grew and content changed, editors decided to put this feature on a different page. Readers complained. They were accustomed to finding their favorite feature in a specific place; they didn't like it when they turned to that page and found a different article.

Not all magazine readers are as precise as the woodworkers who subscribe to *Wood*, but they do demand a certain amount of consistency from their publications. They open the magazine each month with expectations; the successful magazine meets these expectations. Consistency comes in the magazine's format: its writing, design, and graphic

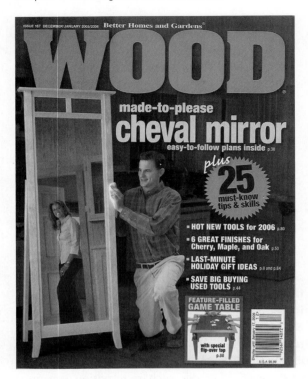

DECEMBER/JANUARY 2006: *Wood* **appeals to a dedicated and specialized audience of home woodworkers, many of whom have subscribed to the magazine for more than 10 years.**

style, and its regular departments, columns, and features.

Consistency, however, does not mean sameness. Readers challenge editors to make the magazine different with each issue, but within a coherent and harmonious structure. The proper balance of consistency and the element of surprise is one hallmark of a quality publication.

Wood magazine eventually covered all common species of wood, and editors were faced with repeating themselves or dealing with obscure types. Repetition wouldn't work with *Wood*'s audience. "Many of our readers have been with us 10 or more years, so when we cover the same topic twice they notice," says editor Bill Krier. So the magazine dropped the wood profiles, but loaded them onto the magazine's website so readers can view them for free.

Krier says that, while magazines need to modify their approach over time, he and his staff try to implement those changes slowly, and explain them to the readers. "Our approach is to be 'evolutionary' in how we change, not 'revolutionary,'" he

says. The success of this approach is mirrored in the success of the magazine: *Wood* is the country's largest woodworking magazine, with a 550,000 circulation, and it continues to enjoy healthy advertising sales and profits.

■ FREQUENCY

Consistency is also attained in the form of regular publication. Magazines may be published weekly, biweekly, monthly, bimonthly, quarterly, or at predetermined, but irregular, intervals throughout the year. Some special editions are published annually.

Wood is published seven times a year—September, October, November, December/January, February/March, April/May, and June/July. Woodworking, Krier says, is a school-year activity, and *Wood* readers are do-it-yourselfers who are involved in outdoor activities in the summer. *The New Yorker* is published weekly, a frequency that may operate against the magazine by building reader guilt. Who can read that many words every week?

■ DEFINITION

When we take all these elements into consideration, we end up with the definition of magazines that will guide us throughout this book:

> Magazines are printed and bound publications offering in-depth coverage of stories often of a timeless nature. Their content may provide opinion and interpretation as well as advocacy. They are geared to a well-defined, specialized audience, and they are published regularly, with a consistent format.

the scope of the medium

You have been job hunting, and told your dad you want to work for a magazine. A look of panic clouds his face. He's thinking, "She'll never work again!" He worries that the field is limited and your prospects correspondingly dim, no matter your brilliance. Don't blame Dad. Like so many members of the general public, he is thinking of only the smallest number of magazines: those we see on the newsstands, or those popular publications we subscribe to and receive in the mail.

This is the mere tip of the magazine iceberg. To get a picture of the scope of the magazine medium, we will briefly look at the different types of magazines being published today and at the size of the contemporary magazine industry.

■ MAGAZINE TYPES

Have you read *Modern Baking, Association Management, Family Ties, Vision,* or *Journal of Soil and Water Conservation?* These all fit the preceding definition of a magazine. The staffs of these publications all put pages together in much the same way. However, their goals are quite different. Magazine professionals classify magazines into three types: consumer, trade, and organization. Understanding these categories gives us a clear and encouraging picture of the breadth of the magazine field.

consumer

Consumer magazines are created primarily for popular consumption. They are sold on the newsstand or by subscriptions and are marketed like any other consumer product. They usually contain advertising; readers are important to advertisers because of their potential as consumers. Most of the largest circulation magazines are consumer publications, such as *Reader's Digest* with 10 million circulation and *Better Homes and Gardens* with 7.6 million circulation.[15] There are fewer consumer magazines than any other type, but individual consumer magazines generally have the largest audiences of all types.

Consumer magazines can be further narrowed into general interest and special interest. General interest titles contain material of interest to a broad audience: for example, *Reader's Digest* and *The Atlantic Monthly.* Special interest magazines focus on a narrow issue, which may be a hobby, issue of concern, or activity: Examples include *American Patchwork and Quilting, Food and Wine,* and *American Hunter.*

A new subset of consumer magazines are the "magalogs" like *Lucky* and *Domino,* and the defunct *Cargo,* which offer consumerism at its most raw, providing readers with ideas on goods to buy and the information on where to buy them. The name magalog comes from the fact that they combine the magazine format with a catalog's content. The essential difference between magalogs and catalogs is that the information in a magalog is created by an editorial staff rather than by a manufacturer or retailer, which gives the reader a broader set of options and a more objective sense of the benefits, or lack of benefits, of specific products.

The sailboat featured on the cover of the May 2005 *Sunset* created a gorgeous and enviable image of sailing through the Hood Canal in Washington State, but the image had far from a happy ending when the boat sunk shortly afterward, during a storm. Salvage crews used the cover to determine the ship's location.

trade

Trade magazines are also called specialized business magazines, or business-to-business magazines. Their content is job related and their audience consists of readers in specific occupations or professions. *Baking Management,* for example, goes to manufacturers and wholesalers of baked goods. Some trade magazines, such as *PC World,* are sold on the newsstand, but most are sold only through subscriptions, which usually go to readers at their workplaces.

According to American Business Media (ABM), a clear majority of executives in all industries—from finance to horticulture—cite these publications as being among the top tools for "helping to build their business and do their jobs better."[16] Occasionally publishers of these magazines offer controlled circulation, in which readers who possess specific occupational characteristics receive the magazine free, because these readers have high appeal to advertisers. The largest circulation trade magazines often have as sizable an audience as their consumer counterparts; the largest, *PC Magazine,* has a circulation of just under 1 million.

MARCH 7, 2006: *PC Magazine* is considered both a trade and a consumer title. As a trade magazine, it is aimed at the information technology professional. As a consumer title, it helps readers control the technology in their daily lives.

Many industries are served by multiple magazines. For example, professional meeting planners have a host of magazines to help them understand their industry and excel at their jobs, including *Association Meetings, Insurance Meetings Management, Small Market Meetings, The Meeting Professional, Successful Meetings, Corporate Meetings and Incentives,* and *Medical Meetings.*

At one time, farm magazines were considered a distinct magazine type, reflective of the importance of agriculture to the American economy. In most cases today, farm magazines operate like trade publications.

organization

Organization magazines fall into three general categories: society and association, public relations, and custom. All are published by organizations for their internal and external constituencies.

Society and Association These magazines usually come as one benefit of membership; examples here include some top names—*Sierra, National Geographic,* and *Smithsonian*—as well as the less well-known *Association Management,* published by the American Society of Association Executives. Some association magazines look and act like consumer magazines, and many boast huge readerships.

The largest circulation magazine in the United States is an association publication: *AARP: The Magazine,* for the American Association of Retired Persons, with a 22.6 million circulation. *National Geographic,* the country's fifth largest title, has a circulation of 5.4 million and is one of our oldest, most respected, and well-known magazines. As a publication of the National Geographic Society, however, its goal is to enhance the operation of that agency, and its format and organizational style are determined by the society. It is available almost exclusively through subscriptions, although in 1998 it became available on selected newsstands in large cities across the county. To get a subscription, you must become a member of the organization. The flagship title has been joined by highly successful offshoots such as *National Geographic Kids* (1.3 million circulation), *National Geographic International* (1 million circulation), *National Geographic Traveler* (733,000 circulation), and *National Geographic Adventure* (427,000 circulation).

Magazines are essential components of an association. Elissa Matulis Myers, former vice president of the American Society of Association Executives, expressed a sentiment in 1995 that still holds true: "For many members, the periodical *is* the association—the monthly visit through the mailbox of colleagues with similar interests." The association magazine, she added, can "unify an industry, profession or interest group. Tightly drawn, a periodical can have remarkable influence for the association and can be a powerful force in support of members."[17]

Association magazines may carry advertising, and most are sold to readers through subscriptions; a few are available on the newsstands. Their general goal, however, is service to the association rather than profit; whatever profit they earn is returned to the association. Dues for new members of the Sierra Club in 2005 were $15 a year; $7.50 of that was earmarked for the organization's magazine, *Sierra.*

Scholarly journals are also association publications and are used by scholars and researchers to share academic information. They differ from other association magazines because the content usually consists of scholarly papers selected by peer review, that is, by a board of scholars or academics. Content is valued because of its contribution to knowledge of the field. Most journals have little or no advertising and go to readers as part of membership in a scholarly or professional organization. Included here are the *ABA Journal*, with 380,000 circulation, and *The New England Journal of Medicine*, with 200,000 circulation. Less well known is *Word Ways: The Journal of Recreational Linguistics*, which offers erudite word games and analyses of the effects of popular culture—computers, MTV, professional sports—on language. *Wilson Quarterly*, published by the Woodrow Wilson International Center for Scholars, has the slogan, "Surveying the World of Ideas." Its content is an eclectic mix of historical analysis, current issues, and gleanings from other scholarly publications.

Journals are often the source of material for consumer magazine articles. Some even study magazines themselves. In 1992, *The New England Journal of Medicine* ran a study that showed a relationship between cigarette advertising and positive articles on smoking. Those magazines that had a great deal of cigarette advertising were also those magazines that tended either to downplay the dangers of smoking, or even to present positive side effects. The authors cited an article from *Cosmopolitan* that suggested smoking might even alleviate endometriosis, a conclusion which, the medical writers noted, had no basis in fact.[18]

Many association magazines, such as *National Geographic*, are also included in lists of consumer magazines; others, such as *Quill*, the magazine of the Society of Professional Journalists, show up in trade magazine lists.

Public Relations Also called corporate communications magazines, these are probably the most ubiquitous of all magazine types. Most large organizations have at least one; some have several. These magazines tell employees what's happening in the organization, explain the organization to clients, and smooth the way for the organization to deal with outside agencies. At one time, these

Why a Magazine? The Iowa Natural Heritage Foundation

The Iowa Natural Heritage Foundation considered changing its 16-page quarterly magazine, *Iowa Natural Heritage*, into a newsletter, hoping to cut costs and, perhaps, reach its 5,000 members more quickly and efficiently. The magazine format won out in the long run. Why? The statewide foundation opted for the magazine because it offers more

■ *value to readers*. The magazine has a pass-along readership of at least three people;

a newsletter couldn't offer that benefit.
■ *depth of content*. A magazine allows the foundation to provide background information that may encourage members to act on the group's agenda: protecting the state's land.
■ *emotion*. A magazine helps the foundation show why it's important to serve as stewards of the land.
■ *opportunity for commentary*. A magazine offers a conve-

nient and credible venue for the foundation's opinions.

What's more, the group found that they would save little money by switching to the newsletter format. Because they use the magazine to build and maintain membership, the foundation staff decided the most effective format for this important communication was the format they'd been using: a magazine. ■

magazines were called house organs to indicate their importance in the communication process of the organization. Included in this group are magazines for nonprofit groups, such as hospitals and universities, as well as magazines produced by and for the government.

Public relations magazines are either internal or external. Internal audiences include employees and retirees; external audiences include clients, governmental agencies, and other companies.

Walgreen World is an internal magazine that goes to 170,000 employees and retirees of Walgreen Co. and includes features on company strategy, employee profiles, and how-to pieces. Its goals are to "deliver information employees find credible and useful, generate feelings of goodwill and unity among employees, and emphasize the importance of customer service in our stores," according to Liz Muhler, manager of employee publications.

FBL Financial Group, an arm of Farm Bureau, produces *Family Ties*, an internal magazine that explains company activities and changes and highlights top employees; it is sent to 2,000 employees and retirees in 15 Midwestern states. The company also produces *Keeping in Touch*, a publication for agents to send to some 95,000 policyholders, offering them information on new products, seasonal reminders on issues such as tax preparation, and wellness tips. It is an imprint publication, produced by FBL for Farm Bureau but imprinted later with individual agencies' names.

Public relations magazines traditionally do not have advertising and are distributed free to readers. They fulfill one of the major objectives of the Public Relations Society of America (PRSA): "To exchange ideas and experience, and to collect and disseminate information of value to public relations professionals and the public."[19]

Custom Also called sponsored publications, these magazines are a type of public relations magazine,

The Magazine Publishers of America initiated an advertising campaign in 2005 to demonstrate the enduring nature of magazines. Participating publishers across the United States ran "faux" covers representing their titles 100 years in the future. Sample cover lines included *AARP*'s "90 Is the New 50," *Esquire*'s "Britney Spears at 70: Still No Pants," and *Family Circle*'s "Mommy, Why Can't We Live on Earth?"

but with a slightly different focus. They are sent to clients as a benefit of purchasing a particular product or service. Like public relations magazines, they seek to present that product or service in a positive light. Unlike public relations magazines, though, they seldom present direct information about the activities of the organization or the direct benefits of the product or service. Most have advertising—usually for the sponsoring organization, but often for other advertisers as well. Most are given to readers free, although some are sold on the newsstand and through subscriptions.

In 2004, more than 32 billion custom magazine copies were circulated. According to the Custom Publishing Council, this segment of magazine publishing has seen a phenomenal growth rate of 168 percent from 2000 to 2004.[20] Many custom titles are created by large consumer magazine publishing houses—Hachette Filipacchi, Meredith Corporation, Hearst Publishing—although the custom divisions usually operate as separate entities, modeled on an advertising agency format, with an emphasis on client as well as reader needs. Others, such as the Journey Group, operate entirely to create custom titles; Journey publishes magazines for nonprofits, including *World Vision*, for the global relief agency World Vision.

Custom publishing is a combination of magazine and marketing expertise, with the emphasis on creating and maintaining brand loyalty. It builds on the positive image consumers have of magazine editors.

"Our research has found that consumers have a special relationship with print," says Brenda White of Starcom USA, which buys print advertising for national clients. "They really trust magazine editors, and they do not classify magazines in specific genres. In my opinion, this is a unique relationship not found in other media, especially electronic."[21]

Automobile marketers are especially keyed to the importance of custom publishing in encouraging repeat purchases of their pricey products. Meredith Integrated Marketing publishes *Jeep* magazine, a travel and lifestyle publication aimed at making the reader—also a Jeep owner—take full advantage of on- and off-road trips. Hachette Filipacchi Custom Media publishes *Mercedes*, for Benz drivers, *Vision* for Cadillac owners, and *Rosso*, for Ferrari folks.

The most visible type of custom publication may be the in-flight magazines produced for major airlines, such as Northwest Airlines' *World Traveler* and United Airlines' *Hemispheres*. These look like consumer magazines but are organized around the interests of airline passengers. Their goal is to keep airline customers happy and occupied while flying. Articles include travel, business profiles, and general features. Special departments include shopping guides and airport maps. These magazines seldom do investigative stories; if they did, one area they would not investigate would be airline crashes.

other types

The vitality of the magazine field is also evident in the various mutations of the magazine, including the following:

Literary Literary publications, such as *North American Review*, publish a steady diet of quality poetry, fiction, literary nonfiction, and literary criticism. Established in Boston in 1815, the magazine is now sponsored by the University of Northern Iowa. *North American Review* promotes itself with the tagline: "Lit Happens." Literary magazines are sometimes called "little" magazines because of their circulations and, occasionally, their page size.

Sunday Supplements Opinions differ on whether these are magazines or not. The largest, *Parade*, has a circulation of more than 35 million. Some newspaper supplements are bound, as is *The New York Times Magazine*. Because these publications, while often of high editorial quality, are simply an added

TV Guide **had more than 200 regional editions with individualized program listings until 2005 when the publication changed its approach, consolidated all editions into one, and focused on entertainment information rather than the details of local program schedules.**

feature of—and are distributed along with—the newspaper, most magazine professionals, including the MPA, consider them newspaper supplements, rather than independent magazines.

Free Urban These narrow-niche publications compete with local newspapers for advertisers and succeed because they provide what the newspaper cannot: a well-defined target audience, a design style that allows a more creative and appealing presentation of their products and services, and, occasionally, better advertising rates. While they often take a magazine approach to design and content, they are usually printed on newsprint and are unbound, making them "magapapers," that is, a combination newspaper and magazine. Many specialized city magazines are entirely supported by advertisers and given to readers free. Des Moines' *City View* magazine takes an alternative view of local and national leaders and issues, even running a column titled "If I Were Abby," in which a local writer revises Dear Abby's advice. *Pulse of the Twin Cities* covers Minneapolis and St. Paul issues; one representative article critiqued "virtuous restaurants"—those that provide organic food, solar power, and employee and community support.

'Zines and E-Zines Low-budget 'zines flourished in the 1990s in print form and were usually created on a home computer, with content on topics such as social opinion, celebrities, science fiction, video games, television, and music. The name is a shortened version of "fanzines," indicating that these publications' roots were in the groupie culture. Increasingly, though, the print versions have given way to e-zines, such as the literary journal *Janus Head*, with original essays, fiction, and poetry.

■ NUMBER OF MAGAZINES

How many magazines exist in America today? It depends on who is counting and what kinds of

The "I"s Have It: Interactive and Integrated

They're complementary concepts, sounding the same but with unique definitions—interactive media and integrated media. Which is which and what means what? These two new departments in American publishing houses are representative of the changes in magazine publishing at the beginning of the 21st century. They're also representative of the confusing rhetoric of a constantly changing world.

Interactive Media

The use of online and digital media to communicate with existing readers and reach out to new ones by offering expanded services beyond the original print magazine is the definition of interactive media. Initially, the term referred to digital versions of print magazines—readersdigest .com, newyorker.com, houseandgarden.com.

As technology improved and Americans got more wired, the interactivity expanded to possibilities limited only by imagination and a decent Internet connection. Now, readers can interact with the magazine staff and with one another, using message boards that help them understand new parenthood and share their health problems and perspectives with one another. On magazine

MARCH 2006: *Better Homes and Gardens* **has earned its rank as one of America's top circulation consumer magazines by providing the country's families with practical information they can use.**

sites now, viewers can experiment with a new hairstyle, choose the right colors for their complexion, and develop a personal fitness regimen.

Meredith Interactive Media, a division within magazine publisher Meredith Corporation, often combines the expertise of more than one magazine for a unique Web offering, such as a weight-loss planner created in 2005 that presented healthy recipes from *Better Homes and Gardens* and diet strategies from *Ladies' Home Journal* in an interactive package that included body mass index (BMI)

calculators and message boards.

Integrated Media

Also called integrated marketing, integrated media refers to client-driven projects that use more than one medium, including custom magazines, advertising inserts, television shows, and special events. These media are marketing tools, based on the concept of branding, or creating a unique and immediately identifiable image of your product or service. Integrated media began when advertisers and publishers combined their talents to create media that served a highly focused audience consisting of the buyers that the marketer wanted to reach with a specialized message. The earliest integrated media were custom magazines, one of the oldest being *Endless Vacations*, the 1.5 million circulation magazine that's been published for more than 20 years for Resort Condominiums International (RCI) vacation ownership exchange.

Integrated media can be also used to promote the magazine itself. To expand the scope of *Premiere, In Style*, or *Entertainment Weekly*, editors show up at the Academy Awards, hosting parties and providing online, televised, and magazine content. Because their brand is directly connected with the

The "I"s Have It (continued)

Oscars, connecting the magazine with the movie industry enhances the publication's image, increases its exposure to audiences beyond its core readership, provides extra service to readers, and provides an economic boost to the magazine through advertising support.

Hachette's Corporate Integrated Marketing, a department of Hachette Filipacchi Media U.S., created a 30-day series of events for advertiser JVC which involved *Premiere, American Photo, Popular Photography and Imaging, Sound and Vision, Home, Elle Decor,* and *For Me.* The events were held in June and July 2005 at the JVC Studio in midtown Manhattan and featured concerts, movie nights, how-to sessions about technology and photography, and demonstrations of new consumer electronics. Editors of the various magazines provided expert information for attendees.

Not all integrated media events are profit based. As a part of *Glamour*'s Love Your Heart campaign, the magazine introduced several products to benefit heart charities: Ralph Lauren Romance Tender Heart fragrance was made exclusively for the campaign, and 10 percent of retail sales at Macy's went to the charity WomenHeart. This was primarily an editorial, not an advertising, venture. ■

MARCH/APRIL 2006: One of the oldest custom magazines, *Endless Vacation* has been published for more than 20 years for Resort Condominiums International (RCI) vacation ownership exchange.

titles are being counted. Some agencies count only consumer magazines, others combine consumer and farm publications, some add newspapers and magazines together, while still others count only association publications. Some magazines aren't included in any lists. It's also difficult to get current lists, as many agencies wait until the end of the year to start counting, so that solid numbers for 2005 might not be available until 2007.

Look at how the following reference books and professional organizations counted magazines in 2005:

- *Ulrich's Periodicals Directory*: More than 186,100 publications worldwide
- *Standard Periodical Directory*: 26,669 U.S. and Canadian periodicals
- *National Directory of Magazines*: 21,266 U.S. and Canadian magazines
- *Magazines for Libraries*: More than 6,850 magazines

- *SRDS Business Publication Advertising Source*: More than 9,300 magazines
- *SRDS Consumer Magazine Advertising Source*: More than 2,700 magazines
- Custom Publishing Council: More than 115,000 custom magazines
- Magazine Publishers of America: 18,821 magazines, of which 7,188 are consumer publications

The memberships of professional media organizations also give a sense of the size of the industry. The MPA represents nearly 240 U.S. publishing companies with approximately 1,400 titles as well as more than 60 international companies. ABM serves 250 member companies with 2,000 member publications.[22] The American Society of Association Executives (ASAE) has more than 23,000 members.[23] A 1996 survey by the ASAE found that half of its members published a periodical.[24] The Society of National Association Publications

(SNAP) produces *Association Publishing*, which serves 1,400 editors, publishers, ad sales managers, circulation supervisors, designers, and production professionals at more than 750 associations.

Whole groups of magazines, however, fall through the cracks in these lists: most public relations magazines, many custom publications, magazines that do not accept advertising, many regional publications, and small or newly created magazines.

No accounting has been done of public relations magazines; estimates by scholars and researchers have ranged from 10,000 to 100,000. The Public Relations Society of America has nearly 20,000 members in 114 chapters. Many of them have editorial duties; others don't. Although magazines are important public relations vehicles, they are usually part of a larger communications strategy, and many organizations do not separate them discretely enough for them to be enumerated.

■ READERSHIP

The size and health of magazines is also determined by the number of people who buy them. Each particular magazine is measured by its circulation, which is the sum of the number of people who buy it on the newsstand and the number of people who buy it through a subscription. A magazine with newsstand sales of 60,000 per issue and with 40,000 subscribers has a circulation of 100,000. And this number, as we've already seen, is only the beginning of an analysis of readership. If that magazine has a pass-along readership of 3.2, it then has 320,000 readers. Table 1.1 offers a glimpse of the leaders in total circulation as well as in subscription and single copy sales. Note that the top five total circulation leaders are also the top five subscription leaders, indicating that strong subscription sales lend a solid boost to overall circulation. By contrast, most of the top magazines in single copy sales do not make the list of total circulation leaders, indicating that they are strong impulse purchases, or are bought for one specific article.

According to the Audit Bureau of Circulation (ABC), the total paid circulation of American magazines added up to 363 million in 2004. Circulation in the 5 years prior to that mirrored the economic seesaw of many American businesses, with circulation peaking at 379 million in 2000, dipping in the 3 subsequent years (361 million in 2001, 358 million in 2002, and 353 million in 2003), with a slight rebound in 2004. Looking at a 10-year span, circulation from 1994 rose steadily until 2000. In fact, total combined circulation in 2004 had just caught up to that of 1994.[25]

■ Table 1.1   Circulation Leaders: Top 10 American Magazines

RANK	PUBLICATION NAME	SUBSCRIPTIONS	SINGLE COPY	TOTAL
1	*AARP: The Magazine*	22,558,000	1,956	22,559,956
2	*Reader's Digest*	9,659,427	469,516	10,128,943
3	*TV Guide**	8,758,689	314,854	9,073,543
4	*Better Homes and Gardens*	7,414,303	219,867	7,634,170
5	*National Geographic*	5,273,053	158,064	5,431,117
6	*Good Housekeeping*	3,851,498	755,302	4,606,800
7	*Family Circle*	3,420,287	877,830	4,298,117
8	*Ladies' Home Journal*	3,837,910	293,333	4,131,243
9	*Time*	3,893,374	157,215	4,050,589
10	*Woman's Day*	3,213,748	801,644	4,015,392

Source: Magazine Publishers of America: http://www.magazine.org/Circulation/circulation_trends_and_magazine_handbook/13222.cfm. Figures from first 6 months of 2005.

*In July 2005, *TV Guide* cut its paid circulation to 4.5 million as part of a revision that included changing the magazine's format and distribution. That circulation might change its place in the top 10.

MAY 22–28, 2006: *TV Guide,* once primarily a program guide with enough regional editions to serve a national audience, eliminated its regional approach when it became an entertainment magazine in 2005.

emerging technology

Competition from television was probably the best thing that happened to the American magazine in the second half of the 20th century; it forced magazines to define themselves and to act on their strengths. Each new communications technology not only brings competition, it also brings the doomsday prophets, who declare the magazine all but dead. Television will kill magazines, they said in the 1950s. It didn't. Cable television will kill magazines, they said in the 1980s. It didn't. The CD-ROM will kill magazines, they said in the early 1990s. It didn't. The Internet will kill magazines, they said in the late 1990s. It hasn't.

Emerging technology, in fact, brings new audiences. As the computer came along, with bells and whistles to threaten magazines, what did the magazine industry do? Start more magazines about computers. The same thing is happening with the Internet and online technology, as demonstrated

by the success of *Wired* magazine, which grew in the era of dot-com growth in the late 1990s, survived when that bubble burst in 2000, and now maintains a healthy circulation of 586,000.

In today's world chock full of media, with competition from television, the Internet, blogs, and other rapidly emerging technology, how can magazines compete? Very well. Those magazines that recognize the inherent strengths of the medium, and use those strengths to fill readers' needs, will be those that survive any onslaught of media competition.

Successful magazines harness the power and energy of new media to supplement their publications and better serve their readers through interactive media and online business practices.

■ INTERACTIVE MEDIA

Digital magazines are important supplements to their print brethren. When Time, Inc., published *Sports Illustrated on Campus* in 2004, they first tested an online version because of the difficulty of reaching college students, especially those at universities without a campus newspaper. Now, the print version is published 26 times a year and the digital version is available through the Internet as well as by downloads. The company also sells a digital version of the *Sports Illustrated* swimsuit issue for $5.99, although the print magazine remains the company's primary focus.[26]

Many large magazine publishers have developed interactive media divisions that create online content as an extension of the print version of a magazine. Meredith Interactive Media creates Web content for Meredith Corporation's consumer magazines, including *Better Homes and Gardens, Ladies' Home Journal, Wood, Country Home, Traditional Home,* and *Midwest Living,* reaching 8 million users monthly and generating 72 million monthly page views.

The Media Industry Newsletter has signaled the importance of interactive, or new, media by printing regular "box scores" of page views of selected websites. In December 2004, ESPN, which publishes *ESPN: The Magazine,* had more than 1.7 billion page views, showing the combined might of magazines, television, and the Web.

The concept of interactive communication is nothing new to magazines. Cullen Murphy, managing editor of one of the country's oldest titles,

The Atlantic Monthly, said in 1996 that today's magazine professionals have the most solid understanding of what audiences want. He wrote on the magazine's site:

> . . . aren't today's publishers the most qualified people to step up to the potential, and the challenge, of interactivity? Of creating new special interest communities and new relationships between reader and expert? Or between reader and reader? The new medium demands organized, vital, up-to-date content. It demands authoritative points of view. The relationship between user and provider requires the very trust that readers bestow on a magazine brand or brands of their choice.[27]

■ ONLINE BUSINESS PRACTICES

In addition to being an important way to link with readers, the Internet also has enhanced the manner in which magazines do business. Online technologies have improved the way magazines communicate with one another, their suppliers, staff members, and freelancers.

The Internet has replaced or supplemented some of the traditional ways magazine staffs do business. Magazines use the Internet to check proofs, find clip art, search for staff members and freelancers, sell subscriptions, do research, and send and receive material. Magazine editors also run ideas past readers on the Internet, asking opinions on cover ideas, articles, redesigns, and magazine focus in general.

In recent decades, many magazines have reduced their full-time staffs to rely more on freelancers than they have in the past. Today's typical magazine freelancer needs a computer and mo-

dem connected to the Internet. She can write in Kermit, Texas, or Keokuk, Iowa, and find major library, government documents, and other research publications on the Internet. She can then sell her ideas, arrange a contract, and send her finished article to her editors electronically. If it snows in Kermit or Keokuk and she's stuck in the house, she can continue to go about her business, connected electronically to her library, publisher, and editor. Her editor in New York may be snowed in as well, but he'll still receive the article electronically and can edit or check facts at home.

What can we expect from magazines in this third millennium? Magazine professionals say, for the short run, we can look for more of the same. The electronic magazine will not replace the printed form. We can soak in the tub with our magazines, take them hiking in the mountains with us, sit down with a cup of tea and relax with them. That's a relationship the computer cannot match. The Internet, like the magazine, has become a storehouse. Furthermore, magazines have expanded into an electronic form. Their strength, however, continues to be in their printed and bound nature, in the comfort level a reader reaches when he settles down with his favorite magazine, puts his feet up, and reads. What Sam Ferber said of magazines in 1979 continues to be true:

> Magazines define who we are and where we fit into society. They delineate the problems with which we are faced and, when they are functioning at their best, provide the range of solutions that are open to us. They remind us that news, or information, is not necessarily understanding. They help us search for meaning in a complex, often bewildering world. Above all, they force us to take the time to reflect when life is moving all around us at a breakneck pace.[28]

notes

1. In 1990, a jury found *Soldier of Fortune* magazine liable for $12 million for publishing an ad: "GUN FOR HIRE: 37-year-old professional mercenary desires jobs. Vietnam veteran. Discreet and very private. Body guard, courier and other special skills. All jobs considered." A businessman used the ad to hire a person to kill his associate. The associate's sons sued successfully; the District Court judge noted that "the publisher could recognize the offer of criminal activity as readily as its readers obviously did." John D. Zelezny, *Communications Law, Liberties, Restraints and the Modern Media* (Belmont, Calif.: Wadsworth, 1993), 95.

2. "The News That Isn't Delivered Day and Night" (ad), *New Yorker* (January 24, 1983), 75.

3. *Black Enterprise Media Kit,* http://www .blackenterprise.com/AboutUsOpen.asp?Source= Aboutbe/15.htm.

 4. "Global Growth Forecast for the World's Magazine Markets," *Magazine World*, International Federation of the Periodical Press, http://www.fipp.com//1396.
 5. David Carr, "Romance, in *Cosmo* 's World, Is Translated in Many Ways," *New York Times* (May 26, 2003), http://ww.nytimes.com/2002/05/26/business/media/26cosm.
 6. *Modern Plastics Worldwide Market and Media Information 2005*, 6.
 7. "How the Economist Made a Million," *Magazine World*, no. 44, International Federation of Publication Publishers, http://www.fipp.com/1667.
 8. Marty Oetting, "Journalism as Commerce," *Service Journalism Dialogue* (November 1988), 5.
 9. Sam Ferber, "Magazines: The Medium of Enlightenment," *USA Today* (July 1979), 43–44.
10. Theodore Peterson, *Magazines in the Twentieth Century* (Urbana: University of Illinois Press, 1964), 442.
11. *The Magazine Handbook: A Comprehensive Guide for Advertisers, Advertising Agencies and Magazine Marketers 2005/06* (New York: Magazine Publishers of America, 2005), 5.
12. Ferber, 44.
13. "The News That Isn't Delivered Day and Night."
14. *Market Facts* (New York: American Business Press, 1996), 7–8.
15. "Top 100 Magazines by Circulation," *Advertising Age*, (December 31, 2004), http://www.adage.com/page.cms?pageId=1110.
16. *Business-to-Business Media Study Final Report*, prepared for American Business Media by Yankelovich Partners and Harris Interactive (October 4, 2001), 57.
17. Elissa Matulis Myers, "The Special Challenge of Association Periodicals Publishing," *A Guide to Periodicals Publishing for Associations*, ed. Frances Shuping (Washington, D.C.: American Society of Association Executives, 1995), vii-ix.
18. Kenneth E. Warner, Linda M Goldenhar, and Catherine G. McLaughlin, "Cigarette Advertising and Magazine Coverage of the Hazards of Smoking," *New England Journal of Medicine* (January 20, 1992), 305–9.
19. *The Blue Book* (New York: Public Relations Society of America, 1996), 10.
20. "In-house Custom Publishing," *Folio:* (February 2005), 45
21. "Custom Magazines Have a Bright Future" (December 2, 2004), http://www.custompublishingcouncil.com/article.php?id=282.
22. http://www.americanbusinessmedia.com/abm/Default.asp.
23. http://www.asaenet.org/asae/cda/index/1,1584,ETI17733_MEN3_NID4067,00.html.
24. *Policies and Procedures in Association Management*, 1996.
25. *The Magazine Handbook*,11.
26. "Supporting Role for Digital Magazines," *Folio:* (February 2005), 12.
27. http://www2.The Atlantic.com/Atlantic/home.htm.
28. Ferber, 43.

for additional reading

Abrahamson, David, ed. *The American Magazine: Research Perspectives and Prospects*. Ames: Iowa State University, 1995.

Click, J. William, and Russell N. Baird. *Magazine Editing and Production*. 6th ed. Madison, Wisc.: Brown and Benchmark, 1994.

Fidler, Roger. *Mediamorphosis: Understanding New Media*. Thousand Oaks, Calif.: Pine Forge Press, 1997.

Ford, James L. C. *Magazines for Millions*. Carbondale: Southern Illinois University Press, 1969.

Husni, Samir. *Samir Husni's Guide to New Consumer Magazines: 20th Anniversary Edition, 2005*. Oxford, Miss.: Nautilus Press, 2005.

Peterson, Theodore. *Magazines in the Twentieth Century*. Urbana: University of Illinois Press, 1964.

Riley, Sam G., ed. *Corporate Magazines of the United States*. New York: Greenwood Press, 1992.

Riley, Sam G., and Gary W. Selnow, eds. *Regional Interest Magazines of the United States*. New York: Greenwood Press, 1991.

Taft, William H. *American Magazines for the 1980s*. New York: Hastings House, 1982.

Wolseley, Roland E. *Understanding Magazines*. Ames: Iowa State University Press, 1965.

chapter 2

the magazine as a marketplace: the role of advertising

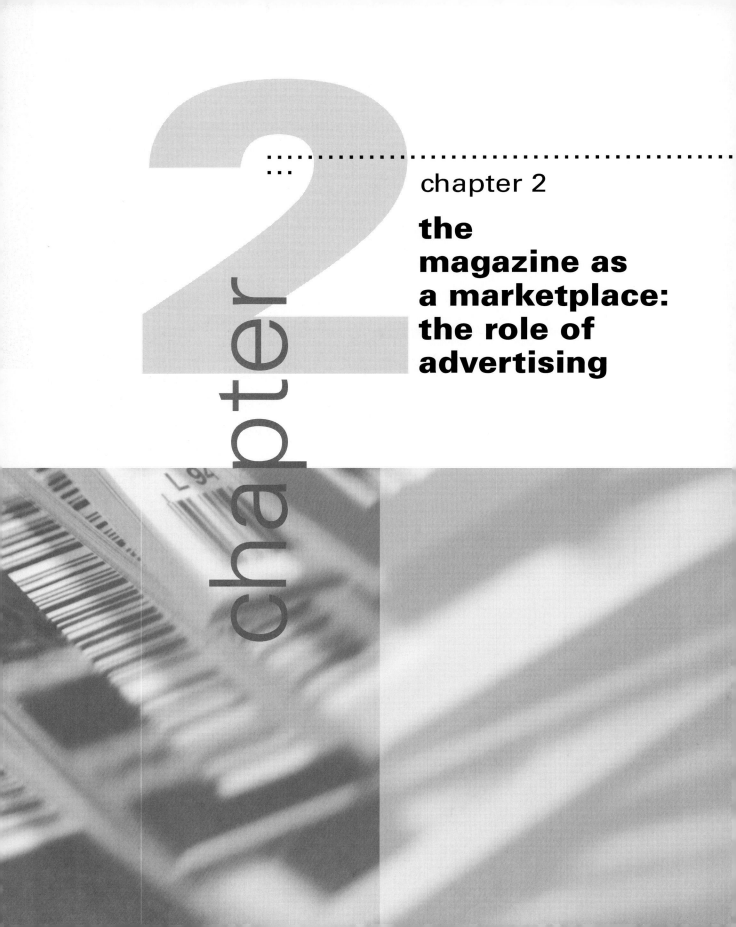

P ete Shepley had a hobby he loved—designing archery equipment. In the late 1970s, he began mass-producing his high-tech bows and turned to magazines for promotion. He advertised in such highly targeted titles as *Bowhunting World* and *Archery Business*. By 1982, he had moved his production out of the barn behind his Tucson, Arizona, home into a 75,000 square-foot plant. By the late 1980s, he had added 100,000 square feet and entered the world of big business. Shepley's hobby had become Precision Shooting Equipment, a leader in the multimillion-dollar bowhunting and archery industry. "Innovation and magazines have been the backbone of our 20 years of continued success," Shepley said in 1996.[1] ▦ Shepley's success hinged on producing a quality product promoted directly to the people who wanted it and could afford it. He chose magazines to reach his consumers because of the effectiveness of special interest titles in reaching a highly defined audience. ▦ As advertising vehicles, magazines are part of our marketing system. Advertising sales people talk about magazines as "buys" and view magazine audiences not just as readers, but as potential markets for their products. Publishers define a successful magazine as one that not only appeals to its audience of readers, but also develops a loyal base of readership that appeals to advertisers. ▦ Advertisers spent $22 billion in magazines in 2004.[2] Even though magazine circulation dipped and swayed in the early part of the 21st century, advertising revenue steadily increased, although at a far slower pace than in the 1990s, with some magazines being hit hard by the magazine recession of the early 2000s. For the first 9 months of 2004, consumer magazines saw a 10 percent increase and trade magazines saw a 1.5 percent increase from the same period the year before.[3]

Advertisers choose magazines because, simply, that's where they find consumers of their products, and advertising rates are determined by the specific characteristics of the magazine audience. Today's major advertisers are manufacturers and retailers of consumer goods such as automobiles and computers; media conglomerates and multi-title publishing houses are the leaders in advertising revenue. Historically, magazines became major players in the ad game when publishers discovered that advertising could help pay the bills, allowing them to lower the cost of the magazine to readers. Some magazine editors, publishers, and even marketers, however, worry about advertiser influence on the editorial product.

why advertisers choose magazines

Advertisers follow readers and, therefore, depend on magazines because of the credibility of the medium, the quality of the reader, and the quality of the product or brand.

JUNE 2006: By advertising in *Bowhunting World,* manufacturers of bows, arrows, and other archery equipment reach a unique and select audience.

■ CREDIBILITY

Advertisers are attracted to magazines because of their halo effect. Readers believe so strongly in their magazines and feel such a solid connection with them that they tend to trust the advertising they carry. A study by Media Choices found that 43 percent of adults ages 18 and over trust magazine advertising, putting it ahead of all other media and at the top of the credibility list. The corresponding figures for trust in advertising in other media are 32 percent for network television, 15 percent for cable television, and only 10 percent for Internet advertising. A Neopets Youth Study determined that teens are less trusting, but still find magazines more credible than other media: 29 percent say they trust magazine advertising. Corresponding figures for youths' trust in advertising in other media are 22 percent for television, 22 percent for radio, and 18 percent for the Internet.[4]

■ READER QUALITY

When advertisers buy space in magazines, they are buying the magazine's audience. In fact, you can

usually determine the characteristics of a magazine's audience just by looking at the ads. Luxury cars are advertised in those magazines that appeal to high-income consumers—*Saveur* or *Condé Nast Traveler*—while minivans are advertised in home and family titles—*Family Fun* or *Parenting.* Magazines appeal to advertisers because of their highly targeted audiences. In general, magazine readers have higher incomes and are better educated than users of other media; magazine audiences are ethnically diverse and show a higher level of commitment and response to editorial and advertising content. Advertising rates are determined by audience characteristics.

highly targeted

When advertisers buy placement in a magazine, they carefully study the readers' demographics and psychographics. Demographics include a precise definition of characteristics such as age, education, income levels, and geographic location. Psychographics include lifestyle issues such as how read-

What Do People Read in the Bathroom?

A study done in 1985 by Simmons Market Research found that one out of every three Americans reads in the bathroom. Based on a survey of 1,000 adults above the age of 18 years, Simmons found that women between the ages of 35 and 49 are "especially avid bathroom readers." Their magazine of choice was *True Story*, founded in 1919.

In rank order, here's what people said they preferred to read:

1. *True Story*
2. *Seventeen* (Simmons said that it "may be that a magazine is brought into the bathroom by a young woman or teenager and then read there by Mom or an older sister.")
3. *Time*
4. *Sport*
5. *Sports Illustrated*

tied {
6. *Money*
   Mother Earth News

8. *Sports Afield*

tied {
10. *Prevention*
   Cosmopolitan

Others listed: *Playboy*, *Popular Mechanics*, and *Reader's Digest*.

On a less scholarly note, blog discussions about bathroom reading in 2005 brought up this motley collection of favorites: *People, The New Yorker, US Weekly, In Touch, Entertainment Weekly*, and *The Nation*. ■

ers feel about classical music, whether they vote, and if they like to travel.

When the Lexus automobile was introduced, the advertising for the new car ran in *AutoWeek* magazine. The Lexus was a luxury car competing against established brands, and the advertising staff looked for the most efficient method of reaching consumers who tend to buy cars often and who have the income to afford a high sticker price. *AutoWeek* readers fit the bill: They owned an average of 4.7 vehicles and, in 1990 when Lexus was launched, earned an average income of $89,300. Equally important was the fact that *AutoWeek* readers are opinion leaders about automobiles, advising others on buying decisions. Richard Anderman, national advertising manager of Lexus, credited the magazine's weekly publication with spreading the news about the new car quickly, making it "an indispensable part of what

has proven to be one of the most successful launches in history."[5]

high income and education

Magazine readers are generally more educated and affluent than the average adult. Research by Mediamark Research, Inc. (MRI) shows that heavy magazine users are adults with college educations, professional or managerial jobs, household incomes above $73,000, and homes valued at nearly $250,000. By contrast, heavy television viewers are less likely to have graduated from college or have professional occupations; they have household incomes at $53,000, with homes worth slightly under $200,000. Magazines are also the medium of choice of "influentials," or those people to whom others go for advice on buying decisions.[6]

Harper's and *The Atlantic Monthly* appeal to an audience of avid readers interested in quality fiction and essays as well as analytical and in-depth nonfiction. Even though they're two of the country's oldest titles—both were started in the 1850s—in recent years their fortunes have been mixed because of a seemingly limited audience base. However, in 1994 both magazines began rebounding; it was the first time in decades that both were in the black. Both saw an increase in advertising and in subscription and newsstand sales. Analysts suggested that the magazines' editorial strength and emphasis on providing top-quality reading material were the keys to their newfound success. Both advertisers and readers rediscovered the magazines that had been around more than a century because both were creatively and effectively reaching the needs of their audience. The trend continues, with *The Atlantic Monthly* showing a 16 percent jump in advertising pages from 2003 to 2004,[7] even though circulation dropped 14 percent in the same time period, from 507,121 to 436,264. *Harper's* circulation is holding steady at around 217,000, which is a deliberately small and highly focused audience. The magazine is a nonprofit entity that now operates in the black, supporting itself with advertising and subscription revenues.[8]

Forty percent of all readers start a magazine at the back, and 67 percent start from some place other than the front of the book.

ethnically diverse

Magazines are naturally positioned to appeal to ethnically diverse readers. Black, Hispanic, and Asian titles serve a highly receptive audience that benefits from editorial content uniquely aimed at their needs and interests. The Selig Center for Economic Growth projects that by 2009 the buying power of these groups will balloon, with African Americans reaching $965 billion, Hispanic Americans reaching $992 billion, and Asian Americans reaching $528 billion.[9] The Magazine Publishers of America (MPA), noting the importance of this audience, has created a series of market profile booklets explaining demographics and psychographics of African American, Hispanic/Latino, and Asian magazine readers.

More than 100 magazines serve the African American audience,[10] including the largest, *Ebony*, with 1.7 million circulation, and *Essence*, with 1 million circulation, plus smaller titles like *Black Issues Book Review*, with 21,843 circulation. Eight out of 10 African American adults read magazines; those readers average 11.9 issues a month, compared with 9.1 issues a month for all U.S. adults.[11]

Hispanic adults represent a growing and increasingly affluent market—the number of Hispanic/Latinos with household incomes higher than $100,000 rose 126 percent from 1991 to 2000.[12] More than 70 percent of Hispanics read magazines, with those reading an average of nine issues a month.[13] This market is served by Spanish-language versions of top magazines—*People en Español*, with 454,265 circulation, and *Glamour en Español* at 72,151—and by specifically targeted titles such as *Hispanic Business* at 237,925 circulation and *Latina* at 353,721.

Almost 75 percent of Asian Americans read magazines, poring over eight issues a month. This is an affluent audience—readers average $62,782 household income a year, compared with the median for all U.S. magazine readers at $54,564.[14] This market is served by more than 120 magazines, including *Audrey*, at 10,000 circulation, and *Asian Week*, at 30,000. While the failure of two top titles, *A* and *Yolk*, initially called into question the viability of the Asian American market as a separate niche, most experts believe magazines for this group have a strong chance of success, especially with younger readers.

committed and responsive

Magazine readers keep their magazines and reread them, with the typical adult spending 45 minutes reading each issue.[15] Magazine readers remember what they read in their magazines—both ads and other specific information—better than newspaper readers remember what was in the newspaper or television viewers remember what they saw on television. Magazine readers are more likely to purchase products they read about in a magazine advertisement than they are products advertised on television. They also are more likely to make purchase decisions or act on information found in magazines than on television. Research done by Affinity Research VISTA Print Tracking Services found that 55 percent of readers took some action as a result of reading an article in a magazine, and 50 percent acted in response to a magazine ad. This included passing the article to a friend (24 percent), saving the article for future reference (23 percent), visiting the advertiser's website (12 percent), purchasing the product (7 percent), and saving the ad for future reference (5 percent).[16]

A study by Yankelovich Partners and Harris Interactive for American Business Media found that business executives are especially receptive to advertising in trade magazines. Fifty-five percent of executives cite business-to-business magazines as influencing or supporting their purchase decisions relating to business.[17]

■ PRODUCT

Magazines are essentially luxury items: Nobody really *needs* a magazine. Imagine living without your favorite title for a year. Chances are pretty good you'll survive. Yet even when you're trying to save pennies, it's still hard to resist that copy of *Entertainment Weekly* with Brad Pitt on the cover.

Most Americans—38 percent—buy their magazines at supermarkets. Increasingly, though, more readers are heading to mass merchandisers such as Wal-Mart and bookstores like Barnes and Noble.[18] Why do readers who are shopping for toothpaste leave the store with a copy of *Self* or *Motor Trend* tucked under their arm? Because of the appeal of the product. They see a cover line that interests them, leaf through the magazine and find an article they want to read, a photo that intrigues them, or a recipe they want to clip.

Advertisers know that readers are loyal to those titles that serve them well. A magazine's economic health hinges on the product. A quality product—be it a magazine or a pair of running shoes—attracts buyers. Conversely, without a quality product, sales eventually drop. In the case of magazines, without product sales, advertising income eventually drops.

Advertisers typically request a right-hand page at the front of the magazine when they can't afford the prime inside front, inside back, or back cover spots. But does it really matter? According to Readex Research, a right-hand page is just a teensy bit more effective—3 percent—than a left-hand page in terms of advertising recall and effectiveness. Being at the front of the book is only 2 percentage points better than being at the back. What does make a difference for ad effectiveness and recall is having a two-page spread and using color.

■ BRANDS

Marketers differentiate between products and brands. The product, they contend, is simply utilitarian, something the buyer values because of how usable it is. A brand, however, implies a specific product image, and means that the consumer has some sort of relationship with that brand. For example, you might go to Sears for your car battery because that's where your parents bought their car batteries. Similarly, you trust *Good Housekeeping* because you grew up with it.

A well-positioned and well-produced brand builds consumer loyalty and allows the creative publisher to create product extensions, or ancillary products.

■ ANCILLARY PRODUCTS

Magazines are increasing their profits by lending their names to related products, such as *Field and Stream* art prints, *Martha Stewart Living* house paint, *Maxim*'s male-oriented fashion bedding, *National Geographic* greeting cards, and *WorkBoat*'s annual International WorkBoat Show. Most of these products are marketing endeavors, created to expand the profitability and advertising reach of the

Confidence in the *Good Housekeeping* Seal of Approval

For advertisers, the strength of a magazine is determined by the degree of confidence readers have in the editorial product. No magazine has been more successful in gaining reader's trust than *Good Housekeeping*, which has operated in a climate of confidence that benefits both readers and advertisers since the turn of the 20th century.

The magazine was an early champion of reliable products for its homemaker readers, creating a *Good Housekeeping* Testing Institute in 1901 as a place to test foods and household products for purity. Then, in 1909, the magazine went a step further with the *Good Housekeeping* Seal of Approval. This was a guarantee that products advertised in the magazine had been "tested and approved by the *Good Housekeeping* Institute" for quality assurance.

Dr. Harvey W. Wiley, a chemist for the Department of Agriculture who spearheaded the passage of the landmark Pure Food and Drug Act of 1906, became the head of the *Good Housekeeping* Institute in 1912. Wiley quickly established the Seal's clout and integrity, making *Good Housekeeping* a trusted family friend to its readers. The Seal of Approval was explained to readers in the June 1919 issue:

> *Good Housekeeping* guarantees its advertisements. *Good Housekeeping* maintains laboratories where all good products are tested and all household appliances are tried out before they are admitted to our advertising pages. *Good Housekeeping* will not accept the advertisement of any kind of a product in which it does not have full confidence. *Good Housekeeping* will not knowingly advertise a good product for a wrong purpose.

Said Wiley upon his retirement in 1929, "*Good Housekeeping* has never advertised any articles unless approved by me. In 17 years more than a million dollars of advertising offered *Good Housekeeping* in my department has been rejected."[1]

The "Seal of Approval" was replaced in 1941 by a "Guaranty Seal" stating that *Good Housekeeping* would give readers a replacement or a refund of money if a product was "not as advertised therein." By 1975, the Seal's guarantee conditions became "A Limited Warranty to Consumers" with *Good Housekeeping*'s promise of "replacement or refund if defective." This change reflected 1975 federal law requirements regulating consumer warranties and guarantees.

The long-standing warranty on products was extended to 2 years from 1 year in 1997. According to publisher Patricia Haegele, the 2-year *Good Housekeeping* Seal warranty is advantageous for both consumers and advertisers. Pointing out that many companies already provide 1-year warranties for their products, Haegele says the 2-year *Good Housekeeping* Seal warranty "gives the consumer an advantage over what they are getting."[2] The Seal continues to provide for the replacement or refund of products that are defective. "No other magazine in the world offers this kind of service to its readers," stated *Good Housekeeping* in its 1997 advertising campaign about the 2-year warranty extension.

In 1999, recognizing that savvy consumers and readers were using the Internet for purchases, the magazine created another layer of review—this time for e-commerce sites. In order to receive the *Good Housekeeping* Website Certification, a site must have clearly defined financial security and privacy policies for credit card

1. Helen Woodward, *The Lady Persuaders* (New York: Ivan Obolensky, 1960): 128.

2. "*Good Housekeeping* to Boost Warranty on Advertised Products to Two Years," *The Wall Street Journal* (August 1, 1997): 12B.

Confidence in the *Good Housekeeping* Seal of Approval (continued)

usage, be easy to navigate, and state all charges, fees, taxes, return, and cancellation procedures up-front. Customer service information has to include the company's name, address, telephone number, and Web address. Of course, *Good Housekeeping* doesn't certify sites that are in bad taste or that sell questionable products. "We look at the overall integrity of the site and ask whether a *Good Housekeeping* reader is going to be happy there," says Sean Sullivan, the magazine's associate publisher.[3]

Unlike the traditional Seal, certification doesn't offer replacement or refund for defective products sold online—unless they separately qualify for Seal approval. "We are not warranty-ing the product. However, we do check the site's financial transaction security and make sure it's up to code. The Seal has always given consumers assurance to buy because we've checked it out," Sullivan says. "Now we're taking this to the next level, saying

it's okay to shop this site because we've checked it out."

It's obvious that the *Good Housekeeping* Seal is a potent advertising tool on several levels. An advertiser must purchase at least a page of advertising a year to be tested; in 2005, a full-page color ad cost $267,780. Products that don't meet the testing standards can't advertise in *Good Housekeeping*. According to a 1999 Roper Starch Worldwide Study, 7 out of 10 consumers surveyed said they were more likely to buy a product carrying the *Good Housekeeping* Seal than a similar product that didn't.[4]

Despite the fact that *Good Housekeeping* has refused products and uncovered misleading claims, ad sales have been enhanced rather than hurt by the Seal. As early as 1952, *Good Housekeeping* refused the lucrative cigarette advertising dollars accepted by other women's magazines. Consequently, it was free to publish such articles as "Can Your Husband's Cigarette Give You Cancer?" without worrying

about advertiser pressure. In an April 1983 letter to the editor, one reader praised *Good Housekeeping* for its refusal to publish cigarette ads, noting that in other women's magazines as much as 12 percent of the ad pages featured cigarettes. Yet in 1983, *Good Housekeeping* was number one among the women's service magazines in both ad volume and revenue with 2,097 ad pages and $127.2 million in ad sales.[5]

Even in the volatile advertising climate of the early 21st century, *Good Housekeeping* has held its own in ad pages while many of its sister women's magazines have lost ground. Publisher's Information Bureau figures put *Good Housekeeping*'s ad pages in 2004 almost even with 2003—down a slight 1 percent. In comparison, *Redbook* lost nearly 12 percent in the same period. *Good Housekeeping* also continues to be one of the top 10 magazines in circulation year after year. ■

3. Jennifer Owens, "*Good Housekeeping* Unveils Web Site Review Program," *Adweek* (May 29, 2000): 68.

4. "Expedia.com Earns *Good Housekeeping* Website Certification Seal" (press release, September 23, 2003), Expedia.com, http://press.expedia.com/index.php?s=awards.

5. *Folio: 400/1984* (October 1984): 329.

original brand, often referred to as the franchise. These extensions are based on the belief that a magazine name, like other brand names, can be franchised, or leased for use on related goods or services.

On its May 1951 cover, *McCall's* introduced its Betsy McCall paper doll. For 40 years, the maga-

zine carried stories about Betsy, accompanied by the cutout doll and new clothes. In 1957, the three-dimensional Betsy debuted. The newest incarnation, however, is for grown-up baby boomers—it's a $75 artist-designed collector's doll. Even though *McCall's* died in 2001, when it was replaced by the short-lived *Rosie*, the allure of the doll lives: In 2005, an original 1957 version was for sale on eBay for $275.

Magazines have traditionally published related books, with the *Better Homes and Gardens New Cook Book*—which started as a premium for subscribing to the magazine—being perhaps the most famous. According to Meredith president and CEO Stephen M. Lacy, for every dollar the company earns from *Better Homes and Gardens* magazine, it earns another dollar from products carrying the *Better Homes* name. Other magazine-related books include such diverse titles as *Oscar Night: 75 Years of Hollywood Parties,* from the editors of *Vanity Fair,* and *Good Things (The Best of Martha Stewart Living).*

The president of Hearst Publishing's magazine division, Cathleen Black, expects editors to consider product extensions a part of their jobs. "Being a magazine editor," she said in 1997, "is more than just literally producing a magazine."[19] Hearst magazines offer a panoply of related products such as *Popular Mechanics for Kids* videos and an interactive asset allocation and investment planning tool from *SmartMoney.*

Trade shows and professional seminars are an increasingly popular ancillary product for business-to-business magazines. *Folio: The Magazine for Magazine Management* sponsors the *Folio:* Show, a conference and exposition held yearly in New York, Chicago, and Los Angeles.

Some publishers see electronic media as essential product extensions, especially for business-to-business magazines. Bob MacArthur, vice president of Primedia Business Magazines and Media, said in 2005 that e-newsletters, virtual trade shows, Internet news blasts, and webiners are the key to economic success for trade magazines and an important way into the readers' and advertisers' hearts. "This is not a matter of cannibalizing readers or content," he said. "Electronic media should be seen as an ancillary product for print, not a replacement."[20]

National Geographic has expanded into television documentaries on its own channel in addition to creating road maps, travel atlases, and national park guides to be sold in retail outlets. Former *National Geographic* publisher Gil Grosvenor, whose family held the reins at the National Geographic Society for five generations, warned that successful branding requires caution. Speaking in 1997, a year after retiring, he said, "Image takes a long time to develop, in our case, 108 years. But images can be destroyed overnight. They are very fragile."[21]

■ ADVERTISING RATES

Advertising rates are based on the size of the magazine audience—its total circulation—and the specific demographics and psychographics of that audience. A magazine with a highly desirable audience that can't be reached easily by other magazines or other media can ask higher rates than a magazine that appeals to audiences easily reached by other media. Food advertisers can reach the American family through television, radio, newspapers, and a variety of magazines, so ad rates for family magazines have to reflect that competitive environment. Manufacturers of commercial boats, however, can reach professional fishermen through only a handful of trade publications, which can therefore ask premium ad rates.

Advertisers determine the actual cost of a magazine ad based on costs per thousand readers, or CPMs, which help them determine the relative value of a magazine ad. The CPM is the cost of the ad divided by the audience delivered, or circulation, divided by one thousand. Advertising professionals use the formula in "CPM: The Little Number with the Big Job."

Calculating the CPM provides basic data, but that gives only a number, not a clear understanding of the overall value of the audience. As the CPM equations demonstrate, *Glamour*'s CPM is more than $40 less than *Marie Claire*'s, so *Marie Claire* must justify this higher rate, which they do by defining their more focused, albeit smaller,

In May 2005, *Men's Journal* ran a special issue on the "100 Greatest Adventures of All Time," including trips to the tropics. One key advertiser: Malarone, an antimalarial drug.

CPM: The Little Number with the Big Job

You are at the grocery store shopping for garbanzo beans. You see a 10-ounce can selling for 65 cents, a 12-ounce can for 78 cents, and an 8-ounce jar for 72 cents. Which is the best deal? Grocers now usually provide a unit cost to help you decide. The 10-ounce and 12-ounce cans sell for the same per ounce—6.5 cents—but the 8-ounce jar is a bit pricier, at 9 cents an ounce. So the cans are cheaper per ounce than the jar.

CPMs operate on the same principle. A CPM is the cost of one unit of advertising. Rather than being an ounce, in the case of the garbanzos, that unit is 1,000 readers. Using CPMs, advertisers can compare the actual cost of reaching 1,000 readers of magazine A versus the cost of reaching 1,000 readers of magazine B.

The term CPM often confuses newcomers, and even some oldcomers. Why is the term not CPT, many ask, if the unit is thousands rather than millions? Because the "M" is the Roman numeral for 1,000. Yes, that is slightly nerdy, but now you can brag that you can talk the language of the ancient Romans—or at least one letter of it.

Publishers and advertisers use the following formula to calculate a CPM:

$$\frac{\text{Total Ad Cost}}{\text{Total Circulation} \div 1,000} = \text{CPM}$$

If an ad costs $10,000 a page for a magazine with 100,000 circulation, the CPM is $100; an ad that costs $100,000 a page in a magazine with 1 million circulation also has a CPM of $100:

$$\frac{\$10,000}{100,000 \div 1,000} = \$100$$

$$\frac{\$100,000}{1,000,000 \div 1,000} = \$100$$

Let's use the formula on two actual magazines, *Glamour* and *Marie Claire*.

Glamour's circulation is 2,397,000, and the cost for a full-page, full-color ad in the magazine is $135,535. Remember that we are dealing with cost per thousand, so we divide the circulation (2,397,000) by 1,000, which gives us 2,397, which is one-thousandth of the total circulation. This is the "M" part of the equation. (Quick hint: Rather than dividing by 1,000, simply lop off the last three digits of the circulation number [2,397,000] and you'll have one-thousandth of the circulation.)

To find the "CP," or the "cost per," figure, we take the advertising rate ($135,535) and divide it by the "M" (2,397).

So, $135,535 divided by 2,397 equals $56.54. *Voila!* This gives us a cost per thousand, or CPM, of $56.54.

The equation form of this is

$$\frac{\$135,535}{2,397,000 \div 1,000} = \$56.54$$

Now, let's compare *Glamour* with a competitor, *Marie Claire*. *Marie Claire* has a circulation of 941,148 and a full-page full-color ad rate of $92,465. We follow the formula:

$$\frac{\$92,465}{941,148 \div 1,000} = \$98.25$$

Marie Claire, then, has a CPM of $98.25.

So, while the one page in *Glamour* is more expensive, at $135,535, compared with *Marie Claire*'s one page cost of $92,465, *Glamour*'s unit cost (remember the garbanzo beans) at $56.54 is a better deal. Why, then, would an advertiser choose a magazine that is so much more expensive per reader? Because *Marie Claire* has a much smaller, but a much better defined audience, giving the advertiser a more precisely defined reader. In much the same way, you might choose to buy the more expensive garbanzo beans because you trust the brand—or would rather have a jar than a can. ◾

readership. Like *Marie Claire*, all magazines must position themselves in such a way that the advertiser sees the depth and breadth of their audience—and they must provide convincing data to support their case.

Publishers increasingly are being asked to provide additional information on and insight into audiences, essentially doing research that was once the responsibility of the advertiser. This happened because of the complexity of the American consumer, heightened competition for advertising pages, and increased dependency on advertising income.

The person who makes $100,000 a year, lives in Texas, and reads *The Atlantic Monthly* is usually a far different beast from the person with the same income and zip code who reads *Spin*. Advertisers want to completely understand the difference so they can spend their advertising dollars—often hundreds of thousands of dollars for a single ad—wooing the right reader. In 2002, Volkswagen went so far as to ask major magazines to provide a perspective of what kind of road trip a typical reader would take if she had a VW Beetle. *National Geographic Adventure, Spin, Blender, GQ, Newsweek,* and *Gourmet* all responded in various ways, from creating videos to personally meeting with the advertisers and sketching a reader's profile.[22]

One clever publisher of a magazine for horse owners calculated a unique audience statistic—cost per horse. Her readers owned an average of eight horses while the competition could boast readers with a measly three. So she determined the cost per horse, marketed that figure, and beat the competition to the finish line.[23]

who advertises in magazines?

The biggest magazine advertisers are automotive manufacturers, who contributed $2.4 billion to the consumer magazine economy in 2004. They were followed by toiletries and cosmetics at $1.92 billion; drugs and remedies at $1.79 billion; apparel and accessories at $1.78 billion; and home furnishings and supplies at $1.73 billion.[24]

The top individual magazine advertisers are large, multinational corporations (see Table 2.1).

■ **Table 2.1** Top Advertisers in 2004 and Their Spending*

Procter and Gamble Co.	$619,724,219
General Motors Corp.	$476,961,423
Altria Group, Inc.	$419,246,045
Ford Motor Co.	$369,360,913
DaimlerChrysler AG	$350,495,367
L'Oreal USA	$328,622,522
Time Warner	$316,095,980
Johnson and Johnson	$305,895,235
Pfizer, Inc.	$243,307,608
Toyota Motor Corp.	$241,472,965

* *The Magazine Handbook*, 22.

The top advertiser, Procter and Gamble, manufactures and distributes household, personal care, food, and coffee products such as Ivory Soap, Crest, Crisco, Charmin, Swiffer, Pampers, and Folgers, and now also distributes prescription drugs such as Asocal, for ulcerative colitis. General Motors, the number two advertiser, dominates transportation on the highways, railways, and skyways by owning Buick, Cadillac, Chevrolet, Hummer, Pontiac, and Saturn, and by producing aircraft engines as well as railroad locomotives and engines. Altria Group, number three, owns Kraft Foods (Maxwell House, Kool-Aid, Ritz crackers, and Post Honey Bunches of Oats) and Philip Morris (Marlboro, Virginia Slims, and English Ovals).

where they advertise

Today's magazine industry is also controlled by large corporations—media conglomerates or multi-title publishing houses. Not surprisingly, these magazine corporations are the leaders in advertising pages and income. At the top is Time Warner, a major publisher of weekly magazines—*People, Sports Illustrated, Entertainment Weekly,* and *Time.* Weeklies can earn more yearly advertising income than other titles because of the frequency with which they are published; they lead in the total number of pages published and, so it follows, they lead in advertising pages and advertis-

■ **Table 2.2** Top Five Publishers in Advertising Pages*

PUBLISHER	REPRESENTATIVE TITLES	2005 AD PAGES
Time, Inc.	*Time, People, Sports Illustrated, Entertainment Weekly, Real Simple*	51 million
Condé Nast	*The New Yorker, Gourmet, Glamour, GQ, Vanity Fair*	25 million
Hearst Corporation	*Cosmopolitan, ESPN, Esquire, Harper's Bazaar*	20 million
Hachette Filipacchi	*Road and Track, Elle, Metropolitan Home, Premiere*	16 million
Meredith Corporation	*Better Homes and Gardens, Ladies' Home Journal, Parents, Successful Farming*	14 million

*Group Publisher's Report January-December 2005/2004 (New York: TNS Media Inteligence, 2006), 2.

ing income. The top companies in advertising pages are shown in Table 2.2.

Advertising revenue translates into a tidy sum for individual titles. The top 10 U.S. magazines in ad revenues in 2004 brought in a combined $5.9 billion, or an average of $590 million per magazine. The newsweeklies were bolstered in 2004 by the presidential election and the second Gulf War, both of which brought increased readership and, therefore, increased advertising. The totals in advertising revenue were, in millions:[25]

People	$898
Sports Illustrated	$806
Better Homes and Gardens	$793
Time	$749
Newsweek	$540
Good Housekeeping	$500
TV Guide	$486
Business Week	$407
Woman's Day	$387
In Style	$364

the birth of advertising in magazines

The first ad in an American magazine appeared the same year the magazine medium appeared in this country: 1741. On May 10 of that year, Richard Brett, deputy postmaster at the Potomac River, ran an ad in Benjamin Franklin's *General Magazine, and Historical Chronicle, For All the British Plantations in America*, for a ferry across the Potomac from Annapolis to Williamsburg.[26] It was small and unobtrusive, typical of advertis-

ing at that time. The earliest American magazines had little or no advertising. What ads appeared were hidden in the back of the magazine. Most were for almanacs or books, and their design resembled that of contemporary classified advertising. Before 1860, the typical business-to-business magazine had only 25 percent advertising, compared with an average of 60 percent today.[27] All this changed during the industrial revolution at the turn of the 20th century that brought mass production, mass distribution, and the potential for mass audiences.

Up to that time, Americans generally bought from people they knew—cheese from the farmer down the road and wool from the mill on the edge of town. When they did shop in retail stores, the goods they purchased were usually locally made and fresh. They bought one pickle at a time from the pickle barrel and a hunk of cheese from the farm in the next county. Few prepackaged goods existed.

Mass production and the growth of the railroads changed all this, starting in the late 1880s. America developed a national, rather than local, economy. The mill in Massachusetts could mass produce and mail its woolens to customers in Wisconsin. The farmer in Wisconsin could send his cheese to Massachusetts. How, though, were producers to educate potential buyers about the quality of their products? How would the buyer be able to differentiate among different cheeses and woolens? Enter the concept of brand names. In 1900, only 1,721 trademarks were registered by the United States Patent Office.[28] Twenty years later that had increased to 10,282. No longer was cheese just cheese—it was a Kraft product. Those woolens were made into scarves sold at newly created retail chains such as F.W. Woolworth or JC Penney.

Magazine Numbers: Who's Counting?

The accuracy of circulation numbers for magazines published before 1914 depended on the integrity of the publisher. There was no system to check the numbers, so a publisher could tell advertisers his magazine reached 100,000 readers and the advertiser would have no way to verify that claim. The Audit Bureau of Circulations (ABC) was created to remedy this problem. Founded by publishers, advertisers, wholesalers, and retailers in 1914, its goal is to issue and verify standardized statements of circulation. Data provided by ABC are now used by agencies that report on magazine statistics.

BPA International was founded in 1931 as Controlled Circulation Audit to audit magazines with less than 70 percent paid circulation. It changed its name to Business Publication Audit of Circulation in 1954 and now audits consumer as well as specialized business magazines.

Standard Rate and Data Service (SRDS) publishes guidebooks that list the consumer and business magazines that carry advertising: *SRDS Consumer Magazine Advertising Source* and *SRDS Business Magazine Advertising Source*. Both books provide a magazine's editorial profile as well as statistics on magazine ad rates, circulation, discounts, and special editions.

Mediamark Research, Inc. (MRI) offers a precise analysis of magazine readers, breaking them into categories such as age, income, time spent reading, and occupations. MRI publishes reports twice a year, based on thousands of personal interviews. Its primary focus is on magazines, although its scope is multimedia. MRI provides estimates of audiences of major consumer publications by demographics and product usage characteristics. MRI also publishes annual studies of business-purchase decision makers, the affluent market, and the top 10 local markets. These provide estimates of demography, magazine readership, audience usage of other media, and marketing behavior. Because MRI is a resource for advertisers, it studies only magazines that carry advertising.

Simmons Market Research Bureau publishes *Study of Media and Markets,* an annual report similar to MRI's. Simmons profiles magazine readership by demography and purchase behaviors through personal interviews. The Publishers Information Bureau (PIB), a division of the MPA, provides analyses of revenue and expenses of major American magazines.

Much of this data is now published online. ■

Mass production and distribution also made the mass circulation magazine possible. Beginning at the turn of the 20th century and continuing until the 1960s, magazines were characterized by huge circulations going to general audiences. Larger circulations could be produced cheaper and distributed farther than in any time in American magazine history. As the only national medium, magazines were the logical conduit for information on brand differences.

Still, some publishers were reluctant to jump on the advertising bandwagon, preferring to keep their magazines unsullied by advertising. Occasionally the issue was more pragmatic than philosophical. At the turn of the 20th century, *Harper's* refused $18,000 for an ad for Howe sewing machines on their back cover because they wanted that space reserved to advertise their own books.[29]

Frank Munsey, though, jumped right in. In the 1890s, Munsey, publisher and editor of *Munsey's* magazine, opened his pages to advertisers at the same time he boosted circulation and distribution. He reached a high volume of readers, which made his magazine appealing to a high volume of advertisers. The amount the advertisers paid for their ads allowed Munsey to reduce the price of his magazine from 35 cents to 10 cents. The low cost made the magazine more affordable to the less affluent, which increased circulation even more. The first 10-cent issue of *Munsey's*, in October 1893, had a 40,000 circulation. By 1895, it had reached 500,000.[30]

Contemporaries didn't look upon Munsey kindly, calling him a magazine "manufacturer" rather than a publisher. Munsey charged a flat CPM of $1. Other magazines printed a set rate, but often gave advertisers a reduction for a variety of reasons. This practice, called rate dealing, had roots in the infancy of magazine advertising. The editor of *The Druggist*, writing in 1859, accused *Druggists' Circular* of accepting "half to two-thirds its published rates."[31] Rate dealing was the precursor to today's practice of "selling off the card," or offering rates lower than those published.

Once Munsey opened the door to advertising, however, other publishers moved right on in, and advertising in magazines has been a given ever since. In 1900 alone, *Harper's* carried more advertising than in its entire preceding 22 years combined.[32]

Magazine advertising income and circulation increased throughout the early years of the 20th century, sometimes with awesome speed. Consider the examples for the *Saturday Evening Post* in Table 2.3.

The April 1929 issue of *Scribner's*, a literary monthly, included ads, all either in the front or the back of the book, for

- Williams Ice-O-Matic Refrigeration: "Always Icy Cold, Never Merely Cool"
- Ciné-Kodak: "Simplest of Home Movie Cameras"
- Union Pacific, offering rail access to "Bryce Canyon, Our Newest National Park"
- Listerine antiseptic, advertised as a shampoo to rid the hair of dandruff
- Burleson Sanitarium, "An Ethical Institution Devoted Exclusively to the Treatment of All Rectal Diseases—EXCEPT CANCER"
- Lucky Strike cigarettes, illustrated with a young flapper, with the ad copy reading: "I'm a 'Lucky Girl' because I've found a new way to keep my

■ **Table 2.3** Advertising Income and Circulation for the *Saturday Evening Post**

YEAR	AVERAGE CIRCULATION	AVERAGE ADVERTISING INCOME
1902	314,671	$360,125
1912	1,920,550	$7,114,581
1922	2,187,024	$28,278,755

* *Group Publisher's Report January-December 2005/2004* (New York: TNS Media Intelligence, 2006), 12.

figure trim. Whenever the desire for a sweet tempts me, I light up a Lucky Strike."

Most advertising in *Scribner's* was for expensive products, illustrating the magazine's affluent target audience. The majority of magazines in the first half of the 20th century, however, were less precisely targeted. Most were huge mass circulation vehicles, going to mass audiences. They were oversized—common cover dimensions were 10 by 12 inches—and fat with editorial content and advertising. The December 7, 1929, issue of the *Saturday Evening Post* was so ad-heavy it weighed nearly 2 pounds. Merchants bought copies of the magazine to use as wrapping paper because it was cheaper than a roll of paper. Many magazine publishers felt they had moved into something of an economic nirvana, with advertising providing a huge new source of income.

Most magazines kept roughly an average 60:40 advertising-to-editorial ratio, which translated into hundreds of ad pages a month for top sellers. For example:

- *Saturday Evening Post*: The October 9, 1954, issue sold for 15 cents and had 152 total pages, with 92 of those in ads, for a 60:40 advertising:editorial ratio.
- *Life*: The October 11, 1954, issue sold for 20 cents and had a total of 196 pages, with 114 of those in ads, for a 58:42 ratio.
- *Look*: The October 4, 1955, issue sold for 15 cents and had 122 total pages, with 66 of those being filled with ads, for a 54:46 ratio.

In 1954, the circulation leaders were general interest magazines with wide appeal. Table 2.4 illustrates how their 1954 and 2004 circulations

■ **Table 2.4**   1954 and 2004 Circulation Figures for General Interest Magazines

MAGAZINE	1954 CIRCULATION*	2004 CIRCULATION†	PERCENTAGE CHANGE
Reader's Digest	11,353,823	10,155,054	(−11%)
Life	5,311,747	not published in 2004	
Ladies' Home Journal	4,869,174	4,114,353	(−15%)
McCall's	4,446,146	no longer published	
Woman's Home Companion	4,315,147	no longer published	
Saturday Evening Post	4,216,017	352,929	(−92%)
Look	3,717,859	not published in 2004	

*Harry Hansen, ed., *The World Almanac Book of Facts, 1954* (New York: World Telegram and Sun, 1954).

†"Top 200 Magazines by Circulation," December 31,2004. *Advertising Age* (June 18, 2005), http://www.adage.com/page.cms?pageId=1110.

compare. Of the top seven magazines in 1954, only three still existed 50 years later—*Reader's Digest, Ladies' Home Journal,* and *Saturday Evening Post.* All of the three remaining titles lost circulation in the half-century span. *Reader's Di-* *gest* dipped 11 percent and *Ladies' Home Journal* dropped 15 percent. The current *Saturday Evening Post* is less than one-tenth the size of its 1954 counterpart. Both *Life* and *Look* were once again revived in 2005, *Life* as a weekly newspaper

NOVEMBER 23, 1936 (Premiere Issue): *Life* magazine celebrated its own beginning with the photo of the birth of a baby, with the caption, "Life Begins."

supplement with a 12 million circulation, and *Look* as a monthly movie magazine, with one test issue in 2005 and a planned 2006 launch. Both are published by Time, Inc. Once competitors, both are now under the same roof.

The fortunes of these magazines were tied to a startling change in the media marketplace beginning in the 1950s. With the advent of television, magazines lost their place as this country's only national medium. Advertisers flocked to television in the 1950s and 1960s because it reached more people than magazines and offered immediacy, drama, and emotion.

By the 1970s, magazines had re-created themselves into smaller, more efficient, and more effective advertising vehicles by positioning themselves as the medium for the specialized audience. Gone were the 2-pound ad-fat bullies. In their place were the streamlined and specialized titles that characterize the industry today.

A study of *Life* provides an intriguing picture of magazines immediately before and after television. Like *Look*, it was a picture magazine, created to take advantage of the newly refined photographic technology. It predated television and did in print what television did in video—showed America pictures of itself.

Life was America's first picture magazine and was published weekly at a cover price of 10 cents. The weekly magazine premiered on November 23, 1936, with a cover photo of Fort Peck Dam in Montana. The first editorial picture inside the magazine was symbolic: a full-page photo of an obstetrician slapping a baby to life, with the headline, "Life Begins." That issue sold out, and customers bought secondhand copies for as much as $1. Within weeks, the magazine was selling a million copies an issue.

Life was founded in 1936 by Henry Luce, who bought the name from a humor magazine. Luce had been highly successful with the launch of *Time* and *Fortune* magazines, and critics wondered why he would bother with a new start-up, instead of resting on his laurels. His excitement for the new magazine, however, was supported—some say initiated—by his wife Clare Booth Luce, and

Research in Brief

Magazine-Made America

One of the most fascinating eras in magazine history came after World War II, when America's culture and economy were transformed by technology and social change. Professor David Abrahamson of Northwestern University charts this change in his book, *Magazine-Made America: The Cultural Transformation of the Postwar Periodical*.

Magazines published immediately after the war, Abrahamson writes, mirrored prewar publications aimed at general audiences and presenting general interest content. By the early 1970s, however, many of America's premier magazines had died: *Collier's*, *Liberty*, and *Woman's Home Companion*. Others faltered: *Life*, *Look*, and *Saturday Evening Post*. According to Abrahamson, "Three principal causes led to these failures: television, mismanagement by publishing companies, and, as a less obvious but important undercurrent, an inability on the part of some of the publications to respond to fundamental sociocultural changes."[1]

Television lured many readers and advertisers away from

1. David Abrahamson, *Magazine-Made America: The Cultural Transformation of the Postwar Periodical* (Cresskill, N.J.: Hampton Press, 1996), 19.

(continued)

Magazine-Made America (continued)

magazines with its promise of more immediate and exciting news and entertainment. However, Abrahamson argues, management decisions made the situation worse. Publishers responded to television competition by trying to increase circulation, even to the extent of exaggerating pass-along readership. In addition, instead of selling advertisers on the quality of their readers, publishers promoted simple numbers, and increased ad rates to boot. So, while advertisers were hesitating about the appeal of magazines in comparison to television, publishers gave them added ammunition: They raised prices so that magazine advertising became increasingly less competitive than television advertising.

Abrahamson provides insight into advertisers' reaction to this dilemma. Wanting to help out magazines in the late 1960s,

General Foods conducted a survey of reader reaction to television and to magazines. The results showed that readers were as likely to respond to magazine advertising as to television. As a result, General Foods, eventually joined by other advertisers, required that all ad buys include magazines. Abrahamson quotes General Foods' executive Archa Knowlton: "We wanted magazines to be able to compete against this monster that was devouring them."[2]

Many of the magazines that faltered or died, though, simply lost sight of their relationships with their audiences and with the changes in those audiences. Social researchers, notes Abrahamson, characterize the 1960s as a time of new attitudes and rules, and "the social and cultural values inherent in, for example, a Norman Rockwell [Saturday

DECEMBER 8, 1934: *Collier's*, a general interest magazine that didn't survive the advent of television, had a robust circulation of more than 2.4 million in the 1930s.

Evening] Post cover, *Liberty's* 'reading times,' or another starlet pictorial in *Life* seemed clearly out of step with the times."[3] ■

2. Ibid., 21.

3. Ibid., 24.

was evident in a memo he sent to staffers 4 months after the first issue: "*Life* has a bias. *Life* is in favor of the human race, and is hopeful. *Life* is quicker to point with pride than to view with alarm."[33]

Life became one of America's most popular and best-read magazines by offering exclusive and timely coverage of the important moments in America's life, advertising itself as being "the showbook of the world." Its photographs often mesmerized a world not yet accustomed to live, breaking news, and they remain some of the best

photographic work ever published of World War II, the Vietnam conflict, and the civil rights movement, as well as the everyday lives of the impoverished as well as the powerful. In 1959, *Life* offered eyewitness stories of the first seven American astronauts; in 1961, it ran a special edition on the inauguration of the young president John F. Kennedy; and in 1963, it ran another special edition on his death. All were printed in the 10.5 × 13.5 inch format that gave photographs plenty of room.

Advertisers loved the magazine because Americans loved it. That relationship began to change in the late 1950s. *Life* continued publishing its impressive photography, but by this time other photographers were on the scene—those with television cameras. The photos *Life* ran were characteristically engaging, but the country had already seen many of the images on live television: John Kennedy, Jr. saluting his father's coffin and the eternal flame being lit at Arlington National Cemetery. In 1969, *Life* published some of the first shots of the moon, but, once again, most Americans had stayed up late to watch the moon walk live on television. Television got to the consumer first.

The magazine continued to grow, however, continuing to believe in the prevalent pretelevision mentality that bigger was better. By 1969, *Life* had a circulation of 8.5 million, and a full-page color ad cost $64,000, which was more than the cost of 1 minute on prime-time television.[34]

In 1972, *Life* ceased publication, a victim not only of television but of high production and postal rates that punished large circulation magazines; the oversized format not only used more paper, but was heavier and, therefore, more expensive to mail. Staff members also argued that the magazine was hurt by poor management and an unwillingness to change content to suit changing times. Whatever the cause of death, few advertisers mourned the magazine's passing; instead, they rode off into the sunset with the Cartright family in *Bonanza*, gambled on *Maverick*, and took heavenly flight with the *Flying Nun*. Food advertisers especially were lured to the new, more colorful and emotional medium that could reach consumers right before dinnertime, when their stomachs were the most susceptible to the television ads' messages.

The passing of *Life* magazine was like a death in the family to its staff. The last issue had one small word printed under the dateline and price: "Goodbye."

This emotion was behind the relaunching of the magazine 6 years later, in October 1978. The new *Life*, once again published by Time/Life, Inc., once again emphasized photography. This time, however, it was a monthly, with a cover price of $1.50, an initial run of only 700,000, and a target circulation of only 2 million—a fourth of its previous size. Ad rates also were quartered, with a full-color page selling for $13,900.

Advertisers in that first "new" issue covered the economic gamut, and included Mercedes-Benz, Lincoln-Mercury, Polaroid, Kmart, and McDonald's, indicating the broad range of the readers. Advertisers were eventually won over by a return of quality photography—this time matched with a smaller, more precise audience of avid readers with above-average education and income—and with significantly lower ad rates. By 1995, a full-page color ad cost $54,600, almost $10,000 less than 20 years before.

That new version of *Life*, while a slim version of its 1960s incarnation, remained a general interest publication, an anomaly in a world of niche titles. With its more affordable rates and more clearly defined audience, it was initially viewed as a good buy by advertisers. *Life* continued as a monthly until 2000, when publication once again ceased. Reports of its death, however, were perhaps premature. Five years later, in 2005, it was revived as a weekly, this time as an insert in 70 news-

> **What magazine is the "hottie" in terms of performance in the advertising marketplace? That accolade belongs to *Vanity Fair* for being on *Adweek*'s Hot List nine times, the most of any magazine in the list's 25-year history. When the list debuted in 1980, selecting the hottest 10 magazines meant looking for those with the biggest increase in ad pages over the previous year. Now *Adweek* gauges advertising performance in terms of pages and dollars by tracking titles over a 3-year period. Publishers Information Bureau category performance figures and circulation also come into play, with media directors weighing in on the amount of media buzz.**

Ms. Magazine: It Just Feels Like Journalism

This is an excerpt from a speech Robin Morgan gave at Drake University in April 1992, when she was editor-in-chief of *Ms.*

Ms. was born in 1972, founded by a group of women including Pat Carbine and Gloria Steinem, who had been active in the magazine world. It never occurred to that first group to try the magazine without advertising because they wanted very much to create a mainstream feminist magazine.

They convinced Clay Felker, at that time owner and publisher of *New York* magazine, to print a small premiere issue of *Ms.* inside of an issue of *New York* magazine. Since *New York* magazine took ads, *Ms.* took ads. That pilot issue was an amazing success, and a year later the full-fledged magazine itself was born. The first issue sold out overnight and they went back to press and it sold out again overnight, and then it was off and running. Clearly it never lacked for readers, and for the next 18 years it would never lack for readers. But then there was the advertising problem.

In 1980, I did an exclusive interview with four Soviet feminist dissidents who had been forced out of the Soviet Union into exile for having published an underground feminist journal. They were all in their late twenties and early thirties. We ran it as a cover story, and it won three journalistic awards. Well, Revlon got upset because the four women on the cover—who had these terrific,

wonderful, strong faces—weren't wearing makeup, and they pulled their ads, and they never came back.

In addition, there was the whole idea of selling the advertising community that feminists were people, that feminists in fact liked children, often had children, often were married people, or some wished to be or some had been, or some might be again, that feminists in fact did not live on air, but often ate things and frequently cooked the things that they ate, that feminists were able to do more than boil water, that feminists drove cars sometimes, that feminists had stereo sets—you name it. The sales force at *Ms.* really educated the advertising world. Some of those saleswomen went on to become quite extraordinary, such as Cathy Black (now president of Hearst Publishing's magazine division).

Ms. was the first to demand that ads be integrated. It was the first magazine to demand, and in many cases to be able to get, advertisers to explore mixed race ads. Same in terms of age. They had a number of remarkable triumphs.

I remember one case in particular. There was a new woman in the *Ms.* ad department, and she'd finally got this account—a liquor manufacturer who had just put forth a new

line of canned, ready-mixed drinks called the Club Line. And then the make-ready (pre-press proof) came in and we're riffling through the magazine saying "Oh this turned out nice, this turned out nice," and I see this ad for the first time, and on the surface of it, it looks like a terrific ad. It shows a gray-haired woman in coveralls, and she's clearly doing some sort of construction work—she's got nails sticking out of the coverall pocket and a hammer in one hand and her hair is kind of tussled. She has one of these cans in her hand and she's tossing it up, and that's all terrific. But the legend emblazoned across the top is "Hit me again, hit me with a Club."

Somehow we had missed seeing the actual ad. The last we heard was that the account had come in but the ad had gotten somehow directly to the art department and had gone off to the printer. We called the printer, but we couldn't pull the ad. We quickly devised a blow-in card, but it was too late to put it in. There was nothing to be done.

So we stopped up our ears and waited, and the letters came. Mailbags of letters. We sent them all over to the advertising agency, and by the next issue we were able to run not only an apology from the magazine, but also an apology from

Ms. Magazine: It Just Feels Like Journalism (continued)

the liquor manufacturer, who had taken the entire account away from the agency. It was around a $2 million account.

What gave that original founding group apoplexy over those 20 years was that fight to get the advertising community to take women as consumers seriously, and then to get them to honor the line that supposedly exists between editorial and advertising because the other women's magazines were not trying that hard anymore, erosion having tired them all out. To make a long story short, by 1987, although again the readers had never flagged, the magazine was tired of the fight with advertisers.

By late 1987, the original group sold the magazine to Fairfax Limited, an Australian-based multimagazine corporation. They were well-meaning, good people with, I think, a profound ignorance of the U.S. women's movement and the assumption that if they could only make *Ms.* jazzy and corporate and appeal to the high-level ranking corporate woman—who of course was off there reading the *Wall Street Journal* —that all would be well. The magazine at first had an enormous amount of capital, for *Ms.*, and at first its subscriptions and its circulation shot way up, close to 500,000, the highest it had ever been.

However, once the first issues were published, readers tired of it very fast, and adver-

tisers still didn't come on board. The curse was still there. The myth of feminism, the stench of feminism was still hovering over this magazine even though you would not necessarily have known it from reading its pages: fashion coverage, a wine column, and an amazing piece on why liposuction was a feminist act. I have a very inclusive vision of feminism, but that one was a stretch for me.

For the first time, the magazine was in trouble with advertisers *and* with readers, and the figures plummeted. I'm beginning to sound like the "Perils of Pauline," but it was like that there for a while. So, while *Ms.* was lying bound on the railroad tracks going, "Ohhh, ohhhh, ohhhh," Lang Communications bought it in 1989. Dale Lang thought he would be acquiring a good subscriber's list for his other magazines, *Working Mother* and *Working Woman*. Lang suspended *Ms.* from the October 1989 issue on because he didn't know what to do with it. It really did seem as if *Ms.*'s time had come and gone, and maybe the most graceful thing to do would be for it to fold its tent and go away.

When the October issue didn't appear, readers started writing. Hundreds of thousands of letters came in to Lang saying, "We want our *Ms.* It's a feminist institution." Well, that really startled all of

Lang Communications, and then at the same point some of the old original group mustered themselves and dusted themselves off and came back in and said, "All right, what if we were to resurrect it as a newsletter? What if we were to resurrect it as a quarterly journal?"

I was asked to come on as editor-in-chief. I made what I thought was a perfectly safe list of absolutely outrageous demands that would permit me to go on with my book writing and my organizing and my traveling and real life. I said, "I will come back this time and run the magazine, but on the following grounds: It must be completely free of all advertising. It must be editorially autonomous from Lang Communications"—in other words, no one at Lang sees this magazine until it's in the mail to subscribers. I want to make it international; I want to have a minimum of six pages of international news in each issue plus at least one major feature. I want to do in-depth investigative journalism, and I want to name names (because now I could if I didn't have advertisers). I want to bring back world-class fiction and poetry. I would suggest not a quarterly but six issues a year, but each to be a double issue of 100 pages of solid copy and art. Those are my terms." To my absolute horror, they met them, and I have not had a chance to wash my hair since.

(continued)

Ms. Magazine: It Just Feels Like Journalism (continued)

That was in December 1989, and my hair is now very dirty. I still have clothes at the cleaners; I haven't had a chance to pick them up.

And *Ms.* is more commercially successful than all the years when it took advertising. As of July 1991, we were already at 200,000 subscribers, and we sell an average of 50,000 to 70,000 copies on newsstands. We are upping the print run on every issue. When this first liberated *Ms.*

came out in July 1990, history repeated itself. We printed a first run of 60,000, and it sold out overnight. We went back to press and we doubled the print run, and it sold out overnight. So then the second issue sold out within 4 days, and the third issue did, and then we began upping the print run. We have virtually 100 percent pay-up on subscriptions, and we were well on our way and self-supporting by the second issue.

The quality of writers and artists that we've been able to publish is the source of my deepest pride. It's a very simple recipe, ultimately. When you have freedom of the press, you get the best damned writers and artists you can. You respect them, and you respect your readers, and then you sit back and shut up and let them talk to each other.

And I have to tell you it feels like journalism. ■

---

papers nationally, with a total circulation of 12 million. This puts the magazine in a unique position of regaining its circulation and advertising strength, but only by piggybacking on newspapers. In general, the place once held by *Life*, as a stand-alone magazine circulation and advertising leader, is now held by specialized titles.

advertising-editorial conflicts

The picture of advertising in American magazines is not all rosy, though. There's another side of this coin. Some of the most contentious conflicts in the magazine publishing world have erupted between the advertising sales staff, with its emphasis on serving the needs of advertisers, and the editorial staff, with its emphasis on serving the needs of readers. Most magazines and advertisers walk this line responsibly, recognizing that what advertisers want are loyal readers, because a quality magazine that serves readers also serves advertisers.

Michael Browner, former head of marketing for General Motors and consultant for American Media, in explaining his advertising strategy in 2004, said the key was to "produce a great magazine with an attractive audience."[35]

Occasionally, though, the line between advertising and editorial blurs when advertisers expect to influence editorial content. The road to profitability can be paved with challenging requests from advertisers: prenotification, complementary copy, or placement adjacent to specific articles. Sometimes an advertiser sponsors an entire issue. Occasionally, an advertiser may request cover treatment, a situation that creates all sorts of difficulties for editors concerned about the magazine's integrity.

■ CLEAR AD-EDIT DISTINCTION

Most magazines separate their advertising and editorial staffs, with the editorial staff planning and developing the magazine, then giving the sales people the information they need to sell the magazine. If a runners' magazine is planning a special series on buying running shoes, for example, the editorial staff does the planning for the issue. The editors, in turn, give information on the series to the advertising sales people, who can then increase efforts to get advertising from shoe manufacturers. The division is clear: The magazine's content is determined by the editors. Magazine staffs often plan editorial content more than a year in advance and give advertisers—as part of a media kit—an editorial calendar, which lists major stories and themes for an entire year's issues. In that way, advertising follows—and supplements—editorial content.

In 2004, Hewlett-Packard bought ad spreads in nearly 30 magazines as part of its award-winning "You + H-P" campaign. They wanted to go one step farther and provide magazine photographers with H-P digital cameras. "Magazine editors said 'no' because of the editorial/advertising separation issues," said Dong Kim, associate media director at Goodby Silverstein and Partners, the Hewlett-Packard advertising agency. "Plus, they didn't feel their readers would appreciate paying for editorial already sponsored by advertisers."[36]

James McGraw, a trade magazine pioneer and one of the founders of McGraw-Hill, believed a quality magazine was one that reported aggressively and did not depend on "write ups from advertisers." A business publication, he wrote in *Electrical World* in 1924, should not be influenced by advertisers, but must "be its own master" and "have no other guides for its opinions and policies but truth and the sound interests of the field it serves."[37]

Alvaro Saralegui, general manager of *Sports Illustrated* in 1997, offered a simple formula: "The way we all believe it works is, you put out a great magazine, you get terrific readers and that will attract great advertisers."[38]

Not so simple, said some major advertisers in 1997. Titleist and Foot-Joy Worldwide canceled nearly $1.5 million in ads in *Sports Illustrated's Golf Plus* supplement in reaction to an April 7, 1997, story on the Nabisco Dinah Shore golf tournament in Palm Springs. The tournament had become, according to the magazine, a "spring break" for some 20,000 lesbians. Wally Uihlein, chairman and chief executive officer of Titleist and Foot-Joy Worldwide, the largest advertiser in *Golf Plus*, called the story "symptomatic of a condescending attitude toward women in golf in general." Managing editor Bill Colson suggested Uihlein respond in a readers' column in the magazine. Uihlein did, but also canceled the ads.

More and more publishers talk about partnerships between magazines and advertisers, contending that blurring the line between advertising and editorial is beneficial to both sides. A magazine that does not make money, they say, does not last. As part of its 50th anniversary celebration of the "*Fortune* 100," *Fortune* magazine partnered with Grey Goose vodka, which created a special *Fortune* martini tied to a customized ad in the anniversary edition.

■ ADVERTISER PRENOTIFICATION

One of the world's largest advertising agencies went a step beyond all this and required prior notice from magazines that plan to publish controversial content. PentaCom, Chrysler Corporation's advertising agency, sent more than 100 magazines a letter in January 1996, which stated:

> In an effort to avoid potential conflicts, it is required that Chrysler Corporation be alerted in advance of any and all editorial content that encompasses sexual, political, social issues or any editorial that might be construed as provocative or offensive. Each and every issue that carries Chrysler advertising requires a written summary outlining major theme/articles appearing in upcoming issues. These summaries are to be forwarded to PentaCom prior to closing in order to give Chrysler ample time to review and reschedule if desired.[39]

This request went far beyond the type of broad content overview offered in editorial calendars and was a blatant effort at censorship by advertisers, who didn't want to know just *what* magazines were covering, but wanted instead to know *how* it was being covered. Colgate-Palmolive provided guidelines to its advertising agencies requiring them to avoid magazine issues with "offensive" sexual content or material the company "considers antisocial or in bad taste," and the Ford Motor Company pulled ads from *The New Yorker* when that magazine didn't tell it about an article containing a four-letter word. *The New Yorker* responded by devising a system to warn some 50 "sensitive advertisers" that the magazine was planning potentially offensive content.[40]

The American Society of Magazine Editors (ASME) responded to the controversy with a position statement issued June 23, 1997:

> The ASME board of directors is deeply concerned about this early-warning trend. Specifically, the ASME board worries that some advertisers may mistake an early warning as an open invitation to pressure the publisher or editor to alter, or even kill, the article in question. We believe publishers should—and will—refuse to bow to such pressure. Furthermore, we believe editors should—and will—follow ASME's explicit principle of editorial independence, which at its core states: "The chief editor of any magazine must have final authority over the editorial content, words and pictures, that appear in the publication."[41]

ASME and the MPA issued a joint statement urging members to refuse to "submit table of contents, text or photos from upcoming issues to advertisers for prior review."[42]

Chrysler responded to the ASME and MPA criticism by backing off from requiring prior review, at the same time suggesting they would place less advertising in magazines. Chrysler spokesman Michael Aberlich said the company responded to industry criticism: "We've said before that if the industry acted together we would abide by it." Nevertheless, he added, Chrysler would "become a lot more conservative" about choosing magazines.[43]

■ COMPLEMENTARY EDITORIAL

Some advertisers believe that if they place an ad in a magazine they deserve a positive mention in the magazine's editorial sections. Gloria Steinem painted a bleak picture of advertiser influence on women's magazines in "Sex, Lies and Advertising," published in 1990 in the first ad-free issue of *Ms.* Manufacturers of food, beauty, and fashion products, she said, expect a "supportive editorial atmosphere" that includes "articles that praise food/fashion/beauty subjects to 'support' and

'complement' food/fashion/beauty ads." Steinem listed the food products the magazine tried unsuccessfully to woo: General Mills, Pillsbury, Carnation, Del Monte, Dole, Kraft, Stouffer, Hormel, Nabisco. *Ms.*, however, ran no recipes, so these advertisers refused to see the magazine as a legitimate advertising buy, even though the readers clearly ate food. *Ms.* was fighting deeply held advertising industry beliefs of the relationship between the editorial and advertising in a women's magazine:

> Food advertisers have always demanded that women's magazines publish recipes and articles on entertaining (preferably ones that name their products) in return for their ads; clothing advertisers expect to be surrounded by fashion spreads (especially ones that credit their designers); and shampoo, fragrance, and beauty products in general usually insist on positive editorial

APRIL 2006: One of the first magalogs to hit the newsstands, *Cargo* appealed to the trendy metrosexual male. In 2006 it became one of the first of the shopping magazines to cease publication.

coverage of beauty subjects, plus photo credits besides.[44]

Complementary editorial is an issue affecting all magazines at one time or another. *Consumers Digest* has been criticized by competitor *Consumer Reports* for ignoring the separation between editorial and advertising. *Consumers Digest*—not associated with *Consumer Reports* in any way—offers a "Best Buy" rating, mimicking *Consumer Reports*' rating of the same name. A *Consumers Digest* "Best Buy" often goes to products advertised within the magazine. The Dodge Neon, for example, not recommended by *Consumer Reports*, earned a "*Consumers Digest* Best Buy." Buyers who don't read closely will mistake that for a "*Consumer Reports* Best Buy," which has to be earned through scientific testing. *Consumer Reports* has trademarked its rating as a "CR Best Buy," but the confusion remains.[45] The primary issue is, of course, whether the rating comes along with an advertising buy.

Women's magazines take advertising placement for granted, and even consider it reader service, telling us what type of blush to use and what shoes to buy. Other magazines have also tested the placement waters—in 2003, *People* ran a piece on Broadway actor Daniel Sunjata, who did a nude scene in the play, *Take Me Out*. To make his body look great in the altogether, the magazine noted, "He uses Oceanus shower gel from the Body Shop."[46] Magalogs like *Domino* are designed completely as shopping vehicles, so advertising placement is a natural for them.

The images of more than 9,000 advertising items and publications dating from 1850 to 1920 can be found on Duke University's Digital Scriptorium website at http://scriptorium.lib.duke .edu/eaa. Titled "Emergence of Advertising in America," the collection covers the roots of the consumer culture, as well as the development of the advertising industry.

■ ADJACENCIES

Occasionally an ad appears next to an article about the product: A window manufacturer ad-vertises its new porch windows right next to an article on the resurgence of porches. Sometimes the editor did not know that the manufacturer would be promoting porch-related products and is honestly chagrined when the ad comes in. If it comes early enough, it can be moved to a less obvious page, or the editorial content can be changed. If it comes in late, though, the editor is stuck.

Sometimes editors suspect that the ad sales representative knew about the content in advance, which is why the ad is late. In that case, the problem happens only once, if the editor and publisher are committed to editorial integrity.

Betsy Carter, former vice president of ASME, agrees that adjacencies are far more common than critics suggest. "Look at fashion magazines or beauty magazines or the women's magazines. It happens all the time," she said in 1997.[47]

Not all adjacencies are the advertiser's idea—and not all advertisers are pleased when placed within certain editorial content. In 2004, *Outside* ran a special Guilty Pleasures issue, which included a feature on "*El Diablo* Made Me Do It," which was peppered with uncharacteristic and explicit—for *Outside*—photographs of women and sexual innuendoes. Advertiser Patagonia objected. Rick Ridgeway, the company's vice president of marketing and environmental initiatives, wrote a letter, which *Outside* published, saying Patagonia was "deeply offended" by the placement of their ad in the feature. "In fact, we're speechless to see ourselves between images of a Hummer on one side and a jet ski on the other, not to mention the babe in each shot," he wrote. "Of course, we didn't have anything to do with either the article or the ad placement, but not all our customers who read *Outside* will know that."[48] *Outside* missed the boat with many readers as well, who wrote to complain that this was not the type of content they wanted from their magazine.

■ ENTIRE ISSUE SPONSORSHIP

Single-advertiser magazine issues have been around for years. *Newsweek* produced a special issue about children in 1996 in which the only advertiser was Johnson and Johnson, and *Time* produced special issues in 1991 and 1996 on heroes in medicine and the frontiers of medicine, respectively, that had pharmaceutical giant and advertising leader Glaxo-Wellcome as the sole advertiser. Chrysler sponsored a special *Time* issue on multiculturalism in 1993.

The New Yorker's August 22, 2005, issue was sponsored entirely by Target Stores and included *New Yorker*-style artwork in the department store's ads, plus a cover with red-and-white beach balls that was a thematic match for the store's target icons. *Chicago Sun-Times* columnist Lewis Lazare lambasted the issue, calling it "the most jaw-dropping collapse of the so-called sacred wall between editorial and advertising in modern magazine history." Lazare also criticized ASME for not responding quickly and vigorously. In response, ASME ultimately issued a statement noting that "our guidelines do call for a publisher's note to readers in single-advertiser issues, and *The New Yorker* has agreed to include such a note when and if they do this again." The magazine remains eligible for National Magazine Awards (NMA), which are awarded through ASME and are the industry's highest honors. Magazines that violate ASME standards have typically been barred from the awards. *The New Yorker* is typically a top NMA winner.[49]

However, advertising and editorial priorities got especially mixed in 1999 when *Time* decided to schedule a sole advertiser for a regularly scheduled—as opposed to additional—issue of the magazine. The first regular issue of *Time* in 1999, with "The Future of Medicine" as its cover story,

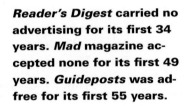

***Reader's Digest* carried no advertising for its first 34 years. *Mad* magazine accepted none for its first 49 years. *Guideposts* was ad-free for its first 55 years.**

had one advertiser: Pfizer, the pharmaceutical giant. That was a first in the magazine industry. While few magazine editors or critics believed that Pfizer shaped the editorial content of the issue, they were troubled about what may be a trend toward having big advertisers sponsor magazine issues on topics of interest to them.

A different spin on the advertising-editorial relationship occurred in 1976 when an advertiser tried to underwrite a series of magazine articles, much as is done in television, where a sole advertiser may sponsor a television program. But the brouhaha that occurred was so loud that only one underwritten article appeared.

The Xerox Corporation paid for a story written by Pulitzer Prize-winning author Harrison Salisbury in the February 1976 issue of *Esquire*. Although *Esquire* selected the author and the topic, Xerox paid Salisbury $40,000 plus $15,000 in expenses to write "Travels through America," a thoughtful essay run in conjunction with the bicentennial fervor sweeping the country. Although Xerox had no editorial control over the article, *Esquire* reaped a 1-year, $115,000 advertising deal from Xerox. Author and essayist E. B. White criticized the arrangement, saying the project was "charting a clear course for the erosion of the free press in America."[50]

■ ADVERTISERS ON THE COVER

The cover of a magazine has traditionally been sacrosanct—"no-ads-allowed" territory. In fact, ASME Guidelines for Advertising Pages and Special Advertising Sections (see page 360) specifically note that cover ads are a violation of ethical principles. Most editors and publishers have no problem toeing this line. "Your cover is your trademark and you shouldn't mess with it," said Oliver Comyn, *The Economist*'s vice president of advertising for North America, in 2003, noting that *The Economist* had not run an ad on its cover in 160 years, "and I don't think we would do it for the next 160."[51]

Comyn was responding to a controversy over a *U.S. News and World Report* cover that had an unusual slash-shaped gatefold containing an ad for the drug Levitra. Technically, the ad did not appear right on the cover, but the magazine was pushing the rules because, with the page open, the drug's logo was right next to the magazine's logo.

Atoosa Rubenstein, editor-in-chief of *Seventeen*, decided to flout the rules completely on the grounds that they should not apply to her magazine. In March 2005, she ran a cover with a sunburst promoting several advertisers: "Hot Bargains! PacSun, American Eagle Outfitters, Forever 21, Old Navy." ASME complained, but Rubenstein did not budge. Instead, she let her ASME membership lapse. *Seventeen* issued a formal statement in response to ASME's complaint: "One of the reasons girls read *Seventeen* is to learn about fashion bargains from today's hottest stores. If what we are doing is a violation of ASME's guidelines, perhaps it is time to reconsider whether they are still relevant and appropriate for all magazines, or if they should be revised for certain categories due to a heightened interest in shopping-related information."[52]

Interestingly enough, the ploy did not even please advertisers that much. Carol Apkarian, vice president of marketing for PacSun, said, "Editorial exposure in a magazine is always something we ask for, but it is not a major decision maker as to whether we go in the magazine."[53]

The matter is not always clear-cut, however. Advertisers regularly provide the props for specialized consumer and trade magazine covers—such as appliances or home products for shelter magazines; CDs for music magazines; clothing for fashion magazines—with the brand names of some products clearly visible. As long as the products used serve the magazine's editorial and design purpose and the advertiser does not pay for placement, most editors see this as serving both the readers and advertisers. Critics, however, see this as being dangerously close to the ethical line.

Some trade magazines offer advertisers special promotions or placement on their covers, believing that advertising is important information for their audiences. Even the media journal *Editor and Publisher* offers regular advertisers special cover options such as stickers and wrappers. *Broadcasting and Cable* sells various "false" covers that either wrap over the actual cover—and include the magazine's logo—or swing out as gatefolds. The magazine does follow ASME guidelines in requiring the word "Advertisement" to appear horizontally at the top of the cover.

responsibility to the reader

Advertising is a bottom line issue, and the bottom line in magazines is the reader. If readers are being served, the magazine is a great vehicle for advertisers. But if readers' needs are considered secondary to advertiser expectations, the magazine is abdicating its responsibility to both groups.

Many readers see no problems with the current state of magazine advertising. A study by Roper Public Affairs found magazine advertising the least interruptive of all media, with only 28 percent of respondents saying advertising gets in the way of their enjoying a magazine. Respondents were less positive about the other media's intrusiveness—with 62 percent saying television advertising was intrusive, 51 percent saying the same for radio, and 49 percent for the Internet. Research by Dynamic Logic found only 8 percent of readers had a negative view of magazine advertising, with 30 percent saying the same for the Web and 19 percent for television.[54]

Wise magazine editors and publishers remember that readers trust in their magazines because they believe in the editorial independence of those in charge. When a magazine loses that independence by agreeing to unreasonable advertising requests, the magazine loses its readers.

Undue advertiser influence not only hurts the magazine, it hurts the advertiser, according to many industry professionals. Readers will desert a magazine that appears to cater too much to advertisers, said *Newsweek* editor and ASME president Mark Whitaker in 2005:

> The reader has to believe that the publication is being edited for the reader, not the advertiser. They're looking for the editor's judgment—when they're not getting it, they'll look elsewhere.[55]

notes

1. *52 More Magazine Success Stories* (New York: Magazine Publishers Association, 1996), 75.
2. "All Media Advertising Expenditures," Mediamark Research Institute, http://www.mriplus.com/cgibin/WebObjects/mriplus.woa/10/wo/pQqdC0ZgE5JzM51QG3GUXw/3.0.37.
3. "U.S. Advertising Expenditures Increase from 2004 Level," *Marketing Today*, http://marketingtoday.com/research/1204/first_9_months_2004.htm.
4. *The Magazine Handbook: A Comprehensive Guide for Advertisers, Advertising Agencies and Consumer Magazine Marketers 2005/06* (New York: Magazine Publishers of America, 2005), 29.
5. *52 More Magazine Success Stories*, 63.
6. *The Magazine Handbook*, 37.
7. "MIN's Weekly Boxscores," *Media Industry Newsletter* (February 14, 2005): 8.
8. Robert Manning, "*Harper's* Magazine: A Survivor," The Nieman Foundation for Journalism at Harvard University, http://www.nieman.harvard.edu/reports/00-3NRfall/Harper's-Magazine.html.
9. Lorrie Freifeld, "Who Is Your Customer?" *License!* (June 2005): 1.
10. "African-American/Black Magazine Readers," in *African-American Market Profile* (New York: Magazine Publishers of America, 2004), 10.
11. Ibid.,12.
12. "Hispanic/Latino Consumer Profile: Young and Increasingly Affluent," in *Hispanic/Latino Market Profile* (New York: Magazine Publishers of America, 2004), 10.
13. Ibid.,12.
14. "Asian-American Magazine Readers," in *Asian-American Market Profiles* (New York: Magazine Publishers of America, 2004), 12.
15. *The Magazine Handbook*, 5.
16. *The Magazine Handbook*, 34.
17. *Business-to-Business Media Study Final Report*, prepared for American Business Media by Yankelovich Partners and Harris Interactive (October 4, 2001), 14.
18. *Magazine Handbook*, 15.
19. Constance L. Hays, "Magazine Chief Shakes Things up at Hearst," *The New York Times* (June 2, 1997): 9.
20. "Flat But Growing" (State of the Industry Panel Discussion, American Society of Business Press Editors, Kansas City Chapter, Overland Park, Kans.), http://www.asbpe.org/chapters/chapter_mtg_recaps_2005/chapkc_02232005.htm.
21. Constance L. Hays, "Seeing Green in a Yellow Border," *The New York Times* (August 3, 1997): 13.
22. Craig Lindsay, "Lights! Camera! Research!" *Folio:* (July 2002): 22.
23. Helen Berman, "Turn Data into Selling Points," *Folio:* (September 15, 2000): 18.
24. *The Magazine Handbook*, 21.
25. "All Media Advertising Expenditures."
26. Frank Luther Mott, *A History of American Magazines, 1744–1850*, vol. 1 (Cambridge, Mass.: Harvard University Press, 1939), 34–35.
27. David Forsyth and Warren Berger, "Trading Places," *Folio:* (March 1991): 85.
28. Theodore Peterson, *Magazines in the Twentieth Century* (Urbana: University of Illinois Press, 1964), 5.
29. Ibid., 21.
30. Ibid., 9–10.
31. Forsyth and Berger, 88.
32. Peterson, 22.
33. Loudon Wainwright, *The Great American Magazine: An Inside History of* Life (New York: Alfred A. Knopf, 1986), 92–93.
34. Betsey Carter, "As Big as *Life*," *Newsweek* (October 2, 1978): 83.
35. "Browner in High Gear as He Shifts from GM to American Media," *MIN's Advertising Report* (April 2004): 2.
36. "H-P Casts Wide Net," *MIN's Advertising Report* (April 2004): 1.
37. Roger Burlingame, *Endless Frontiers: The Story of McGraw-Hill* (New York: McGraw-Hill, 1959), 122.
38. Constance L. Hays, "Titleist Withdraws Advertising in Dispute with *Sports Illustrated*," *The New York Times* (April 28, 1997): D10.
39. G. Bruce Knecht, "Magazine Advertisers Demand Prior Notice of 'Offensive' Articles," *The Wall Street Journal* (April 30, 1997): A1.
40. Ibid., A1.
41. "ASME Expresses Deep Concern about Advertiser 'Early Warnings,'" (news release, June 23, 1997).
42. Bruce Knecht, "Chrysler Drops Its Demand for Early Look at Magazines, *The Wall Street Journal* (October 15,1997): B1.
43. Ibid., B1.
44. Gloria Steinem, "Sex, Lies and Advertising," *Ms.* (July/August 1990): 19.
45. Rhoda Karpatkin, "What's a Best Buy?" *Consumer Reports* (July 1996): 5.
46. Simon Dumenco, "Make it Stop!" *Folio:* (October 1, 2003), http://foliomagarticle.asp?magazinearticleid=184047&magazineid=125&siteID=@&releaseis=11651.
47. Jeff Garigliano, "*Notorious* Lives Up to Its Name," *Folio:* (October 1, 1997): 20.
48. "Letters," *Outside* (December 2004): 22.
49. Nat Ives, "ASME Scolds *New Yorker* for Target Issue," *Advertising Age* (September 13, 2005), http://www.adage.com/news.cms?newsId=46051.
50. "25 Good Ideas—and a Few Really Bad Ones," *Folio:* (April 1, 1997): 48.
51. Jeff Bercovici, "Is That an Ad on the *U.S. News* Cover?" *Folio:* (October 20, 2003), http://foliomag/newsarticle.asp?Newsarticleid=2699773&SiteID=2&magazineid.
52. "Teen Mag Mash Up," *YPulse.com* (March 4, 2005), http://ypulse/archives/2005/03/teen_mag_mash_u.php.
53. Ibid.
54. *The Magazine Handbook*, 26.
55. "Product Placement's Latest Cameo," *Folio:* (January 2005): 15.

for additional reading

Abrahamson, David. *Magazine-Made America: The Cultural Transformation of the Postwar Periodical.* Cresskill, N.J., Hampton Press, 1996.

Burlingame, Roger. *Endless Frontiers: The Story of McGraw-Hill.* New York: McGraw-Hill, 1959.

Peterson, Theodore. *Magazines in the Twentieth Century.* Urbana: University of Illinois Press, 1964.

Wainwright, Loudon. *The Great American Magazine: An Inside History of* Life. New York: Alfred A. Knopf, 1986.

Woodward, Helen. *The Lady Persuaders.* New York: Ivan Obolensky, 1960.

chapter 3

the magazine as a historical document: trends over time

Today's newsstands cradle the great-great-grandchildren of America's magazine pioneers. *Harper's* magazine is the offspring of *Harper's Monthly,* the country's oldest continuous consumer title,[1] first published in June 1850. The Harper brothers—Fletcher, James, John, and Joseph—were successful book publishers who decided a literary magazine would be a good way to keep their printing presses busy. They also started *Harper's Weekly,* which provided a rich illustration of American civilization through engravings, woodcuts, and cartoons from 1857 until 1916. More than 150 years later, the Harper name still graces the cover of one of America's most respected magazines. ▪ *The Atlantic Monthly,* our second oldest continuous consumer magazine title, saw its first press run in November 1857. It was started by writers with the age-old pursuit of an audience. The magazine succeeded and so did the writers, whose works today fill American literature classes: Ralph Waldo Emerson, Harriet Beecher Stowe, Oliver Wendell Holmes, and Henry Wadsworth Longfellow. ▪ *Cosmopolitan* dates back to 1886 and originally carried this tagline: "The world is my country and all mankind are my countrymen." Like *Harper's* and *The Atlantic Monthly,* it was one of the quality journals of opinion and the arts that characterized magazines started after the Civil War. Its contemporary incarnation is, likewise, representative of its era, encouraging sexual freedom and individual expression. The magazines in Table 3.1 have lasted for a century or more.

■ **Table 3.1** The Magazine Century Club

DATE ESTABLISHED	MAGAZINE	DATE ESTABLISHED	MAGAZINE
1812	*The New England Journal of Medicine*	1885	*American Rifleman*
1821	*Saturday Evening Post* (died 1969; reborn 1971)*	1885	*Good Housekeeping*
		1886	*Cosmopolitan*
1835	*American Banker*	1886	*The Sporting News*
1845	*Scientific American*	1886	*Progressive Farmer*
1846	*Town and Country*	1887	*Sports Afield*
1850	*Harper's*	1888	*National Geographic*
1857	*The Atlantic Monthly*	1891	*American School Board Journal*
1865	*The Nation*	1892	*Vogue*
1867	*The Locomotive*	1893	*Sierra*
1867	*Harper's Bazaar*	1895	*Field and Stream*
1872	*Publishers Weekly*	1895	*Automotive Industries*
1872	*Popular Science*	1898	*Sunset*
1873	*Tobacco Reporter*	1898	*Outdoor Life*
1877	*American Machinist*	1898	*America's Pharmacist*
1880	*American Fruit Grower*	1900	*American Journal of Nursing*
1883	*Ladies' Home Journal*	1902	*Popular Mechanics*
1883	*Journal of the American Medical Association (JAMA)*	1903	*Redbook*
		1904	*American Nurseryman*
1884	*The Christian Century*		

*When revived as a quarterly in 1971, *Saturday Evening Post* specialized in nostalgia. Currently, the magazine is published six times a year by the Benjamin Franklin Literary and Medical Society and concentrates on articles about health and medicine.

These magazines are survivors in a media world that rewards creativity, tenacity, and adaptability. Unfortunately, numerous magazines stumble and fall because they cannot successfully refocus or reinvent themselves. But even magazine dinosaurs provide insight into a particular time and place in society. The magazine's role in American history is secure: For more than 260 years, magazines have shown themselves to be an enduring medium.

the beginning

In 1741, the first American magazines were established within 3 days of each other, the result of intense rivalry between Benjamin Franklin and Andrew Bradford. That event in Philadelphia foreshadowed the future competitiveness and challenges of the magazine industry. Bradford's *American Magazine, or A Monthly View of the Political State of the British Colonies* preceded Franklin's equally wordy *The General Magazine, and Historical Chronicle, For All the British Planta-*

tions in America. However, Franklin had the idea first. Bradford's magazine lasted just 3 months; Franklin's survived for 6 months. They were followed by other titles to satisfy an 18th-century audience enthralled by this new medium that differed significantly from books and newspapers.

No magazines published between 1741 and 1800 lasted more than 18 months, and 60 percent of the periodicals started between 1741 and 1794 did not survive even the first year. Noah Webster, who published several magazines before finding success with his dictionary, said in 1788, "The expectation of *failure* is connected with the very name of a Magazine."[2]

Today's magazines have more optimistic publishers and a lower mortality rate, with more than 40 percent of new magazines surviving the critical first year.[3] Hundreds of magazines are now developed every year—in 2004 alone, 1,006 new magazines were launched.[4] By contrast, only 98 magazines were published during the entire 18th century.[5] These early American magazines were victims of a variety of influences. As early as 1828, an article in the *New-York Mirror* stated: "These

JANUARY 1741: Like most 18th-century magazines, Benjamin Franklin's *The General Magazine, and Historical Chronicle, For all the British Plantations in America,* lasted only a few months.

Even when magazines have longer life spans—*Scientific American* and *Town and Country* are more than 160 years old, while *The Nation* is the oldest continuously published weekly, since 1865—there will always be survivors and failures.

Five factors have had an ongoing impact on the magazine industry from 1741 to the present: (1) literacy and education, (2) content, (3) appearance, (4) transportation and delivery, and (5) production and technology. Within these categories, structural and cultural shifts have appeared that can be studied as trends over time. Table 3.2 demonstrates these factors.

For example, the audience of literate readers since 1741 has moved from small, elite, upper-class groups, to middle-class masses with leisure time, to well-educated, special interest niches.

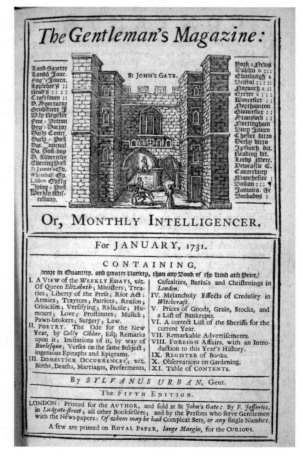

JANUARY 1731 (Premiere Issue): Publisher Edward Cave was the first to use the word "magazine"—referring to storehouse—in connection with *The Gentleman's Magazine* in London, England.

United States are fertile in most things, but in periodicals they are extremely luxuriant. They spring up as fast as mushrooms, in every corner, and like all rapid vegetation bear the seeds of early decay within them." The article continued its plantlike analogy of new magazines:

> They put forth their young green leaves in the shape of promises and prospectuses—blossom through a few numbers—and then comes a "frost, a killing frost," in the form of bills due and debts unpaid. . . . This is the fate of hundreds; but hundreds more are found to supply their place, to tread in their steps, and share their destiny. The average age of periodicals in this country is found to be six months.[6]

British Magazines Take Precedence by a Decade

When Edward Cave produced *The Gentleman's Magazine* in England in February 1731, it was the first publication to call itself a magazine. Periodicals featuring essays, journals, verse, and fiction had been around since the late 1690s. But Cave, departing from the popular periodical format of essays and journals used by Richard Steele's *Tatler* and Joseph Addison's *Spectator,* offered something different. Cave's publication featured useful news, miscellaneous extracts, and various articles—or "tydings"—taken from the leading publications of the day. In that sense, it was more like a *Reader's Digest* in its eclectic choice of content, which ran the gamut from the literary to the political, from the critical to the biographical. A new concept for British readers was Cave's "The Monthly Intelligencer," a regular department with short excerpts—vital statistics (births, deaths, marriages), book lists, foreign and domestic news, and current prices—taken from different newspapers.

Cave promised his new magazine would live up to its name before the first issue even appeared. His January 30, 1731, advertisement in the *Universal Spectator* announced the content of *The Gentleman's Magazine* as being:

A Collection of all Matters of Information and Amusement:
Compriz'd under the following Heads, viz.
Publick Affairs, Foreign and Domestick,
Births, Marriages, and Deaths of Eminent Persons,
Preferments, Ecclesiastical and Civil.
Prices of Goods, Grain and Stocks.
Bankrupts declar'd and Books Publish'd
Pieces of Humour and Poetry
Disputes in Politicks and Learning.
Remarkable Advertisements and Occurrences.
Lists of the Civil and Military Establishment.
And whatever is worth quoting from the Numerous Papers of News and Entertainment,
British and Foreign; or shall be Communicated proper for Publication. With Instructions in Gardening, and the Fairs for February.[1]

Dr. Samuel Johnson, the leading literary scholar and critic of the period, wrote numerous articles, biographies, essays, and literary tidbits for *The Gentleman's Magazine.* By 1744, the circulation of the magazine had reached 10,000, and Johnson became Cave's assistant as well as his chief reporter, writer, and editor.

Soon other successful publications with the storehouse approach were started. *The London Magazine* and *The Monthly Review* were two rivals to *The Gentleman's Magazine* by the middle of the 18th century. Of course, these magazines were read in the American colonies. In fact, *The Gentleman's Magazine* was one of the primary sources for material published by both Benjamin Franklin and Andrew Bradford in their new magazines.

Historians have pointed out that Franklin and Bradford had no intention of publishing anything but a British magazine in America. Certainly, they took the majority of their editorial content from British periodicals and copied their profitable formats. Bradford acknowledged the profit motive in the January 1741 issue of his *American Magazine:* "The Success and Approbation which the MAGAZINES, published in *Great-Britain,* have met with for many Years past, among all Ranks and Degrees of People, *Encouraged*

1. C. Lennart Carlson, *The First Magazine: A History of* The Gentleman's Magazine (Providence, R.I.: Brown University, 1938): 30.

British Magazines Take Precedence by a Decade (continued)

us to *Attempt* a Work of the like Nature in *America.*"[2]

Presenting a favorable picture of the American colonies to England and Europe was an equally strong reason for starting a magazine. Bradford wrote that he desired *"That the Parliament and People* of Great Britain, *may be* truly *and* clearly *informed of the Constitutions and Governments in the Colonies,* whose great Distance from their Mother-Country seems, in some sense, to have placed them out of her View."

2. Andrew Bradford, "The Plan of the Undertaking," *The American Magazine, or A Monthly View of the Political State of the British Colonies* (January 1741): i.

Magazine content has reflected changing attitudes as editorial copy segued from ponderous treatises about government and politics interspersed with sentimental musings by anonymous authors, to signed general interest articles with a muckraking agenda, to an emphasis on fiction, to the current domination of nonfiction and service journalism. The magazine's appearance has mirrored the impact of design innovations as the look of the book shifted from a type-heavy, plain document; to one with limited use of woodcuts, drawings, and varying typefaces; to a merger of design and type with photographs, color, and large page sizes; to a design-driven appearance reflective of fast-paced lifestyles. Transportation and delivery, influenced by geography and government postal regulations, have dramatically affected circulation's pendulum from low to widely expanded to intentionally reduced. Finally, production and technological innovations have led magazines from provincialism to mass consumption as the first national communications medium and as a multimillion dollar business.

literacy and education

One of the most consistent correlations reflected in American magazine readership over time is the literacy rate. Literacy and formal education are the cornerstones for an audience of readers. Class and income also influence magazine readership. However, the only statement that can be made about magazines and their readers with any certainty is that the number of readers is seldom static. Instead, magazine audiences evolve and shift as different societal influences and individual interests come into play.

■ 18TH CENTURY: EDUCATED ELITE

Eighteenth-century magazines were few in number because there were few readers. In 1741, the British colonies in America had a population of about 1 million. Fifty years later, the population had increased to about 4.5 million. Although there was no universal education, it's been estimated that approximately 60 percent of the male population in colonial America from 1650 to 1750 was literate, based on whether they could sign their wills.[7] Female literacy during the same period was considerably lower, around 30 percent.

There were differing attitudes toward literacy in the colonies. The southern colonies—Georgia, North Carolina, and South Carolina—were primarily agricultural and did not have compulsory education laws. Such laws had been enacted in New England, where many dissident religious groups migrated, to ensure that everyone could read the Bible. The middle colonies—Virginia, Maryland, New York, and Pennsylvania—with their mix of commerce and church, also appreciated educated readers. But Massachusetts, with its Puritan heritage that particularly valued male literacy, had the highest literacy rates. Ninety percent of all men were literate by 1790 in Suffolk and Middlesex counties in Massachusetts.[8] So it's not surprising that when magazines were established during the late 18th century, they were found in cities such as Boston, New York, and Philadelphia. In comparison, about 50 percent of the adult males in the other colonies could read and write.

■ **Table 3.2** Magazine Trends

	1741–1800	1801–1865	1866–1889	1890–1920
Longevity	Less than 18 months	Decades		
Numbers	Few titles	Thousands launched		
			Boom Years	
Audience	Few readers Mostly male Educated elite High income	Rising literacy Male and female readers Rising middle class	Compulsory education Middle class	High school education Mass audience More leisure
Content	Assorted miscellany Few bylines Reproduce British articles	Variety Bylined articles American literature Specialized business press	Biographies Serializations Short stories Long essays	General interest Muckraking Advice
Appearance	Plain Few illustrations Type heavy Small type size	Hand-tinted illustrations Woodcuts Copperplate engravings	Photography	Fine illustrations Increased photos Color Larger page sizes
Delivery and transportation	Up to postmaster Reader pays postage Mostly northeast Philadelphia key city By foot, horse, carriage	More indulgent postal rates Publisher pays postage To frontier's edge New York key city Improved roads	Second-class mailing West past Mississippi River Railroads	Rural free delivery Coast to coast
Production and technology	Hand-set type Hand-operated press Handmade paper Costly to produce	Machine-set type Mechanical press	Cheap wood pulp paper	Improved machinery Halftones Four-color printing Faster, cheaper to produce
Circulation	Very low, about 500 By subscription	Higher, up to 40,000	Exceeds 100,000	Hits 1 million Newsstand single copies
Cost	Very expensive	Affordable	Affordable	Cheap

However, literacy was almost universal among wealthy males, wherever they lived.

During the 18th century, the average periodical's circulation was 500; only about half were fully paid subscriptions. A high income was necessary for magazine readership, and barter, rather than cash, was the prevailing economic unit until after the American Revolution. Both Bradford's and Franklin's magazines sold for 1 sterling shilling. The wage for a colonial artisan, such as a carpenter, was 2 shillings a day during this period. Few people wanted to pay half a day's wages for a magazine, and most laborers had to work 4 or 5 days to earn enough for a year's subscription to a maga-

zine. Imagine paying what you would earn if you received $10 an hour for a 40-hour work week ($400) for a 1-year subscription to a magazine, and you can see why magazines were not widely purchased during the 18th century. Dock workers and laborers weren't interested in the price of wheat or the latest essays about drawing room manners. Clearly, early magazines were aimed at specific social and economic groups with some discretionary income—gentlemen and merchants, as opposed to farmers and laborers.

Because relatively few women were well educated, audiences for 18th-century American magazines were assumed to be male, which was re-

1921–1959	1960–1979	1980–2000
Death of some quality magazines	Many start-ups and some surprising failures	Continued growth
Literate		Readers as consumers
Demographically targeted		Niche audience
High income	Discretionary income	
Shorter articles		
Departments	Specialized departments	Custom publications
Tighter writing	Specialized topics	More service topics
More fiction		Less fiction
Photo-heavy	More color	Anything goes
	Smaller page size	
Reduced rates	Postal reorganization	Increased postal costs
	Increased rates	
Coast to coast		
Newsstands		
Supermarkets and bookstores		Niche distribution outlets
	Inflation and increased production costs	Computers cut costs
		Desktop publishing
		Computer-to-plate (CTP)
Slick, coated paper		Slick and some recycled paper
		Digital production
In the millions	Intentionally reduced	Variable
Subscription and newsstand		
Inexpensive	Inflationary	Affordable

flected in the heavy dose of political, commercial, agricultural, scientific, and moral topics found within a publication's pages. Women were perceived as not being interested in those topics, a perception reinforced by the few female magazine subscribers. In a study of the readers of *New-York Magazine* in 1790, David Paul Nord, a journalism professor at Indiana University, discovered that 98 percent of the 370 subscribers were male; only seven women were subscribers in their own names.[9] Furthermore, nearly 50 percent of the readers were professionals, primarily lawyers and physicians, or merchants, bankers, and brokers. The subscription list included the names of old,

moneyed families still familiar to New Yorkers today: Roosevelt, Van Rensselaer, Beekman, and Livingston. President George Washington, Vice President John Adams, and Chief Justice John Jay were subscribers, as was the mayor of New York, Richard Varick.

Shopkeepers and artisans made up the rest of the readers of *New-York Magazine* in 1790. Broadway was the main address for shopkeeper subscribers with their taverns, tobacco shops, bookstores, livery stables, and hardware stores. Artisans identified themselves as carpenters, printers, sea captains, barbers, shoemakers, bakers, tailors, and watchmakers. Most worked in the commercial district, and some headed craft organizations and committees.

The fact that subscribers ranged from "gentle-men" to "glover," according to Nord, suggests "the importance of reading as a form of participation in the new social order of post-revolutionary America." At this time, the heartbeat of New York City revolved around trade, and many shopkeep-ers and artisans clearly had aspirations for culture and a better life. They showed this by subscribing to *New-York Magazine*, priced at $2.25 per year, during a time when a typical New York working man made 50 cents a day. Nord states, however, that if the price was "somewhat aristocratic," the content was not elitist and ranged from the arcane to the earthy.

While *New-York Magazine* positioned itself as a publication designed to "contribute greatly to dif-fuse knowledge throughout a community and to create in that community a taste for literature," other publishers saw a need for magazines that would provide highly detailed and useful informa-tion to a concentrated group of readers. *The South-Carolina Price-Current*, established in 1774, marked the start of the specialized business press. As the first magazine to reach a specialized business audi-ence, it informed readers of price quotes for buying and shipping the staples of the day, such as wheat,

Research in Brief

Portrayal of Women in 18th-Century Magazines

Feminists argue that the media's backlash toward the women's rights move-ment began at the Seneca Falls convention in 1848; men saw the emergence of women into public life as a threat to male dominance in politics, business, society, and the family. Conse-quently, male editors started to depict women as unfit for public life and as being "unnatural" in their desire to define them-selves in new ways. Author Su-san Faludi says the message was no different during the 1970s and 1980s.[1]

Media historian Karen List, a professor of journalism at the University of Massachusetts, places the backlash date con-siderably earlier. List says the first media backlash against women's involvement and visi-bility in society occurred during the 1790s in the days of the new American republic.[2] She reached this conclusion after studying 15 magazines pub-lished in Philadelphia during the last decade of the 18th century.[3] List used the original magazines as windows on the past, to reveal what actually was written, as opposed to what historians suspect may have happened.

American women were ac-tively involved in the revolu-tionary fight against England, taking on jobs as printers, blacksmiths, and undertakers while their husbands fought at Valley Forge and Yorktown. Women competently ran the farms and shops; some even practiced law and medicine. In short, many women, mainly upper- and middle-class white women, began to define themselves as individuals who

1. Susan Faludi, *Backlash: The Undeclared War Against American Women* (New York: Crown Publishers), 1991.

2. Karen List, "The Media and the Depiction of Women," in *The Significance of the Media in American History*, ed. James D. Startt and Wm. David Sloan (Northport, Ala.: Vision Press, 1994): 106–28.

3. List has done extensive research on late-18th-century magazines and newspapers. Among her numerous articles about the role of women as revealed in the publications of the new republic, these three are particularly relevant: Karen K. List, "Magazine Portrayals of Women's Role in the New Republic," *Journalism History*, 13, no. 2 (Summer 1986): 64–70; Karen K. List, "The Post-Revolutionary Woman Idealized: Philadelphia Me-dia's 'Republican Mother,'" *Journalism Quarterly*, 66, no. 1 (Spring 1989): 65-75; and Karen K. List, "Reflections on Realities and Possibilities: Women's Lives in New Republic Periodicals" (paper presented at the annual meeting of the Association for Education in Journalism and Mass Communication, Boston, Mass., August 1991).

Portrayal of Women in 18th-Century Magazines (continued)

had public lives. But after the war, they were told to go home and forget about their political progress and business participation; they were told to become once again dependent wives and loving mothers with private rather than public lives. They were given this message through the magazines being published during the last decade of the 18th century.

List writes that "the groundwork for the media's depiction of women was laid in the 1790s, almost 60 years before the women's movement began, and the media since that time have often conveyed the same thinking on women's place that appeared in these publications 200 years ago."[4] Although the new nation was founded in Enlightenment ideology, a free and equitable society belonged to white men only. Mary Wollstonecraft may have argued for the extension of democracy to women, but the men of the new republic and the magazines they published glorified marriage, worshipped motherhood, and supported domesticity.

Two main themes could be found in magazines of the 1790s, reports List: "First, women generally lacked the ability to get on in the public world because they were different from and inferior to men. Second, women could not find happiness through autonomy

but only through affiliation with others, preferably husbands and children." Even *Ladies Magazine,* the first magazine directed exclusively to female readers, supported the superiority of men and the need for women to submit. The role of women in the new nation was to nurture their husbands and educate their sons in the virtues of republican government. In other words, the only power women had was through their relationships in the home.

List points out that while historians have suggested that early magazines merely held up a mirror to national life, the reality was that the magazines authoritatively told women to achieve a particular ideal. Her opinion is that the tone of 18th-century magazines was "one of paternalistic lecturing." The content arbitrarily and stridently stressed the status quo. List says women were stereotyped as "giddy nonentities" who were to blame if their husbands were unfaithful. A sentence from the September 1792 issue of *Ladies Magazine* makes the point: "A husband may, possibly, in his daily excursions, see many women he thinks handsomer than his wife; but it is generally her fault if he meets with one that he thinks more amiable."

Women did not engage in conversation, but gossiped, tattled, and tittered. As for

friendship, a woman's best friend was her husband; other women were viewed as rivals. Those women who were held up as role models in the magazines were either fictional, exotic, or long dead and political, such as Queen Elizabeth I and Lady Jane Gray. The lives and situations of real, contemporary women who might have deviated from the ideal were not depicted since almost all the essays, articles, and letters were written by men.

Why, List asks, did magazines harp so continuously on women's compliant domestic role if they did not fear some deviation from it? Although most women chose not to challenge convention, some did move outside the narrow boundaries of "republican motherhood" embodied in the magazines of the 1790s. Historians are still finding out about these exceptions, since the press of the day seldom wrote about them. Only occasionally was there an article in a late-18th-century magazine where women were portrayed as rational beings capable of finding the truth and acting on it.

Concludes List, "No matter what their effect may have been, the periodicals clearly attempted to influence the course of women's development, and in so doing, they provided a basis for thinking on women's progress that would recur for the next two centuries." ■

4. List, "The Media and the Depiction of Women," 110.

hog's lard, ginseng, wax candles, and beer. Armed with that knowledge, readers could make business decisions that were timely and exclusive. This became the formula for success in the specialized business press, which would grow as more and more men became better educated.

As for women, those who lived in Boston were likely to have a 60 percent literacy rate by 1787, versus 45 percent for women living in rural areas.[10] In 1784, *The Gentleman and Lady's Town and Country Magazine* became the first magazine to appeal to women readers with a stated editorial policy that featured "the elegant polish of the Female Pencil, where purity of sentiment, and impassioned Fancy, are happily blended together."[11] She was a married woman who knew her place was at home, caring for husbands and children—or brothers and sisters if she was unmarried. As an educated woman, it was her responsibility to teach children "rationally and carefully, preferably by example" the proper republican values of a new nation.[12] Female readers were provided an editorial diet of etiquette, morality, instruction, and amusement, all designed around the notion that a woman's place was in the home. Published in Boston, the magazine reached as far north as New Hampshire, southwest into Connecticut, and south toward Rhode Island.

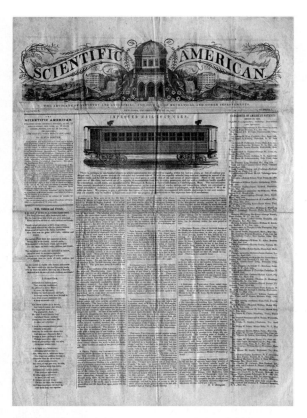

AUGUST 28, 1845 (Premiere Issue): *Scientific American,* **which began as a weekly trade newspaper devoted to inventions and patents, is now a monthly magazine in which scientists and experts write about scientific discoveries and technological innovations for the general public.**

■ 19TH CENTURY: RISING LITERACY

By 1800, with a more stable society in place and a larger population density concentrated in existing cities and newly formed towns, literacy rates across the fledgling United States rose to 75 percent.[13] In general, literacy was higher in the northern and eastern states than in the southern or western ones. Literacy was particularly low along the frontier, where individual settlers were concerned primarily with clearing forests and building log homes. They were unable to support schools, while residents of "older" states had both the resources and the time to offer educational opportunities.

By 1830, when the United States stretched from the Atlantic Ocean across the Mississippi River, followers of President Andrew Jackson began making a connection between education and citizenship. Recognizing that an industrialized America needed laborers who could think, read, write, and add, Jacksonian Democrats argued that literacy was a birthright. They supported numerous workingmen's associations that urged a public primary education for every child and the systematic establishment of common schools throughout the United States. Compulsory education laws were passed by a number of states following the Civil War, and by 1880, school attendance laws and their enforcement were on the books.[14]

After the Civil War, literacy was no longer the domain of the well-educated few; education had become the foundation for the development of the great American middle class. Nowhere was this relationship stronger than in women's magazines. *Godey's Lady's Book,* under the direction of Sarah Josepha Hale and Louis A. Godey, influenced women's manners, morals, and milieu in polite society for much of the middle 19th century. Hale was a forceful advocate of education for women, child welfare, and national recognition of Thanksgiving. However, she avoided discussion of abolition, slavery, and women's suffrage; literate ladies, according to Hale, were not supposed to be concerned with such issues.

Nineteenth-century magazines addressed their reader with such flattering adjectives as "gentle," "genteel," and "moral." While this might be expected in the women's magazines being published, even publications with predominantly male subscribers, such as *The Atlantic Monthly, Harper's, Scribner's,* and *The Century,* assumed that literate, educated audiences wanted a genteel mixture of romantic and practical content in their magazines. Middle-class sensibilities were enshrined in material that tended to be sentimental, optimistic, and nationalistic. These 19th-century magazines were merely matching the dominant educational values and traditions of the day.

As America's population dramatically increased in size and diversity, due to immigration, and in both agrarian and industrial income, due to productivity, so did the number of magazines. From 1825 to 1850, as many as 5,000 American magazines were launched. Their chances for survival were better than those of 18th-century start-ups because salaried jobs and a rising middle class went along with the country's great expansion westward. There simply was more money to spend throughout the 19th century. This eliminated the income problem faced by 18th-century publishers who often took eggs, corn, or butter as payment for their publications. Nineteenth-century magazines were solid entrepreneurial ventures grounded in cash paid by individuals who appreciated the publications' professional, personal, and patriotic value.

The specialized business press made strong contributions to the literate American's life during the middle of the 19th century. Matching the rise in education was a burst of technological improvements prior to the Civil War that demanded more informed managers and workers, with both turning to such publications as *American Mechanics Magazine.* Specialized agricultural magazines for farmers, law journals for attorneys, scientific periodicals for physicians, and magazines devoted to covering specific industries—mining, metals, printing, pharmaceuticals, railroads, and banking—were started. Many are still around, such as *American Banker, Tobacco Reporter,* and *American Machinist.* These early specialized business and trade magazines recorded the diversification and progress occurring in a variety of occupations and fields.

Although men were likely to be regular readers of the specialized trade magazines, well-to-do ladies devoured sentimental fiction and were prime targets for magazines that recognized women's homemaker interests and increasing amounts of leisure time, such as *Godey's Lady's Book, Ladies' Repository,* and *Peterson's Magazine.* Reading clubs, literary societies, and lending libraries were established by women who read as much for entertainment as they did to expand the confines of their traditional roles as wife and mother. Turn-of-the-century magazines such as *Ladies' Home Journal, Woman's Home Companion,* and *McCall's* recognized the liberated needs of middle-class women. These magazines took the

JUNE 1784: *The Gentleman and Lady's Town and Country Magazine,* like most 18th-century magazines, looks gray and dull by today's standards, with two narrow columns of type set in Caslon Old Style and no illustrations.

lead in the emergence of a national magazine industry because of their scope and range of readers. By 1903, *Ladies' Home Journal* became the first magazine to reach 1 million readers; others were not far behind.

For much of the 19th century, magazine readers tended to be concentrated in the northeast portion of the United States, as were most publishing headquarters. New York, the largest city in 1860, accounted for one-third of all magazines published then.[15] Although Boston had a smaller population than Philadelphia, where such popular magazines as *Saturday Evening Post* and *Peterson's Magazine* were headquartered, Boston was considered the rival to New York's publishing excellence because of *The Atlantic Monthly, North American Review, Youth's Companion,* and *Christian Examiner.*[16] New York continues to be the magazine media capital today, with Los Angeles in second place, and Chicago ranking third. Philadelphia takes fourth place—Boston is no longer one of the top 10 magazine publishing centers.

■ 20TH CENTURY: NICHE AUDIENCES

"The reading of magazines," wrote William B. Cairns in 1921 when he was associate professor of American literature at the University of Wisconsin, "has come to be far more common than the reading of books. Thousands of persons who would resent the imputation that they are lacking in culture read almost no books at all. . . . No home, however, in which there is pretence of intellectual interest is without magazines, which are usually read by all members of the family."[17]

If magazines were capable of reaching just about every American during the 20th century, it was because of a greater appreciation for their content. Magazine reading, which depends on an educated audience, became ubiquitous during the 20th century as increasing numbers of Americans attended and completed high school. In 1920, only 32 percent of young peo-

Most Americans can recite the first stanza of "Mary's Lamb," but very few know that the 24-line poem beginning "Mary had a little lamb" was written in 1830 by Sarah Josepha Hale. Hale, a widow with five children, was best known as the editor of *Godey's Lady's Book*, the most successful women's magazine of the early 19th century.

ple ages 14–17 were in school, but by 1950, more than 77 percent were attending high school.[18] College enrollments continued to rise, slowly from 1900 to 1920, spurting between 1920 and 1940, dropping a bit during World War II, and jumping after 1946. A study of readers in 1923 found that 97 percent of the respondents with a college degree read magazines; 83 percent of those with a high school education did so; and just 57 percent of those with less than an 8th-grade education were magazine aficionados.[19] Almost 40 years later, a 1960 study found that regular magazine readers included 86 percent of all college-educated respondents, 68 percent with a high school education, and only 41 percent with a grade school education.[20]

Today's college-educated adults continue to read more magazines than the average American adult. "You have more educated people today than at any other time in history," said Clay Felker, founder of *New York* magazine and of the Felker Magazine Center at the University of California at Berkeley Graduate School of Journalism, in 1995.[21] "People want and need historical perspective."

Magazines have been successful in providing that historical perspective to a literate audience. However, today's publishers consider audience demographics, psychographics, and buying behavior to be as important as literacy. This has resulted in magazine niche marketing and fragmentation of various social attributes according to age, education, income, occupation, and geography. In the 1960s, audience specialization became the name of the magazine game, with four new magazines appearing for every one that folded. Specialized magazine debuts increased in the 1970s to take advantage of every new constituency and micro-market interest group that appeared.

This concept of specialization began at the start of the 20th century and coincided with a shift in how the literate reader was addressed. Gone were "gentle readers." An audience of hungry consumers had taken their place. During the early years of the 20th century, Cyrus Curtis, publisher of *Saturday Evening*

MARCH 1876: Many historians consider *St. Nicholas* **to be the best magazine for children ever published, yet it failed to evolve with the needs of its readers and died in 1943.**

Post and *Ladies' Home Journal*, was among the first to understand the relationship between the audience as reader and the audience as consumer—and to link that concept to advertising. According to media historian Douglas B. Ward, Curtis, *Saturday Evening Post* editor George Horace Lorimer, and *Ladies' Home Journal* editor Edward Bok argued that their turn of the 20th century publications "reached the elite of American society—people with culture and, most important, people with money."[22] Through advertisements in the trade press intended to entice big-ticket companies such as Packard and Pierce-Arrow automobiles, they depicted a specific kind of reader: "the intelligent, the earnest and the progressive." *Saturday Evening Post*, while appealing to men and women, concentrated on male readers in its promotions during the 1910s and 1920s. Said Lorimer, the *Post* reaches "two classes of men: Men with income,

and men who are going to have incomes, and the second is quite as important as the first to the advertiser."

Although *Ladies' Home Journal* was "designed for the home loving," Bok delineated readers by income during the first two decades of the 20th century because he recognized the relationship between income and discretionary spending. From 1918 to 1919, for example, only 3 percent of the population earned more than $2,500 per year; 71 percent of them purchased magazines.[23] However, the majority of the population, 55 percent, had a yearly income between $1,200 and $1,800. Almost half of them, about 48 percent, bought magazines.[24] Bok positioned *Ladies' Home Journal* as primarily reaching those families with yearly incomes of $1,200 to $2,500.

Ward points out that income, education, and literacy had been the key factors in determining magazine development until the start of the 20th century. But now, in trying to tap the ever-expanding middle class, Curtis specified only "worth-while white families" in an advertising piece in 1922. Blacks and recent immigrants were excluded from consideration as regular readers of either *Saturday Evening Post* or *Ladies' Home Journal* because, in general, they had low literacy rates and even lower incomes. Even native-born white families were eliminated as a target audience unless they lived in "accessible" cities or affluent suburbs.[25]

According to Ward, even though the *Post, Journal,* and other similar large-circulation magazines were considered "mass" magazines because they reached a national audience, in many ways they "were closer to a niche market in that they represented only a fraction of the population—a fraction targeted and defined by income" and literacy.[26]

content

A reader is drawn to a magazine's content and appearance for a variety of reasons: aesthetic, pragmatic, whimsical, sensational, or ideological. While the format of a magazine hasn't changed that much—a magazine published in 1775 or 1875 generally resembles today's publications—the content and the way it is presented have changed dramatically. Early magazines were little wrens, plain and content-heavy, with few artistic embellishments and little to no advertising. In comparison, most of today's magazines are screeching peacocks. Their colorfully written editorial pages are filled with so many photographs and illustrations that the line between ad and editorial is not always distinguishable.

■ 18TH CENTURY: ASSORTED ARTICLES

Eighteenth-century magazines were literally storehouses of material, mostly gathered from British magazines, books, and pamphlets. About three-fourths of the content of 18th-century American magazines was lifted from English publications and reprinted in their entirety, generally without credit because there were no copyright laws. Yet there existed a strong nationalistic orientation because of the inclusion of colonial state and regional political documents. From the start, the content of a magazine was considerably broader than that of a local newspaper. About one-third of Franklin's *General Magazine* was devoted to proceedings of parliament and state assemblies. Essays about currency concerns, historical sketches, firearms manuals, and "Extracts from New Books, Pamphlets, etc. Published in the Plantations" made up the rest.

The 1758 editorial profile of the *New England Magazine of Knowledge and Pleasure,* written in verse, is reflective of the varied and eclectic content of early publications:

> Old-fashioned writings, and Select Essays,
> Queer Notions, Useful Hints, Extracts from Plays,
> Relations Wonderful, and Psalm and Song,
> Good Sense, Wit, Humour, Morals, all *ding dong;*
> Poems and Speeches, Politicks and News,
> What *Some* will like, and other *Some* refuse;
> Births, Deaths, and Dreams, and Apparitions too;
> With some Thing suited to each different Geû
>   [view]
> To Humour *Him,* and *Her,* and *Me,* and *You.*[27]

Despite the miscellany, early editors primarily were interested in influencing opinion in the colonies and in England; the perception in Europe was that New World folks were raw, rude, and rambunctious. Colonial publishers wanted to depict American social and political life in a favorable light—and were able to do so because they also were the editor, the primary author, and the printer. Consequently, articles tended to be lengthy and unsigned.

When revolutionary ideas began to ferment, magazines quickly reflected increasingly strong political and partisan views. During this period, magazines helped unify the colonies and fanned the patriotic fervor of the people, resulting in a much greater influence than their low circulation figures might indicate. Magazines were cherished; every page was read closely by many individuals.

Contributors to 18th-century magazines included every great thinker and statesman of early American history: George Washington, Alexander Hamilton, John Jay, John Hancock, Thomas Paine, Benjamin Franklin, John Quincy Adams, Noah Webster, Mathew Carey, and Isaiah Thomas. However, the vast majority of early magazine writers did not receive credit for their work because there were no professional writers. Writing for money was frowned upon as unbecoming to ladies and unsporting for gentlemen. This attitude probably had its roots in Puritan beliefs that modesty was its own reward, particularly when writing one's opinion about art or literature. When bylines were given, initials, Greco-Roman names like Minerva and Romulus, and popular pseudonyms of the period, such as Frank Amity or Jemima Loveleap, often were used.

■ 19TH CENTURY: MATERIAL MANIA

Led by Joseph Dennie's *Port Folio,* considered the first significant and successful literary magazine to be published after 1800, magazines became broader in content, with sentimental fiction, plays, essays, and poetry added to expected articles about industry, education, agriculture, economics, science, and politics. Education, enlightenment, and entertainment were the legs of an increasingly successful industry. Popular publications of the magazine boom years from 1825 to 1850 included *North American Review, New-York Mirror,* and *Saturday Evening Post.* British authors, particularly Sir Walter Scott, George Byron, Samuel Taylor Coleridge, and William Wordsworth, were widely read in America. However, a number of magazines, such as *Graham's* and *Knickerbocker,* preferred to support the American literature of Washington Irving, Edgar Allan Poe, Nathaniel Hawthorne, and John Greenleaf Whittier. Indeed,

Roll Call of Famous Authors

From the start, *The Atlantic Monthly* identified its mission as providing the best in "literature, politics, science and the arts" to its readers. The magazine accomplished its goal by publishing the work of the most noted writers of the day, year after year after year. The following authors were all published in *The Atlantic Monthly*:

1858	Henry David Thoreau, "Chesuncook"
1860	Walt Whitman, "Bardic Symbols"
1862	Julia Ward Howe, "Battle Hymn of the Republic"
1863	Henry Wadsworth Longfellow, "Paul Revere's Ride"
1866	Frederick Douglass, "Reconstruction"
1869	Harriet Beecher Stowe, "The True Story of Lady Byron's Life"
1875	Mark Twain, "Old Times on the Mississippi"
1897	Theodore Roosevelt, "Municipal Administration: The New York Police Force"
1900	Kate Douglas Wiggin, "Tuppenny Travels in London"
1901	John Muir, "Hunting Big Redwoods"
1902	Jack London, "Li Wan, the Fair"
1915	Robert Frost, "A Group of Poems"
1923	Woodrow Wilson, "The Road Away from Revolution"
1929	Emily Dickinson, "Poems"
1932	John Maynard Keynes, "The World's Economic Outlook"
1933	Edith Wharton, "Confessions of a Novelist"
1940	Gertrude Stein, "The Winner Loses; A Picture of Occupied France"
1947	Dylan Thomas, "In Country Sleep"
1948	E. B. White, "Death of a Pig"
1956	John Steinbeck, "How Mr. Hogan Robbed a Bank"
1957	Ernest Hemingway, "Two Tales of Darkness"
1959	James Thurber, "The Porcupines in the Artichokes"
1963	Martin Luther King Jr., "The Negro Is Your Brother"
1964	Sylvia Plath, "The Wishing Box"
1969:	Margaret Atwood, "A Night in the Royal Ontario Museum"
1973	Annie Dillard, "The Force That Drives the Flower"
1973	Gabriel Garcia Marquez, "Death Constant Beyond Love"
1976	John Cheever, "The President of the Argentine"
1979	William Faulkner, "Evangeline"
1982	William Least Heat Moon, "Blue Highways"
1984	Benjamin Spock, "School Reform: Coercion in the Classroom Won't Work"
1989	Amy Tan, "Two Kinds"
1992	John Updike, "The Brown Chest"
1995	William Zinsser, "Doin' the Chameleon"
1996	Garrison Keillor, "The Poetry Judge"
1997	Arthur Schlesinger Jr., "A Man from Mars"
1999	Garry Wills, "Lincoln's Greatest Speech"
2000	Nadine Gordimer, "The Generation Gap"
2001	Louise Erdrich, "Sister Godzilla"
2002	A.S. Byatt, "Raw Material"
2004	William F. Buckley Jr., "Aweigh"
2005	Christopher Buckley, "The Flirty Dozen"

literature, both prose and poetry, dominated magazine content until the 1890s, and even through the 1950s many consumer publications carried several short stories and poems per issue.

By the 1830s and 1840s, paid editors and by-lined contributors became the norm. A new class of writers developed who called themselves "magazinists" because they made their living by editing or writing for magazines. Nathaniel Parker Willis was the most successful, praised during his lifetime as the pre-eminent magazine writer and editor in the United States and Europe. Ironically, though Willis became a wealthy man as a professional writer, he is not as well remembered for his achievements as is his contemporary, Edgar Allan Poe, who received much less money from the same magazines. For example, both Poe and Willis wrote for *Godey's Lady's Book, Graham's,* and *New-York Mirror.* However, Willis received as much as $11 per page for his prose from *Graham's,* while Poe's payment was only $4 per page. By 1842, Willis was earning $1,500 a year—which was more than the salary of the governor of Connecticut—from four monthly magazines for which he wrote clever, short sketches about picturesque places. In comparison, Poe earned just $300 in 1843.[28]

Following the Civil War, magazines that had fought for the abolition of slavery, such as *The Liberator,* died once they no longer had a cause to support. However, other magazines rushed to fill the gap. In 1867, the editors of *The Round Table* wrote about a "mania" of magazine start-ups, which they predicted would spend itself only "by every successful writer's becoming possessed of a magazine of his own, or by the exhaustion of names for new essays—a contingency which seems by no means remote when we find old titles revived."[29] *The Round Table*'s editors itemized

World-famous artists have created variations of their trademark landscapes and images for magazine covers. Erté's June 1936 cover for *Harper's Bazaar* is Art Deco at its most elegant with his use of a slinky, sinuous tie to suggest a speeding automobile for the "Travel and Resort Fashions" issue. Salvador Dali's June 1939 bridal cover for *Vogue* is eerily similar to his renowned "Persistence of Memory," while Roy Lichtenstein's May 24, 1968, *Time* cover of Robert Kennedy reeks of the artist's colorful Pop Art comic book style.

some of the new magazines, which included "trash" such as *Kitchen Corners, Chambermaid's Delights, Prize Fighter's Joys,* and *Tattler's Teapots,* as well as "newcomers of a more than respectable character":

We have new quarterlies of Law, of Medicine, of Speculative Philosophy; new monthlies of Natural History, of Art, of Music, of Numismatics, of the Davis Family; a publication of some sort and of some merit from nearly every live college in the country; our first creditable fashion weekly; numberless admirable innovations in juvenile journalism; three presentable weeklies whose business is to wrangle with ability over the tariff—all these and more like unto them, coming from almost as many parts of the country.

The number of religious publications doubled between 1865 and 1885, while the number of specialized business publications quadrupled in the three decades following the Civil War. The overall number of magazines available increased from 700 in 1865 to 3,300 in 1885, according to census figures. As many as 9,000 magazines were published during the period, now with an average life span of 4 years. The number of magazines continued to accelerate. By 1890, there were more than 4,400; by 1895, more than 5,100. And 1900 rang in the new century with more than 5,500 magazines.

Specialized trade and business magazines in particular took advantage of the reader-as-consumer movement. Useful information was the focus of business publications, as stated by Rufus Porter, founder of *Scientific American:* "Our readers have already learned that instead of detailing stories and narratives to the full extent of words and phrases for the purpose of filling up our columns, our custom is to curtail and abbreviate, giving the pith and substance of a story in as few words as possible."[30]

By the end of the 19th century, it would have been difficult to find a trade, profession, or industry without at least one magazine devoted to it. Indeed, magazine historian Frank Luther Mott commented that only bootblacks, nursemaids, and janitors lacked individual publications by 1885.[31] By 1921, when Standard Rate and Data Services (SRDS) produced the first listing of trade and business magazines, there were 1,235 publications covering a variety of fields. Leading the list of categories was "Medical and Surgical," with 95 magazines, followed by "Automotive" with 60, "Export Trade" with 47, "Financial and Banking" with 46, and "Drugs, Pharmaceutics, etc." with 33.[32]

Companies began publishing their own sponsored magazines as public relations tools as early as 1847 when *Mechanic* was founded by the H. B. Smith Machine Company of Smithville, New Jersey. One of the oldest corporate communications

magazines still being published today was founded after the Civil War. *The Locomotive,* established in 1867, belongs to the Hartford Steam Boiler Inspection and Insurance Company (HSB).

Trade, professional, and corporate magazines took a businesslike approach to their editorial content, stressing application and utility in straightforward language. Consumer magazine content tended to be high in tone, stressing quality fiction and biographies, although there seemed to be an abundance of religious and sentimental points of view in women's magazines. Biographies were popular because Americans wanted to be reassured that their past was glorious, despite the vicissitudes of the recently fought Civil War.

Various magazines also maneuvered to take advantage of readers' interest in fiction, which still was influenced by such English writers as Thomas Hardy, Charles Dickens, Wilkie Collins, and George Eliot. Their novels were run serially and offered as "serious" reading, while the short story was considered entertainment designed to be read

Urban Humor in 19th-Century Magazines

Magazine historian Frank Luther Mott was nothing if not thorough. Each of his five volumes about magazine history detailed the business of magazine publishing and the parade of leading magazines. Every volume also included voluminous information about the artistic, educational, political, social, literary, scientific, religious, philosophical, agricultural, and recreational content of magazines that flourished and failed over time.

So it's not surprising to find that Mott, when discussing humor as a literary device, compiled a list of the standard urban jokes to be found in 19th-century magazines. He called his list of 22 jokes "urban comedy" and said that while the material may have been worn, "most of them bloom perennially."[1] Unfortunately, he didn't include the content of any of the jokes. But the following 10 titles suggest that many of them have mutated only a little

bit and now can be found on Internet joke websites.

The wedding night joke
The newly rich joke
The unwelcome suitor joke
The old maid joke
The drunkard's return joke
The bashful suitor joke
The sleeping policeman joke
The black eye joke
The peddler (salesman) joke
The love letter joke

1. Frank Luther Mott, A History of American Magazines, 1850–1865, vol. 2 (Cambridge, Mass.: Harvard University Press, 1957), 178–9.

aloud in a family circle in the parlor. In the period after the Civil War, the short story was sentimental and romantic, recounting suffering, exploitation, poverty, and even abuse in terms of moral fortitude—yet there always was eventual triumph. Humor frequently was found in magazines as fillers, departments, and entire stories. Urban humor parodied social and cultural fads, follies, and functions, while frontier humor, especially in dialect, was popularized by Mark Twain, who knew just how far to go with his exaggerations. Twain's "The Celebrated Jumping Frog of Calaveras County" was first published in *Saturday Press,* which was established in 1857 as a humor magazine.

During the 1890s, when industrial turmoil and crowded cities became social problems, muckraking and service articles dominated many magazines' tables of content. Edward W. Bok offered advice and information to the women's market, stating that *Ladies' Home Journal* was edited for "the intelligent American woman rather than to the intellectual type."[33] Women who read *Ladies' Home Journal* could find material about everyday concerns both in and out of the home, as well as advertisements that offered labor-saving products and practical housekeeping remedies. Other women's magazines soon followed Bok's mix of information, advice, fiction, and advertising—a content base that continues to be successful today.

Magazines for children and young people flourished, with *Youth's Companion,* founded in 1827, leading the field for many years. *Youth's Companion,* designed to amuse and instruct children, featured the works of Rudyard Kipling, Jack London, Jules Verne, and Alfred Tennyson. The emphasis was on action and adventure, with a strong moral tone that shut out anything related to sex, crime, or violence. The writing was of such high quality that many adults also read the magazine.

Youth's Companion reached young readers through a special circulation device: It was one of the first magazines to give premiums for annual subscriptions. Children could receive toys ranging from dolls to miniature printing presses if they obtained new or renewed subscriptions. The list of available premiums was so extensive that it filled 36 pages of each October's issue. Circulation soared, from 385,000 in 1885 to more than 500,000 in 1898. Nevertheless, *Youth's Companion* failed in 1929, a victim of the uninhibited amusements of the 1920s. The editors were unable to meet the new interests of youth, who found radio

more exciting and the fledgling motion picture industry more entertaining.

St. Nicholas, with its lavish illustrations and stories by Mark Twain, Robert Louis Stevenson, Louisa May Alcott, and Theodore Roosevelt, is considered by many historians to be the best magazine for children ever published in America. Established in 1873, *St. Nicholas* defined a child's magazine as a playground, rather than a restrictive playpen, and avoided the moralistic tone of most children's magazines. Despite its beautiful printing and numerous pictures, *St. Nicholas* died in 1943, unable to keep up with children's changing tastes. Both *Youth's Companion* and *St. Nicholas* died because they did not evolve with the needs of their readers. See Table 3.3 for other quality magazines that are no longer published.

■ 20TH CENTURY: SUBTLE SPECIALIZATION

Probably the most dramatic change in content came in the 1920s. Three magazines—*Time, Reader's Digest,* and *The New Yorker*—were created in response to shifts in attitudes toward work and leisure time following World War I. Each periodical offered new approaches to reading in a fast-paced society. While other magazines were publishing long pieces about immigration or labor strife, along with serialized romances, westerns, and mysteries, *Time* and *Reader's Digest* chose to focus on brevity and the need to know. *The New Yorker,* on the other hand, created an urban magazine product that oozed brilliance and critical style.

Henry Luce and Briton Hadden founded *Time* in 1923 because they believed busy Americans were poorly informed. Newspapers, they said, were unorganized and random in their content, making it difficult for people to understand what was happening in the world around them. *Time's* content was driven by four key concepts, which continue to be followed today: (1) The week's news would be organized logically in short departments; (2) while both sides of a story would be told, *Time* would be evaluative and interpret what the news meant; (3) writing would be crisp, curt, and complete; and (4) emphasis would be on the personalities who made the news. The weekly news magazine was a new animal, grounded in a group journalism approach where field corre-

■ **Table 3.3** Gone but Not Forgotten: Some Significant Magazines of the 18th and 19th Centuries

MAGAZINE	DATES PUBLISHED
The American Magazine, or A Monthly View of the Political State of the British Colonies	1741–1741
The General Magazine, and Historical Chronicle, For All the British Plantations in America	1741–1741
South-Carolina Price-Current	1774–1774
The Royal American Magazine	1774–1775
Pennsylvania Magazine	1775–1776
United States Magazine	1779–1779
The Gentleman and Lady's Town and Country Magazine	1784–1784
The Columbian Magazine	1786–1792
The American Museum	1787–1792
New-York Magazine	1790–1797
Ladies Magazine (also published as Lady's Magazine)	1792–1793
Port Folio	1801–1827
New-York Mirror	1823–1842
American Mechanics Magazine	1825–1826
Youth's Companion	1827–1929
Godey's Lady's Book	1830–1898
The Liberator	1831–1865
The American Railroad Journal	1832–1837
Southern Literary Messenger	1834–1864
Graham's	1840–1858
Merry's Museum	1841–1872
Peterson's Magazine	1842–1898
Frank Leslie's Illustrated Weekly	1855–1922
Harper's Weekly	1857–1916
The Century (initially Scribner's Monthly)	1870–1930
St. Nicholas	1873–1943
Woman's Home Companion	1873–1957
McCall's	1876–2001
Scribner's Magazine	1887–1939
Collier's	1888–1957
Munsey's	1889–1929
McClure's	1892–1929

spondents gathered data that would be organized and rewritten by editors in New York. Articles in *Time* seldom had bylines, but they did have perspective—Luce's particular ideas on politics, government, economics, and philosophy shaped each issue for many years.

A different kind of editorial shaping was done by DeWitt Wallace and his wife Lila Acheson Wallace, who created *Reader's Digest* in 1922. Magazine digests were not new—magazines during the 18th century and well into the 19th century frequently reprinted articles from other publications, sometimes with, but mostly without attribution or payment. The Wallaces got written permission to reprint articles, and later paid both the publisher and the author for the option. That in itself was groundbreaking. But what really made *Reader's Digest* different was that the Wallaces condensed material only if it contained three characteristics: (1) applicability and value for readers, (2) lasting interest to the extent that it was worth reading a year later, and (3) optimistic constructiveness. Finding the right mix of perennially optimistic articles was easy for DeWitt Wallace, who stated, "I simply hunt for things that interest me, and if they do, I print them."[34]

DeWitt Wallace claimed he could eliminate as much as 75 percent of an article and still publish a piece of substance, style, and authority. That brevity

was a great service to busy readers, who could read 31 articles each month selected from a myriad of leading magazine sources. The first *Reader's Digest*, dated February 1922, set the tone for all that followed, with articles from such popular magazines as *The Atlantic Monthly, Ladies' Home Journal, Scientific American, Popular Science, Delineator, Theatre Magazine, Scribner's, House Beautiful, Good Housekeeping, The Nation's Business, McClure's,* and *Physi-*

Research in Brief

Magazines and Memory

Magazines operate on two levels: (1) as newsstand marketing tools that attract readers to reach for the latest issue because they are drawn by the image or words on the cover, and (2) as cultural artifacts that reflect societal norms and demographic trends, mirroring gender interests, ethnic concerns, and current events. On both levels, magazines serve as memory aids with artistic and popular implications. They show us the way we are and the way we were, pinpointing where individuals and groups are in terms of power and influence at a particular point in time.

Magazine scholar Carolyn Kitch of Temple University argues that magazines interpret the past and actively construct America's historical memory. She points out that magazines are "both an encyclopedia (for instance, think how many homes contain shelves of *National Geographic*) and an identity statement" for many readers.[1] The result is that consumer magazines in particular have become repositories of national culture. Kitch's memory research—about magazine anniversary issues, generational identities, and how dead celebrities are mourned and new heroes created—is the focus of her book *Pages from the Past: History and Memory in American Magazines*.

The book incorporates a broad cultural and textual perspective, weaving sociology, anthropology, history, psychology, semiotics, and journalism into a narrative about the public history function of 60 magazines. Kitch explains how magazines—ranging from *The Atlantic* to *Vibe* —consciously construct cultural narratives that build on the past and shape the present and future. These cultural narratives, with symbolic characters and story-telling codes, have become part of society's collective memory. Kitch details the role of magazines as "important social commentators on American life, as well as public historians of national culture."[2]

She stresses how *Time, Newsweek, U.S. News and World Report,* and *Life* packaged the 20th century into thematic decades focusing on six "core plots": the virtue of individualism, the rise of the underdog, the downfall of greedy or immoral individuals, the triumph of democracy, the survival of small towns, and the positive side of technology. Kitch points to *Time* 's six-part "People of the Century" series and *Newsweek*'s three-part "Voices of the Century" series as examples of how the stories of great events are told through extraordinary and ordinary people. Traditional journalistic objectivity is abandoned by writers and editors in these

1. Kitch, Carolyn. *Pages from the Past: History and Memory in American Magazines.* (Chapel Hill: University of North Carolina Press, 2005): 8.

2. Ibid., 11.

Magazines and Memory (continued)

special issues "in favor of a voice that was meant to establish their authority as national leaders and to forge a personal bond with their readers."[3]

Kitch demonstrates that the September 11, 2001, tragedy created a narrative template for dealing with disasters. The new American hero is the fire*man* (not the politically correct fire-*fighter*). Kitch's take on the creation of a 21st-century working-class mythology builds on Janice Hume's studies of media constructions of 19th-century heroes and notes the inclusion of military rhetoric to the theme of ordinary men in extraordinary situations. According to Kitch, "The focus on firemen enabled journalistic media to quickly rewrite the story of September 11 from one of vulnerability, fear, and death to one of strength, courage, and survival."[4]

Kitch argues that because we "know" and identify with celebrities as a result media stories, it makes sense that we publicly mourn them through commemorative editions and tributes. She examines the deaths of 20 celebrities over a 40-year period, including Frank Sinatra, John Lennon, Princess Diana of Wales, and John F. Kennedy Jr., who were covered by magazines as disparate as *People, Rolling Stone, The New Yorker,* and *U.S. News and World Report.*

"Counter-memory" is the key to understanding the role of magazines for African Americans, an under-researched topic. Kitch focuses on the historical content in *Ebony* and *American Legacy,* examining "the activist claim that African-Americans can thrive in the present only with an understanding of the past."[5] She points out that both magazines often document the past while challenging what the public remembers about it. This dual process highlights unique black experiences while at the same time showing the reality of race and place in America for much of the 19th and 20th centuries.

Magazines have articulated and identified key social trends revolving around the Greatest Generation, Baby Boomers, Generation X, and Generation Y. Kitch focuses on 20 cover stories that reported on the various generations and their reinterpretation of life changes, asking whether magazines are really reflecting social identities or creating them because of the marketing value of the generational labels.

Kitch turns to nostalgia magazines, studying 30 consecutive issues of *Good Old Days* and *Reminisce* and raises "the question of why a certain vi-

sion of the past emerges, with clear and consistent symbols, themes, and narratives in a reader-interactive medium."[6] More important, Kitch notes that nostalgia magazines are critical sites of cultural-identity construction for senior citizens and particularly older women. She asks what it is about the pull of nostalgia for today's young adults who yearn for a "simpler" past.

Finally, Kitch shows how magazines have celebrated their institutional birthdays as a way of defining national memory. Anniversary issues—whether they are produced by *Gourmet* or *Sports Illustrated*— "conflate their own past with the American past."[7] In particular, these special issues define themselves, editorially and graphically, as historical keepsakes as they personalized their past along with historical events and individuals.

In *Pages from the Past,* Kitch alerts scholars that amnesia may occur as magazines retell and retool certain events. Although stories may be "redrafted" by journalists, media memory doesn't have to be the antithesis of history. Through magazines, we share a memory and a history of the way we were, the way we are, and the way we're likely to become. ■

3. Ibid., 16–17.

4. Ibid., 53.

5. Ibid., 92.

6. Ibid., 153.

7. Ibid., 157.

cal Culture. Adding to the distinctiveness of the content was the appearance of *Reader's Digest.* It was small enough to fit in a jacket pocket or handbag at a time when most magazines were considerably larger.

In their intentional brevity of content, both *Time* and *Reader's Digest* capitalized on a trend that had started around 1900. While 19th-century magazines featured very long essays and rambling short stories, early-20th-century editors began running shorter articles to match the busier urban lives of their readers. David Graham Phillips, author of "The Treason of the Senate" (*Cosmopolitan*, March 1906), one of the most famous muckraking articles of the early 20th century, wrote about the demise of long essays in a 1903 article in *Success:* "The wise editors won't have them any more, because the people won't read them and won't even take magazines that get the reputation of harboring them." Phillips cited impatience on the part of the "present generation," whose only interests were the "here and now."[35]

Phillips's observation was prescient: Only two of the four general interest literary magazines popular at the turn of the century have survived. *The Century,* an elegant magazine that demanded a long, focused, attention span, and *Scribner's Magazine,* which competed as a less costly literary option that was strong in biography and autobiography, died during the 1930s.[36] *The Atlantic Monthly* and *Harper's* have managed to survive to this day as thoughtful literary magazines, but with considerably fewer readers and clout than they once had.

The third 20th-century magazine start-up to have a long-lasting effect on content was *The New Yorker,* established by Harold Ross in 1925. If the Wallaces were folksy and inspirational, Ross was witty and acerbic. Ross's distinctive approach to content in a metropolitan magazine is forever immortalized in *The New Yorker's* prospectus:

> *The New Yorker* will be a reflection in word and pictures of metropolitan life. It will be human. Its general tenor will be one of gaiety, wit and satire, but it will be more than a jester. It will not be what is commonly called sophisticated, in that it will assume a reasonable degree of enlightenment on the part of its readers. It will hate bunk. . . . Its integrity will be above suspicion. It hopes to be so entertaining and informative as to be a necessity for the person who knows his way about or wants to.
>
> *The New Yorker* will be the magazine which is not edited for the old lady in Dubuque. It will not be concerned in what she is thinking about. This is not meant in disrespect, but *The New Yorker* is a magazine avowedly published for a metropolitan audience and thereby will escape an influence which hampers most national publications. It expects a considerable national circulation, but this will come from persons who have a metropolitan interest.

Ross demanded perfection from his writers, and *The New Yorker* revolutionized editorial content through its individualistic essays, droll cartoons, biting criticism, plotless short stories, wry humor, ironic fragments used as fillers, and interpretive profiles. Then and now, *The New Yorker, Time,* and *Reader's Digest* lead the way as successful, long-term survivors by giving readers precisely the kind of content they want.

appearance

Most of today's magazines are visual entities, filled with colors, photos, illustrations, varied typefaces, and assorted graphic tricks. The words are so closely intertwined with the designs that it is hard to imagine that a magazine was ever anything but slick, vibrant, and glossy. However, the appearance

---

The 1927 silent movie *It* was a romantic comedy about an article in *Cosmopolitan* that dealt with sexual attraction. The month the movie was released, the magazine ran the same cover and article featured in the movie. This was some 40 years before Helen Gurley Brown took over the magazine and made it a periodical version of her book, *Sex and the Single Girl.* In 1927, *Cosmopolitan* was a respected general interest family magazine and not for "fun fearless females" wanting to read about turn-on tricks and passionate positions.

of the magazine has changed significantly over the years, from a dull all-type document to one that is design-driven to reflect the expectations of readers who want to be dazzled visually by images as well as by content.

■ 18TH CENTURY: DEFICIENT DESIGN

Although the content of early American magazines was engaging and diverse, the look was merely serviceable. Indeed, reading magazines published prior to 1825 took a great deal of concentration and determination. Capitalization, punctuation, and spelling were capricious. The type size for articles was a minuscule 6 or 7 points (about the size of today's classified advertisements), and type was densely set by hand. Most 18th-century printers used Caslon Old Style as their typeface, which is the font used in the Declaration of Independence. While patriotic, it is a difficult typeface for today's reader to comprehend: the "long s," which resembles a lowercase "f," was used; for example, "blessings" looked like "ble*ff*ings."

The concept of basing design on a two-page spread was unknown. A thin rule typically separated the end of one article and the beginning of the next. Placement of headlines and bylines was inconsistent. Even serialized articles ended arbitrarily rather than at an exciting moment to be continued. Graphic design was nonexistent until the 1830s; there were few type embellishments and limited type variation of size or family. A 1784 issue of *The Gentleman and Lady's Town and Country Magazine* reveals the standard look of late 18th-century magazines: gray and boring because just two narrow columns of type filled the 5¾ by 8¾ inch page.

Most 18th-century magazines measured about 5–6 inches by 8–9 inches per full page. Franklin's early magazine had one of the smallest type page of the day, measuring a mere 3⅛ by 6¼ inches on a full page measuring 4 by 6⅝ inches. Bradford's magazine was larger in size, measuring a full 5 by 8 inches. However, Bradford's first issue ran 34 pages, while Franklin published 76 pages.

Stiff, rough, rag paper was used. The paper stock of these early magazines has turned out to be surprisingly durable. Most are still intact, though yellowed and crumbling a bit around the edges. You can find many of the earliest magazines in the American Antiquarian Society Library in Worcester, Massachusetts.

The quality of printing varied from copy to copy because magazines were printed from hand-set type on hand-operated wooden presses. The title page or cover generally was illustrated with a crude woodcut, although some magazine publishers of the 18th century could afford to print the more detailed copperplate engravings laboriously done by hand.

The Royal American Magazine, established in Boston in 1774 by Isaiah Thomas, was the first periodical to use illustrations on a regular basis. Over a 15-issue run, a total of 22 engravings were published in *The Royal American*, with Paul Revere's political cartoons appearing regularly. One of Revere's most popular engravings was "The Able Doctor, or America Swallowing the Bitter Draught" in the June 1774 *Royal American*. That engraving showed a half-naked "America" held down by a bewigged and robed judge while "Parliament" forcibly poured tea from the spout of a teapot into her mouth. It was a clear reference to the British taxation of tea.

But most publishers felt the use of woodcuts or copperplate engravings to break up long pages of text was simply too expensive and time-consuming to produce. In the first issue of *The Gentleman and Lady's Town and Country Magazine*, publishers Job Weeden and William Barrett apologized

According to Trumbull White, *Redbook*'s first editor in 1903, the magazine got its name because "red is the color of happiness." The connection still holds true today, with *Redbook*'s website stating, "*Redbook* continues to help young working mothers pursue happiness, bring balance to a busy life and focus on what matters most to them."

for the lack of a "frontispiece and other plates," which they "could not obtain."[37]

■ 19TH CENTURY: ENGRAVED EMBELLISHMENTS

By the early 1800s, magazines were using at least an inch of white space around the type page and a larger type size of at least 8 points for the body copy. Headlines, clearly delineating copy, tended to be in 10- or 12-point boldface with all capital letters. In format, magazines of the period from 1825 to 1855 tended to look like books, with a one-column width.

The migration of English engravers to America during the early 19th century greatly improved the look of magazines. The use of sketches, drawings, and engravings became more prevalent, resulting in more attractive pages than had been found in 18th-century magazines. By 1809, *Port Folio* began publishing one copperplate engraving with each monthly issue, usually miniature scenes from the novels of Sir Walter Scott. Other magazines, such as *Graham's* and *Peterson's,* used numerous steel and copperplate engravings in each issue.

Fashion and flower copperplate engravings often were highlighted with watercolors individually applied by hand. *Godey's Lady's Book* led the way here beginning in 1830, with publisher Louis A. Godey eventually hiring 150 women to color pages by hand. The published plates in *Godey's Lady's Book* were so lovely that many readers cut them out, framed them, and hung them in parlors and bedrooms. You still can find framed pages from *Godey's Lady's Book* in antique stores throughout the country, selling for upwards of $50 each. Hand-etched copper and steel engravings were very expensive; editors at *New-York Mirror* wrote that large plates cost $1,000 apiece.[38] That meant a publisher sometimes paid more for an illustration than he did for all the literary content in a single issue. An advertisement in *Godey's Lady's Book* in 1831 stated that "the publishers have expended for Embellishments alone upwards of SEVEN THOUSAND DOLLARS" during the first 18 months of publication.[39]

Woodcuts were cheaper to use, but for many years were crude in detail and utilitarian in design. They also didn't last as long as steel plates, which were more durable than copper ones. By 1835, engraving on wood blocks had improved considerably in detail, delicacy, and durability. Wood engravings became more frequent because they were more cost efficient, at about $30 each, compared to the several hundred dollars required for each average-sized steel plate.

During the Civil War, a variety of illustrations depicted life and death on the battlefield. Mathew Brady's photographs of war scenes and national leaders during the Civil War could be found in some magazines as wood engravings of the original photographs. Artists had to carefully etch out the relief image of each scene, a task that took considerably more time than it did for Brady to set up his camera and snap. Most Civil War illustrations in the magazines of the day were grim battlefield sketches by artists who were called "picture correspondents." *Harper's Weekly* offered a variety of Civil War images, with artist Winslow Homer specializing in camp life while cartoonist Thomas Nast drew sentimental works, such as "Santa Claus in Camp" for the magazine's Christmas 1862 issue. Nast's later political cartoons for *Harper's Weekly* were dark and satirical, focusing on corrupt politicians and urban social ills in the 1870s.

During the 1880s, fine illustrations of beautiful young women became a popular form of pictorial content in magazines. Charles Dana Gibson was famous for his "Gibson Girl," who appeared in magazines as wide ranging as *Collier's, Cosmopolitan,* and *Saturday Evening Post* from 1887 until prior to World War I. Harrison Fisher and James Montgomery Flagg were other artists who drew lovely, all-American girls for women's magazines. The works of all three often were framed and hung in homes; many of their portraits were made into posters. Clearly, magazines were contributing to both the artistic and decorative instincts of their readers.

■ 20TH CENTURY: POPULAR PHOTOGRAPHY

Photography didn't revolutionize the appearance of magazines until the 1890s, when improved printing presses and the invention of the halftone brought the costs of production down. With photography, both the artist and the engraver were eliminated because the print could be rephotographed onto a sensitized plate and an acid bath could create the contrasting points needed in the final plate. Wood engravings became a dinosaur art form.

More and more magazines began using halftones to embellish articles. *McClure's,* for example, included photographs from the lives of famous men in its "Human Document" series, while *Munsey's* used the nude female to illustrate a department titled "Artists and Their Work." Photographs were still black and white, yet the images were nonetheless dramatic. *Collier's* news photographs of the 1898 Spanish-American War established the publication as the premier picture magazine of the time. *Collier's* also led the way in color illustration with the publication of Maxfield Parrish's imaginative series of Arabian Nights drawings from 1906 to 1907. Women's magazines, such as *Ladies' Home Journal,* also featured Parrish's ethereal and dreamlike images and landscapes on their covers.

Better paper quality, improved printing capabilities, and lowered costs all resulted in a vastly improved physical product. Soon after the turn of the 20th century, the photographic halftone cost just $20 to produce, while a full page fine-line wood engraving cost up to $300. Magazines featured more photography, more color, more attention to the layout of pages, and more design tricks. Two publications are responsible for critical turning points in the visual appearance of magazines.

Gilbert Hovey Grosvenor was editor of *National Geographic* in December 1904 when he learned from the printer that he was short on copy for the next issue—furthermore, he lacked any manuscripts to fill the space. Grosvenor told the story of his eventual good fortune in his 75th anniversary salute to the magazine, appropriate titled "The Romance of the *Geographic.*" Grosvenor wrote:

> By sheer chance I received in the mail 50 beautiful photographs of Lhasa, the mysterious capital of Tibet, on the very day that I urgently needed 11 pages of material for the January 1905 issue. The Russian explorers who took the pictures offered them free. So I filled the entire 11 pages with the photographs, raiding the Society's slim treasury to make the plates.[40]

Grosvenor said he expected to be fired by the magazine's board of directors for filling so much space with just photos. But when the magazine ap-

JANUARY 1905: Readers stopped editor Gilbert Hovey Grosvenor to tell him how much they enjoyed the *National Geographic* article with its extensive use of photos of Lhasa, Tibet.

peared, people stopped Grosvenor on the street to congratulate him on the Lhasa photo spread. That incident led him to run more and more photos in *National Geographic.*

In the April 1905 issue, Grosvenor published 138 photos depicting the Philippines, which had been sent to him by his cousin William Howard Taft, who was governor general of the islands.

Readers were so enamored of the issue that a second printing was ordered. Membership in the National Geographic Society soared from 3,662 in January 1905 to 11,479 by the end of the year.

Equally significant were the photos in the July 1906 issue: the first "flashlight pictures" of wild animals in their natural habitats. Grosvenor published 74 animal photos on 50 pages, with just 4 pages of text. It's not surprising that *National Geographic* was the first to run hand-tinted photographs of Korea and China in November 1910 and the first true color photograph in 1914.

With each new photographic delight, the circulation of *National Geographic* grew. This was noticed by other magazines, which began increasing the number of photos issue by issue. During the 1920s, fashion and high society magazines, particularly *Vogue* and *Vanity Fair*, enthusiastically embraced photography, as did *Harper's Bazaar* and *Town and Country*.

But it wasn't until November 1936 that a full-fledged modern picture magazine appeared on the newsstands: Henry Luce's *Life*. Unlike earlier magazines that had photos to illustrate copy (such as *Collier's* and *Frank Leslie's Illustrated Weekly*), *Life* used pictures to tell the story. Through the camera lenses of staff photographers Margaret Bourke-White, Alfred Eisenstaedt, Peter Stackpole, and Thomas McAvoy, *Life* introduced a whole new genre in content and form to the magazine industry: photojournalism.

Life wouldn't be the only picture magazine game in town for long. *Look* appeared in January 1937, and although it also was a picture magazine, there were fundamental differences in content. *Life* used photos that highlighted news and information, while *Look* opted for shots that were sensational and entertaining.

Adding photos and more color to editorial pages not only contributed to the physical improvement of magazines, they also affected the visual literacy of readers, who became more demanding. During the 1930s and 1940s, art direction became a factor in magazine design. Art directors were added to a staff that had long been top-heavy with editors and writers, and this contributed to a significant evolution in the visual component of magazines.

Under the creative eyes of such art directors as Alexey Brodovitch at *Harper's Bazaar* and Mehemed Fehmy Agha at *Vogue* and *Vanity Fair*, magazine pages finally had a sense of unity, conti-

nuity, and most important, style. Observers pointed out that for Brodovitch, magazine design was "a musical feeling, a rhythm resulting from the interaction of space and time—he wanted the magazine to read like a sheet of music. He and [editor] Carmel Snow would dance around the pages spread before them on the floor, trying to pick up the rhythm."[41] In general, magazines became bolder in their design and more dramatic in their appearance through the use of large blocks of white space. This trend continues today.

transportation and delivery

Transportation is dependent upon geography, terrain, and location, while delivery is influenced by postal regulations. Both factors affect a magazine's range and reach in terms of circulation and impact. While transportation facilities showed continual improvement, mail delivery was hampered by costly and capricious laws that did not always favor the early magazine industry.

■ 18TH CENTURY: LIMITED RESTRAINTS

When Bradford and Franklin established the first magazines in 1741, the American colonies stretched about 1,200 miles from northeast to southwest along the Atlantic Ocean. Although the colonies went inland as far west as 1,000 miles, most of the development was concentrated along the Atlantic seaboard. The population of the colonies was about 1 million people, with Philadelphia as the midpoint between New England and the Carolinas. By 1783, when the United States was recognized as a nation, 13 states extended north to Canada, west to the Mississippi River, and south to Florida. But during all of the 18th century and well into the 19th century, magazine readership was centered in a narrow strip from Boston to Baltimore.

Transportation was either by foot, by horse, or by carriage during the 18th century. Roads were poor, and the stagecoach averaged only 2 miles an hour. The journey from Boston to New York, a distance of 208 miles, took a stagecoach 8–10 days. As late as 1789, postal roads, where post offices were located and used by mail carriers, were few, numbering only 75 and scattered over a thousand miles of terrain. Through the late 1780s, most post roads ran along a north-south axis near the Atlantic seaboard.

The colonies had enjoyed a postal system since Queen Anne's Act of 1710, but no specific provisions had been made for carrying magazines in the mails. Each postmaster had considerable discretion over what could and could not be sent. Ben Franklin was the postmaster for Philadelphia in 1741, which explains why his magazine lasted 3 months longer than Bradford's. Franklin allowed post riders on horseback to carry his magazine, but not his rival's. Magazines were bulkier and heavier than newspapers and letters, and were often rejected because of space.

Even when stagecoaches carried mail, space and weight were at a premium. When allowed to use the mails, magazines were charged more than newspapers for the same service. The cost of postage was paid by the reader, directly to the post riders or postmasters. For the first 50 years of American magazine publishing, individual postmasters determined whether periodicals would be delivered, although some magazine publishers used independent "news carriers" for distribution.

Although postmasters may have been capricious, their approach was more favorable for magazine delivery than the Postal Act of 1792. This act allowed newspapers to be mailed for 1 cent postage for a distance of up to 100 miles, and 1.5 cents for more than 100 miles. This was a fraction of the cost of letters, which cost 6 cents per sheet for delivery up to 30 miles. Yet, a typical newspaper was four times larger than the one sheet of paper used for letters.[42] Nothing was said about magazines, and this was interpreted by postmasters as meaning they now could charge magazines the much higher letter rates.

Two popular magazines were hurt by the Postal Act of 1792. Both the *Columbian Magazine,* established in 1786, and *The American Museum,* started in 1787, had exceeded the typical magazine's life span because they were original and ambitious: new magazines for a new nation. Both publications collected and published Revolutionary War documents, letters, and essays so everyone could become familiar with the great thinkers of the war years. Some historians consider *The American Museum* to be the most important American magazine of the 18th century, because it reached a circulation of more than 1,200, which was enormous for the time period. Yet, despite the insight and obvious appeal of the two magazines, both died in 1792, victims of the postal system. Neither magazine could afford the new prohibitive and unequal postal rates.

A more indulgent postal law was passed by Congress in 1794 that recognized the importance of magazines and lowered their costs significantly. This resulted in an increasing number of magazine start-ups and was a factor in the magazine boom that occurred during the 19th century. However, it did not alleviate the expenses associated with magazines for readers. A 64-page magazine delivered more than 100 miles cost 8 cents postage. Eight cents in 1794 would buy a chair or pay the wages of a cleaning woman for a day. The postage fee was in addition to the subscription cost of a magazine. Many readers simply refused to pay for their magazines upon delivery, which affected the fortunes of magazine publishers. Consequently, some editors even printed the names of debtors in each issue in an attempt to shame delinquent readers into paying for the magazine.

> **In 1929 you could have purchased a "perpetual subscription" to *Time* for $60 that could be passed on to your heirs forever—or until *Time* went out of business. More than 100 subscribers are still taking advantage of that deal, which, unfortunately, is no longer available.**

■ 19TH CENTURY: POSTAL IMPROVEMENTS

By 1800, the United States had a much improved road system linking many communities. Postal roads were extended inland, and the government began to build federal highways. The famous Erie

Canal across New York State from Buffalo to Albany, completed in 1825, established the destiny of New York City as the biggest city and the center of American communications. Railroads began to be laid westward by the Baltimore and Ohio Railroad, offering another way for mail to reach readers. Unfortunately, postal rates did not decline as roads improved or as other transportation modes developed.

In 1825, Congress connected magazine postage to size and distance, at 1.5 cents per octavo sheet (per eight pages printed on a single sheet of paper) for up to 100 miles, and 2.5 cents for greater distances. This meant that a 96-page magazine paid 18 cents per issue for postage up to 100 miles and 30 cents for greater distances—or rather, subscribers paid. Yet newspapers, regardless of size, still paid a maximum of 1.5 cents for delivery anywhere in the country. Because of the extra cost of mailing a magazine more than 100 miles, circulation tended to remain concentrated in the northeast portion of the United States.

Newspapers sent fewer than 30 miles were mailed free. Some magazines tried to get newspaper classification, even calling themselves newspapers. Finally in 1845, Congress abolished the distance factor, fixing the rate by weight at 2.5 cents for the first ounce of weight and 1 cent for each additional ounce. Most monthlies weighed between 5 and 6 ounces, so this meant a reduction in postal costs (see Table 3.4). That typical 96-page magazine now cost between 6.5 cents and 7.5 cents to mail.

Magazine circulations continued to be low, ranging from a few hundred up to the 40,000 claimed by *Godey's Lady's Book* in 1849. Readership tended to be concentrated east of the Mississippi River. Circulation figures are hard to determine, but it's estimated that the average during the 1850s was about 7,500.

Magazine publishers continued to lobby for reduced rates, and a significant turning point occurred in 1852, when postal rates dropped again. The average 96-page magazine that weighed 5 ounces had cost 6.5 cents to receive under the 1845 Post Office Act; now it would cost 1.5 cents to send. More fundamental was that the 1852 Post Office Act allowed postal fees to be paid at the mailing office, and publishers decided it would be better policy to absorb the cost of postage at that point. No longer would subscribers have to prepay the postage sum on a quarterly basis at their post offices.

Following the Civil War, another round of magazine expansion began, with as many as 9,000 periodicals established. These now had an average life of 4 years. Transportation channels for distribution were greatly facilitated when the East and West Coasts were connected by rail in 1869; tracks laid from the east by the Union Pacific joined those from the west laid by the Central Pacific at Promontory Point, Utah. Magazines became more national in approach, and circulations regularly began to exceed 100,000. Between 1865 and 1885, more than 30 magazines boasted having circulations of 100,000 or more. Among them were *Youth's Companion, Harper's Monthly, Godey's Lady's Book,* and *Peterson's.*

The most important postal date in conjunction with the modern magazine is 1879, when special second-class mailing privileges were given to magazines. Delivery had long been a major, if not the

■ **Table 3.4** Early Magazine Postage Costs

YEAR	MAGAZINE SIZE	DISTANCE	COST TO MAIL
1794	64 pages Weight not a factor	Up to 100 miles More than 100 miles	6 cents 8 cents
1825	96 pages Weight not a factor	Up to 100 miles More than 100 miles	18 cents 30 cents
1845	96 pages 5 ounces in weight	Any distance	6.5 cents
1852	96 pages 5 ounces in weight	Any distance	1.5 cents
1885	Any size Second-class privileges	Any distance	1 cent per pound (16 ounces)

major, problem facing publishers. For the first time, the federal government in effect subsidized magazine delivery. The Postal Act of 1879 meant that magazines could be mailed from coast to coast at the same low cost newspapers had long enjoyed. Scores of magazines were then developed and designed for the average working man and woman, as opposed to the more prosperous urban professional who previously had been the primary audience.

Postage rates for second-class mail dropped again in 1885, to 1 cent per pound, and in 1897, the rural free delivery system was instituted. Both developments helped farm, agriculture, and women's periodicals. Magazines now could reach every corner of the nation, and circulations soared to the millions. Delivery and transportation costs were more than covered by advertising revenue. Most magazines were sold by subscription, although newsstand single-copy sales became a more important factor after publishers began distributing their magazines to dealers through independent wholesalers during the 1890s.

■ 20TH CENTURY: COMPLEX COSTS

Transportation and delivery systems became linked to production and technological improvements that grew out of the Industrial Revolution. Postal regulations became more complex; starting in 1917, editorial matter was charged a flat rate, while advertising pages were zoned and cost accordingly. Since the 1950s, one of the concerns in magazine budgets has been to allow for rising second-class postage rates. Consequently, after years of increasingly higher circulations, many publishers found it prudent to deliberately cut back or reduce circulation numbers after the 1960s.

The Postal Reorganization Act of 1970 took away the power to set rates and classifications from Congress and made the post office an independent regulatory agency. This quasi-government agency, the United States Postal Service (USPS) with its Postal Rate Commission, now sets rates, reviews mail service, and investigates complaints. Greatly increased second-class rates were established in 1970, but were phased in over a 10-year period. By 1980, after a decade of runaway inflation, postal rates had increased more than 400 percent.

In 1970, subscriptions accounted for 71 percent of magazine sales, with single-copy purchases ac-

counting for the remaining 29 percent. By 1990, that figure was 80 percent subscriptions and 20 percent single-copy sales. In 2000, 84 percent of total magazine circulation sales came from subscriptions, with single-copy sales accounting for the remaining 16 percent.[43] Postal rate hikes, whether or not they occur under the rubric of reform, have a major impact on a magazine's economic health. Although no rate increase is ever welcome, publishers say they prefer moderate, steady increases that are phased in over several years over a single whopping price increase.

Another economic factor for magazine publishers was a shift in distribution outlets from the stand-alone outdoor newsstand (one on every corner in major cities like New York and Chicago), to supermarket and convenience store checkout counters and bookstores, to specialty or niche retail outlets. In 1999, Wal-Mart chopped the number of magazines being sold in its stores by as many as 2,200 because of poor efficiency and sales performances. Titles that were selling only one or two copies in a store simply weren't wanted.[44] Specialty consumer titles like *Sea Kayaker* went to kayak shops in order to reach impulse buyers, who have long driven newsstand sales. Many hobby and crafts magazines moved to arts and crafts stores—niche distribution outlets—where consumers were looking for scrapbooks, patterns, and scale models as well as information about how to include the latest border, stitch, or stripe.

"A lot of new, really niche titles can't get significant distribution through the traditional wholesaler system," said John Morthanos, vice president of single-copy sales for Primedia Special Interest publications, in 1999, adding that "as titles become more vertical, mass outlets become less relevant."[45] Just as magazines have become more segmented, so have the shopping habits of consumers. It's not surprising that the biggest retail outlet for *This Old House* is Home Depot and not a traditional grocery store.

production and technology

· ·

Increases in the amount of leisure time, shorter work weeks, appliances that lightened household chores, transportation improvements, and significant changes in technology and production all had an impact on American magazines.

■ 18TH CENTURY: INTENSIVE HAND LABORS

An enormous amount of labor was needed to produce a magazine during the 18th century. Printing a magazine was slow, hard work done by hand. Printing presses were virtually the same in the 18th century as they had been in 1448, when Johannes Gutenberg created moveable type. The cumbersome wooden press used by Franklin and Bradford in 1741 was still based on the screw-operated press devised by Gutenberg when he printed the Bible in the mid-15th century. More than a dozen distinct operations were needed to turn out a single page. Type was set by hand, one letter, one line, one page at a time. Then the page form would be broken up so the type could be used again—and again.

Paper also was made by hand from rags and scraps of linen cloth. Ink, too, tended to be produced by the printer using lampblack and boiled linseed oil, with each printer having his own "secret" formula. Although the first ink factory was established in America in 1742, its output was limited and costly.

In order to have consistent quality and quantity of paper and ink as well as the best type and presses, those American printers who could afford it imported their printing necessities from England. With the Revolutionary War, however, England embargoed all paper and printing equipment. Consequently, magazine publication came to a standstill during the American Revolution.

■ 19TH CENTURY: MASS PRODUCTION PROCEDURES

Mass production methods were introduced to printing during the last 10 years of the 19th century: timed production scheduling, conveyor systems, and assembly lines. The slow flatbed press that printed merely one sheet at a time gave way to the steam-powered press in 1822, then to the swifter rotary press in 1847, and finally, by 1871, to the web perfecting press capable of simultaneously printing both sides of a continuous roll of paper. Color printing was part of the production process by the 1860s.

For illustrations, magazines no longer had to depend on sketches that were laboriously copied, expensively engraved on copper or wood, and then colored by hand. With new photoengraving techniques, photographs became common. In 1886, the Mergenthaler Linotype machine revolutionized publishing by eliminating the need to set type by hand. The Linotype could do the work of seven or eight hand-typesetters faster and more efficiently.

Papermaking techniques also improved as publishers moved from the costly handmade linen pulp of the 18th century to cheap wood pulp during the mid-19th century, to elegant, yet affordable, slick and coated sheets in the 20th century. The result was that technology allowed for attractive magazines to be turned out at a low unit cost, again leading to lower prices for the magazine reader. Today, some environmentally conscious publishers are turning to recycled paper, although it is not always an economical decision.

■ 20TH CENTURY: TECHNOLOGICAL TECHNIQUES

The 20th century brought more technological improvements to the magazine industry. E-mail, online bill paying, and faxes changed the expectations of subscribers as well as publishers. Increasingly readers began subscribing or renewing their subscriptions online rather than by direct mail. Digital photography became a source for editorial and advertising color images, eliminating the darkroom with its chemical smells and stains.

Computer and satellite technology narrowed the amount of time needed to accept advertising as well as to print fast-breaking stories. That same technology, along with demographic information, encouraged publishers to target narrowly defined, niche audiences through selective binding as early as 1982.

Scientific American offers an excellent example of the steps a magazine takes in adapting to technology. According to Richard Sasso, who was associate publisher and vice president of production at the time, the first desktop, or computer-assisted, issue of *Scientific American* was published in 1978. By 1989, the art and production departments were using Macintosh computers to their fullest capacity, with editors switching to Macintosh in 1991. All departments were networked by 1993.

In October 1994, the first computer-to-plate (CTP) test took place: 16 pages were produced using all digital information. No film was shot and no negatives were made for those pages. According to Sasso, the quality of CTP technology was excellent, and editors agreed to try it with an entire issue. The convincing argument for editors was that 3–5 days could be cut from the editorial schedule using CTP. Advertisers could also send material in later than normal.

The January 1995 issue of *Scientific American*, touting "The Computer in the 21st Century" on the cover, became the first true digital web-offset magazine. All ads and editorial in the 200-page magazine were produced without film. Apple Computer supplied the ads, 22 full color pages in digital form. Said Sasso, "It was a first for the web offset magazine industry."[46]

By the end of 1995, 70 million copy pages had been produced for the magazine using CTP. *Scientific American* announced it would begin accepting digital advertising, but Sasso said there were no takers at first. However, by the March 1996 issue, half of the ads were supplied as digital data.

The new platform slowly gained acceptance in the magazine industry during the late 1990s. By 2000, digital editorial and advertising material—produced without film—was the norm at the majority of magazines being published. CTP, with its filmless workflow, has eliminated much of a publisher's prepress bill and allowed for content alternations to occur in hours rather than days.

Sasso encouraged the use of CTP because it meant better quality, lower costs, and faster editorial turnaround time. As with any technological innovation, some publishers were quicker to adapt than others. Sasso observed in 1998 that education, communication, and a lot of cooperation were needed.

Those words are almost a mantra for the magazine field. Throughout history, the constantly evolving magazine remains a vehicle for communication and a marketplace of ideas. Or, as Art Cooper, *GQ*'s editor-in-chief from 1983–2003, explained it: "A magazine is a living thing, not a museum. The magazine that doesn't continue to change is going to perish."[47]

notes

1. Some historians cite *Town and Country* and *Scientific American* as the oldest magazine titles. However, both started as newspapers. *Town and Country*, which celebrated its 150th anniversary in October 1996, began in 1846 as a weekly newspaper titled *National Press*, then changed its name to *Home Journal* 9 months later. *Town and Country* did not receive its current name until 1901. *Scientific American* was established as a weekly newspaper in 1845, and didn't evolve into a monthly magazine until 1921.
2. "Acknowledgements," *American Magazine* (February 1788): 130.
3. Bob Hershfeld, "Improbable Mission," *Folio:* (April 2004): 30.
4. Samir Husni, "New Titles," Mr. Magazine, http://www.mrmagazine.com/titles.html.
5. William Beer, C*hecklist of American Magazines, 1741–1800* (Worcester, Mass.: American Antiquarian Society, 1923).
6. "American Periodicals," *New-York Mirror* (November 15, 1828): 151.
7. Lee Soltow and Edward Stevens, *The Rise of Literacy and the Common School in the United States: A Socioeconomic Analysis to 1870* (Chicago: University of Chicago Press, 1981), 34–51.
8. Kenneth A. Lockridge, *Literacy in Colonial New England* (New York: W. W. Norton, 1974), 13.
9. David Paul Nord, "A Republican Literature: A Study of Magazine Reading and Readers in Late-Eighteenth-Century New York" (paper presented at the annual meeting of the Association for Education in Journalism and Mass Communication, Norman, Okla., August 1986).
10. Lockridge, 38–42.
11. Job Weeden and William Barrett, "To the Public," *Gentleman and Lady's Town and Country Magazine* (May 1784): 4.
12. Sara M. Evans, *Born for Liberty: A History of Women in America* (New York: Free Press, 1989), 65.
13. Soltow and Stevens, 51.
14. Ibid., 51.
15. Frank Luther Mott, *A History of American Magazines, 1850-1865*, vol. 2 (Cambridge, Mass.: Harvard University Press, 1957), 103.
16. Ibid., 106–7.
17. William B. Cairns, "Later Magazines," in *Cambridge History of American Literature,* vol. 3, ed. William Peterfield Trent, John Erskine, Stuart P. Sherman, and Carl Van Doren (New York: G. P. Putnam's Sons, 1921), 299.
18. Carl F. Kaestle, Helen Damon-Moore, Lawrence C. Stedman, Katherine Tinsley, and William Vance Trollinger Jr., eds. *Literacy in the United States: Readers and Reading Since 1880* (New Haven, Conn.: Yale University Press, 1991), 283.

19. Ibid., 193.
20. Paul F. Lazarsfeld and Patricia Kendall, "The Communications Behavior of the Average American," in *Mass Communications,* ed. Wilbur Schramm (Urbana: University of Illinois Press, 1960), 432.
21. Stephen G. Smith, "From the Editor: The Bond Between a Magazine and Its Readers," *Civilization* (May/June 1995): 6.
22. Douglas B. Ward, "The Reader as Consumer: Curtis Publishing Company and Its Audience, 1910–1930," *Journalism History* (Summer 1996): 47.
23. Kaestle, 172.
24. Ibid., 172.
25. Ward, 52.
26. Ibid., 53.
27. Isaiah Thomas, *The History of Printing in America* (New York: Weathervane Books, 1970, from the second edition printed by the American Antiquarian Society Library, 1824), 284.
28. Frank Luther Mott, *A History of American Magazines, 1741–1850,* vol. 1 (Cambridge, Mass.: Harvard University Press, 1939), 494–513.
29. "The Magazine Galore," *The Round Table* (November 23, 1867): 337.
30. David Forsyth and Warren Berger, "Trading Places," *Folio:* (March 1991): 82.
31. Frank Luther Mott, *A History of American Magazines, 1865–1885,* vol. 3 (Cambridge, Mass.: Harvard University Press, 1957), 133.
32. American Business Press website (June 16, 1998), http://www.americanbusinesspress.com.
33. Edward Bok, *The Americanization of Edward Bok* (New York: Scribner's Sons, 1920), 374–75.
34. "The Common Touch," *Time* (December 10, 1951): 64.
35. Wm. David Sloan and James D. Startt, *The Media in America: A History,* 3rd ed. (Northport, Ala.: Vision Press, 1996), 472–73.
36. *Scribner's Monthly* was founded in 1870 and published as a literary magazine until 1881 when it was sold because of a difference of opinions between the book publishing Scribners (Charles Scribner's Sons) and the magazine publishing Scribners (Scribner and Company). The magazine's name was changed to *The Century* under a new publisher and editor; *The Century* died in 1930. The book publishing Scribners promised not to start another magazine within 5 years. Their *Scribner's Magazine* was established in 1887 and died in 1939.
37. Weeden and Barrett, 4.
38. "American Periodical Literature," *New-York Mirror* (January 4, 1834): 215.
39. *Godey's Lady's Book* (July 1831), back cover.
40. Gilbert Hovey Grosvenor, "The Romance of the *Geographic*," *National Geographic* (October 1963): 565.
41. "*Harper's Bazaar* at 100," *Print* (September/October 1967): 46.
42. Kielbowicz, Richard B. *News in the Mail: The Press, Post Office, and Public Information, 1700–1860s* (New York: Greenwood Press, 1989): 33–36.
43. Magazine Publishers of America, "Circulation Trends: Historical Subscriptions/Single Copy Sales," http://www.magazine.org/circulation.
44. Joanna Lowenstein, "The Shift to Specialty Distribution," *Folio:* (June 1999): 65.
45. Ibid., 71.
46. Richard Sasso, "The Art of Magazine Production," Stanford Professional Publishing Course, Palo Alto, Calif. (July 27, 1997).
47. Keith J. Kelly, "Magazines Put on New Face," *Advertising Age* (November 28, 1994): 8.

for additional reading

Angeletti, Norberto, and Alberto Oliva. *Magazines That Make History.* Gainesville: University Press of Florida, 2004.
Bainbridge, John. *Little Wonder or, the* Reader's Digest *and How It Grew.* New York: Reynal and Hitchcock, 1945.
Bok, Edward. *The Americanization of Edward Bok.* New York: Scribner's Sons, 1920.
Canning, Peter. *American Dreamers: The Wallaces and Reader's Digest: An Insider's Story.* New York: Simon and Schuster, 1996.
Cohn, Jan. *Creating America: George Horace Lorimer and the* Saturday Evening Post. Pittsburgh: University of Pittsburgh Press, 1989.
Edgar, Neal L. *A History and Bibliography of American Magazines, 1810–1820.* Metuchen, N.J.: Scarecrow Press, 1975.
Elson, Robert T. *Time Inc.: The Intimate History of a Publishing Enterprise, 1923–1941.* New York: Atheneum, 1968.
———. *The World of Time Inc.: The Intimate History of a Publishing Enterprise, 1941–1960.* New York: Atheneum, 1973.
Ford, James L. C. *Magazines for Millions: The Story of Specialized Publications.* Carbondale: Southern Illinois University Press, 1969.
Forsyth, David P. *The Business Press in America, 1750–1865.* Philadelphia: Chilton Books, 1964.
Harper, J. Henry. *The House of Harper: A Century of Publishing in Franklin Square.* New York: Harper and Brothers Publishing, 1912.
Janello, Amy, and Brennon Jones. *The American Magazine.* New York: Harry N. Abrams, 1991.
Lapham, Lewis H., and Ellen Rosenbush, eds. *An American Album: One Hundred and Fifty Years of* Harper's Magazine. New York: Franklin Square Press, 2000.
Mott, Frank Luther. *A History of American Magazines, 1741–1850.* Vol. 1. Cambridge, Mass.: Harvard University Press, 1930.
———. *A History of American Magazines, 1850–1865.* Vol. 2. Cambridge, Mass.: Harvard University Press, 1938.
———. *A History of American Magazines, 1865–1885.* Vol. 3. Cambridge, Mass.: Harvard University Press, 1938.
———. *A History of American Magazines, 1885–1905.* Vol.

4. Cambridge, Mass.: Harvard University Press, 1957.
———. *A History of American Magazines, 1905–1930.* Vol. 5. Cambridge, Mass.: Harvard University Press, 1968.

Nourie, Alan, and Barbara Nourie, eds. *American Mass-Market Magazines.* Westport, Conn.: Greenwood Press, 1990.

Peterson, Theodore. *Magazines in the Twentieth Century.* Urbana: University of Illinois Press, 1964.

Prendergast, Curtis, with Geoffrey Colvin. *The World of Time Inc.: The Intimate History of a Changing Enterprise, 1960–1980.* New York: Atheneum, 1986.

Richardson, Lyon N. *A History of Early American Magazines, 1741–1789.* New York: Octagon Books, 1978.

Schneirov, Matthew. *The Dream of a New Social Order: Popular Magazines in America, 1893–1914.* New York: Columbia University Press, 1994.

Swanberg, W. A. *Luce and His Empire.* New York: Charles Scribner's Sons, 1972.

Tassin, Algernon. *The Magazine in America.* New York: Dodd, Mead, 1916.

Tebbel, John. *The American Magazine: A Compact History.* New York: Hawthorn Books, 1969.

Tebbel, John, and Mary Ellen Zuckerman. *The Magazine in America, 1741–1990.* New York: Oxford University Press, 1991.

Thurber, James. *The Years with Ross.* Boston: Little, Brown, 1957.

Weber, Ronald. *Hired Pens: Professional Writers in America's Golden Age of Print.* Athens: Ohio University Press, 1997.

Wood, James Playsted. *Magazines in the United States.* 2d ed. New York: Ronald Press, 1956.

———. *Of Lasting Interest: The Story of the* Reader's Digest. New York: Doubleday, 1958.

Zuckerman, Mary Ellen. *A History of Popular Women's Magazines in the United States, 1792–1995.* Westport, Conn.: Greenwood Press, 1998.

chapter 4

the magazine as a social barometer: political and cultural interaction

n 1877 when Thomas Edison fine-tuned the phonograph and was ready to show his invention to somebody outside his shop, whom did he choose? The editor of *Scientific American*. When fans begged mystery writer Arthur Conan Doyle to bring back Sherlock Holmes, whom he had killed off in 1893, what medium did Doyle use to usher in the long-awaited return of the detective? The magazine *Collier's*, in a story that appeared in the September 26, 1903, issue. In 2005, when W. Mark Felt, who was assistant director of the FBI during the Nixon Administration, decided to reveal that he was Watergate's "Deep Throat" after keeping his identity a secret for more than 30 years, he turned to *Vanity Fair*. Depending on their generation, young men have used *National Geographic*, *Playboy*, or *Maxim* as their introduction to the female form. Young women have read *Seventeen*, *Sassy*, or *Cosmopolitan* for advice on how to deal with those young men. Their parents read *Parents* or *Psychology Today* to try to figure it all out. ■ Magazines are lively and engaging societal resources, affecting the world around them and, in turn, being affected themselves by that world. The social influence of magazines is as diverse as the magazines themselves. Magazines such as *The New Yorker*, *Ebony*, *Glamour*, and *Utne* have influenced their worlds by the nature of the information they present as well as by the way they present that information. The world is different in a variety of ways because magazines exist. ■ That world is far from static, though. Just as magazines influence society, they are influenced by it. Magazines are born, die, shrink, grow, and change their appearances and audiences because of a host of developments within society. As society changes, so do magazines.

the interaction of magazines and society

Do magazines mirror society or does society mirror magazines? An easy answer would be "both." A more complete explanation, however, would recognize magazines as active members of a complex society, leading the discussion in many cases, but allowing others in society to take the action that will cause change. Change only happens when the messages magazines present find a receptive ear in society. Conversely, those messages may not be heard without the help of magazines.

Your family, education, religious background, job, geographic location, political beliefs, gender, cultural history, and a host of other factors cause you to react differently from your neighbor and similarly to your best friend when faced with information from a magazine. For example, you may base all your computer purchases on ratings from *Consumer Reports*, while your neighbor swears by *PC Magazine*. Your sister trusts *The Nation*; you trust *National Review*. You get your sports information from *Sports Illustrated*; your brother turns to *ESPN: The Magazine*. We all live our lives differently—we're all surrounded by different phenomena—so we react differently to the media and they affect us differently.

The phenomenistic approach to the study of magazines takes all these differences into account and recognizes that magazines are but one influence in a whole universe of influences. Named by mass communications researcher Joseph Klapper,[1] this theory grew out of scholars' frustration with their attempts to prove specific, absolute media effects. Those effects, Klapper suggested, were difficult to isolate because the media aren't isolated entities. They are, instead, phenomena operating within a system of other phenomena.

In 1987, *Hustler* magazine was sued for publishing an article titled "Orgasm of Death," which explained autoerotic asphyxia, the practice of masturbating while hanging oneself, supposedly to increase pleasure. It began with examples of deaths caused by the practice and included a warning against trying the act. It also, however, included information on how to do it. At least one young man tried the act after reading the article, and died. The issue of *Hustler* with the "Orgasm" article was found at his feet. The boy's mother and his close friend sued the magazine and were

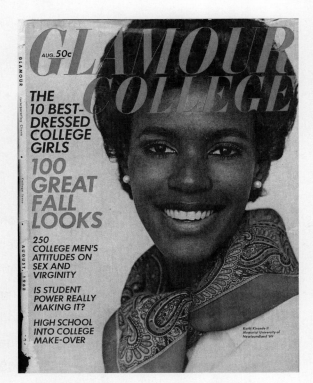

AUGUST 1968: With this issue, *Glamour* became the first major women's magazine to place a black woman on the cover.

awarded $200,000 in damages. The judgment was reversed, however, by the federal court of appeals, which noted the lack of evidence that the article by itself could have caused the death.[2] What was the effect of that article? The magazine did provide the information, but it was just one phenomenon. It, alone, was not responsible for the reader's actions, but it did have an influence.

To study the interaction between magazines and society, it is necessary to break society into smaller segments and analyze those segments. We can study the political and cultural nature of magazines through four perspectives: magazines as political influences; political influences on magazines; magazines as cultural influences; and cultural influences on magazines.

magazines as political influences

The voice magazines give to political causes—mainstream and alternative, popular and unpopular—may be one of the medium's most important influences. The diversity of magazines makes them, in total, a balanced voice that speaks for liberal as well as conservative viewpoints, for groups who seek to change society as well as those who advocate maintaining the status quo. While *National Review* focuses on the shortcomings of liberal Democrats, *The Nation* looks at errors in the ways of conservative Republicans.

As political influences, magazines are agenda setters and advocates. Agenda setters influence change, often unintentionally, simply by calling public attention to an issue. The term agenda setting began to be used by 1960s media scholars who were still searching for a way to isolate and analyze media effects, and it represented an important change in approach.[3] Until that time, theorists had been looking at the ways in which the media made us think, with brainwashing being an early concern. The focus in agenda setting theory is on the belief that the media do not tell us *how* to think, they tell us what to think *about.*

Magazines act as agenda setters when they identify and frame the issues on which society focuses. They tell the public, in essence, that something is important and should be discussed. Magazine journalists, agenda setting theorists believe, do not directly cause social change. They provide information that may motivate others to enact change.

Changes influenced by agenda setters may be direct or indirect, for good or for ill. Magazines were setting the public agenda long before the term was coined. In the past, agenda setters have been called muckrakers; today they're likely to be called investigative reporters.

In other cases, magazine staffers can be advocates for a cause affecting their audience. Advocates can also be agenda setters. In fact, in most cases, agenda setting is an advocate's goal.

■ AGENDA SETTERS

Magazines set the public agenda by their emphasis on the major as well as the minor. When *Education Week* magazine runs a state-by-state critique of the nation's schools, it sends school boards across the country scurrying, some heading for the press room to crow about their accomplishments, others to the back room to figure out an excuse for their poor rating. When *Money* magazine ranks the tax burdens of individual states, legislators

throughout the nation huddle in strategy sessions, often discussing ways to change the tax structure that led to a low evaluation.

You'll see examples of agenda setting throughout this book, ranging from *Playboy*'s creation of Playmates to *Glamour*'s fashion don'ts. The very existence of titles such as *Latina* and *Audrey* set the nation's agenda by stressing the importance of groups within society, in these cases Hispanic and Asian American women.

Seldom is the case for agenda setting so clear and so strong, however, as it was with Rachel Carson's environmental writing. In 1960, Carson, a journalist and biologist, wrote a series of articles for *The New Yorker* about the dangers of pesticides, specifically DDT. Carson's work, titled "Silent Spring," also was published in a book of the same name. Based on meticulous research and articulated with grace and detail, *Silent Spring* is credited with causing the ban on DDT use and production in this country and is seen by many as the seed that eventually grew into the Environmental Protection Agency. *The New Yorker* in this case was an agenda setter. It brought forth a topic to discuss and let society as a whole make its own decision on how to deal with the issue.

Carson's *Silent Spring* demonstrated how chemicals were contaminating the food chain, leading to health dangers such as cancer and to possible genetic effects that might not be known for generations. It led the nation into a debate on the issue, with articles in *Time, Consumer Bulletin,* and *Saturday Evening Post* broadening the discussion.[4] By 1970, state and federal legislation severely restricted the use of DDT. By 1980, the use of DDT was eliminated in the United States and limited in Third World countries. In addition, chemical companies reacted to Carson's criticisms by producing less dangerous chemical pesticides and by directing agrochemical research toward the creation of pesticides that are used in smaller doses and with less frequent application.[5]

Carson was not universally supported, however. *Time* called her work "oversimplified" and suggested she might do more harm than good with "her emotional and inaccurate outburst." Edwin Diamond, writing in *Saturday Evening Post*, also called Carson "emotional" and said that, thanks to her, "a big fuss has been stirred up to scare the American public out of its wits." Likewise, this discussion of Carson's ideas became part of the public agenda, although final action was left to politicians. Carson's role was to get the country talking, and she did: The discussion of chemical pesticides continues, more than 40 years after Carson sat down at her typewriter.

Trade magazines, likewise, can be effective agenda setters. *Aviation Week and Space Technology* has long been acknowledged as the leader in aerospace information. Dating back to pre-World War I daredevil days of flight, the magazine devotes page after page to all facets of aircraft production, the airline industry, and both defense and civil aerospace concerns.

Whenever a new aircraft is developed at home or abroad, when an airline reconfigures its seat pitch, or when an airplane crashes, *Aviation Week and Space Technology* authoritatively tells readers what it means from a technical point of view. Its coverage of the 1986 *Challenger* explosion, with

photos of the spaceship's solid booster spraying stray fire at the external tank, was studied closely by aerospace insiders and by outside experts.

The publication maintains a staunch independence from the industry it covers and is regularly quoted by newspapers and television network news programs. Military coverage has long been dominant in the magazine's pages. The 1991 Persian Gulf War (Operation Desert Storm), however, was the first time *Aviation Week and Space Technology* covered a military conflict as a breaking news story, while also relating technical and operational air aspects.[6]

Possibly the best-known agenda setters were the muckrakers, the early investigative reporters who wrote in magazines at the turn of the 20th century: journalists such as Ida M. Tarbell, Lincoln

Research in Brief

Agenda Setting

In July 1962, the *Journal of the American Medical Association (JAMA)* published an article by Dr. C. Henry Kempe on "The Battered Child Syndrome." In the decade before the article, mass circulation magazines carried only three articles on child abuse. In the decade following the article, these same magazines published 28 such articles, a 900 percent increase. What's most important, however, is that Kempe gave a phenomenon a catchy name: battered child syndrome. Ultimately, through significant media use, this name became part of our language.

In *Making an Issue of Child Abuse*, media scholar Barbara

Nelson studied this phenomenon.[1] Nelson noted that the news magazines—*Time* and *Newsweek*—were the first to run articles on Kempe's research, and *Saturday Evening Post* and *Life* followed with articles within months. Kempe was always listed as a source. All articles took Kempe's slant, emphasizing the medical rather than the criminal aspects of the "syndrome." What had been seen as an activity was now seen as a disease—treatable and preventable. The battered child syndrome, a phrase invented in 1962 and introduced to the public through *JAMA*, had become the defining term.

One magazine—*JAMA*, the organization magazine for the medical industry—led the way as the source for other magazines. It also led the way for newspapers and television. The syndrome appeared on *Dragnet* as well as on *Dr. Kildare* and *Ben Casey, M.D.*—the 1960s forerunners of *Grey's Anatomy* and *ER*—and was the subject of 16 stories in *The New York Times* in 1964 alone.

The child abuse issue reached consideration in state legislatures and in Congress, Nelson maintains, due in part to "sustained coverage in professional journals, popular magazines and newspapers." ■

1. Barbara Nelson, *Making an Issue of Child Abuse: Political Agenda Setting for Social Problems* (Urbana: University of Chicago Press, 1984).

Steffens, and Ray Stannard Baker. The term muck-rakers was coined in 1906 by President Theodore Roosevelt, who compared such writers to "the Man with the Muckrake" who dug through the filth without seeing the positive side of life in John Bunyan's *Pilgrim's Progress*.[7] Generally supportive of the reforms encouraged by muckrakers, Roosevelt nevertheless became frustrated with the intensity of the movement. His frustration no doubt grew out of the tempestuous mood of social change fostered by the articles.

Tarbell's series on "The History of the Standard Oil Company" chronicled John D. Rockefeller's often ruthless treatment of employees and competitors; it took her 5 years to research. Steffens outlined local political corruption in New York, Minneapolis, and St. Louis in "Shame of the Cities." Baker wrote a treatise on employment practices and working conditions titled "The Right to Work." All three had segments of their work published in the January 1903 issue of *McClure's*, the issue that is generally regarded as the first breath of the muckraking movement. Magazines such as *Collier's*, *Cosmopolitan*, and *Hampton's* also jumped on the muckraking bandwagon, which rolled along until roughly 1912.

Even the top women's magazines at the start of the 20th century engaged in muckraking. *Good Housekeeping*, *Woman's Home Companion*, *McCall's*, and *Ladies' Home Journal* took the position that a woman's sphere—her influence or place in society—could go beyond the traditional home environment. With women's magazines forging a link between the narrow confines of the home and the larger "national household," a proper Victorian lady could address housekeeping issues facing the whole community. The women's sphere argument allowed middle-class women and their magazines to respond to and participate in the muckraking movement.

Professor Kathleen L. Endres of the University of Akron has argued that writers for the top four women's magazines of this period did not just illustrate scandalous situations. They also were expected to offer solutions to the ills they reported, while continuing to support the prevalent conservative view of women as homemakers and nurturers.[8] The homemaker who would not tolerate adulterated food in her own kitchen—rotten apples used in commercial jellies, milk with formaldehyde as a preservative, or vanilla extract laced with wood alcohol—could protect her fam-

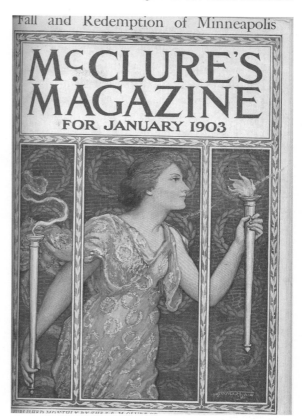

JANUARY 1903: This issue of *McClure's* included investigative articles by muckrakers Ida M. Tarbell, Lincoln Steffens, and Ray Stannard Baker.

ily through intelligent shopping. And because, as the "perfect" wife and mother, she was the primary consumer of the period, she waged war against corrupted food at the national level through her purchases. The women's magazines, by telling readers how to shop, elevated domestic concerns to national consciousness.

Good Housekeeping was the first to enter the fight against the misrepresentation of products, setting up a Good Housekeeping Testing Institute in 1901 as a place to test foods and household products for purity. By 1906, the magazine was providing monthly reports of brand-name foods that met its standards for purity, as well as annual summaries to be used as guides to safe shopping. Similarly, *Ladies' Home Journal* crusaded against the patent medicines used by women to doctor themselves and their families. Unknown to users, many patent medicines with reassuring names like "Carney's Common Sense Cure" or "Children's Comfort" contained high percentages of alcohol or addictive narcotics (opium, morphine, codeine, laudanum). Medical surveys revealed that by 1900 as many as two-thirds of American opiate addicts were women.

Both magazines urged existing women's clubs and leagues to show support for a national pure foods act by contacting their legislators. Magazines also offered free "kits" to women to help them mobilize public opinion. In 1906, the federal Pure Food and Drug Act was enacted.

Yet early 20th-century readers did not always endorse women's magazines in their muckraking approach. *Ladies' Home Journal* lost 75,000 subscribers in 1906 after printing an editorial about the dangers of venereal disease, a topic that was seldom discussed.[9]

Scholars have credited muckrakers as a whole with the passage of child labor laws, workmen's compensation, the Pure Food and Drug Act, and the development of congressional investigations. Tarbell, though, thought the muckraker title unfair. She argued with Roosevelt that *McClure's* writers "were concerned only with the facts, not with stirring up revolt."[10] Muckraking magazines, Tarbell wrote in her autobiography, "sought to present things as they were, not as somebody thought they ought to be. We were journalists, not propagandists; and as journalists we sought new angles on old subjects."[11]

■ ADVOCACY

The ability to expose dangerous or unhealthy situations continues to be a powerful aspect of magazines' editorial mix. Many of today's writers and editors are likely to practice advocacy journalism: taking an editorial stand that enables readers to become more aware of social concerns, empowers them, and urges them to act.

Following America's involvement in the Vietnam War during the late 1960s and early 1970s, magazine editors began to react to major societal concerns—about the environment, the homeless, drugs, and gun control—by choosing to go beyond covering an issue to advocating specific support for a cause. This was a break with the traditional journalistic mandate that editors must offer objective analysis and verifiable opinions if they were to maintain editorial perspective, balanced coverage, and their readers' trust.

Although some popular historians identify advocacy journalism as a product of the post–Vietnam War period, the advocacy role has long been a key part of American magazines. *Editor and Publisher*, founded in 1884 as a national trade magazine, offers an early illustration. The period from 1870 through the 1920s was one of unprecedented growth for newspapers as well as magazines. It was also a time when journalists began viewing their job as a profession with ethical standards and educational requirements rather than a trade.

Editor and Publisher's pages were filled with articles and editorials encouraging professionalism and calling on the press to become accountable for its actions. Professor Mary M. Cronin (now Lamonica) of Bridgewater State College has studied the role of the trade press in promoting early professional values and ethics among journalists. She points out that *Editor and Publisher* regularly used the term "profession" in articles and frequently praised politically independent newspapers during its first 15 years of publication.[12] According to Cronin, the first major crusade by *Editor and Publisher* occurred in 1902 and was aimed at stamping out fake news stories. Journalists supported that crusade, as well as others led by *Editor and Publisher*, including campaigns for higher salaries needed to attract loyal, reliable, and intelligent workers. Today's *Editor and Publisher* continues to advocate such professional standards as honesty, accuracy, political independence, and morality, while urging readers to honor their watchdog function.

Magazines occasionally go beyond their pages to promote specific causes of importance to their field or their audience. Editors and staff members of these magazines may choose to take a leadership role in societal concerns. In 1988, for example, *Metropolitan Home* pushed beyond editorial objectivity and lent its name to a project to raise both money for and awareness of AIDS. After much discussion about the ethics of advocacy, the editors agreed that the design community had been affected by AIDS and to ignore it was unconscionable.

The project originally involved charging the public $10 each to view showcase rooms designed by some of the world's best interior decorators and artists in a five-story house on Manhattan's Upper East Side. The money raised would go to the Design Industries Foundation for AIDS (DIFFA). But the editor at the time, Dorothy Kalins, soon realized that "we could never raise enough just by putting people through the house, so we decided

the magazine's personality

ike people, successful magazines have personalities that reflect their philosophies, energy, wisdom, and wit. The cover is a magazine's statement of its identity, as the following examples demonstrate.

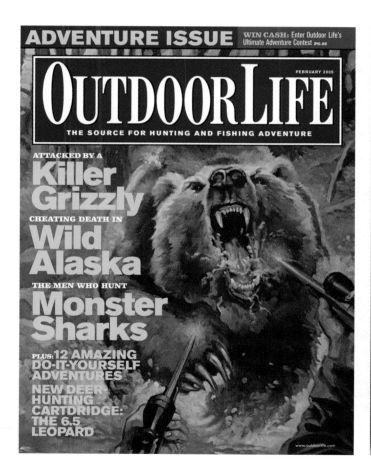

FEBRUARY 2006 and JANUARY/FEBRUARY 1996: Which bear would you want to protect? The cuddly fellow on the *Sierra* cover, of course. The *Outdoor Life* snarling Kodiak, meanwhile, sends you searching for your gun. It's all part of each magazine's plan. *Sierra*, the magazine of the Sierra Club, is aimed at individuals who advocate the importance of maintaining our natural environment. *Outdoor Life*, "The Sportsman's Authority," includes hunters in its audience.

TONS OF USEFUL STUFF — AUGUST 1997

Men's Health®

Train for GREAT SEX

The Hard-Body Diet

SLEEP YOUR WAY TO SUCCESS (pg. 74)

Amazing Abs→
How This Guy Did It

10 FASTEST WORKOUTS

FREE EXERCISE POSTER INSIDE

AUGUST 1997: *Men's Health* filled a marketplace need by offering personal service for men, a content area that had previously been limited to women's magazines. The distinctive black-and-white cover photograph sets the magazine off from its competitors. Originally, the cover model's face was obscured so the emphasis could be on the man's amazing abs. Eventually, more and more of the model was shown, but the abs remained a focal point.

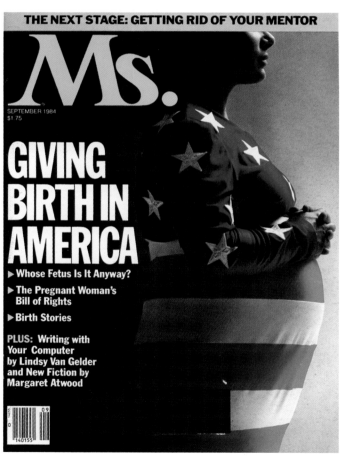

JULY/AUGUST 1997 and SEPTEMBER 1984: *Ms.* celebrated its 25th anniversary by reprinting the cover of its July 1972 premiere issue. The Wonder Woman theme demonstrated the magazine's focus on feminist issues as well as its ability to be playful. In the 1980s, the magazine was more serious, but the focus on women's rights was front and center, as was its ability to challenge cultural assumptions and symbols.

SUMMER 2006 and NOVEMBER/DECEMBER 2005: *Tricycle: The Buddhist Review* is an international quarterly that explores Buddhist activity and its influence on Western life. The covers are a mix of Western and Eastern images, type, and symbols. *Today's Christian Woman* appeals to contemporary women through cover stories such as this one, featuring singer/songwriter Twila Paris, a 46-year-old first-time mom and worship leader. The simple and clean format matches the magazine's philosophy by emphasizing the message.

50 WAYS TO ADD SABOR TO CHRISTMAS

$3.95 try me! only $1.99

Latina

10 Daring & Dazzling
Latinas

Eva Longoria
Tops our list of
Mujeres of the Year

You're hired!
The best jobs for
you in 2006

Work those curves!
Perfect party outfits for caderas & booties—any size latina.com
DEC. 2005 / JAN. 2006

COLLECTOR'S EDITION **OUR BIGGEST ISSUE EVER!**

ESSENCE

CELEBRATING **35** YEARS

**BE INSPIRED
GET STRONG
BE BLESSED**
The Best Time
Ever to Be a
Black Woman!

ON THE COVER
Mo'Nique
Fantasia
Alicia Keys
Angela Bassett
Iman
and Our Own
Susan L. Taylor

INSIDE
Queen Latifah
Halle Berry
Beyoncé
Yolanda Adams
Whoopi Goldberg
Raven-Symoné
and Others

essence.com MAY 2005

The Beautiful Ones
35 of the Most Remarkable
Women in the World

DECEMBER 2005/JANUARY 2006 and MAY 2005: *Latina* is a dual-language magazine for today's Hispanic woman, reaching one of the fastest-growing ethnic groups in the United States. Eva Longoria of *Desperate Housewives* fame is an appropriate cover—and role—model. The 35th anniversary issue of *Essence* demonstrates the staying power of the title, which offers African American women advice and inspiration and emphasizes readers' mindsets rather than their age or income. This issue supports the editorial philosophy of helping the reader "look good—and to feel as good as she looks."

FEBRUARY 21, 1925 (Premiere Issue), and DECEMBER 2005: Eustace Tilley—a fictitious dandy—is one of the most-recognized trademarks in American history as a symbol of *The New Yorker*. He was introduced on the magazine's first cover and since then has regularly appeared on its anniversary covers and shows up every week atop the magazine's "The Talk of the Town" department. By contrast, the very real Willie Nelson on *Texas Monthly* demonstrates one version of what it means to be Texan.

JUNE 1985 and SEPTEMBER 12, 2005: The young Afghan girl with mesmerizing eyes on *National Geographic*'s cover so intrigued photographer Steve McCurry that he returned to Afghanistan 17 years later to tell her story and updated the photograph, which then appeared on the cover of the magazine's April 2002 issue. *Time* magazine's trademark red border is much emulated, but there remains only one original. The tragedy of Hurricane Katrina's effect on New Orleans is dramatized by a poignant photograph emphasized by a stark black background.

REAL SIMPLE

| life made easier |

The new classics:
10 timeless pieces to
buy now, wear forever

The fit-anywhere home office

Quick fixes for common
makeup mistakes

3 big sleep problems, solved

Smart shopping secrets
from the pros

plus the best:
tote bags
online art
black pants

SEPTEMBER 2005 $3.95US $4.95CAN

www.realsimple.com AOL keyword: real simple

SEPTEMBER 2005: True to its name, *Real Simple* is known for clear, precise design that celebrates the beauty of simplicity and encourages readers to dig in, dream, and create. Highly stylized photography tells the story and beguiles the eye, in this case, with monochromatic colors and a wardrobe waiting to be worn.

to hold a gala charity ball for 1,000 people to celebrate the opening."[13] Editors found themselves planning an auction, gathering items, publishing a catalog, seeking corporate sponsors, and asking for donations in addition to producing three of the largest issues in *Metropolitan Home*'s history.

What was the result of all their hard work as advocates for AIDS awareness? Including *Metropolitan Home*'s donation of 5 percent of its ad revenues from a special show house issue, more than $1 million was raised. DIFFA netted $800,000 from the project.

"I believe magazines are very potent communications tools and they should take a leadership role," Kalins said, adding that the issue being tackled should relate to legitimate concerns of the readers and be within the editorial scope of the magazine.[14] "In our case, readers could get interested in the issue because it showed rooms by David Hockney and Michael Graves and people they never would have seen. We were serving the basic reasons that readers came to *Met Home*, which is that we were showing them great designs."[15]

Kalins summarized the advocacy experience: "Beating people over the head with an issue would be very inappropriate. When magazines work best, there is a sacred bond between the reader and the thing that is held in the hand. You have to treat that relationship with great care. Otherwise you're just using the magazine as a platform, and I feel this is a terrible misuse."

But the advocacy role is troubling to many editors. At what point does a magazine become a social force simply by presenting ideas? Gregory Curtis, editor of *Texas Monthly* from 1981 to 2000, argued, "There is a boundary between good coverage and advocacy. When you cross that line, people will begin to think that you have an ax to grind."[16] For many editors, magazines should not step beyond covering issues of concern to readers, nor should magazines lead the charge.

political influences on magazines

The political realm, in war and in peace, has driven editorial coverage since the earliest magazines began publication. At important periods in American history, wartime issues drove editorial coverage; at other times, peacetime political shenanigans kept magazines buzzing. America's political climate changed, as the country moved from conservative to liberal, back to conservative again, and as political activism forced a focus on minority rights and redefined the roles of women and men.

Among the major political movements to push their way onto magazines' pages were colonial concerns of independence, slavery and abolition surrounding the Civil War, the 1950s cold war anti-Communism hysteria, the civil rights movement, the counterculture of the Vietnam era that challenged government authority, the constitutional crisis of Watergate, and the feminist activism that changed the way women saw their lives and their magazines.

Not all magazines embraced all these issues; some embraced none of them. Some of these movements spawned their own magazines, often alternative in structure and content. In other cases, mainstream magazines took a position that might have seemed to run counter to their traditional editorial stance.

■ INDEPENDENCE

During the colonial period, the vital political questions of the day—King George's War, the French and Indian War, treaties with Indian tribes, territorial expansion, shipping routes, taxation, and the relationship with England—filled page upon page of magazines published in Philadelphia, Boston, and New York. Of particular concern to many colonists was their role within the British Empire, especially when they had to follow laws made thousands of miles away. Although most early editors tried to steer clear of independence issues and party connections, by 1770 political essays and articles were clearly either Whig (reflecting American grievances and questioning the crown's domination of colonial affairs) or Tory (pro-England).

By 1772, growing discontent among American colonists led by John Adams, Thomas Paine, and Isaiah Thomas precluded any but anti-British political views in the few magazines being published. Indeed, between 1772 and 1783, only three magazines were published in America: *The Royal American Magazine*, with engravings by Paul Revere, January 1774 to March 1775; *Pennsylvania*

Magazine, January 1775 to July 1776, with the last issue including the text of the Declaration of Independence; and *United States Magazine*, the first to refer to the colonies as united states, January 1779 to December 1779.[17] For all practical purposes, magazine printing halted as colonists fought for their independence from England.

The new republic ushered in more mature, varied, and insightful magazines as Americans turned their thoughts from war to peace after 1800. This led to what many historians have dubbed a golden age of magazines, from 1825 to 1850, when as many as 5,000 magazines were launched.

ABOLITION

The next major political event to affect magazines occurred during the Civil War period. Anti-slavery magazines such as *The Liberator* spoke out as early as 1831. Once war appeared imminent, magazines responded to prevailing political attitudes that were revealed as Yankees and Confederates clashed on American soil. Magazines published in the South, such as the *Southern Literary Messenger*, lined up squarely for secession and lost their Northern subscribers. Yet magazines published in the North did not fare much better, as they lost Southern subscribers and faced soaring printing costs.

The outstanding magazine for eyewitness accounts of the Civil War was *Harper's Weekly*, which hired a team of correspondents, artists, and photographers to cover the conflict. Their reports immediately placed the images of war into the hands of a reading public far away from the front lines. However, *Harper's Weekly* soon found itself in a political quandary as a result of its photography. Federal Secretary of War Edwin Stanton thought the horrific images gave aid and comfort to the enemy and ordered the publication to cease. But editor Fletcher Harper convinced Stanton that *Harper's Weekly* was actually a powerful political tool for the Union, showing the military strength and economic resolve of the North. The ban was lifted.

Harper's Weekly's detailed Civil War coverage is so important that an interactive electronic database, "HarpWeek: The Civil War Era 1857–1865," was created in 1997 to allow students and scholars to study the magazine's stories of that era. *Harper's Weekly*'s coverage of the Reconstruction period (1866–1877) and the Gilded Age (1876–1912) also

are available as full-text electronic databases. The total cost of the nine-segment set covering 1857–1912 is $84,200 for a research institution; smaller colleges with fewer than 2,500 students pay only $28,100.

THE COLD WAR

The cold war, a metaphor which reflected a battle between democracy and Communism, also affected magazine coverage, particularly in terms of how the specialized business press covered military and aviation developments. In its December 22, 1947, issue, *Aviation Week* (the title was expanded to include space technology in 1958) scooped the national and world media with the revelation that the U.S. Air Force had broken the sound barrier in a rocket-powered experimental plane. The magazine was accused of revealing top secret information to the Soviet military and was the focus of an investigation by the FBI and the Justice Department. Subscription records revealed Russian names, undoubtedly Soviet intelligence officers who assiduously read the magazine for its detailed data.

Although *Aviation Week* was not prosecuted because no federal laws had been violated, the Truman Administration tightened secrecy codes and information access. Yet the magazine continued to irritate the U.S. government, with articles pointing out that the Soviet-built MiG-15 could outmaneuver America's first jet fighter.

The cold war found Americans worrying about the threat of Communism in their own backyards. Red Scare paranoia culminated in the House Un-American Activities Committee investigations led by Senator Joseph R. McCarthy of Wisconsin during the 1950s. McCarthy's Communist witch hunt dragged many authors, actors, and directors into the Congressional limelight. In 1956, playwright Arthur Miller was among those cited for contempt of Congress for refusing to name past associates who might have been members of the Communist Party.

Author John Steinbeck eloquently questioned the morality of the investigations in a June 1957 *Esquire* essay: "If I were in Arthur Miller's shoes, I do not know what I would do, but I could wish, for myself and for my children, that I would be brave enough to fortify and defend my private morality as he has." However, it would not be until after the death of McCarthy in 1957 that assessments of "the most dangerous man in America" began appearing. Richard H. Rovere's "The Frivolous Demagogue," in the August 1958 issue of *Esquire*, was one of the most thoughtful, revealing, and longest, at six pages of dense copy with no photos.

■ CIVIL RIGHTS

Mainstream magazines such as *Look* and *Life* took on the fight against racism, offering pictorial representation of the real world of segregation, the day-to-day lives of American blacks, and the civil rights movement in its infancy.

In 1938, while the country was still reeling from the effects of the Great Depression, and astute observers were looking with worried eyes at growing unrest in Europe, *Life* was looking at the heart of the country, with a 14-page photo essay titled "Negroes: The U.S. Also Has a Minority Problem." Featuring the work of premier photographer Al-

fred Eisenstaedt, the feature included photos of 20 distinguished black Americans, and offered comments on their contributions to American culture. It also acknowledged the social structure that kept these achievements from the public eye.[18]

In 1956, *Life* covered a bus boycott in Montgomery, Alabama. Under a photo of the man who had yet to reach national prominence ran the line, "Boycott Director, Rev. Martin King, head of association which guides it, is mugged after arrest."[19]

Look, likewise, covered the civil rights movement in the 1950s. The April 30, 1957, issue included an eight-page article on "Eight Klans Bring New Terror to the South," written by author Fletcher Knebel and Pulitzer Prize–winner Clark Mollenhoff. Chronicling a resurgence of Klan activity—100,000 new members had joined since the Supreme Court outlawed school segregation in 1954—the article described clandestine Klan meetings and local sheriffs who looked the other

JANUARY 14, 1964: One of the most enduring images from the civil rights movement is this Norman Rockwell illustration for a *Look* article about desegregation in Little Rock, Arkansas.

Reactions to Race and Rights

In 1966, *Look* won the first annual National Magazine Award for "skillful editing, imagination and integrity, all of which were reflected particularly in its treatment of the racial issue during 1965."[1]

The magazine's audience, however, was not always receptive. Letters to the editor after the April 30, 1957, publication of a story about the Ku Klux Klan story revealed a mixture of revulsion for the Klan and anger at *Look* for "brainwashing." One reader asked if *Look*'s editors wanted to have mulatto descendants; another said the magazine was biased and vindictive; still another wrote, "All people are not equal and white people have a right to pick their friends." Nevertheless, many readers wrote to praise the piece, calling the Klansmen hypocrites and expressing shock at the Klan's activities, especially at the number of ministers who were active members.[2]

Publisher and *Look* founder Gardner Cowles wrote in his autobiography that publication of articles about civil rights issues brought hundreds of "the most violent letters calling us 'nigger lovers' and everything else you can think of." Cowles also maintained that certain advertisers "steadfastly refused to use *Look* solely on the basis of its human rights coverage."[3]

Although the picture magazines were offering portraits of the country during change, their approach sometimes missed the mark. Historian Loudon Wainwright noted that *Life*'s 1938 essay on the country's "minority problem," while unusual and impressive for the time, was replete with stereotypes and occasionally racist cutlines. One photo of men picking cotton was captioned, "Tote dat barge. Lift dat bale." Nevertheless, it was well received because it was one of the first times such topics were discussed in the mainstream press. Jazz great Duke Ellington wrote, "I believe this is one of the fairest and most comprehensive articles ever to appear in a national publication."[4]

1. "Coverage of Racial Troubles Earned New National Journalistic Honors," *The Look Years* (Cowles Communications, 1972): 78.

2. "Letters to the Editor," *Look* (June 11, 1957): 26.

3. Gardner Cowles, *Mike Looks Back* (New York: Gardner Cowles, 1985): 204.

4. Loudon Wainwright, *The Great American Magazine: An Inside History of* Life (New York: Alfred A. Knopf, 1986): 100.

way. Cross burnings, Klansmen dressed in hoods, and the angry face of the Rev. Alvin Horn, Alabama grand dragon of the Klan, were depicted. A month earlier, in the March 19 issue, *Look* had taken a more positive approach. "Los Angeles: A Race Relations Success Story," profiled Willard Johnson, a young black man who was elected president of the UCLA student body. When school desegregation was enforced in Little Rock, Arkansas, Knebel was again on the scene with "The Real Little Rock Story" in the November 12, 1957, issue. Probably the magazine's most famous civil rights statement was also about Little Rock desegregation: a poignant illustration by Norman Rockwell, showing a young black girl, dressed primly in white, carrying her school supplies, walking solemnly but proudly into school, flanked by U.S. Marshals.[20]

Perhaps it was time for blacks to present their own picture of the world. In 1942, while black people were still prohibited from trying on hats in Atlanta department stores or staying in hotels in downtown Chicago, the time came for a magazine devoted to black readers. Using his mother's furniture as collateral for a $500 loan, John H. Johnson founded *Negro Digest*. Soon it had a circulation of

50,000 readers a month, although at first distributors told him they didn't "handle colored books because colored books didn't sell," Johnson wrote in his autobiography.[21]

Johnson showed his political savvy in 1943 when he convinced Eleanor Roosevelt to contribute to an ongoing series, "If I Were a Negro." White authors, including Orson Welles, Pearl Buck, and Marshall Field, already had answered difficult questions such as would they want their children to wait another generation for quality education. But Johnson craved a bigger editorial attraction—an exclusive from the wife of the president of the United States. Mrs. Roosevelt wrote in the October 1943 cover story that if she were a Negro, she would "have great patience and great bitterness." Circulation leaped to more than 100,000 with that single issue.

Johnson's *Ebony*, a picture magazine established in 1945 with the stated goal "to emphasize the positive aspects of black life," placed the day's political realities in tandem with what readers wanted.[22] Said Johnson, "Black people wanted to see themselves in photographs. We were dressing up for society balls, and we wanted to see that. We were going places we had never been before and doing things we'd never done before, and we wanted to see that. . . . We intended to highlight black breakthroughs and pockets of progress. But we didn't intend to ignore difficulties and harsh realities." An examination of *Ebony*'s 50-plus years of publication reveals that Johnson consistently has chosen to take the political high road by emphasizing the brighter side of black life rather than by publishing articles critical of black problems.

When Johnson died in 2005 at the age of 87, he was eulogized as a magazine publisher who shaped history. U.S. Senator Barack Obama of Illinois said, "Only a handful of men and women leave an imprint on the conscience of a nation and on the history that they helped shape. John Johnson was one of these men." Indeed, many of the speakers at Johnson's funeral emphasized how *Ebony* and *Jet* changed the way black Americans thought of themselves at a time when the advertising world and popular culture depicted them as Aunt Jemima, Uncle Ben, Prissy, Mammy, and Buckwheat.

"John Johnson put a human face on African people," said the Rev. Jesse Jackson, activist founder of the Rainbow/PUSH Coalition. "He changed the face of American journalism. The media projected us as less intelligent than we were, less hardworking, less patriotic, more volatile, less worthy. But John Johnson affirmed us with a clear mirror and clear water. We were not ugly—the water was dirty, and the dirty mirror gave distorted images of who we really were."[23]

■ VIETNAM ERA

A new kind of political consciousness and literary dissent developed during the 1960s and 1970s that resulted in a degree of criticism not often seen in the mainstream American press. The harsh realities of the Vietnam War caused numerous underground and alternative magazines to spring up in response to governmental and military actions at home and abroad.

From roughly 1964 to 1973, the underground press reacted to changes occurring in society that were, for the most part, politically driven. The period from 1967 to 1969 was particularly dramatic:

> Demonstrations grew from 100,000 one year to 1 million two years later. Students went from peaceful petitioning to seizing university buildings all in the same period. Black nationalists overtook the civil rights movement, and strident radical declarations were met with systematic police violence. In Vietnam, the United States went from rosy predictions of "the light at the end of the tunnel" to the devastating Tet offensive that forced Lyndon Johnson from office.[24]

Ramparts, Counter-Spy, and *High Times* served the counterculture generation through an editorial milieu that challenged authority, particularly the CIA, and supported readers who inhaled, swallowed, or snorted drugs other than alcohol.

Of course, established alternative magazines such as *The Progressive* and *Mother Jones* and liberal publications such as *The Nation* and *The New Republic* also criticized the war and the government, but in less strident terms. Even religious magazines responded to the growing ideological split in society over the Vietnam War. Researcher David E. Settje compared how two prominent Protestant periodicals, *Christianity Today* and *The Christian Century*, reacted to the Vietnam War.[25] According to Settje, the conservative, evangelical *Christianity Today* presented prowar opinions in support of the various presidential administrations, while the liberal *The Christian Century* argued for an end to American involvement and supported most types of war resistance. Yet both magazines cautioned about total trust of Communists and vilified the Soviet Union. The two magazines reflected American worries about the cold war, while debating U.S. involvement in Southeast Asia.

Similarly, *Aviation Week and Space Technology* was skeptical of American involvement in the Vietnam War, objecting to President Lyndon Johnson's air war. The magazine urged an all-out, uninterrupted air campaign rather than Johnson's stop-and-start approach after breaking the news that the Soviet Union was shipping surface-to-surface missiles to North Vietnam. Yet for the most part, the magazine supported the war effort and the military personnel in combat.

Women's magazines took a different approach to the Vietnam War. *Ladies' Home Journal* recognized its "unique position as representative of millions of American women" by offering its readers a forum for expressing concern about the 1,500 American military personnel who were prisoners of war and missing in action. In the December 1970 issue, *Ladies' Home Journal* published a petition in cooperation with the National League of Families of American Prisoners and Missing in Southeast Asia, and asked for reader signatures. More than 60,000 readers signed the petition and sent it to the magazine. Among the signers were Joyce Carol Oates, Katherine Anne Porter, Senator Margaret Chase Smith, and Martha Mitchell. The response "was among the greatest in our publishing history," wrote the editors in an April 1971 open letter. Addressed to North and South Vietnamese officials, the letter proposed a meeting in Paris between "a small group of *Journal* editors and reader representatives" with representatives of the North Vietnamese and Provisional Revolutionary Governments.[26]

The petitions were delivered to the Paris peace talks by *Ladies' Home Journal* editor John Mack Carter and co-managing editor Lenore Hershey. "Did we make a step toward peace? Time will tell," wrote the editors in the July 1971 issue, adding:

> We had a commitment. We honored it. We do not know if we changed anybody's mind. But we do know that as the only magazine to speak in a nonpolitical, humanitarian way in behalf of our readers, we were continuing a long history of public service. If we have not brought peace closer, and

brought home our men from Southeast Asia, let the record show that at least we tried.[27]

■ WATERGATE

The period following the June 1972 discovery that burglars hired by the Republican Committee for the Re-Election of the President had been caught breaking into the Democratic National Committee offices at the Watergate apartment-hotel complex came to be known as Watergate. During 1973 and 1974, *Time* magazine put Richard M. Nixon on the cover 14 times during the unraveling of the Watergate plot. More than 20 other *Time* covers were devoted to the Watergate personalities, hearings, trials, and aftermath. Indeed, the first editorial published by *Time*, in November 1973, called for Nixon to resign for the good of the country.[28]

The two other weekly news magazines, *Newsweek* and *U.S. News and World Report*, also hammered home that this was one of the gravest constitutional crises in the nation's history. Opinion publications such as *The Atlantic Monthly* and *Harper's,* and political journals such as *The Nation* and *National Review* also commented extensively on the scandal.

Even magazines written for women responded to the heightened interest in Watergate by interviewing the spouses of indicted White House aides, such as Maureen "Mo" Dean. Never before had so many magazines devoted so much space for so long to a single topic.

■ FEMINISM

During the same period, feminist magazines also developed in response to changes in society. Many feminist magazines had their roots in the women's political movement of the 1970s and stretched from scholarly to popular in tone, content, and audience. Only a few had a significant national distribution, but their grassroots impact was impressive at a time when women were beginning to seek and achieve equality in the workplace.

Feminist magazines eschewed advertising that depicted women as sex objects and turned away from the argument that women have only one goal: to find a man. Titles of note included *Aphra, Chrysalis, Lesbian Tide, Lilith,* and, of course, the longest-lived feminist magazine of all time, *Ms.*

Feminist magazines were not always as radical or as bitter as the underground periodicals, but they still had an uncompromising approach to an enormous range of issues of importance to women. To reread these publications is like taking an immersion course in feminist activism. The breadth and depth of coverage is striking, including information about women's studies courses, health issues, economic solutions, legal strategies, and programs to assist women outside the mainstream of society, as well as fiction and poetry. Although underpaid secretaries, overworked waitresses, women in poverty, women in prison, Native American women, black women, and women in the developing world tended to receive more attention than white female executives, all were embraced by this niche.

■ SEPTEMBER 11, 2001

If you went to a newsstand or bookstore or supermarket checkout during late August or early September 2001, you saw celebrity after celebrity smiling at you from magazine covers. The interest in celebrities was at an all-time high and showed no sign of slowing down, for celebrity journalism had invaded fashion, news, music, sports, and hobbies. Every conceivable magazine seemed to feature a celebrity on the cover and inside the editorial pages. Not only were celebrities dominating magazine covers and content, but celebrities also were starting their own magazines. Oprah Winfrey's *O: The Oprah Magazine,* which blasted onto the newsstands in April 2000, was a hot commodity; also popular was Rosie O'Donnell's *Rosie,* which swallowed the 124-year-old *McCall's* that spring. Mary-Kate and Ashley Olsen offered *Mary-Kate and Ashley* to teens, while Martha Stewart's *Martha Stewart Living* had recently celebrated its 10th anniversary.

It was obvious that columnist Ellen Goodman had made a keen observation in 1999 when she said, "There's been a generational transition from a country that looked up to heroes to a country that gaped at celebrities."[29]

On September 11, 2001, when the hijacked airplanes crashed into the World Trade Center and the Pentagon, some September issues were still available, but October issues were starting to hit the newsstands. Harry Potter was flying on the cover of *Vanity Fair*'s 374-page October issue. *More*'s October issue focused on Isabella Rossellini,

while *Cosmopolitan* promoted "Our Most Outrageous Lust Lessons."

As the World Trade Center was collapsing and people were escaping from the Pentagon, editors at the newsweeklies—*Time, Newsweek,* and *U.S. News and World Report*—were the quickest to rush Manhattan disaster photos and stories to print. Other weekly and biweekly magazines, such as *The New Yorker, People,* and *Fortune,* were able to respond within the week. But most of the monthly magazines—with their longer lead times—already had closed out their November issues and some were putting finishing touches on December layouts when the attacks occurred. October issues for the monthly magazines were already arriving in mailboxes and newsstands.

On September 11, *Time*'s editors were working on the September 24 issue when the tragic news came in. They immediately decided to produce a special advertising-free, 52-page issue devoted to the attacks. By September 13, newsstands were displaying 3 million copies, and 4 million copies had

SEPTEMBER 14, 2001: *U.S. News and World Report* published a special report on the attacks of September 11, 2001. A newsstand-only version was advertising-free.

been mailed to subscribers. *Newsweek*'s editors did the same thing, producing an advertising-free 68-page issue by September 13; however, *Newsweek* distributed its 3 million copies only on newsstands.[30] This was about six times the typical number of newsstand copies. Both magazines featured World Trade Center images. *U.S. News and World Report* also produced a 54-page advertising-free special issue with the World Trade Center crash image; it also was distributed to newsstands only.

All three newsweeklies sold out their special editions. The result was that newsstand sales of *Time, Newsweek,* and *U.S. News and World Report* all leaped to more than 10 times their average levels the week after September 11, setting new records.[31] And newsstand sales in subsequent weeks remained several times higher than their usual levels.

An ominous all-black cover that barely revealed outlines of the twin towers was used by *The New Yorker*, where editor David Remnick and his staff spent 4 days tearing up the planned September 24th issue to devote space to the attack and its aftermath. The magazine was published with just one cartoon on the contributor's page; the only other time *The New Yorker* was devoid of cartoons occurred in the August 31, 1946, issue devoted entirely to John Hersey's "Hiroshima."

Working on a short deadline in order to put their special issue on the newsstands, *People* failed to notify advertisers of their last-minute decision to dump regular content and concentrate on September 11 stories and photos. Some advertisers were appalled to find their ads opposite photos of bloodied victims and other images of terror in the September 24, 2001, issue.

An ad for Kraft's Oasis energy bar that read, "The airline loses your luggage. You have an excuse to buy a whole new wardrobe" was opposite an article about people escaping from the World Trade Center and a photo showing people running away from the crash site. A two-page spread for Kraft's Honey Nut Shredded Wheat that poked fun at the nutritional content of airline peanuts was opposite a full-page photo of a bloodied victim. A Kraft spokeswoman said about the two ads: "We were very shocked and disappointed and concerned. The ads were very inappropriate in this tragic and horrific situation."[32] She said Kraft would have pulled the ads had they been given the opportunity.

The president of the *People* magazine group said it never crossed her mind to unilaterally pull advertising that had been scheduled weeks earlier; after all, issues of *People* covering tragic events such as the Oklahoma City bombing had carried ads.[33]

Other magazines scrambled to make appropriate changes to later issues and considered advertising content. *Fortune*'s publisher pulled more than 60 pages of ads from the October 1 issue as not being "appropriate in this environment."[34] Some of the technology and finance ads featured the World Trade Center, while others included airplanes; also pulled were airline and oil company ads. At a rate of $76,000 for a color page, that was a potential loss of more than $4 million.[35]

Some magazine editors assumed that Americans' fascination with celebrities would die, or at least lessen, following the September 11 tragedies. In an interview on September 18, *Vanity Fair* editor Graydon Carter predicted, "There's going to be a seismic change. I think it's the end of the age of irony. Things that were considered fringe and frivolous are going to disappear."[36]

By implication, the days of pure celebrity voyeurism were gone. The belief seemed to be that the terrorists attacks would lead to a kinder, gentler world, with less satire and black comedy, less pre-

> **Robert Kincaid, heart-throb hero of *The Bridges of Madison County*, was described as a *National Geographic* photographer. Readers, however, didn't quite understand that the book was fiction. Hundreds of fans wrote to *National Geographic* asking which issues contained Kincaid's work. The magazine responded in detail in an article, "Reel to Real," in August 1995: *National Geographic* photographers spend decades preparing an acceptable portfolio before they get an assignment and spend months shooting one story. Calendar photographers, like Kincaid, they noted, need not apply.**

Magazine Deaths and Terrorist Acts in 2001

Even before September 11, the year 2001 had been a difficult one for publishers, with advertisers slashing budgets to reflect the slowing economy, particularly in the technology and financial sectors. On the day before the World Trade Center terrorist attack, an article in *The New York Times* had discussed the challenges facing magazine publishers: Newsstand sales were down; wholesale distributors (the people who stock the newsstands) were losing money; and advertising revenue already had dropped so drastically since the first quarter of 2001 that publishers were characterizing the magazine industry's economic climate as a depression.[1]

In fact, total ad pages for the top 200-plus magazines audited by the Publishers Information Bureau (PIB) were down more than 9 percent for the first three quarters of 2001. Only a handful of titles—including *Bride's, Modern Bride,* and *Bride's Guide*—avoided a drop.[2] Many magazines—including *Rolling Stone, Time, Business Week, U.S. News and World Report,* and *Good Housekeeping*—had started cutting staff in an effort to stem what looked to be a flat or red ink year for 2001.

A number of popular magazines already had folded before September, although some were still were on the newsstands when the terrorist attack occurred. Others were already at the printer in September and wouldn't reach the newsstands until November. The proximity to September 11 made the deaths of the following magazines appear to be a result of the terrorist events:

- *George*
- *Working Woman*
- *Family PC*
- *Individual Investor*
- *Family Money*
- *Industry Standard*
- *Mode*
- *Brill's Content*
- *Lingua Franca*
- *Expedia*
- *Travelocity*
- *MH-18*
- *Asiaweek*
- *Family Life*
- *Mademoiselle*

In reality, they died because magazine publishers decided to cut what they perceived to be poor-performing titles (either in terms of advertising or circulation) as a way of reducing costs during a recessionary period. Publishers were cautious by the fourth quarter of 2001

and were reducing their estimates for year-end earnings.

After September 11, with the nation and the economy filled with anxiety and fear, advertisers were looking for reasons not to spend money, making ad budgets decline even more. The overall advertising ad page drop for the magazine industry during 2001 was almost 12 percent, which was the worst decline in a single year in almost 25 years.[3]

Certain categories of magazines had far greater than a 12 percent drop in the number of advertising pages and advertising revenue. Hardest hit—with up to 50 percent drops—were business and personal finance magazines, airline magazines, luxury magazines, and travel magazines. Only teen magazines showed a substantial gain, while women's service magazines had a modest increase.[4]

Although some magazines had stronger than usual newsstand sales following September 11, most ended up posting losses of millions of dollars for 2001 because of declining advertising revenues. A lot of advertisers simply pulled out of the November and December issues. ■

1. Alex Kuczynski, "Summer Over, Editors Face Grim Return," *The New York Times* (September 10, 2001), C7.

2. Joe Fine, "Magazine Ad Pages Decline 9.2%," *Advertising Age* (October 22, 2001), http://www.adage.com/news.cms?newsId=33212.

3. Keith J. Kelly, "Mag Ads Tumbled 11.7%," *New York Post* (January 11, 2002), http://nypost.com/business/37585.htm.

4. Joe Bercovici, "2001 Magazine Ad Page Drop: 11.7%," *Media Life* (January 2, 2002), http://www.medialifemagazine.com/news2002/jan02/jan05/5_fri/news1friday.html

tense and skepticism, less cynicism and detachment, and more curiosity, optimism, faith, and hope. In other words, there would be less celebrity gossip and celebrity voyeurism in the media market and more about the seriousness and preciousness of life. The media might even be more patriotic and less blasé.

The inclusion of the American flag on magazine covers became almost standard after September 11. The last time the flag was shown so frequently on magazine covers was in July 1942, when America's magazine publishers joined together to inspire the nation by featuring the American flag on their covers.

Carter, who had almost closed the November *Vanity Fair* when the attacks occurred, decided to include a separate advertising-free 54-page edition titled "One Week in September" that showed tired firemen on its cover. Unfortunately, the special edition seemed at odds with the regular November issue it was paired with. This was *Vanity Fair*'s second annual "music issue" devoted to rock, pop, hip-hop, folk, country, and punk music stars who were shown on a three-part pull-out cover shot by celebrity photographer Annie Leibovitz.

Most of the women's magazines were unable to make significant changes to their November issues, settling instead for an editorial comment from the editor or publisher. Only a few women's magazines were able to add a cover line or an article for the November issue. *O: The Oprah Magazine* kept its perky signature cover shot of Winfrey for November, but added this cover line: "After Shock: Comfort in the Face of Disaster."

The December issues of women's magazines included fewer stories about glittering gifts and fancy foods and numerous uplifting profiles of firefighters and other heroes. For the first time in *Latina*'s 7-year history, real-life women were featured on the December 2001 cover: a hospital paramedic, an American Red Cross volunteer, and a police officer who were in New York City on September 11. All of the women's magazines, as well as all of the teen magazines, had some variation on "how you can cope

Time's inventive use of language has resulted in new words being added to the American vernacular. Socialite, guesstimate, televangelist, male chauvinist, and op art are all words coined by Time that caught on. Words used by Time that didn't make it include cinemoppet, cinemactor, Broadwayfarer, nudancer, sexational, politricks, and newshawk.

with our national tragedy." A low-key approach—stressing the need to make time for what matters and helping readers achieve balance in difficult situations—was taken by most of the women's magazines.

"What the U.S. Crisis Means to Black America," was *Ebony*'s December response to September 11, with nine pages of text and photos about the emotional and economic impact for minority-owned businesses operating near the World Trade Center. However, despite an above-the-logo cover line for that article, two of the stories and the cover photo highlighted celebrities.

By December 2001, covers for monthly magazines had lots of celebrities gazing out at readers. *Vanity Fair* had Brad Pitt; *More* had Lauren Hutton; *GQ*, Will Smith; *Marie Claire*, Michelle Pfeiffer; and *Psychology Today*, Carrie Fisher. *People* was already back in its usual celebrity mode by mid-October; having devoted three covers to terrorism's effects and aftermath, *People* magazine went back to its usual celebrity treatment. Said then-managing editor Carol Wallace, "I think readers still care about the rich and the famous. We are a news feature magazine, but we're not in the market to become *Time* or *Newsweek*."[37]

As 2001 drew to a close, *Time*'s editors faced their annual "Person of the Year" decision and selected New York Mayor Rudy Giuliani. Many media critics were disappointed by the choice, arguing that Osama bin Laden was the individual who had the greatest impact for good or for ill for 2001 (the determining factor for selection as "Person of the Year").

magazines as cultural influences

Magazines help us choose our kitchen colors and Christmas trees, raise our children and our standards, save our marriages and our money. Open the pages of a magazine and it opens the world to

The Alternative Magazine: Building Community

Jay Walljasper was editor of *Utne Reader* (later shortened to *Utne*) when he gave this speech at Drake University in 1994. During his leadership from 1980, when the magazine was founded, until 1995, *Utne* was nominated for the National Magazine Award in the general excellence category for 1994, 1991, and 1987. Today, Walljasper is an editor-at-large for *Utne* and a regular contributor to *The Nation*.

There's a richness to this country, but sometimes it gets reduced in the media to oversimplifications about "what Americans think" or "what Americans do." What thrills me about alternative journalism is the recognition of our culture's diversity and that we don't speak with a single voice. There are a number of points of view on any subject. There's not just one single truth. To know the way it is, we need to take a lot of testimony from lots of different kinds of people.

Alternative journalism tends to reject the notion of objectivity. Objectivity is a concept that journalism borrowed from the physical sciences. It means a reporter can discern the truth by viewing a situation in a detached, clinical manner. While this may work in physics, in journalism it's impossible. No reporter can be truly objective. As human beings, we're shaped by innumerable forces in the world. Those forces tend to influence how we filter the news. It's dishonest to pretend there are no biases, when in fact every reporter has them.

I make a distinction between the facts and objectivity. Objectivity is more a state of mind. The facts are tangible things that we can talk about. The alternative press relies upon the facts just as much as the mainstream press does, but if we offer our own opinions on a subject, we admit it rather than hiding behind the cloak of objectivity. Every word you choose when you're writing a story gives you the opportunity to bring your point of view to it. What the alternative press says is we call them as we see them; we're not playing any word games.

So, is the alternative press impartial? No, it's probably not. But we offer something more important: a sense of passion. What we delight in doing at *Utne Reader* is mixing things up a little bit. We'll run a story, and then we'll run another story that may totally disagree with the first story. In fact, we may even hire someone to write a story that disagrees with the first story, and we may put in another story that brings in the third point of view or fourth point of view. We defy the notion that there are only two sides to every story. We assume there are at least 11, but it's probably more like 174. What we look for are the points of views that don't get presented in the mainstream media.

The process of putting together *Utne Reader* is pretty simple. About 2,000 publications come into our office each month. It's our job to sift through these different publications. If you want to see the diversity of American life, you should be looking at all the publications I look through. We get pacifist journals from the desert of Arizona. We get gay publications from Oregon. We get publications about psychobotany, which is the study of plants you can eat and have hallucinations with. We get a lot of church publications. As we look through these different publications, what we're really looking for are the stories that we're not seeing in *The New*

APRIL 2006: *Utne*, formerly *The Utne Reader*, achieved success by building community through alternative journalism.

(continued)

The Alternative Magazine: Building Community (continued)

York Times, not seeing on CNN. We want the important news behind the headlines, the news that didn't make it into the mainstream media.

We want to reinstill the notion of community in American life. A magazine is sometimes a community in and of itself. If you read personal ads in the newspapers, you'll notice people convey a sense of who they are by saying, "I'm a *Spin* magazine kind of person," or "I love *The New York Review of Books*."

We write a lot about community in our magazine, but it isn't always a community that is the subject of the article. We have coverage about how to save the public schools, because that's one of the basic things that ties a community together. We write about the need for new transportation policies, because we can't have a cohesive community if the only time people see each other is through windshields. We try to foster community with our promotion of salons where people meet face to face and talk about what's on their minds. We promote the notion of the urban village. We try to recreate what was good about the simpler world that we used

to live in, and hopefully not repeat what was bad about it.

In his book *Moral Fragments and Moral Community,* Larry Rassmussen, a Lutheran pastor and theologian at the Union Theological Seminary in New York City, discusses what he calls the elements of community. These elements also make a good list for the elements of a successful magazine, showing the tie between community and magazine.

The first element is historicity, or a sense of historical continuity. The most important thing for a magazine to have is a clear identity from issue to issue. *Newsweek* has to have a different identity from *Time,* because if they're interchangeable, why do you care whether you pick up one or the other? Each magazine has to carve out its own identity. That's a function of community.

Another element is mutuality, which means open-ended obligation. There's an obligation in putting out *Utne Reader.* It's an obligation to publish a magazine that people find interesting. On the crassest level you pay money and you get a magazine, but there's an exchange about ideas and sensibilities

involved which is central to magazines.

Rassmussen identifies plurality as another element to community. This equals the fact that there isn't just one single voice on a magazine. There's usually a community of people who put out a magazine.

An additional element in community is autonomy. A magazine has to have its own independent voice.

Participation is important for communities and magazines both. It's been proven in survey after survey that one of the most highly read sections of any publication is the letters, because people can participate that way in magazines.

Finally, integration is an element of community; integration is balance. That's important in a magazine as well. A magazine that just makes the same point over and over again doesn't have that much to offer.

What keeps me interested in journalism is that notion of reaching people as part of a farflung community. When you're thinking about a career in journalism, you might not be thinking about the idea of community, but it's something that's part of the job. ∎

us. It helps us build our foundation, our beliefs. From the homespun humor of "Life in These United States" in *Reader's Digest* to the ribald raciness of *Playboy's* "Advisor," magazines reflect and transmit our cultural standards.

When social conditions reach a certain fever, or mass, you can be certain that a magazine will come

along to either tell you about it or persuade you to follow its moral or ideological stance. Magazines are cultural artifacts, and, as such, are as complex as our society. They are natural community builders; they create the symbolic meaning that we use to interpret our world; and they present pseudoworlds and pseudoevents we often mistake for reality.

■ COMMUNITY BUILDERS

Throughout history, magazines have connected people with common interests and concerns, and they have forged a solid bond through shared knowledge. As magazines target increasingly narrow audience segments, they can address increasingly special needs and interests.

The communities magazines help build run the cultural gamut, but their vitality is well demonstrated by titles that give voice to groups previously unheard, such as gays, lesbians, and the disabled. Community building, however, is not limited to narrow social groups. Businesses, trades, and organizations use magazines to rally colleagues and members around causes and issues.

Perhaps most important, magazines help readers relate to one another, building reader-to-reader relationships. The ways in which magazines help readers build communities are as common as letters to the editors, as unusual as the creation of actual face-to-face groups, and as high-tech as the development of online relationships.

giving voice to groups

The Advocate, Out, Curve, and *Girlfriends* speak the language of and focus on the issues faced by their gay and lesbian readers, in addition to dealing with real-world issues everybody faces. Magazines reaching this group have been around for decades—*The Advocate* was started in 1967—but the number of titles mushroomed in the late 1990s and, like magazines for all other groups, became more specialized.

Advertisers' acceptance of these magazines may herald a larger social acceptance. It may, also, simply be good economic sense: This audience has the income and purchasing patterns that appeal to Madison Avenue. According to the Gay Press Report, produced annually by New York advertising agency Prime Access, Inc., and the gay and lesbian media placement firm Rivendell Media, the total buying power of gay, lesbian, and bisexual Americans is projected at $610 billion for 2005.[38] Overall, 2004 ad spending in gay and lesbian publications was up 28.4 percent versus the previous year, reaching $207 million. The 2004 report stressed that gays and lesbians prefer to purchase brands that advertise directly to them and they demonstrate higher brand loyalty than do their straight counterparts.

MAY 2006: Like many magazines that assume an advocacy role in service to their readers, *The Advocate* is a resource for the gay and lesbian community.

Reflecting the increasing interest in gay and lesbian publications, the Gay Press Report noted that spending for the gay and lesbian publications jumped 182 percent between 1996 and 2004, while consumer magazine spending had an overall increase of only 35 percent. In general, the gay and lesbian press is growing three times faster than mainstream consumer magazines, which have seldom made it a point to reach straight, gay, and lesbian readers.

Some analysts say the gay and lesbian market is 20 million strong, whereas others say it's less than half that size. Whatever the size, it is increasingly visible and affluent, with $610 billion buying power in 2005.[39] The market is now served by a spectrum of gay and lesbian magazines—close to 100 in 2005, according to the Magazine Publishers of America (MPA)—that focus on news, lifestyles, travel, fashion, parenting, art, and humor. Readers of gay and lesbian magazines tend to be urban, well educated, professional, and affluent. *The Advocate*, a news magazine that reaches both gay and lesbian readers, has a median household income of $90,000; 90 percent of *Curve*'s lesbian readers are college graduates; and half of *Passport*'s gay and lesbian travelers spend between $1,500 and $3,499 per person on vacations.[40]

Other gay and lesbian titles are more specialized, such as *Echelon* for gay, lesbian, bisexual, and transgender (GLBT) business professionals and entrepreneurs; *Instinct* with its humorous approach to trends and fashions for gay men who want a magazine that identifies itself as a mix of the mainstream magazines *Details* and *Jane* (but funny and clever); and *Gay Parent* for the more than one in four gay and lesbian households who are raising children.

Likewise, the disabled are increasingly recognized as a viable audience. Brigham Young University professor emeritus Jack A. Nelson has identified the period following World War II, when a large number of war wounded returned home to try to live normal lives, as a turning point.[41] The oldest monthly magazine, *PN/Paraplegia News,* for those with spinal injuries, was founded in 1946 by the Paralyzed Veterans of America to meet the informational needs of veterans. Today the magazine serves anyone who uses a wheelchair. Another magazine in the field is *Palaestra*, established in 1984 as a comprehensive magazine covering sports, physical education, and recreation for those with disabilities that include, but are not limited to, limb loss, blindness, cerebral palsy, deafness, dwarfism, mental retardation, and spinal cord injuries. The magazine is a top resource for information about the Special Olympic and Paralympic Games. Even more specialized is *Hearing Health*, a quarterly publication established in 1985 by the Deafness Research

A single magazine article can have multiple lives, writer Jon Krakauer discovered. His first-person reporting about a blizzard on Mount Everest that killed eight climbers was published in the September 1996 issue of *Outside*. The 17,000 word article, "Into Thin Air," won the 1997 National Magazine Award for reporting, then avalanched into a television movie on ABC later that year, with Krakauer as the main character. Krakauer expanded his article into a book, also called *Into Thin Air*, which became a 1997 *New York Times* hardback best seller. The book later topped the charts as a nonfiction paperback. Krakauer's definitive tale of death reached multiple media audiences in a little more than a year.

Foundation that provides consumer information about hearing aids, cochlear implants, tinnitus, assistive listening devices, and disability rights, as well as the latest research, technology, and trends revolving around hearing loss.

According to Nelson, publications targeted to the disabled build a sense of identity and community, provide information, and advance an activist agenda. Certainly, the passage of the Americans with Disabilities Act (ADA) in 1990 contributed to many start-ups, including *Ability* (1992) for Americans with a wide range of disabilities and *inMotion* (1992) for people with limb loss, their families, and the professionals who care for them.

The 2005 SRDS *Consumer Magazine Advertising Source* lists only six magazines in its disabilities classification, although Nelson points to a directory published in late 1995 that identified 70 disability magazines. Many publications focusing on disabilities are published by nonprofit foundations and organizations that don't advertise. The MPA listed 47 disability magazines being published in 2005.

businesses, trades, and organizations

Specialized business magazines, because they are aimed at readers as members of a clearly defined trade or occupation, exist, in many cases, specifically to build relationships. In February 1988, *Hardware Age* provided a valuable service to its readers, largely independent hardware retailers, who were facing a common enemy: Wal-Mart. The large chain was offering prices so low that Main Street retailers couldn't match them; the result was the failure of many local businesses. *Hardware Age* issued a call to competitive action, suggesting that independent store owners regularly advertise and promote the fact that they provide better and more varied service from knowledgeable clerks. The magazine also suggested local retailers change their hours to be open the same hours as Wal-Mart. Editor-in-chief Jim Cory, who wrote the story, said the result was wiser and more competitive local store owners who were equipped to compete.

Six years later, *Hardware Age* went to Spokane, Washington—considered an economic microcosm of the country as a whole—to study the potential battle between the independents and the fast-growing Home Depot chain. Editors commissioned a study of hardware consumers to determine their shopping preferences. Because Home Depot had not yet entered the Spokane market, local retailers were the shoppers' favorites, although many consumers were aware of Home Depot from other cities. The magazine studied why consumers were loyal to the independents—in most cases, because of service—and again suggested the local stores promote that difference.[42] That series won a prestigious 1995 Neal Award from the American Business Media.

The magazine changed its name to *Home Improvement Market* in 1998 to better reflect its audience, but folded a few years later, along with many small independent retailers who couldn't compete with the "big box" retailers. It was a sign of the times.

Association and organization magazines exist largely to build communities. The National Audubon Society hopes its magazine, *Audubon*, will help differentiate itself from the Sierra Club and the National Wildlife Federation. These two other groups have the same hopes for *Sierra* and *National Wildlife* magazines.

Long known for its annual model search contest, *Seventeen* decided to try something trendier in 2005—a reality television show on MTV. Seventeen attractive young women, ages 18–21, shared a Manhattan loft apartment as they faced tests based on their intelligence, loyalty, and honesty over 10 episodes. The winner, chosen on the last show, walked away with a paid internship at *Seventeen*, a college scholarship, and an appearance as the magazine's February 2006 cover model. "Every editor's dream is to have a television show," said *Seventeen*'s editor-in-chief Atoosa Rubenstein, who created the show, served as executive producer, and made the final elimination decisions, but without saying, "You're fired."

Public relations and custom magazines are information sources as well as advocacy vehicles for readers within the organization and outside of it. Their audiences include employees, customers, clients, and others within the field and in related agencies. *USAA Magazine* talks to active and retired members of the military and their families who use the company's insurance, banking, and financial services, showing them the company cares and piquing their interest in new programs and resources.

reader-to-reader relationships

Some magazines take community building a step farther by establishing reading groups, study circles, salons, and, most recently, supper clubs to bring like-minded people together. As early as the 1960s, study circles were formed by readers of *Commentary*, a Jewish opinion magazine. In the 1980s, *Tikkun*, a magazine of liberal Jewish thought, sponsored more than 40 reader discussion groups throughout the United States.[43] In 1991, *Utne Reader*, which summarizes and publishes articles from more than 2,000 alternative media sources, formed groups it called neighborhood salons. *Utne Reader* (now titled *Utne*) advertised the salons in its pages and in mailings to readers, who were asked to write to the magazine expressing interest. More than 8,000 readers responded and asked to be matched up with other *Utne* readers in their community. A movement was born. At its peak in 1995, the Neighborhood Salon Association had 25,000 participants in approximately 600 salons meeting monthly throughout the United States and in foreign countries. Eventually, *Utne* decided to bow out

The Reader and *Country Home*

Country Home editors regularly connect with readers as they plan new issues and evaluate existing ones. Some methods they use are the following:

Focus Groups

Country Home uses the focus group approach when testing the water for change in the magazine. In September 2004, the staff wanted to freshen and evolve the magazine to keep pace with trends in design, shopping, magazine publishing, and lifestyle by introducing a new graphic design and new editorial departments. The staff conducted four sessions in four cities across the country, meeting with small groups of subscribers and nonsubscribers who met the profile of readers *Country Home* wanted to attract to the magazine. Editors heard verbatim how readers live; their current needs, aspirations, and future plans; and what they want from a magazine.

E-mail and Letters

The staff at *Country Home* reads and responds to correspondence from readers. Every letter is placed in a notebook and reviewed with the staff. Reader comments have an important impact on the editorial direction of the magazine.

Quantitative Benchmark Studies

An in-depth type of research, quantitative benchmark studies typically are carried out every few years, and are much like a report card. Most recently, *Country Home* did a mail survey of subscribers, testing everything from content mix to individual story titles and topics.

Hitting the Streets

Country Home staffers meet personally with readers in a variety of formal and informal events. Editors attend trade shows, press events introducing new products, and industry seminars. Staffers work with a national network of field editors who stay plugged into what's happening in their areas—looking for great homes, shops, and restaurants. Editors are well positioned to provide a national perspective because of this network and the fact that they're headquartered in the Midwest. Sandra Soria, executive editor of *Country Home*, says, "I truly feel this prevents New York myopia and allows for editors who produce more relevant magazines for readers."

Diving into the Database

Meredith Corporation, the publisher of *Country Home*, has a substantial database of readers. Analysts run profiles of readers for demographic and psychographic information.

Digesting Secondary Research and Tapping Internal Experts

If *Country Home* staff members aren't reading the latest marketing books, trends magazines, and trend research, they aren't doing their jobs.

Hiring a Staff That Lives the Life with Passion

Country Home editors live like their readers, and they have a passion for the lifestyle and aesthetic the magazine represents. Having this type of connection is the starting point that makes all of the preceding modes of staying in touch both interesting and personal. ■

---

of overseeing the salons, leaving members to continue on their own. In an era of disappearing communities, national magazines give neighbors a chance to meet one another, creating a printed and bound replacement for the front porch.

In one of the latest wrinkles in community building, *Cooking Light* has transformed a reader's idea into informal get-togethers across the country where readers cook meals using recipes from the magazine, then dine together in *Cooking Light* supper clubs. The idea originated with Amy Lai Fong, a reader in Alameda, California, who organized the first one in 1999 in the Bay Area on her own, without the magazine's participation. Then in 2000, *Cooking Light* published an article about the concept and thousands of readers began forming their own clubs, finding one another on the magazine's website.

Taking the concept a step further, *Cooking Light* began sponsoring more than a dozen formal events in major cities across the United States in conjunction with McCormick, the spices and seasonings company, and 31 other advertisers such as Modavi's Woodbridge wines and Alaska seafood. This transition from a reader initiative to a promotional event is being dubbed "experiential marketing." "There is nothing as effective, as long-lasting, as giving the advertiser and the reader an opportunity to shake hands with us over a period of time," says Christopher C. Allen, vice president and publisher of *Cooking Light*.[44]

Although experiential marketing moves the magazine from the static page and into a tangible experience, some publishers are concerned that they may alienate readers if the events become too commercialized. "Having started with the readers, it's not like the supper clubs were part of a marketing plan," says Mary Kay Culpepper, editor-in-chief of *Cooking Light*. "We're pretty careful about honoring the grass-roots way they started, keeping the readers at heart."

In the letters to the editor section of many magazines, readers sometimes share more with one another than they do with their families. During the 1950s and 1960s, farm women, who often were isolated from traditional women's social groups found in towns and cities, wrote about personal, political, and business issues via letters to the editor in *The Farm Journal* and *The Farmer's Wife*. According to Amy Mattson Lauters of the University of Minnesota, their letters showed "women's discouragement with their domestic roles and pride in their roles as businesswomen on farms."[45] Topics discussed by women focused on family life, education, reproduction, individualism, and the importance of farming as a business in a larger global arena. Men's letters, on the other hand, tended to center around government aid to farmers, agricultural techniques, farm surpluses, and which political party did more for farmers.

In its early years, *Ms.* showed readers that women throughout the country were experiencing similar frustrations. The letters were such important documents that editor Mary Thom collected them in a book, *Letters to Ms.* Readers of *The Mother Earth News,* likewise, connected through the letters columns. Letters were answered in the magazine by "Mother" and readers were referred to as Mother's "children." One reader, writing in the third issue, May 1970, suggested a readers' convention. Several others asked for information on communes. Another, writing in the fourth issue, July 1970, said "Hey, we're a movement? I thought I was the only one."

Other relationships bloom online, where *Better Homes and Gardens* readers share recipes, *Wired* readers share philosophies, and *Utne* continues its salons electronically in the Café *Utne* virtual community. The community bond also can be created through humor. In 1995, two users of the *Better Homes and Gardens* website were sharing recipes for muffins. One reader got waylaid because of her pets, and sent this message, which made the magazine's food staff chuckle:

> Sorry I took so long to reply back but my dog had pups so I've been very busy. They turned out really good. The only thing I'm going to change is instead of putting them in the muffin pans I'm going to put them in a pie plate or cookie sheet so the outside will be softer. Mine came out kind of hard on the outside but they were much softer on the inside.

■ SYMBOLIC MEANING

Magazines give symbolic meaning to our world in the images they present in images and words. *Gourmet* pictures the perfect apple pie, *Sports Illustrated* the ideal athlete, *Architectural Digest* the exquisitely decorated vacation cottage. Who would want to make the pie if *Gourmet* showed a burned crust and drooping center? How could we aspire to sports success if we had before us an image of a couch potato? Who would want to mimic the look of a cottage decorated with pictures of dogs playing poker?

The study of these symbolic messages, or semiotics, is as old as Western civilization, with origins in Plato and St. Augustine and more recent popularization by Sigmund Freud and Claude Lévi-Strauss. The premise of semiotic theory is that all communication is symbolic and these symbols are brimming with cultural meaning. Semioticians believe any culture can be defined and understood by studying its symbols.[46] A study of magazines is a study of our culture. Look at *Esquire* from 1950, and you'll not only read the news of that year, but you'll also wade into the social mores, trends, and styles of the time.

In magazines, symbolic messages are created in words as well as in images. The cover lines tempt us: "Lose 10 Pounds by Christmas," "Great Pecs in a Month," "What Your Lover *Really* Wants." The assumption is that we're flawed—overweight, dumpy, and sexually deficient—and that by reading the articles we can improve ourselves. Photographs illustrate the perfection we try to achieve.

Psychologists say we would be healthier mentally if the images in magazines were more attainable—if the bodies pictured were rounder, the homes were less perfect, the sexual standards saner and safer.

Editors realize, though, that readers often look for the fantasy that magazines present. By presenting the ideals to which we aspire—a great pie, a fantastic body—magazines provide us with a world that motivates us. We often buy magazines to enter that world and use those images to improve ourselves. This fantasy world is created not just by the editorial content of magazines, but by the advertising as well.

Some magazines present contradictory written messages from page to page. For example, one issue of *Woman's Day*, like many women's magazines, contained two weight-related cover lines: "10 Diet Rules to Break and Lose Weight" and "Dress Thinner." Pictured on the cover was an "Easy to Make Sunflower Cake." The cake, a delicious combination of pound cake and cookies, packs a hefty 744 calories into each piece. Where does that fit into a healthy diet?

Do these images affect us? Consider this: This book is being written in a house that one of the authors first saw on the pages of *Better Homes and Gardens Home Plan Ideas*. She saved the magazine, looking at the house regularly and imagining it as her own. A year later, she called a builder and signed a contract to build the house. The house has been standing for 14 years now, and the author has written three articles about it so far for *Better Homes and Gardens* Special Interest Publications. Other readers looked at the images in those articles and called the author to talk about the house they saw in words and pictures. They, too, were planning to build it.

Research in Brief

Mixed Messages on Women

Of special concern to magazine researchers are images of women in editorial content as well as advertising. Are these images negative or positive? Researchers' assessments are mixed, as are the images themselves.

As in all areas of magazines, editorial goals and audiences determine the type of images presented. In a study done in 1985, researchers divided women's magazines into two types: traditional—such as *McCall's* and *Family Circle*—and nontraditional—such as *Working Woman* and *New Woman*. The traditional magazines more frequently presented women in conventional occupations such as homemakers or nurses.[1]

Temple University professor Carolyn Kitch notes that in the "golden age of illustration," the first three decades of the 20th century, women were either depicted as "girls"—most notably, the Gibson Girl drawn by Charles Dana Gibson for *Collier's* magazine—or as mothers.[2] The girls, she notes, were drawn by men—Gibson,

1. J.A. Ruggerio, and L.C. Weston, "Work Options for Men and Women in Women's Magazines: The Medium and the Message," *Sex Roles* (Vol. 12, 1985): 535–547.

2. Carolyn Kitch, "Maternal Images in the Age of the Girl: The Work of Jessie Willcox Smith and Other Women Artists in Early Twentieth-Century Magazine Illustration" (paper presented at the annual meeting of the Association for Education in Journalism and Mass Communication, Anaheim, Calif., August 1996).

Mixed Messages on Women (continued)

Howard Chandler Christy, and John Held Jr. The mothers were drawn by women, the most prolific being Jessie Willcox Smith, who drew nearly 200 covers for *Good Housekeeping* between 1917 and 1933.

Moreover, Kitch says, the girls "bore little relationship at all to flesh-and-blood females." Some were bathing beauties; others, like Held's flapper, were caricatures— "skinny, flat-chested and hipless." The female illustrators, in contrast, drew realistic images of women as mature adults. Smith and other women illustrators, Kitch maintains, offered readers an "alternative view of womanhood" that was "consistently respectful."

Much research on the portrayal of women in magazines has dealt with advertising content. Researchers at Texas Tech University studied magazine advertisements from late 1994 to early 1995 and found that women were most often portrayed as decorative objects or

entertainers.[3] They duplicated research done in 1971 and found that images of women were even less representative of reality in 1995 than they were in 1971. The researchers studied *Cosmopolitan, Redbook, Glamour, Self, Shape, Gentleman's Quarterly, Esquire, Men's Journal, Men's Fitness, Business Week, Vanity Fair, Better Homes and Gardens, People,* and *Time.* These were chosen because of their wide appeal to both male and female audiences.

The researchers found that almost 25 years later women were still portrayed in stereotypical homemaker roles or as decoration, holding a bag of potato chips, for example, even though they had no direct connection to the product. Men continued to be pictured as professionals, managers, or administrators, while the women were shown predominantly as homemakers and parents.

But the story isn't that simple. In *The Beauty Myth,* author Naomi Wolf paints a seem-

ingly contradictory picture of women's magazines as keepers of the flame of women's rights as well as dangerous stereotypers of women's lives. She pinpoints substantial differences between advertising and editorial content, and takes these magazines to task for creating an unrealistic image of women in photos, beauty articles, and advertising.

However, Wolf emphasizes that these messages often are offset by other editorial decisions. In fact, she praises the editorial content of women's magazines and considers these publications as a whole "the only products of popular culture that change with women's reality, are mostly written by women for women about women's issues, and take women's concerns seriously." Wolf calls them "potent agents of social change" and says they "have popularized feminist ideas more widely than any other medium—certainly more widely than explicitly feminist journals."[4] ■

3. Diana Cornelius, Christine Thompson, Wayne Melanson, and Christen Zelaya, "The Portrayal of Women in Magazine Advertising: A Content Analytical and Comparative Study" (paper presented at the annual convention of the Association for Education in Journalism and Mass Communication, Anaheim, Calif., August 1996).

4. Naomi Wolf, *The Beauty Myth* (New York: William Morris and Company, 1991): 70–72.

pseudoworlds

Closely related to the images in magazines is the concept of the pseudoworld. Journalist Walter Lippmann coined the term to refer to a world of the media's creation, which has little, if any, connection to reality.[47] In today's magazines, it's a

world where Madonna changes personae five times a year, where the Barrymores act from generation to generation, where men and women are healthy, well dressed and, usually, middle class and white. And it's a world where all this matters. The world portrayed in many magazines, however, is not the world in which most people live. The

Sex and the Single Magazine

The sexual revolution of the 1960s would have been a mere skirmish without magazines. More explicit language appeared in magazines in response to a loosening of morality. Treatment of sexual topics, once ignored or draped with euphemisms, became the norm in magazines. Articles about orgasms and erections appeared alongside pumpkin pie recipes and shopping tips. The magazine leaders of the revolution were *Playboy* and *Cosmopolitan*.

Begun in 1953 by a young *Esquire* staffer who asked for a raise and was rejected, *Playboy* was not only a magazine but also a social phenomenon. That young man, Hugh Hefner, became renowned for parties at his Playboy Mansion, and for his womanizing. He also made a fortune by expanding the magazine franchise, creating national *Playboy* clubs, with entry by keys and service by women barely dressed as *Playboy* bunnies. The women who starred in his magazine were the young, buxom Playmates of the Month, a cottage industry of their own, with calendars and television specials. Along the way, Hefner mainstreamed barroom humor and made modeling nude into a socially accepted activity to which college women throughout the country aspired.

Playboy clashed with social and economic reality in the 1980s, however, when a conservative mood hit the country politically, and when other, brasher magazines such as *Penthouse* outdid it in the soft pornography category. A boom in men's health and lifestyle magazines made some of the articles in *Playboy* somewhat passé. But a larger concern was that the magazine's readers, who had been in their late twenties and early thirties when the magazine was started, were aging along with founder Hefner. Hefner's daughter Christie now runs the company, a phenomenon in itself: a woman who lives the feminist ideal of the successful professional by running a magazine that was the bane of feminists' existence.

In the late 1990s, *Playboy's* dominance in the men's market was challenged by several "lad" magazines that were exported in name and content from England. *Maxim* made its American debut in 1997. Until *Maxim*, the assumption was that guys in the highly desirable 18- to 34-year-old age group didn't buy magazines. According to the *Ragan Communications Media Relations Report*:

Pictorial mags like *Playboy* and *Penthouse* were too blatant for many men to buy (at least publicly), and *GQ* and *Esquire* were considered too fashion-oriented and too literary, respectively. *Maxim* came into the market saying, "We're a magazine for men who don't think about anything except sex, cars, music, beer, and gadgets." *Maxim* made a smart move in deciding not to use blatant nudity in its editorial so a guy can buy it and leave it on his coffee table, and his girlfriend won't get angry at him.[1]

What distinguishes *Maxim* from other men's magazines is its raunchy, fraternity house sense of humor. *Maxim* mocks everyone and everything, including itself ("Date Out of Your League: Pickup Tips So Good You Won't Believe Your Luck!"), on the cover and inside the magazine (three pages on how to "beat the crap out of somebody" have the *Maxim* lad bashing a Gandhi look-alike). It's not surprising to find such *Maxim* cover lines as "Sex Express! How to Spot the Girl with a Condom in Her Purse"; and "Jump-start Your Sex Life! We Even Show You

1. "'Lad Mags' Reach Young Men with Money to Burn," *Ragan Communications Media Relations Report* (February 28, 2002). http://www.ragan.com/mrr.

Sex and the Single Magazine (continued)

Where to Put the Alligator Clips!" That kind of editorial isn't found in *Playboy*, with its thoughtful interviews with eminent statesmen and popular entertainers ranging from Jimmy Carter to Jimmy Kimmel and fiction by Ian Fleming, John Updike, and Kurt Vonnegut.

Advertising Age placed *Maxim* 31st in total advertising and circulation gross revenue in 2004, with a circulation of 2,517,126.[2] While *Playboy* has a larger circulation, at 3,051,344, its revenues are lower, resulting in a rank of 44th on the *Advertising Age* list. Plus, *Playboy* appeals to an older demographic, with many of the "lads" considering it to be the magazine that their fathers read. *Maxim* places third among best-selling magazines in college bookstores and is the number one men's lifestyle magazine in that age group.[3] Consequently, it makes sense for *Maxim* to state on the spine of every issue that it is "the best thing to happen to men since women."

In 1965, when motherhood and apple pies dominated the women's magazine category, *Cosmopolitan* did an about-face, from a staid general interest magazine into a sexy, sophisticated relationship guidebook that spoke to newly liberated women during the sexual revolution. The force behind the metamorphosis, Helen Gurley Brown, modeled the magazine after her successful book, *Sex and the Single Girl*. Her advice to *Cosmopolitan* readers was clear: "The fact is, if you're not a sex object, that's when you have to worry. To be desired sexually, in my opinion, is about the best thing there is."[4]

Editor-in-chief Brown called her idealized 18- to 34-year-old reader "the *Cosmo* Girl" and each issue featured a gorgeous model whose notable neckline either plunged to the waist or tickled the chin in see-through filmy fabric. If this sounds like a description of a *Playboy* Playmate, that image wasn't far from Brown's mind: "A guy reading *Playboy* can say, 'Hey, That's me.' I want my *Cosmo* Girl to be able to say the same thing."[5]

Readers were encouraged to make themselves into the women who would marry the chairman of the board. As the feminist movement gained momentum, *Cosmo* girls not only were angling to marry the chairman—but to be one, too.

Under Brown's leadership, *Cosmopolitan* became the best-selling young women's lifestyle magazine in the world. When Brown retired in 1997 at age 73, the "*Cosmo* Girl" label was dropped in favor of the "Fun Fearless Female" designation that currently drives the magazine. Still the leading young women's magazine after more than 30 years, *Cosmopolitan*'s formula remains provocative, titillating, and sexy. The covers continue to feature fabulously beautiful, busty women (although more celebrities than models appear now, such as Jennifer Lopez, Britney Spears, and Sarah Michelle Gellar), and the cover lines perpetually emphasize sex ("100 Sex Tips from Guys"; "Have More Fun in Bed"; "7 New Pulse-Pounding Positions"). Obviously, the fun fearless female is beautiful and bold—she still doesn't wait for a man to make the first move, no matter what that move might be.

In its annual list of the top 300 magazines, *Advertising Age* ranked *Cosmopolitan* 10th in total advertising and circulation revenue for 2004. As of December 31, 2004, *Cosmopolitan*'s total paid circulation was 2,982,508. Its nearest category competitor, *Glamour*, ranked 24th in total advertising and circulation revenue and had a total paid circulation of 2,397,508. Even more significant, *Cosmopolitan* sells out on the newsstands, issue after

2. "Magazine 300," *Advertising Age* (September 26, 2005): S–1.

3. "Recovery or Recession," *College Store Executive* (September 2004): 26–32.

4. R. Roberts, "The Oldest Living *Cosmo* Girl," in *Messages 4: The Washington Post Media Companion*, ed. T. Beell (Boston: Allyn and Bacon, 1997): 46.

5. L. Ouellette, "Inventing the *Cosmo* Girl: Class Identity and Girl-style American Dreams," in *Gender, Race, and Class in Media: A Text-reader*, eds. G. Dines and J. M. Humez (Thousand Oaks, Calif.: Sage, 2003): 120.

Sex and the Single Magazine (continued)

issue, for full cover price; it consistently is number one in single-copy sales, according to the Audit Bureau of Circulations. *Cosmopolitan* also is the number-one-selling title in college bookstores, as it has been for the past 25 years.

Today's media buyers have noticed the similarity between *Maxim* and *Cosmopolitan* in terms of cover designs and messages, saying the two publications have a "boyfriend and girlfriend-like relationship." Priya Narang, senior vice president and media director of De-Witt Media in New York, is more direct: "*Cosmo* is like *Maxim.*"[6]

Actually, *Cosmopolitan* goes farther than *Maxim*, at least in terms of the cover lines. A study of a year's worth of covers of both *Maxim* and *Cosmopolitan* revealed that while both magazines emphasized sex on their covers, *Cosmopolitan* had more cover lines associated with sexual content than did *Maxim*. However, *Maxim* depicted women as sexual objects in terms of image position and clothing, while *Cosmopolitan* did not. All of *Maxim*'s cover women were shown partially nude or with very minimal clothing, while all of *Cosmopolitan*'s cover women had on sexy yet traditional clothing that could be worn in public. ∎

6. M. Davids, "Let's Talk about Sex," *Brandweek* (October 25, 1999): 16.

pseudoworld created by magazines is largely populated by beautiful people, usually celebrities.

The pseudoworld created by consumer-based media is a world in which the proper use of the proper product buys prestige and social acceptance. *Mountain Bike* offers advice on which bike to buy, *Outside* shows us the body we need to ride that bike, *Shape* tells us to avoid last year's biking shorts styles, and *Health* advises us to build our biking muscles with the right vitamins, although those change from month to month, as do biking fashions and fitness regimens.

Media critic Michael Parenti offers an explanation for the pseudoworld phenomenon. The American media, he says, tend to "favor personality over issue, event over content, official positions over popular grievances, the atypical over the systemic."[48]

pseudoevents

A corollary to the pseudoworld is the pseudoevent, named by historian Daniel Boorstin[49] to refer to the superhyped events the media create, then cover as though they had evolved on their own. A magazine cover can be viewed as an event: Put a model on that cover and she starts dating rock stars; put a rock star on the cover and his career takes off.

Magazines select our best and worst cities, celebrities, schools, investments, cars, computers, and people, and these selections become fodder for other media stories. A city chosen as one of *Money* magazine's most livable becomes the headline of newspaper stories across the country, and the selection becomes the chamber of commerce's biggest asset. Likewise colleges and universities recommended by *U.S. News and World Report* are then perceived as the top schools, because the magazine made them so. It's even better if *Barron's* also names them a "Best Buy."

Celebrities, again, are the highlight of pseudoevents. Who reads *People*'s list of the most intriguing people other than celebrity watchers? Writer Martha Sherrill got so frustrated with writing celebrity profiles that she decided to create her own celebrity and see what happened. She went beyond the pseudoevent and created a pseudoperson. The result was a mythical starlet, Allegra Coleman. Coleman was *Esquire*'s November 1996 cover model, seducing readers with the cover line: "Forget Gwyneth . . . Forget Mira . . . Here's Hollywood's Next Dream Girl. The Allegra Coleman Nobody Knows." Nobody knew Allegra because she didn't exist. The cover model was actually Ali

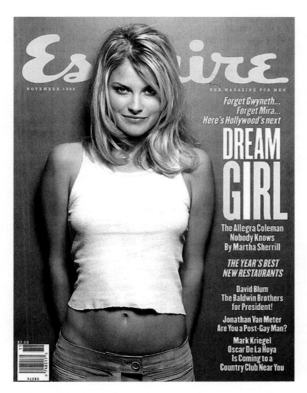

NOVEMBER 1996: This *Esquire* cover story on Allegra Coleman was supposedly about a hot new movie star; in reality, she didn't exist.

Larter, an actress who, the magazine said, "is the perfect expression of the movie industry today and its cult of instant celebrity." The model's role in the pseudoworld became oddly real, though, when she began getting calls from modeling and theatrical agents. "I think she's going to get a little career," *Esquire*'s then editor-in-chief Edward Kosner said. "Isn't that the ultimate irony?"[50] Maybe. Or maybe the irony was the realistic self-involved tone of the article, which starts like so many "I'm-amazing-because-I-was-right-there-with-her" profiles:

> She is laughing, and in my head she is smiling, and she's thinking, holding a notion, the whole thought of her life and her stardom in her laugh. Allegra Coleman is sitting in her old white bathtub of a car, her old Porsche, older than she is, even older than I am. She is speeding. The road is winding. . . .

Kosner called the piece "a brilliant parody of the brainless celebrity fluff that fills the media these days, and her article—a work of fiction from beginning to end—provides an occasion for all of us in the media to cast a fresh eye on celebrity mania."[51] How fresh that eye actually is might be open to discussion. In justifying Sherrill's piece, the magazine's public relations newsletter stated, "One of the roles of *Esquire* ever since the magazine's founding more than 60 years ago is to identify and examine what's happening in the culture."[52] That's all well and good, but should any cultural examination be based on fiction?

cultural influences on magazines

The 20th century was a time of intense cultural change. After World War II, the population boomed, the economy blasted off, leisure activities mushroomed, and affluence spread more than ever before throughout society. As the century moved on, ethnic groups increasingly left their mark on the culture and demanded that their voices be heard.

The 40-hour work week, a product of labor unions' political activism during the 1920s and 1930s, became standard in the 1970s, leading to more leisure time, though not necessarily more reading time with magazines. A 1938 Gallup Poll found Americans' favorite way to spend an evening was reading, followed by going to the movies/theater, and dancing.[53] By 1974 the answers to the same question put watching television as first choice, followed by reading, and then dining out.[54] In 1986 respondents told Gallup their first choice was watching television, followed by a tie between resting and reading. In 1992 and 1999, Gallup polls found that 40 percent of adults and 70 percent of teenagers said they spend too much time in front of the television.

Two audiences have dominated the magazine marketplace during the last half of the 20th century and are expected to continue to do so well into the 21st century: baby boomers and racial and ethnic groups. These groups are the two most significant forces shaping U.S. society now and in the future. A third audience began mushrooming in importance after 1980: the youth market consisting of teens and children in grades 1–8.

■ BABY BOOMERS

The baby boom produced about 4 million babies a year between 1946 and 1964, adding 78 million people to America's population. Today's first baby boomers have hit 60 years of age, and this fact alone represents a shift from a youth culture to a middle-aged culture, although baby boomers in general tend to feel, act, and buy much younger than their actual age. Magazines that established themselves as the voices of youth, like *Rolling Stone*, have had to decide whether to shift their focus to match their older, but still loyal, readers, or to stay with the age group they know—and cater to a smaller audience.

Some magazines have made it a point to go after the 50-plus market, including *AARP: The Magazine*, the largest circulation magazine with more than 22 million readers, and *More* for women, launched in 1998. Reaching a long-neglected market, *More* promotes itself as an alternative to traditional women's magazines and as a matter of editorial policy will not allow a model under the age of 40 to appear on its pages. Rejecting articles

FALL 2005: *Country Gardens* **extends the definition of home to the outdoors, which is of special appeal to baby boomers.**

about tighter tushes in 10 days, *More* discusses hormone replacement therapy, cashing in on retirement nest eggs, and starting fulfilling second careers. Covers are dominated by baby boomer celebrities with a mature glow: Jessica Lange, Jodie Foster, Sela Ward. *More*'s median age is 48 for readers, a household income of more than $113,500, and a total asset value of more than $876,000.[55]

Unfortunately, advertisers historically have been reluctant to tap into the mature market, preferring to concentrate on the 18–34-year-old group. Yet the Generation X baby busters (born 1965–1976), who followed the boomers, and Generation Y (born 1977–1994) simply don't have the volume of buying power that their predecessors had at their age and continue to have a generation later. The estimated spending power of baby boomers is more than $2 trillion, while Generation X and Generation Y combined reach only $923 billion.

Advertisers have failed to recognize the buying power of the 50-plus market. This is despite the fact that "the median age of new car buyers is now over 50," says Jim Fishman, publisher of *AARP: The Magazine*, adding that the magazine doesn't get as much automobile advertising as it should.[56] Additionally, the 50-plus market continues to be the fastest growing market segment, according to U.S. Census data: from 76.1 million in 2000 to 97.1 million by 2010. That's an increase of more than 27 percent in just 10 years.

From the time they graduated from college in record numbers, boomer readers have been touted as being more educated, more affluent, and more interested in pursuing the good life than the previous World War II generation, many of whom came of age during the Depression of the 1930s. Most revealing is the fact, however, that 60-year-old baby boomers don't act like their parents did at that age. In fact, boomer models Christie Brinkley and Cheryl Tiegs state that "50 is the new 30." Indeed, as Fishman observes, "A lot of these people are going to live until 100. You've got to fill that time somehow."[57] Magazine publishers who can correctly predict the desires, needs, and behaviors of aging boomers (who are resistant to the mature market label) will do well, say futurists.

What are some of the potential magazine topics likely to interest and excite baby boomers over the next decade? Health, shelter, personal finance, and leisure are the four horsemen of the boomer apocalypse, as evidenced by a growing number of successful launches and ongoing prosperity of established consumer and trade titles in those areas.

health

Women traditionally have kept on top of health concerns through the various service departments in the slew of women's beauty, fashion, and service magazines being published. Special health titles for women, such as *Shape, Fit, Self,* and *Fitness* are a slice of the niche, which is no longer the exclusive domain of female readers. Men's magazines such as *Men's Journal, Men's Health,* and *Men's Fitness* also have jumped on the service journalism bandwagon and are dispensing advice ranging from hiking to hair care.

Long-time top circulation titles in the health and fitness market include *Prevention* (a boomer itself, with a birth year of 1950), at more than 3.3 million, and *Health,* at more than 1.4 million. *Prevention* in particular is perfectly positioned to reach baby boomers—the median age of readers is 52. Hard-core and gloomy in tone with a "health nut" image during the 1950s and 1960s, today's *Prevention* has a "can-do approach." Along with mainstream articles such as "Head off Migraines Before They Start" and "Seven Foods That Boost Fat Loss," *Prevention* offers the exercise moves found on its pages in fitness videos like "3-2-1 Workout." Readers also are encouraged to take the *Prevention* Walking Challenge involving walker-friendly marathons around the country; editors put together a 6-month training program that even beginning walkers could do and provide weekly online tips as well as answers to training questions. The magazine also practices what it preaches—staffers walked with 19 readers, mostly female, ranging in age from 25 to 65 in the Marine Corps Marathon in Washington, D.C., in October 2005.

A 2005 survey of 1,081 brands in terms of likeability and awareness among respondents ages 13–49 years found many magazines on the list. Research firm Genius Insight reported that *Martha Stewart Living* was the top-ranked magazine brand in terms of awareness (97th), but *Time* led all magazine brands in terms of likeability (469th). *TV Guide* was the highest ranking magazine among the more than 1,000 brands, at 268th.

Health also dominates the business and trade magazine category, with health care and pharmaceutical publications having a separate advertising book devoted to them in the *SRDS Business Publications Advertising Source.* There you'll find more than 1,500 medical, surgical, dental, nursing, hospital administration, drugs, pharmaceutical, and health care titles, including *The New England Journal of Medicine, Surgical Rounds, Dental Products Report, RN, Medical Economics, Drug Topics,* and *Contemporary Long Term Care.*

shelter

Home has long been where the heart is, and the shelter magazines show no signs of slowing down. Futurists predict that as more and more boomers enter their fifties and sixties, they'll want to spend more time at home. The home service magazine category has been extremely active in the last several years. According to *House Beautiful* publisher David Arnold, more than 117 magazines in the market have the word "house" or "home" in the title.[58]

Typical of the boomer influence on the shelter category was *Apartment Life's* title change in 1981 to *Metropolitan Home.* The change, which included a complete makeover, reflected the fact that the magazine's baby boomer readers were beginning to disdain the apartment renter nomenclature and were purchasing co-ops, condos, lofts, and townhouses in cities across the nation. Editors wanted to reflect the boomer audience's desire for a more upscale, refined, mature look in their more spacious abodes. After all, by 1986 their median household income was $81,900 and their median home value was $184,200.[59] These readers were no longer 1970s radicals. They had settled down to comfortable affluence.

Home ownership is now at a record high of 67 percent, and nearly 1 million homes a year have major improvements done on them. So it was no surprise that *This Old House*, one of the highest-rated series on public television, was translated into a magazine offering. *This Old House* was launched in 1995 as a joint venture between Time, Inc., and WGBH of Boston, the producer of the program. The tone of the magazine matches that of the PBS show, while successfully filling the fixer-upper niche in the shelter market. Most shelter books deal with finished space, but *This Old House* walks more than 950,000 readers through the entire process. It is the number-one-selling magazine at home centers.[60] It joins *Old-House Journal* and *The Family Handyman* in a home improvement niche position between traditional home service publications such as *House Beautiful* and *Home* and magazines providing professional level, in-depth information about residential building and remodeling, such as *Fine Homebuilding*.

Lately, however, the baby boomers' obsession with home and shelter has been fed by popular TV shows such as *Extreme Makeover: Home Edition*, *Trading Spaces*, and the HGTV Channel. This has led to a whole new generation of shelter magazines since 2000 that focuses on a more relaxed decorating philosophy. These include *Cottage Living*, which offers itself as a metaphor for a relaxed, comfortable, and cozy approach whether you live in a cottage or not; *Domino*, which puts a shelter spin on the shopping format of *Lucky*, and *O at Home*, coattailing on the Oprah brand and stressing that you live your best life at home.

"We've always known that the home category was an important part of our readers' lives," said *O* vice president and publisher Jill Seelig in 2004. "Research shows that *O* readers spent more than $8 million in the last year alone on home remodeling."[61]

Gardens and outdoor patios are a natural extension of the homebody lifestyle. After baby boomers put finishing touches on the inside of their homes (how many times can you reupholster that chair or repaint that wall?), it's logical to turn to the adjacent outdoor areas. Titles here include *Country Gardens*, *Fine Gardening*, and *Horticulture*.

Paralleling the consumer interest in shelter are trade magazines focusing on architecture, construction, air conditioning, plumbing, hardware, interior design, floriculture, and landscape and garden supplies. The hundreds of titles listed in *SRDS Business Publications Advertising Source* range from *Builder* and *Construction Specifier* to *Nursery Retailer* and *Landscape and Irrigation*.

personal finance

Boomers are turning 50 at the rate of seven every minute and will continue to do so until 2014. They currently control 70 percent of total net worth in the United States, according to the Federal Reserve Board. Consequently, a logical top baby boomer interest is the consumer business and finance sector, long dominated by *Forbes*, *Fortune*, and *Business Week*. Other business titles of note include *Entrepreneur*, *Black Enterprise*, and *Inc.*, which all tend to stress business-to-business advertisements and feature articles focusing on corporate image and management issues for an audience of business people.

However, the most intriguing aspect of this category has been its movement into the lifestyle and service-oriented personal finance niche. Baby boomers are moving from being spenders to savers as they age and worry about financing their children's college education, caring for their own aging parents, and having enough money for their own retirement. This shift in focus has affected the magazines they want to purchase and read. *Worth*, *Money*, *SmartMoney*, and *Kiplinger's Personal Finance* have taken advantage of the boomers' new attitude and emphasize financial planning in terms of better savings and wiser investments. They also often add a dose of lifestyle attitudes and approaches in the forms of health tips, food lists, and physical exercises as they advise readers on how to accumulate, manage, and spend their personal wealth.

Carrying the luxury lifestyle and personal wealth merger to the *n*th degree is the *Robb Report* franchise, with magazines devoted to luxury cars, boats, aircraft, vacation homes, luxury homes, home entertainment systems, and motocycles (easy, but very, very wealthy, riders who spend $50,000 on motorcycles). *Robb Report* readers have an average annual income of $1.1 million and a net worth of more than $5 million.[62]

Business and finance ranks just behind health as a mega-classification in the trade magazine category in *SRDS Business Publication Advertising Source*. This is where you'll find magazines devoted to business concerns (*Industry Week*), banking (*American Banker*), finance (*Institutional Investor*), insurance (*Business Insurance*), and legal issues (*ABA Journal*).

leisure

Leisure, desired by all and consumed most avidly and sumptuously by the well-to-do baby boomer, is the wild card in the deck. Pinpointing leisure magazines is a matter of determining prevailing trends and interests.

Leisure-oriented magazines take the attitude that the general magazine is dead and that audiences want highly specialized magazines to read. Consequently, leisure titles—all competing for variations in the same educated, affluent niche—range from *Cigar Aficionado* for stogies stokers to *Fine Woodworking* for crafty carvers to *hr: Watches Magazines* about the workings of fine timepieces for collectors, professionals, and wearers of expensive wristwatches. Leisure magazines tend to be expensive: *hr: Watches Magazines* has a hefty cover price of $9.95, topped only by *Robb Report*'s $9.99 figure. *Fine Woodworking* costs $7.99, while *Cigar Aficionado* puffs a price of $4.95. The average cover price of a magazine on the newsstands in 2004 was $4.40.[63]

Of course, there are less opulent and less outrageous leisure and lifestyle offerings for the middle-class reader, baby boomer or not. Leisure magazines account for the myriad growth of special interest magazines each year. In the 20-year period from 1985 to 2005, the top three magazine categories showing the most growth were crafts, home, and cooking, according to magazine analyst Samir Husni of the University of Mississippi.[64] However, the standard categories in the leisure market continue to prosper. For example, the big three travel magazines, *Condé Nast Traveler*, *Travel and Leisure*, and *National Geographic Traveler* have maintained their high circulations even with the advent of more focused titles like *Arthur Frommer's Budget Travel*, *Caribbean Travel and Life*, and *Islands*. Association magazines also fill the leisure niche, particularly in the travel field, where state, regional, and national automobile associations cover American destinations and resorts.

For every new sport or hobby that becomes popular, you can be sure that a magazine won't be far behind. *Snowboarder* is one magazine that developed only after snowboards had found acceptance on popular ski slopes, while soccer magazines are growing along with the sport. Magazines serve every conceivable craft or hobby, and thrive despite competition for a narrow slice of the reader pie. For example, Teddy bear collectors can choose between *Teddy Bear Review* and *Teddy Bear and Friends*, while numismatists have a wider currency to pick from, with *World Coin News*, *Coins*, *Coinage*, *Coin World*, and *Coin Prices*. Guitarists can strum through *Acoustic Guitar*, *Guitar Player*, *Guitar World*, *Just Jazz Guitar*, *Freestyle Guitar*, *Guitar One*, *Vintage Guitar*, *Fingerstyle Guitar*, and *Play Guitar*. Many guitar magazines found on newsstands are from the United Kingdom: *Bass Guitar Magazine*, *Classical Guitar*, and *Guitarist*, for example.

A surge of interest in poker on television on the ESPN and Bravo channels has led to a boomlet in gambling magazines since 2003. Only *Card Player* has been in the game since the late 1980s; the latest "hand" dealt since 2003 includes *All In*, *Bluff*, *Poker Pro*, and *Woman Poker Player*.

In the business and trade magazine area, technology magazines have both leisure and personal/finance overtones, due to the computer, telecommunications, software, and electronic engineering explosion. Many fall into the business-to-business classification and are listed in *SRDS Business Publications Advertising Source*. For example, three circulation leaders in the specialized trade genre that cross over to consumer readership are *PC Magazine*, *PC World*, and *Macworld*.

The circulation of narrowly focused, special interest magazines can range from a few thousand to more than a million. Between 1995 and 2005, the number of interior design and decoration magazines more than doubled, from 85 to 183; ditto the number of dog magazines from 41 to 92. The leisure categories of golf, collectibles, and guns and firearms also showed double-digit increases during that decade.[65]

■ RACIAL AND ETHNIC SHIFTS

Magazines for African American, Hispanic, and Asian American audiences have been around for decades, but the number of titles boomed during the 1990s. That's when census data confirmed increasing numbers of ethnic groups with the income and advertising patterns that appealed to Madison Avenue. During the 1960s and 1970s, *Ebony, Jet, Essence, Black Enterprise,* and *Hispanic Business* struggled to convince advertisers of their readers' purchasing power, educational savvy, and professional status. By 1990, advertisers' acceptance of magazines for ethnic and minority groups not only heralded a larger social acceptance, it also was good economic sense.

In 1996, Population Reference Bureau researcher Carol J. De Vita predicted, "Within the next 25 years, about one in three Americans will come from a minority background, and by the middle of the 21st century, the size of the 'minority' population should just about equal the size of the non-Hispanic white population."[66]

By 2020, the Hispanic population is expected to exceed 60 million, while the Asian population should more than double in size to 21 million. African Americans will reach 42 million by 2020, but the pace of growth will be slower than for the other two. What does this mean for the magazine industry? More magazines will be launched that specifically target Hispanics, African Americans, and Asian Americans. However, many minorities were born during the baby boom years and have acculturated themselves to the same values, interests, and lifestyles as white boomers.

hispanic titles

The phenomenal growth of the Hispanic population in the last quarter of the 20th century and continuing into the 21st century has been an important demographic trend, resulting in a significant growth in the Hispanic middle class. The 1990 census was the first time Americans could choose to identify themselves as Hispanics, and 23 million did. By 2002, Hispanics outnumbered the African Amercians for the first time in history, according to the U.S. Census; by 2050, Hispanics are expected to comprise 30 percent of the entire U.S. population. (Nomenclature is a problem when discussing the Hispanic magazine market in the United States. Identifying names for this group have included Latin, Latin American, Latino, Mexican, Mexican American, Chicano, and Spanish, with Hispanic being acknowledged as the most inclusive.)

For years there have been Spanish-language versions of *Reader's Digest, Cosmopolitan, Harper's Bazaar, Good Housekeeping,* and *Popular Mechan-*

JANUARY 2006: *Siempre Mujer* **is a lifestyle and shelter magazine for the burgeoning market of Hispanic women living in the United States**.

ics distributed throughout Latin America and the Caribbean, as well as major Spanish-language publishers such as Editorial Televisa, the largest publisher of Spanish-language magazines in the world. These magazines see their readership as Spanish-speaking and largely foreign; *Reader's Digest Seleccions* is the longest-lived Spanish-language publication in the United States, established in 1940. However, publishers also are specifically targeting Americans of Hispanic background through magazines written in English or a mix of English and Spanish. Taking the bilingual and bicultural editorial approach are *Latina* and *Estylo,* two women's fashion and lifestyle magazines, as well as *El Andar,* a literary magazine that's heavy on analytical commentary and investigative reporting. *Catalina, Latina Style, Hispanic Business,* and *Hispanic* are published in English. There are more than 100 English-language, bilingual, and Spanish-language magazines targeting Hispanics.

Latina, established in 1995, was the first women's lifestyle magazine to focus on Hispanic women. Founder Christy Haubegger, who is of Mexican descent, explained, "I remember being 10 years old, standing in the checkout line at the grocery store with my adoptive mother and examining the women's magazines. I noticed a lack of people who looked like me. I wondered why there weren't any magazines for Hispanic women."[67]

Hispanic Business is older than *Latina*, having been established in 1979 specifically for Hispanic CEOs, managers, and professionals. The first to target business readers in its minority group, *Hispanic Business* is considered the key information source for and about Hispanic business in the United States.

People en Español is the number one Hispanic magazine in advertising and circulation revenue, and has been a powerhouse ever since its launch in 1997. *People en Español* grew out of *People's* success with a special Southwest edition cover story about popular Mexican American singer Selena who had been murdered in Texas. That edition sold 442,000 copies in a single day, and a special Selena "tribute" memorial issue sold a million copies.[68] *People en Español* is one of the most successful brand extensions in the magazine market with a circulation of more than 454,000.

Previously, the most successful mass market Hispanic title was a Spanish-language publication, *Mas*. During the late 1980s and early 1990s *Mas* had a newsstand circulation of 680,000, and a full-page ad cost $20,000.[69] "We were the *Time* magazine, the *Vanity Fair*, the *Vogue* of the American Hispanic," said former publisher Roger Toll. Started by Univision, the Spanish-language television network, *Mas* was shut down in 1993 when Mexican media giant Televisa purchased Univision.

People en Español, *Latina*, and *Selicciones* are the only magazines targeted to Hispanics to make the *Advertising Age* Top 300 Magazines list in terms of gross advertising and circulation revenues. Yet all three lag behind such black titles as *Essence*, *Ebony*, *Jet*, and *Black Enterprise*. Hispanic-oriented magazines—there are about 60 being published in the United States today, not counting locally distributed titles—are finding readers, but they continue to struggle to develop advertising revenue.

There's still room for more magazines, say media analysts. Publishers and advertisers have to been slow to acknowledge that one size doesn't fit all. Instead of seeing Hispanic magazine publishing as a single niche, media critics say publishers need to develop niche magazines for Hispanics. "Advertisers in the past were guilty of approaching the marketplace as monolithic. There's a great deal of diversity within the diversity," says Paul Hunt, vice president and media director of GlobalHue, a multicultural marketing communications agency.[70]

Meredith Publishing Group took that segmented approach with the 2005 start-up of the Spanish-language magazine *Siempre Mujer* ("Always Woman") in the lifestyle and shelter category, rather than launching a *Better Homes and Gardens en Español*. "That would have been much easier," says Ruth Gaviria, *Siempre Mujer*'s publisher. But she argues it wouldn't necessarily have been the right move, adding that the *Siempre Mujer* reader is either foreign born or speaks Spanish in the home. "This woman is imbued in two worlds: traditional and adopting American values. She is buying her first home, getting an education. All of these first time opportunities. We needed to grow up with this reader. It is very difficult to do that with a magazine that serves a different reader."[71]

black titles

Black magazines are the longest-lived minority publication group in the United States, with the first one, *Mirror of Liberty*, established in 1838. The total number of magazine titles specifically reaching African American readers has remained above 100 since 1996 and covers a variety of genres, including fashion, entertainment, business, and religion. Magazines for African Americans have been the most successful in responding to changing demographic and marketing shifts, moving into niche and specialty titles as early as the 1970s, when dozens of black titles were launched. Unfortunately, having start-up dollars, an editorial niche, and a specialized audience are only a small part of the magazine success equation, particularly in a recessionary period, such as occurred during the late 1970s. Many magazines—not just black ones—failed to survive. Among the black magazines that died were *Gentleman of Color*, *Miss Black America*, *Black Perspective in Music*, *Bronze Thrills*, *Black Sports*, *Black Tennis*, and *Black Politician*. Very little has been written about these magazines, and finding them for study is difficult; no detailed census of black magazines exists. Few of those magazines were archived by libraries either.

Various labels have been used to identify magazines for African American audiences over the years, starting with "colored" and ending with "black." In his Pulitzer Prize–winning history of American magazines, Frank Luther Mott referred to "Negro" magazines, which was the preferred term in formal and academic writing before and after the Civil War; "colored" was used in informal writing and in conversations during much of the 18th, 19th, and 20th centuries. The debate over terminology didn't escalate until the 1960s, when a variety of words came and went: colored, Negro, Negro-oriented, Black, Afro-American, Aframerican, nonwhite, people of color, African American, and black (lowercased). By the late 1980s, African American and black appeared to be the frontrunners in the name game. U.S. Census terminology is both Black and African American; however, most magazine publishers and editors use Black or black in their titles or references to readers and issues. In this book, African American is used when referring to audiences; black is used when referring to the publications, their content, and their overall approach.

Magazine researcher Lillie Fears of Arkansas State University estimates that more than 150 black magazines are being published in the United States today; identifying and finding all of them is problematic. "Black magazines have tended to be overlooked when studying the black press," said Fears at a conference in 1999. "The last major survey of black magazines and readers was done in 1969."[72]

Titles for African American readers grew in the 1990s while, at the same time, advertising pages in established black magazines—*Ebony, Essence, Jet,* and *Black Enterprise*—increased. Editors of both new and established magazines for the African American audience say the market can hold still more titles, and point to the lack of images of African Americans in mainstream magazines as a reason for introducing new publications.

Magazines for African Americans always have been more in tune with the nuances and needs of baby boomers than have magazines for other ethnic groups. For example, *Heart and Soul* merges articles about health, fitness, finance, and spiritual well-being for African American women. *Brides Noir* offers the bridal experience for the bride of color. Numerous magazines for African American women have been created over the years, including *Black Elegance, Honey,* and most recently, *Suede.* None has had the staying power of *Essence,* which has led the market for African American women since 1970.

Likewise, magazines for African American men also have had numerous contenders, including *Code,*

Smooth, and *Savoy,* dubbed "the black *Vanity Fair.*" The highly praised *Savoy,* for the affluent 30-something professional, shut down in 2003 but is now back on the newsstands in 2005. *King,* subtitled "the illest men's magazine ever," is the current leader in the young urban black men's lifestyle category.

Two particularly interesting niche publications are *American Legacy* and *Black Issues Book Review.* Both magazines are ambitious in scope, with elegant writing and production values. *American Legacy,* subtitled "The Magazine of African-American History and Culture," is published quarterly in a joint venture with the American Heritage division of Forbes, Inc. *American Legacy*'s founding publisher, Rodney J. Reynolds, knew there was a market for "a history magazine that would make blacks proud of their heritage, not only as blacks but as Americans" in 1995.[73] *American Legacy* encourages African Americans to celebrate their history every day; the magazine is a premier resource of black history and culture. *Black Issues Book Review,* established in 1998, is devoted entirely to books by or about black authors as well as trends in publishing.

Vibe carved a special niche among black men and women in their twenties when it hit the newsstands in 1993 as the cultural purveyor of the hiphop music scene. Its dramatic covers featuring Whitney Houston, Tupac Shakur, Kanye West, and Nelly reach young trendsetters who thrive on the culture, fashion, and sounds of urban music. Although 31 percent of *Vibe*'s audience is Caucasian, the magazine says it reaches more people of color ages 18–24 than any other magazine, and that 61 percent of African American teens read the publication, more than any other magazine.[74]

In 2005, *Vibe* decided to expand its reach by publishing a beauty and fashion magazine in recognition of the 50 percent of its audience who wanted articles about cutting-edge fashion and beauty trends for urban "fashionistas who worship hip-hop chic." *Vibe Vixen* was a hit, with the magazine receiving 300 e-mails within the first week and 2,400 responses to the in-book and online surveys.[75]

asian titles

More than 11 million Asian Americans now live in the United States. This group had the highest growth rate of any ethnic group between 1990 and 2000, a 72 percent increase compared to an increase of 13 percent for the general population.

The two largest Asian groups are Chinese and Filipinos, with the three fastest-growing groups being Asian Indians, Bangladeshi, and Pakistani. The 2000 Census was the first time people were given the option of identifying themselves as more than one race, and almost 2 million said they were Asian and another race. (The use of the term Asian here follows the broad U.S. Census definition, which includes the Far East, Southeast Asia, and the Indian subcontinent, including India, China, Japan, the Philippines, North and South Korea, Cambodia, Thailand, Vietnam, Malaysia, Bangladesh, and Sri Lanka.)

In general, Asian Americans have higher education and higher earnings relative to their numbers than other ethnic or minority groups. They also are more likely to hold high technology and professional jobs and, on average, also outspend other ethnic groups. Media analysts describe Asian Americans as having "demographics from heaven" because of their high disposable incomes.[76] Yet the market is underserved, with fewer marketers specifically targeting Asian Americans compared to Hispanics and African Americans.

Although there are more than 120 magazines for Asian Americans, most of them segment readers by their country of origin, such as China, Vietnam, Korea, the Philippines, India, and Japan. For example, *Filipinas* has reached Filipino Americans since 1992, while *KoreAm Journal* has targeted Korean Americans since 1990. Both *Filipinas* (18,665 circulation), and *KoreAm Journal* (12,000 circulation) are published in English, reflecting the fact that 83 percent of Asian American adults speak English only or very well. However, many magazines for specific Asian groups are "in-language" titles that publish in native languages. This results in small circulations and limited appeal for national advertisers who want to target a less fragmented demographic.

Although there are numerous Asian languages and dialects, English is the unifying language among Asian Americans and their magazines. Affluent Asian Americans in the 18–35 age bracket tend to be American born and prefer English as their written and spoken language. So far, only a handful of magazines have been targeted to the larger, "national" Asian American group.

A. Magazine, a lifestyle book covering news, politics, and culture reached more than 100,000 readers when it died in 2002 after a 13-year publishing run. *Yolk,* with comedian Margaret Cho on the inaugural 1994 cover, was edgy and political as it sought "NewGenerAsian" readers across the country. The magazine folded in 2003 after revamping itself into an entertainment, lifestyle, and pop culture magazine.

For now, the top national titles are *Audrey* and *Asian Week. Audrey,* a bimonthly lifestyle and fashion magazine for Asian American women nationwide, hit the newsstands in 2003 with a 10,000 circulation. *Asian Week,* established in 1979 as an English language national newsweekly for Asian Pacific Americans, positions itself as "the link for American born Asians to better understand their community. It has become a bridge for Asian immigrants to mainstream American culture. Likewise, it is the primary vehicle for mainstream America to learn of the concerns and aspirations of one of the country's fastest growing communities."[77]

Media analysts have been cautious about this market for more than a decade. Said one media buyer in 1995, "I think the Asian market is a sleeping giant. There's a great potential for the upscale segment of the Asian population that advertisers will find desirable, but nobody's paying attention to it yet."[78]

"It's definitely a tight market," says Sam Lau, advertising manager at *Audrey.* "It is still a struggle. We are dependent on advertising, and if there is an ethnic budget, it usually goes to Hispanics first, then African-Americans, then maybe in-language Asian media."[79]

other ethnic and racial groups

Although the MPA puts the number of ethnic magazines at 534, finding a breakout of the ethnicities is virtually impossible. The *SRDS Business Publications Advertising Source* "Ethnic" category, with just 25 listings, includes magazines as disparate as *American Indian Report, Irish America Magazine,* and *Italian American,* as well as a handful of Spanish-language titles and English-language titles for Hispanic audiences. Others, such as *Primo* for Italian Americans and *German Life* about German culture, seem more for the outsider than the particular ethnic group.

■ YOUTH

Following the demise of *Youth's Companion* and *St. Nicholas,* the two most significant magazines for young readers during the 19th and early 20th centuries, the youth market was neglected. Only a handful of magazines targeted young people and had a presence on newsstands in the 1950s, 1960s, and 1970s: *Seventeen, Young Miss,* and *Teen* for teen girls; *Jack and Jill, Highlights for Children,* and *Humpty Dumpty* for toddlers. Publishers and associations such as Scholastic, Inc., and the National Wildlife Federation concentrated on reaching the youth market through schools. Then, in the late 1980s, new consumer magazines for young people began mushrooming. Three contributing factors caused publishers to gravitate to this audience: Baby boomers were having children; the youth market was becoming an economic force with significant spending power; and magazines for youngsters could be viewed as a petri dish for growing future subscribers.

children's titles

The turning point for children's magazines occurred between 1987 and 1989, when magazines for children (as young as 2 and as old as 12 years) nearly doubled in number, from 85 to 160.[80] Although half of them were designed as teaching aids for the classroom, the fastest-growing crop were junior versions of adult magazines, such as *National Geographic World,* relaunched in 2002 as *National Geographic Kids,* and *Sports Illustrated for Kids.*

More significant for advertisers, discretionary income for the kids themselves is significant. Children between the ages of 8 and 12 years—"tweens"—spend $19 billion annually, with most of that disposable income given to them by their parents and grandparents.[81] Not only do children have more money of their own to spend, they have more influence over household spending on food, beverages, vacations, and even cars—more than $150 billion worth of goods.[82] Although today's tweens were born using technology, they also like to read: Fifty-two percent say they play video games in their free time, while 29 percent say they read magazines.[83]

The range of magazines for children ages 8–12 includes glossy, trendy publications such as *Nickelodeon* and *Disney Adventures,* highly specialized ones such as *Young Dancer* and *Ranger Rick,* as well as serious literary and scientific offerings such as *Stone Soup* and *Muse.* Kids' magazines that are spin-offs of successful adult titles—*Time for Kids, Sports Illustrated for Kids, National Geographic Kids,* and *MAD Kids*—are expected to bring young readers to the grown-up franchise as they mature.

There are even magazines for the youngest audience, in the 2–6 year age bracket: *Ladybug* and *Nick Jr. Magazine* encourage children to get into the reading habit early. *Nick Jr.,* from the Nickelodeon channel, takes a two-pronged approach, with the front half of the book written for parents and the back half for kids. The paper stock is different; the back half is meant to be written on, with puzzles and games to complete, alone or with Mom or Dad.

teen titles

Teens ages 12–19 had a soaring increase in numbers between 1990 and 2000, a 17 percent growth that outpaced the rest of the population. Numbering more than 32 million, the current teen market is also the most multicultural in U.S. history. Like their younger brothers and sisters, teens have significant discretionary income and influence their parents' spending on both large and small products. At ages 12 and 13, teens have about $1,500 in yearly discretionary income to spend, a figure that rises to nearly $4,500 by the time they are 16 and 17. According to U.S. Census figures, teens spent more than $112 billion in 2003.

As many as 8 out of 10 teens read magazines, which translates into more than 19 million readers.[84] For years, the big three in the teen market were *Seventeen, YM,* and *Teen,* reaching millions of teen girls who spend millions of dollars on clothes, shoes, and CDs. Lifestyle or service magazines for teen boys haven't been successful; *MH-18,* a bimonthly offshoot of *Men's Health* for boys 13–18 lasted only a year. Teen boys don't gravitate to the larger general interest topics of fashion and beauty that dominate girls' magazines. Teen boys are more likely to read videogame and motorcycle magazines such as *Electronic Gaming Monthly, Game Informer,* and *Dirt Rider.*

The successful launch of *Teen People* in 1998 and its blockbuster newsstand performance—circulation more than doubled from half a million to 1.2 million copies after just 10 issues—reinvigorated the entire teen category. That was followed by the 1999 launch of *CosmoGirl* as another example of a spin-off title capitalizing on a long-established franchise name. Publishers see such spin-offs as "incubators for future readers." Cathleen Black, president of Hearst Magazines, says *CosmoGirl* is a way "to graduate them up to the big sister publication when they're older."[85]

MAY 2006: *Seventeen* has been a standard in the teen magazine market since its birth in 1942.

of earlier years. Bathing suit sections in *Seventeen, Teen People, CosmoGirl,* and *Teen Vogue* often show young women with thick thighs and flabby abs. "It's not going to help my reader if we only show girls who are size 6's," says Atoosa Rubenstein, editor of *Seventeen.* "Everyone is beautiful. It's just a matter of confidence and we try to show that."[86]

By running photos of teens with believable dimensions rather than waif models, teen magazines emphasize realistic images. Additionally, they are dealing with weightier topics than in the past, often with a new level of frankness that acknowledges that teens are more mature and more independent than previous generations.

In their role as both shapers and reflectors of American society, magazines have made a critical impact on each century's readers and writers. In December 1846, Edgar Allan Poe, himself an influential magazine editor and freelance writer, wrote in *Graham's American Monthly Magazine of Literature and Art:*

> Whatever may be the merits or demerits, generally of the Magazine Literature of America, there can be no question as to its extent or influence. The topic—Magazine Literature—is therefore an important one. In a few years its importance will be found to have increased in geometrical ratio. The whole tendency of the age is Magazine-ward.[87]

The teen branding frenzy continued into the 21st century, with the launches of *ElleGirl* in 2001 and *Teen Vogue* in 2002. These ate away at the market once owned by *Seventeen, YM,* and *Teen,* with *Teen Vogue* absorbing *YM* in 2005.

These teen magazines feature girls of all shapes and sizes now, not just the pencil-thin size 2 models

The idea of creating culture continues to resonate in the 21st century. An updated version of Poe's eloquent statement comes from Hugh Roome, president of Scholastic, Inc. Said Roome, "They say magazines are the cockroaches of media—we'll survive whatever changes come, even nuclear war."[88]

notes

1. Joseph Klapper, *The Effects of Mass Communication,* 2d ed. (Glencoe, Ill.: Free Press, 1961).
2. John D. Zelezny, *Communications Law, Liberties, Restraints and the Modern Media* (Belmont, Calif.: Wadsworth Publishing Company, 1993), 95.
3. Maxwell McCombs and Donald Shaw, "The Agenda-Setting Function of Mass Media," *Public Opinion Quarterly,* 36 (Summer 1972): 176–85.
4. Edwin Diamond, "The Myth of the 'Pesticide Menace,'" *Saturday Evening Post* (September 28, 1963), 16–18; "Pesticides: The Price for Progress," *Time* (Sep-

tember 28, 1962), 45–48; "Can Human Beings Withstand the Barrage of Economic Poisons?" *Consumer Bulletin* (October 1962), 36–37.
5. Gino Marco, Robert M. Hollingworth, and William Hollingworth, *Silent Spring Revisited* (Washington, D.C.: American Chemical Society, 1987).
6. Kathleen L. Endres, ed. *Trade, Industrial, and Professional Periodicals of the United States* (Westport, Conn.: Greenwood Press, 1994): 72–84.
7. Arthur Weinberg and Lila Weinberg, *The Muckrakers: The Era of Journalism That Moved America to Reform:*

PROM: BE THE PRETTIEST GIRL THERE!

Seventeen

love

New Section!

Find Your Soul Mate

May 2006

Pink "I'm A Stupid Girl Every Other Day"

The Best Fashion And Styling Ideas

653 Ways To Stand Out (In A Good Way)

PLUS: Outfits Guys Love

When GOSSIP Hurts see page 108

YOUR PERIOD What's Normal, What's Not

17 REAL LIFE Why So Many Girls At This High School Are Getting Pregnant

The Most Significant Magazine Articles of 1902–1912. (New York: Simon and Schuster, 1961), 58.

8. Kathleen L. Endres, "Women and the 'Larger Household': An Examination of Muckraking in Women's Magazines" (paper presented at the annual meeting of the Association for Education in Journalism and Mass Communication, Atlanta, Ga., August 1994). Later published as "Women and the 'Larger Household': The 'Big Six' and Muckraking," *American Journalism*, 14, nos. 3–4 (Summer-Fall 1997), 262-82.

9. James Playsted Wood, *Magazines in the United States,* 2d ed. (New York: Ronald Press, 1956), 119–20.

10. Ida M. Tarbell, *All in the Day's Work: An Autobiography* (New York: Macmillan, 1939), 242.

11. Ibid., 281.

12. Mary M. Cronin, "A Master for the Watchdog: The Progressive Era Trade Press' Role in Promoting Professional Values and Ethics Among Journalists" (paper presented at the annual meeting of the Association for Education in Journalism and Mass Communication, Boston, Mass., August 1991).

13. Richard Edel, "How 'Passionate Commitment' Raised $1 million for AIDS," *Advertising Age* (May 24, 1989), 34.

14. Richard Edel, "Advocacy Picks Up Steam," *Advertising Age* (May 24, 1989), 34.

15. Edel, "How 'Passionate Commitment,'" 74.

16. Edel, "Advocacy," 40.

17. Lyon N. Richardson, *A History of Early American Magazines, 1741–1789* (New York: Octagon Books, 1978), 163–210.

18. Loudon Wainwright, *The Great American Magazine: An Inside History of* Life (New York: Alfred A. Knopf, 1986), 100–101.

19. Ibid., 235.

20. Gardner Cowles, *Mike Looks Back* (New York: Gardner Cowles, 1985), 151; and "The Fifties," *The Look Years* (Cowles Communications, 1972), 22–23.

21. John H. Johnson, *Succeeding Against the Odds* (New York: Warner Books, 1989), 125.

22. Ibid., 156–7.

23. Tara Burghart, "Hundreds Attend Publisher's Rites," *San Antonio Express-News* (August 16, 2005), 4A.

24. Bob Hippler, "Fast Times in the Motor City: The First Ten Years of the Fifth Estate, 1965–1975," in *Voices from the Underground: Volume 1, Insider Histories of the Vietnam Era Underground Press,* ed. Ken Wachsberger (Tempe, Ariz.: Mica Press, 1993), 18.

25. David E. Settje, "The Vietnam War, the Cold War, and Protestants: How *The Christian Century* and *Christianity Today* Reflected American Society in the 1960s" (paper presented at the annual meeting of the American Journalism History Association, London, Ontario, Canada, October 1996).

26. "An Open Letter to," *Ladies' Home Journal* (April 1971), 50.

27. "The Power of a Woman," *Ladies' Home Journal* (July 1971), 46, 152.

28. Elizabeth Valk Long, "To Our Readers," *Time* (May 2, 1994), 4.

29. Ellen Goodman, "JFK Jr. More Than Just Another Celebrity," *San Antonio Express-News* (July 23, 1999), 5B.

30. Keith J. Kelly, "Bin Laden Book Due Early," *New York Post* (September 19, 2001), http://nypost.com/business/4457.htm.

31. David D. Kirkpatrick, "Newsweeklies Run to Keep Up on Tricky Turf," *The New York Times* (October 24, 2001), C1, C9.

32. Ibid., B12.

33. Matthew Rose, "In Its Rush, *People* Neglects Advertisers," *Wall Street Journal* (September 19, 2001), B12.

34. "Magazines Change Plans," *ASJA Newsletter* (October 2001), 3.

35. Ann Marie Kerwin, "Print Proves Mettle," *Advertising Age* (September 17, 2001), 26.

36. Seth Mnookin, "In Disaster's Aftermath, Once-Cocky Media Culture Disses the Age of Irony," *Inside.com* (September 18, 2001), http://www.inside.com/product/Product.

37. Ann Oldenburg, Kelly Carter, and Jeannie Williams, "Celebrity World Lights Up: Journalists, Stars Step Gingerly to Avoid Offense," *USA Today* (October 4, 2001), 1D.

38. Prime Access, Inc., and Rivendell Media, "2004 Gay Press Report," http://www.gaymarket.com/gaypressreport2004.pdf.

39. Rivendell Media, Inc., "How Big Is the Gay Market?" http://www.rivendellmedia.com/news/gaymarket.pdf.

40. Sandra Yin, "Coming Out in Print," *American Demographics* (February 2003), http://www.gaymarket.com/news/coming_out_in_print.html.

41. Jack A. Nelson, "Disability Magazines: The Search for Identity and Empowerment" (paper presented at the annual meeting of the Association for Education in Journalism and Mass Communication, Anaheim, Calif., August 1996).

42. Jim Cory, "The Spokane Story," *Hardware Age* (October 1994): 30–52.

43. Jonathan Rabinovitz, "Attempted Comeback for the Literary Salon," *New York Times* (April 13, 1992), B2.

44. Stuart Elliott, "Read the Magazine, Then Eat the Meal," *New York Times* (August 30, 2005), http://www.nytimes.com/2005/08/30/business/media.

45. Amy Mattson Lauters, "'We Are Legion': Community-building and *The Farmer's Wife*, 1955–1962" (paper presented at the annual convention of the American Journalism Historians Association, San Antonio, Texas, October 2005).

46. Kaja Silverman, *The Subject of Semiotics* (New York: Oxford University Press, 1983).

47. Walter Lippmann, *Public Opinion* (New York: Macmillan Publishing, 1922).

48. Michael Parenti, *Inventing Reality: The Politics of News Media,* 2d ed. (New York: St. Martin's Press, 1993), 191.

49. Daniel Boorstin, *The Image: or What Happened to the American Dream* (New York: Atheneum, 1962).

50. "Unlike Madonna, She's Fake, But Not Icky," *Des Moines Register* (October 28, 1996), 2.

51. "*Esquire* Spoofs Celebrity Journalism," *Esquire News* (October 23, 1996), 1.

52. Ibid., 2.

53. Edward W. Barrett, "Sex, Death and Other Trends in Magazines," *Mass Media and Society,* 2d ed., ed. Alan

Wells. (Palo Alto, Calif.: Mayfield Publishing, 1975), 35–37.

54. Ibid., 37.

55. *More* 2005 Media Kit, http://www.meredith.com/mediakit/more.

56. Michael Shields, "Mag Spotlight: *AARP*," *Media Post's Media Daily News* (November 29, 2004), http://www.mediapost.com/PrintFriend.cfjm?articleId=280310.

57. Ibid.

58. Michael Shields, "Shelter Skelter: Home Mag Category Goes Nuts," *Media Post's Media Daily News* (November 3, 2004), http://www.mediapost.com/PrintFriend.cfjm?articleId=276733.

59. Kathleen L. Endres and Theresa L. Lueck, eds. *Women's Periodicals of the United States: Consumer Magazines* (Westport, Conn.: Greenwood Press, 1995), 225–29.

60. *This Old House* 2005 Media Kit, http://www.thisoldhouse.com/toh/advertising.

61. Mickey Alam Khan, "*O at Home* Hits Newsstands as Hearst Widens Francise," *DM News* (May 12, 2004), http://www.dmnews.com/cgi-bin/artprevbot.cgi?article_id+27687.

62. *Robb Report* 2005 Media Kit, http://www.robbreport.com.

63. *The Magazine Handbook: A Comprehensive Guide for Advertisers, Advertising Agencies and Consumer Magazine Marketers 2005/06* (New York: Magazine Publishers of America), 13.

64. "Samir Husni: Most Notable Launches Since 1985," *The Circulator* (August 3, 2005) (e-newsletter).

65. "Top 10 Magazine Categories 1995–2005," Magazine Publishers of America, http://www.magazine.org/editorial/editorial_trends_and_magazine_handbook.

66. Carol J. De Vita, "The United States at Mid-Decade," *Population Bulletin*, 50, no. 3, 17.

67. "Ones to Watch: Christy Haubegger," *Folio:* (April 15, 1999): 54.

68. Marie Arana-Wood, "Magazines, Latinos Find Themselves on the Same Page," *Washington Post* (December 5, 1996): A23.

69. Ibid., A24.

70. Jenna Schnuer, "Home, Sports, Health Titles Are Announcing the Call for Segmentation," *Advertising Age* (January 31, 2005): S-10.

71. Michael Shields, "Meredith Goes En Casa, Launches Shelter Book Aimed at Hispanics," *Media Post's*

Media Daily News (January 27, 2005), http://www.mediapost.com/PrintFriend.cfm?articleId=289158.

72. Lillie Fears, "Research Review: The Black Magazine in America" (a paper presented at the Southwest Symposium annual conference of the Southwest Education Council for Journalism and Mass Communication, Jonesboro, Ark., November 1999).

73. Deirdre Carmody, "Two New Black History Magazines Seek Out a Niche Within a Niche," *New York Times* (February 13, 1995): C6.

74. *Vibe* 2005 Media Kit, http://www.vibe.com/magazine/about_us.

75. "*Vibe* Declares *Vibe Vixen* a Success," press release (June 24, 2005), http://www.vibe.com/magazine/press_room/2005/06.

76. Gilbert Cheah, "Fulfillment's Neglected Niche," *Folio:* (March 15, 1998): 37.

77. *Asian Week* 2005 Media Kit, http://www.asianweek.com/mediakit.

78. Chris Beam, "Asian-American Titles Take Off," *Folio:* (June 1, 1995): 27.

79. Michael Shields, "*Yin* Yang: Asian Title Signals Big Asian Mag Bang," *Media Post's Media Daily News* (June 14, 2004).

80. Laurence Zuckerman, "Tapping the Kiddie Market," *Time* (April 24, 1989): 74.

81. Robyn Greenspan, "The Kids Are Alright with Spending," *ClickZ Network* (September 16, 2003), http://www.clickz.com/stats/sectors/demographics/print.php/3077581.

82. Mercedes M. Cardona and Alice Z. Cuneo, "Retailers Reaching Out to Capture Kids' Clout," *Advertising Age* (October 9, 2000): 16.

83. Paul Kurnit, "The Elusive Tween: Here today, Here Tomorrow?" Playthings (November 1, 2005): 1.

84. "Teens, Magazines, and Media," *Teen Market Profile* (New York: Magazine Publishers of America, 2004): 10.

85. Alex Kuczynski, "Keeping Magazines All in the Family," *New York Times* (March 29, 1999): C12.

86. Colleen Long, "Teen, Women's Magazines Now Featuring Females of All Shapes and Sizes," Associated Press (August 9, 2005), http://web.lexis-nexis.com.

87. Edgar Allan Poe, *Marginalia* (Charlottesville: University Press of Virginia, 1981): 139.

88. "Manage and Prosper Through Change," *Folio:* (July 2001): 10.

for additional reading

Carson, Rachel. *Silent Spring*. Boston: Houghton Mifflin, 1962.

Damon-Moore, Helen. *Magazines for the Millions: Gender and Commerce in the* Ladies' Home Journal *and the* Saturday Evening Post, *1880–1910*. Albany: State University of New York, 1994.

Endres, Kathleen L., ed. *Trade, Industrial, and Professional Periodicals of the United States*. Westport, Conn.: Greenwood Press, 1994.

Endres, Kathleen L., and Therese L. Lueck, eds. *Women's Periodicals in the United States: Consumer Magazines*. Westport, Conn.: Greenwood Press, 1995.

——— eds. *Women's Periodicals in the United States: Social and Political Issues*. Westport, Conn.: Greenwood Press, 1996.

Johnson, John H. *Succeeding Against the Odds*. New York: Warner Books, 1989.

Kitch, Carolyn. *The Girl on the Cover: The Origins of Visual*

Stereotypes in American Mass Media. Chapel Hill: University of North Carolina Press, 2001.

Marco, Gino, Robert M. Hollingworth, and William Durham. *Silent Spring Revisited.* Washington, D.C.: American Chemical Society, 1987.

Pearman, Phil, ed. *Dear Editor: Letters to* Time *Magazine, 1923–1984.* Salem, N. H.: Salem House, 1985.

Polsgrove, Carol. *It Wasn't Pretty Folks, But Didn't We Have Fun? Surviving the '60s with* Esquire*'s Harold Hayes.* Oakland, Calif.: RDR Books, 2001.

Regier, C. C. *The Era of the Muckrakers.* Chapel Hill: The University of North Carolina Press, 1932.

Rennie, Susan, and Kirsten Grimstad. *The New Woman's Survival Sourcebook.* New York: Alfred A. Knopf, 1975.

Scanlon, Jennifer. *Inarticulate Longings: The* Ladies' Home Journal, *Gender and the Promises of Consumer Culture.* New York: Routledge, 1995.

Solomon, Martha A., ed. *A Voice of Their Own: The Woman Suffrage Press, 1840–1920.* Tuscaloosa: University of Alabama Press, 1991.

Streitmatter, Rodger. *Sex Sells: The Media's Journey from Repression to Obsession.* Cambridge, Mass.: Westview Press, 2004.

Tarbell, Ida M. *All in the Day's Work: An Autobiography.* New York: Macmillan, 1939.

Thom, Mary. *Letters to* Ms., *1972–1987.* New York: Henry Holt, 1987.

—— *Inside* Ms.: *25 Years of the Magazine and the Feminist Movement.* New York: Henry Holt, 1997.

Wachsberger, Ken, ed. *Voices from the Underground: Volume I, Insider Histories of the Vietnam Era Underground Press.* Tempe, Ariz.: Mica Press, 1993.

—— ed. *Voices from the Underground: Volume 2. A Directory of Sources and Resources on the Vietnam Era Underground Press.* Tempe, Ariz.: Mica Press, 1993.

Walker, Nancy A., ed. *Women's Magazines, 1940–1960: Gender Roles and the Popular Press.* New York: Bedford/St. Martin's, 1998.

Weinberg, Arthur, and Lila Weinberg. *The Muckrakers: The Era of Journalism That Moved America to Reform: The Most Significant Magazine Articles of 1902–1912.* New York: Simon and Schuster, 1961.

Wilson, Harold S. McClure's *Magazine and the Muckrakers.* Princeton, N.J.: Princeton University Press, 1970.

Wolf, Naomi. *The Beauty Myth.* New York: William Morrow, 1991.

Wood, James Playsted. *Magazines in the United States,* 2d ed. New York: Ronald Press, 1956.

PART **two**

PART TWO

the
magazine's
blueprint

chapter 5

conceptualizing the magazine: formulas for success

n 1983, *Harper's* magazine seemed to be at the end of its 133-year life. It was losing nearly $1 million a year and circulation was dwindling. Subscriptions were sold at discount rates to buyers who felt little loyalty to the finished product; advertisers saw small appeal in a title that seemed to have outlived its usefulness. *Harper's* was on life support, and magazine experts waited for the inevitable: The venerable old title would soon follow *Century* and *Scribner's* to the magazine cemetery. ■ It didn't happen. ■ *Harper's* editors responded to the crisis by refashioning an innovative magazine that is now as representative of its time as the original publication was when it was launched in 1850. It was the magazine's fifth revision. What the editors did was retool the editorial philosophy, or mission statement, and redraw the formula of the magazine. In the process they introduced elements, such as the *Harper's* Index and Annotation, which tapped the national mood so well they were eventually emulated by other magazines. ■ It's a process all successful editors follow, in one way or another, to create a package that every reader wants: consistency with an element of surprise. The magazine field is a highly competitive and harsh market; only those publications with clear philosophies and formulas succeed. Often the title is the strongest indication of the magazine's focus. Magazines with long lives, like *Harper's,* reformulate themselves regularly, following life cycles built around audience growth and change.

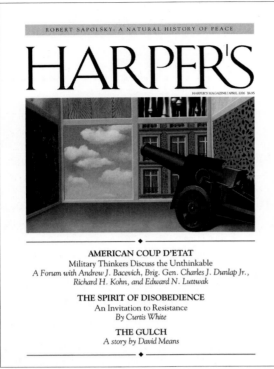

APRIL 2006: One of the country's oldest magazines, *Harper's* has mastered a winning formula. The magazine consistently wins top literary and journalistic awards.

magazine success and failure

Bob Anderson was a high school student in 1966 when he personally stapled together a 28-page magazine on his favorite sport. He spent $100 on that first *Runner's World* and started a whole new field of magazines. He lured 350 subscribers that first year; the magazine, now owned by Rodale Press, has a circulation of 586,000. In 1978, Anderson explained his success: "I had an idea I believed in—I'm a dedicated runner myself, and I knew there were a lot of others like me—and I started small."[1]

Compare that with *You*, a magazine started in 1977 with the enigmatic philosophy:

> We're definitely not about celebrities, not about bionic people, not about fantasy lifestyles that aren't available. . . . We're about people taking responsibility for their own lives, people taking part

in the personal revolution going on coast to coast. And we're saying, "That's great, get some happiness in your own life and maybe you'll bring it to others, too"[2]

Disco music outlived *You*, which lasted less than a year. Editor Rick Bard talked about investors who never materialized, and said his problem was not "readjusting my budget accordingly." Unenthusiastic supporters, however, were probably a symptom of a magazine with a vague direction.

Have you read *Politicks and Other Human Interests*? Few others did, either. The magazine started in 1977 and was gone in 1978. According to editor Thomas Morgan, "A magazine for the community of political activists in the country was necessary in a period when there was so much political apathy." Started with $900,000 private money, the magazine lost more than $1 million. Why did it fold? Morgan talked about the magazine's "cash-flow concept" and said, "We didn't develop circulation fast enough to attract advertisers."[3] The base problem, however, was in the concept. You can't make kids love broccoli and you can't make people who don't care about politics read a political magazine, especially one with a misspelled title.

Sometimes, though, magazines with illustrious careers and award-winning histories fail. *High Fidelity*, launched in 1958, published its last issue in 1989; readers with remaining subscriptions received copies of *Stereo Review*, which ultimately merged with *Video* magazine to create *Sound and Vision*. The titles tell all. We no longer talk about high fidelity, or even just about stereo; now, the focus is on the entire audio-video package.

In 1976, magazine consultant James Kobak said the primary reason for the failure of most magazines was lack of reader interest and a loss of editorial focus, which could kill previously successful magazines as times and audience interests change.[4] A major error in publishing new magazines, he said, is in creating titles nobody wants, titles that are of interest to the staff but which hold little appeal to a larger group of readers.[5] The editor may be a member of the audience, but he may be the only one in the audience.

Harlan Logan, publishing consultant for *Scribner's*, looked at the problem in the 1940s, during the era of the large, general interest magazines and, not surprisingly, emphasized audience less than analysts studying contemporary special interest magazines. Nevertheless, his conclusions often mirror those of modern scholars. Magazines failed, he said, because they lacked an "editorial reason for existence," a "clearly defined editorial pattern," and a solid advertising base.[6]

Researcher Milton Hollstein surveyed magazine publishers in the 1960s in search of the reasons for magazine success. His respondents said magazines failed because of "managerial inexperience or incompetence."[7] Writer Christopher Byron provided perhaps one of the best examples of the influence of management on a magazine's success or failure in a study of *TV-Cable Week*. That magazine suffered, he said, from the "business school orientation" that created a product geared not to the reader's needs but, rather, to the needs of the MBAs who started it.[8] These needs included making use of analytical skills taught at Harvard and making a mark on the corporate environment. Instead of relying on editorial talent, skills, and connections with the audience, the managers relied only on the numbers.

The perspectives of these scholars create a picture of the reasons for a magazine's success. In rank order, they are

1. A highly focused editorial philosophy;
2. A clearly defined formula;
3. A thorough understanding of and connection with the audience.

These elements exist within a supportive structure that includes adequate financial support, a well-planned marketing and distribution system, and solid management. All the money in the world, however, cannot save an ill-conceived magazine.

editorial philosophy

Editors differ on what they call their statement of goals. Some call it an editorial philosophy, some call it a mission statement, some call it nothing at all but know intuitively what it is.

An editorial philosophy is a magazine's focus. Just as we develop our own personal philosophies, which differentiate us from our friends and serve as the basis for our personalities, a magazine has a driving philosophy which, if strongly defined, gives the publication its identity and personality. An editorial philosophy explains what the magazine is intended to do, what areas of interest it covers, how it

will approach those interests, and the voice it will use to express itself. It is highly specific.

Harper's philosophy, developed in 1984, still guides the magazine today. That philosophy was explained in a 1992 essay by then-editor Lewis Lapham:

> The magazine set itself the task of asking questions. Instead of attempting to provide approved answers, the magazine said, in effect, look at this or imagine that—see how much more beautiful and strange and full of possibility is the world than has been dreamed of by the philosophers at *Time* or NBC. The proposition assumed the complicity of a reader willing to concede that for the time being it was enough to assemble the pieces of the puzzle and to try to figure out what goes with what.
>
> The revised text of the magazine introduced an anthology of new forms . . . intended to convey a sense of the world's ambiguity and surprise.[9]

The magazine was redefined as "an interpretative instead of an investigative instrument" that would help readers place information into "some sort of plausible context or intelligible sequence." Lapham acknowledged that readers had information coming at them from all directions—cable and network television, newspapers, magazines—and needed help making sense of it all. *Harper's* editors also recognized that helping readers conquer the information glut could be not only educational, but also fun. The result: an organized hodgepodge of essays, excerpts, discussions, and fiction. Circulation has rebounded, from 140,000 in 1983 to 229,000 in 2005. Advertisers include Lufthansa, Sony, and Subaru. And readers are engaged, carrying on their own energetic dialogue on the magazine's letters pages. Some lambaste Lapham for his liberal views, others for his selling out to conservatives. Having offended both sides, the magazine is promoting national discussion of the significant issues of the day: religion, technology, the media, and politics.

Harper's clearly redefined its nature and its scope, and that redefinition serves as the staff's organizing force. It provides direction for editorial planning as well as for advertising sales.

Dorothy Kalins, founding editor of *Metropolitan Home, Saveur,* and *Garden Design,* suggests editors write down their philosophy, or mission statement, then convince everyone on staff of its value. She says the philosophy is especially important with the advertising staff, and says she explains magazine content to advertisers in the context of the magazine's philosophy, noting why an article was written or designed a particular way. This helps advertisers understand the magazine and keeps potential complaints to a minimum. "Nothing that happens on a magazine," Kalins says, "should happen by accident."[10]

Anne Graham, former editor of *Internal Auditor*, published by the Institute of Internal Auditors, says a cogent editorial philosophy is especially important for an association magazine, in that it "heightens awareness of the magazine's role, contributes to organizational success, and inspires support for magazine initiatives."[11]

The statement of philosophy serves as the guide in developing a new magazine and keeps an existing magazine on track. It defines the purpose of the magazine, the type of content that will serve that purpose, and the voice the magazine will use. Essential to the philosophy is an understanding of the magazine's target audience. All this is built on a title that embodies the magazine's image and identity.

■ TITLE

A good title positions the magazine, and it does so with as few words as possible. It is short, direct, and clear. It also should be timeless, able to grow old with the magazine. Titles can position the magazine vertically, indicating that it gives in-depth coverage of a narrow topic, such as *Brew Your Own* magazine. Or it can position the magazine horizontally, indicating that it covers a wide range of topics, such as United Airline's in-flight magazine, *Hemispheres*.

Many magazines can make their point quickly and succinctly, such as *Ms., Money, Southern Lumberman*, and *Student Lawyer*. Some trade and organization magazines often require longer, more detailed names, such as *Advances in Skin and Wound Care* and *Pharmaceutical and Medical Packaging News*. Some magazines show their attitude upfront, such as *Bust* and *Bitch*. And some go straight to the heart with humor, such as the pet magazine *Bark*, with the tag line: "Dog is my co-pilot."

Mike Lafavore, founding editor of *Men's Health*, calls that magazine one of the few titles in the men's field that position the magazine. When you pick up *Men's Health*, you know exactly what you're getting. This is less true of *Esquire*. What is

APRIL 2006: *Pharmaceutical and Medical Packaging News* **is a controlled circulation publication that serves two industries—the pharmaceutical and the medical— just as its name implies**.

an esquire, and what can you expect from one? Actually, an esquire is a lawyer, and the name for the magazine came about serendipitously when *Esquire*'s founding editors were searching for a title and received a letter from their lawyer. After the lawyer's name was the word *esquire*. That summed up the attitude the editors were seeking, and a title was born. It came just in time: The editors had toyed with the names *Beau* and *Stag*, and had even completed a prototype with the name *Town and Gown*.

Facts was the planned title for the new weekly magazine being created by Henry Luce and Britton Hadden. But neither was crazy about the name. One night, Luce was riding the subway home, reading ads that shouted, "time to change" and "time to retire." He knew then it was time to retitle his magazine: *Time*.

Garden Design was a trade magazine title when Dorothy Kalins and her partners bought it in 1994 and repositioned it to become an upscale consumer publication. And the title did just what Kalins wanted it to do: focus on the design elements, not the growing, of the garden. *Entertainment Weekly* takes two words to spell out the magazine's focus as well as its frequency. *Glamour* uses only one word to demonstrate content as well as tone.

In 1967, Jann Wenner considered calling his new magazine *The Electric Newspaper*. Instead, he wisely chose the name *Rolling Stone*, which has weathered the passage of time. Eponymous titles such as *Harper's, Forbes,* and *Utne* are great for those entrepreneurs with unique names that can easily be pronounced.

■ MAGAZINE PURPOSE

Whether working with an established magazine or a new launch, the essential question to ask is Why does this magazine exist? Magazines may inform, interpret, entertain, advocate, and provide service.

inform

Magazines whose function is primarily to inform include the news magazines and many trade titles that provide basic day-to-day industry information to professionals. *Time* and *Newsweek* writers follow the same news stories as newspaper and television reporters. *Medical Device and Diagnostic Industry* covers regulation and market information for professionals who develop, design, manufacture, and manage medical products. *National Geographic* informs us about the world and its people, *Saudi Aramco World* informs us about the history and culture of the Arab and Muslim world.

interpret

Many journalists are still uncertain about the place of interpretation in a field heralded for its objectivity. Interpretation, however, helps readers make sense of a complex world. Readers head to *Money* and *Kiplinger's Personal Finance* because they want those magazines to help them make some sense of their finances. In its series "The Plague Years," which later became a book, *Rolling Stone* helped readers understand a relatively new disease: AIDS.

entertain

Content that entertains makes readers laugh, smile, or simply relax. *Reader's Digest* has long provided readers with "Humor in Uniform," "Laughter, the Best Medicine," and "Life in These United States." The goal of these departments: entertainment. *Mad* exists primarily to entertain although, as is the case with most humor, it offers pointed social commentary.

advocate

Advocacy goes beyond interpretation into taking a position on not only what *is*, but what *should* be. *Sierra* is a strong advocate for the environment and *AARP: The Magazine* for the rights of older Americans.

provide service

Service articles help readers take action that betters their lives. How-to articles are included here, but service goes beyond simply telling us how to firm our abs or file our taxes. Service pieces provide the information and incentive to build a model airplane, bake a cake, travel to Budapest, sleep better, get along with our parents, and find the loves of our lives. *Mamm* steers readers through the medical and legal rights of women with cancer, and *Smart Computing* helps readers get along with the digital dictator on their desks.

Better Homes and Gardens implants service in its editorial philosophy:

> *Better Homes and Gardens* knows what millions of Americans care about most: those they love and the home that brings them together. We understand that the desire for a happy, healthy home life impacts countless individual decisions and actions every day. *Better Homes and Gardens* is a trusted friend women and men turn to when making those choices for their family, themselves, and their home. With a unique perspective that spans the generations, we provide ideas, information, and inspiration for a well-lived and meaningful life.
>
> Better isn't only our name, it's our promise.

Most magazines provide a combination of these five functions. Individual magazines, however, develop their unique identity by determining which purposes might take precedence and which will be secondary. *Harper's* primary purpose is to interpret, but it also informs and entertains. *Emerge* is an advocate, while it also provides service. *Modern Baking* informs and advocates. *The American Spectator* informs and interprets.

The more explicit the statement of purpose, the better the philosophy and, therefore, the better the magazine's direction. The purpose, of course, has to be logically tied to a need or interest in the broader society. Kalins, who is now executive editor of *Newsweek*, says the successful magazine "catches a wave in the culture. Something big has to be happening out there that your magazine relates to."

Garden Design, for example, is about how gardening "informs our lives," Kalins says. When she began planning the magazine in 1994, she says, "Baby boomers were beginning to garden, to look for the substance beneath the style. They knew nothing about the garden except that they wanted to be there." *Garden Design* was "the first magazine to treat the garden as a state of mind as well as a place to be."

The magazine's philosophy is also clearly defined by what it is not. Kalins says *Garden Design* is not a "root ball" magazine—it's not about *how* to garden. Kalins advises new editors not to be so arrogant as to think they can do something better than the competition. "Do something different," she says.

■ TYPE OF CONTENT

How is a magazine's purpose to be achieved? What is its character and overall slant? What special mood or tone does it capture? The answers to these questions help determine the type of editorial, design, and advertising content that will characterize that magazine.

editorial

If it is an entertainment publication, is that entertainment straightforward and practical, as in *Games*? Or satirical, as in *Mad*? Does the magazine inform people on how to do things of a practical nature, as does *Wood*? Does it inform about general weekly events, as do *Time* and *Newsweek,* or does it cover only business news, as does *Business Week*? Is the advocacy going to be forthright, as in *The Advocate* or does the magazine have an under-

MAY 2006: The British edition of *Men's Health* demonstrates the international appeal of the title, which is published in more than 40 countries.

stated political point of view, as is the case now with *Mother Earth News,* or even *Harper's?*

Kalins notes that magazines that succeed have a "compelling editorial strength." The reader expects a specific kind of content served in a specific style. The successful magazine does not disappoint.

Mike Lafavore says he conceived *Men's Health* to provide readers with personal service. Before the magazine's start in 1988, he says, "men had never been treated to service journalism." He regularly read his wife's copy of *Glamour* and asked why men couldn't have a magazine like that. The personal service emphasis, he said, makes *Men's Health* stand out in a field that previously offered men information only on "cars, tools, science." Although Lafavore is no longer with the magazine, it continues his concept, providing tips on keeping in shape, building relationships and creating a fulfilling life. Lafavore calls this a "benefit-oriented approach." Today's men, he says, "feel their lives are out of control. Service journalism gives them a sense of private control." And it works: The magazine now has a worldwide circulation of nearly 4 million, with 32 editions in 40 countries.

Mamm and *Poz*: Helping Readers Survive

Poz magazine was launched in April 1994 as a response to the growing AIDS threat. It's a health magazine for people with a life-threatening disease and carries the tag line: "Health, Hope and HIV." Its founding philosophy was twofold:

- To improve and extend the lives of people facing long-term or life-threatening illnesses by providing the first-rate treatment information needed for survival.
- To bridge the gap between the mainstream media's coverage of AIDS and HIV health issues and the technical, professional and medical media (newsletters and journals) which cater to select audiences.[1]

The magazine is published 11 times a year with a circulation of more than 150,000, and has a companion publication, *Poz Focus*, which deals with HIV issues in the black community; audience and writers are all doctors. The magazine's web-site offers readers a chance to interact with one another through discussion boards and *Poz* Mentor, an online support group for those just diagnosed with HIV.

Mamm, launched in 1997, serves readers who have been diagnosed with breast cancer. Its founding philosophy:

> *Mamm* is a bimonthly women's health and features magazine focusing on cancer prevention, treatment and survival. *Maam* gives its readers the essential tools and emotional support they need before, during and after diagnosis of breast, ovarian and other women's cancers. Offering a mix of survivor profiles, the latest treatment information, investigative features, alternative treatments and cutting-edge news, *Maam* informs, inspires and entertains. *Maam*'s editorial demonstrates first-hand that life goes on after

APRIL 2006: *Poz*—an abbreviated reference to "HIV positive"—is a health magazine for people with life-threatening diseases.

> diagnosis—with strength, elegance and humor.[2]

Mamm, with the tag line, "Women, Cancer and Community," is now published 10 times a year. Its website offers support groups, news updates, and a calendar of cancer-related telephone workshops on issues such as clinical trials, nutrition, and therapy options. ■

1. *Poz* (Media Kit, 1997).
2. *Mamm* (Media Kit, 1997).

design

A magazine's look is essential to its concept. Just as the way you dress represents who you are, so, too, the way a magazine dresses defines what it is. Although not all editors include design concepts in their editorial philosophy, they have a strong sense of what look will best achieve their purposes. How does the magazine look, and why does it look that way?

Does the magazine make generous use of white space? Is it type-heavy? Are photographs used for information or illustration, or both? Does it always use large photos? Sometimes? Never? How much color does the magazine have? Does it use spot colors? Where? How? Why?

Wired, Harper's, and *Men's Health* have such distinctive looks that a reader would recognize the magazines even if their names were hidden. *Wired's* look is bold and experimental, trying new tricks: It's a format that offers few constraints and is built around bright colors, sometimes neon tints, in type as well as illustrations. The dull coated paper stock sets it apart from the crowd of traditional magazines with glossy pages. The logo, which resembles a movie marquee, looks electrical. The magazine and its readers are similarly plugged-in. At the same time, *Wired* provides reader service with explanatory photographs clarifying the text, and articles organized logically to suit an audience that has grown up with MTV and computers. Reading the magazine is like using the computer.

Reading *Harper's* is more like reading a book or listening to an engaging speaker. Every month, the magazine cover features a small horizontally cropped photo surrounded by a sea of white space. The rest of the cover is type-heavy, giving article titles, subtitles, and bylines. The message: This is a magazine for people who like to read and are open to new ways of viewing the world. Inside, the magazine has a highly formulaic design, with an emphasis on text that allows the occasional illustration to shine and encourages the reader to think and make up her own mind about what all this means.

Men's Health demonstrates its service approach in a lively but straightforward design with photographs of men whose physiques the reader hopes to emulate. Under his editorship, Lafavore began a policy of using no celebrities on the cover to avoid the impression that the magazine is about that person, rather than about the reader. This decision was a reaction to a reader who criticized the man on one cover. "I could beat him up," the reader said. Lafavore said he made sure after that to choose a model who could beat the reader up.

advertising

Readers assess the identity of a magazine not only through its editorial but also through its advertising content. What's more, they hold the editors responsible for that ad content. Advertising should do more than simply match a magazine's audience demographics and psychographics. It should match the philosophy. A magazine that doesn't want cigarette ads, waif-thin models, red meat, or liquor should say so upfront. The advertising and editorial staffs should be singing the same song.

The editorial philosophy is also the best defense against advertisers who expect special treatment of their products, or who cringe at a magazine's coverage of topical events or issues. Often, an ill-defined advertising philosophy will cause the editorial staff to self-censor material. In other cases, it causes advertisers to pull out because their perception of the magazine is different from the editors' vision.

Arthritis Today, published by the Arthritis Foundation, has an Advertising Standards Committee that approves all ads. The committee may ask for a sample of a product to be advertised, including a list of ingredients and specifications.

Good Housekeeping has turned down ads for handguns designed for women, editor-in-chief Ellen Levine says, because they did not suit the magazine's philosophy. The magazine was also one of many to refuse a Shake'n Bake ad that would have placed a chicken leg in the middle of a page, wrapped by copy; the resulting design would have served the advertiser but not the reader, Levine said. The reader would have to try to navigate around an odd invasion of the page, while the advertiser would benefit because the reader's eye would have to keep going back to the product. The magazine even lost the Campbell's soup account in 1997 because food editors used too little creamed soup in the recipes they published. "It's an ongoing dance," Levine says.[12]

Harper's has also battled friction between the magazine's editorial and advertising interests. In 1992, former section editor Alexandra Ringe criticized a system in which, she said, the editorial staff tiptoed around advertiser interests. "I found that we were censoring ourselves before advertisers were even shown something that might be objectionable."[13] Writer Allan Gurganus, who has won a National Magazine Award for work published in *Harper's,* alleged in 1997 that Lapham refused to print his story, "30 Dildos," because of concerns the title would offend advertisers. Lapham said advertisers were not the issue. "I thought it would put readers off the story," he said of the title. "It was offensive."

Lapham acknowledged that the magazine has had dissatisfied advertisers. "But," he said, "it's after the fact, not beforehand."[14]

In 1913, *The Merchants' and Manufacturers' Journal* of Baltimore published an essay by Condé Nast, founder of the publishing house that bears his name and publishes titles such as *Vogue, Glamour, Vanity Fair,* and *Gourmet.* Nast clearly articulated the appeal to advertisers of what he called "Class Publications":

> The exact value of any particular class publication to any given advertiser depends entirely on the accuracy with which it performs its duty of selecting possible buyers in his line, which, in turn, depends upon the degree of authority accorded the editorial side of the publication within its own class, and on the methods by which circulation is obtained. And in the judgment of this, each publication must, of course, rest entirely on its own merits.[15]

advertising hybrids

Advertising hybrids have complicated advertising-editorial dynamics, at the same time adding a boost to the magazine economy. One reason for the healthy growth in magazine advertising discussed in chapter 2 is the creative use of hybrid advertising forms such as advertorials, inserts, and outserts.

Advertorials An advertorial combines articles and advertising in a magazine supplement sponsored entirely by the advertiser. Advertorials began regularly appearing in magazines in the 1970s and have stirred up their own storm of controversy. At the outset, many were written and designed by magazine staff members, so readers could not tell where the magazine editorial ended and where the advertising began. In response, the American Society of Magazine Editors (ASME) developed guidelines that require that advertorials be clearly labeled as advertising supplements and that their design be

noticeably different from the design of the magazine. Advertorials can be as short as 4 pages and as long as 32. They are produced separately from the magazine and then bound in. Many look like mini-magazines, even with covers.

Advertorials can be an important income stream, but how well do they serve the reader? Advertorials are neither inherently evil nor inherently good, but their use does require forethought. When dropped right in the middle of an article, they are intrusive. When placed between articles, they can blend with other editorial. More than one advertorial in an issue can seriously hurt the magazine's flow, no matter the location.

Advertorial content can actually serve the reader. Health advertorials can provide important supplementary information in a women's magazine; travel advertorials can offer service information for the readers of a general interest title.

Inserts An insert is an ad created and produced by the advertiser; it comes to the magazine already printed and is then bound into the magazine. An insert is noticeable because it is often printed on different paper from the rest of the magazine and might even be a different shape. Advertisers are increasingly using inserts to capture the attention of readers, especially among the media-savvy Generation X and Generation Y. *People* magazine ran an insert featuring a bottle of Aquafina formed partially out of bubble wrap. Producers of the WB drama *Supernatural* created an ad with flickering lights, music, and comments from cast members. The insert, which appeared in *Rolling Stone* and *US Weekly,* was intended as "something that is just not going to sit on your coffee table," said Lew Goldstein, co-president of marketing for the network.[16]

The omnipresent cologne ads with scented samples are usually inserts. Other inserts advertisers have used include computer CDs, holograms, pop-ups, and stand-alone booklets. *Healthy Kids en Español* ran a 12-page booklet titled "Viva la Actividad!" that contained health and exercise tips for kids, courtesy of McDonald's.

If she were stuck on a desert island and could choose only one magazine to read, Fleur Cowles, founding editor of *Flair*, said, "I'd start one."

Ad-Free Magazines

Several contemporary magazines have made a conscious decision to avoid advertising because it conflicts with their mission. *Consumer Reports* editors believe advertising would compromise the editorial integrity of a magazine that tests and evaluates consumer products. Not depending on advertising means the staff can present an unflattering report on a product without risk of offending advertisers. *Ms.* accepted advertising for nearly 20 years, but ran headfirst into advertiser opposition to the magazine's articles on such topics as battered women and abortion; the magazine is now ad-free and is published by the not-for-profit Feminist Majority Foundation. *Highlights for Children* avoids advertising because of a desire to keep commerce from competing with the magazine's educational function.

Some relatively recent magazine launches, though, have been advertising-free simply because of the publisher's preference. August Home Publishing in Iowa and Reiman Publishing in Wisconsin are multimillion dollar enterprises built primarily on circulation, or income from readers. August Home's flagship magazine, *Woodsmith*, is ad-free, as are its newer starts, *Cuisine at*

Home, *Garden Gate*, and *Shop-Notes*. Founder Don Peschke says he simply didn't want to bother with advertising when he first started publishing. Advertising costs money to get, he notes, and he had very little of that at the beginning. He also had a staff of one, and felt he'd be better served by spending all his time creating and promoting the magazine to and for readers, rather than advertisers. August's renewal rates are enviable—75–85 percent of *Woodsmith* readers typically renew.

Peschke started *Woodsmith* in 1979 when he was unemployed. "I was thinking I was going to build up my portfolio for when I went out to get a real job," he said in 1993. In the first 2 years of the company's existence, Peschke paid himself no salary. In the third year, he rewarded himself with $6,000. In 1985 and 1986, the company made *Inc.* magazine's lists of fastest-growing privately held companies. August Home now employs more than 125 people, and the company's operations fill three office buildings. When the company purchased *Workbench* in 1996, it kept that magazine's format, which included advertising.

Reiman's titles, including *Country*, *Country Woman*, *Farm and Ranch Living*, *Craft-*

APRIL 2006: The ad-free *Cuisine at Home* challenges the assumption that magazines need advertising income to succeed.

ing Traditions, *Reminisce*, *Taste of Home*, *Birds and Blooms*, and *Country Discoveries* are the brainchildren of Roy Reiman, founder and publisher, who says the ad-free decision has paid off in reader loyalty. The company's first publication, *Farm Wife News*, published in 1970, attracted 84,000 subscribers in only 3 months and with only one promotional mailing to 400,000 rural women. The reason for the staggering response—women who received the initial mailing told their friends who told their friends. In 2 years, subscribers topped 340,000, fueled largely

Outserts An outsert is a preprinted publication that contains advertising and may also include editorial material. An outsert differs from an insert in that it is not bound into the magazine. It is mailed to subscribers with the magazine, the two being connected inside a shrink wrap. Some outserts are also included in shrink wrap in newsstand copies, but that causes an obvious problem: Readers cannot then browse through the magazine.

Trade magazines use outserts to mail readers information on trade shows sponsored by the magazine; travel titles use them for special tours; and women's magazines use them for beauty or health material.

■ VOICE

A magazine's identity is most easily defined by its voice—that is, the tone and tenor of articles and graphics. A magazine with a well-defined voice not only offers the reader consistency and imagination, it can also give advertisers the opportunity to develop unique ads that match the magazine's voice.

Lafavore says the voice of *Men's Health* is of the "wise guy buddy who knows everything." The August 1997 issue featured a man with washboard abs and a cover line offering the reader "Amazing Abs: How This Guy Did It," with a red arrow pointing to the model. Inside, the article started with an off-the-cuff conversation: "Hey, pal, how'd you get those abdominal muscles?" It gives an easy-to-follow plan for how the cover model— whose last name was actually Guy—built his body.

Don Peschke of *Woodsmith* invented a "little old woodworker named Don" as the voice of his magazine. All articles in *Woodsmith* are in first person, and are from the point of view of this idealized Don. When readers visit the magazine, as they often do, they come asking for Don. When the magazine was in its infancy in the 1980s, visitors were met with the 30-something Peschke and were a tad bewildered. Where was that old man who spoke so convincingly about woodworking?

Jay Walljasper, editor-at-large of *Utne*, says the magazine speaks with a "contrarian voice" and has a "set of values as well as a gadfly role," which means it challenges authority but within responsible bounds. In 1996, the magazine was redesigned and the tone was changed to what Walljasper saw as being "gadfly for gadfly's sake." The Summer 1996 issue ran a cover line on "The Familiar Face of Fascism" with a foil insert for the reader to see his own reflection. "That wasn't us," Walljasper says. Readers hated the redesign and the magazine has returned to its original contrarian tone.

editorial formula
···

The editorial formula ties all the elements of a magazine together logically and coherently, in a readable, usable package. It's the practical application of the editorial philosophy, and it offers a blueprint for each issue of the magazine. It defines the type of content staff members will use in implementing the editorial philosophy. It details the specific subjects with which the magazine will deal and defines how much emphasis will be given to each subject. Like the philosophy, the formula should be written down and should be highly detailed and specific.

Questions editors ask when planning a formula are the following: How many pages will the magazine typically be? What is the advertising-to-editorial ratio? How many continuing departments will the magazine have? What will they be? How long will department stories be? How many feature-length articles will the magazine have? What types of articles will they be? How long will they be? Will the magazine include fiction? Poetry? Photo essays? Any other special content? How will this content be organized?

Developing an editorial formula is as simple as it is vital. A worksheet for an editorial formula looks something like this:

- Number of total pages:
- Number of pages of advertising:
- Number of pages of editorial, including cover, masthead, and table of contents:
- Number, if any, of pages of continuing departments and columns:
- Number of feature pages:
- Breakdown of feature material, including types of articles, the number of each type, and their length:
- Names of continuing departments, plus a description of what each department will cover, how many articles may be included and their length:
- Placement of content:

■ ADVERTISING AND EDITORIAL PAGES

The successful magazine staff determines in advance how many pages it will target for advertising and how many for editorial. This is stated in terms of advertising-editorial ratio as well as total num-

Affluent Americans are their own narrow niche. Readers of *Barron's* magazine earn an average $140,000 a year and have total assets of more than $1.5 million. *Absolute* magazine goes to New Yorkers with an estimated annual income of at least $500,000 and, marketers hope, a taste for vodka.

ber of pages. An advertising-editorial ratio of 60:40 means a magazine has 60 pages of advertising for every 40 pages of editorial. If that magazine has 100 pages, 60 contain advertising and 40 contain editorial. If it has 120 pages, 72 are advertising and 48 are editorial.

The magazine staff must determine how many pages it can reasonably sell to advertisers and how many pages it needs for the level of content it has planned. The ideal ratio and number of pages usually is the result of trial and error and reaches a balance after a magazine has been published for several years.

The best advice when starting a new magazine is to study the competition. What is the audience size of the closest possible competitor? How similar is the new magazine to that competitor? How different? What are the competition's ad and circulation rates, number of ads run, number of pages, and advertising-editorial ratio?

Competition includes magazines, newspapers, and broadcast programs that reach the new magazine's target audience as well as other media that cover the same type of content. The television show *Entertainment Tonight* preceded *Entertainment Weekly* and demonstrated that regular coverage of television, music, and film news would appeal to advertisers. Personal finance columns ran in newspapers nationwide before the launch of *Worth*, and advertisers sought placement on its pages because of its appeal to a select audience.

What advertisers are missing from the competition that could be lured to a new magazine? Could this new magazine reach a larger audience? Or a smaller audience with more targeted information? *Time* and *Newsweek* have long covered health issues, but not with the detail provided by *Men's Health* or *Women's Health*.

Media that successfully serve the target audience will also appeal to the same advertisers, whether or not the content is at all similar. McDonald's traditionally advertises heavily on family-oriented television programs and has become a presence on

The *Entrepreneur*ial Spirit: Dissecting a Philosophy and Formula

Many magazines state their editorial philosophies on their websites, usually as part of subscription or advertising information. Most often, it is one element in the magazine's media kit, which is aimed at advertisers. *Entrepreneur* magazine's philosophy, as stated in its 2006 Media Kit, covers the publication's purpose, type of content, and voice:

> Written for busy entrepreneurs who want practical—not theoretical—information, *Entrepreneur* offers real-life solutions for entrepreneurs with growing companies. The magazine gives readers concise, hands-on advice so they can get in, get out and back to business. Expert columnists cover the latest developments in technology, money, management and marketing, highlighting products, services, and strategies to help readers run better businesses. In *Entrepreneur's* more than 40 monthly columns and features, readers learn from other entrepreneurs who have successfully solved their growth challenges. The magazine also analyzes current issues, news, and trends from the unique perspective of the entrepreneur.

Its audience is equally well defined:

> *Entrepreneur* readers are owners of established and growing companies who turn to *Entrepreneur* for guidance in taking their businesses to the next level.

> Total Audience—
> 2,175,000
> Median Age—41 Years
> Median Household
> Income—$77,235
> Owner/Partner—63%
> Involved in Purchase
> Decisions—91%
> Average Gross
> Revenue—$15.5 million

Entrepreneur's formula is complex, with a well-organized mix of features, departments, and columns organized around five content areas, each of which has a series of monthly columns. The formula is listed under "Editorial Overview" in the magazine's media kit:

Smarts

> The magazine's opening section, Smarts, updates readers on current news and trends in the world of business, as seen from the entrepreneur's perspective. From serious analyses of business issues to humorous looks at the latest business fads, Smarts gives readers a quick update on their world.

> *Monthly columns:* Biz Travel, Books, Capitol Issues, Flash, Hot Seat, It Figures, Snapshot, Tech Toy, What's the Point?, Wheels, Women.

Technology

> Technology enables entrepreneurs to compete with big business on an equal playing field. That's why the editors of *Entrepreneur* devote one third of the total editorial package to technology issues. From hardware to software, Internet to wireless computing, *Entrepreneur* delivers the news, insights, and information savvy entrepreneurs need to make smart purchasing decisions.

> *Monthly columns*: Buyer's Guide, Cool Clicks, Digital Edge, Hot Disks, Net Profits, Solutions, Wireless.

Money

> Money is the lifeblood of every business—and *Entrepreneur* shows readers how to raise it, how to manage it, and how to keep

(continued)

The *Entrepreneur*ial Spirit (continued)

it flowing. For entrepreneurs seeking smart advice on managing both business and personal finances, *Entrepreneur* provides a perspective that other magazines don't—the entrepreneur's.

Monthly columns: Dollar Signs, Funds, Personal Finance, Raising Money, Tax Talk.

Management

Today's entrepreneur faces a vast array of management challenges—from human resources issues to laws and regulations governing business. *Entrepreneur* is the how-to business management manual, with information-packed editorial that provides the growing business perspective on these pressing issues. With seven regular columns

exclusively dedicated to the subject of management, readers know they can rely on *Entrepreneur* as a comprehensive resource that answers all of their most important questions.

Monthly columns: Creative Zone, Insurance, Legal, Real Deal, Smart Moves, Staff Smarts.

Marketing

It takes more than a great product or service to achieve business success. *Entrepreneur*'s marketing experts keep readers up-to-date on the latest trends and strategies in sales, marketing, advertising, and public relations—all the tools they need to help their businesses flourish. From creating ads that get results to staking out new target

markets, *Entrepreneur* offers advice every entrepreneur can use to market more effectively.

Monthly columns: A+ Ads, Breakthrough, Net Sales, Retail Register, Sales Force, Sales Success, Tactics.[1]

A magazine's formula, which is the implementation of its philosophy, evolves over time; its most recent incarnation is demonstrated in the magazine's table of contents. Not all elements of a formula, however, are included in each issue, and some issues have additional elements. The January 2006 *Entrepreneur* table of contents includes a special section on franchises and one feature on the future of the web and one on a scientific guide to using brain power. The departments follow the editorial formula. □

1. "Editorial Overview," *Entrepreneur Media Kit*, http://www.entrepreneur.com/mediakit/1,6710,,00.html?sect=Mag_Overview.

Latino channels, so it is not surprising that they would advertise in *Healthy Kids en Español*.

■ DEPARTMENTS AND COLUMNS

Departments offer consistency to readers by providing smaller articles, essays, and columns that offer updates, details, and perspectives on a wide variety of predetermined issues. These are grouped together under one common topic area, so that an individual department may have as few as one article and as many as several dozen. These whet the reader's appetite for the longer features, and they

also satisfy the need for a broad range of topics. The staff knows exactly what departments it must fill every issue, and the readers know which to expect. Well-planned and executed departments are often the easiest way for a magazine to maintain consistency.

Columns are a type of department, in that they regularly appear and are consistent in their approach, if not always in their content. They are often signed essays or opinion pieces, and are usually no longer than a page in length.

Early American magazines had few, if any departments or columns. *Scribner's, Century,* and *McClure's* simply began each issue with one long feature and followed that with another long feature, consistent with their booklike approach. Articles then looked like chapters in a book.

Changing reader habits as well as the move toward specialized titles and more service journalism led to the growth of department articles beginning in the 1960s. Partially to compete with television, magazines began offering shorter articles. At the same time, specialized titles began finding that the small pieces brought readers quickly into the magazine and allowed the staff to add late-breaking information. Service-related departments—quick recipes, hobby tips, shopping guides—earned high reader appeal. Departments are now a staple in most magazines. Columns likewise have become increasingly popular. News magazines feature columnists who provide a perspective on the news; health and women's magazines include first-person views in their columns; and Generation X and Y magazines include columns with a personal take and tone.

The first question to ask when planning the editorial formula is Do departments and columns belong in the magazine? If the answer is yes, ask what kinds of departments fit the magazine's editorial philosophy and will fill the needs of its audience? What kinds of columns? Not all have to appear in every issue, but a consistent group of departments and columns should regularly appear. News magazines, for example, are highly departmentalized around broad topics such as "Politics," "The Arts," and "Business." One issue may have no articles on business, while another issue may have three. Throughout the span of a year, however, the business department appears in a majority of the issues.

The second fundamental question is What kinds of content will these short articles regularly cover? Some departments are built entirely of service articles, others of interpretive pieces; still others have a mix of article types. Department titles should give an immediate indication of what's included in that section. Cute, evasive titles such as "Dimensions" and "Frames" are an indication of an ill-conceived department. What is a dimension

and what will the audience gain from reading about one? To-the-point names, such as *People*'s "Picks and Pans," are meaningful and, therefore, successful. There's no confusion in the reader's mind about what to expect on those pages: a series of reviews on current music, movies, books, and television shows. Department names should be the same from issue to issue and the length of department pieces should be consistent. Columns are usually based on the perspective of the writer, so their content might vary from issue to issue, but the reader should know that she can regularly expect a specific viewpoint from a regular columnist.

The third question is What will be the length of department articles and columns? Departments can be snippets of fewer than 50 words, or longer pieces that take up a whole page. Typically, department articles are shorter than 500 words. Often, one department includes a range of lengths: perhaps two pieces under 50 words, three at between 150 and 200 words, and one at 500–600 words. This range, however, should be consistent. Columns usually have one dedicated page.

"Picks and Pans" are consistently between 150 and 200 words each, with five to eight items, plus illustrations, taking up a page. *Men's Health*'s "male-grams" department, by contrast, is a 20-page section that contains a lively mix of articles from under 100 words to more than 1,000, with some pages consisting of only one article, and others composed of 8–10 articles. *Newsweek*'s "My Turn" is a one-page column containing an essay written by a different reader every week.

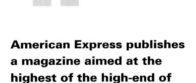

American Express publishes a magazine aimed at the highest of the high-end of its credit card users. It's so exclusive it has no name.

■ FEATURES

Features are the bread and butter of a magazine. They're the content readers take time to sink their teeth into. The features in any given issue connect logically as well as aesthetically and emotionally. Over time, those features create the backbone of the magazine.

Planning for features often begins 1–2 years before publication. Editors look for topical issues, but offer the writers enough time for planning, research, and development.

Features provide spark to a magazine by the diversity of their content and length. Some magazines plan, for example, for one major service article, one profile, and two general features. Others go for one long feature—3,000–5,000 words—surrounded by smaller features at 1,000–1,200 words.

Features have shrunk in word length throughout the past century and now average fewer than 2,000 words. They range, however, from 1,000 to more than 10,000 words. The longest magazine features are typically 5,000–8,000 words, but a few magazines—*The New Yorker, Esquire,* and *Sports Illustrated*—have features that may exceed 10,000 words.

For a start-up, the essential questions are the following: What kinds of feature articles will be included? What kind of content will full-length articles cover? How does the magazine define a full-length article? The formula for features should be specific enough to offer the reader—and the staff—some direction, but broad enough to give everybody some room to move around.

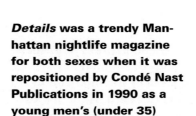

Details **was a trendy Manhattan nightlife magazine for both sexes when it was repositioned by Condé Nast Publications in 1990 as a young men's (under 35) fashion periodical.**

■ PLACEMENT OF CONTENT

There's no one "right" way to organize all this material as long as it follows a plan. Some magazines are entirely departmentalized, some have a mix of departments and features, and some combine department articles and features on similar topics into regular sections.

Think of the magazine structure as a house. The cover is the front door; the departments, the entryway; and the features, the bigger rooms. You want that front door to look inviting enough for the reader to walk in. Once in, you want her to be delighted and intrigued by what is elsewhere in the house. Then you want her to roam from room to room easily, following her own pace, being satisfied by what she finds, and curious about what's ahead. Perhaps she'll go through one room twice, to study it better, because she finds it especially appealing.

Just as the interior design of a house makes it comfortable and reflective of the owner's personality, so too should the design of the magazine make the reader's stroll through its pages easy and pleasurable. You want a visitor to your house to sit down every now and then and just look around, perhaps at the paintings you've hung, the color of the walls, the heights of your ceilings, the shapes of your windows, and the view outside. You want her to know, just by looking around, whose house she is visiting, you want her to be comfortable, and you want her to know she's welcome.

A good magazine host plans for a smooth and comfortable pacing from article to article. A short article after a longer article gently encourages the reader to keep reading. A design with consistent signposts tells her when one department ends and another begins and helps the reader follow the articles from page to page. Editorial jumps—in which the continuation of an article that began in the middle of the magazine "jumps" to the end—are like serving a guest coffee in the kitchen and telling her to go through the bathroom, down the basement stairs, through the laundry room, and out the back door if she wants cream and sugar. That cream and sugar better be mighty good for her to make that trek.

Departments are usually placed either in the front of the book (FOB) or the back of the book (BOB). Advertising is often sold for placement in specific departments. In other cases, it is sold to be placed anywhere in the front or back, with ad contracts, then, requesting FOB or BOB placement. Those few advertisers with no preference simply ask for a run of the book (ROB) placement.

Many departments have both advertising and editorial material on a single page. These pages, called "A and E," for advertising and editorial, may change from day to day during the final stages of a magazine's production, as editorial pages are dropped to make room for advertising, or added to replace ads that don't materialize.

Features are usually structured according to wells, or blocks of editorial material unbroken

Harper's Formula: A Tool of Success

A significant part of the successful repositioning of *Harper's* is a direct result of retooling the magazine's formula. Regular departments of the magazine include "*Harper's* Index," "Readings," "Annotation," "Essay," and "Story." Each of these elements has a clearly articulated goal and consistent design and placement:

- The "Index" is a list of current statistics, juxtaposed against other statistics to give a quick glimpse of contemporary culture:

  Number of Pepsi products plainly visible in a May television ad for Arnold Schwarzenegger: 5
  Chance that a U.S. company monitors the e-mails of at least some employees: 1 in 3[1]

  Editor emeritus Lewis Lapham calls this a "plumb line" built on "our American faith in numerical measurement."[2] This is one full page in each issue. Its design is identical from issue to issue: one full page, type only, copy centered on the page, topped with an all-caps, no-nonsense headline: "Harper's Index."

- "Readings" are miscellaneous gleanings from such diverse sources as edited versions of governmental repots, Fox News Radio interview transcripts, Target Corporation's training manual, websites, personal letters, and, of course, books and other magazines. "Readings" take up 16–18 pages per issue. They run in a continuous two-column flow, with an italicized introduction, and with identical type treatment for headlines of each separate article. Interspersed through the department are quirky art photos and illustrations, which stand on their own as content, unrelated to the articles.

- "Essay" is an article-length analysis of a contemporary issue, which runs for 7–9 pages and is usually illustrated with interpretative art.

- "Annotation" is a double-page spread with photos and annotated text putting the illustrated material into contemporary context. In December 1995, the magazine ran "Out of the Closet, and into Never-Never Land" about gay magazines that, the writers maintained, trivialized the politics they were purporting to cover in colorful and glossy publications that serve more as marketing vehicles than as serious perspectives on issues. The spread featured the cover of *Out* magazine connected with arrows to editorial comments on the magazine's sanitized version of gay life and emphasis on celebrities. The "Annotation," while regular, is not offered in every issue. The photo of the subject to be discussed takes up the majority of the spread, with paragraphs of comment placed around the edges of the illustration. It looks a bit like the illustrations in your car's owner's manual that point to individual parts of your dashboard and tell you which switch does what.

- "Story" covers the short fiction for which the magazine has historically been known. Stories range from 10 to 15 pages in length.

- Other regular elements include "Letters" (2–4 pages), "Notebook" (Lapham's essay, 2–5 pages), "Reviews" (7–10 pages) and "Puzzle" (a full page).

- Advertising in each issue ranges from 88 to 100 pages, including the covers. The inside front cover, inside back cover, and back cover—called by advertisers the second, third, and fourth covers—have full-color ads. Average advertising-to-editorial ratio in 2005 was 20:80. ■

---

1. *Harper's* Index," *Harper's* (August 2005): 11.

2. Lapham, 9.

by advertising. A monowell structure means that all feature material is placed together, usually in the center of the magazine, and all ads are either in the front or back of the book. American magazines used this structure when advertising first began appearing after the Civil War, keeping an obvious separation between advertising and editorial material. *National Geographic* has a monowell structure.

More common is a multiwell structure, in which editorial material remains unbroken in smaller wells throughout the magazine. Advertising appears between wells. This maintains the integrity of the editorial material while allowing advertising to be placed in the middle of the publication. *Saveur, Harper's,* and *The Atlantic* use a multiwell structure. Some magazines, such as *Cosmopolitan,* modify the multiwell approach by adding jumps to longer pieces.

Nest **magazine, which billed itself as a "Quarterly of Interiors," took a nonformulaic approach to its pages, giving readers a unique editorial and design take on interior design in each issue, with no standardized front of the book, back of the book, or feature well. The magazine's innovative approach to content earned it the admiration of loyal readers and a host of awards. Unfortunately, that wasn't enough to keep it afloat. In 2004, after 92 issues, the magazine folded.**

audience

Before a magazine is even published, the editors have to define the way in which the magazine's content is geared to the needs, interests, and motivations of its audience.

Although advertising is sold based on a clear delineation of reader demographics and psychographics, much editorial material is created based on the editors' inherent understanding of their audience. This understanding goes far deeper than the numbers created by the research department; it derives from a savvy editor's gut feeling.

In many cases, the editor *is* the reader, and the magazine is aimed at the editor's tastes, which nicely mesh with the tastes of the larger audience. Don Peschke wanted to subscribe to a magazine with step-by-step instructions on woodworking. When he couldn't find one, he started *Woodsmith.*

Gloria Steinem and Patricia Carbine saw no magazine doing what they envisioned *Ms.* could do, so they started one.

International versions of American magazines have to make the transition from one culture to another. The *Men's Health* in Slovenia looks like the American version, but has less emphasis on fitness and more on sex because Slovene men are highly athletic and, unlike their American brothers, don't need a magazine to help them get in shape. The Russian version of the magazine has had hard-hitting articles on drugs and alcohol, which are problems facing men in that country. The Finnish edition of *Cosmopolitan* rejected Britney Spears as the cover model of its "Fun, Fearless Female" issue in favor of a Finnish woman with whom readers of that country could relate. The Hong Kong *Cosmo* uses Asian models and is heavy on local celebrities.[17]

As new audiences develop, astute magazines find ways to speak to those audiences. The alternative politics of the late 1960s and early 1970s brought magazines for those movements: *Mother Earth News, Rolling Stone,* and *Ms.* The growth of magazines for Generation X readers in the 1990s has been a response to the same type of audience growth. *Details, Bikini, Wired, Vibe, Accent,* and a host of national, regional, and local magazines began to hit the newsstands in the early 1990s, aimed at Americans born from 1961 to 1981. James Truman, *Details* editor-in-chief, said in 1992 that his readers, like him, were "tremendously cynical because they know the media is most often talking to them to sell them something."[18] In 1993, *Advertising Age* named *Details* "Magazine of the Year," saying it had "established itself as the leading vehicle to reach Generation X."[19]

The newest generation, Generation Y, has been greeted with an exploding number of teen titles, many of them aimed at 12–17-year-old girls— *Teen People, Teen Vogue, CosmoGirl.* The maga-

Research in Brief

Teens Got *Sassy*, Advertisers Got Nervous

Sassy's concept was simple when it entered the teen magazine market in March 1988: It would use more contemporary language and be more direct in issues such as sex than were the three dominant magazines in the market: *Seventeen*, *YM*, and *'Teen*. As Jane Pratt, the founding editor of *Sassy*, explained, "We'll talk to readers as peers rather than as some authority figure. . . . Teenagers will be told the truth, without euphemisms or apologies."[1]

Within 6 months of the magazine's start-up, circulation jumped from 250,000 to 400,000 paid subscribers. By October 1994, *Sassy*'s circulation was more than 800,000.

While a student at Trinity University in San Antonio, Texas, Debra Ceffalio studied *Sassy* from 1988 through 1996 to determine its impact on the teen magazine market.[2] Ceffalio points out that the magazine quickly became a sensation because of its sexual frankness, breezy language, and unique relationship with its readers. Although *Time* magazine dismissed *Sassy*'s editorial voice as "pajama-party journalism,"

teen readers appreciated the first name relationship with writers Jane, Catherine, Karen, and Christina. Said editor Pratt (who, at 25, was only a few years older than her readers): "Other magazines have, like, a stereotypical or idealized vision of teenagers. Maybe what parents or teachers would like. Not really what teenagers are about, you know."[3]

Ceffalio's study of *Sassy* reveals an editorial staff closely in touch with its readers. For example, in September 1990, a reader wrote in wondering how a magazine that advised girls to "lighten up" about their body image could run an ad aimed at women who wanted sexier bodies. Pratt wrote that the editors really had no control over the advertising but that the ad also had made her stomach lurch. Ceffalio notes that an editorial response openly criticizing a published ad would not have been found in any of the more traditional teen magazines.

Sassy challenged the status quo that most teen magazines supported by running stories about "When We Were Depressed," "Nine Things About

America That Make Us Want to Scream and Throw Stuff," and "And They're Gay," a sympathetic, accepting profile of two young lesbian couples. *Sassy* also dedicated 43 percent of its editorial content to lifestyle and general interest issues, such as an article on the Persian Gulf War titled "The Iraq Thing," which ran in the February 1991 issue. With the subtitles "What Sadam is irked about" and "Why some Americans feel dissed enough to go to war," this article explained an important world event in the readers' own iconoclastic language.

The magazine's frank sex information set *Sassy* apart from its competitors, who, writes Ceffalio, tended to couch coverage of sexual issues in judgmental terms, if they wrote about sex at all. *Sassy* ran articles about the pros and cons of virginity, getting turned on and how to handle it, and "The Truth About Boys' Bodies." These topics got rave reactions from readers, but advertisers eventually weighed in with a thumbs down following a massive letter-writing campaign launched by two mothers from Wabash, Indiana, who were

1. Geraldine Fabrikant, "Magazine to Pursue Teenagers," *New York Times* (May 3, 1988): sec. 4, p. 26.

2. Debra Ceffalio and Sammye Johnson, "Teenagers Get *Sassy*, 1988–1996: A Case Study of the Teen Magazine Market," *Southwestern Mass Communication Journal* 13:2 (1998): 1–11.

3. Suzanne Daley, "*Sassy*, Like, You Know, for Kids," *New York Times* (April 11, 1988): sec. 4, p. 8.

(continued)

Teens Got *Sassy*, Advertisers Got Nervous (continued)

dismayed by the sexually candid articles. The campaign threatened to boycott the products of companies who continued to advertise in *Sassy*. By late 1988, at least nine major accounts, led by Levi's along with Maybelline and Cover Girl cosmetics, had pulled their ads from the magazine. To save itself, *Sassy* was forced to tone down its articles.

Ceffalio believes this marked the beginning of the end for *Sassy*, although the magazine kept its strong editorial position among teens as long as Jane Pratt remained at the helm. *Seventeen, YM,* and *'Teen* began copying ideas first seen in *Sassy* —using slang, including the personalities of the staff in editorial comments, having a less preachy approach to topics, and providing a clean look through design makeovers. But they did not emulate the emphasis on sex.

Pratt left *Sassy* in late 1994 after the magazine was sold to Petersen Publishing, owner of competitor *'Teen.* Trying to revive *Sassy*, which had experienced economic difficulties ever since the advertising boycott, Petersen hired a new staff to revamp the magazine in a more traditional fashion. This "new" *Sassy*, which debuted in August 1995, lacked the irreverent edge of its predecessor. Stated new editorial director Catherine Ettlinger, "We have underage girls reading

this magazine. We are responsible. We are mainstream. We are not out to shock. We'll never be sassy gratuitously."[4]

Readers of the original *Sassy* quickly noticed the editorial difference, says Ceffalio. In the January 1996 issue, *Sassy* published a page of letters from disgruntled readers pining for the "old" *Sassy.* "Without Jane Pratt and Co. this magazine is boring, repetitive and just like any other one on the shelf," one reader complained. Many readers expressed a feeling of abandonment: "You have sucked every ounce of what the 'old' *Sassy* stood for out of the magazine. This magazine contains nothing but superficial garbage that needs to be thrown away forever. How could you do this to us? We depended on *Sassy* month to month for advice, security and most of all, a good friend."

Readers began canceling their subscriptions. In response to the barrage of negative letters, the new *Sassy* staff told readers, "Get over it! Get a clue! Get a life!" because "Jane's gone."

In a few months, even *Sassy* was gone. In December 1996, Petersen Publishing folded *Sassy* into *'Teen*. All that was left of the original *Sassy* was a 10-page section titled "*Sassy* Slant," offering the latest "hot bits on style, stars, gossip, bands and guys." Although the layout for this section was rem-

iniscent of the original *Sassy*, the mixture of cheekiness, bravado, and vulnerability that resulted in the *Sassy* personality was missing. Then, in August 1997, a totally redesigned *Teen* (*sans* apostrophe) hit the newsstands—with no evidence of *Sassy* to be found anywhere in its editorial pages.

Ceffalio's study highlights the fact that all teen magazines speak to an audience that is vulnerable. Teenage girls often are obsessed with beautiful bodies and boys and are plagued by stress, self-esteem problems, and eating disorders. *Sassy* proved that because teenagers look to magazines for support and friendship, establishing a bond of trust between the staff and readers can be a key to success. *Sassy* also demonstrated that young girls want to be treated as intelligent young women who are interested in a wider variety of topics than previously had been covered by teen magazines.

By becoming a friend to teenage girls, *Sassy* found a niche in what previously was considered a saturated market. At the time of *Sassy*'s death, the teen category was led by *Seventeen, YM,* and *Teen.* Ceffalio says these magazines seemed content to focus on celebrities, boys, beauty, and fashion rather than hard-edged issues like suicide or sexual abuse. *Sassy*'s frank style of

4. Mark Adams, "The Mainstreaming of *Sassy*," *Mediaweek* (July 10, 1995): 18.

Teens Got *Sassy*, Advertisers Got Nervous (continued)

writing no longer was embraced by the three teen magazine leaders.

While the title may be gone, its influence is not. Atoosa Rubenstein, founding editor of *CosmoGirl*, interned at Lange Communication, publisher of *Sassy*, when she was in college. "I loved the personality I got from it," she says of *Sassy*. *CosmoGirl* occasionally follows the *Sassy* tradition, such as

running an honest and poignant first-person article by a teen mother in one of the magazine's early issues. "The message wasn't' don't have sex,' because it's not my place to say that," Rubenstein said about the piece. "But to say, 'the girl went through this, she made one mistake and her life was changed.'"[5]

As for Jane Pratt, she headed her namesake maga-

zine, *Jane*, for nearly 8 years, stepping down in September 2005. *Jane*, which premiered in September 1997, did the same thing for women ages 18–34 that *Sassy* did: talk to them in an irreverent, edgy tone and make them feel good after reading the magazine. Pratt left *Jane* with a healthy circulation of 700,000. ■

5. Handelman, M72.

---

zines understand that this is an audience that recognizes when it is being talked down to, so the editors work to strike a balance between fun and substance. The tone of *CosmoGirl* was set by founding editor Atoosa Rubenstein, who shared with her readers the fact that she missed her own senior prom. "I don't mind sacrificing or embarrassing myself as long as someone learns something from me or feels better about herself," Rubenstein said. "They get a real sense of empowerment and inspiration to know that I was just a regular girl like them."[20]

The survival of Generation X and Y magazines is dependent on the vitality of the audience, which could mature and buy houses in the suburbs at any time, as happened to the audiences of several noteworthy 1960s and 1970s start-ups, including *Rolling Stone* and *The Mother Earth News*.

anatomy of a failure

Flair is one of the most popular magazine failures in American history and provides an excellent case history of the importance of editorial philosophy, formula, and audience. *Flair* lasted only 12 issues,

from February 1950 to January 1951. Nearly 50 years later, in 1997, *Flair*'s editor Fleur Cowles published a collection of the magazine's most popular features in a $250 book titled *The Best of Flair*. The book sold out and went to a second printing. Fleur, *Flair*, and the book were the topic of articles in 1997 in *Vanity Fair*, *Mirabella*, and newspapers throughout the country.

Flair was a design innovator, boasting production tricks that would make 1990s publishers quiver: vertical and horizontal half-pages, a variety of paper stocks, die-cut covers, accordion inserts, and foldouts. Publisher Gardner (Mike) Cowles—who was married to Fleur at the time—also published the then-successful mass circulation *Look*. Mike said he suspended publication of *Flair* because of high production costs. Fleur Cowles blamed the death additionally on poor marketing techniques.[21]

Flair took a bewildering planning route, with regular changes in concept. In September 1948, Mike Cowles spoke of creating a "new man's magazine" that would combine various elements of *Esquire*, *Field and Stream*, *Outdoor Life*, and *Holiday*. He offered Arnold Gingrich, founding editor of *Esquire*, the opportunity to work with Cowles Publishing to start such a magazine. However, Gingrich said Mike Cowles lured him to work on a

AUGUST 1950: *Flair* **magazine pulled out all the production stops available during its brief life in 1950. These horizontal half pages allow the reader to match different skirts and blouses.**

"left-wing Republican magazine" and that Fleur "flanked us by turning it into what was commonly regarded as a pansy's home journal."[22]

In early stages, content included cuisine, which was later dropped and replaced with literature. Humor was included at one point, and theater drifted in and out as a content category. Consistent throughout is an emphasis on the arts, fashion, and "decoration."[23]

Planning for design was more clearly articulated than planning for editorial content. A memo dated April 1, 1949, calls the magazine a "large and luxurious publication of distinctive format." Moreover, it adds, because the magazine "is itself a thing of beauty, it furnishes in its each appearance its own excuse for being."

The first issue of *Flair* was published in February 1950. In it, Fleur Cowles used a handwritten note to explain the magazine to readers. Her plan emphasized variety and graphic experimentation rather than editorial information:

There have been great adventures in paper and in printing and in the presentation of the graphic arts in the last decade . . . unhappily, few of them for the public at large. I have longed to introduce a magazine daring enough to utilize the best of these adventures. A magazine which combines, for the first time under one set of covers, the best in the arts: literature, fashion, humor, decoration, travel and entertainment.

This copy of *Flair* shows that it can be done; it is proof that a magazine need no longer be stolidly frozen to the familiar format. *Flair* can, and will, vary from issue to issue, from year to year, assuring you that most delicious of all rewards—a sense of surprise, a joy of discovery. For the young in heart, men and women, I believe our efforts will help give a vital contemporary direction and fullness to American life.[24]

When *Flair* folded, *Time* magazine noted that "journalists (no doubt including Mike Cowles) knew the real trouble: In striving valiantly for the unusual, *Flair* had too little old-fashioned journalistic flair itself."[25] *Newsweek* said the magazine was "perhaps more famous for the hole in its cover than its contents."[26]

Geared to a sophisticated audience interested in the arts, fashion, and travel, *Flair* was positioned against 10 magazines aiming at the same audience: *House and Garden, House Beautiful, Vogue, Harper's Bazaar, Holiday, The New Yorker, The Atlantic Monthly, Harper's, Saturday Review of Literature,* and *Town and Country.* An April 1, 1949, planning paper discussed the hazards of too close a resemblance to these magazines and suggested humor as a point of difference. Humor, the paper noted, was "completely lacking in all magazines in this field"—an odd comment that ignored the highly developed humor for which *The New Yorker* was justifiably famous.

The Cowleses projected a circulation of 200,000, but the debut issue had only 31,000 subscribers.[27] By the end of the year, this had grown to only 90,000.[28] The magazine sold 245,000 copies at its peak.[29] By the end of 1950, according to Mike

Cowles, losses before taxes were roughly $2,485,000, a loss of nearly 75 cents per copy sold.[30]

Flair contained advertising for upscale products such as diamonds, minks, and designer clothing, but the magazine did not see eye-to-eye with advertisers. Fleur Cowles requested custom-designed ads "in keeping with *Flair*'s content," but ad agencies saw too little profit in creating ads for only one magazine. Agencies avoided the magazine, she said, because it was "too new in format to be judged by any but the trail-blazers."[31]

The Cowleses' plan was to market the magazine using direct mail to "carefully selected lists," which would include book club subscribers, club women, career women, professionals, and college gradu-

ates. That results of tests to such readers were successful, especially from purchasers of "quality," or high-priced, items.

Fleur suggested a cover price of 60 cents, setting the magazine apart from the competitors, which were still selling for 50 cents. She said the magazine needed a select direct-mail appeal to an elite readership and a higher selling price. Ultimately, though, the magazine was primarily marketed through the same mass market newsstands used by its sister publication, *Look*, and was sold for the standard 50 cents.

Not only was it unclear what *Flair* was to be, it was unclear why it was to be. The two major managers, Fleur and Gardner Cowles, presented both

Flair Meets *Flaunt*: Twins Born 50 Years Apart?

Ever since *Flair* magazine died in 1951, founding editor Fleur Cowles has believed that her magazine brainchild was an idea just waiting for some adventurous souls to make it happen again.

In 1999 it did. *Flaunt* was an end-of-the-millennium reprise of the 1950s *Flair*. The design and production similarities of these magazine twins that were born half a century apart are obvious: die-cut and embossed covers; double covers; horizontal and vertical half pages; small booklets bound in; and a constantly changing logo design.

Content, however, is a different matter. *Flair* emphasized contemporary arts and fashion that now look almost naive and innocent. *Flaunt* is another matter. On its pages, young

people wrap their lithe, barely clothed bodies around one another; old women wrap their wrinkles in the newest fashions. Young and old look hip rather than happy. Both magazines represent their eras. The postwar *Flair* represents a country excited about having a surplus of money and goods. It was a country of growing families, growing hope, and growing, if somewhat tacky, suburbs. The status quo was the ideal in this culture. The clothes, humor, designs, and general content of *Flair* represented a spirit of experimentation that contradicted this leave-it-be attitude. The magazine represented the dichotomy of change in a don't-rock-the-boat culture. *Flaunt* came along in 1998 when Americans looked at the world

through the lens of the celebrity; sex was no longer revolutionary; the youth culture defined fashion. *Flaunt* continues to push a social envelope that was already wide open.

APRIL 2006: ***Flaunt*** **is the design and production reincarnation of the 1950s** ***Flair.***

conflicting and inconsistent messages about the magazine they were planning and producing. The third manager, Arnold Gingrich, seems to have been shut out of the editorial process despite his success as a founding editor of *Esquire*.

The success of *Flair* depended on Mike Cowles's understanding of magazine publishing and Fleur Cowles's understanding of the luxury market. Mike Cowles's only regret seemed to be in starting the magazine in the first place. He said he doubted he would have done so if Fleur "hadn't been such a persuasive saleswoman." He said he was reluctant to publish the magazine because neither he nor Fleur had experience in producing a luxury magazine. His final assessment: "I'm sure I should never have started publishing *Flair*."[32]

In her memoirs, Fleur Cowles reflected on the failure of the magazine: "The money *Flair* lost will probably never again be available on the same basis. It was put into my hands by Mike Cowles to prove that artistic effort can be commercial—which for good or bad reasons it wasn't and may never be." She contended that the magazine was marketed poorly: "No magazine was ever sold by such mistaken methods." *Flair*, she said, was "born to the right parents but reared by the wrong nannies."[33]

JANUARY 1970 (Premiere Issue): *The Mother Earth News* advocated a back-to-the-land philosophy in the early 1970s with practical articles for those who wanted a simple rural life.

launches and life cycles

Magazine analysts say that a magazine has a chance of long-term success if it can last at least 3 years. The figures on how many magazines last that long are a bit blurred, because magazines are launched with great fanfare but often die quiet deaths. The field is so risky that the Small Business Administration bylaws prohibit loans for publishing.

Magazines are generally launched in three ways: on the newsstand, by subscription, or a combination of the two.

Newsstand launches can be an easy tool for large publishers. *People* was launched on the newsstand and remains a strong newsstand title. When a publication does well in newsstand sales, as was the case with Meredith Corporation's *Country Home* and *Traditional Home*, it may be launched as a subscription title. Large publishers have the distribution system already in place and have already developed relationships with wholesalers and retailers, allowing their titles to get placement

on the newsstand. Smaller or new publishers, however, have no such benefit and are well advised not to depend only on newsstand distribution.

When he was National Geographic Society president and editor, Alexander Graham Bell hoped to increase newsstand sales of *National Geographic* in 1898, 10 years after its launch. No luck. The magazine's legendary success came when Bell hired Gilbert Grosvenor, who revamped the magazine, added photographs, and made it an appealing perk of membership in the society.

Subscription launches offer some interesting benefits available only to magazines. Publishers can ask for payment before a reader even sees the publication, giving the publisher up-front funds for expenses. The costs of subscription launches can be daunting, however, because they often include buying a mailing list, and producing and mailing an expensive brochure. Again, large publishers have the advantage because they have the operating capital.

But even the giants were once small and had to start somewhere. Innovation, in fact, is often the entrepreneur's advantage. When John Shuttleworth started *The Mother Earth News* in 1970, he knew where his readers might be—at anti-Vietnam War rallies. He headed to the rallies himself, gave away free magazines with subscription cards included, and sure enough, he ended up adding to his readership. Not satisfied with that, he wrote to other magazines offering a free ad in his magazine in exchange for an ad in theirs, at a time when he had fewer than 1,000 readers. Jann Wenner of *Rolling Stone* took Shuttleworth up on the offer, and gave the magazine a needed boost in subscriptions.

Stephen Osborne and Mike Bradley left full-time jobs in advertising sales at Cahners Publishing, put their life savings on the line, and took on second mortgages to launch *Pharmaceutical and Medical Packaging News* through controlled circulation. Approaching the market with the entrepreneur's unique vision, they saw that most medical and pharmaceutical titles were highly vertical—either narrowly dealing with medical issues or narrowly dealing with pharmaceutical issues. The men decided to go "diagonal" and combine the two fields. Launched in 1993, the publication was in the black within 2 years, with 1995 ad revenue exceeding $1 million.[34]

The launch is just the first step; if a magazine is to keep walking, it needs to keep putting one foot in front of the other with a targeted publishing strategy. The life cycle of a magazine depends on editors who keep aware of readers' needs and social trends, and who can fine-tune the magazine to deal with the vagaries of markets and social momentum.

The conditions that precede and follow the magazine's start-up—that is, the social context in which magazines operate—are important determinants of a magazine's success. Likewise, as the audience changes, the magazine must respond to that change.

O: The Oprah Magazine, **a spin-off of the popular television show, was one of the fastest and most successful start-ups in magazine history, but magazines as offshoots of broadcast shows are nothing new. In 1926,** *Kitchen Klatter* **magazine premiered as a complement to the radio show of the same name that was broadcast in six Midwestern states. At its peak, the magazine had a circulation of 90,000.**

How does a magazine respond to changes in society? How do such changes affect the nature of the magazine's audience as well as the nature of the magazine's content? And how do publishing realities—the necessity of making money—affect the magazine and its relationship with its audience?

A magazine and its audience develop through the same social history. Magazines have life cycles that are cyclical and unique to the magazines' relationships with their audiences. Not all magazines go through all steps of the life cycle. Some die early; some defy the odds and live on and on; some die and are restarted.

Nevertheless, looking at the patterns of a magazine's life as cyclical helps us make some sense of how a magazine and its audience change over time. The steps of this life cycle are

- emergence of the audience.
- creation of the magazine.
- growth and change.
- refocus or death.

The Mother Earth News has gone through an entire life cycle, from birth to death; after death, it started a new cycle.

■ EMERGENCE OF THE AUDIENCE

Before the magazine is started, the audience already exists. The founders of the magazine are usually members of this audience. John and Jane Shuttleworth, founding editors of *The Mother Earth News*, were self-sufficient Ohio farmers.

America was born as an agrarian nation, so in many ways *Mother's* audience was as old as the country. *The Mother Earth News* emerged as the voice of the back-to-the-land movement of the 1970s. Other magazines were already serving small pockets of this audience by providing articles on living simple and self-sufficient lives on the land and showing respect for the environment: *Farm Journal, Vocations for Social Change, Popular Mechanics,* and

Motorhome Life. Audience members profiled in the first issues of *The Mother Earth News* had left urban jobs for rural areas in the 1940s and 1950s—20–30 years before the magazine was born.

■ CREATION OF THE MAGAZINE

The creation of the magazine pulls these individuals together. The editor is closely connected with the magazine and with the audience.

The first issue of *The Mother Earth News* was published in January 1970. John Shuttleworth said he and his wife started the magazine armed with several filing cabinets full of material "on people who have successfully walked away from the system and started living life on their own terms." The first issue was printed on newsprint and was type-heavy, with some black-and-white line drawings and photos. It sported a black-and-yellow cover with a drawing of a sun and the cover line, "a new beginning." The table of contents page introduced the magazine's tag line: "*The Mother Earth News* . . . it tells you how," and the magazine was promoted as showing readers "how to do more with less." The language throughout the magazine is representative of the 1970s counterculture, with words like "pad" and "groovy" used regularly. The magazine was referred to as "Mother," almost as though it were a person rather than a publication.

John Shuttleworth wrote to readers in a friendly neighbor voice full of 1970s counterculture rhetoric. In May 1970 he penned a "Statement of Policy" to readers:

> There are many paths to the Clear Light and we are all pilgrims. MOTHER exists only to present the HOW of alternate life styles not normally considered in our modern society. That's "lifestyles" not "style." Each individual must choose the way that is proper for him. We can only help to make a meaningful selection possible. Peace.[35]

Readers began their connections with one another in the Letters section of the second issue. Letters were answered in the magazine by "Mother," and readers were referred to as "Mother's" children. One reader, writing in the third issue, May 1970, suggested a readers' convention. Several others asked for information on communes.

The magazine became so popular that Shuttleworth had to rein in readers who had begun to make pests of themselves. By the ninth issue, a year and a half after the magazine was started, Shuttleworth made a plea to readers that indicated the popularity of the movement as well as his exhaustion and frustration with his role as the "Mother" of the movement:

> Please! Folks, we love you . . . but please, please don't "just drop by" Mother's offices this summer expecting to find "a place on the floor" on which to spread your bedroll. We ain't got such a place."

The magazine had not only solidified the audience, it had helped it become a family: connected, supportive, and, occasionally, bickering. In December 1973, after one especially emotional debate about a letter defending "law-abiding hunters," Mother wrote in a parental voice: "For one final, last time . . . I think both sides are right and both sides are wrong on this argument and this is the last time—for now—that I want to see name-calling and finger-pointing."

■ GROWTH AND CHANGE

To grow, the magazine strives to reach a broader audience. As part of the process, the magazine may look more to advertising to help generate revenue. If not done with care, this makes the magazine less of a voice of the community it helped solidify because it may become more attuned to the needs of advertisers than to readers. At the same time, the success of the magazine leads to the development of other magazines with similar content to serve the audience. The founding editor or editors may leave the magazine, perhaps selling it.

By the sixth issue, November 1970, *The Mother Earth News* had grown to 124 pages; a year later it was regularly 132 pages. The masthead, which originally listed only the Shuttleworths and a few friends, expanded and listed the contributors alphabetically, so the Shuttleworths' names came at the end of the list. In 1975, the magazine's motto was changed to "More than a magazine—a way of life."

Early advertising in the magazine was black and white, consisting of homesteading books and organic products, often offered by people profiled in articles. At the beginning, Shuttleworth said he was trying to restrict advertising to 15 percent or less of every issue. Color ads started appearing in the magazine in 1975, but were still related to self-sufficiency. Advertising increased gradually through the years, but editorial seriously outdistanced advertising. Ads were for home-based businesses, log cabins, seeds and gardening materials, and occasionally even Jack Daniel's whiskey.

The Mother Earth News agenda had seeped into the American consciousness by the late 1970s: *Better Homes and Gardens* ran articles on woodstoves and dome houses, and architects were designing high-cost, high-quality underground and solar homes. In 1978, Congress authorized a solar tax credit to encourage the building of new solar homes—long a staple of the magazine's content—and the integration of solar technology into existing homes.

The mythical "Mother" continued answering letters although, as the magazine aged, fewer letters rated an answer than in early years. Content changed dramatically in the late 1970s, with emphasis on energy conservation, home building, remodeling, and organic gardening. Letters about communes disappeared, but readers were still willing to share what they had, although they were often looking for a profit. One letter offered readers the chance to buy moccasins at 20–40 percent off wholesale prices. Others offered supplementary information on previously published articles and gave suggestions for environmentally sound lifestyles.

Increasing stress colored Shuttleworth's columns, however, as he regularly talked about working 14-hour days and never having a vacation. Finally, in October 1978, he gave up the editorship of the magazine, and in 1980 he sold it to staff members.

The energy crisis of the 1970s fueled interest in the magazine's self-sufficient focus.[36] In 1980, the magazine ran roughly one page of advertising to every five pages of editorial, a formula that continued until 1985, when ad pages for the year totaled 300. Circulation grew from 490,000 in 1977 to 939,000 in 1979, going slightly over 1 million in 1980, 1981, and 1982. By 1983, however, energy conservation was no longer as great an issue with the American public, and *The Mother Earth News'* circulation moved downward again, to 911,000. It inched down farther, to 893,000 by 1985.[37]

In 1985, the magazine was purchased by Owen Lipstein, founder of *American Health,* who was optimistic about increasing ad revenues because *The Mother Earth News* had "never been sold to

Madison Avenue." It was, he said, like "a new launch." The motto was changed again, this time to "the original country magazine."[38] In the September/October 1985 issue, one reader was so comfortable with the magazine he referred to it as "Mom."

■ REFOCUS OR DEATH

As social and economic realities change over time, the magazine's relationship with the audience may reach a critical point, at which some readers accuse the magazine of failing its original audience and others accuse it of not changing enough to suit changing times. This forces either a change in the magazine or in its target audience. Failure to successfully refocus leads to the death of the magazine. No matter what the fate of the magazine, however, the audience remains in some form, having changed as society has changed. This audience may be served by some version of the original magazine, or it may have moved to other magazines more suited to its changed needs.

The 1980s were possibly the antithesis of the era in which *The Mother Earth News* was born. The ideal of living on less was replaced by the goal of accumulating more. The concept of country became associated with decorating, collecting, and living *on* the land, but not *off* it. Wall Street was king, and the term "yuppie" came to characterize many of the baby boomers who no longer were interested in activism but, rather, aspired to high-paying jobs and expensive houses and cars. Condos had replaced communes.

By the mid-1980s, as the magazine came under Lipstein's control, much of the country was comfortably entrenched in a consumerism mentality. Many of the changes in the magazine after 1985, then, reflect not only a changing culture but also changing ownership and a changing perception of readers. Lipstein succeeded in promoting the magazine to advertisers. *Advertising Age* named *The Mother Earth News* one of the 10 "hot" magazines of 1988.

The same year, *Adweek* named *The Mother Earth News* one of the 10 hottest small magazines. According to *Adweek,* the magazine saw a 33.5 percent increase in ad pages in 1988 and a 38.7 percent increase in ad revenue. The magazine Lipstein was promoting, however, was different from the one the Shuttleworths had started. *Advertising Age* defined the magazine's focus in explaining its strength: "The continued strong interest in home and property will bode well for *The Mother Earth News,* the once back-to-the-land hippie journal that has been redesigned for yuppies." Lipstein was obviously so comfortable with this characterization he used it in promotional material for the magazine.[39]

The back-to-the land movement was partially subsumed by the environmental movement of the late 1980s, and *The Mother Earth News* became one of many voices of that movement. However, as one of many environmental magazines, the magazine competed with old standards such *Audubon* as well as new starts like *E.* As a country magazine, *The Mother Earth News* also competed with the growing number of country magazines—*Country Living, Country Home, Country,* and *Country Journal.*

A successful new start-up of the late 1980s, *Utne Reader* (later changed to simply *Utne*), may have brought the alternative magazine concept full circle. Promoting itself as "the best of the alternative press," *Utne Reader,* like the early *The Mother Earth News,* was a storehouse of alternative information from other publications.

In a column in the magazine's January/February 1990 issue, editor Bruce Woods acknowledged that *The Mother Earth News* lost readers in the mid-1980s, but said these were people who were concerned only with the energy crisis and who disappeared when the crisis faded. The solid core of readers, he said, were different; they didn't change their "ideals with the seasons," but maintained their interest in the environmental movement and in *The Mother Earth News* as a "how-to" publication of that movement. He makes no reference to the back-to-the-

land movement. Woods presented the magazine as a practical guide for the ecologically concerned.

Letter writers, however, disagreed, saying the magazine looked like it was "aimed at 'eco-yuppies'" and had become a "bordello for lawnmowers." In 1990, the motto was changed simply to "The original," dropping all reference to country. "The original," however, had become just one magazine among many doing the same thing. It had lost its special focus, its appeal to the frontier spirit, to individual initiative, and to the ideals of a simpler life. Articles appearing in *The Mother Earth News* could have appeared in many other country, environmental, or women's magazines.

The Mother Earth News celebrated the 20th anniversary of the magazine and of Earth Day with the March/April 1990 issue. The logo was changed to a lighter, airier typeface. The tone of the articles was professional but removed from the audience. Articles concerned the environment, but how-to tips were usually limited to the letters column. First person was occasionally used, but in a clean, professional—certainly not chatty—tone. Covers became more dramatic and less homey. For example, the May/June 1990 issue featured a "radical fisherman" in a bright yellow slicker silhouetted against an ominously dark sky and blue-black water. Most cover models were still unknowns, but Willie Nelson popped up in May/June 1987 in an article on Farm Aid.

After Issue 125, September/October 1990, the magazine ceased publication for a year. That issue featured a moody cover with a young couple—mother holding the baby, father drawing water from the well, with sunbeams drenching the whole family. The magazine looked like a poetic version of *Audubon.* Lisa Quinn, public relations

The inaugural issue of *The New Yorker,* February 21, 1925, had 36 pages, 8.3 of which were advertisements. Its contents included seven cartoons, one a full-page and one a double-page spread; twelve works of fiction; three poems; one profile; and the Talk of the Town. In announcing that it is "not edited for the old lady in Dubuque," editors noted that it would not be "engaged in tapping the Great Buying Power of the North American steppe region by trading mirrors and colored beads in the form of our best brands of hokum."

representative for *The Mother Earth News*, said readers "freaked out" over the new issue, saying it was too urban and too slick, and canceled their subscriptions.[40]

As with many magazines, the death of *The Mother Earth News* was gradual and was based on business decisions. But at the heart of the magazine business is the audience. Without audience connection, a magazine has no reason to exist. When *The Mother Earth News* lost that, the rest was inevitable.

The magazine survived nevertheless. In August/September 1991, the magazine was reintroduced with its former motto, "The Original Country Magazine." The "News from Mother" column speaks of audience reaction to the magazine's 1989–1990 changes and eventual death:

> You rightly told us that the last three or four issues didn't deliver useful tips and practical information on how to live wisely and responsibly in the country. One subscriber compared her disillusionment with the new MOTHER to the way she felt when John Lennon was murdered. You knew it and we knew it: MOTHER no longer was MOTHER. . . .

Although the back-to-the-land movement had faded as an artifact of the 1970s, the interest in back-to-the-land issues remained. Americans still see nature and the country as a refuge from urban problems and as a means of reconnecting with traditional roots. Essentially, then, the magazine came full circle, returning to its roots while changing its approach to match changes in its audience and society as a whole. That audience has retained its back-to-the-land ideals, but has modified them with some 1990s realism. The "new" *Mother Earth News*—the magazine no longer includes "*The*" in its title—is geared to a new audience, one that existed before its restart. The difference in this incarnation of the cycle is that the magazine itself had a hand in creating that audience. In addition, *Mother Earth News'* redevelopment exists in an environment full of other magazine voices competing for that audience.

Now owned by Ogden Publishers of Topeka, Kansas, and published six times a year, *Mother Earth News* reaches a circulation of more than 325,000. Its innovative website offers a look at all of the magazine's 200-plus issues, starting with the January 1970 inaugural edition.

living to a ripe old age

Harper's is now in its second century and *Mother Earth News* is in its fourth decade. *Harper's* bears little resemblance to the booklike publication launched in 1850. Perhaps the Harper brothers are rolling in their graves at what has happened to their creation. What has happened is that it has kept its emphasis on fiction alive, one of only a handful of magazines doing so, and it has outlasted all other American magazines. *Mother Earth News* is far more glossy and colorful than Shuttleworth's original creation, but it still tells readers how to compost and live responsibly with and off the land.

Meanwhile, *Flair* exists only as a remarkable historical artifact. The innovations *Flair* introduced still fascinate American audiences and designers, even those born long after the magazine died.

Just as cars and clothing change over time, so must magazines. *Harper's* was introduced at a time when women wore bustles; *Flair* came along in an era in which wearing mink was chic rather than dangerous; and *Mother Earth News* took full advantage of its hip-hugging trendiness. Those original magazines would fit in today's society, perhaps, if women still wore basketlike contraptions on the backs of their skirts, tiny mink heads around their shoulders, and chartreuse beaded pants hanging beneath their navels.

Harper's and *Mother Earth News* stayed alive by responding to change. Magazines, Lapham said in 1992, need to move with the same speed as other forms of communication:

> The ubiquity and accelerating speeds of the mass media had accustomed a generation of readers to the techniques of film, to shorter texts, to the abrupt juxtaposition of images as distant from one another as Madonna and Barbara Bush. Any publication that hoped to reflect the spirit of the age was obliged to align itself with a sensibility formed as much by the watching of MTV as by the reading of Marcel Proust.[41]

notes

1. William J. Garry, "The Winners . . . and the Losers," *Free Enterprise* (August 1978): 40.
2. Ibid., 41.
3. Ibid.
4. James Kobak, "The Life Cycle of a Magazine," *Magazine Publishing Management* (New Canaan, Conn.: Folio Magazine Publishing, 1976), 35.
5. James Kobak, "How to Destroy a Magazine: Let Me Count the Ways," *Magazine Publishing Management* (New Canaan, Conn.: Folio Magazine Publishing, 1976), 43.
6. Theodore Peterson, *Magazines in the Twentieth Century* (Urbana: University of Illinois Press, 1956), 43.
7. Milton Hollstein, *Magazines in Search of an Audience* (Magazine Publishers Association, n.d.), 25.
8. Christopher Byron, *The Fanciest Dive* (New York: W.W. Norton, 1986), 272.
9. Lewis Lapham, "Notebook," *Harper's* (October 1992): 7.
10. Dorothy Kalins, "Positioning: The Mission of Your Magazine," Stanford Professional Publishing Course (Stanford University, Palo Alto, Calif., July 21, 1997).
11. Anne Graham, "Mission Statements Light the Way," *Folio:* (March 15, 1995): 47.
12. Ellen Levine, "The Editor's Business," Stanford Professional Publishing Course (Stanford University, Palo Alto, Calif., July 24, 1997).
13. Fred Kaplan, "Stopping the Presses," *Boston Globe* (July 16, 1997): E2.
14. Ibid.
15. Condé Nast, "Class Publications," *History: The Condé Nast Publications* (New York: Condé Nast Publications, n.d.): 12.
16. Brian Steinberg, "Gimmicky Magazine Inserts Aim to Grab Page Flippers." *Wall Street Journal* Online (August 8, 2005), http://online.wsj.com/public/article/0,,SB112346384833807207–XFCvTjZIi3u8qxtcjDr5Bt1sIkl_\20060808,00.html.
17. David Carr, "Romance, in Cosmo's World, Is Translated in Many Ways," *New York Times* (May 26, 2002), http://www.nytimes.com/2002/05/26/business/media/26COSM.html.
18. Laura Zinn, "Move over Boomers," *Business Week* (December 14, 1992): 79.
19. Keith White, "How *Details* Magazine Turned Me into a Rebel Consumer," *Washington Monthly* (April 1994): 18.
20. David Handelman, "*CosmoGirl!* Defines the Fun, Fearless Female—Junior Division," *Folio:* (March 6, 2000): M74.
21. All references to correspondence and prepublication material on *Flair* comes from The Cowles Collection, Cowles Library, Drake University, Des Moines, Iowa. Much of this material is undated. Dates, when available, are cited.
22. Arnold Gingrich, *Nothing but People: The Early Days at Esquire* (New York: Crown Publishers, 1971), 180.
23. Patricia Prijatel and Marcia Prior–Miller, "An Analysis of the Failure of *Flair* Magazine (paper presented at the annual convention of the Association for Education in Journalism and Mass Communication, Boston, Mass., August, 1991).
24. Fleur Cowles [Untitled], *Flair* (February 1950): 23.
25. "No *Flair*," *Time* (December 11, 1950): 67.
26. "*Flair*'s Finish," *Newsweek* (December 11, 1950): 57.
27. "Sugar and Spice," *Newsweek* (January 30, 1950): 46–47.
28. "No *Flair*," 67.
29. Herbert Raymond Mayes, *The Magazine Maze* (Garden City, N.Y.: Doubleday, 1980), 199.
30. Gardner Cowles, *Mike Looks Back: The Memoirs of Gardner Cowles, Publisher of* Look *Magazine* (New York: Gardner Cowles, 1985), 115.
31. Fleur Fenton Cowles, *Friends and Memories* (New York: Reynal and Company, in association with William Morrow and Company, 1978), 53.
32. Gardner Cowles, 116
33. Fleur Fenton Cowles, 55.
34. Lorraine Calvacca, "No Guts, No Glory," *Folio:* (February 1, 1996): 48.
35. "A Statement of Policy," *The Mother Earth News* (May 1970): 9.
36. "The Story of *Mother Earth News*," *The Mother Earth News* (March/April, 1990): 98.
37. *The World Almanac and Book of Facts* (New York: Newspaper Enterprise Association, 1977). Also, almanacs for 1979, 1980, 1981, 1982, 1983, and 1985.
38. "American Health Repositions *The Mother Earth News*," *Folio:* (February 1986): 59.
39. Promotional flyer from *The Mother Earth News*, n. d.
40. Personal discussion, October 12, 1990.
41. Lapham, 6.

for additional reading

Abramson, Howard S. *National Geographic: Behind America's Lens on the World.* New York: Crown Publishers, 1987.

Burlingame, Roger. *Endless Frontiers, The Story of McGraw-Hill.* New York: McGraw-Hill, 1959.

Byron, Christopher. The *Fanciest Dive.* New York: W.W. Norton, 1986.

Cowles, Fleur, ed. *The Best of* Flair. New York: Harper-Collins, 1996.

Cowles, Fleur Fenton. *Friends and Memories*. New York: Reynal, in association with William Morrow, 1978.

Cowles, Gardner. *Mike Looks Back: The Memoirs of Gardner Cowles, Publisher of* Look *Magazine*. New York: Gardner Cowles, 1985.

Gingrich, Arnold. *Nothing but People: The Early Days at Esquire*. New York: Crown Publishers, 1971.

Handbook of Magazine Publishing, The. Stamford, Conn.: Cowles Business Media, 1996.

Kobak, James B. *How to Start a Magazine*. New York: M. Evans, 2002.

Mayes, Herbert Raymond. *The Magazine Maze*. Garden City, N.Y.: Doubleday, 1980.

Reiman, Roy. *I Could Write a Book*. Milwaukee, Wisc.: Grandhaven Group, 2005.

chapter 6

magazine business plans: determining the bottom line

used to use words like 'lead' and 'grammar,'" *Good Housekeeping* editor-in-chief Ellen Levine told a group of magazine professionals in 1997. "Now I use words like 'margins' and 'revenue.'" Levine is typical of today's editor who goes on advertising sales calls, carefully studies the magazine's profit-and-loss statement, and has a voice in circulation price hikes. ▊ Magazines that last in today's marketplace are managed by individuals, on both the editorial and business sides, who have a day-to-day understanding of the intricacies of their publication's budget. ▊ This is even more true of new magazines. Keith Clinkscales, president and general manager of ESPN Publishing, is a Harvard MBA whose first job was as a credit analyst. His career includes starting Vanguard Media, which launched *Honey*, *Heart and Soul*, and *Savoy* magazines. He oversaw the launch of *Vibe* in 1993 and saw the magazine grow from an initial circulation of 100,000 to 700,000 by the time he left in 1999. Before joining *Vibe*, he was a founder of *Urban Profile*, a magazine that targeted 18–34-year-old African American males. His success at that magazine, in fact, was what caught Time Warner's eye and caused them to lure him to their publishing house as the force behind the launch of *Vibe*. One of Clinkscales's many talents is the development of business plans that work.

APRIL 2006: *Vibe*, launched in 1993, built financial success by growing its circulation as well as by the creation of a one-hour late-night talk show, the development of an industry trade show, and the publication of books related to the magazine's focus on urban music and its multicultural proponents and trendsetters.

In the summer of 1997, Clinkscales helped a group of magazine editors, writers, designers, publishers, and ad sales people create a business plan for a hypothetical magazine. The group was part of the Stanford Professional Publishing Course, and participants who might have once considered themselves strictly word or picture people were using their calculators, computers, and heads to build an economic structure. Many, in fact, had come to the course primarily to learn about the business side of magazines.

The group's goal was to launch a magazine with a $300,000 investment. Clinkscales guided the professionals through revenues and expenses, adjusting one to make the other work. He chided an editor from *National Geographic* who had budgeted herself a $100,000 salary for the new magazine and told her to scale it down to $60,000.

Clinkscales reminded the group that, even though the start-up was modest, they could not likely get a loan for it. The money, he said, would have to come from mortgaging their houses, maxing their credit cards, and borrowing from friends. When he launched *Urban Profile,* Clinkscales asked a group of his friends for $300 each, and he threw a party for 3,000 people, who attended at $15 a head.

The Stanford group eventually came up with a 20,000 circulation bimonthly magazine that would sell on the newsstand for $5.95, have a full color ad rate of $8,000 a page, would be produced for 75 cents an issue, and be headed by an editor whose salary was more modest than she had planned.

How did they do it? By following standard magazine economics.

The key to a magazine's economic foundation is the business plan, which outlines the publication's strategy and tactics and helps lure investors to a new magazine. It is built on a financial structure that is common to all magazines, and it follows budget procedures that have been well tested in the industry. To understand how to create a business plan, it's important to first understand the basic components of a magazine's budget.

the magazine budget

A magazine must eventually earn more than it spends. That's the simple part. More complex are the revenue streams on which magazines depend and the costs associated with those revenues. Table 6.1 is an overview of the areas of income and expenses in a typical magazine, illustrated with figures representing budgets of 129 national consumer, trade, and association magazines for 2004.

We'll use Table 6.1 as our base in the following discussion of magazine budgets. That is, when we refer to the "average" magazine, we are referring to the averages of these 129 consumer, trade, and association magazines. Likewise, when we refer to percentages, we mean the percentages derived from these 129 magazines. The data in Table 6.1 give us a way of imagining magazine economics. Recognize, of course, that actual amounts can vary significantly from one magazine to another and from year to year on the same magazine.

■ REVENUE

The magazines in Table 6.1 derived 54 percent of their revenue from advertising, 45 percent from

■ **Table 6.1**   Magazine Revenues and Expenses

	TOTAL/000	AVERAGE/000	PERCENTAGE OF TOTAL REVENUE
REVENUE			
Net advertising revenues	$4,933,673	$38,246	54%
Gross subscription revenues	$2,922,807	$22,657	32%
Gross single-copy revenues	$1,176,799	$9,122	13%
List rental revenues	$45,645	$354	1%
Total magazine revenues	**$9,078,924**	**$70,379**	**100%**
EXPENSES			
Advertising			
Total advertising expenses	$857,368	$6,646	9%
Subscription			
Total subscription expenses	$1,887,981	$14,636	21%
Single copy			
Total single-copy expenses	$594,232	$4,606	7%
Editorial			
Total editorial expenses	$924,140	$7,164	10%
Production			
Total production expenses	$1,554,882	$12,053	17%
Distribution			
Total distribution expenses	$1,037,887	$8,046	11%
Administrative and other operating costs	$720,607	$5,586	8%
Total magazine costs	**$7,577,097**	**$58,737**	**83%**
Operating profit	**$1,501,827**	**$11,642**	**17%**

Note: Columns 1 and 2 are reduced by thousands, or by three digits, so that the total revenue of all magazines, listed as $9,078,924 should be multiplied by a thousand, for the final figure of $9.08 billion. Column 1 shows actual income and expenditure amounts of all 129 magazines combined. Column 2 is an average of the 129 magazines and thus provides figures for one "average" magazine. Column 3 demonstrates relative percentages: the percentage of individual revenue lines to total revenues, and individual expenses to total costs. For example, the average magazine earns a total revenue of $70 million a year, $38 million of that from advertising. Advertising then accounts for 54 percent of that revenue. Total profit is shown as a percentage of total revenues. Total revenues add up to 100 percent, and total costs add up to 93 percent of that, leaving a 17 percent total operating profit.

Source. Magazine Publishers of America, 2004–2005. Figures based on responses from 129 consumer magazines prepared for Magazine Publishers of America.

circulation and 1 percent from list rentals. Circulation income includes subscriptions—which account for 32 percent of revenues—and single-copy, or newsstand, sales—which account for 13 percent. The average magazine earned $38.2 million a year from advertising and $31.8 million from circulation—$22.7 million of that from subscriptions and $9.1 million from single-copy sales. It sold its lists of subscribers to other magazines, organizations, and marketing firms for $354,000.

Circulation revenue is counted according to gross receipts—that is, revenues before costs are deducted. In the case of advertising, however, net revenue is counted, which is revenue after commissions for sales people and discounts for advertisers have been deducted. All circulation expenses and some additional advertising-related costs are listed as expenses.

Table 6.1 is based on the assumption that magazines will have advertising income. Because ad-free magazines have no ad-related income, they build their overall income on circulation revenues and list rentals.

■ EXPENSES

To earn money, magazines have to spend money. In the process, they become huge employers and users of goods and services, thus pumping billions of dollars back into the economy.

The direct costs associated with earning advertising and subscription income for the magazines in Table 6.1 added up to more than a third of the magazines' expenses: advertising 9 percent, subscriptions 21 percent, and single-copy sales 7 percent, for a total of 37 percent. Other costs included editorial at 10 percent, production at 17 percent, distribution at 11 percent, and administrative and operating costs at 8 percent.

advertising

The average magazine in Table 6.1 spent $6.6 million to earn its $38.2 million advertising revenue. That is, for every advertising dollar earned, the magazine spent 17 cents for selling, research, and promotion. Expenses include advertising salaries, development and production of media kits, and research and creation of audience demographic and psychographic profiles. Ad-free magazines, of course, have none of these expenses.

subscriptions

The average magazine in Table 6.1 spent $14.6 million to earn its $22.7 million in subscriptions. That is, for every subscription dollar earned, it spent 64 cents on subscription costs. Expenses include postage, creation and development of promotional materials such as direct mail flyers to potential subscribers, reminder mailings to current subscribers, and commissions to outside agencies, or fulfillment houses, which manage subscriber accounts.

single copies

The average magazine in Table 6.1 spent $4.6 million to earn $9.1 million. That is, for every dollar earned on the newsstand, the magazine spent 51 cents on single-copy costs. Expenses include commissions to wholesalers who provide the magazines to the newsstand, commissions to newsstand sellers, and special promotions for individual issues.

editorial

Even though those of us who have spent our lives in the editorial ranks believe editors are the center of a magazine's universe, in the economic world, editors make up less than 10 percent of the budget. The average magazine in Table 6.1 spent $7.1 million on editorial expenses. Costs include salaries for editorial staff members and for freelance writers, designers, editors, photographers, and artists.

production

The manufacturing of the product itself takes up 17 percent of the expenses of the magazines in Table 6.1. The average magazine spent $12 million on production. Costs include production salaries, printing the magazine, paper, and prepress such as color separations, desktop printing, and press proofs.

distribution

Getting the magazine to the readers made up 11 percent of the budget for the magazines in Table 6.1. The average magazine spent $8 million on distribution. Costs include in-house distribution salaries, commissions given to wholesalers (outlets that sell to retailers) and retailers (outlets that sell directly to consumers), plus postage to subscribers.

administration/operating costs

This catch-all category covers everything from heating bills to computer systems to executive and administrative salaries. The average magazine in Table 6.1 spent $5.6 million on administration. Costs include offices, the requisite office equipment, the people to run the offices, and the people to run the publishing house. As technology increasingly moves into all aspects of business, more and more overhead costs include computer hardware and software, training in their use, and regular upgrading.

operating profit

The amount left over after expenses have been deducted from income is the operating profit, which rests at 17 percent. For the average magazine in Table 6.1, that meant the following:

Total Revenues:	$70,379,000
Total Costs:	$58,737,000
Total Profit:	$11,642,000

Profit, of course, varies from magazine to magazine, and within individual titles from year to year. New magazines may operate at a loss for as long as 5 years. Established magazines may have a banner year at 12 percent profit, followed by a leaner one at 8 percent profit.

the business plan

A business plan offers a clear statement of the magazine's strategies and tactics. It demonstrates the interconnectedness of the product and its economics. A business plan typically defines the product through the editorial philosophy, formula, and audience, as well as an outline of staff structure. The marketing plan and the summary of profitability are the primary economic planning sections of the plan.

A typical business plan would follow this outline:

Title: Use chapter 5, "Conceptualizing the Magazine," as a guide.

Magazine type: Consumer, trade, association, public relations, custom. Use the definitions in chapter 1, "The Magazine as a Storehouse."

Editorial philosophy: Purpose, type of content, and voice. Use the definitions in chapter 5, "Conceptualizing the Magazine."

Editorial Costs per Page

One way to determine magazine expenses is by computing the average editorial cost per page. This is the cost of all editorial material divided by the number of pages. The problem with this is that not all publishers define "editorial material" the same way. Some include staff and freelance expense for editors, writers, designers, and photographers; others use only freelance costs, with staff salaries included in overall operating costs.

Editorial costs per page, then, can vary from publisher to publisher and magazine to magazine, depending on what expenses are included and the type of content on the page. Meredith Corporation, publisher of titles such as *Better Homes and Gardens, Country Home, Ladies' Home Journal,* and *More,* has editorial costs per page ranging from $1,500 to $2,500. This includes only freelance manuscript and art costs, plus color separations, not staff costs, according to Karla Jeffries, vice president of finance and administration of Meredith's Magazine Group. *More* and *Ladies' Home Journal* are at the high end of this range because they deal with celebrities and fashion, which can mean high-ticket photography and editorial.

August Home Publishing, with magazines such as *Cuisine at Home* and *Woodsmith,* has editorial costs per page between $2,600 and $3,000, according to *Cuisine* editor John Meyer. This range includes the use of numerous intricate drawings and step-by-step photos, plus significant research, design, and development costs. Staff and freelance costs and related expenses are included. ■

Audience: Demographics and psychographics. Use chapter 2, "The Magazine as a Marketplace," and chapter 5, "Conceptualizing the Magazine."

Identity/comparisons with competitors: How is the magazine different from those that appeal to the same audience or that deal with the same content? What does the new launch do that is not already being done? Use chapter 5, "Conceptualizing the Magazine."

Formula: Three to five tables of contents to show the editorial breakdown and the types of departments and features to be included in each issue. Use the worksheet in chapter 5, "Conceptualizing the Magazine," as a guide.

Organizational plan: Staff size, organization chart, job duties, and the place of the magazine within the organization, if applicable. Use chapter 7, "Magazine Structures," as a guide.

Marketing plan and executive summary of profitability: Decisions on promotion, frequency, circulation, distribution, and budget.

the marketing plan

A marketing plan is the strategy, or specific plan of action, for breaking into the market. It explains how the magazine will be promoted to readers and advertisers and how it will stand out among the other magazines competing for attention and income. It also includes decisions on frequency; costs of subscriptions, single copies, and advertising; and distribution.

■ ADVERTISING PROMOTION

The primary advertising sales tool is the media kit, which is a direct promotion of the magazine to advertisers, who use it to compare a magazine against other magazines and other media. The media kit must reflect the magazine's identity. It is part of the magazine's promotion plan, and it sells the magazine as a brand.

printed media kits

The most common form of printed media kit is a folder with multiple pockets for brochures, back issues, and other printed sales tools. *The History*

Channel Magazine kit not only sells the readership of the magazine, but also explains its partnership with the History Channel. Typical of other printed media kits, it includes:

- several recent issues of the magazine.
- an editorial statement, which includes the magazine's mission.
- an advertising rate card, with costs for all possible configurations of ads, specific ad sizes available, total circulation, number of subscribers, average newsstand sales, regional editions available, and regional sales rates.
- demographic and psychographic details on the magazine's audience, including readership rates and pass-along readership data.
- an editorial calendar, showing what types of articles will be covered in future issues.
- an information sheet from the Audit Bureau of Circulations (ABC).
- an insertion order.
- a letter from the publisher and a background sheet on the editor.

A media kit may also include articles about the magazine that have appeared in other publications.

online media kits

Many magazine media kits are available online, and can be downloaded as a PDF file. *Lucky* magazine's media kit starts with the mission statement: "*Lucky* is America's ultimate shopping magazine. 100 percent shopping—and nothing else. The best to buy in fashion, beauty and living. The voice of a friend you love to take shopping. Choices, not dictates. Price points ranging from high to low. Buying info for every item featured."

Online media kits include the same elements as their printed brethren. Some media analysts suggest that online kits cost less than 10 percent of a printed kit to produce.

■ CIRCULATION PROMOTION

A magazine must also be promoted to readers. Because this builds circulation, it is referred to as circulation promotion. A successful circulation strategy is to build in efficiency. Large circulations are not automatically a sign of success, nor are small

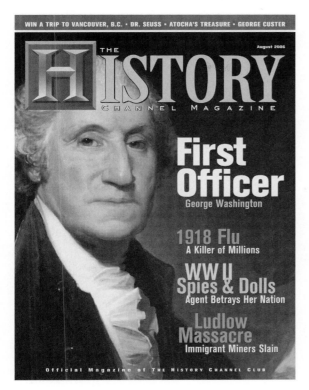

WIN A TRIP TO VANCOUVER, B.C. • DR. SEUSS • ATOCHA'S TREASURE • GEORGE CUSTER

August 2006

THE HISTORY
CHANNEL MAGAZINE

First Officer
George Washington

1918 Flu
A Killer of Millions

WW II
Spies & Dolls
Agent Betrays Her Nation

Ludlow Massacre
Immigrant Miners Slain

Official Magazine of THE HISTORY CHANNEL CLUB

AUGUST 2006: One benefit of a printed rather than online version of *The History Channel Magazine*'s media kit is a recent copy of the magazine. The media kit also explains the magazine's relationship with the television channel.

circulations necessarily a sign of failure. Well-targeted magazines are aimed at readers who make the difference to the bottom line, whether the readership is 20,000 or 2 million.

New readers can come from a variety of sources. Magazines depend on direct marketing for new business; this includes direct mail, advertising in other media, the Internet, and insert cards. Direct marketing includes a mechanism for reader response—a printed or online form to fill out, a number to call to subscribe, a coupon to send in.

Most publishers use some form of incentives. These may include free magazines, test issues, sweepstakes, and "value-added" offers. Publishers hope to maintain existing readers through renewals.

direct mail

Direct mail can be the most efficient way of matching a magazine with its audience. Because subscriptions usually get to the reader through the

mail, direct mail is a logical approach to selling subscriptions. Magazines, catalogs, public television stations, associations, even grocery stores sell mailing lists of specific demographic groups. List houses, which advertise in the back of most industry publications, serve as brokers for a variety of different lists. Many publishing houses have list kits, which look like media kits but that sell lists of readers of their publications.

Eighty percent of publishers use some form of direct mail, but many actually lose money through this source. In 2005, about 78 percent of publishers lost $13.90 for each new subscriber gained through direct mail. Why do it? Because, in the long run, subscribers who renew are a source of revenue and because numbers drive advertising rates, and the more readers, the higher the possible ad rate.[1]

The successful direct mail piece has a clear and consistent message and format that sells the magazine as a benefit to the reader. A typical direct mail package includes an envelope, a lift device ("Yes, I would like to subscribe to *Your Magazine*"), a brochure, a letter, and a response envelope. The cost varies, depending on the complexity of the package, and can range from less than 50 cents to more than $1.

A less expensive method is the double or triple postcard. One part of a double card includes the sales message; the other is a response card. Postage is prepaid, and the card is preaddressed, so the subscriber simply has to mark a box and drop it in the mail. While less expensive, these usually work well only with established titles that do not need the explanatory material usually included in the most expanded package.

Texas Parks and Wildlife experimented with a three-paneled card that offered more information on the magazine than possible on a standard card. Ultimately, 1.6 percent of those receiving the triple card ended up subscribing, compared to 1.37 percent of those who received the double card.[2]

Some 67 percent of first-time subscribers the typical magazine originally reached through direct mail will ultimately pay for the subscription—which means a 67 percent pay-up rate.[3]

the internet

Magazines are increasingly using their websites to sell subscriptions. The costs can be minimal for any magazine that already has a website. Some magazines offer Instant Digital Fulfillment, which gives the subscriber immediate access to a digital magazine once she has paid, while she waits the traditional 4–6 weeks for the print publication to arrive in the mail. The Internet has traditionally been especially effective for publications aimed at the heavy computer users of Generation X and Generation Y, but the success of the medium has spread to publications for all ages and interests.

Lucky magazine offers a digital free-offer to any-one who fills out a subscriber form; this has in-creased the number of completed forms, giving the magazine a list of possible subscribers at a fraction of the cost of direct mail. *Bon Appetit* offers a digital sample of the magazine on their home page. Those interested complete a form, which includes their e-mail address. The magazine confirms the sample by e-mail and then can track whether the user has read the issues; follow-up e-mails are tailored to that readership. This has resulted in significantly in-creased orders from new readers.

FEBRUARY 2006: *Lucky* **promotes itself to readers as a shopping buddy.**

Internet subscribers have a 63 percent pay-up rate.[4]

other media

Magazines can also reach their audiences using other media. Network television may be too broad a medium for a specialized magazine, but some cable television shows can be good buys. Radio and newspapers may be too local for a national promotion, but it's possible to buy ads in groups of stations or newspapers. The magazine also can be pitched in other magazines, especially maga-zines of organizations to which large numbers of the audience might belong.

It also may be possible to swap ads with other magazines—that is, offer one or more ads in the new magazine in response for an ad in an existing magazine. Hearst Communications teases like-minded readers of one of their magazines with of-fers for their other titles: *Seventeen* subscribers can get a 6-month trial to *CosmoGirl*; *Cosmopolitan* subscribers can get 6 months of *Marie Claire*.

insert cards

Those annoying little cards that clutter your fa-vorite magazines and fall all over the floor are there for a reason: They work. They are used by readers who have already selected the magazine on their own, so they go directly to a qualified and in-terested audience. Typically, an issue with high newsstand sales will yield high rates of insert card returns because it has higher initial readership and a higher pass-along readership.

Insert cards may be bound in (attached to the binding), or blown in (unattached to the binding) the issue. They work equally well for consumer, trade, and association magazines and are some-times the choice for magazines with limited pro-motion budgets.

Insert cards have a 54 percent pay-up rate.[5]

subscription offers

Publishers often offer free subscriptions in the hopes that once the magazine gets into the sub-scriber's home, the reader is hooked and will want to keep the publication coming. Ray Reiman, founder of Reiman Publications, whose titles

Reader's Digest Keeps Riding the Culture Wave

Successful magazine start-ups reflect the political, social, and economic climate of their times and can demonstrate why a particular type of journalism began at a particular time and place. Magazine historian Carolyn Kitch of Temple University says *Reader's Digest*'s success exemplifies how a magazine can succeed by remaining a key player in mass culture, in this case for more than 80 years.[1]

On the heels of World War I, the 1920s ushered in flaming flappers, jazz-age speakeasies, and disillusioned youth. A probusiness economy supported mass production in factories, leading to uniformity and conformity on and off the job. For the first time, more people lived in cities than in rural areas; look-alike housing developments flourished, and even furniture and accessories were similar, thanks to Sears, Roebuck and Company. "America and Americans First" was the motto of the day. This was accompanied by an increase in nativism and racism, as exemplified by the 1924 National Origins Act that severely restricted immigration from non-English speaking countries.

The time was ripe for a magazine that matched how people were thinking. Kitch cites historian Paul Boyer's explanation for founder DeWitt Wallace's roaring success with *Reader's Digest:* "What Ford [did] in automobile manufacturing, Wallace [did] in publishing. Ford gave Everyman a car he could drive, [and] Wallace gave Everyman some literature he could read; both turned the trick with mass production." By adapting assembly-line techniques to the production of a magazine, Wallace made *Reader's Digest* emblematic of America during the 1920s.

The prototype *Reader's Digest*, with 31 articles filling 64 pages of copy, was rejected by publishers all over the country. So Wallace and his wife, Lila Acheson Wallace, decided to produce the new magazine themselves. Kitch studied the first issue to determine its appeal to a 1922 reader. She found articles that clearly matched the prevailing attitudes and assumptions of the time:

■ lots of lists (24 articles took this form).
■ articles touting America's scientific progress (aerial photography to promote property sales) and science trivia (how fireflies light up).
■ emphasis on self-improvement ("Be More Popular and Make More Money" and a guide to effective complaining).
■ reliance on expert advice (from Thomas Edison about the qualities of a good business executive).
■ scientific arguments to justify nativism: One article said broad-hipped, short-legged, immigrant women with "necks like prize fighters" were producing three babies for every one borne by "the beautiful women of old American stock." The racist result: "The moment we lose beauty we lose intelligence."
■ articles disapproving of women who were childless or who kept "the apron strings" tied to teenage sons ready to go out in the world and become men.

Also in the first issue were human interest fillers, a personality profile, and a round-up, or catch-all, department. Along with self-help, scientific progress, and relationship pieces, these would set the

1. Carolyn L. Kitch, "'Of Enduring Interest': The First Issue of the *Reader's Digest* as a 'Snapshot' of America in 1922—and Its Legacy in a Mass-Market Culture" (paper presented at the annual meeting of the Association for Education in Journalism and Mass Communication, Anaheim, Calif., August 1996).

(continued)

Reader's Digest Keeps Riding the Culture Wave (continued)

tone for future issues. The prose was straightforward and conversational and the editorial voice was optimistic, two welcome changes of pace from the grim realism of many magazine articles of the Roaring Twenties. *Reader's Digest* offered subscribers editorial consistency in a world of increasing turmoil, and, with its compact size, instant recognition.

Kitch's reading of the September 1995 through December 1995 issues shows ongoing similarities to themes discussed in that first issue. Also enduring is the magazine's constructiveness—no matter what the problem, an answer can be found. Kitch points out that innovative editorial devices found in the first *Reader's Digest*, such as the list format and expert bylines, are now

standard fare in modern consumer magazines.

Reader's Digest has been attacked as being shallow and insulting to the American public, yet the magazine's reduction of information and ideas obviously met a need for its readers from the 1920s to the present day. Kitch says this is because "the social and cultural phenomena that made the *Digest* a welcome new idea in 1922—the forces of urbanization, mass production, information explosion, and the busyness of daily life—are still with us in 1996."

Originally a product of a specific time and place, *Reader's Digest* continues to thrive, although some themes, like nativism, have been moderated by time. The 1922 formula established by *Reader's Digest* remains popular at home and around the world. Today the

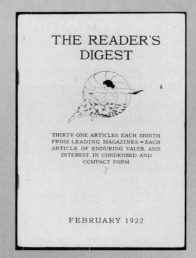

THE READER'S DIGEST

THIRTY-ONE ARTICLES EACH MONTH FROM LEADING MAGAZINES • EACH ARTICLE OF ENDURING VALUE AND INTEREST, IN CONDENSED AND COMPACT FORM

FEBRUARY 1922

FEBRUARY 1922 (Premiere Issue): A solid editorial philosophy provided *Reader's Digest* with a foundation that has lasted more than eight decades.

magazine reaches 10 million readers in the United States and is sold in more than 60 countries in 19 languages. ■

---

include *Country, Country Woman,* and *Reminisce,* built a multimillion dollar business by sending premiere issues with a letter.

Publishers offer two ways for potential subscribers to respond: soft offers and hard offers:

Soft offer: Yes, please send me a free issue of XYZ magazine at no risk or obligation to subscribe. If I like it, I'll pay $12 for 12 issues (including my free issue). If I don't, I'll write cancel on the bill you'll send, return it and owe nothing, and the free issue is mine to keep with your compliments.

Hard offer: Yes! Please enter my subscription to XYZ magazine and bill me for a year (12 issues at $12).

Soft offers might attract more interest, but hard offers typically result in more subscribers. Hard offers are especially successful online, fitting in easily with the online culture of easy credit card use. Still, even in direct mail campaigns, publishers are increasingly asking readers to ante up immediately.

Since 1998, the use of direct mail hard offers has increased, and the pay-up rates have increased by 32 percent. In 2004, *English Home* tested two mailings, both offering six issues at $24.95. The soft offer had a response rate of 3.8 percent, but only about half of those—around 1.5–1.6 percent—ended up subscribing. In comparison, 2.1 percent of those receiving the hard offer subscribed.[6]

Keith Clinkscales learned a lesson about audience appeal while promoting *Vibe*. The magazine, partially funded by well-known music producer Quincy Jones, sent a mailing out to potential subscribers, which included a letter from Jones. Readers looked at the letter, Clinkscales said, and asked, "Why does Quincy Jones need money from *me*?"

test issues

Publishers often create one or two test issues—actual printed magazines, with advertising content—to get an idea of subscription sales possibilities and newsstand draw. They analyze the sales results and reader reactions to determine whether the magazine should be launched as is, modified, or scrapped. Potential readers get an actual magazine to study.

In other cases, publishers will dry test, that is, send only a direct mail package announcing the magazine before the creation of an actual publication. *Latina* did a prepublication test mailing to 70,000 names, then refunded the money sent in by potential subscribers. They didn't have an actual magazine to send them yet. In the process they found enough interest to warrant the 1996 launch of the magazine.[7]

To sell advertisers and other investors on dry-tested magazines, publishers create prototype issues, or professional-quality mock magazines. These may or may not include actual articles, but they do include representative cover lines, titles, and pull-quotes. Photos are usually picked up from another publication—easy to do for companies that produce multiple titles—and advertising may come from ad agencies at no cost, or may also be picked up from other titles. The goal of a

Direct Appeals

In promoting their publications to readers, innovative magazine staffs take advantage of social trends, political calendars, fashion styles, and just about anything that might connect a potential reader with the publication. Some examples:

- *Time* magazine replaced the word "Professional" with the phrase "Senior Citizen Rate Offer" on a mailing piece and dropped the offer from $29.95 to $29. The senior offer came with a desktop organizer for home use rather than the handheld organizer offered to professionals. The senior offer was 40 percent more successful than the professional offer.
- During the 2004 presidential elections, *The New Republic* sent a direct mail piece with a plain white envelope stating "Get *The New Republic* Free This Election Season," offering 12 free weekly issues. Instead of an order form, the magazine sent the reader to a URL. The subscriber had to give a credit card number, which was charged if they didn't cancel after 12 issues.
- *Latina* magazine pushed the concept of a hard offer a tad by giving subscribers a chance to receive a red satin cosmetic bag quicker if they paid immediately.

Other, more general tricks that can create a connection with a potential reader, include the following:

- Stamps look more real and personal than metered mail.
- First-class stamps get to the reader faster than third class, but seldom have an effect on the response rate.
- An address printed right on the envelope is more effective than a label.
- Classy paper—soft white book and antique finishes—works better than cheaper and thinner slick white. ∎

prototype is to show advertisers and other investors how the proposed title will look.

Successful magazine launches include budgets for an advertising staff that will take a prototype of the proposed magazine to potential advertisers and get commitments for future advertising. When *Wood* was still in the planning stages, founding editor Larry Clayton took a prototype to woodworking conventions and sold potential advertisers on the new magazine.

sponsored circulation

Magazines can sell subscriptions through third-party, or sponsored circulation agencies, such as sweepstakes and subscription houses. This is often a good deal for the agency, but less of a deal for the publisher. Organizations such as Publishers' Clearinghouse get a percentage of the sale of each magazine as an incentive. Sometimes called "dirty subscriptions," sweepstakes can yield high response rates but lower payment rates than non-sweepstake subscriptions. While sweepstakes may provide the magazine with loyal readers, more often they're the source of one-time trials from consumers who are looking for a bargain and hoping to see Ed McMahon after the Super Bowl. Interestingly, sweepstakes offers don't have to be significantly lower than the normal subscription price to work.

In 2005, the ABC disqualified circulation numbers from some subscription agencies, such as EBSCO Consumer Magazine Services and InFlight programs because, once the publisher paid the agency, there was no profit left, meaning the resulting subscriptions were not actually paid. ABC instituted new rules requiring all paid circulations to result in some profit to the publisher, meaning that paid subscriptions were, therefore, paid.

Successful new partnerships have replaced some of the reliance on sponsored subscriptions. *Sports Illustrated* and *Entertainment Weekly* are sold to Ticketron customers, a neat fit with sports and entertainment buffs.

Ida Tarbell's history of the Standard Oil Company cost *McClure's* magazine around $4,000 per article and Lincoln Steffens's stories on American cities cost $2,000 each. Both were published in *McClure's* January 1903 issue.

value added

Publishers often send extra goodies as incentives for buying their magazine: A "Hidden Pictures Calendar" from *Highlights for Children*, a retirement planning book from *Kiplinger's,* canvas duffle bags from *American Artist.* After 9/11, the nature of premiums changed: Scissors and knives were replaced by security devices such as radios with flashlights and sirens.

renewals

The source of the original subscription affects the renewal rate. Renewals from direct mail range from 35–50 percent. That is, 35–50 percent of those who subscribed to the magazine through a direct mailing will renew once their subscriptions expire. Insert cards bring 50–60 percent renewals. The Internet is still too young as an original source of subscriptions, but analysts suggest it will end up rivaling direct mail at a much lower cost. Hard offers bring healthier renewal rates than soft.

To cut costs and improve efficiency, publishers promote multiple-year subscriptions for renewals. Much of publishing is built on renewal rates. In general, renewals cost less money than new business. It costs about 50 cents to send an average renewal bill for a magazine—the average cost of a direct mailing. That bill sent to an existing subscriber, however, could be the publisher's only cost, while the direct mailing often has to be followed up with a bill. Subscribers who sign up online can usually be reached by e-mail, significantly reducing the cost of the renewal reminder.

■ FREQUENCY

To be economically viable, magazines should be published at least four times a year. Magazines published less frequently have trouble building an advertising or subscription base and getting news-

MARCH 2006: In 2007, *The Atlantic Monthly* celebrates its 150th anniversary. Despite its name, it is published only 10 times a year.

stand placement. Common publication schedules are weekly, biweekly, monthly, bimonthly, and 10 times a year.

Time, *Newsweek*, and *Business Week* choose the weekly frequency because they provide a great deal of timely material and compete more directly with other media produced daily, such as newspapers and television. Other titles such as *Coin World*, *US Weekly*, *The Nation*, and *The New Yorker* publish weekly to provide interpretation and analysis on breaking news and issues.

Fortune is biweekly—published every 2 weeks—which the publishers believe gives the magazine the impact of a weekly, but with the luxury of having twice the time for production.

Monthly titles, including *National Fisherman*, *Glamour*, and *Texas Monthly*, offer readers and advertisers regular coverage, but at a slower pace that allows them to reduce staff and production costs and gives them more lead time for development of stories.

Jewish Voice Today, *Military History*, and *PC Tools* are bimonthly—published every two months.

The *Wilson Quarterly* is just that: published four times a year.

Some magazines customize their frequencies: *The Atlantic Monthly* is published 10 times a year. Although *Sports Illustrated* is technically a weekly, it is published only 50 weeks a year. *Cowboys and Indians* is published eight times a year.

Karla Jeffries, vice president of finance and administration of Meredith Publishing's Magazine Group, said the decision to increase frequency from 6 to 10 times a year is primarily ad driven. Usually, the company cannot increase the subscription cost enough to justify the added production costs. Subscription buyers, Jeffries said, simply do not see enough value in added frequency to pay for it. That is, if they get a magazine six times a year for $12, they are paying $2 per issue. At that rate, they would have to pay $20 a year for 10 issues. Their magazine, then, would have gone from costing $12 to costing $20 a year; the shock of the increased cost is not offset by the benefit of the four extra issues.

The 10 times a year frequency is often a substitute for a monthly schedule. January and July are slow advertising sales months for these magazines, so they print combined January/February and July/August issues.

■ ADVERTISING RATES

Ad income is projected by determining ad rates, advertising-to-editorial ratio, CPMs, and discounts.

full-color ad rate

New publishers may look wistfully at the ad rates for major magazines—$279,450 for a full-color page for *Sports Illustrated*, $135,500 for *Glamour*, and $124,645 for *Rolling Stone*. The important consideration is how much the competition charges, and how closely a new launch can approximate the value given by that competitor. Like newsstand and subscription rates, these can be tested, but the tests are not scientific. Generally, they depend on committed ad sales people getting the magazine's message to advertising agencies and product managers.

A new magazine might start with a low advertising rate or increase discounts for new advertisers

Public Relations Techniques: Innovation Sells

Public relations experts find ways to make the magazine newsworthy so that it is covered as a news event in the media. These experts send out publicity releases to the other media and plan special events and promotions to emphasize, or even create, newsworthy issues related to the magazine. The limits of magazine public relations extend to the limits of the staff's creativity.

Publicity Releases

A newsworthy magazine might merit a mention in the other media, especially in the many "What's New" or "People in the News" departments in newspapers, magazines, and on television. Newsworthiness might be found in content, staff, the magazine's history, its offices, in how it matches contemporary social norms, or in how it marches to a different drummer.

Talk Show Appearances

Never underestimate the power of Oprah. What unique, lively, quirky, heartwarming, or otherwise newsworthy stories does the new magazine offer that might appeal to a local, regional, or national talk show audience?

Special Events

Magazines may sponsor a cooking contest with the proceeds going to the homeless. Or organize a concert of bands on the rise. Or plan an expedition to the Grand Canyon de-signed specifically for urbanites. An essential element of these events is that they are newsworthy. Wouldn't *60 Minutes* love to watch a group of well-dressed New Yorkers skid down the rim of America's largest canyon?

Special Promotions

A magazine might create a board game based on the magazine's philosophy, offer design worksheets for fledgling designers based on the magazine's grid, or give schools a special discount for using the magazine in discussion groups. All have the basic goal of getting the magazine into as many readers' hands as possible. ■

to get the magazine rolling. Occasionally publishers offer virtually cost-free advertising for the first few issues, in return for the promise that the advertiser will buy space in future issues. This is especially true in test issues. Some advertisers jump at this; others avoid it. No advertiser wants to be in a dead magazine—or being caught in the casket with the corpse, as advertising people poetically call it.

advertising pages per issue

This is part of the magazine's formula. A magazine with an advertising-to-editorial ratio of 40:60 would have 40 pages of advertising and 60 of editorial for every 100 pages.

cost per thousand

Cost per thousand, or CPM, is the cost for an advertiser to reach 1,000 readers. CPMs help advertisers determine the relative value of a magazine ad. (See chapter 2 for a more thorough explanation.) Rates are based on a full-color, full-page ad running in the magazine only once. If an ad costs $10,000 a page for a magazine with 100,000 circulation, the CPM is $100, meaning it costs $100 to reach 1,000 readers. An ad that costs $100,000 a page in a magazine with 1 million circulation also has a CPM of $100, so it also costs $100 to reach 1,000 readers. *Outside* has a verified circulation of 650,000 and a full-page, full-color ad rate of $73,670, yielding a CPM of $113. (Here's the math: 650,000 divided by 1,000 equals 650, or 650 thousand readers. Divide $73,670 by 650 and you'll get $113, or a cost of $113 for 1,000 readers.)

Publishers want the highest CPM they can manage, and ad buyers want the lowest. Advertisers will pay a premium, however, for a premium audience. *Vibe* has a CPM of $104, *Rolling Stone* $96, and *Maxim* $76. All are dwarfed, however, by some controlled circulation titles. *WorkBoat*, for example, has 25,000 circulation and a $3,090 ad page rate, for an enviable CPM of $124. *Pharmaceutical and Medical Packaging News*, which goes to a small but elite audience of 20,000 buyers of medical equipment, supplies, and services, sells a full-page black-and-white ad for $4,315 a page, meaning a CPM of $216. Add $850 per page for each additional color.

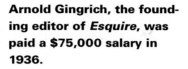

Arnold Gingrich, the founding editor of *Esquire*, was paid a $75,000 salary in 1936.

rate base

Advertisers buy readership, so ad costs are based to a great degree on number of readers. A magazine with 100,000 verified readers has a rate base of 100,000. Because a magazine must publish for a year before it is audited by the ABC, the rate base for the first issues is a projection. It must be an honest projection, however, or the magazine will lose whatever advertisers it has attracted, if they find that the 100,000 rate base they were promised is actually 50,000. Had the ad buyers planned for 50,000 to begin with, many of them would be satisfied.

Average Discount Advertisers seldom pay full rate for an ad. How much is discounted per ad should be determined when the magazine is still in its planning stages. Advertising discounts are usually determined by frequency of ad placement. An advertiser who advertises in six issues pays less per ad than the advertiser who takes out an ad for only one issue. All magazines offer some sort of frequency discount.

Outside's 2005 full-color full-page rate for one-time placement was $73,670. For placement 12 times, this was reduced to $65,565, meaning a discount of 11 percent.

Discounts may also be given based on the advertiser's or magazine's special circumstances. These are determined by what the market will bear and are not listed in the rate card. If you're the first magazine in your class and advertisers see that they can get to readers who are simply not accessible elsewhere, they may pay a premium. Conversely, if you're in a crowded field, you may have to offer discounts to lure some advertisers; that is, your sales people may "sell off the card," or sell the ads for less than they are listed on the rate card.

Occasionally, a magazine faces the challenge of "selling the category," or convincing advertisers that a need—and readership—exists for such a magazine. *Ms.* had to sell advertisers on a whole new audience of women consumers who were looking for products advertisers hadn't yet considered targeting at women—cars, computers, and investments.

Average Advertising Revenue per Page This is the ad rate per page minus the discount. An ad that sells for $3,500 per full color page with a 40 percent discount brings in $2,100 per page.

■ CIRCULATION RATES

American newsstands sold some $3 billion in magazines in 2004 and subscribers paid more than $7 billion a year for their magazines.[8] How does a magazine determine this cost to readers? It's a complicated formula based on reader income, the state of the economy, discounts, the advertising-to-editorial ratio, and supply and demand.

reader income

In 1932, *Esquire* was founded to appeal to the man of the "new leisure class," a fellow who clearly had money in addition to time. The magazine sold for a princely 50 cents, compared with the popular *Saturday Evening Post*'s cover price of 5 cents.[9] *Esquire*'s first issue sold out.

Buying Versus Starting a Magazine: A Dollars and Cents View

Assuming you have a few million dollars and you can't figure out what to do with it, should you buy an existing magazine or start your own? Start-ups offer publishers and entrepreneurs a creative challenge and reward. From a strictly fiscal perspective, though, accountants consider the following issues.

Buying

Publishers who purchase an established magazine usually pay roughly 10 times its yearly operating profit. If it has an operating profit of $30 million, the standard purchase price would be $300 million. Some publishers have purchased magazines for 15–17 times their profit, but it is hard to recoup those costs. Variables specific to individual publishers can affect the purchase price. A buyer who might be able to reduce costs and improve profit might be willing to pay more for a magazine. Large publishing houses can reduce production costs though lower paper costs and better printing bids because they have bargaining clout with printing plants. They can also reduce staff members by consolidating service people with those already in the company.

Starting

Publishers expect a new magazine to operate in the red until its fifth year. Then, they look at the profit they can make after that and consider what opportunities they would have lost because they were losing money on the title. It can take up to 12 years to really see an overall profit, when cumulative costs and lost opportunities are factored in. By then, though, the publisher can sell the magazine at a nice profit.

Establishing the Brand

When starting a magazine, a publisher has to build brand recognition and loyalty. When buying an existing title, that is already done. ■

The cost of a magazine is directly related to the audience's ability to pay. *Architectural Digest* can ask $6 per issue because its readers are in America's top income tiers. *TV Guide*, by contrast, sells to a middle-class audience for a middle-of-the-road $1.99 an issue. Magazines for Generation X buyers recognize that this young audience has a good deal of purchasing power, with *Wired* selling for $4.95.

state of the economy

As the economy changes and other products increase in price, so do magazines. In 1970, when one of the authors bought her first *Ms.* for $1, she also bought a brand-new avocado-green Chevy Nova for $3,000. Interestingly, the magazine is still intact, settled comfortably in a file drawer, while the Nova has long since rusted away. The current *Ms.* on her coffee table has a $5.95 cover price, while the 1994 hunter-green Honda Civic EX in her garage sported a sticker price of $17,000. Soon the 1970 *Ms.* will be worth more than the Honda.

Average single-copy prices increased 64 percent from 1994 to 2004 (from $2.81 to $4.40) while subscription prices decreased 9 percent (from $28.51 to $25.93),[10] demonstrating the deep discounts publishers offer to subscribers.

Smart magazine entrepreneurs match their magazine launches with the economy. In a "down market," when other consumer goods are selling poorly, chances are a magazine won't sell well, either. The growth in magazines for personal investing, for example, was a logical development in the 1990s, when personal income was up.

There's always an exception, however. *Esquire* was started in 1933 at the deepest depths of the

Finding Fulfillment

Several companies nationwide are in the business of serving subscribers of magazines throughout the country. Called circulation fulfillment houses, they process all subscription-related paperwork: billings and renewals, memberships, label preparation, postal presorting, and subscription file updating. They offer customer service to subscribers and create circulation projections for publishers. In many cases, when you contact your favorite magazine about a subscription, you're dealing with a company that has no connection with producing that magazine.

Some large companies do their own fulfillment, but increasingly it is cheaper to hire the work done by an outside company. One of the largest fulfillment houses, Communications Data Service, or CDS, grew out of the fulfillment department of *Look* magazine, in Des Moines, Iowa. When the magazine folded, the fulfillment staff continued its service to outside clients. CDS now serves more than 400 magazines and 150 million subscribers.

Other large houses include Swet Information Services, which works with 65,000 publishers worldwide; Kable News Company, which serves 400 magazines and more than 100 subscribers; and Strategic Fulfillment Group, which manages more than 32 million customer names. ■

Great Depression. Its founders expected to sell it through men's clothing stores—using the magazine almost as a catalog—with only a handful going to newsstands. The demand was so great on the newsstand that the magazine's staff took the copies out of the stores and sold them on the newsstand.

Fortune, one of America's primary business magazines, likewise saw its start in 1930, only months after the stock market crashed. Readers who were losing their fortunes needed help and perspective. For a financial magazine, the timing was excellent.

subscription discounts

Subscription prices are often discounted so that subscribers pay only 50–60 percent—and sometimes only 10 percent—of what they would pay if they bought the magazine on the newsstand. Many editors challenge this practice because they believe the discounts cheapen the value of their magazine and increase the magazine's reliance on other sources of income, primarily advertising.

People showed a profit in 18 months. Sports Illustrated took 9 years to show a profit, at a loss of $20 million. Both were started by Time-Life and are still published by the same company, which is now Time Warner.

advertising-to-editorial ratio

Magazines determine up front how much advertising will subsidize the magazine. While it might seem logical that magazines with low ad pages would have higher cover prices than magazines with a high number of ad pages, such is not always the case, as anybody who reads *Cosmopolitan*, *Harper's Bazaar*, or *Elle* knows. It all depends on what the market will bear.

supply and demand

Readers can influence the cost of a magazine through their interest in a particular title. In 1970, *Ms.* was founded with an economic philosophy that maintained that readers, not advertisers, should pay the bulk of the magazine's costs, so the editors slapped on a cover price of $1. This compared with 39 cents for *Woman's Day*. *Ms.* was the first magazine of its kind, and readers signed up because it offered information and perspective not available elsewhere at the time. That first issue of *Ms.* sold out.

Magazine prices change with the times, as do prices of all consumer goods. Some magazines, though, like *Esquire* and *Ms.*, start out by pushing the envelope with a high price on an initial issue. Readers follow, and so do other magazines. Competitors sniffed when *Ms.* expected readers to spend $1 an issue. When readers anted up, these competitors turned around and raised their own prices.

At least one media critic pointed out in retrospect that Watergate encouraged *Time* and *Newsweek* to raise their cover prices. After all, the news magazines were selling the latest Watergate revelation week after week during an inflationary period when prices of everything—bread, candy bars, cigarettes—were rising. So why not the cost of news? Wrote media critic Edwin Diamond: "In April 1973, when Nixon fired John Dean, the price of a trial subscription to either [*Time* or *Newsweek*] was pegged at 16 cents. By the fall, when the Senate Watergate hearings in the summer of 1973 had run their course, the *Newsweek* and *Time* trial-subscription price had reached 20 cents. A year later, when the House Judiciary Committee began debating articles of impeachment, the trial-subscription price hit 30 cents and the newsstand price 60 cents."[11]

According to *Newsweek* circulation director Robert Riordan, "It was a seller's market for us. We decided to seize the day."[12] By the end of 1974, *Newsweek* had reached a pricing structure of 37.5 cents per copy to subscribers and 75 cents on the newsstands; *Time* was close

at 35 cents for subscribers and 75 cents on the newsstand. The coverage of Watergate resulted in a circulation profit center for both magazines.

■ SUBSCRIPTIONS AND MEMBERSHIPS

Americans buy most of their magazines through subscriptions: Only 14 percent are sold on the newsstand, and 86 percent are sold through subscriptions.[13] Increases in postal rates have deeply affected magazine distribution. A Magazine Publishers of America Postal Committee has worked with Congress to privatize postal delivery and to make postal price setting more flexible and less time-consuming.

Most trade and organization titles are subscription-only, with the exception of some mass interest titles such as *Adweek, MacWorld,* or *Smithsonian.* Many trade publications are built primarily on controlled circulation. Association magazines depend on memberships. Both trade and association publications may have paid subscribers as well.

controlled circulation

Subscribers of *WorkBoat* magazine pay nothing for the magazine because they are highly appealing buyers of products advertised within the magazine. The magazine earns 98 percent of its income from advertising because manufacturers of commercial boats and related equipment know the magazine provides them with a select audience of readers who are buyers—commercial fishermen. Subscribers must sign a form validating the fact that they are in the fishing business.

Trade publications spend a great deal of time qualifying readers. It pays off for them, though, because they know exactly the size of their audience when they are producing the magazine and have to print only the quantity of magazines they'll actually need.

Martha Stewart Living stock doubled while she was in prison. It rose from $17 when she went to prison in October 2004 to $34 when she was released in March 2005.

MARCH 2006: Because it reaches a premium audience, *WorkBoat* **can ask a premium rate for advertising.**

memberships

While association magazines are supported by readers in the form of memberships, some associations go beyond membership and make their publications available to nonmember subscribers. Membership does have its privileges, though, and in some instances, access to the online version of a print magazine is limited to members only. A subscription to the print and online versions of *Food Technology* magazine is part of the membership of the Institute of Food technologists; for online access, nonmember subscribers have to register a second time. *AAUW Outlook*, the magazine of the American Association of University Women, goes to 100,000 members and to 550 nonmember subscribers, most of which are libraries.

The circulation numbers of association magazines may be small, but they can be mighty, as is the case with *Communication World*, published by the International Association of Business Communicators, with 13,000 members across the globe, 57 percent of whom hold leadership positions in corporations, the government, educational institutions, and associations.

■ DISTRIBUTION

The greatest product in the world has little value if it can't get to the consumer. Getting magazines to their readers has been a struggle for magazine publishers, with distribution costs increasing decade after decade.

single copy

Thirty-eight percent of single-copy sales are made in supermarkets, where magazines are one of the most profitable product categories. National chain stores such as Kmart and Wal-Mart, however, are rapidly becoming the dominant retailers of magazines.[14]

Magazine distribution was restructured significantly in 1996, when the number of wholesalers who delivered magazines to the newsstands was drastically reduced. Retailers are getting increasingly picky about the titles they will sell and the wholesalers they will use to get those titles to the racks. Wal-Mart, which had been using 154 wholesalers, cut down to 3 in 1997.

The implications of this change is that magazine quality is more and more important, as is cover price. Smaller publishers are finding it more difficult to get on the newsstand. Retailers are also receiving more of the cover price. At the beginning of the 1990s, retailers had received 20 percent of the cover price; by 2004 the gross profit was 33.6 percent.

Consumer marketer Baird David recommends a 3:1 ratio between cover price and the promoted cost of the magazine in direct mail materials. That is, a magazine that promotes itself to potential subscribers at $14.99 for 12 issues is promising each issue for $1.25. Multiply that by three, and you get a cover price of $3.75. Baird says publishers can safely round this up to $3.99, but no higher.[15]

Another single-copy option is direct distribution, or selling the magazine through specialty stores either instead of or in addition to selling it through newsstands. *Cigar Aficionado* is sold through cigar stores, *Print* at art stores, and *The Source* at record stores. All are also sold on the newsstand.

Publishers offering controlled circulations are required by the Postal Service to show proof that more than 50 percent of all mailed magazines go to qualified subscribers.

sell-through rates

Newsstand marketing is an inexact science. One newsstand may sell only half its copies of an individual title, while another may not have enough to fill demand. The number of copies given to the newsstand divided by the number of copies sold is the sell-through rate. A magazine that gives 10,000 copies to the newsstand and sells 5,000 has a sell-through rate of 50 percent. According to John Harrington, publisher of *The New Single-Copy Newsletter*, the industry-wide average sell-through rate is 34 percent.[16]

The premiere issue of *Latina* sold 200,000 copies on the newsstand, which was a 40 percent sell-through. In 2004, *Maxim* had a 44 percent sell-through average, and its competition, *FHM*, averaged 43 percent.[17]

Controlled circulation magazines have no sell-through problem because their readership numbers are predetermined.

executive summary of profitability

The section of the business plan that offers an overview of finances is called the executive summary of profitability. It builds directly on the marketing plan, and it typically spans 5 years. Some experts recommend using modeling software to create this executive summary. Plug in the numbers you know and the programs can help determine related costs and income. Modeling software can project direct mail or insert card response rates, the

Using outside auditing firms can significantly improve a magazine's bottom line. Some Hispanic titles have shown reluctance in taking this step, but recent research demonstrates that audits can give a magazine more clout and credibility. Consistently audited Hispanic publications sold an average of $2.5 million in advertising in 2004, while those that are occasionally audited sold an average of only $1.3 million. Hispanic publications that have never been audited sold an average of only $560,000.

relationships between ad and circulation revenue, and costs associated with each.

The magazine profiled in the business plan executive summary of profitability in Table 6.2 is a new launch that loses money the first 4 years and shows a profit the fifth year. This plan is based on the belief that it costs money to make money and that a series of planned losses can be the basis for substantial profit. The magazine loses money while it establishes itself.

For the first 2 years, the magazine will be bimonthly—published six times a year—which gives it a regular presence on the newsstand and in reader mailboxes while at the same time eliminating the costs associated with more regular production; as reader and advertising loyalty grow, the magazine's potential for profit grows, and its frequency is expanded to 10 times a year.

The magazine starts with a circulation of 100,000, based on comparisons of competing magazines. It grows steadily to a goal of 275,000 in the fifth year, again based on the track records of similar magazines. Throughout the 5 years, subscriptions outnumber newsstand sales. In the first year, the difference is negligible—55,000 subscriptions sold versus 45,000 in newsstand sales. By the fifth year, however, the magazine sells almost twice as many copies through subscriptions as by the newsstand—180,000 subscriptions versus 95,000 newsstand sales. The logic of this approach is that new buyers will find the magazine initially on the newsstand, develop product loyalty, and become subscribers.

■ INCOME

The subscription price begins at $12 a year for 6 issues and grows to $24 when the magazine expands to 10 issues a year. Initially, then, the subscriber pays $2 an issue. This grows to $2.40 an issue as the magazine grows in size and popularity. The

■ **Table 6.2**   Business Plan Executive Summary of Profitability

	PERCENTAGE	YEAR 1	PERCENTAGE	YEAR 2	PERCENTAGE	YEAR 3	PERCENTAGE	YEAR 4	PERCENTAGE	YEAR 5
Number of issues per year		6		6		10		10		10
Total circulation		100,000		150,000		200,000		250,000		275,000
Number of subscribers		55,000		91,000		132,000		170,000		180,000
Number of newsstand sales		45,000		59,000		68,000		80,000		95,000
Subscription price		$12		$12		$24		$24		$24
Cover price		$2.95		$2.95		$3.50		$3.50		$3.95
Ad:Edit ratio		40:60		40:60		50:50		50:50		50:50
Advertising pages per issue		40		48		60		70		70
Editorial pages per issue		60		72		60		70		70
Total pages		100		120		120		140		140
CPM		$70.00		$70.00		$70.00		$70.00		$70.00
Rate base		100,000		150,000		200,000		250,000		275,000
Full-color ad rate		$7,000		$10,500		$14,000		$17,500		$19,250
Average discount		40%		36%		36%		36%		34%
Average ad revenue per page		$4,200		$6,720		$8,960		$11,200		$12,705
Revenues										
Subscriptions	32	$660,000	31	$1,092,000	33	$3,168,000	31	$4,080,000	29	$4,320,000
Single-copy sales	19	$398,250	15	$522,150	12	$1,190,000	11	$1,400,000	12	$1,876,250
Advertising	49	$1,008,000	55	$1,935,360	55	$5,376,000	59	$7,840,000	59	$8,893,500
Total revenues	**100**	**$2,066,250**	**100**	**$3,549,510**	**100**	**$9,734,000**	**100**	**$13,320,000**	**100**	**$15,089,750**
Expenses										
Advertising	23	$475,000	22	$788,000	20	$1,991,000	20	$2,670,000	16	$2,414,000
Subscriptions	25	$517,000	25	$886,000	24	$2,351,000	24	$3,156,000	22	$3,320,000
Single-copy sales	16	$331,000	12	$432,000	11	$1,023,000	10	$1,307,000	10	$1,509,000
Editorial	10	$207,000	10	$345,000	10	$958,000	10	$1,340,000	10	$1,509,000
Production	18	$372,000	18	$642,000	18	$1,773,000	18	$2,413,000	17	$2,565,000
Distribution	11	$227,000	11	$375,000	11	$1,090,000	11	$1,454,000	11	$1,660,000
Administrative costs	8	$165,000	8	$275,000	8	$797,000	8	$1,089,000	8	$1,207,000
Total expenses	**111**	**$2,294,000**	**105**	**$3,743,000**	**103**	**$9,983,000**	**101**	**$13,429,000**	**94**	**$14,184,000**
Net income (loss)		**($227,750)**		**($193,490)**		**($249,000)**		**($109,000)**		**$905,750**
Cumulative income (loss)		($227,750)		($421,240)		($670,240)		($779,240)		$126,510

cover price increases slightly from a rather low $2.95 to an equally reasonable $3.95. The staff's philosophy is that subscribers and newsstand buyers should pay similar prices for the magazine. If this noble philosophy doesn't pan out, the subscription price can be reduced and the newsstand price increased.

Subscription income was determined by multiplying the subscription rate by the number of subscribers. In the first year, this was $12 × 55,000, for a yearly subscription income of $660,000. Single copy income is a little trickier because of retailer and wholesaler discounts. In Table 6.2, single copy income was determined by multiplying the cover price by the frequency by the number of single copy sales. For the first year, this is $2.95 × 6 × 45,000, for gross single-copy income of $796,500. Magazines don't see this gross income, however; they see the net income, or income after the discounts are paid to the retailers and wholesalers. In Table 6.2, the total discount was computed at 50 percent, so the single-copy income of $675,000 was reduced by half, for a net income of $398,250.

The magazine begins with an advertising-editorial ratio of 40:60, which balances out to 50:50 by the fifth year. The magazine grows slightly in pages throughout the 5 years, from a total of 100 to a total of 140. The second and third years have the same total pages—120—but a different ad:edit ratio, so the second year has 48 ad pages, and the third year has 60. The magazine staff feels it is important to start with a magazine that is close to the size of the final, established magazine. The product, after all, must be substantial if it is to appeal to a growing base of readers.

The CPM remains standard at $70, which is the CPM of other magazines reaching the same audience. The ad rate increases as circulation increases. In the first year, the rate base is 100—based on 100,000 projected circulation (55,000 subscription and 45,000 newsstand)—and, therefore, the ad rate is $7,000 ($70 CPM × 100 rate base). As the rate base grows, so does the ad rate, to a final $19,250 in the fifth year ($70 CPM × 275 rate base). The magazine projects an initial advertising

discount of 40 percent, which drops in 5 years to 34 percent. Initially, the discount provides advertisers with an incentive for multiple ad placements. The incentive becomes less sizable as the magazine's reputation and reader loyalty grow. The ad income per page is the actual ad rate minus the discount. In the first year, the $7,000 per page rate is reduced by 40 percent, or $2,800, to yield final ad income per page of $4,200.

■ EXPENSES

Projections of magazine expenses require an ability to look into the economic future while understanding and remembering the past. Magazine staffers study past performance, analyze future trends, and use this information to build an economic plan that guides the creation of a financially feasible magazine.

Expenses are based on revenue. If you want to spend $1 million printing a magazine, you'd better have a lot more than that million in revenue—usually $5–$7 million. New magazines must spend proportionally more on advertising, subscription, single copy, and distribution than established magazines because they are paying to sell themselves to new readers, advertisers, wholesalers, and retailers. Editorial costs are usually proportionally the same for a new start-up as for an established magazine, although some new magazines may offer staff members a percentage of the profits in exchange for lower initial salaries. Some administrative costs can be reduced by renting low-cost offices and putting off major equipment buys.

Production costs are probably the least stable expenses, therefore the most difficult to project. Magazine budgets have been decimated when paper prices have risen or when production technology has changed and required new equipment.

One tenet should serve as a guide when determining expense projections: A magazine will always cost more than you think.

In creating expense projections, staff members have to determine how much they can reasonably

Immediately after September 11, 2001, publishers eliminated plain envelopes in direct mail promotions, in response to the public's fears of contaminated letters.

Magazine Salaries: A Glimpse at the Field

Today's magazine salaries are reflective of a field that includes both paupers and princes. Many lucrative jobs exist in New York City, which has one of the highest costs of living in the country; magazine professionals there need significantly higher incomes to be able to live at the same level as their counterparts in the heart of the country. The West—principally San Francisco and Los Angeles—are providing competitive salaries that have knocked New York out of position as the best-paid area for magazine editors. The Northeast brings the top salaries for advertising sales directors, however, with the West at the bottom of the scale.

Folio: magazine annually surveys editors, art directors, circulation directors and managers, production directors and managers, and ad sales directors throughout the country and uses that data to report on average trade and consumer magazine salaries, ranked according to variables such as job title, magazine size, the editors' years of experience; and region of the country.

Some highlights from the 2005 *Folio:* survey, looking at the top editorial and advertising positions, follow. Unless otherwise noted, salaries are means, or averages.

Editorial Director

Consumer magazines: $97,000
Business-to-business
  magazines: $85,900
Highest reported for consumer
  magazines: $250,000
Highest reported for business-
  to-business magazines:
  $160,000
Geographic differences:
  West: $101,300
  South: $93,100
  Northeast: $84,700
  Midwest: $81,000
Gender differences:
  Males: $90,000
  Females: $85,000
Age variables:
  9 years or less in industry:
    $60,300
  10–19 years in industry:
    $86,300
  More than 20 years in
    industry: $97,900
Company revenue:
  Less than $3 million:
    $68,300
  $3 million to $9.9 million:
    $91,500

$10 million or more:
  $97,200[1]

Advertising Sales Director

Consumer magazines:
  $90,400
Business-to-business
  magazines: $90,600
Geographic differences:
  Northeast: $109,600
  Midwest: $73,100
  South: $70,100
  West: $73,300
Gender differences:
  Males: $93,100
  Females: $75,000
Experience variables:
  9 years or less in industry:
    $75,300
  10–19 years in industry:
    $91,100
  20 or more years in
    industry: $91,300
Company revenue:
  Less than $10 million:
    $63,100
  $3 million or more:
    $108,500[2]

To determine a salary range based on location, experience, and company size, try the online salary calculator from *Folio:* at http://www.readexsurvey.com/ foliosalcalc/salary.asp. ■

1. Matt Kinsman, "*Folio*'s 2005 Editorial Management Salary Survey," *Folio:* (August 1, 2005), http://www.m10report.com/index.php?id=396&backPID=396&tt_news=1074.

2. "*Folio* 2004 Advertising Sales Survey," *Folio:* (August 31, 2005), http://www.m10report.com/index.php?id=396&backPID=396&tt_news=1150.

limit expenses in one area to support costs in another and how much loss they can sustain for how long. Magazines with major investors also have to present a plan that shows a significant enough profit in time to encourage investors to take a risk.

Clinkscales said the business plan "answers the most important question of the investor, namely, How much and when are you going to pay me back?"

Table 6.2 demonstrates expense projections for a new magazine, plus an explanation of how those projections were determined. All expenses are based on total projected revenue. The staff determines how much income the magazine can make and bases expenses on that income. Projected expenses in Table 6.2 are modeled on industry standards, based on the percentages given in Table 6.1.

However, Table 6.1 represents established magazines and shows an overall profit for an established title of 17 percent. That is unrealistic for a start-up, so Table 6.2 gets the magazine into the black more realistically by year 5, with a 6 percent profit. It will take several more years for it to reach the industry standard of 17 percent. In fact, some industry critics charge that this large a profit is unethical and goes to CEOs and stockholders, rather than to the staffs that create the magazine. Magazines owned by large publishing houses typically require a larger profit—to pay corporate overhead and stockholders—than independently owned publications that do not have this extra layer of costs.

The established magazines in Figure 6.1 spent an average of 9 percent of total revenues on advertising. The start-up magazine in Table 6.2 spends 23 percent on advertising in its first year, when it is trying to develop a presence, and decreases that yearly, ending up spending 16 percent on advertising in its fifth year, when it is more established.

The percentages used in Table 6.2 are projections, or hypothetical figures based on the best assumptions available at the time and interpreted as wisely as possible. Because business plans are readings of the future, they have to be as honestly close to reality as possible. That reality can change, however, as the economy bumps up or down.

The magazine loses money for the first 4 years, spending more than it can make. It spends proportionally more (a higher percentage than the industry standard) on advertising, subscription, and single-copy costs in the first few years to build its audience base. Costs for editorial, production, distribution, and administration remain proportionally the same through the 5 years.

The percentages of revenue projected as expenses in the first year follow. All expenses, except for the final operating income or loss, are rounded to the nearest 1,000. (For example, advertising expenses are actually $475,237.50, but we rounded this to $475,000 to simplify things—at least a little.)

Advertising: 23 percent (.23 × $2,066,250 total revenue = $475,000)

Subscriptions: 25 percent (.25 × $2,066,250 = $517,000)

Single Copy: 16 percent (.16 × $2,066,250 = $331,000)

Editorial: 10 percent (.10 × $2,066,250 = $207,000)

Production: 18 percent (.18 × $2,066,250 = $372,000)

Distribution: 11 percent (.11 × $2,066,250 = $227,000)

Administration: 8 percent (.08 × $2,066,250 = $165,000)

Total Costs: 111 percent (1.11 × $2,066,250 = $2,294,000)

Operating Loss: 11 percent (.11 × $2,066,250 = $227,750)

Operating loss can also, of course, be determined by subtracting expenses from income:

$$\begin{array}{r} \$2{,}066{,}250 \text{ projected income} \\ - \underline{\$2{,}294{,}000 \text{ projected expenses}} \\ (\$227{,}750 \text{ operating loss}) \end{array}$$

By the fifth year, expense percentages have changed to:

Advertising: 16 percent (.16 × $15,089,750 total revenue = $2,414,000)

Subscriptions: 22 percent (.22 × $15,089,750 = $3,320,000)

Single Copy: 10 percent (.10 × $15,089,750 = $1,509,000)

Editorial: 10 percent (.10 × $15,089,750 = $1,509,000)

Production: 17 percent (.17 × $15,089,750 = $2,565,000)

Distribution: 11 percent (.11 × $15,089,750 = $1,660,000)

Administration: 8 percent (.08 × $15,089,750 = $1,207,000)

Total Costs: 94 percent (.94 × $15,089,750 = $14,184,000)

Operating Profit: 6 percent (.06 × $15,089,750 = $905,000)

Operating profit can also, of course, be determined by subtracting expenses from income:

$15,089,750 projected income
− $14,184,000 projected expenses
$ 905,750 operating profit

Because we rounded the figures, we end up with an extra $750 that shows up when we do the straight subtraction, but not when we do the percentages. This is a downside of rounding numbers, but the simplification is worth the occasional discrepancy.

For the first year, the magazine loses 11 percent. Losses are reduced until the magazine earns a small profit in the fifth year. The magazine loses 5 percent in the second year, 3 percent in the third year, and 1 percent in the fourth year. It earns a 6 percent profit in the fifth year. By the sixth and seventh years, the magazine should aim for at least a 9–10 percent profit.

The final year profit, though, is not the end of the story. Each year's loss must be added to the previous loss for a cumulative loss or profit. In this case, the magazine loses $227,750 the first year, $193,490 the second, $249,000 the third, and $109,000 the fourth, for a cumulative loss over the 4 years of $779,240. When the magazine finally makes a profit in the fifth year, the cumulative loss is subtracted from the $905,750 profit for a cumulative gain of $126,510.

The business plan, Clinkscales said, is a process, not a destination, and it will change several times before a new magazine is actually launched. A good plan must be flexible.

Most important, he said, is that the plan should be built on a quality product. A well-conceived and articulated editorial philosophy and formula are the heart of the business plan. "Without the product, you have nothing," Clinkscales said. "It is virtually impossible for good business to save a bad product."[18]

notes

1. "Direct Mail—the Good News and the Bad," *Circulation Management* (October 12, 2005), http://circman.com/Circulation_Management_Article.445+M51ff8649e97.0.html?&tx_ttnews[swords]=in%20the%20mail.
2. Meghan Hamill, "What's New in the Mail," *Circulation Management* (June 1, 2005), www.circman.com/ar/Circulation_Management.445%20M5af87d8b4cb.0.html?&tx_ttnews%5Btt_news%5D=102-76k.
3. "Direct Mail," *Circulation Management* (October 12, 2005), op. cit.
4. Ibid.
5. "Direct Mail," *Circulation Management* (October 12, 2005), op. cit.
6. Hamill.
7. Lambath Hochwald, "Circulation Secrets," *Folio:* (February 1, 1996): 57.
8. *The Magazine Handbook, A Comprehensive Guide for Advertisers, Advertising Agencies and Consumer Magazine Marketers 2005/06* (New York: Magazine Publishers of America, 2005), 14.
9. Phillip Moffitt, "Esquire from the Beginning," *Esquire* (June 1983): 13.
10. *The Magazine Handbook*, 13.
11. Edwin Diamond, "The Mid-Life Crisis of the Newsweeklies," *New York* (June 7, 1976): 56.
12. Ibid.
13. *The Magazine Handbook*, 16.
14. "Magazine Wholesaler Restructuring," *MPA Consumer Marketing Newsletter* (Spring 1996): 1.
15. "Newsstand Sales Continue Their Upward Trend," *Circulation Management* (April 2005): 24.
16. Stephanie D. Smith, "Men's Startups Tweaked to Bulk Up Sales," *Mediaweek.com* (October 8, 2005), http://www.mediaweek.com/mw/news/cabletv/article_display.jsp?vnu_content_id=1001262188.
17. Ibid.
18. Keith Clinkscales, "The Economics of Magazine Publishing," Stanford Professional Publishing Course (Stanford University, Palo Alto, Calif., July 28, 1997).

for additional reading

Compaine, Benjamin M. *The Business of Consumer Magazines.* White Plains, N.Y.: Knowledge Industry Publications, 1982.

Greco, Albert. *Advertising Management and the Business Publishing Industry.* New York: New York University Press, 1991.

Marino, Sal. *Business Magazine Publishing: Creative Ideas on Management, Editorial, Selling Space, Promotion . . . and Boosting Profits.* Lincolnwood, Ill.: NTC Publishing, 1993.

Woodard, Cheryl. *Starting and Running a Successful Newsletter or Magazine.* Berkeley, Calif.: Nolo, 2004.

chapter 7

magazine structures: staff organization

The magazine workplace has changed significantly since the days of Benjamin Franklin, when the editor was also the printer, the publisher, and the proprietor, and it continues to change. While magazines historically have functioned as vehicles for information, interpretation, entertainment, advocacy, and service, their creation is usually a business decision. Their day-to-day success depends not only on editorial quality, but also on business acumen. The professionals who run today's magazines are managing complex businesses; their decisions must go beyond the creation of the physical product.

MAY/JUNE 2003: Meredith Publishing, a division of Meredith Corporation, publishes more than 24 subscription magazines, in addition to special interest and custom publications. The company began when founder E. T. Meredith published the first issue of *Successful Farming* in 1902.

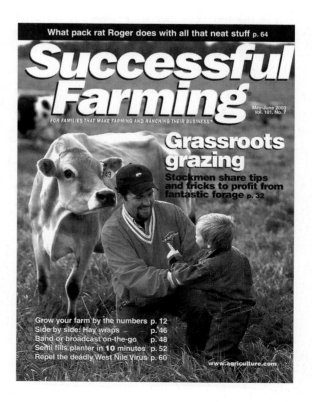

What pack rat Roger does with all that neat stuff p. 64

Successful Farming

FOR FAMILIES THAT MAKE FARMING AND RANCHING THEIR BUSINESS

May-June 2003
Vol. 101, No. 7

Grassroots grazing

Stockmen share tips and tricks to profit from fantastic forage p. 32

Grow your farm by the numbers p. 12
Side by side: Hay wraps   p. 46
Band or broadcast on-the-go   p. 48
Semi fills planter in **10** minutes p. 52
Repel the deadly West Nile Virus p. 60

www.agriculture.com

who's running the show?

All magazine staffs have to complete the same basic tasks—planning, writing and editing articles, designing pages, overseeing the manufacture of the finished product, promoting the magazine to advertisers as well as to readers, managing audience needs, and making sure the bills are paid.

Look at magazine mastheads: On one magazine, a single individual may do it all, with help from outside agencies and freelancers. Another magazine may need hundreds of staffers. Some important staff members, without whom the magazine would be doomed, are never named on the publication's pages. What's more, there's little consistency in magazine job titles and the duties associated with them. A senior editor at one magazine may have the responsibilities of an associate editor at another magazine. An advertising manager at one company may be the marketing director at another.

It's a constantly changing mix, as well. The job of editor has shifted dramatically in recent years, and with it, the roles of the rest of the staff. Nevertheless, the editor's role remains pivotal. Twenty years ago, magazine consultant John Fry explained the importance of the editor in giving form to the rest of the staff, in words that remain true today: "A successful magazine is characterized by a strong editor who supplies its central thrust. There is no room for weakness or uncertainty in defining what the editor does. To some extent, then, everyone else's job description follows."[1] Figures 7.1 and 7.2 illustrate the organizational structure of a multiple magazine publisher and the staff hierarchy of one of its publications.

The size, frequency, and content of a magazine, as well as its place within a corporate structure, determine the size and structure of its staff. A weekly magazine needs a large staff and is more likely to have staff writers and photographers than magazines published less frequently. A quarterly, by comparison, may rely on a regular pool of freelancers and purchase its illustrative material from a photo house. A highly departmentalized magazine might need several department editors, while a magazine with mostly feature material may have none.

The traditional division of labor at a magazine falls into four areas: editorial, advertising sales, circulation, and production. Editorial involves the magazine's content—its features, departments, and illustrations from the cover to the last page. The advertising sales staff has the responsibility of selling ad space in the magazine and for marketing and promoting the title. The circulation department is concerned with getting and keeping readers, whether they are newsstand buyers or regular subscribers. Production staffers cover the printing and technological concerns of equipment, paper, color, binding, and delivering the magazine to the newsstand or the home. However, this traditional approach doesn't allow for the evolving roles of magazine staffs and the need for fluidity in the workplace. It assumes that every magazine has four departments, when there are many small magazines that may not even have four full-time employees because many functions are outsourced to freelancers or special service companies.

Consequently, it makes more sense to divide magazine staffs into two major groups: the creative side and the business side. The creative side develops the magazine's content—articles, artwork, photos, and design. The business side consists of advertising, marketing, circulation, distribution, and

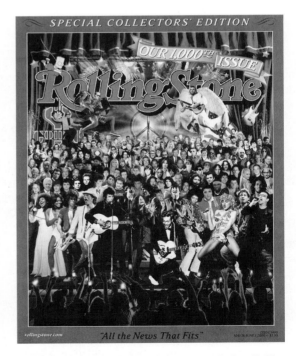

MAY/JUNE 2006: Wenner Media is named after *Rolling Stone* **founder Jann Wenner, who created the magazine in 1967. Wenner also publishes** *US Weekly* **and** *Men's Journal.*

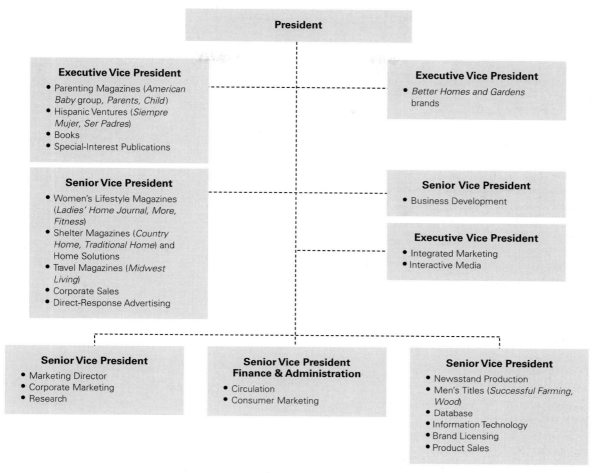

FIGURE 7.1 Meredith Corporate Organization Chart. Meredith Corporation, Des Moines, Iowa, publishes consumer, trade, custom, and corporate communication magazines. The company's publishing group organization chart illustrates the complexity of a multiple-title publishing house, with 24 consumer magazines, more than 150 special interest titles, plus custom magazines and websites. Because Meredith is a multimedia company, the magazine group is just one section of a more complex system, with a series of vice presidents who oversee corporate development, finance, and broadcasting. In addition to consumer titles such as *Better Homes and Gardens, Family Circle, Fitness, Ladies' Home Journal,* and *Country Home,* Meredith publishes the trade title *Successful Farming.* The Integrated Marketing group publishes custom magazines such as *Jeep, On DirecTV,* and Iams pet food's *Your Dog* and *Your Cat.* The Interactive Media group consists of online versions of the company's print titles.

production. Both sides report to the publisher. In large publishing houses with more than one magazine, there may be a president or chief executive officer who is the ultimate decision maker. At a small magazine, decisions may be shared by both the editor and the publisher. Regardless of the staff's organization, a magazine's creative side and business side work together for a common goal.

The job titles and descriptions that follow are those typically found at a large or midsized consumer or trade magazine. Smaller consumer,

trade, and organization magazines are less likely to have the entire hierarchy of titles and may have collapsed several job responsibilities into a few positions.

■ PRESIDENT AND CEO

Chief executive officer (CEO) is the top title in America's corporate structure. It is a corporate title, not a traditional magazine one, so only magazines

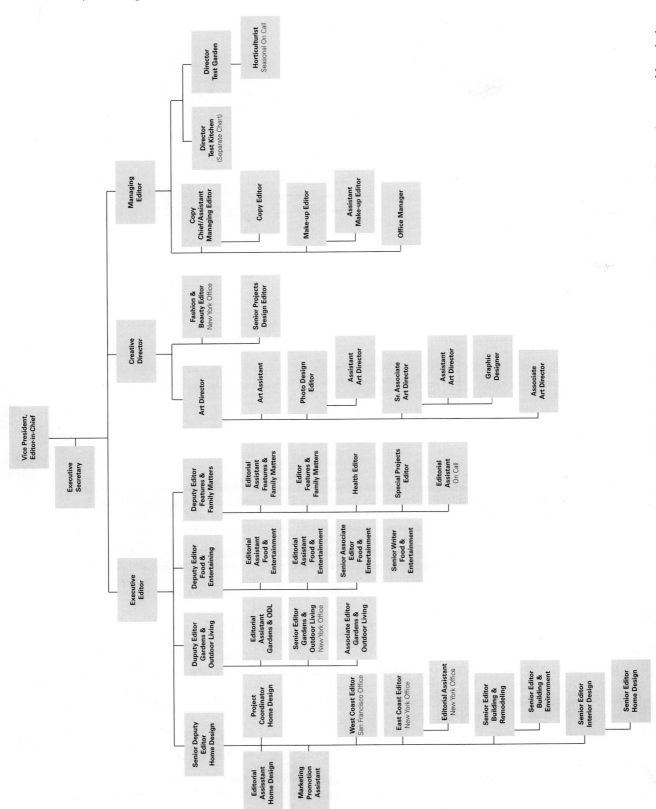

FIGURE 7.2 *Better Homes and Gardens* Editorial Chart. The *Better Homes and Gardens* editorial chart breaks out the positions needed to produce one of America's largest circulation magazines. The magazine has a test kitchen and a test garden, in addition to standard magazine job positions.

Typical Magazine Job Titles

Business Positions

President/CEO
Publisher
Circulation Director
Marketing Director
Public Relations Director/
   Promotion Director
Production Director*
Advertising Sales Director
Assistant Publisher/Business Manager
Research Director*
Advertising Sales Representative

Creative Positions

Editor-in-chief/Editor
Managing Editor
Executive Editor
Creative Director
Art Director
Senior Editor/Section Editor
Associate Editor/Assistant Editor
Copy Editor
Online Editor
Staff Writer
Photographer
Contributing Editor
Editorial Assistant/Fact Checker
Freelancer

*Depending on the magazine, this may be considered a business position or a creative position.

that are part of a larger company have these positions on their mastheads. The title of president is also a corporate designation and implies leadership over a major section of the organization. Sometimes the president is also the CEO; at other times the president reports to the CEO.

◼ PUBLISHER

This is typically the top business job on a magazine. The publisher has final responsibility for the magazine's profitability, which includes budgeting, strategic planning, and advertising development. Publishers combine business acumen with an understanding of the importance of a magazine's relationship with its audience and its advertisers.

Traditionally, publishers have moved up the ranks from advertising sales, where they learned how magazines build a profit base through readership and advertising. Publishers can move up from the editorial side, which is logically the case with a

privately owned company where the publisher may be the editor who started the magazine.

Multiple magazine publishing houses may have a group publisher who is responsible for several magazines. Group publishers at companies like Hearst may have 12 or 13 publishers reporting to them.

◼ EDITOR-IN-CHIEF/EDITOR

This is the top creative job on a magazine. At some magazines, the top title may be editor-in-chief, while at others it may be editor, or even editorial director. Whatever the title, this key person is the creative force behind the magazine.

Today's editor-in-chief or editor (the titles are interchangeable, and it's a moot question why one may be chosen over the other as the name for the top title) is expected to be more than a creative and visionary editorial architect. As the top editorial player, the editor reports to the publisher and

APRIL 2006: *Time* magazine is the flagship publication of Time, Inc., the publishing arm of Time Warner. The company, started when Henry Luce first published *Time* in 1923, publishes more than 145 consumer titles.

formula. He does this by maintaining continuity with the past, while also adding an element of surprise and excitement. The final decision on what articles and artwork to assign and to accept, and what graphic approach best suits the magazine rests with the editor-in-chief.

The best magazine editors infuse their magazines with their own personalities. They look ahead for what the audience might need in 1 or 2 years, and plan an exciting and involving way to provide it. Good editors read their competition, and lots of it, and spend their lives with their ears open to the delights, vagaries, oddities, and thrills of the world around them.

manager

The editor-in-chief is the primary magazine "boss," managing the creative staff as well as the magazine itself. At a big-circulation magazine, a

works with her in planning a budget; he works with advertising sales people and the public relations manager to provide the information they need to sell the magazine; and he works with the managing editor in making assignments. Not surprisingly, the editor-in-chief must be a successful manager of both staffers and freelancers. Increasingly, the position also has marketing implications, including building relationships with advertisers and creating brand extensions. Some editors may emphasize the visionary aspects of their jobs; others may focus primarily on being managers; and others see their marketing roles as of primary importance. Personal strengths and interests aside, today's magazines need editors who combine all three functions.

visionary

The editor-in-chief is responsible for shaping the magazine's content to suit its editorial philosophy and audience and for determining the magazine's

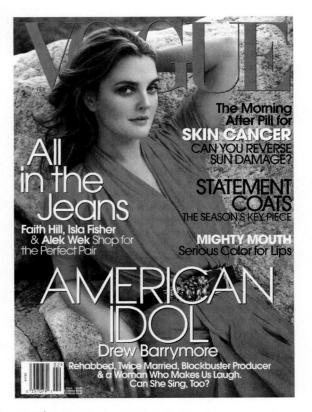

FEBRUARY 2006: Condé Nast Publications, a part of Advance Publications and publisher of more than 30 consumer titles, traces its roots back to 1915, when founder Conde Nast took over *Vogue*.

Long Live *The New Yorker:* An Editorial Genealogy

Since its founding in 1925, *The New Yorker* has had just five editorial monarchs reigning over the content of a magazine that many historians believe is one of the finest of the 20th century. Emperor Harold Ross (1925–1951), King William Shawn (1952–1987), Prince Robert Gottlieb (1987–1992), Queen Tina Brown (1992–1998), and Prince David Remnick (1998 to present) are the royal players in *The New Yorker*'s editorial genealogy.

The wordy and cerebral magazine was founded by 33-year-old Harold Ross, a "tramp journalist" who hopped freight trains from town to town and worked on dozens of newspapers before achieving success as editor of the Army's *Stars and Stripes* newspaper during World War I. Identified as an abrasive, boorish hick from the West by *New Yorker* contributor Brendan Gill, Ross nevertheless had the acumen to create a magazine for the most exciting city in America. *The New Yorker*'s rise to prominence as a national publication for a metropolitan audience was due to Ross's ability to surround himself with the best and the brightest of the famous Algonquin Round Table: Robert Benchley as drama critic, Dorothy Parker as book

reviewer, Katharine Angell White as fiction editor, and E.B. White and James Thurber as general editors and writers.

Ross himself was quirky, awkward, and unsophisticated, but his editorial style was eloquent, precise, and grammatically exact. From the start, Ross gave *The New Yorker* an urbane and urban tone, which readers and writers loved. And Ross loved his writers as long as they avoided language that was intellectually stuffy, self-consciously literary, or sexually connotative. Editorial content could be detached, whimsical, or even humorous—Ross liked cartoons—but the magazine had to be taken seriously. That Ross took it seriously was evident by the amount of money he budgeted for editorial, about $400,000 a year during the Depression.

As an editor, Ross demanded accuracy and he was known for his long, detailed comments on manuscripts. The fact-checking department he created still has the reputation for being the best in the magazine industry.

Ross hand-picked his editorial successor, William Shawn, who joined the staff in 1933 as a "Talk of the Town" reporter when he was 26 years old. By 1939, Shawn was managing

editor and he became editor after Ross's death in December 1951. Quiet and unassuming outside the office, Shawn was a powerful editor who molded *The New Yorker* for more than 30 years into a magazine that combined the best of journalism and literature.

According to *The New York Times* book critic John Leonard, "Shawn changed *The New Yorker* from a smarty-pants parish tip sheet into a journal that altered our experience instead of just posturing in front of it."[1] In the April 22, 1985, "Notes and Comment" section, Shawn laid out the editorial philosophy he had been following for years: "Amid a chaos of images, we value coherence. We believe in the printed word. And we believe in clarity. And in immaculate syntax. And in the beauty of the English language."

Shawn's editorial style was simple: He read every word published in *The New Yorker,* from original typescript to page proofs. Unlike Ross, who sent detailed memos to his staff, Shawn dealt directly with the two-dozen full-time editors and about 140 fiction and nonfiction writers who worked on contract. He personally edited Rachel Carson's *Silent Spring* and Truman Capote's *In Cold Blood*.

1. Eric Pace, "William Shawn, 85, Is Dead; *New Yorker*'s Gentle Despot," *New York Times* (December 9, 1992): 1A.

(continued)

Long Live *The New Yorker:* An Editorial Genealogy (continued)

Writers said Shawn was patient and supportive, allowing them to work at their own pace while providing an atmosphere that encouraged creativity. As Shawn explained: "No writer or artist is ever given an order. When a journalistic writer undertakes a new project, it is always done in full agreement with the editor; the two have to bring to it the same enthusiasm. And no editing is ever imposed on a writer; every editorial suggestion is presented in the form of a question, and is settled by agreement between writer and editor."[2]

When the Fleischmann family, who had funded *The New Yorker* from the start, sold the magazine to Advance Publications (owners of *Vogue, Mademoiselle, Glamour, Vanity Fair,* and *GQ,* among others) in 1984, insiders suspected Shawn's days as editor were numbered. They were right. In 1987, the 80-year-old Shawn was forced to retire and an outsider, 55-year-old Robert Gottlieb, was named editor.

Gottlieb, who had been president of Alfred A. Knopf and was a respected book editor, did not make as many changes in *The New Yorker* as magazine watchers anticipated. He added color to the editorial pages in the 64th anniversary issue in February 1989—for the first time since 1926, when a two-

page color cartoon ran. He tried to appeal to a younger audience through trendy book excerpts, more foreign coverage, new sections, and listings such as "Edge of Night Life" about late-night clubs. However, Gottlieb was not interested in revolutionizing *The New Yorker,* and he turned out to be a conservator who refused even to lunch with major advertisers or talk to them about his vision of the magazine.

That was a problem, for *The New Yorker* was in trouble, selling an average of 20,000 copies per week at the newsstand, versus its 1950s heyday of 100,000 newsstand copies a week. Not only was circulation down, but so was advertising. The solution was to bring in a new editor to sit on the throne.

Tina Brown earned her tiara at *Vanity Fair* by reviving a literary icon into what some critics described as a celebrity-driven, upscale *People.* Brown had long been a master of generating media buzz: She put a naked and pregnant Demi Moore on *Vanity Fair* 's cover. So it wasn't surprising that Brown threw tradition out the window at *The New Yorker* when she took over in 1992. The table of contents was expanded, bylines went to the front of stories, pieces on movie stars were carried, articles were shortened, a letters

to the editor department was initiated, and controversial illustrations appeared on the covers while large photos ran on the editorial pages. Brown's goal was to add more variety to the editorial mix, make the magazine more timely and topical, and include an offbeat and irreverent tone to shorter, peppier pieces. Said Brown, "It's part of a pattern of reimagining and recreating *The New Yorker* while keeping the most important things intact."[3]

Brown's detractors said she took *The New Yorker* downmarket, making it a vulgar celebrity magazine for insiders. They said the magazine was no longer elegant and that it had lost its quality of timelessness. Supporters, however, said the magazine was livelier, trendier, and more interesting. Brown dismissed most of the criticism, saying, "Anyone who talks about the lack of timelessness isn't reading the magazine. If they were reading it, they would see that the pieces I'm publishing are exactly those kinds of pieces that were previously published, but are now being mixed up with other kinds of pieces."[4] And despite all the talk about short articles, there were still long, 25,000-word pieces.

Certainly *The New Yorker* looked different under Brown, and that may be what critics

2. William Shawn, "Notes and Comments," *New Yorker* (April 22, 1985): 35–36.

3. Robert D. McFadden, "Eustace Tilley's on Vacation, and, My What a Stand-in," *New York Times* (February 15, 1994): B3.

4. Deirdre Carmody, "Tina Brown's Progress at *The* New *New Yorker*," *New York Times* (April 12, 1993): C2.

Long Live *The New Yorker:* An Editorial Genealogy (continued)

responded to, rather than content. The 1993 Valentine's Day cover of a Hasidic man kissing a black woman, which shocked and offended many readers, turned out to be a top seller. Circulation went up under Brown, yet the magazine still lost millions of dollars each year.

Reinforcing her reputation as the celebrity queen of buzz, Brown left *The New Yorker* in July 1998 to head her own multimedia venture in affiliation with Miramax Films. David Remnick, author of more than 100 articles for the magazine over a period of 6 years, was named editor. Remnick, who received a Pulitzer Prize in 1994 for his book, *Lenin's Tomb,* hasn't imitated Brown's celebrity approach. When he took over the title, he said he would miss being a writer, but added, "An editor needs to be in the chair, editing and reading, or out and about meeting with writers, and that's where you'll find me from now on."[5]

As for his plans for the magazine, Remnick said, "In the next several years *The New Yorker* will have a fuller engagement with the world. We're in a crazy Gilded Age of money, money, money, and we want to get much more of that story. And though we want to cover the unique aspects of our city, we also want to have a global reach." He stresses high-quality, brilliantly written pieces, pointing out, "There's no reason why the level of writing can't be extraordinarily high in every arena. Ostensibly glitzy subjects such as fashion can be written with the same intensity and skill as coverage of Bosnia or Rudolph Giuliani."

But along with expanded reporting and deeper literary writing, Remnick hasn't forgotten the cartoon tradition. "Cartoons are our signature," he said, "probably the first thing people read, and we want to treat them well." He often features more cartoons in larger

spaces, covering a half page and even a full page.

The magazine's 80th anniversary edition, February 14–21, 2005, was a 262-page double issue that paid homage to the magazine's past luminaries, with a cover cartoon strip by artist Chris Ware that featured the magazine's iconic figure Eustace Tilley watching a butterfly through his prince-nez, back page art by Saul Steinberg, and a memoir by Roger Angell about his stepfather, the legendary *The New Yorker* writer and editor E.B. White.

In assuming the editorship of one of America's most respected titles, Remnick said, "Americans are surrounded by a blizzard of information. If you were inclined to lose your mind you could stay on the Internet all day. In the middle of this blizzard *The New Yorker* should stand as a place of clarity, coverage, intelligence, reliability— and hilarity. We don't want to forget hilarity." ■

5. Stefan Kanter, "David Remnick: 'We Don't Want to Forget the Hilarity,'" *Columbia Journalism Review* (September/October 1998): 43.

---

good manager provides direction for his large staff and then gets out of the way by delegating as much work as possible. At a smaller magazine with a two- or three-person editorial staff, the editor is more likely to be a hands-on manager who works with the staff individually and as a group to control the direction of the magazine. Whatever the magazine's size, the editor-in-chief is responsible for staff relations and communication, editorial supervision, planning, and public relations.

Good editors nurture talent and find the right people to be both editors and writers. The editor-

in-chief strives to create an environment in which they can all do their best work together. Two magazine editorial heavyweights, Tina Brown and Anna Wintour, discussed the editor's role on the PBS television program *The Charlie Rose Show* in 1998.[2]

Brown, who left her job as editor of *The New Yorker* in July 1998 to start the short-lived *Talk* magazine in affiliation with Miramax Films, said she believed a good editor fosters teamwork over a period of several years: "I think it takes, really, that long for an editor to grapple with all the forces at play, learn what her team is best at, form that team, forge that team, create an identity, and then have you all dancing on the same team."

Wintour, editor-in-chief of *Vogue*, emphasized that an editor is responsible for hiring and encouraging quality staff members: "I'm always looking to the people that I work with for a sense of news and for a sense of journalism because I don't feel that a magazine can be a coffee table book. It has to have a sense of urgency to make people want to pick it up every month. So, you need very competitive, newsy, journalistic people working for you that are inspiring to you and to everyone who works with you. One's always looking for young people who want to push the envelope a bit and tell you that you're an old fuddy-duddy and that we have to move on. I think it's really being open to other voices and listening to what they have to say."

marketer

Because today's magazines are viewed as brands that can be extended and franchised, the editor-in-chief is expected to think beyond the magazine into new products and publishing opportunities. Cathleen Black, president of Hearst Magazines Division, instructs her editors to think like marketers by growing, leveraging, and expanding their titles, which she sees as "incredible franchises."[3] Conferences, books, and one-shot issues are just a few possibilities. "Being a magazine editor is more than just literally producing a magazine," she says.[4]

Today's editors are expected to be entrepreneurial market authorities who know what their readers want. This leads to credibility both inside the company and within the magazine industry. This has led to editors going on advertising calls with the sales people. Their function there, however, is to educate the advertiser on the magazine; the sales staff handles closing the sale.

Good Housekeeping editor-in-chief Ellen Levine likes to call on advertisers, because, she says, she believes in the "care and feeding of major advertisers." She'd rather meet with the product manager than with an advertising agency representative, however, because the product manager has a clearer idea of his product and how it might mesh with *Good Housekeeping* content.

Anna Wintour, editor of *Vogue*, was hit by a tofu pie thrown by members of People for the Ethical Treatment of Animals (PETA) at a fashion event in Paris in 2005. PETA members said they were objecting to the magazine's decision to run fur ads while refusing PETA's anti-fur messages.

■ MANAGING EDITOR

Often called a magazine's "sergeant," the managing editor may have the toughest job on staff, spending half his time on managerial duties, half on editorial. Enforcing deadlines, hiring and firing staff and freelancers, and keeping the magazine generally on track and on schedule are all the responsibility of the managing editor, who reports directly to the editor-in-chief. In some cases, a managing editor may write articles, edit, and generally jump in to fill whatever needs exist.

It is the managing editor's responsibility to see that all work progresses efficiently and gets done by deadline. The managing editor must be aware of all problems and use discretion in either dealing with them immediately or consulting the editor-in-chief. The editor-in-chief must be made aware of all problems eventually, however.

The managing editor works with the senior, associate, or departmental editors to assign and track all articles and keeps in contact with these editors from start to finish. He works with the art director in ensuring that all design and photography is well executed, on time, consistent, and appropriate for the magazine. He works with the production director to develop production deadlines and to make sure these deadlines are met. The managing editor is usually the last person to see the magazine before it goes to print.

At many Time, Inc., magazines, the managing editor actually functions as the editor-in-chief. This is a legacy from the days of Henry Luce, when there was only one top editor in the company: Mr. Luce. Now, John Huey is editor-in-chief of Time, Inc., which puts him at the top of every masthead,

Out and About: Why Employees Quit

Organizational consultant and author Leigh Branham cites these as the seven reasons people leave a company:[1]

1. The job or workplace was not as expected.
2. A mismatch between the job and the person.
3. Too little coaching and feedback.
4. Too few growth and advancement opportunities.
5. Feeling devalued and unrecognized.
6. Stress from overwork and work-life imbalance.
7. Loss of trust and confidence in senior leaders.

1. Branham.

from *Time* to *Fortune* to *Sports Illustrated for Kids.* The person who really runs the individual magazine is the managing editor.

EXECUTIVE EDITOR

Some magazines have an executive editor in place of a managing editor. More complex magazine staffs have both positions.

The executive editor, who reports to the editor-in-chief, often balances the work of the editor; the role of the executive editor is, therefore, often defined by the qualities of the editor. "If the editor is an authority and writer, but has a distaste for administration, for example, clearly the next person in the chain of command should be strong in areas of budgeting, scheduling, and sensing how to carry out assignments coming from the editor. For this reason, we see on more and more mastheads today the title of 'executive editor,'" said consultant John Fry.[5]

CREATIVE DIRECTOR

The creative director is the liaison between the editorial and design staffs and between design and production. The creative director, who reports to the editor-in-chief, assures that all editorial and design content is in the proper tone and style. Next to the editor-in-chief, this person is the keeper of the magazine's personality. Not all magazines have a creative director, but it is an important position for highly visual titles.

ART DIRECTOR

The art director oversees the look of the magazine, assuring that design is consistent with editorial philosophy, logical and readable, and appealing to the audience. The art director manages all design and photography assignments and makes sure the resultant material is well executed, on time, consistent, and appropriate for the magazine. On a larger magazine, the art director often designs the cover and features pages and oversees cover shoots, managing a staff that may include a deputy art director, an associate art director, or an assistant art director. At a small magazine, however, the art director might be the only full-time design employee; he might use freelance designers to help provide layout variety.

The art director, who reports to the editor-in-chief, works with the production director to determine production deadlines and to make sure these deadlines are met. The art director, top staff editors, and production director work together on the break-of-the-book, planning a budget, submitting requests for quotes, and selecting a printer. When the inevitable differences arise between editors and the art director, they must work together to reach a compromise, basing decisions on editorial philosophy and audience. Should they reach an impasse, the editor-in-chief has the final say at most magazines.

■ SENIOR EDITOR/SECTION EDITOR

This position has a variety of functions on American magazines and may have a variety of names, including feature editor, department editor, beauty editor, fashion editor, and so on. In general, the senior editor helps assign all articles, making sure the writer understands the topic, angle, length, tone, and other specifics, and works with the writer throughout the process to assure quality and efficiency.

The senior editor works with the top editors in determining what articles to assign and how to approach them, and works with writers to make sure the end product suits the magazine's needs. However, the final decision on what articles to use rests with the editor-in-chief; the senior editor seldom

Research in Brief

Magazine Careers 1850–1926: Inhospitable Climate for Women

What was it like to be a woman magazine writer or editor between 1850 and 1926? How did popular magazines of the period portray journalism as a career for women? To find the answer to these questions, Professor Agnes Hooper Gottlieb of Seton Hall University analyzed dozens of articles written by women journalists about their experiences, as well as features discussing the field in general. She looked at such popular consumer magazines as *Collier's, Harper's Weekly, Harper's Bazaar, The Arena,* and *The Atlantic Monthly,* as well as the journalism trade journal *The Journalist.*[1]

Although women had worked as editors, writers, and even publishers of magazines since the 18th century, Gottlieb points out that it wasn't until 1870 that the U.S. Census established a category for women who made their living as journalists. That year, there were just 35 women in this new category, or less than 0.6 percent of all working journalists. By 1900, 2,193 women defined themselves as journalists. Between 1920 and 1930, the number of women reporters and editors doubled to 14,786. What kind of welcome did these women receive at magazines?

Some women were lured to magazine journalism, notes Gottlieb, because they wanted to defy societal conventions. Others thought it was a good place to meet a man. And some "women also thought, mistakenly as we all know, that journalism was easy," Gottlieb says.

Despite a few tales of romance and adventure, Gottlieb found that magazines of the day painted an inhospitable picture of the climate for women reporters:

Women journalists recounted stories of editors who paid them less than men who did similar jobs, who tried to take sexual advantage of them, who printed articles but then refused to pay for them, and who treated them pejoratively and as interlopers in their newsrooms. The women told of the drudgery they were assigned to because of their sex and about how journalism spoiled their rosy

1. Agnes Hooper Gottlieb, "Grit Your Teeth, Then Learn to Swear: Women in Journalistic Careers, 1850–1926" (paper presented at the annual meeting of the American Journalism History Association, Louisville, Ky., October 1998).

Magazine Careers 1850–1926 (continued)

attitudes and made cynics out of the best of them.

It definitely was not easy being a magazine editor or writer during the 75-year period from before the Civil War until after World War I. Ironically, even male editors of magazines devoted to women, which included articles written by women, made discouraging comments about women as journalists. In a 1901 article in *Ladies' Home Journal,* editor Edward Bok discouraged women from journalistic careers, saying the field "tends to make a woman too independent, too free, too broad. It establishes her on a footing with men that is not wise; it gives her opportunities that are not uplifting."

Other male editors argued that it was "unseemly" for a woman to be out at all hours, in all kinds of weather, and in the company of men without a chaperone. Many male writers tended to feel uncomfortable competing against women for stories, plus they resented the "glory" some women received for some articles. Yet as early as 1889, *The Journalist* dedicated a 24-page issue to women journalists to signal the acceptance of women within the ranks. The trade magazine's editor, Allan Forman, urged women to drop the use of pen names and to build solid reputations as professional reporters.

Gottlieb reports that women writers were honest about the traits needed to succeed in the field of journalism. An article by Cynthia May Westover Alden in *Frank Leslie's Popular Monthly* described the following attributes needed by a woman reporter in 1898: "Conscientiousness, fidelity to truth, absence of hypersensitiveness, common sense in dress, self-confidence, and exemption from the hypochondriacal tendency to which so many women are prone." Eleanor Hoyt, who wrote regularly for *Collier's,* noted in an article in *Current Literature* in 1903 that women needed "good health, more than average intelligence, dogged persistence, and indomitable pluck."

Women who succeeded as magazine journalists were driven by a passion to write, an ability to write well, and a need to earn money. Gottlieb says that "uniformly among women journalists of the 19th century can be found an absence of family money and a real need for the woman to support herself, her parents and/or her children. This group of scribblers who turned to journalism often had never married or, if married, often divorced."

In 1901, *Ladies' Home Journal* asked 42 female working journalists whether they would approve of their daughter working in the same field. Thirty-nine said they would not approve. By the 1920s, attitudes had changed. When *Collier's* asked a woman journalist hypothetically if she'd let a younger sister be a reporter in 1922, the enthusiastic response from the journalist was "I have one and she is." Foreign correspondent Dorothy Thompson, asked to write about women journalists overseas for *The Nation* in 1926, stated there was "nothing extraordinary" about a woman in the job. She said she was surprised this would be cause for comment, adding, "The see-what-the-little-darling-has-done-now attitude ought to be outlawed."

Genevieve Jackson Boughner, author of the 1926 book *Women in Journalism: A Guide to the Opportunities and a Manual of the Technique of Women's Work for Newspapers and Magazines,* listed dozens of possibilities for women, including society editor, home-making writer, fashion reporter, columnist, and magazine editor. Women were no longer a rarity on magazine editorial staffs.

According to Gottlieb, magazines were an appropriate forum for the debate about careers for women in journalism. Although many articles highlighted negative aspects—discrimination, low pay, and harassment—they nonetheless pointed out that some women succeeded as journalists, which popularized and glamorized the field. Additionally, Gottlieb notes, these magazine articles are invaluable primary sources from and about women journalists who left no other record of their work experiences. ■

assigns an article without first consulting the editor-in-chief. The senior editor also often writes articles, usually major feature pieces. The senior editor may report to either the editor-in-chief or to the managing editor.

■ ASSOCIATE EDITOR/ASSISTANT EDITOR

These two positions, while separate on the masthead, often have similar duties, which include writing, editing, or assigning material for front-of-book (FOB) or back-of-book (BOB) departments, and writing heads and subheads. The major distinction between the two is that, often, assistant editors have more administrative duties and associate editors have more management responsibilities.

An associate editor may have the responsibility for a department, usually at the front of the book, and may have additional editorial duties, such as writing the table of contents and article titles and subtitles. Associate and assistant editors typically report to the senior editor.

■ COPY EDITOR

The copy editor reads every article, caption, headline, blurb, and teaser in the magazine, correcting all errors in grammar, usage, punctuation, and style. The copy editor follows the magazine's style, which may be customized, or may follow University of Chicago style or Associated Press (AP) style. The copy editor, who is in charge of creating style guidelines when special problems arise, reports to the managing editor.

The copy editor also looks for problems with clarity and organization and corrects these if possible. When problems seem too massive, the article is returned to the writer, through the senior or associate editor. The copy editor helps the senior or associate editor critique articles in terms of tone, con-

tent, and development of the assigned topic. Problems in these areas are dealt with by the managing editor or senior editor, with input from the copy editor.

■ ONLINE EDITOR

This position is one of the newest to surface in the magazine hierarchy over the last decade. A similar title would be website editor. The online editor typically creates and maintains the magazine's website, serves as the liaison between the print magazine staff and the online staff, and assigns or creates online content. The online editor, who reports to the editor-in-chief or to the managing editor, may have an assistant who edits online material and creates online content.

■ STAFF WRITER

Fewer and fewer magazines today have staff writers. Those few individuals lucky enough to spend their lives as staff writers are talented professionals who have experience with the magazine and are entrusted with the more difficult, comprehensive articles. Staff writers consult with the managing editor or senior editor, to whom they report, in determining appropriate articles for the magazine and also help with headlines, pull-quotes, and captions.

From 1984 to 2004, *Time* reduced its staff by 15 percent and *Newsweek* cut its by 50 percent, according to the Project for Excellence in Journalism. The biggest hit was taken by lower-ranking editors. The number of contributors and contributing editors increased during the same period.

■ PHOTOGRAPHER

Only a handful of magazines have staff photographers, such as *National Geographic, Newsweek,* and *The Washingtonian.* Most photographers are freelancers. Both staff and freelance photographers work under the direction of the art director or creative director, who makes photography assignments based on consultation with staff editors and writers. Photographers are responsible for all aspects of an assignment they are given. This includes scheduling; finding models, equipment, and props as needed; getting photo releases; shooting the assignment; and doing reshoots as necessary. Photo-heavy magazines may also have a photo editor, who is the liaison between the photographer and the art director or creative director.

■ CONTRIBUTING EDITOR

Contributing editors are freelancers rather than staff members. Despite their title, contributing editors tend to be writers who are experts in the field the magazine covers. Regular freelancer writers with whom the magazine wants to maintain a relationship may be given this title. They report to either the managing editor or senior editor.

■ EDITORIAL ASSISTANT/FACT CHECKER

This is a common entry-level position, especially for New York–based magazines. The editorial assistant does some administrative work such as research, making copies, even filing for other staffers. Some magazines have one editorial assistant for every two to three editors. These staffers open and answer the mail, so they're often the most knowledgeable about magazine gossip. Some editorial assistants write short BOB or FOB articles and may do an occasional sidebar or two. Most people stay in these positions for 1 or 2 years, pay their dues, then move up.

Often, the editorial assistant is also the fact checker, who makes sure all information presented in articles is correct. The fact checker starts with the assumption that all writers are liars, and asks for verification for everything that is not common knowledge. This includes the spelling of names, the wording of quotes if the quote doesn't ring true to the fact checker, and all other information presented as fact. It is the fact checker's responsibility to contact sources for verification when the writer's notes do not contain adequate information. The fact checker rewrites portions of articles when it is possible to correct errors with a minimum of rewriting. When major changes are needed, the fact checker consults with the managing editor, senior editor, or associate editor, who are responsible for getting the rewrite done.

MARCH 2006: August Home Publishing got its start in 1979 when founder Donald Peschke started *Woodsmith* magazine. The company also publishes *Cuisine at Home, Garden Gate, ShopNotes,* and *Workbench.*

■ FREELANCE WRITER/DESIGNER

With budget cutbacks and the trend toward outsourcing, more magazines are using freelance writers and designers than ever before. Freelancers usually work for a variety of magazines, striving for financial security through consistent assignments from the same titles or publishing houses. Most successful freelancers already have been staff members on a magazine, where they learned the ropes, fine-tuned their talents, built their reputations, and established contacts. Depending on the magazine's structure, freelancer writers may report to the managing editor or senior editor, and occasionally to the associate editor. Freelance designers report to the art director.

■ CIRCULATION DIRECTOR

Circulation directors are essential to the financial success of a magazine because they connect the magazine to readers. It is the job of a circulation

From Intern to Editor-in-Chief in Just 6 Years

Atoosa Rubenstein became the youngest editor in Hearst Magazines' history when she was named founding editor of *CosmoGirl* at the age of 26. How did she get her dream job in publishing? Rubenstein shared her "Five Ways to Be an Editor-in-Chief by Age 26" in a *Student Press Review* interview with a Coral Gables, Florida, high school reporter:

Step 1: Dream big.
Step 2: Get experience.
Step 3: Look for internships.
Step 4: When you get the assistant job, be an amazing assistant.
Step 5: Trust yourself.[1]

Rubenstein followed steps two and three by landing her first internship at *Sassy* while still an undergraduate at Barnard College. "I did my job as if it were the most important thing in the world, and no task was too small," Rubenstein said. "I would practically follow the people from *Sassy* into the bathroom, just so that they would notice me and know that I was there."

After graduating in 1993, Rubenstein followed step four by taking a job as a fashion assistant at *Cosmopolitan* and working her way up to senior fashion editor. In 1999, she trusted in step five by launching *CosmoGirl*, which was named *Adweek*'s start-up of the year in 2000 and one of *Advertising Age*'s top five magazines for 2001.

"Ignorance is bliss," said Rubenstein about starting up *CosmoGirl*. "I was 26 years old, I didn't know any better. I didn't know what could happen if we failed. I just worked, worked, worked, and luckily it all went well."[2]

In 2004, Rubenstein's biggest dream came true when she became editor-in-chief of *Seventeen*, the oldest of the teen magazines and the leader in advertising and circulation revenue. ■

1. Carolina Vester, "Atoosa Rubenstein Outlines 'Five Ways to Be an Editor-in-Chief by Age 26,'" *Student Press Review* (August 6, 2003), http://www.studentpressreview.com/media/paper421/news/2003/08/06/ConventionStories/Atoosa.Rubenstein.Outlines.five.Ways.To.Be.An.Editor.In.Chief.By.Age.26-449400.shtml.

2. Taylor K. Vecsey, "Atoosa Rubenstein: A New Challenge," *The East Hampton Star* (September 11, 2003), http://www.easthamptonstar.com/20030911/feat1.htm.

director not only to take care of existing readers, but also to find new ones. In a nutshell, the circulation director manages all paid circulation and is responsible for expanding readership through creative use of databases, analyzing single-copy and subscription programs, defining and exploring new areas of potential readership, and maintaining a high renewal rate. The circulation director reports to the publisher. Increasingly, circulation directors are moving into top management.

Larger publishing houses may have a circulation manager as well as assistants to support the circulation director. However, some magazines hire outside fulfillment agencies to take care of circulation, finding it cheaper and more efficient to hire a group of experts than to train their own staffs. The circulation director is the liaison between the magazine and the fulfillment house.

■ MARKETING DIRECTOR

The marketing director is primarily responsible for publicity and promotion for the magazine, with the goal of selling the magazine to readers and advertisers. This includes promotional programs to generate ad sales and increase circulation. At some magazines, the marketing director is responsible for all budgeting and analyses of circulation programs, list rentals, and rate base planning and maintenance. The marketing director reports to the publisher.

■ PUBLIC RELATIONS DIRECTOR/PROMOTION DIRECTOR

The public relations (PR) director or promotion director is responsible for creating media kits and overseeing other special promotional efforts that create and maintain the identity of the magazine in the eyes of readers and advertisers. At a small magazine without a public relations or promotion director, the media kit would be the responsibility of the marketing director. The PR or promotion director reports to either the publisher or to the marketing director.

■ AD SALES DIRECTOR

The ad sales director manages a staff of ad sales representatives, and is ultimately responsible for generating advertising in the magazine. His job includes researching and analyzing data on existing and potential audiences, creating ad sales support material, developing ad rates, overseeing ad sales contacts, finalizing contracts with advertisers, and scheduling ad placement. In large publishing houses, he may supervise advertising branch managers located throughout the United States. The ad sales director may report either to the publisher or to the marketing director.

■ AD SALES REPRESENTATIVE

Ad sales representatives make the actual calls on advertisers, connecting the magazine with the needs and interests of the advertiser. They service and maintain their current accounts and are responsible for finding new business. Ad sales representatives report to the advertising director.

■ PRODUCTION DIRECTOR

The production director is the magazine's technical director and manages the break-of-the-book. She is responsible for maintaining production effi-

ciency, helping staff members format material on the computer as needed, and assuring that all pages are completed—precise and technically accurate. The production director makes sure as much work as possible is done before the final deadline, preparing pages on the computer as articles and photographs are completed. The production director gets all advertising and editorial material to the printer on time and in proper form, and oversees the magazine's press run. Occasionally, she also is in charge of distribution, getting the magazine to subscribers and newsstands from the printer.

The production director generally reports directly to the publisher, although at some magazines, she reports to the editor-in-chief or to the art director. Some large magazines have a production manager who reports to the production director. In this case, job duties are shared by the two individuals.

Cosmopolitan **editor-in-chief Kate White has written three mystery novels while on the job at** *Cosmo,* **including** *If Looks Could Kill, 'Til Death Do Us Part,* **and** *Over Her Dead Body,* **using characters who resemble real-life industry biggies.**

■ ASSISTANT PUBLISHER/ BUSINESS MANAGER

In conjunction with the publisher, to whom she reports, this individual is primarily responsible for the magazine's budget, which entails cost control, financial planning and analysis, and profit-and-loss reviews. The assistant publisher formulates general business policy, makes salary and wage proposals, and sees that the magazine's bills are paid and its debts collected. She supervises internal office management as well as operations of ad sales, circulation fulfillment, and editorial and advertising promotion. On small magazines, this individual also may be the circulation director or public relations director, or both.

■ RESEARCH DIRECTOR

Only large publishing houses have research directors. In smaller operations, research is done by the editor or marketing director or by an outside agency. Typically, a research director researches the nature of the magazine's audience, which includes analyses of audience behaviors; plans and manages focus groups; presents focus group results to the staff; and makes recommendations for the magazine's response to audience attitudes. The research director either reports to the publisher or to the editor-in-chief.

A 1998 study by the American Business Press found that few magazines today have a single individual serving as research director: only 5 among 965 audited trade publications had a research director.[6] It wasn't that the research function was missing, but that it had become the responsibility of someone in advertising sales or marketing as a result of organizational downsizing.

magazine ownership

Magazines are published by some of the largest businesses in America. Many make profits for thousands of investors, while others must only make enough to keep one owner happy. Some magazines are nonprofit, while others see profit as part of the larger corporate picture. Increasingly, the single consumer or trade magazine, published by a single publisher, is disappearing, while conglomerates and group publishers are growing. Successful titles are sold almost weekly, and huge corporations sell entire groups of magazines, then buy others. Some of the largest publishing houses are privately owned; others are public properties with responsibility to stockholders. Ownership varies depending on the type of magazine, with different business structures possible for consumer, trade, and organization magazines.

■ CONSUMER AND TRADE MAGAZINE OWNERSHIP

Many consumer and trade magazines are largely a product of a single individual's vision, even though the financing may come from other sources. In 1923, Henry Luce and Briton Hadden offered stock in their fledgling *Time* magazine to supplement their own investment. Their magazine is now part of the giant Time Warner media conglomerate and remains a public offering sold on the New York Stock Exchange.

In 1925, Harold Ross's *The New Yorker* was bankrolled by Raoul Fleischmann, who was the sole owner. Today, *The New Yorker* is still privately owned—by S. I. Newhouse Jr. and his brother Donald as part of their Advance Publications media empire, which also includes Condé Nast Publications.

A magazine's ownership defines the way decisions are made. Consumer and trade magazines may be publicly owned or privately owned.

publicly owned

Publicly owned magazines are traded on a stock exchange and must be responsive to their stockholders, who are looking for as large a return on their investment as possible. This adds an extra level of financial accountability to the magazine staff. Those investors may or may not care about editorial quality, but they are seriously interested in profit. Publicly held magazines must publish their earnings in annual reports, and their editors have to report to corporate officers as well as a board of directors. It's Wall Street leading the dance, and magazines have to follow.

Some publicly owned magazines grow to become part of a conglomerate, dealing with a variety of media—and then some. Time, Inc., which includes such consumer magazines as *Time, Sports Illustrated,* and *People,* is now part of Time Warner, which also owns HBO, CNN, Warner Brothers, theaters, theme parks, and music production houses. Meredith Corporation owns consumer magazines such as *Better Homes and Gardens, Ladies' Home Journal,* and *Successful Farming,* as well as broadcasting stations, custom publications, and special ancillary products. McGraw-Hill Companies owns *Business Week* and *Aviation Week and Space Technology,* plus Standard and Poor business ratings services, textbook publishers, television stations, and JD Power and Associates. Hanley Wood publishes business-to-business magazines with an emphasis on the building trades, including *Builder, Replacement Contractor,* and *Tools of the Trade.*

privately owned

Privately owned companies do not have to publicize earnings. A single individual, a family, or a

Some Top Magazine Publishing Houses

The following are some privately owned and publicly owned publishing houses, along with a representative sampling of some of their magazine titles.

Privately Owned

Advance Publications

Condé Nast
  Architectural Digest
  Allure
  Vogue
  Glamour
  Self
  Lucky
  GQ
  Vanity Fair
  The New Yorker
  Wired
Fairchild
  Jane
  W
  Details
  Brand Marketing
  Modern Bride

Hearst Corporation
  Cosmopolitan
  Redbook
  Good Housekeeping
  Esquire
  Country Living
  Seventeen
  Harper's Bazaar
  Popular Mechanics
  Marie Claire
  Town and Country

Wenner Media
  Rolling Stone
  Men's Journal
  US Weekly

Strang Communications
  Charisma
  Ministries Today
  New Man
  Christian Retailing
  Vida Cristiana

Publicly Owned

McGraw-Hill Companies
  Aviation Week and Space Technology
  Business Week

Hanley Wood
  Builder
  Replacement Contractor
  Tools of the Trade
  Residential Architect
  Digital Home
  American Dream Homes
  Custom Home

Meredith Corporation
  Better Homes and Gardens
  Ladies' Home Journal
  Midwest Living
  Country Home
  Traditional Home
  Fitness
  Wood
  Successful Farming
  Family Circle
  American Baby

Time Warner
  Time
  Fortune
  Sports Illustrated
  Business 2.0
  People
  Entertainment Weekly
  InStyle
  Southern Living
  Sunset
  Real Simple

group of private investors may choose to keep the company off the stock exchange for a variety of reasons. They may enjoy the autonomy and secrecy of private ownership, they may not trust corporate buyers, or they simply may not have enough cash flow potential to go public.

Advance Publications owns not only *The New Yorker*, but also the Condé Nast group of magazines, which includes *Glamour, GQ, Vanity Fair, Vogue,* and *Mademoiselle*. Other large privately held magazine publishers are the Hearst Corporation, August Home Publishing, and Wenner Media. Hearst, started by William Randolph Hearst and still owned by the Hearst family, publishes such titles as *Cosmopolitan, Good Housekeeping, Redbook,* and *Esquire.* August Home, owned by founder Don Peschke, publishes *Woodsmith, Cuisine at Home, Garden Gate, ShopNotes* and *Workbench.* Wenner Media, owned by founder Jann Wenner, publishes *Rolling Stone, US Weekly,* and *Men's Journal.*

Many small, niche magazines are privately owned. Strang Communications Company publishes five evangelical Christian magazines—*Charisma, Ministries Today, New Man, Christian Retailing,* and *Vida Cristiana* (in Spanish), as well as religious books and educational materials. Founded by Stephen Strang in 1975, the Florida-based publishing company also produces religious conferences.

Some industry insiders say that privately held magazines can take financial risks other publishers would shudder at. The buzz in publishing circles was that Newhouse bought *The New Yorker*—for $168 million—for the prestige of the title, and allowed it to lose tens of millions of dollars a year. Because Newhouse is not accountable financially to any outsiders, he can spend as much money as he wishes. It is, after all, his money.

At one point in the late 1990s, Condé Nast was known for its top editorial perks, including condos, limousines, and clothing allowances for editors. No publicly held publisher could justify that to a stockholder.

Magazine insiders have said that *Glamour* was traditionally Condé Nast's healthiest title and that Hearst's *Esquire* lost money for years. Because private companies can keep successes and failures a secret, these comments cannot be validated. The success of both Condé Nast and Hearst titles can be measured by audited circulation or by the number of ad pages. Certainly, their titles are successful on the newsstands, but because of discounts given to advertisers, it is difficult to determine total profits and losses.

■ ORGANIZATION MAGAZINE OWNERSHIP

Association magazines usually are published by nonprofit entities; often, however, the magazine operates as a profit center. Public relations magazines have corporate parents, which may be publicly or privately owned. Custom magazines are marketing tools, and may be outsourced by an organization's marketing department; they are often produced by publishers of other consumer or trade titles.

association magazines

Association members are like stockholders; they essentially own the organization and are concerned about its success. Consequently, members have a stake in the way in which their association's publication is run. They differ from stockholders significantly, however, in that they typically are more interested in the content of the magazine and the way it serves the organization than in profit. The money the magazine makes is plowed back into membership benefits and into the work of the association.

Many association publications make a substantial amount of money, but because they are produced by nonprofit organizations, they are viewed as service to the membership rather than as profit centers. Many association magazines bring in advertising as well as subscription income, all of which goes back to the association.

Perhaps the most famous fact checker was played by Michael J. Fox in the movie *Bright Lights, Big City,* based on novelist Jay McInerney's 1984 fictitious account of life at a magazine that looked suspiciously like *The New Yorker.*

A New Family of Jobs

New technology has created evolving media, most notably online magazines. It has also created new job titles that sound and act like their print equivalents, but which have their own unique challenges and expectations.

Editor-in-Chief, Interactive Media

The editor-in-chief of Meredith Interactive Media oversees such online magazines as *Fitnessmagazine.com*, *Parents.com,* and *Americanbaby.com*, ensuring that all sites represent the original brand and are appropriate interactive extensions of the print magazine. This includes brainstorming new online features that build the business, engage users, drive ad revenue, and increase magazine subscriptions. David Kurns, who was the first person in the company to hold this position, said the job differs from that of a print editor in that a Web editor is in charge of the entire online experience, making sure, for example, that ads don't interfere with user navigation. While print magazines have a logical flow—page 2 clearly follows from page 1—Kurns said he had to worry about more complex navigational issues on his Web magazines to create an experience that was informative as well as enjoyable, and created business. Kurns called the Meredith Interactive Media structure a "new job family." Each online title has a site director, who is responsible for day-to-day content creation and production. Some sites have senior editors, others have associate editors, and others have editors; most have a producer, which is the equivalent of a production staffer on a print magazine.

Design Editor/Web Producer

As a college student at Drake University, Travis Daub was recognized across campus for his signature cowboy hat. Now, as design editor of *FP*, or *Foreign Policy*, he wears a multitude of hats. On the print magazine, a publication of the Carnegie Endowment for International Peace, he is a combination art director and production manager, designing the look of the magazine and seeing it through to production. He is also producer of the publication's website, which he helped design.

"As an organization we're pouring more and more resources into the Internet, and we're seeing great returns," he says. "We don't pretend to have the marriage of magazines and the Internet figured out, but we've made great progress."

Editorial Media Director

At August Home Publishing, editorial media directors manage multimedia information that appears in the company's magazines, websites, and other media, including television and webcasts. John Meyer, editor of *Cuisine at Home*, also doubles as an editorial media director for the company's food-related media. "It's very similar to a brand manager in the business world," Meyer says. Print, he says, is just one way to deliver information. "We have to be able to keep up with technology to deliver our message in a format that will appeal to" evolving audiences. Formats include "the Web, television, videos, video magazines, and who knows what else," Meyer says.

public relations magazines

Public relations magazines are one arm of a corporation and are generally published out of public relations, corporate communications, or human resources departments. They take their identity from the corporation and exist at the will of the corporation's management. Generally, content decisions in these magazines are made in conjunction with managers or boards of directors, not by the editors alone. When upper managers understand the goals and intricacies of the magazine, the editor's job can be smooth sailing. Often, however, management has no idea of what a magazine is, how it operates, or how it can contribute to the organization's goals. It is often the job of the editor to educate upper management on these issues.

Although the editor must make decisions based on what's good for the organization, this does not mean avoiding controversy. It may mean taking a proactive stance and being frank about problems and concerns. As with all magazines, decisions should be based on the needs of the audience. The management and the editor must make sure they agree on what those needs are.

Chronicle, the magazine of Des Moines University, formerly the University of Osteopathic Medicine and Health Sciences, has to be responsive to two groups: the university administration, which provides the budget, and the students and alumni who are readers and who ultimately provide many of the university's funds through tuition and gifts. Editor David Krause gets approval of the magazine's content from university administrators, who have the final say. If Krause disagrees with administrators' decisions, the best he can do is argue that the magazine fills the needs of two of the university's major constituencies. For example, when the university came under local media scrutiny because of financial improprieties of one president and the short tenure of a replacement, Krause ran both an article and an editorial about dealing with change.

When Liz Muhler, editor of Walgreen's internal magazine, *Walgreen World,* decided to redesign the publication, her first step was to look at the corporate mission statement and interview corporate officers. She asked them such questions as What is the main purpose of the magazine: employee recognition? company news? feature articles? Do you think the magazine currently is fulfilling that purpose? What do you like about the magazine? What would you change?

Next, Muhler studied management's responses along with responses from a questionnaire randomly sent to employees. "What these two pieces of information showed," she says, "was that people needed company information about business goals and expansion, but they also wanted employee recognition. So, as a compromise, we are developing a bimonthly newsletter geared solely toward employee recognition and trying to use the magazine for business stories." Of course, the proposed editorial plan and budget had to be presented to Muhler's department head for approval and then circulated among upper management levels for their approval.

Straight Arrow Publishing was the original name of the parent publishing company of *Rolling Stone.* Founder Jann Wenner picked that name in 1967 when he was 21 years old; he even included a small Boy Scout logo as part of the name. The Boy Scout logo disappeared in 1978, but Wenner didn't get around to changing the name of his private publishing house until 1993. Said Wenner of the switch to Wenner Media, "Straight Arrow seems sort of out of date, sort of archaic. The name Wenner Media just reflects the modern reality of what we are and what we do. It positions us for our

custom magazines

Custom magazines are external marketing tools designed to reach an existing database of consumers of a specific product or service. A custom magazine is usually an outsourced operation, which means it is created by an agency outside of the sponsoring organization. Rather than creating its own magazines, DaimlerChrysler contracted with Meredith Integrated Marketing to produce titles such as *Jeep* and *Dodge.*

The advertising implications of a custom magazine are significant. While the publication looks and feels like a consumer magazine, implicit in its publication is a marketing pitch. The creation of custom publications often resembles the creation of an advertising campaign, in which the agency offers concepts and content, but the client has the final say.

Custom magazines are created by contractual agreements, which may last several years. The magazine is owned by the organization, not by the custom publisher. At the end of the contract, the client may choose to take the magazine to another publishing house. Like advertising agencies, custom publishing houses can win or lose clients in a heartbeat.

mergers and acquisitions

America's trend toward mega-corporations seriously affects the quality of the magazine environment. The advertising-editorial conflict is exacerbated when the same large corporations own different product categories, some of which magazines seek, others of which they avoid. And editorial decisions can be influenced by corporate conflicts of interest because of corporation ownership of magazines as well as the products or services those magazines cover.

■ CORPORATE CONFLICTS OF INTEREST

Time Warner owns Warner Brothers film studios and television networks, including Home Box Office, CNN, Warner Brothers Studios, Turner Network Television, and Castle Rock Entertainment. It also owns AOL Instant Messenger, MapQuest.com and has partial ownership of amazon.com. Then there are the magazines, such as *Time, Entertainment Weekly, People, Fortune,* and *Sports Illustrated.* So, what happens if *People* editors want to pan a Warner Brothers movie, or *Time* wants to critique the dubious social effects of text messaging, or *Fortune* wants to analyze the economics of the entertainment industry?

Fairness and Accuracy in Reporting (FAIR), a media watchdog group, reported that writer and analyst Graef Crystal lost his job at *Fortune* in the early 1990s after writing about the compensation packages of Time Warner executives.[7] More common, however, are "sins of omission," when magazines choose to sidestep an issue entirely to avoid trodding on corporate toes.

Time has traditionally had a clear separation of advertising and editorial, which has served the news magazine and its publishing brothers and sisters well. Since the Time Warner merger, Time, Inc., magazines have worked toward an editorial balance, occasionally criticizing Warner executives and products, occasionally speaking positively about both. In all cases, when referring to various subsidiaries of Time Warner, the magazines make their interrelationship clear. CNN reporters, when covering any Time Warner products, include a line that explains that they are owned by the same company.

Variations on a Title

The continuation of magazine coverage of specialized topics and the expansion of custom titles and international editions have created a 21st-century crop of job titles that evolve as magazine structures expand and diversify. Sometimes new titles grow out of political or economic stresses—some companies do not allow for substantial raises with a promotion, so a person who is doing an impressive job and deserves a reward, or who is getting wooed by another publisher, gets a fancier title to do essentially the same work. This may, for example, turn a garden variety senior editor into the senior editor of features.

(continued)

Variations on a Title (continued)

Deputy Editor/Director

Wendy Naugle was promoted from health director of *Glamour* to deputy editor, health, in 2004. She says, "Almost every health story comes through my office before it goes to our editor-in-chief. At many large magazines, deputies are a way to help handle the copy flow. In essence, my job is a mix of big- and small-picture stuff. I'm trying to catch anything that an associate/articles/senior editor might miss in the editing process, and also look at the bigger picture of things: how this health story fits with other health—and beauty and news and even fashion—stories in the magazine. I also think of long-range partnerships, Web programs, and other ideas to help extend the brand and our position as a health authority in the magazine industry as well as elsewhere—I like people in the halls of science to think we have the best health coverage, too."

Integrated Marketing Editor

Rick Jost, editor of *Jeep* magazine, says his job differs significantly from that of many other Meredith Corporation editors. Meredith Integrated Marketing creates *Jeep* as a custom publication for DaimlerChrysler. The client has final say on all aspects—text, photos, layouts, and the covers. Jost and the other members of Meredith's *Jeep* team often finalize the front-cover art only a few weeks before the magazine is printed. At Meredith's consumer magazines, this decision often is made months in advance.

Entertainment Editor

Nicholas Fonseca has worked his way up the ladder of *Entertainment Weekly*, starting as an American Society of Magazine Editors intern while in college. After graduation, he joined the magazine as an editorial assistant, where he opened mail, answered phones, and did editorial research. He had the chance to pitch story ideas and write stories and, in his final year as an editorial assistant, wrote the magazine's "Monitor" section every week.

He was promoted to a correspondent position, writing and reporting for the "News and Notes" section, where he says he gave "the magazine's take on anything from a show's cancellation to an actor's death to a film's big flop. The correspondent period at *Entertainment Weekly* is typically seen as the first time you are free to generate and execute your own stories—a time to stake your claim if you want to graduate to writing longer feature stories. It's also a good time to build up your contacts." Correspondents work in New York, but spend 3-month hitches in Los Angeles to work in the magazine's West Coast bureau.

Fonseca's next promotion was to staff writer, where he got to write feature-length pieces, work for a particular section of the magazine, and generate and execute feature stories. "This was the period in which I got to write my longest and most involved stories. As a staff writer, I also covered Sundance, the Oscars, and the Emmys for the magazine" he says.

His most recent promotion was to the position of staff editor, where he works closely with one of the assistant managing editors and the staff of writers on the television beat to plan and execute feature stories. "Right now," he says, "we're planning a cover story on the NBC sitcom *The Office*, and it's my duty to work with the publicist on setting things up, keeping in contact with the writer to make sure that things are flowing smoothly and questions are being answered, and working side-by-side with our photo and art/design departments."

Fonseca works with the staff to brainstorm headlines, captions, and secondary headlines for stories. He also line-edits all feature stories about television. ■

■ PUBLISHERS OWNING ADVERTISERS

When a magazine chooses to avoid cigarette advertising, it may offend the owner of Kraft Foods. Why? Because the Altria Group, which owns cigarette manufacturer Philip Morris, also owns Kraft, with products such as Maxwell House coffee and Ritz crackers. So the magazine that wants Maxwell House advertising but wants to avoid cigarette ads has to deal with the same corporation to woo one while rejecting the other.

Or how about the magazine that publishes an article that finds fault with the chemical ingredients in the Swiffer mop? Writers do a good job, preparing an accurate, balanced, and fair report. Oops! Watch out for Procter and Gamble, manufacturer and distributor of Swiffer, in addition to Ivory Soap, Crest, Crisco, Charmin, Pampers, and a laundry list of major consumer goods. That article could cost the magazine some of its largest advertisers.

Procter and Gamble spent $620 million in American magazines in 2005; Altria Group, spent $419 million. Those are big worms dangling on the advertisers' hooks. In the 1980s, when *Ms.* was still trying to win advertisers to its side, Procter and Gamble refused to be in any issue of the magazine that included material on "gun control, abortion, the occult, cults, or the disparagement of religion" as well as those covering sex or drugs. Those guidelines virtually eliminated *Ms.* as a Procter and Gamble buy.[8] When *Ms.* ran afoul of Clairol's executives for running an article about Congressional hearings on the toxicity of hair dyes, it also lost ads from parent company Bristol-Myers, which owned Windex, Drano, and Bufferin.

Imagine the editor facing her boss, the publisher, and explaining the loss of $150,000 for one page of advertising. What will she do to make it up? Multiply that loss by 12 issues—and that editor is looking at losses in the millions of dollars. Assume the magazine is a monthly title, and the losses are potentially in the billions. Any editor would shudder at that potential.

The confident editor, backed by a supportive publisher and a magazine with high reader and advertiser appeal, can take the high road and argue that serving readers is the best way to serve advertisers. What happens, though, when the publisher is not supportive or when the magazine is having trouble selling ad pages? The publisher might be willing to live with the prospect of offending one

advertiser. Offending a huge corporation full of major advertisers is another, and far more ominous, matter.

A magazine that has trouble filling its ad pages probably has problems beyond advertiser influence. In this case, it's especially important to reassess and define the magazine's direction, and educate the ad sales staff on that direction.

Kathie Robinson, publisher of *NFPA*, the magazine of the National Fire Protection Association, acknowledged in 1998 that "mergers and acquisitions are cutting into the number of separate advertisers we previously had. Our advertisers are extremely loyal, but a highly competitive market is becoming even more so. We try to give our ad reps everything we can to help them out."[9]

NFPA's editorial staff meets with the ad staff weekly to share information, and the two staffs work together to create a strong media kit and a solid editorial calendar, to which they adhere. The editorial staff listens to ideas from the ad staff, but makes the final editorial decision without editorial input.

the work environment

Over the last 15 years, the magazine landscape has changed significantly. Downsizing, outsourcing, and restructuring have eliminated many middle management jobs. Job titles have changed, as have the responsibilities inherent in both creative and business positions. The days when an individual could specialize in a narrow skill—as a writer, an editor, or even an accountant—are largely gone. Today's staffs have to have broad skills and adaptable constitutions that allow them to work in a constantly changing environment with regularly evolving technology. Some of today's Web editors are working in a medium that did not even exist when they first entered the magazine workforce. Certainly, at small magazines, editors must be generalists—in technology, content, budgeting, and management—who can do a variety of things with little support staff. Even at larger publishers, the editor's job is like a magnet, collecting more and more work and responsibility over time, with less and less help.

Changes in ownership as a result of more financial players becoming involved in publicly owned

Women Wielding Power at the Top[1]

In an industry based on the written word, women are just as likely to hold the pen as men. Some of the most famous women of 19th-century American history have owned, operated, or edited women's magazines: Amelia Bloomer, Elizabeth Cady Stanton, Susan B. Anthony, Ida B. Wells, Jane Grey Swisshelm, and Rosa Sonneschein. Significant 20th-century editors have included Margaret Sanger, Elizabeth Tilberis, Ruth Whitney, Frances Lear, Grace Mirabella, Myrna Blyth, Jean LemMon, Patricia Carbine, Gloria Steinem, and Robin Morgan. Through the decades, then, magazine mastheads have listed notable women in top editorial positions.

Sarah Josepha Hale, who founded *Ladies' Magazine* in 1828, was one of the earliest great magazine editors. Hale merged her publication with Louis Godey's *Lady's Book* in 1837, creating *Godey's Lady's Book,* which became famous for its elegant essays and hand-colored fashion plates. Serving as editor for 50 years, Hale encouraged and published the works of women writers while also crusading for education for women.

Another significant early magazine editor and publisher was Mary Barney, who offered a forum for women to express their views on matters both political and literary. Barney wasn't interested in producing a "lady's" magazine primarily concerned with home life and fashion, a formula made successful by Hale. Barney's *The National Magazine; or, Lady's Emporium,* dismissed the stereotype that "women writers had a very real limitation in the common feeling that feminine talents did not present learned treatises on such abstract subjects as philosophy, religion, government, and history." From the first issue in November 1830, Barney provided discerning and thought-provoking articles about religious history ("The Inquisition") and transportation ("Baltimore and Ohio Rail Road"), rather than the pious poetry, etiquette hints, and sentimental page-turners anticipated by many women at this time.[2]

Miriam Leslie took over her husband Frank Leslie's magazine empire following his death in 1880 and legally changed her name to Frank Leslie in order to retain control. *Frank Leslie's Illustrated Weekly* became a financial success in 1881 as a result of the magazine's coverage of the assassination of President James A. Garfield. Certain that Garfield would die, Miriam Leslie had a special edition printed in advance that was rushed to the streets within minutes after his death. Supposedly, she earned $100,000 a year as editor and publisher. Upon her death in 1914, she left $1 million to the women's suffrage movement as well as a reputation of feminine competence and independence during the Victorian era.

Gertrude Battles Lane, who was editor of *Woman's Home Companion* from 1911 to 1940, sent women to France to cover World War I and to Geneva to cover the International Women Suffrage Alliance after the war. *Time* magazine wrote about Lane's "editorial showmanship," pointing out that in 1936, *Woman's Home Companion* had the largest circulation of all women's magazines. In 1959, Lane's salary of $52,000 was the highest paid to a woman editor—an article in *The New York Times* observed that it probably was among the highest paid to men as well.[3]

1. Excerpted from Sammye Johnson, "Women's Salary and Status in the Magazine Industry," in *Women in Mass Communication*, 3d ed., ed. Pamela J. Creedon and Judith Cramer (Thousand Oaks, Calif.: Sage Publications, 2006).

2. Sammye Johnson, *"The National Magazine; or, Lady's Emporium,"* in Kathleen L. Endres and Therese L. Lueck, *Women's Periodicals in the United States: Consumer Magazines* (Westport, Conn.: Greenwood Press): 243–53.

3. Kathleen L. Endres, *"Woman's Home Companion,"* in Kathleen L. Endres and Therese L. Lueck, *Women's Periodicals in the United States: Consumer Magazines* (Westport, Conn.: Greenwood Press): 444–55.

Research in Brief

Women Wielding Power at the Top (continued)

Although Oprah Winfrey and Martha Stewart are high-profile celebrities with successful magazines and even more successful media conglomerates, many of the top women publishers and editorial directors of today's magazines are relatively unknown to the public. But their impact on the magazine industry is significant.

Ann S. Moore oversees the world's leading magazine company as chairman and chief executive officer of Time, Inc., whose 150-plus magazines (including *Time, Sports Illustrated, Fortune, People,* and *Entertainment Weekly*) reach a total audience of more than 340 million readers worldwide and account for nearly a quarter of total advertising revenues of U.S. consumer magazines. Christie Hefner, daughter of *Playboy* founder Hugh Hefner, has been chief executive officer of Playboy Enterprises, Inc., since 1988. Cathleen Black, president of Hearst Magazines, has been called "The First Lady of American Magazines" and "one of the leading figures in American publishing over the past two decades" by *Financial Times*.

Black manages the financial performance and operations of 19 of the largest and most successful magazines in the industry, including *Cosmopolitan, Redbook, Esquire, Good Housekeeping, Seventeen, Harper's Bazaar, Marie Claire,* and *Popular Mechanics*. She also oversees 145 international editions of those magazines in more than 100 countries.

Reaching the top positions in any industry takes time. Black started in advertising sales at *Holiday* and *Travel and Leisure* in 1970 and was involved in the launch of *Ms.* magazine in 1972; she took the job at Hearst in 1996. Moore has been at Time, Inc., since 1978; she was named to her current position in 2002.

A 30-year veteran in the magazine industry, who has worked at six different consumer magazines in her climb to the top as a senior vice president and publisher of a major women's magazine, said recently, "In the 1970s, most of the people in magazines were men, but there's been a gradual shift since then. In general, more men work in business books than women. Because

of the content, more women work at women's consumer magazines." According to a vice president and publisher on the business-to-business side of the magazine industry, "Right now, we've got a full generation of women working at magazines, and there's going to be more. Women only really started working at magazines 20 years ago. So there are more women working every year, which helps. Eventually, everything will be equal."

The highest paid editor in the magazine industry in 2005—possibly the highest paid print journalist anywhere—is Bonnie Fuller, editorial director for American Media and the mastermind of a slick new look and attitude for *Star*. Fuller, who has held top editorial positions at *YM, Marie Claire, Cosmopolitan, Glamour,* and *US Weekly*, is reported to have a $3 million yearly compensation package consisting of $1.5 million salary, $1.5 million equity stake, circulation incentives up to $900,000 per year, and such perks as car service and health club expenses. ■

publishing houses have led to increasing financial pressures on publishers. Editors are being told their magazines must be both editorially creative and financially solvent. Editorial formulas must also take into account cash-flow needs and growth. Brand extensions, or ancillary activities, sometimes produce more revenue than the magazine itself.

Table 6.1 on "Magazine Revenues and Expenses," presented in Chapter 6 (see page 167), provides a demonstration of how the magazine industry has changed since the first edition of this book. In the first edition, which represented 1998 numbers, the average operating profit for the 129 magazines surveyed was 10 percent. In this edition, which represents 2004 numbers, the average operating profit was 17 percent. That increased profit has to come from somewhere, and it is often seen in increased stress on magazine staffs who are expected to serve readers and advertisers with an existing magazine while planning ancillary products, including spin-off titles, managing international editions, and overseeing Web products.

Technology also has affected both the creative and the business sides of magazines. Editors now edit on page design programs, so they need to be as adept at software such as InDesign as they are at grammar and punctuation. Designers are doing more of the work once left to printers and outside agencies, such as color correcting. "PhotoShopping" has become as much a magazine word as "Googling."

The addition of websites may or may not be accompanied by the addition of a staff to create them, especially on small magazines. That means editors now have two publications to oversee, with the online magazine creating day-to-day stress from readers with the expectation of immediate gratification.

Magazine staffs may no longer be located in the same state, much less on the same floor, so communication can be complex, with e-mail the preferred mode of discussion, bringing with it the confusion, frustration, and, occasionally, anger related to miscommunication. Strangely, people e-mail from one office to another, feeling so busy they can't get up and communicate personally with another human being down the hall.

This technical connectivity is good news for freelancers or staffers who want to work from home. Anyone with a computer can be in touch with every aspect of a magazine's business environment with the touch of a key. Telecommuting has become as commonplace as the subway as a way to get to the office. This also means, however, that many staff members are never away from the job, but are connected electronically throughout the day to other staffers, readers, advertisers, and anybody with access to their e-mail account.

The move to hire more and more freelancers helps a magazine's bottom line, but can come at the expense of the staff, which has to manage outside writers and designers who may or may not actually comprehend the magazine's mission. Editors can spend several days rewriting the work of a freelance writer who collected the essential information but who wrote a piece that lacks the magazine's style and tone. In other cases, sadly, editors have to back up and even do additional research to replace dull quotes or vague details. Art directors have to redo designed pages that ignored the magazine's grid structure or color palette.

The race to make more profits for shareholders has resulted in what some consider wage inflation at the top, with CEOs being paid in the millions. Others say the competition for such people is fierce and their compensation has to be connected to the huge stresses that come from the expectations to keep the company increasingly profitable nationally and internationally. Plus, with huge responsibilities come huge risks, and highly paid staffers can be ex-staffers fairly quickly.

Still, treating people well and creating a supportive work environment pays off financially at all levels. According to Leigh Branham, author of *The 7 Hidden Reasons Employees Leave*, research "supports the fact that positive cultures and good people management practices are leading indicators of business performance. In fact, the stock growth of the public companies selected in *Fortune*'s '100 best places to work' during the years 1998 to 2003 outperformed the Standard and Poor average 125 percent to 25 percent."[10]

notes

1. John Fry, "Supereditor: Making the Myth Work," *Folio:* (January 1987): 156.
2. *The Charlie Rose Show*, PBS (August 25, 1998), Show #2233.
3. "40 for the Future," *Folio:* (April 1, 1996), 35.
4. Constance L. Hayes, "Magazine Chief Shakes Things up at Hearst," *New York Times* (June 2, 1997): 1B.
5. Fry, 157.
6. Barbara Love, "How Our Jobs Have Changed," *Folio:* (April 1, 1998): 52.
7. "Where's the Power: Newsroom or Boardroom?" *Extra: The Magazine of FAIR* (July/August 1998): 23.
8. Gloria Steinem, "Sex, Lies, and Advertising," *Ms.* (July/August 1990): 26.
9. Anne Graham, "Peace Overtakes the Ad/Edit Conflict," *Folio:* (July 1998): 89.
10. Leigh Branham, "Q and A with the Author of *The 7 Hidden Reasons Employees Leave,*" *Keeping the People Report* (Winter 2005), http://www.keepingthepeople .com/newsletter/vol-03-winter-2005.html.

for additional reading

Branham, Leigh. *The 7 Hidden Reasons Employees Leave: How to Recognize the Subtle Signs and Act Before It's Too Late*. New York: Amacom, 2004.

Gill, Brendan. *Here at* The New Yorker. New York: Random House, 1975.

Kunkel, Thomas. *Genius in Disguise: Harold Ross of* The New Yorker. New York: Random House, 1997.

Mehta, Ved. *Remembering Mr. Shawn's* New Yorker: *The Invisible Art of Editing*. Woodstock, N.Y.: Overlook Press, 1998.

Ross, Lillian. *Here but Not Here*. New York: Random House, 1998.

PART

three

PART THREE

the
magazine's
content

chapter 8

molding the magazine's content: editorial style

When *Newsweek* began in 1933 as a news magazine alternative to *Time*, it had a hyphen between the two syllables of its name and seven photographs on the cover to depict an important event for each day of the week. *Newsweek* has dropped the hyphen and the seven photos as part of its news digest approach. Other cosmetic changes have occurred over the years, but *Newsweek*'s underlying character remains the same: Editorially, it's not *Time*. ■ *Newsweek*'s character is reflected in how editorial content—the departments and features—is molded in terms of topic, angle, style, and approach, as well as the amount of research and authority that goes into each piece. Readers are drawn to a magazine's editorial package, to the vibrant and engaging article mix that distinguishes one publication from another. While some readers may occasionally pick up a magazine because of a single department, a successful publication needs a core readership that transcends any particular article. This reader loyalty starts with a single issue and builds up over time. Readers eventually look for certain types of articles in every issue and gravitate toward magazines that provide a particular approach or way of covering topics. ■ Norman Cousins, who was editor of *Saturday Review* for 30 years, from 1940 to 1971, believed that "reader loyalty is based on the continuing maintenance of certain standards, not just on past performance." A magazine's readership, Cousins said, "rests on the quality of the relationship between editors and readers. Readers must feel respected and valued; they must feel that they are not just keys on a cash register but partners in an ongoing venture."[1]

FEBRUARY 17, 1933 (Premiere Issue): The first issue of *Newsweek*, originally called *News-Week*, demonstrated its editorial approach on the cover, which featured seven photographs, one for each day of the week. Each photograph highlighted a significant aspect of current news, which revolved around the implications of Hitler's advances in Germany.

article types

A magazine's editorial content provides that ongoing venture from issue to issue. Specific article types occur in both the feature and department sections of magazines: service, profile, investigative reporting, essay, and fiction. The length and depth of coverage, as well as the editor-in-chief's inclinations toward a particular approach, generally determine whether the article becomes a department or a feature. Some features aren't obviously a particular type or may be a blending of types; these are referred to as "general features" by magazine editors.

Service, profile, and investigative articles typically are grounded in objective, balanced reporting that includes a context for verifiable, in-depth facts and quotes gathered from myriad sources.

While some essays follow an objective path, most are intensely personal and interpretive. Fiction—short stories and novels—is the least frequent type of content found in today's magazines. Yet many of the most engaging nonfiction articles use the tools of fiction, including narration, dialogue, description, point of view, characterization, and personification.

■ SERVICE

Early in the history of *Better Homes and Gardens*, founder Edwin T. Meredith coined a phrase that melodiously summed up his vision of what service was in a magazine: "No fiction, no fashion, no piffle, no passion." "Piffle" was the buzz word in the 1920s for trivial nonsense that was of little worth; "no passion" referred to a lack of sentimental short stories.

The definition of service journalism was updated in 1987 by Byron T. Scott, then the Meredith Chair of Service Journalism at the University of Missouri in Columbia: "Service journalism is needed information delivered in the right medium at the right time in an understandable form, and intended for immediate use by the audience."[2] James Autry, editor of *Better Homes and Gardens* from 1970 to 1981, preferred to identify service journalism as "action journalism" because "it is journalism that goes beyond the delivery of pure information, to include the expectation that the reader will *do* something as a result of the reading."[3]

With that definition in mind, today's service pieces include expert yet practical advice, how-to information, and news and trends that empower readers and their families. While the content of service pieces may seem more micro and local than macro and global, "they can have a tremendous impact: They can change the way readers think or act, alter the way they spend time or money, influence style, eating habits and travel plans, improve relationships, diminish biases," argues Pamela Fiori, editor-in-chief of *Town and Country*. She continues,

> Service magazines help the reader cope—with aging parents or one's aging self, an alcoholic co-worker, a serious illness, unemployment, change of address or change of life. They might even inspire the reader to contribute to society—by volunteering his or her services, by writing to Con-

THE BUSINESS TOOL FOR REAL ESTATE PROFESSIONALS

REALTOR
MAGAZINE

Countdown to NARdi Gras p. 14
Digital cameras from $250 to $1,500 p. 50

THE POWER OF INTERNET MARKETING
Blog for business growth
Turn leads into profits
p. 33

MAY 2006: As the publication of the National Association of Realtors, *Realtor* magazine provides service information on managing a successful real estate business.

gress, by joining a local environmental group. Or closer to home, by spending more time with the kids.[4]

Though once narrowly associated with women's concerns and issues, service articles now can be found in most consumer, trade, and organization magazines, as ongoing departments and stand-alone features. Service articles demand accuracy and credibility in the depiction of material that is easy to read and understand. Graphic devices are important tools in service formats: lists, boxes, bullets, charts, maps, graphs, calendars, and diagrams abound in order to highlight information for the reader.

expert advice

The service article dates back to the advice-giving departments established in 1883 by Louisa Knapp Curtis, the first editor of *Ladies' Home Journal.* She followed the long-established editorial formula found in successful women's magazines of the mid-19th century, such as *Godey's Lady's Book* and *Peterson's Magazine,* and featured serialized novels and short stories for entertainment along with articles on motherhood, housekeeping, and fashion for women. However, the backbone of *Ladies' Home Journal* was in the household hints departments and special homemaker features written by women for women.

The women writers who suggested better ways of cleaning, cooking, needlework, and interior decorating were considered experts in their fields. They all had many years of experience in successfully managing a home; some, like *Ladies' Home Journal* contributing household editor Christine Frederick, took a scientific approach to housekeeping, based on business and engineering principles being adopted in factories. Frederick believed women's work would be more efficient if counters and sinks were the right height, if kitchens had good light and ventilation, and if tasks were systematically organized. In almost every issue, Frederick wrote about "the new housekeeping," which saved steps in the kitchen, whether it was washing dishes, canning fruit, or preparing dinner for eight couples.

Clearly, the content of *Ladies' Home Journal* revolved around expert domestic advice as indicated in the "Practical Homekeeper" subtitle to the title. At *Ladies' Home Journal,* the practical homemaker was urged to be efficient and professional—and to take advantage of the many new appliances and products being developed specifically for the home.

When Edward Bok became editor in January 1890, the service function of *Ladies' Home Journal* already was well established. A sharp businessman and brilliant editor, Bok expanded the service departments and made the magazine an exciting blend of commerce and education. During his 39 years as editor, Bok constantly consulted his readers through informal surveys, encouraged them to write letters to the editor, and consistently responded to their wants and desires.

In his third-person autobiography, Bok described his concept of service and its development: "Step by step, the editor built up this service behind the magazine until he had a staff of thirty-five editors on the monthly payroll; in each issue he proclaimed the willingness of these editors to answer immediately any questions by mail; he encouraged and cajoled his readers to form the habit

Marriages Still Being Saved by *Ladies' Home Journal*

Ladies' Home Journal touts its "Can This Marriage Be Saved?" department as "the most enduring women's magazine feature in the world." The long-running column, which peeks into the problems of married couples every month, first appeared in January 1953.

For 30 years, "Can This Marriage Be Saved?" was written by Dorothy Cameron Disney, a pioneer marriage advice counselor and columnist. Her technique was to take the troubled couple out to dinner to learn about their marital woes, then interview each separately. No identifying names or details were ever used, and Disney contacted counseling agencies and therapists throughout the United States for source material.

What distinguished Disney's advice column was her use of

intimate "he said/she said" dialogue about money problems, jealousy, infidelity, and sex, followed by her down-to-earth advice. Because of its candid language, "Can This Marriage Be Saved?" was said to be how many girls of the 1950s learned about sex.

In the 100th anniversary issue of *Ladies' Home Journal* in 1984, Disney wrote, "The columns seem to represent a chronicle of the many changes in the institution of marriage— and the fascination it holds." She concluded that of all the marital problems she came across, "the single greatest pitfall of all times is the inability of husband and wife to communicate. 'He (or she) never listens' is universal."

Still timely today—the January 2006 issue stated: "He hates his job and it's ruining our

MARCH 2006: The longevity of *Ladies' Home Journal's* "Can this Marriage Be Saved?" department demonstrates the enduring relationship readers have with their magazines.

marriage"—and still following the same format, "Can This Marriage Be Saved?" is even a registered trademark. ■

of looking upon his magazine as a great clearing-house of information."[5]

For example, in the March 1914 issue, readers could find advice on dealing with warts and moles, preparing ham 38 different ways, repairing fences, dressing a baby in winter, and furnishing a five-room apartment for $500. Queries about proper dating etiquette with men as well as questions about sticky social situations and cultural conundrums were answered in the regular "Girls' Affairs" column. In the ongoing department "What Other Women Have Found out About Economy in the Kitchen," 24 readers shared their tips: Use bread crusts to grease pans, dip the knife in boiling

water before cutting a slice of butter, and jot down the costs of each item on the recipe card.

The success of the service approach quickly became evident. Bok pointed out that when the practice of personally responding to every reader by return mail "was finally stopped by the Great War of 1917–1918, the yearly correspondence totaled nearly a million letters."

To the service format, then, Bok brought reader participation and trust in the editorial message, creating a magazine that became "a vital need in the personal lives of its readers" because it was grounded in information. Or, in today's parlance, it was "news you can use." The women's service

A Little Extra on the Side: Sidebars and Tip Boxes

Today's readers are accustomed to messages with multiple points of entry. Members of Generations X and Y especially tend not to be linear thinkers, preferring their articles in bits and bytes that allow them to go in multiple directions while reading. Sidebars and tip boxes spread information around the page for a lively package that can add depth and breadth to standard articles.

A sidebar consists of editorial material that supports a feature. Sidebars can be short, secondary articles that provide an in-depth look at one aspect of the topic the feature introduced; a list of bulleted points providing additional details; or even a short profile of a person introduced in the feature. The same person usually writes the sidebar and the main article. Sidebars appear on the same pages as the feature they support, but the two are graphically separated, usually with rule lines, color tints, or both. Sidebars can be as small as a paragraph or as large as a double-page spread. In an article on personal investing, a sidebar could provide sample budgets, short profiles on successful young investors, or a time line showing how an investment grows over several decades.

A tip box offers service information to support a feature or department article. Tip boxes typically consist of bulleted points that provide additional resources, suggestions for action, or extra ideas, with very little narrative copy, if any. Tip boxes, as their name implies, are usually boxed either by rules or color blocks. A tip box for the personal investment article might include tips on how to save money to invest or a list of websites that provide investment work sheets.

approach pioneered by *Ladies' Home Journal* was followed by other popular women's magazines. The largest in circulation and most successful practitioners in the category became known as the "seven sisters" magazines: *Better Homes and Gardens, Family Circle, Good Housekeeping, McCall's, Redbook, Woman's Day,* and of course, *Ladies' Home Journal.*

The seven sisters are now six with the demise of *McCall's,* and the service article is no longer exclusive to women's magazines. Other publications have adopted the service approach and made it their own.

Sunset magazine is an example of how the service approach spread beyond women magazines. It was established in 1898 by the Southern Pacific Railroad to challenge the assumptions of Eastern magazines such as *The Atlantic Monthly* about the West: that the region was a land of get-rich-quick schemers and not for respectable families. Stories about the wonders of the West and short stories by Zane Gray, Jack London, and Bret Harte domi-

nated the pages of the magazine. Then, in 1929, a new owner who had been an advertising executive with *Better Homes and Gardens* decided to turn *Sunset* into a service magazine that gave newcomers to the West information about the best in Western living. Articles about the four lifestyle categories of food, home, garden, and travel became the basic service format for the regional magazine that the magazine continues to follow today.

In 1996, then-editor-in-chief Rosalie Muller Wright said *Sunset*'s strength is service to readers, pointing out that the magazine has three people who spend each day fielding phone calls from readers. Said Wright, "Far and away the largest number of them are from people who recently bought their first home. They've got a scrubby little garden; they want to do something with it, what can they do? Well, that's what we're here for. Service, service, service."[6]

Service articles can be found in consumer magazines as disparate as *Glamour, Men's Health,* and

Baby Talk. The National Magazine Awards category for personal service honors excellence in service journalism, specifically advice or instruction that helps readers improve the quality of their lives.

Glamour's 1997 National Magazine Award-winning two-part series about health management organizations is a fine example of the content and approach found in a service article. "Is Managed Care Good for Women's Health?" by Leslie Laurence and "Making Managed Care Work for You" by Tessa DeCarlo, which ran in the August and September 1996 issues, respectively, provided a clear and compelling examination of HMOs and their effects on consumers. The articles were designed to inspire action and to provide the information needed to act.

The 2004 National Magazine Award winner in the personal service category went to a special report on heart disease that appeared in the July/August 2003 issue of *Men's Health*. Judges said readers were given "a defibrillating jolt of service journalism" with "A Tale of Three Hearts" by Peter Moore, "100 Ways to Live Forever" by Adam Campbell and Brian Good, and "Death by Exercise" by Lou Schuler. Continuing the heart metaphor, judges

added, "This package doesn't miss a beat. Palpitating photography and graphics enhance the ultimate reader service: a chance for a longer life."[7]

Baby Talk won the 2005 National Magazine Award in the personal service category for its article about breast-feeding in the August 2004 issue. The judges clearly pinpointed what made the article a quintessential service one: "In 'You *Can* Breastfeed,' Kristin O'Callaghan mixes useful advice, knowing humor and accessible prose to demystify one of the more complex experiences of new motherhood. Presenting seven common challenges faced by most breastfeeding moms—the piece artfully sets a comforting, we're-all-in-the-same-boat tone while offering highly practical tips for nursing moms."[8]

Expert advice in business-to-business magazines operates on a similar level, but it's not as personal and intimate. Instead, it is designed to help people in their professions. Robert Freedman, editor of *Realtor Magazine*, says, "Magazines in the construction industry must write about why remodelers are going for honed stone countertops rather than flamed granite, and what the tricks are of mastering installation." The bottom line, Freed-

---

How to Improve Editorial Content

Good Housekeeping editor-in-chief Ellen Levine has 10 tips for improving editorial content that she's been following ever since she became a magazine editor:

1. Cut story lengths; readers are impatient.
2. When you can't find news, try to create it by conducting surveys.
3. Sex still sells.
4. Give readers information unavailable elsewhere.
5. Strive for exclusive stories.
6. Don't focus on winning awards.
7. Lists of information are popular.
8. Don't rely on "proven" formulas for editing magazines.
9. Always be nice to advertisers.
10. Remember your magazine can make readers' lives better or worse with what it publishes.[1]

1. "Editors Air Their Views About Print," *ABC News Bulletin* (December 1987): 9.

man says, is that business magazines have a "central role in the exchange of best practices within a business or industry."[9]

how-to information

It's not enough to simply advise in service journalism; explanation, interpretation, and suggestions for future action must be included, usually through the inclusion of how-to-do-it information. Along with who, when, and where, the what, why, and how are thoroughly documented, as problems are solved or possibilities discussed.

What a reader finds applicable and of value in a service-oriented magazine like *Wood* are articles on how to use tools safely, such as "Spotlight on Tablesaw Safety" that began: "In 1975, more than 5,000 woodworkers lost fingers in tablesaw accidents." According to editor Bill Krier, each issue is filled with "projects you can build without hassle (thanks to our step-by-step, fully illustrated how-to instructions); informative articles on shop skills and techniques; jigs and fixtures you can build; handy shop tips; hard-hitting tool and product reviews (complete with brand-name recommendations); and fascinating feature articles covering the world of wood."[10] With its emphasis on detailed, shop-tested instructions, *Wood* reaches all skill levels, from novice to fine craftsman.

Reader's Digest **has published more than 100,000 jokes since its first issue in 1922 and paid more than $25 million to readers for their contributions to "Laughter, the Best Medicine" and "Humor in Uniform."**

Sunset often includes the how-to approach when it goes beyond the backyard relationship with readers to cover national environmental concerns, as in its February 2005 article on "Paradise Saved: 10 Newly Preserved Western Treasures, Waiting for You to Enjoy Them."

"Editors aim to make their trade publications central to their readers' professional success, but the extent to which they succeed in that ambition depends in large measure on how well they handle how-to articles," says Kimberly Sweet, editor of *Professional Remodeler.* "More than any other content, how-to articles are a way of providing information that readers take away from the publication and apply directly to their work."[11]

How-to articles cover details in a show-and-tell approach. When *Success in Home Care* chronicled a day in the life of a nurse in an article about time management and productivity in the May/June 2003 issue, an actual page from the nurse's day planner was included. Editors also included a blank daily activity log that readers could photocopy for their own use.

Travel magazines are built almost entirely around the how-to service approach. With almost unlimited where-to-go and when-to-go globetrotting possibilities, destination pieces can be developed that attract armchair travelers and adventurous vacationers. Both groups of readers want consumer information, entertaining copy, and lush descriptions of the settings. They also want accuracy. Recognizing this, *Condé Nast Traveler*'s "truth in travel" stance has led the way toward a more critical viewpoint and voice in travel pieces. Readers now can learn which beaches are dirty and which cities are safe from terrorist acts.

Travel pieces have been a magazine staple since the 18th century. As early as 1784, a travel article about the South Seas was serialized for three issues in *The Gentleman and Lady's Town and Country Magazine.* The first issue of *Port Folio* featured John Quincy Adams's "Journal of a Tour through Silesia" in January 1801; the journal ran during most of the year. Later, travel articles by Mark Twain in *The Century* and *The Atlantic Monthly* and by Ernest Hemingway in *Life* and *Esquire* took a subjective and anecdotal tone. But they still performed a service for readers in terms of where-to-go in order to escape from the mundane and ordinary and featured informative you-are-there descriptions of places and people.

Some magazine scholars argue that travel articles, because of their descriptive nature, are closer to profiles, especially when geographic, social, political, and economic data are included. *National Geographic*'s pieces are often so exhaustively in-depth that "service," with its implication of quick accessibility and utility, seems a misnomer. Additionally, there's a strong literary tradition to be found in travel articles by Jan Morris and Paul Theroux, who both write in an impressionistic yet highly detailed tone about exotic locales. Their work could be described as safari-style new journalism.

Articles in travel magazines range from *Travel and Leisure*'s expensive monthlong jaunts to distant and exotic destinations to the affordable 4-day travel tips found in *Arthur Frommer's Budget Travel,* appropriately subtitled *Vacations for Real People.* The practical, bargain-orientation of *Arthur Frommer's Budget Travel* is almost 180 degrees away from the "aspirational" luxury travel magazines dominating the travel market. Founded by travel advice guru Arthur Frommer, the magazine focuses on service to readers who prefer to spend an average of $1,000 to $2,000 on trips, as opposed to $10,000 or more.[12]

news and trends

Trade and association magazines are particularly dedicated to the news and trends aspect of service. Dennis W. Jeffers, a journalism professor at Central Michigan University who studied service journalism in *Angus Journal,* a publication of the American Angus Association, says, "Technical and educational information relating to specific practices of members is featured in these magazines in the hope that members will read it and then take specific action to adopt 'new and improved' methods or techniques."[13] According to Jeffers, readers of association magazines like *Angus Journal* "clearly indicate that 'service' content in the form of management information has the highest priority." He says that feature stories and personality profiles are not what the majority of readers want, although editors include such material to provide variety. Above all, association readers want content that is useful.

Useful service content for trade and organization magazine readers is news—about government regulation and legislation, market trends, technological and research innovations, and new products that might be helpful to one's business or profession. Most specialized business press service pieces focus on solving practical problems.

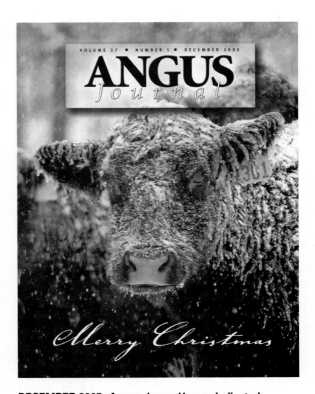

DECEMBER 2005: *Angus Journal* **has a dedicated readership of cattle breeders—which they call "our Angus family"—who look to the magazine for industry news and trends.**

The writers' guidelines for *Internal Auditor,* the publication of the Institute of Internal Auditors, explain what are considered to be good articles:

One basic criterion for any good manuscript is whether or not the author has something of value to say: Does the manuscript provide information others might need or value? The best catalyst for a good article is likely to come from one's own internal audit experiences. Individuals who have found a way to audit a new high-risk area or to simplify report writing, for example, have information others want and will avidly read. Articles falling under this category include case studies that describe actual procedures or methodologies used at a particular organization or discussions of audit challenges that offer solutions, using actual or hypothetical examples. Articles that are theoretical in nature or are based on academic research should include practical applications. Manuscripts based on studies or surveys, for example, should draw conclusions from the research, analyze the impact on the profession, and offer insight or advice that will be useful to readers.[14]

Awards: A Measurement of How Well Magazines Serve Their Readers

Receiving recognition from their peers is a great incentive for many writers and editors, although awards are hard to quantify. Awards often motivate people to perform at their highest level—the pride factor—and awards can be marketed in media sales kits and other promotional pieces to highlight market status.

Peer approval is often measured by awards from the American Society of Magazine Editors (ASME), which annually presents the National Magazine Awards, and the American Business Media, which hands out the Neal Awards. Both competitions are considered among the most prestigious in the magazine industry and are often referred to as the Pulitzers of the magazine world.

What does it take to bring home one of those awards—and what does it mean to the magazine's bottom line?

Lew McCreary, editorial director of CXO Media, whose *CIO* magazine won Grand Neal Awards in 2003 and 2004, says it may be tempting to keep awards in mind when making article assignments, but that's not the secret to success. You have to keep your reader first

and foremost. "Be intensively responsive to what your readers need. Most awards programs recognize an intimate understanding of the audience," McCreary says.[1]

Since being named *Esquire*'s editor-in chief in 1997, David Granger has guided the magazine to seven National Magazine Awards, most recently for feature writing in 2005. "The large part of the judging process in the general excellence awards is whether a magazine serves its mission statement and readers. If you create a magazine that thrills and serves your readers, that goes a long way."[2]

Alfred Rosenblatt, managing editor *IEEE Spectrum,* which has won four National Magazine Awards, talks about the effects of the honor: "It shows we are well regarded by our peers. It is more than symbolic. It's motivation. It is something our editors can aspire to. It's like an Oscar for writers."[3] *IEEE Spectrum* is the flagship magazine of the IEEE, or Institute of Electrical and Electronics Engineers, Inc., an international professional association for the advancement of technology ranging from aerospace systems, computers and

telecommunications to biomedical engineering and consumer electronics.

While adding prestige to the magazine, though, awards are not a clear indication of the magazine's economic health. Ellen Levine, editor-in-chief of *Good Housekeeping*, says awards are a "wonderful thing for editors and ad salespeople to talk about. But I've seen editors accept awards and then get fired the next month. And I have yet to meet an advertiser who buys a page because you won an award."[4]

Advertisers are wary of awards. "We have to remember it's the magazine community, not the readers, who are voting. As much as we might want to believe there's a carryover effect with the reader, we have to marry the winning of the award with other indicators of reader appreciation," says Ellen Oppenheim, executive vice president and chief marketing officer of the Magazine Publishers of America (MPA). Prior to joining MPA in 2001, Oppenheim was senior vice president and media director at Foote, Cone and Belding advertising agency in New York.[5] ∎

1. "Six Steps to Winning Magazine Awards," *Folio:* (May 2005): 20.
2. Ibid., 20.
3. "Winning Responses," *Folio:* (April 15, 1994): 28.
4. Constance L. Hays, "Award Puffs Magazines' Egos but Fails to Bolster Ad Sales," *The New York Times* (April 28, 1997): C7.
5. Ibid., C7.

■ PROFILE

Articles concentrating on the lives and achievements of famous, infamous, and ordinary individuals have been published since American magazines were established in 1741. The word "profile" was coined by *The New Yorker* during the 1920s and even registered. But the magazine wasn't rigorous in maintaining its rights and use of the word passed into everyday use as an article detailing an individual's life and showing who that person is. The profile has a variety of approaches: biography, *The New Yorker* profile, personality sketch, question and answer (Q & A), no interviewer, and institutional.

biography

During the 18th and 19th centuries, biographies of famous statesmen—and a few women—took a linear approach from birth to death. Alexander the Great, Napoleon Bonaparte, George Washington, and Abraham Lincoln were some of the historical figures whose lives appeared in magazines. "The last half of the present century has developed an extraordinary mania for heroes and hero worship," wrote adventurer C. Chaillé-Long in the *North American Review* in May 1887, when discussing the number of biographies found in magazines then.[15]

Successful businessmen and financiers such as John Jacob Astor and John D. Rockefeller, as well as sports figures such as Babe Ruth, were predominant biographical subjects after the turn of the 20th century. While these biographical articles were long, detailed, and often comprehensive, they lacked honesty and candor.

the new yorker profile

Harold Ross, founder of *The New Yorker,* wanted to run a shorter, more focused form of the biography in his new magazine. Critic Wolcott Gibbs, writing in 1943, observed that *The New Yorker* profile gradually developed "from its very feeble beginnings [in the 1925 first issue] to its present remarkably thorough form" because of Harold Ross's "ferocious curiosity about people."[16]

Under Ross, the profile became a probing biographical study. Ross didn't want an impression of an individual, such as would be found in a short

MAY 15, 2006: *The New Yorker* **introduced the profile form in the magazine's first issue in 1925. The profile— a name coined by** *The New Yorker* **founder Harold Ross, remains a staple of the magazine's editorial mix.**

personality sketch. He wanted "a family history, bank reference, Social Security number, urinalysis, catalogue of household possessions, names of all living relatives, business connections, political affiliations, as well as a profile."[17] Writers were expected to interview not just the individual, but his or her family, friends, enemies, professional colleagues, and even servants. The profiles were so long they sometimes appeared in four to six installments. The result often was provocative and profound. To be profiled in *The New Yorker,* said critic Clifton Fadiman, individuals merely had to have "made a success, not of their bank-balances, but of their personalities."

The New Yorker profiled the famous and the infamous. Some scholars consider Lillian Ross's May 13, 1950, *New Yorker* profile of Ernest Hemingway to be one of the most controversial magazine articles ever published. Taking the "I am a camera" approach, Ross provided a detailed account of what it was like to spend 2 days with the famous novelist: "I tried to describe as precisely as possible how Hemingway, who had the nerve to be like nobody else on earth, looked and sounded when he was in action, talking, between work periods—to give a picture of the man as he was, in his uniqueness and with his vitality and his enormous spirit of fun intact."[18]

Hemingway fans hated the piece. One critic wrote, "It was widely thought to be a 'devastating' portrait of the writer as an over-the-hill borderline alcoholic, whose mock-Indian lingo and constant baseball and boxing references were sad affectations."[19]

Ross, who later republished the Hemingway profile in two of her books, *Portrait of Hemingway* and *Reporting*, defended her work:

> When I wrote the Profile, I attempted to set down only what I had seen and heard,

and not to comment on the facts or express any opinions or pass any judgments. However, I believe that today—with the advantage gained by distance—almost any reader would see that although I did not reveal my viewpoint directly, implicit in my choice and arrangement of detail, and in the total atmosphere created, was my feeling of affection and admiration.

She pointed out that Hemingway himself liked the piece and wrote to reassure her that "some people couldn't understand his enjoying himself and his not being really spooky; they couldn't understand his being a serious writer without being pompous."

Only a handful of magazines today—including *Vanity Fair, Esquire,* and *Sports Illustrated*—have the space and stamina to follow the demanding *New Yorker* profile form, which often ran thousands of words. Most editors use the word profile to indicate an article that's less comprehensive than a biography, more in-depth than a sketch, but

The entire 80 years of *The New Yorker* are available on searchable digital videodiscs that allow each page of the magazine to be displayed either singularly or in pairs. A viewer can search on any disc for an author, artist, title, subject, or cover, or by key words. Readers can also go directly to the pages with cartoons. According to editor David Remnick, "Ninety percent of our subscribers say they read the cartoons first, and the rest would be lying."

not as exhaustive as a *New Yorker* piece.

personality sketch

Although it's an axiom that people like to read about people, the long profile form is not as prevalent as it once was. The trend now is toward the short, tightly focused personality sketch that was honed by *People* magazine, established in 1974. *People*'s personality sketches may be as short as 1,000 words in length, taking only a page or two of space, while celebrity cover interviews often run multiple pages. Many of *People*'s thumbnail profiles revolve around "hot" entertainment celebrities, although there are always stories about ordinary people whose lives provide an emotional impact or who have been thrust into the news for one heroic reason or another.

question and answer

Some magazines prefer the question-and-answer, or Q & A, approach to profiles. *Saturday Evening Post* took a tightly focused, short Q & A angle during the late 1950s and most of the 1960s for a series titled "I Call On" by Pete Martin. Martin "called on" movie stars ranging from Bing Crosby and Zsa Zsa Gabor to Jack Lemmon and Shirley MacLaine. Most of the low-key interviews took place in the stars' homes, where respondents felt comfortable being informal and amusing.

Playboy offers another variation on the Q & A, with its monthly question-and-answer format involving many hours of taped interviews with an individual. *Playboy* likes to talk to powerhouse celebrities from the political, entertainment, and literary arenas. Interviews have ranged from Tom Clancy to Tom Cruise and from Betty Friedan to Joyce Carol Oates. *Playboy*'s first interview, in September 1962, was with jazzman Miles Davis; it was conducted by a young writer named Alex Haley. Haley, who did 10 interviews for *Playboy,* including the Rev. Martin Luther King Jr., Cassius Clay (boxer Mohammed

The Two-page, 800-word *People* Profile

In the introductory note of the March 4, 1974, premiere issue of *People Weekly* magazine, managing editor Richard B. Stolley explained the magazine's philosophy: "*People* is a magazine whose title fits it perfectly. There is nothing abstract about our name. *People* is what we are all about. Journalism has, of course, always noted and dealt with people. But we dedicate our entire editorial content to that pursuit."

In focusing on celebrities as well as ordinary men and women, Stolley stressed that the magazine would "concentrate on the individuals rather than the issues, on the force of personality, on what's happening to human beings and how those human beings react."

In order to follow that mandate, a formula was developed for the bread-and-butter feature of the magazine: the two-page, 800-word profile. That piece is extensively researched, exhaustively fact-checked, and painstakingly edited and re-edited multiple times by full-time fact checkers, says executive editor Cutler Durkee.

"We have high standards. We get it right," Durkee says.

Gerald Grow, a journalism professor at Florida A & M University, visited with the editors of *People* in 2005 to learn more about the magazine's story structure.[1] According to Grow, *People* has "a boilerplate approach to stories, with people telling their story in a colloquial style, to hook the reader with photo, typography, and lede."

That approach results in the following story structure for *People* profiles:[2]

- *Anecdotal opening*: A reflective story, revealing scene, or provocative quote that grabs the reader. It has its own appeal and its own "kicker" ending that sets up the story.
- *"Billboard"* paragraph: Explains what the story is about and why we are reading it now. It pulls the reader further into the story.
- *Body*: Tells the rest of the story, generally taking about three paragraphs in a two-page profile.
- *Biography*: Falling about two thirds of the way into the story, a brief chronological overview covers such information as "He was born in. . . ." The *People* formula eschews putting the biography near the top, which is where most writers would be tempted to place it. The assumption is that readers aren't interested in back-

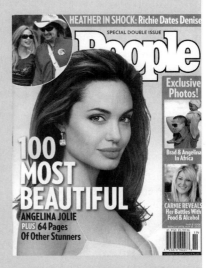

MAY 8, 2006: Using a well-defined editorial process, *People* magazine tells the stories of celebrated as well as unknown Americans.

ground unless they are first interested in the person.
- *Ending*: Can be anything that provides a definite, satisfying close to the story, such as a clever final quote from the individual, or even an ironic parting shot from the writer.

People distinguishes itself "by not being gratuitously nasty or harassing its subjects," says Durkee. "The heart and soul of it is good writing"—and a template that blends straight journalistic reporting and literary techniques to tell a good story. ■

1. Gerald Grow, "Professional Development Tour of New York Magazines 2005," http://www.longleaf.net/ggrow/NY05.
2. Gerald Grow, "Professional Development Tour of New York Magazines 2002," http://www.longleaf.net/ggrow/NYTrip02.

Ali), and Quincy Jones, had the tables turned when he was interviewed in January 1977 shortly after completing *Roots.*

Individuals who commit to a *Playboy* "interview of record," as the editors call it, must agree to an extended session that can range from 6 to 40 hours over a period as long as 6 months. Writer Larry DuBois spent 2 years interviewing actor Robert Redford—an hour here, an hour there—before the piece appeared in the December 1974 issue. Each Q & A is prefaced by a comprehensive introduction that tells where and when the interview took place, sets the tone of the profile, and establishes the parameters of the dialogue.

The published Q & A is not a simple linear transcript of the conversation; it is a judiciously edited piece that gets at the heart and soul of the subject. The journalist-interviewer serves as the magazine's voice: probing, yet neutral.

In a 1998 Internet chat, founder Hugh Hefner identified the *Playboy* interview as his favorite recurring feature (after the centerfold, of course). Said Hefner, "The one that stands out first is the interview with Jimmy Carter in the '70s [November 1976] because it became the major source of controversy before the election and he got elected." Hefner also lists the Martin Luther King Jr., Fidel Castro, and Malcolm X interviews as memorable, adding, "They are a source of great journalistic pride for me."[20]

no interviewer

In 1884, *The Century* began a series that featured the first-person Civil War experiences of surviving generals—Grant, McClellan, Sherman, Beauregard,

Fly Rod and Reel is a maverick among fly-fishing magazines due to its publication of a "fiction issue" every year since 1988. The Robert Traver Fly-fishing Fiction Award is given to "a distinguished original work of short fiction that embodies an implicit love of fly-fishing, respect for the sport and the natural world in which it takes place, and high literary values." In addition to having the story published in the magazine, the winner receives $2,500. Rhett Ashley, who had never published a piece of fiction before entering the contest and winning in 2005, wrote about two guys marooned at a women-only fishing camp in the wilds of Alaska. That must have been some fish story.

Johnston, and Longstreet—from both sides of the Mason-Dixon line, as well as the remembrances of unmilitary types like Mark Twain. Editors saw the series as a way of reconciling the North and South without any frills or moralizing. The "Civil War Series" ran monthly for 3 years, from November 1884 through November 1887, making it the longest running article in magazine history. The series resonated with the nation; subscribers said they felt a catharsis after reading each issue. *The Century*'s circulation jumped from 127,000 to 225,000 in 1885, and newspapers across the country discussed the series' impact. The series and resulting book earned more than $1 million for the magazine.

That approach, eliminating the interviewer altogether, is still part of the profile pantheon of possibilities. *Vanity Fair, Vogue,* and *Premiere* ran "dear diary" jottings by, respectively, singer Madonna (while filming *Evita* in Argentina), novelist Tama Janowitz (while adopting a Chinese baby), and actress Glenn Close (while filming *101 Dalmatians*). Other magazines let celebrities interview themselves, such as "Nobody Does It Better: Sharon Stone on Herself" in *Harper's Bazaar* and "The Unbelievable Truth About Mel Gibson. By Mel Gibson" in *US Weekly.*

institutional

At the other end of the profile spectrum are the institutional profiles of small and large businesses that are the staples of trade and organization magazines. Here the focus is on the company, as an institutional personality, rather than the people who run it. According to business press researcher Patrick Clinton, case studies and site visits are profile forms found in the trade press that increase

Longevity, Celebrity, and Topicality in Special Issues

Magazine anniversaries and deaths of celebrities lend themselves to special magazine issues, although an entire issue can be devoted to just about any topic. Advertisers like special issues because they have longer shelf lives on the newsstands than the regular weekly or monthly magazine. Another plus is that readers save special issues and refer to them time and again, weeks, months, and even years after their purchase.

Following the death of Princess Diana of Wales in August 1997, magazines as varied as *TV Guide, Entertainment Weekly, Harper's Bazaar, People, Life, Newsweek,* and *Time* all devoted special issues to a tribute. Some magazines have special issues already planned for speedy publication upon the death of a celebrity. Far from being exploitative, tribute issues generally accentuate the positive and play down the negative in individuals' lives. Readers of all ages see tribute issues as prized keepsakes.

Magazine anniversary issues also are popular collectibles. *Playboy*'s 25th anniversary issue in 1979 was a hefty 414 pages, while *Cosmopolitan*'s 20th in 1985 (starting the count in 1965 when the "*Cosmopolitan* girl" was articulated by Helen Gurley Brown) was a whopping 484 pages. The cover of a

magazine anniversary issue often shows miniatures of previous covers: *Time* followed this approach for both the 60th (1983) and 75th (1998) anniversary issues, as did *People* for its 20th (1994), *Vassar Quarterly* for its 70th (1986), *Massage* for its 10th (1995), *Ebony* for both its 40th (1985) and 45th (1990), and *Town and Country* for its 150th (1996).

National Geographic produced a 12-page foldout of 360 thumbnail-sized covers for its 100-year anniversary in 1988. *Sports Illustrated* reprinted all 2,548 covers in a special issue in 2003 and pointed out that Michael Jordan was the most frequent covered individual and the New York Yankees the most covered team.

However, the 60th anniversary issue of *Life* in October 1996 literally covered the most visual territory through its dramatic use of Rob Silvers's trademarked Photomosaic image, which revealed Marilyn Monroe's face in relief via his arrangement of old *Life* covers. Using a special computer program at the MIT Media Laboratory, Silvers considered hundreds of aspects (color, shape, texture, contrast) of *Life*'s 2,128 covers to create the larger image of Marilyn Monroe. If you stand a few feet away from the cover, Monroe's face "pops out" in a striking resemblance to the famous 1953

Alfred Eisenstaedt portrait of the blonde bombshell.

The entire August 31, 1946, issue of *The New Yorker* was devoted to "Hiroshima" by John Hersey. The 31,000-word piece, about the city's destruction by the atomic bomb as seen through six characters, was a first for *The New Yorker* and led the way for magazines to focus on a single topic or story in one issue. When Hersey died in 1993, one obituary said "Hiroshima" was "the most famous magazine article ever published." In March 1971, virtually the entire *Harper's* was devoted to "The Prisoner of Sex," Norman Mailer's macho musings on the women's liberation movement.

The New Yorker has run entire issues—cover, contents, and cartoons—devoted to fiction, film, fashion, and women as part of the regular year's subscription. Annual special editions, such as *Sports Illustrated*'s swimsuit issue and *Seventeen*'s back-to-school issue primarily attract single-issue buyers, some of whom go on to become regular readers.

Newsweek, Time, and *U.S. News and World Report* regularly put out special issues devoted to such topics as medicine, retirement, or education that aren't part of their weekly cycle; these special issues are received by regular subscribers. Beginning in 1995, all

Longevity, Celebrity, and Topicality in Special Issues (continued)

three newsweeklies produced major special issues revolving around the end of the 20th century and start of the 21st. All three recapped the 20th century by focusing on noteworthy individuals and historic events and how they affected the lives of ordinary Americans. However, *Life*'s 1997 special issue went several steps further by focusing on the most important events and people of the millennium—looking at the past 1,000 years in terms of technology.

Special issues devoted to the September 11, 2001, terrorist attack on the World Trade Center generally sold out on newsstands. Plus, *Time*, *Newsweek*, and *U.S. News and World Report* all produced retrospective issues a year later.

Trade magazines are big producers of special issues because publishers count on the extra revenue from both regular and new advertisers. Additionally, publishers like the extra money that comes in from

reader orders for back issues and reprints following special issues. New product guides, trade show and convention exhibitions, and buyers' directories are frequent special reports developed by trade magazines. *Advertising Age* publishes well-received special reports on magazines several times a year, while *Adweek*'s hottest magazines and editor of the year issue is eagerly awaited every March. ■

readers' understanding of an industry. Consequently, profiles of new buildings are highlighted in *Building Design and Construction*, quarries are visited in *Rock Products*, and bakery solutions are illustrated in *Baking and Snack*.

Consumer magazines also publish institutional profiles, such as *Entertainment Weekly*'s National Magazine Award-winning "The Seinfeld Chronicles," which dominated the May 30, 1997, issue. The cover story and more than a dozen accompanying articles examined the popular television show, *Seinfeld*, rather than honing in on the individual actors. Of particular interest was the "Obsessive-Compulsive Viewer's Guide to All 148 Episodes," from season 1–8, with a plot synopsis, analysis of key scenes, historic moments, critique, and "final grade." The institutional approach provided readers with more than they would ever want to know about a single television sitcom.

■ INVESTIGATIVE REPORTING

Dating back to the muckrakers, today's investigative articles continue to be imaginative and enterprising pieces that tackle major social and political concerns through intensive interviews and insightful interpretations. Many investigative articles

tackle topics of significant public interest in an attempt to make a difference. In 1991, *Family Circle* won a National Magazine Award for its investigation of environmental health hazards in Jacksonville, Arkansas. Titled "Toxic Nightmare on Main Street," the August 14, 1990, article by Stephanie Arbarbanel was a direct descendant of muckraking era articles in women's magazines which exposed the health dangers of patent medicines.

"The True Story of John/Joan," a 19,000-word article by John Colapinto that appeared in the December 11, 1997, issue of *Rolling Stone*, exposed a different kind of health danger. Colapinto traveled more than 20,000 miles over a period of 8 months for interviews with more than 40 people for his behind-the-scenes investigation into the question of nature versus nurture in determining gender identity. The resulting report about sex-reassignment surgery on infants—focused on the story of one young man—whose genitals are irregular or have been damaged by accidents won the 1998 National Magazine Award for reporting. Colapinto's article later became a best-selling book, *As Nature Made Him: The Boy Who Was Raised as a Girl*.

Most investigative articles perform a watchdog function, which particularly suits business and trade magazines. For example, the July 1995 issue of

Research in Brief

Hidden Biases in Editorial Content

More than half of all magazine research published in academic journals centers around editorial content analyses. Magazine researchers have studied the coverage of AIDS in men's magazines, analyzed presidential campaign accounts in news magazines, documented the progress of feminism during the 1920s, deconstructed the work experiences of short-story heroines in the 1940s, investigated racial attitudes in civil rights articles of the 1960s, and compared the coverage of sexually transmitted infections in popular men's and women's magazines in the late 1990s and early 2000s.

The analysis of the editorial content of magazines is extremely accessible—at its most basic level, a researcher needs only a topic, a consistent way of coding or counting what is being studied, and the magazines themselves. However, at its most sophisticated level—as the following three studies show—a researcher may reveal hidden biases and shatter myths about editorial content.

Joseph P. Bernt, a professor at Ohio University's E. W. Scripps School of Journalism, was curious whether trade magazines were doing a better job than other media in balancing race and gender in their editorial and advertising pages. Pointing out that trade magazines play an important role in America's economic and business life, Bernt also wondered if the business magazines' percentages matched race and gender numbers found in the overall labor force. Therefore, he studied editorial and advertising photographs, mastheads, and bylines in 164 trade magazines to see how many Asians, blacks, whites, men, and women appeared.[1] His analysis of race and gender diversity in trade magazines revealed that editors underrepresent blacks and women.

Bernt found that whites were overrepresented in trade magazine editorial, cover, and advertising photography and that men were dominant as both staff members and writers. Whites make up about 86 percent of the labor force, yet they were found in 95 percent of the photos. Men represent 55 percent of the 1990 U.S. labor force, but they were dominant in 75 percent of the photos. Clearly, people of color and women were not being represented in the numbers expected if diversity and balanced representation were important factors.

Bernt says his research has practical implications for trade magazines interested in global expansion. Calling attention to studies that predict jobs increasingly will be filled by people of color and women, Bernt argues, "To retain the attention and respect of tomorrow's work force—to continue to inform and train that work force—trade periodicals must allow their readers to find themselves and their colleagues in their pages."

Barbara Straus Reed, a professor in the Department of Journalism and Mass Media at Rutgers University, has done numerous studies on how magazines have presented health issues, such as breast cancer and eating disorders. In 1995, Reed and coauthor Christine Morrongiello evaluated just how accurately consumer magazines interpreted scientific

1. Joseph P. Bernt, "Race and Gender Diversity in Trade and Business Periodicals as Reflected in Editorial and Advertising Images, Mastheads, and Bylines" (paper presented at the annual meeting of the Association for Education in Journalism and Mass Communication, Washington, D.C., August 1995).

2. Christine Morrongiello and Barbara Straus Reed, "The Accuracy of Breast Cancer Reports in Consumer Magazines" (paper presented to the annual meeting of the Association for Education in Journalism and Mass Communication, Washington, D.C., August 1995).

Hidden Biases in Editorial Content (continued)

and technical information about breast cancer and how they presented it to readers.[2] They studied 232 articles in five consumer magazine areas: science, women's, news weekly, health/sports/fitness, and alternative/journals of opinion and compared their content with original research reports about breast cancer. Among the magazines studied were *Ladies' Home Journal, McCall's, Redbook, Vogue, The Nation, The New Republic, Prevention, Health,* and *Science News.*

Reed and Morrongiello found that breast cancer articles in consumer science magazines contained the lowest number of errors compared to the other magazines studied. They also found that errors of omission (incomplete information about results or methodology, lack of full identification of a source or research team members, or lack of attribution of fact to a source) were more likely than errors of commission (misstatement or misquoting of fact or report, misleading headline, or speculation treated as fact). Omission of sources and omission of relevant information about results were the most common errors, particularly in women's and alternative magazines. The bottom line: Consumer science magazines such as *Prevention, Health,* and *Science News* may be the best

source for information about health research and medical news.

Professionals in the field also study magazine content, often to satisfy their own curiosity. Sometimes that information becomes news that may make a difference in changing attitudes or deflating myths.

Wondering whether women's bylines appeared less frequently than men's, Ruth Davis Konigsberg, a deputy editor at *Glamour,* began counting bylines in *Harper's, The New Yorker, The New York Times Magazine, Vanity Fair,* and *The Atlantic.* In a period from September 2005 through November 2005, she tallied 324 male bylines and 99 female ones.[3]

When told of the ratio at *Vanity Fair,* 34 men to 12 women, editor Graydon Carter said, "We don't assign stories based on gender, but now that Ruth Davis Konigsberg has helpfully shown us the error of our ways, henceforth all assignments will be equally balanced between the sexes." Cullen Davis, managing editor of *The Atlantic* (61 male bylines to 18 female ones), said "The byline imbalance is endemic in public affairs magazines. At *The Atlantic* we are aware of the problem and have been actively taking steps to address it." Editors at *The New Yorker* (98

male bylines to 27 female bylines), *Harper's* (28 male to 6 female), and *The New York Times Magazine* (103 male to 36 female) declined to comment.

Konigsberg's results are displayed on a website, www.womeTK.com that is updated on a regular basis. By the end of January 2006, reflecting bylines in the five magazines from the September 2005 through the February 2006 issues, the ratio was 651 men to 216 women, with men still outnumbering women about 3:1.

"It started as a personal pet peeve," Konigsberg said, adding that the website is unrelated to her job at *Glamour.* "I thought someone should really be keeping track of it. I'm interested in starting a conversation."

In a similar study, bylines in the nation's top political and intellectual magazines were calculated using the ProQuest database from October 2003 through the end of May 2005 by Jennifer Weiss for *Columbia Journalism Review.* That research revealed that bylines are heavily male, with women writers occasionally shut out of entire issues. Weiss reported the following byline ratios: *National Review,* 13:1 (male to female); *Foreign Affairs,* 9:1; and *The New Republic,* 8:1.[4] ■

3. Julie Bosman, "At Some Magazines, Men Appear to Rule the World," *The New York Times* (November 7, 2005), http://www.nytimes.com/2005/11/07/business/07gender.html.

4. Weiss, Jennifer, "Gentlemen's Club," *Columbia Journalism Review* (July/August 2005): 14.

Sales and Marketing Management reported on the practice of sales people taking customers to topless bars, noting that this wasn't fair to women in the sales business. The article—titled "That's Entertainment?"—won a 1996 Neal Award for best investigative piece.

Detailed investigative articles tend to exceed 5,000 words and sometimes are serialized over several issues. They frequently are touted on magazine covers as major features. Two currents flow in the river of investigative reporting: literary journalism and new journalism.

literary journalism

American literary journalism includes the work of such historic figures as Stephen Crane, Jacob A. Riis, Theodore Dreiser, Mark Twain, Lincoln Steffens, Richard Harding Davis, and John Reed. They started out as newspaper reporters whose work evolved into longer, more interpretive forms that were published in such top magazines of the day as *Saturday Evening Post, McClure's, Scribner's,* and *The Atlantic Monthly.*

The American literary journalism approach stressed the use of novelistic detail that was realistic rather than fanciful. Yet it also had an immediacy in its use of the standard news-gathering techniques of interviews, documentation, and observation. Literary journalism has been defined as "nonfiction printed prose whose verifiable content is shaped and transformed into a story or sketch by use of narrative or rhetorical techniques generally associated with fiction."[21] In a literary journalism piece, style is a critical component to the structure and organization of language. Although this approach flourished from the late 1880s into the 1920s, the genre dwindled with the Depression. Magazine editors wanted straight investigative news reporting— just the facts, ma'am—to match the no frills American mood.

It was an editor's worst nightmare come true, said *Ms.* editor-in-chief Marcia Ann Gillespie when the May/June 1996 issue of *Ms.* hit the newsstands. The problem: "feminism"—a word frequently used in the magazine known for its long involvement in the women's movement—was misspelled on the cover. The 48-point-high headline, for the 19-page lead feature, proclaimed "Mothers and Daughters: Honest Talk about Feminisim & Real Life."

new journalism

It wasn't until the mid-1960s that some writers chose to shift from the mainstream, traditional investigative style that dominated most magazine reporting. Such writers as Gay Talese, Gloria Steinem, Tom Wolfe, Joan Didion, Norman Mailer, Hunter S. Thompson, Truman Capote, and Jimmy Breslin returned to many of the traditions of literary journalism, but dubbed their looser, more personal structure "new journalism." According to Tom Wolfe, new journalism resulted in greater flexibility and required "saturation reporting" because of the writer's willingness to immerse himself in the story being told and to become part of it with first-person commentary.

Wolfe identified four central devices that characterized new journalism: constructing events by moving from scene to scene rather than from fact to fact; recording dialogue in its entirety; presenting events through the thoughts and emotions of the subject at the time of the happening; and recording the everyday habits, manners, gestures, and clothing that reveal an individual's status in life. The two most controversial aspects of new journalism were the presentation of the subject's interior monologue, revealing a person's inner thoughts at a certain time, and the very personal intrusion of the author into the story. Many new journalism pieces revolved around the famous or near-famous as writers attempted to reveal the private side to the public persona. Or as Wolfe put it:

The result is a form that is not merely *like a novel.* It consumes devices that happen to have originated with the novel and mixes them with every other device known to prose. And all the while, quite beyond matters of technique, it enjoys an advantage so obvious, so built-in, one almost forgets what a power it has: The simple fact that the reader knows *all this actually happened.*[22]

David Sumner, a journalism professor at Ball State University, explains how the new journalism originated in such magazines as *Rolling Stone, Esquire, Harper's,* and *New York.* The genre that emerged between 1965 and 1975 was a departure from traditional investigative articles that stressed objectivity above all else. The use of "I" by the authors matched the mood of a society experiencing upheaval ranging from civil rights marches and antiwar draft card burnings to the effects of the women's movement and the hippie counterculture. However, Sumner also argues that the inroads of television in the 1960s encouraged a group of innovative editors to take experimental risks with their magazines. Sumner writes, "High-circulation, general interest magazines such as *Saturday Evening Post* and *Collier's* had already closed, while *Life* and *Look* faced declining circulations and revenues. For many magazines, especially *Esquire* and the fledgling *New York* and *Rolling Stone,* experimentation held the key to survival."[23]

Sumner quotes *New York* founding editor Clay Felker as stating in a 1996 telephone interview that television played a role in editors' deciding to try out the new writing approach:

> What new journalism did was to recognize that there was new competition for print. That competition was television. That brought the news to people quicker than a daily newspaper or a national newsmagazine. And so what you had to do was give another interpretation. You had to present the news in a more emotional, interpretive conceptual context. And also it had to be more dramatic and emotional so that the reader not only got the intellectual argument behind it, but the reader was connected emotionally to the story.

Sumner points out that a few key magazines made a difference in journalism history by experimenting with new forms and publishing such controversial nonfiction as Hunter S. Thompson's "Fear and Loathing" series during the 1972 presidential campaign in *Rolling Stone,* Tom Wolfe's "Kandy-Colored Tangerine-Flake Streamlined Baby" in *Esquire,* and Norman Mailer's "The Steps of the Pentagon" in *Harper's.*

Contest Categories as a Learning Tool

A contest is more than just receiving an award. Contests are also a good way to study what style, storytelling approach, or technique was used in the winning entry.

The National Magazine Awards, administered by the American Society of Magazine Editors (ASME), are given to any magazine edited, published at least four times a year, and sold in the United States. National Magazine Awards take

the form of a copper elephant, a reproduction of an Alexander Calder stabile called "Ellie." The awards cover 17 categories:

General Excellence
■ Recognizes overall excellence in magazines in six circulation categories (under 100,000; 100,000–250,000; 250,000–500,000; 500,000–1,000,000; 1,000,000–2,000,000; over 2,000,000). It honors the

effectiveness with which writing, reporting, editing, and design all come together to command readers' attention and fulfill the magazine's unique editorial mission.

Personal Service
■ Recognizes excellence in service journalism. The advice or instruction presented should help readers improve the quality of their personal lives (covering such topics as health,

(continued)

Contest Categories as a Learning Tool (continued)

medicine, psychology, relationships, family, careers, or personal finance). Pieces that include practical information are preferable to straight narrative.

Leisure Interests

■ Recognizes excellent service journalism about leisure-time pursuits. The practical advice or instruction presented should help readers enjoy hobbies or other recreational interests (e.g., sports, travel, fashion, interior decorating, design, food, crafts, or arts and entertainment).

Reporting

■ Recognizes excellence in reporting. It honors the enterprise, exclusive reporting, and intelligent analysis that a magazine exhibits in covering an event, a situation, or a problem of contemporary interest and significance.

Public Interest

■ Recognizes journalism that has the potential to affect national or local policy or lawmaking. It honors investigative reporting or groundbreaking analysis that sheds new light on an issue of public importance.

Feature Writing

■ Recognizes excellence in feature writing. It honors the stylishness and originality with which the author treats his or her subject. Freshness counts, and brevity is not a negative.

Profile Writing

■ Recognizes excellence in profile writing. It honors the

vividness and perceptiveness with which the writer brings his or her subject to life. Interviews are eligible, but pieces co-authored by the profile subject are not.

Essays

■ Recognizes excellence in essay writing on topics ranging from the personal to the political. Whatever the subject, emphasis should be placed on the author's eloquence, perspective, fresh thinking, and unique voice.

Columns and Commentary

■ Recognizes excellence in short-form political, social, economic, or humorous commentary. It honors the eloquence, force of argument, and succinctness with which the writer presents his or her views.

Reviews and Criticism

■ Recognizes excellence in criticism of art, books, movies, television, theater, music, dance, food, dining, fashion, products, and the like. It honors the knowledge, persuasiveness, and original voice that the critic brings to his or her reviews.

Magazine Section

■ Recognizes the excellence of a regular department or editorial section of a magazine, either front- or back-of-book, and composed of a variety of elements, both text and visual. Judges will select finalists based on the section's voice, originality, design, and packaging.

Single-topic Issue

■ Recognizes magazines that have devoted an issue to an in-depth examination of one topic. It honors the ambition, comprehensiveness, and imagination with which a magazine treats its subject.

Design

■ Recognizes excellence in magazine design. It honors the effectiveness of overall design, artwork, graphics, and typography in enhancing a magazine's unique mission and personality.

Photography

■ Recognizes excellence in magazine photography. It honors the effectiveness of photography, photojournalism, and photo illustration in enhancing a magazine's unique mission and personality.

Photo Portfolio/Photo Essay

■ Recognizes a distinctive portfolio or photographic essay. It honors either photos that express an idea or a concept (including portraiture or specially produced layouts on fashion, food, decorating, crafts, travel, design, the arts, etc.), or documentary photojournalism shot in real time. Although photo essays accompanied by text will be eligible, they will be judged primarily on the strength of the photographs. Real-time shots that are manipulated or digitally altered are not eligible.

Fiction

■ Recognizes excellence in magazine fiction writing. It

Contest Categories as a Learning Tool (continued)

honors the quality of a publication's literary selections.

General Excellence Online
- Recognizes outstanding magazine Internet sites, as well as online-only magazines and blogs, that have a significant amount of original content. To qualify, a site's primary function must be to inform or entertain rather than to sell products or promote a business (i.e., online stores and advertiser sites are not eligible). The site must also convey a distinct editorial identity, particularly if it is within a larger corporate site, and create a unique magazine environment on the Web. Selection of links (if any, plus supporting context and commentary) should show discernment, but the linked content itself will not be judged here. Editorial material must be clearly delineated from sponsored content, advertising and product sales, as prescribed in ASME's "Best Practices for Digital Media."

The New Yorker is the biggest winner in the 40-year history of the National Magazine Awards, walking away with 44 Ellies between 1970 and 2005. Along with four General Excellence Awards (400,000–1,000,000 category), *The New Yorker* has won in reporting, fiction, feature writing, essays, public interest, reviews and criticism, and profile. *The Atlantic* comes in second with 19 awards; *Esquire* is third with 16.

The Jesse H. Neal National Business Journalism Awards competition is open only to editors of specialized business media, produced by companies belonging to the American Business Media. Neal Awards are ribboned medallions reminiscent of Olympic gold medals. They are given to individual editors, not to publications. All Neal Awards are divided into three categories based on gross advertising/circulation revenue classifications: less than $3 million, $3–$7 million, and more than $7 million. The Grand Neal, considered the pinnacle of business-to-business editorial achievement, is chosen from among the Neal winners in all 12 categories:

Best Single Article
- Any carefully researched, in-depth article dealing with subjects, events, or developments of importance to the publication's readers and industry. The article may include sidebars.

Best Subject-related Series of Articles
- Any carefully researched series of two or more in-depth articles dealing with subjects, events, or developments of importance to the publication's readers and industry. Subject-related articles appearing either in a single issue or in different issues belong in this category.

Best Staff-written Editorials or Opinion Columns
- Four editorials or opinion columns written by a member or members of the full-time editorial staff. The submissions may address a single subject or may cover a variety of subjects. This is the category for opinion journalism.

Best Department
- Four examples of a single, regularly recurring department from four different issues. News-related departments are eligible. Include the Table of Contents (TOC) for each issue in which the selections appear. The department must be clearly labeled as such in the TOC. The department can be brief or lengthy, but its format must be distinct from feature articles and consistent from issue to issue.

Best How-to Article or Subject-related Series of How-to Articles
- Article(s) informing readers how to do their jobs better, more efficiently, more productively, and so on. The emphasis should be on direct instruction of the reader rather than on case studies or examples, although they may be used in the articles.

Best News Coverage: Dailies and Weeklies
- Breaking or timely coverage of an event or issue of importance to the publication's

(continued)

Contest Categories as a Learning Tool (continued)

readers and industry. This can be one article, a series of articles, or a combination of articles from the print and Web editions.

Best News Coverage: Other Frequencies

■ Breaking or timely coverage of an event or issue of importance to the publication's readers and industry. This can be one article, a series of articles, or a combination of articles from the print and Web editions.

Best Single Theme or Special Issue of a Magazine or Newspaper/News Tabloid

■ Bonus or series-numbered issues or stand-alone supplements devoted to a single theme or subject. The theme or subject must be evident on the cover or front page; the feature well must be devoted to the theme. Any advertorials within the issue must be clearly identified as such to the reader of the publication.

Best Single Issue of a Magazine

■ An issue that best exemplifies the overall mission and reflects the magazine's typical format. It must be part of the regular publishing cycle, distributed to the full circulation. Any advertorials within the issue must be clearly identified as such to the reader of the publication.

Best Single Issue of a Newspaper/News Tabloid

■ An issue that best exemplifies the overall mission and reflects the publication's typical format. It must be part of the regular publishing cycle, distributed to the full circulation. Any advertorials within the issue must be clearly identified as such to the reader of the publication.

Best Start-up Publication

■ New, stand-alone periodicals.

Best Website

■ Business-to-business journalism produced online under the magazine's editorial control.

When it was first established in 1955, the Neal Awards competition had only 22 entries. Fifty years later, there were 1,168 entries, reflecting both the growth of business-to-business magazines and the importance of the awards. The 2004 Grand Neal Award winner was *CIO* magazine for an article about a disastrous 4-day crash of a hospital's computer network, while the 2005 Grand Neal went to *Baseline* for a chilling story about how inferior radiation dosage software led to the deaths of several patients. Multiple honors in 2004 and 2005 went to *CSO* and *Editor and Publisher*. Marianne Dekker Mattera, editor of *Medical Economics*, holds the record for the most Neal Awards won. ■

■ ESSAY

Essays are the oldest of magazine article types, dating back to the English periodicals of the 18th century. Essays have always been slippery beasts, being commentary on manners, morals, modes, and matters of everything from architecture to zoology—in voices ranging from serious to slapstick. All magazines of the 18th and 19th century printed essays that essentially were the opinions of the educated and the elite. Early essays had little research or documentation to back up the author's personal experiences and thoughts. For example, in an October 1784 essay in *The Gentleman and Lady's Town and Country Magazine,* Judith Sargent Murray, writing under the pen name of Constantia, described her plan for the education of young women in "Desultory Thoughts upon the Utility of Encouraging a Degree of Self-Complacency, Especially in Female Bosoms." In women's magazines of the early to mid-19th century, most essays explored sentimental concerns of women: a lady's character, a wife's sacrifice, a mother's love. Magazines with a predominantly male audience at this time published essays about meditation and repose, city life versus country life, and dialectical encounters with people of different classes and ethnicity.

The modern essay found in 20th-century magazines, however, is a more challenging approach to topics that affect readers' public and private lives. Editors expect essayists to provide wit and imagination as well as examination, dissection, and contemplation of events and ideas grounded in a believable authority. Pulitzer Prize-winner Annie Dillard, a contributing editor to *Harper's* who also has written for magazines as varied as *Cosmopolitan, Sports Illustrated, The American Scholar, Travel and Leisure,* and *The Atlantic Monthly,* describes the essay's function: "The essayist does what we do with our lives; the essayist thinks about actual things. He can make sense of them analytically or artistically. In either case he renders the real world coherent and meaningful, even if only bits of it, and even if that coherence and meaning reside only inside small texts."[24]

Today's essays fall into two broad types, critical and personal. A magazine's content may lean more toward one type than the other, but the approach is popular in both departments (short form of 1,000 words or less) and features (long form of more than 2,500 words). Editorial and opinion columns may follow either the critical or the personal essay form.

One writer sold the same story to four different magazines. Author Ted Schwarz wrote four different versions of Kathy Miller's tragic story of being struck by a car while crossing a street. The teenager literally was knocked out of her shoes and socks; doctors gave her little chance of regaining consciousness, much less ever walking because muscles were torn from her legs. Months later, Miller had relearned to talk and walk, and eventually became a competitive long-distance runner. Schwarz told the compelling story from four different perspectives, with publication in *Family Circle, Seventeen, Success,* and *Today's Christian Woman.*

books and movies in *The New Yorker* generally are built around a theme. For example, film critic Pauline Kael's frank, wickedly witty, and passionate discussions of just-released movies transcended the term "review" because of the thematic approach she took. For example, she once linked *On the Waterfront, East of Eden,* and *Blackboard Jungle* under the title "The Glamour of Delinquency" to show how the literary theme of alienation had invaded the mass culture medium of film. For many years, her work appeared in *Life, Vogue, The Atlantic Monthly, Film Quarterly, McCall's, Mademoiselle,* and *The New Yorker.*

personal

Personal essays are just that: individualistic, often one-of-a-kind exercises in tone, topic, and territory. Personal essays, unlike critical ones, tend not to have an obvious thematic center, but they do have a point. They often ramble, metaphorically growing from small to large and back again in connections that are charming in the hands of a skilled writer. A popular topic in the personal essay genre is outdoor life and all of its ramifications: natural history, the environment, the wilderness, ranching, farming, and camping. Annie Dillard has distinguished herself in this area, as have John McPhee, Edward Abbey, and Gretel Ehrlich. Their works have appeared in *Time, The Atlantic Monthly, Harper's, New Age Journal, Antaeus,* and *The New Yorker,* to name a few.

Lauren Hillenbrand's account of her years-long battle with a devastatingly virulent chronic fatigue syndrome won the National Magazine Award for essays in 2004. But this wasn't just a personal medical story; how she wrote the 2001 best-seller *Seabiscuit: An American Legend* is part of the moving

critical

Critical essays tend to discuss literature, plays, and the arts in general. Unlike the thumbs-up, thumbs-down scorecard reviews found in a *Premiere* or *Entertainment Weekly,* critical essays of essay published in the July 7, 2003, issue of *The New Yorker.* Bruce Vilanch's "Notes from a Blond" column in *The Advocate* takes a personal approach to gay and lesbian topics with more than an occasional tongue in cheek because of his background as a comic writer for Bette Midler, Billy Crystal, Andy Williams, and the televised Oscar awards presentations.

editorials

Editorials and opinion columns generally fall under the essay rubric, where they offer a splendid way to strengthen ties with readers. For trade and business magazines, opinion columns and editorials are where professional issues, ethics, and standards are debated and put before the readers. Former *Internal Auditor* executive editor Anne Graham urges association magazine editors to avoid writing editorials that rehash the material found inside each issue: "Editorials can be powerful agents for persuading, inspiring, illuminating, informing and connecting with readers." She says the best editorials are "highly personalized—the more personal, the better."[25]

The American Business Media's Neal Awards include a category for best staff-written editorials. *Meat and Poultry* executive editor Keith Nunes, who has won in this category, says, "An editorial has to take a strong position. And it must prompt discussion in the industry."[26]

Consumer magazines are less likely to publish editorials; the National Magazine Awards doesn't even have a category for this form. At most consumer magazines, the editor's page could offer a bully pulpit, but only a handful of editors use it to expound on an issue. More likely, they promote the articles inside the current issue, detail how a particular story was researched, or share an anecdote about a writer or photographer.

■ FICTION

Serialized novels, short stories, and poems were a dominant part of magazines for many years, occupying a significant amount of space as early as 1741. Fiction could be found in just about every magazine published during the 18th and 19th centuries.

The role of magazines in supporting book publishing was recognized as early as 1885, when a leading book publisher testified before a Senate committee: "It is impossible to make books of most American authors pay unless they are first published and acquire recognition through the columns of the magazines. Were it not for that one saving opportunity of the great American magazines . . . American authorship would be at a still lower ebb than at present."[27] Magazine editors also praised magazines' role in promoting and popularizing fine literature. In 1908, *Harper's* editor, Henry Mills Alden, proclaimed: "With scarcely an exception, every distinguished writer of books during this period has been also a contributor to magazines. Periodical literature has done more for the American people than any other."[28]

serialized novels

Serialized novels became especially popular following the Civil War. Magazines published the serialized works of England's greatest writers—Charles Dickens, William Thackeray, and Wilkie Collins—as well as popular American novels by Henry James, William Dean Howells, Edward Everett Hale, and Bret Harte. By the 1870s, it was not unusual to find as many as three different serial installments running in *The Atlantic Monthly.* Other general magazines of the period, as well as all women's magazines, carried at least one chapter of a serialized novel per issue. Some magazines, such as *The Galaxy,* regularly carried fiction in more than one-third of their editorial content.

short stories

By the 20th century, the short story, with its tighter framework and compact narrative form, had become the primary type of magazine fiction. In 1919, the weekly *Saturday Evening Post* published 308 short stories, while the monthly *Harper's* ran 60. Consequently, some magazine historians credit *Saturday Evening Post* with making the short story a medium of mass culture by publishing hundreds of mysteries, westerns, romances, and even science fiction every year. Yet the *Post* also ran serious works, publishing more than 60 short stories by F. Scott Fitzgerald, and took a chance on William Faulkner long before other magazines did.

After World War II, fewer and fewer editors published novels in the face of the short story's popularity. *Town and Country* serialized Evelyn Waugh's *Brideshead Revisited* in 1945 and *Life* published Ernest Hemingway's *The Old Man and the Sea* novella in a single issue in 1952. *Rolling Stone*'s publication of all 31 chapters of Tom Wolfe's *The Bonfire of the Vanities,* from July 19/August 2, 1984 through August 29, 1985, harked back to the Dickens tradition of a lengthy serial.

More recently, *Time* published a serialized novel by Caleb Carr, author of such historical thrillers as *The Alienist* and *Angel of Darkness*. This was a first for *Time,* which had occasionally published excerpts from fiction and nonfiction books, but had never published an entire novel in serial form. *Killing Time* ran in five special issues focusing on "Visions of the 21st Century" (November 8, 1999; February 21, 2000; April 10, 2000; May 22, 2000; and June 19, 2000). *Killing Time* was published in hardback by Random House in November 2000.

excerpts

Today's magazines are more likely to run excerpts of nonfiction books, such as Gail Sheehy's *Understanding Men's Passages* in *Men's Health* and Bob Woodward's *The Choice* in *Newsweek.* *The New Yorker,* on the other hand, often prints an adaptation of a piece of fiction rather than an excerpt. This process involves taking sections of the book and creating a similar, but shorter, whole.

The decline in consumer magazine fiction occurred with the decline in mass market magazines during the 1950s and 1960s. Only a handful of consumer magazines now publish serious short stories on a regular basis: *The New Yorker, The Atlantic Monthly, Harper's, Playboy, Esquire,* and a few others. Fiction doesn't directly attract advertisers, so publishing it requires a major commitment on the part of a consumer magazine; trade and organization magazines rarely run fiction.

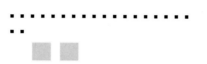

Truman Capote spent 6 years interviewing people in Holcomb, Kansas, including the two killers of the Clutter family for "Annals of Crime: In Cold Blood," which ran as a four-part series in the September 25, October 2, October 9, and October 16, 1965, issues of *The New Yorker*. Published as a book later that year, *In Cold Blood* has been called "the first successful nonfiction novel" because of its use of literary devices.

"There are very few magazines that pop up and start publishing good fiction," said former *Texas Monthly* editor Gregory Curtis, who has been a judge in the National Magazine Award fiction category. "Those magazines that value fiction as an integral part of the magazine have always assumed that their readers are buying the magazine for the totality of the magazine and that totality includes fiction. Magazines that publish good fiction must have the confidence of the main editor."[29]

Literary journals and quarterly reviews, or "little magazines" supported by universities, such as *Kenyon Review,* are the primary outlet for writers of fiction, poetry, and prose. These publications tend to pay their writers poorly, if at all; sometimes payment is in copies.

Currently, there are more literary magazines—about 1,000— being published than at any time in history.[30] The literary magazine landscape ranges from *The Threepenny Review* with 9,000 subscribers to *Quick Fiction* with a print run of 900. Most literary magazines have an average readership of 2,000 and annual budgets of less than $10,000.

Jeffrey Lependorf, executive director of the Council of Literary Magazines and Presses, says, "If you're interested in experimental poetry, there's a journal for you. If you're interested in Southern culture, there's a literary magazine for you."[31] The council has 217 magazine members across the United States; New York and California are home to more than half of the magazines.

According to Wendy Lasser, editor of *The Threepenny Review,* which was founded in 1980 and recently published its 100th issue, "We benefit in some ways from the crassness of the culture. The Tina Brown years at *The New Yorker* were golden years for us. She commissioned all these pieces and she'd get them and they were too literary for *The New Yorker.*"[32]

Readers Don't Care About Bad Journalism

Letters to the editor are designed to offer feedback from the magazine's readers to the editors. A look at the letters in most magazines reveals a preponderance of congratulatory and positive comments reflecting agreement with previous articles; occasionally a negative observation or angry remark is made. Some topics set readers off more than others. *Time*'s 1973 *Last Tango in Paris* cover story, about the erotic movie starring Marlon Brandon, generated the most reader mail ever received by the magazine—12,191 mostly angry letters. The second highest number of letters—5,180—came in response to *Time*'s selection of Iran's Ayatollah Khomeini as 1980 "Man of the Year."[1]

What do letters to the editor say about reader reactions to whether magazines are doing a good job of upholding journalistic standards and ethics? Brian Thornton, a professor in the Department of Communications at Northern Illinois University, studied magazine letters to the editor to learn more about the ongoing conversation about journalistic standards conducted by magazine readers, and how that conversation has changed over time.

"People hate journalism and journalists nowadays," Thornton said, pointing to public opinion surveys, articles in reporting trade magazines that discuss the animosity between reporters and readers, and cover stories in consumer magazines such as *The Atlantic Monthly* explaining "Why Americans Hate the Media." He reasoned that "this glut of articles about Americans' rampant dislike of the press might lead one to believe this anger would find its way into letters to the editors in today's magazines. And it would seem that if letters to the editor in popular magazines from the beginning of this century were compared to modern letters, there would be much more comment in this era about how the media need to get their ethical house in order."[2]

Thornton found that only a handful of researchers have even studied letters to the editor, although they play an important role as a magazine department and they offer content information about readers' likes and dislikes to editors. So he set out to study all letters to the editor published between 1982 and 1992 in 10 magazines *(The Atlantic Monthly, Forbes, Harper's, Life, The Nation, The New Republic,*

Newsweek, The Progressive, Time, and *U.S. News and World Report)* and compare them to letters to the editor published between 1902 and 1912 in 10 popular magazines then *(Arena, Collier's, Cosmopolitan, Everybody's, Harper's Weekly, The Independent, Ladies' Home Journal, McClure's, Munsey's,* and *World's Work)*. That meant a total of 43,976 letters to the editor to read, with 41,822 of them appearing from 1982 through 1992.

He discovered only 3.5 percent of the letters from 1982 through 1992 discussed magazine journalistic standards or such qualities as truthfulness, honesty, and accuracy. In sharp contrast, 30 percent of the letters from the muckraking period between 1902 and 1912 debated journalistic standards and qualities.

Thornton said the implications of his findings pose important questions: Why has the number of letters to the editor about magazine journalistic standards declined? Does it mean that today's readers are uninterested in the good and bad qualities of journalism? Why do they say they are angry about the way journalists go about their business, but

---

1. "Dear Idiots," *Time* (March 9, 1998): 182.

2. Brian Thornton, "The Shrinking Debate over Journalistic Standards: Where Have All the Letters (to the Editor) Gone?" (paper presented to the annual meeting of the Association for Education in Journalism and Mass Communication, Anaheim, Calif., August 1996).

Readers Don't Care About Bad Journalism (continued)

comment only on the accuracy of an article without engaging in a comment about journalistic standards? What has caused this indifference or alienation, which is in great contrast to the letters of the muckraking period, which nevertheless show an affection for the press amidst the criticisms?

Thornton continues to study letters to the editor as a way of examining the voice of magazine readers and as a historical record reflecting their attitudes toward societal change. He hopes the research "may contribute to a deeper understanding of muckraking, audience reaction then and now, and the discussion of journalistic standards among today's journalistic audience." ■

the editor and the reader

Norman Cousins argued that there were two general theories about editors and the way they edit for their readers:

> One is that an editor should engage market research to find out what readers want to read. The other is that an editor must edit to please himself or herself. If there are enough people who share his or her tastes, the latter method is apt to be more successful. If there are not enough people to share those tastes, the editor should get out of the way and make room for someone else.[33]

In his final comments as editor of *Saturday Review*, in 1971, Cousins wrote, "The one thing I learned about editing over the years is that you have to edit and publish out of your own tastes, enthusiasms and concerns, and not out of notions or guesswork about what other people might like to read."[34]

The role of the editor as a middle person between the article and the reader is an important one. In a 1994 speech, Reginald K. Brack Jr., then chairman of Time, Inc., observed: "Editors—those gifted middle-men and women—are the difference between the stock tables and *Fortune* magazine. The difference between the box scores and *Sports Illustrated*. The difference between the Wednesday food coupons in the newspaper and *Martha Stewart Living*. The difference between an on-line bulletin board and *Wired* magazine."[35]

Former *Time* editorial director Ray Cave says editors should give readers what they ought to read as well as what they want to read. "As editor, I make the choice of subject matter in a magazine, but I still must make the reader want to read it," Cave says. "In this respect the editor is a packager, a con man, a huckster and a whole lot of other things that journalists don't want to think they are."[36]

Because editors are expected to understand and fulfill the expectations of their readers, some editors want to hedge their bets through extensive market research about reader thoughts, attitudes, and habits. Yet editors also are concerned that research can lead to focusing on the lowest common denominator, much as network television does.

Helen Gurley Brown, who edited *Cosmopolitan* for 32 years until 1997 and now is editor-in-chief of international editions, agrees that too many editors try to edit by feeling the pulse of their readers. "Everybody is researching himself to pieces to find out what to do in life, and depending on others to give the answers for what the editor-in-chief should be finding out for herself/himself. You can't edit a magazine by committee. It's not a democracy," Brown explains. She says surveys can tell you where you went the most wrong or the most right with an issue, and that information can be helpful. But, she adds, in the final analysis it all boils down to basic gut instinct and intuition.[37]

Or, as Cave puts it, "What matters most is not what the editor puts into a publication, but what the reader takes away."[38]

National Geographic's Editorial Standards

In the March 1915 issue of *National Geographic,* editor Gilbert H. Grosvenor published a list of standards, or seven guiding principles, to give readers a sense of the editorial path he followed:

1. The first principle is absolute accuracy. Nothing must be printed that is not strictly according to fact.

2. Abundance of beautiful, instructive, and artistic illustrations.

3. Everything printed in the Magazine must have permanent value, and be so planned that each magazine will be as valuable and pertinent one year or five years after publication as it is on the day of publication.

4. All personalities and notes of a trivial character are avoided.

5. Nothing of a partisan or controversial character is printed.

6. Only what is of a kindly nature is printed about any country or people, everything unpleasant or unduly critical being avoided.

7. The contents of each number is planned with a view of being timely. Whenever any part of the world becomes prominent in public interest, by reason of war, earthquake, volcanic eruption, etc., the members of the National Geographic Society have come to know that in the next issue of their Magazine they will obtain the latest geographic, historical, and economic information about that region, presented in an interesting and absolutely non-partisan manner, and accompanied by photographs which in number and excellence can be equaled by no other publication. ■

notes

1. "How to Win and Hold Reader Loyalty," *Media Management Monograph,* no. 6 (February 1979): 7–8.

2. Byron T. Scott, "Service Journalism: Toward a Heuristic Agenda: A Speculative Paper" (paper presented at the midyear meeting of the Association for Education in Journalism and Mass Communication, Washington and Lee University, Lexington, Va., March 1987).

3. Ibid.

4. Pamela Fiori, "Celebrating Service Magazines," *Folio:* (May 1992): 78–79.

5. Edward Bok, *The Americanization of Edward Bok* (New York: Charles Scribner's Sons, 1920), 174.

6. John Burks, "At *Sunset,* Another Day Is About to Dawn," *New York Times* (October 7, 1996): C9.

7. American Society of Magazine Editors, "39th Annual National Magazine Award Winners Announced" (press release, May 5, 2004), http://www.magazine.org/editorial/about_asme/press/releases/7046.cfm.

8. American Society of Magazine Editors, "40th Annual National Magazine Award Winners Announced," (press release, April 13, 2005), http://www.magazine.org/Press_Room/MPA_Press_Release/11624cfm.

9. Robert Freedman, ed., *Best Practices of the Business Press* (Dubuque, Iowa: Kendall/Hunt Publishing, 2004): 1.

10. Bill Krier, "Editor's Welcome," *Wood,* http://www.woodmagazine.com/wood/story.jhtml?storyid=/templatedata/wood/story/data/206.xml.

11. Freedman, 83.

12. Rolf Maurer, "Travel on the Cheap," *Folio:* (June 1998): 31–32.

13. Dennis W. Jeffers, "Service Journalism in the Association Magazine: A Case Study of the *Angus Journal*" (paper presented at the annual meeting of the Association for Education in Journalism and Mass Communication, Portland, Ore., July 1988).

14. "*Internal Auditor* Writers' Guidelines, http://www.theiia.org/?doc_id=544.

15. C. Chaillé-Long, "Heroes to Order," *North American Review,* (May 1887): 507.

16. John E. Drewry, " A Study of *New Yorker* Profiles of Famous Journalists," *Journalism Quarterly,* vol. 23, no. 4 (December 1946): 372.

17. Russell Maloney, "A Profile of *The New Yorker*," *Saturday Review of Literature* (August 30, 1947): 30.

18. Lillian Ross, *Portrait of Hemingway* (New York: Simon and Schuster, 1961), 14.
19. Kevin Kerrane and Ben Yagoda, eds., *The Art of Fact: A Historical Anthology of Literary Journalism* (New York: Scribner, 1997), 129.
20. "Chat with Hugh M. Hefner, *Playboy* founder and editor-in-chief," April 21, 1998, http://www.playboy.com/features/hef/1998-04-21-hmh.html.
21. Thomas B. Connery, ed. *A Sourcebook of American Literary Journalism: Representative Writers in an Emerging Genre* (New York: Greenwood Press, 1992), xiv.
22. Tom Wolfe and E. W. Johnson, eds., *The New Journalism: With an Anthology* (New York: Harper and Row, 1973), 34.
23. David Sumner, "*Esquire, Harper's, New York, New Yorker,* and *Rolling Stone*: Innovators of the 'New Journalism'" (paper presented at the annual meeting of the Association for Education in Journalism and Mass Communication, Anaheim, Calif., August 1996).
24. Annie Dillard, "Introduction," *The Best American Essays 1988* (New York: Ticknor and Fields, 1988), xvii.
25. Anne Graham, "The Power of a Good Editorial Page," *Folio:* (Special Sourcebook Issue, 1998): 226–27.
26. "Editorials: The More Opinionated, the Better They Are," *Folio:* (June 1999): 10.
27. Frank Luther Mott, *A History of American Magazines, 1741–1850,* vol. 1 (Cambridge, Mass.: Harvard University Press, 1939), 3.
28. Henry Mills Alden, *Magazine Writing and the New Literature* (Freeport, N.Y.: Books for Libraries Press, 1908, reprinted 1971), 49.
29. Deirdre Carmody, "The Short Story: Out of the Mainstream but Flourishing," *New York Times* (April 23, 1991), B2.
30. Felicia Lee, "A Little Journal for Nearly Every Literary Voice," *New York Times* (December 27, 2004), E1.
31. Ibid., E1.
32. Ibid., E1.
33. "How to Win and Hold Reader Loyalty," 8.
34. Norman Cousins, "Final Report to Readers," *Saturday Review* (November 27, 1971): 32.
35. Reginald K. Brack Jr., "Magazines and a New Ethic of Communication" (speech given at Acres of Diamonds Award Luncheon, New York, N.Y., October 31, 1994).
36. Ray Cave, "Good Journalism vs. What Sells," *Folio:* (December 1987): 177.
37. "Editing a Magazine: 'It's Not a Democracy,'" *Folio:* (August 1, 1996): 9.
38. Cave, 177.

for additional reading

· ·

Applegate, Edd, ed. *Literary Journalism: A Biographical Dictionary of Writers and Editors.* Westport, Conn.: Greenwood Press, 1996.

Capote, Truman. *In Cold Blood.* New York: Random House, 1965.

Clinton, Patrick. *Guide to Writing for the Business Press.* Lincolnwood, Ill.: NTC Business Books, 1997.

Connery, Thomas B. *A Sourcebook of American Literary Journalism: Representative Writers in an Emerging Genre.* New York: Greenwood Press, 1992.

Edgren, Gretchen. *The Playboy Book: Forty Years.* Los Angeles: General Publishing Group, 1998.

Fadiman, Anne. *Ex Libris: Confessions of a Common Reader.* New York: Farrar, Straus and Giroux, 1998.

Freedman, Robert, ed. *Best Practices of the Business Press.* Dubuque, Iowa: Kendall/Hall Publishing, 2004.

Golson, G. Barry, ed. *The* Playboy *Interview.* New York: Playboy Press, 1981.

———, ed. *The* Playboy *Interview: Volume 2.* New York: Perigee Books, 1983.

Kael, Pauline. *I Lost It at the Movies.* Boston: Little, Brown, 1965.

Kerrane, Kevin, and Ben Yagoda, eds. *The Art of Fact: A Historical Anthology of Literary Journalism.* New York: Scribner, 1997.

Ladies' Home Journal editors, with Margery D. Rosen. *Can This Marriage Be Saved?* New York: Workman Publishing, 1994.

Mailer, Norman. *Armies of the Night.* New York: New American Library, 1968.

Marino, Sal. *Business Magazine Publishing.* Lincolnwood, Ill.: NTC Business Books, 1992.

Playboy *Interviews: Selected by the editors of* Playboy. Chicago: Playboy Press, 1967.

Ross, Lillian. *Portrait of Hemingway.* New York: Simon and Schuster, 1961.

Smith, Sarah Harrison. *The Fact Checker's Bible: A Guide to Getting It Right.* New York: Anchor, 2004.

Thompson, Hunter S. *Fear and Loathing on the Campaign Trail '72.* San Francisco: Straight Arrow Books, 1973.

Wolfe, Tom. *The Electric Kool-Aid Acid Test.* New York: Farrar, Straus and Giroux, 1968.

———. *The Kandy-Colored, Tangerine-Flake Streamlined Baby.* New York: Farrar, Straus and Giroux, 1965.

———. *Radical Chic and Mau-Mauing the Flak Catchers.* New York: Farrar, Straus and Giroux, 1970.

Wolfe, Tom, and E. W. Johnson, eds. *The New Journalism: With an Anthology.* New York: Harper and Row, 1973.

chapter 9

**creating the
magazine's
look: designs
for readability**

From 1934 until 1958, the page layouts at *Harper's Bazaar* were orchestrated by art director Alexey Brodovitch to have a musical feeling and a rhythm that would carry the reader through the magazine like a series of dance steps—a tango here, a cha-cha there, with a waltz or a polka for variety. Brodovitch expected magazine design to have spontaneity, vitality, and movement. Yet he also provided unity and continuity through the use of large amounts of white space and consistent typefaces, and through his treatment of the open magazine as a two-page spread. Mehemed Fehmy Agha, who designed *Vogue* from 1929 through 1942, also created a distinctive look for that magazine. Agha stressed the synergy between editorial copy and design by cutting across the spine of *Vogue* to unite two single pages into one double-page spread through the use of photo bleeds across margins and gutters. ■ Both Brodovitch and Agha instinctively understood what makes magazine design different from that in books and newspapers: a reader focuses on two pages at a time as the frame of reference. Earlier art directors used the two-page spread as a design unit, but they didn't push the horizontal envelope the way that Brodovitch and Agha did. For Brodovitch and Agha, the two-page spread naturally led to other two-page units to create a depth and continuity that transcended each two-dimensional sheet of paper.

They also designed with a clear understanding of their magazines' editorial missions, so that each issue had a strong visual identity. During Agha's tenure, *Vogue* was dedicated to presenting fashion reporting and was a showplace of fashion photography. At Brodovitch's *Harper's Bazaar*, fashion pictures were shot on location with models in action; articles about fashion trends were tempered by the writings of Virginia Woolf, Eudora Welty, and Carson McCullers. The two magazines were, and continue to be, rivals for readers interested in women's fashion and style. More important, their visual identities still honor the legacies of Agha and Brodovitch.

A strong visual identity helps differentiate a magazine from its competitors. *Vibe* and *Rolling Stone* are both music culture magazines. They both have distinctive design looks, and no one would confuse an issue of *Vibe* with its stress on urban hip-hop music and cover celebrities who stare directly into the camera lens and challenge the reader to stare back with *Rolling Stone*'s striking photography and trendy yet sophisticated design. Both magazines have won numerous awards for design and photography, as well as the National Magazine Award for General Editorial Excellence.

A magazine's visual identity derives from its editorial mission; in a very real sense, form follows function here. Design is integral, not incidental, to a magazine's editorial voice. If there's a lack of clarity in the editorial content, there's also likely to be weakness in the visual element.

Magazine design has to offer both change and continuity to readers. On one hand, the magazine must look familiar from issue to issue, with thoughtful, planned content to aid in reader recognition. At the same time, the magazine can't appear boring or static. The integration of words and pictures—the use of titles, photos, cutlines, illustrations, cartoons, and infographics—has to consider readers' content expectations as well as their willingness to be challenged through the manipulation of key design principles.

Design consultant Jan White believes a magazine's design character "is defined by the underlying styling system, which is a subtle mix of titles, logos, slugs, display type, body copy type, spacing, columns, and color. Its success depends on disciplined self-control of the patterning, which causes the reader to say, 'Of course, it couldn't be any other way.'"[1]

Eric Utne, founder of *Utne*, likes to recall a conversation he had with anthropologist Margaret Mead when he considers magazine design. Mead told him there was "a difference between entertaining readers, which she defined as giving them what they wanted, and delighting readers, which she said was giving them what they didn't know they wanted."[2]

form follows function

The function of a magazine has little to do with art and much to do with business, which is determined by a magazine's mission or philosophy. That's why editors and art directors talk about designing a page rather than decorating it. It's also why there's a difference between magazine editorial page design and advertising design. An advertising designer has to catch the reader's attention just once, while a publication designer has to grab that reader over and over, from page to page, and from issue to issue. Design helps readers navigate their way through the pages to find the articles they want to read; it also lures them to articles they may not have intended to read. While design may be what holds a magazine together into a unified package, design alone doesn't keep readers coming back. Think of design as the means and editorial content as the important end result.

Jan White, who has designed the format of hundreds of magazines, says, "The purpose of editorial design is not to make a handsome piece, but a piece that *says something*. Good design should make the reason for publishing the message flare off the page at first glance. This should be the editor's primary goal."[3]

This is why the editor and the art director have to work as a team, with the editor defining and articulating each story's message to the art director, who then determines which visual tools will quickly, clearly, and effectively transmit that message to the reader. The magazine's raw material—white space, type, pictures, color—is shaped into an intellectually consistent and visually pleasing whole.

That visual whole, or the magazine's visual identity, typically is enhanced by a visual hierarchy found in every spread. This hierarchy is based on how most readers skim a story—generally the pictures first, then the title, perhaps over to the

art in american magazines

America's magazines have long enjoyed a close relationship with contemporary artists, from Salvador Dali to Annie Leibovitz. The magazine cover itself is an art form; when that cover showcases museum-quality art, it becomes part of America's cultural heritage. This section offers a brief walk through 20th-century American magazine covers that featured world-famous artists who created variations of their trademark images and landscapes.

SEPTEMBER 1904: Artist Maxfield Parrish offered fantasy and drama through beautifully illustrated magazine covers for *Ladies' Home Journal* at the turn of the 20th century. This image is an example of a poster cover with no cover lines to take away from the image; also known as an art cover, the poster cover was often framed and hung on living-room walls.

DECEMBER 7, 1929: Illustrator Norman Rockwell drew more than 300 covers for *Saturday Evening Post*. This particular issue was so ad-heavy that it weighed nearly two pounds. Merchants bought extra copies to use as wrapping paper because it cost less than a roll of paper.

Flair

February 1950

THE MONTHLY MAGAZINE   FIFTY CENTS

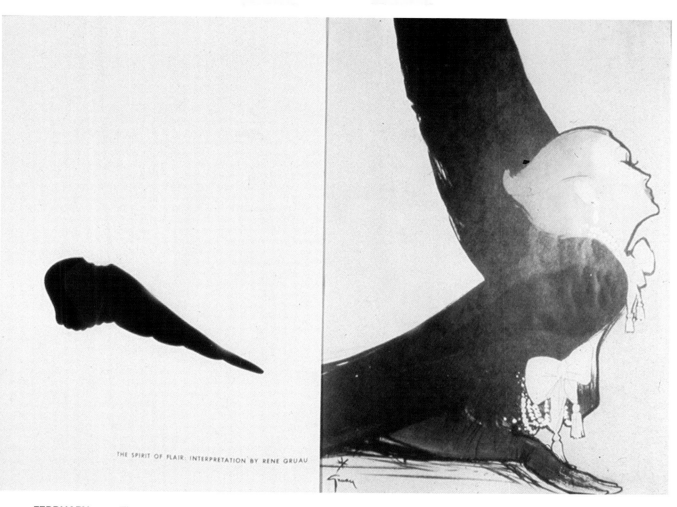

THE SPIRIT OF FLAIR: INTERPRETATION BY RENE GRUAU

FEBRUARY 1950: The cover of the premier issue of *Flair* was—like all subsequent issues in the magazine's year-long run—embossed and die cut. The illustration forming the die cut was modeled after a favorite pin owned by editor and founder Fleur Cowles. Through the hole formed by the die cut, readers could see the second sheet of the cover, which contained a drawing titled *The Spirit of Flair* by René Gruau.

JUNE 1, 1939: Salvador Dali's surrealistic bridal cover for *Vogue* is eerily similar to his renowned *Persistence of Memory* painting.

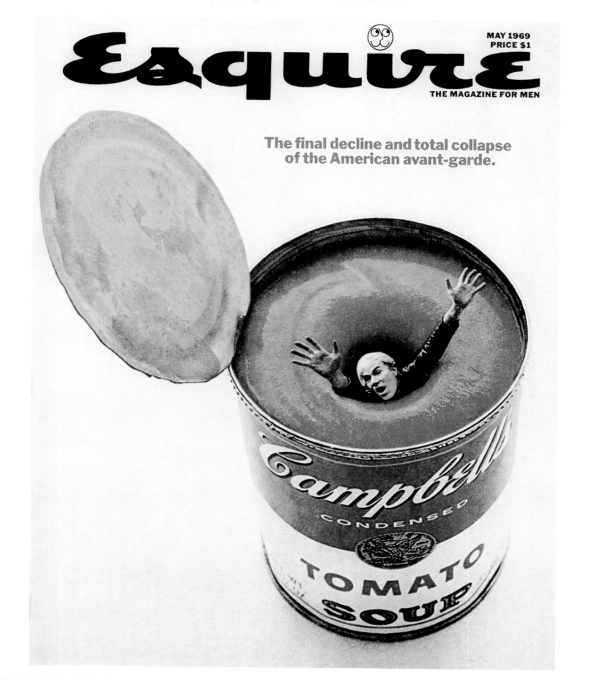

Esquire

MAY 1969
PRICE $1

THE MAGAZINE FOR MEN

The final decline and total collapse
of the American avant-garde.

MAY 1969: Andy Warhol took the Campbell's soup can to the level of pop art in the 1960s by painting it in giant, realistic detail. To symbolize the death of the avant-garde, *Esquire* spoofed the artist's work by showing him drowning in the can he made famous.

JANUARY 22, 1981: *Rolling Stone:* A panel of 52 magazine editors selected *Rolling Stone*'s cover of John Lennon and Yoko Ono as the top magazine cover of the past 40 years. Lennon said Annie Leibovitz's photo of him and his wife "captured our relationship perfect." Lennon was killed shortly after the photo was taken.

You Say Title and I Say Headline

The terminology used to discuss design readout matter—the titles, subtitles, cutlines, subheads, and other words that draw a reader into the body copy—varies from magazine to magazine, and often depends on whether the editor-in-chief majored in journalism or English. Many magazine editors have an English, or book background, although some come to the field from journalism and mass communications programs or the features departments of newspapers. Art directors often have some newspaper experience as part of their publication background.

This is not a definitive list, and there are instances where the newspaper term may dominate, particularly in the use of caption for the name of the text matter that accompanies illustrations. The term cutline dates back to the 19th century, when magazines used woodcuts as illustrations; the cutline was the material identifying what was in a woodcut.

Magazine	Newspaper	Magazine Definition
Logo	Nameplate, flag, banner	**Logo:** The design of the magazine's name.
Cover lines	Main head	**Cover lines:** Short titles, also called sell lines, that appear on the cover of a magazine.
Title	Headline, head, display type	**Title:** Identifying words that usually go above the start of an article or story and provide information as to the article's topic and content.
Subtitle	Deck, drop head, subhead	**Subtitle:** Words that immediately follow the title and that are usually located just below the start of an article; subtitles provide additional clues as to the nature of the article.
Pull-quote	Panel quote, pull-out, breakout, callout	**Pull-quote:** Words pulled from the article that are used as a design element to break up large blocks of text.
Subhead	Slug	**Subhead:** Short phrases or words used to provide organizational information between paragraphs.
Cutline	Caption	**Cutline:** Words underneath a photo that provide information about the image or its context.
Dingbat	Endmark	**Dingbat:** A small design device at the end of each article.
Initial caps	Large initial letter, drop-in	**Initial caps:** The first letter of a word used in a large size to make it stand out.
Byline	Byline	**Byline:** Identification of the author of the article.

cutlines or pull-quotes, then back to the subtitle. Key hierarchical elements, such as the photo or title, generally provide instantaneous communication with the reader and are the subliminal equivalent of an article saying "Read me."

Today's readers are visually sophisticated, and they expect design to be effective, efficient, and engaging. A magazine with a strong visual identity and a clear visual hierarchy has a design that creatively juxtaposes words and images, features and departments, and articles and advertisements. The result is a sequential organization—most of the time. Magazine design is not rigid, and rules are broken every day. When discussing design principles, the phrase "everything's relative" must be recited as if it's a mantra.

On the one hand, most art directors agree that every page should have a single important element that pops out at the reader. On the other hand, not all magazines have a visual hierarchy that quickly draws the reader into the layout and into the article. *Ray Gun* and *blue* were two magazines lacking a hierarchy on their pages: Typed lines ran across each other, into the gutter, and turned upside-down on top of images until nothing was distinguishable on a page.

David Carson, who designed both magazines, challenges how people read magazines. He often takes the constant visual barrage of images, messages, advertisements, and graffiti seen or heard while walking down the street or watching television, and renders them on paper. Carson's lack of a hierarchy in magazine page design is based on his belief that art directors tend to underestimate the sophistication of magazine readers and that readers are willing to view a magazine as graphic performance art.

According to magazine art director Rhonda Rubinstein, Carson's contortionist and iconoclastic approach as art director of *Ray Gun* from 1992 to1995 let readers "experience the raucous confrontation of type and image slamming onto the page."[4] At its peak, *Ray Gun*, which died in 2001, won a slew of awards; the American Center for Design called Carson's designs for the magazine "the most important work coming out of America." Carson, who now has his own design consulting firm, has been called one of the world's most distinctive and innovative typographic voices.

the coming of age of magazine design

The acceptance of an "anything goes" design approach among readers, editors, and art directors is a recent phenomenon. The evolution of magazine design cannot be separated from changing patterns of reader interest that developed following World War II—from an acceptance of broad, general editorial content to a demand for highly spe-

cific, informative niches and topics. The audience drives both editorial content and visual identity, and art directors have had to respond to the specific challenges that arose with a new generation of readers who were experiencing a fast-changing environment at home and at work.

■ DESIGN GOLDEN AGE

Design historian William Owen dubs the period from 1945 to 1968 as the golden age of magazine design. He points out that magazine design matured quickly, with a short adolescence of less than 50 years from the introduction of the halftone as a regular photographic entity at the turn of the 20th century.

the innovators

The golden age of magazine design was preceded by three innovative designers: T. M. Cleland, who created *Fortune*'s modernistic and functional format; Mehemed Fehmy Agha, who gave a new graphic language to *Vogue* and *Vanity Fair;* and Alexey

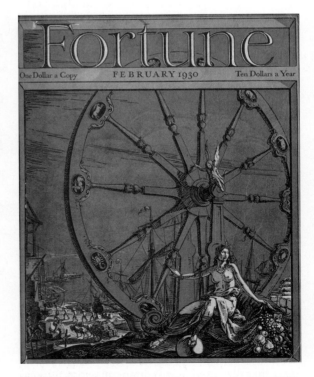

FEBRUARY 1930: In this issue, innovative designer T. M. Cleland introduced his design of *Fortune* magazine, which he said should be "in accord with the best principles of fine bookmaking."

Brodovitch, who brought a sense of music and rhythm to the pages of *Harper's Bazaar*. These three greatly influenced the work of the golden age art directors.

Cleland laid out his design approach to *Fortune* in the February 1930 first issue:

> The design of *Fortune* is based upon its function of presenting a clear and readable text profusely illustrated with pictures, mostly photographic, in a form ample and agreeable to the eye. It is planned upon an economic scale which permits it to go toward that end beyond the technical limitations of most periodicals. . . . The size and proportions of the magazine are designed to give scope to its illustrations and text without crowding and margins to its pages which shall be in accord with the best principles of fine bookmaking.[5]

The 14 inch by 11.25 inch *Fortune* had a commanding physical presence: Averaging 200 pages, the magazine weighed in at 3 pounds due to the use of heavy, uncoated paper stock. The design stressed simplicity and consistency throughout the magazine via the use of the same typeface (Baskerville, which dates back to the 18th century), and the use of a thick 4-point rule around all the oversized photos. This was a departure from the myriad typefaces, borders, and small photos found in many magazines of the time in their attempt to be exciting. Clearly, *Fortune*'s design matched the serious business topics being covered and the "less is more" philosophy of the time.

Agha's deliberate union of two single pages into one double-page spread by crossing the gutter was a new and dramatic way of making photos larger and bolder, as was his penchant for fanning action photos sequentially across a *Vanity Fair* or *Vogue* page to suggest movement. He eliminated column rules and decorative borders, simplified typography, and used lots of white space at the margins of pages. Agha demanded and achieved an elegant perfection in his layouts; in fact, "elegance" was the word used by peers to describe his work.

Brodovitch is considered the dean of art directors by many magazine designers. According to Owen, "Most of the techniques used in contemporary magazine design were pioneered or exploited at some time or another by Brodovitch— an undogmatic and instinctive rather than rational designer, who obsessively pursued change and modernity, and whose watchword was 'Make it new.'"[6] Brodovitch used handheld cameras,

overexposed photographs, and image repetition long before Andy Warhol burst onto the art scene. Brodovitch's cover for the August 1940 *Harper's Bazaar* repeats a woman's face with blue, green, red, and yellow colored lips, predating Warhol's variously colored Marilyn Monroes in a far more lyrical and powerful format. Plain backgrounds with large photos and ragged type were juxtaposed with inanimate and animate forms to give depth to the pages. A sense of pacing is strong in Brodovitch's work. That's because he viewed the page as three-dimensional rather than two, depicting depth along with height and width.

the heirs

A number of photographers and art directors were the heirs of Cleland, Agha, and Brodovitch, and became key players during the golden age of magazine design. Concentrated in New York City, "designers of this period were distinguished primarily by their positive commitment to information design in the popular press, and were hidebound neither by stylistic fetish nor slavish adherence to the typographic dogma which sometimes encumbered European contemporaries," said Owen.[7] Some names to remember here are Otto Storch of *McCall's;* Bradbury Thompson of *Mademoiselle;* Henry Wolf of *Esquire, Harper's Bazaar,* and *Show;* and Alexander Liberman, who followed Agha as art director for all the Condé Nast magazines, including *Vanity Fair* and *Vogue.*

Storch, who was art director of *McCall's* from 1954 until 1967, reinforced the idea that copy, art, and typography were one unit; he was particularly adept at linking typography with photography for a unique design approach. For example, to illustrate an article titled "Why Mommy Can't Read," those words were written on the lens of a pair of eyeglasses. In "The Forty-winks Reducing Plan," a woman is shown reclining on her side on a cutaway mattress made of type, with the words of the article curving along her body from the pillow to her feet. Storch also regularly built two-page spreads around a single bleed photo—extending past the edge of the page—that served as both the background for the text and its illustration.

Thompson found new applications for type while at *Mademoiselle* from 1945 to 1959. He experimented with type both as an illustrative tool and as an alliterative form to create movement, volume, place, and mood. Plus, he used large horizontal and vertical grids to fashion layouts dominated by blocks of primary color, mimicking the paintings of the Dutch artist Piet Mondrian.

Wolf, who served as art director at *Esquire* (from 1952 to 1958), *Harper's Bazaar* (from 1958 to 1961), and *Show* (from 1961 to 1964), took a surrealistic approach to his pages. To illustrate *Esquire*'s July 1958 cover story about "The Americanization of Paris," Wolf shot a photo of a packet of "instant vin rouge" being poured into a goblet of water. Although it was meant to satirize the spread of American conveniences and customs, letters were sent to the editor asking where instant wine could be purchased. A May 1959 *Harper's Bazaar* cover touting "The Wonders of Water" found Wolf creating a refracted image of a woman's face in a large glass of water; the real face loomed behind the glass. Where the logo touched the glass, it, too, was refracted.

Liberman had the title of editorial director at *Vogue* and *Vanity Fair*, which allowed him to take a journalistic approach to design and to recognize the need to meld commercialism and circulation sales with fine art. He liked dramatic layouts that were classically bold and crudely aggressive at the same time. That was possible at fashion magazines where the photograph or illustration of clothing had to speak as loudly as the copy describing each garment.

Speaking in 1958, Wolf said the fashion magazine offered

> the highest form for art direction: it is the art director's ideal showcase. The fantasy inherent in fashion stimulates creative designing, and furthermore, the photography and its layout are the means of "talking" fashion. Since the picture can and must say it all, the copy in a fashion magazine plays a subordinate role. What a rare privilege for an art director! The only objective to present something visually beautiful![8]

But even when accentuating the visual, art directors from 1945 to 1968 wanted a gestalt, or integration of various parts into a functional unit. A gestalt occurs when editorial and design are in harmony, so that the layout's whole—the spread—is greater than the sum of its individual parts (copy, title, subtitle, photos, cutlines). With a gestalt, the design reflects or builds upon the editorial content by helping to tell the story rather than just embellishing it.

The golden age of design, then, clearly linked all the elements of a page into a synergistic whole. Preliminary editorial conferences defined the feature copy and thinking that went behind each piece; design was supposed to express the concepts and ideas of each article. Next, the art director worked with photographers, illustrators, and graphic artists to plan and to visualize how the material could be presented imaginatively. Advertising tended to be clustered at the front and back of the magazines, and departments were few. There usually was an editorial block, or well of 40–50 pages to work with, and although stories had to jump to the back of the magazine, most had a lavish start of four or five pages.

The assumption was that readers spent an unhurried, relaxing visit with their favorite magazines, and they would become absorbed by the visual and verbal spectacle on each page. Adding to the elegance and drama was the large size of the magazines themselves, averaging 10.125 inches by 13.125 inches. Although lavish, physically imposing, and slick, there nonetheless was always a sense of logic to the most opulent pages produced during the period from 1948 through 1967.

■ DESIGN TURNING POINT

Many designers believe the launch of *New York* in 1968 was an important turning point in magazine design. Founder Clay Felker says *New York*'s design and content were based on his belief that magazines had to compete in new ways for readers' time and attention. Certainly, there was enough going on in American society during the late 1960s to co-opt leisurely reading: the Vietnam War, civil rights sit-downs, women's liberation marches, and the increasing dominance of television in telling the stories of the day all affected the kinds of magazines being developed. Some pundits were even predicting the death of the magazine as a significant communication medium.

The time was right for highly specialized, smaller scaled, tightly formatted magazines like *New York* that took readers' needs into account. Calling the design formula simple enough to work on a weekly basis yet sophisticated enough to compete for a busy metropolitan reader, Felker explained how it worked:

> It was a magazine that had to give the reader a feeling of getting something out of the magazine just

If It's Ljubljana, It Must Be *Cosmopolitan*

Ljubljana, the capital of Slovenia, is a cosmopolitan city whose history dates back to the Roman Empire, where Armani suits are sold in pricey boutiques in refurbished medieval shops, and where stylishly thin women navigate cobblestone streets in 4-inch heels. On nearly every block in the city center, the visitor can expect not only an outdoor café or bar, but also a bookstore or newsstand. The magazines on sale throughout the city are as much of a mix of new and old as the city itself. *Mladina*, the leftist magazine that was an important voice of opposition to Communism in the 1980s, sells next to a sexy issue of the Slovenian *Cosmopolitan*. Residents of this tiny mountain nation are avid readers who even buy their magazines from street vendors as they sit in their cars at busy intersections.

Slovenian publications are written in Slovene, a language regularly spoken only by the country's 2 million residents and distinct from that spoken by the country's southern neighbors, Croatia and Serbia, although all have similar Slavic roots. The newsstand duel between the Slovenian and the Croatian editions of *Cosmopolitan* demonstrates the distinct but similar language and culture between Croatia and Slovenia—and illustrates the strength of the Slovene market economy. The Croatian *Cosmopolitan* was launched in 2000 and was sold successfully on newsstands in Slovenia, whose citizens can easily read Croatian. When the Slovene *Cosmopolitan* was launched in 2001, however, Slovene readers quickly deserted the Croatian version, and it was ultimately taken off the stands in Slovenia.

The economics of scale in Slovenia are difficult to comprehend using an American model to study Slovene magazines. The Slovene *Cosmopolitan* is a healthy and successful title, even though it has a circulation of only 25,000. Its market penetration, however, is impressive, with 1 out of every 80 Slovenes buying the magazine. Its pass-along readership of four means the magazine is read by one of every 20 Slovenes. The Slovene versions of *Cosmopolitan*, *Playboy*, and *Men's Health* are in the top 5 percentiles for penetration of their respective brands worldwide.

Editor and publisher Bostjan Jevsek, whose company publishes titles including *Men's Health*, *Cosmopolitan*, and *Playboy*, lists his rules for a good cover: It must be powerful and intriguing; cover lines must offer an exact promise that the magazine can fulfill; numbers are a staple in service magazines and celebrities are an option for lifestyle titles; images should reflect the content of the magazine and cover lines should reflect the editorial mix; and cover lines can highlight minor as well as major articles.

In this, he is following the lead given by the American publishers with whom he works. He is also challenging widely held Slovene magazine assumptions that only top stories should be listed in cover lines and that the cover should be the last thing created. He is striving to push cover development to an earlier phase of the magazine production process. It is no longer the last task the editors tackle, he says, but it is still "not at all the first thing."

Each Slovene edition of an American title has its own cover style. Scantily dressed beautiful women are always on the cover of *Cosmopolitan*. So

Excerpted from Patricia Prijatel, "A New Culture of Covers: Slovenian Magazines in Transition," *Journal of Magazine and New Media Research*, vol. 5, no. 1 (Fall 2002), http://www.bsu.edu/web/aejmcmagazine/journal/archive/Fall_2002/Prijatel.htm.

(continued)

If It's Ljubljana, It Must Be *Cosmopolitan* (continued)

far, no Slovene women have been used as cover models because the cost of photography forces editors to use pickup photos from other Hearst International magazines. Sometimes celebrities make the cover, but not always. Editors must send the covers to New York City for approval. Usually the only change is that the American staff "spices up" the cover lines, editor Lidija Petek says.

The cover of *Men's Health* always has a handsome and fit young man, undressed from the waist up, looking at the camera. Covers show "the joy of life," Jevsek says. Images come from Rodale Publishing—often from other international rather than American editions. Cover lines are written by Slovene editors, then translated into English for review by editors in Pennsylvania. Rodale strictly protects its brand and often changes cover lines. The Slovene brand has more emphasis on sex than on health, which matches the market need. Slovenes, like other Europeans, are fairly liberal about sex and are, in general, a healthy lot.

Many *Playboy* cover models have been Slovenian, but other European and some South American women have also been featured. Editors prefer not to use women from the American *Playboy*. "They are plastic, artificial, always blond with big breasts," Jevsek says. Brazilian models are a favorite as they are often shot in a natural setting such as the beach, as opposed to the studio shots regularly featured in the American edition. Many Slovenian women are interested in posing for the American *Playboy* but not the Slovenian one, where relatives, boyfriends, and bosses would all know should she pop up in the buff on the corner newsstand.

American concepts do not always translate neatly into Slovene. For example, "Make Her Want You" works well on the American *Men's Health.* The phrase, though, simply does not translate into Slovene. "Make" has only a pragmatic meaning in the Slovene language and refers to making a cake or a cup of coffee. It has no real meaning in the more esoteric and theoretical sense of influencing a

woman's heart. To get the idea of "Make Her Want You," the Slovenian editors would have to invent a new construction that would be the length of a full sentence and would lack the punch and energy necessary for a cover line.

English words seldom are used on Slovene covers beyond the names of the magazines themselves. "Seks," however, is a staple on *Cosmopolitan* and *Men's Health*. Slovene has no "x," so the "ks" is required for the correct pronunciation. The *Playboy* interview is translated into "*intervju*," as the "j" in Slovene has a "y" sound.

Because *Cosmopolitan* has sold well in the past, it gets premium space in kiosks and bookstores—it is difficult to walk through the center of Ljubljana without confronting the magazine several times. And, because it gets prominent display, *Cosmopolitan* continues to sell well, in the age-old cycle of success breeding success. After all, not even the best-designed cover can sell a magazine unless readers can see it, which is the pragmatic bottom line wherever magazines are sold. ■

by paging through it—without reading anything, on the surface. And then if they decided to read something more, they would get another experience on a deeper level. It had to operate on two levels and it had to operate very quickly. We assumed that the readers we had didn't have a lot of time; we had to get our message across very quickly, to intrigue those readers enough to get them to read the

magazine in the subsequent paging through. We designed the magazine with that in mind.[9]

Founding design director Milton Glaser said he created *New York* according to an assumed attention span of 7 minutes, which, he observed, "coincided exactly with the interval between television commercials during most TV programs. So we designed *New York* to be read by somebody with that temperament, for the television generation. It had constant interruptions—titles, subheads on every page, everything was designed for easy access."[10]

New York moved away from the graceful, sweeping, primarily visual approach of the golden age to compartmentalized pages that eliminated jumping features to the back of the magazine and allowed advertising to run throughout the publication rather than just in the front and back. A lot more text, including sidebars, filled each page. Glaser's design format was very functional: Readers knew precisely where to go to get information and they could get it in short but dense chunks without having to jump to the back of the magazine to find it.

Wildly colorful psychedelic art was balanced by such type paraphernalia as initial caps, column rules, boxes, and a variety of decorative types for feature titles, although standing department heads tended to use traditional typefaces. Reverse type, bolded first sentences, and squared off, boxed-in pages became the norm. There were fewer bleed photos and more illustrations, along with a willingness to break the sweeping unity of type and image used earlier.

Many city and regional magazines copied *New York* down to the last dingbat detail. Magazines as disparate as *Esquire, Playboy, Redbook,* and *Adweek* began playing around with what some critics called "fusspot" typography and flat graphic design. However, the 1960s and 1970s were about letting go and experimenting, even if there was a surprisingly homogenous quality to the "revolution." So why should magazines be any different?

An estimated one in five U.S. adults will read, or at least look at, the annual *Sports Illustrated* swimsuit issue. Men buy the magazine to eyeball drop-dead gorgeous models revealing a lot of flesh in provocative poses. However, women see the issue as the most extensive catalogue of swimsuit trends being published. According to swimsuit manufacturers, having their suit on the cover or in the issue guarantees a sell-out for that particular item. So who *really* benefits from the swimsuit issue?

■ COMPUTERS AND DESIGN

The real revolution was still to come, and it was a technological one in 1984 that forever changed the magazine design process. In that year, the first generation Macintosh computer was introduced by Apple; type letterforms were primitive dot matrixes, and graphic choices were limited. But it was clear that an innovative tool had arrived on the art director's desk, one that was transformed into a powerful graphic desktop by the late 1980s.

As an interactive tool, computers enable text to be edited and designed on screen simultaneously. All the components of design choice—words, photos, illustrations, typefaces, colors, textures, rules, and boxes—are integrated into a single system. This does not necessarily make magazine design easier, nor does it make the process faster. Design combinations and choices still have to be made, but now the possibilities are almost limitless.

The late Henry Wolf called the computer a "seductive piece of equipment that too easily facilitates excess."[11] Referring to the golden age of design, Wolf said, "In my world, the idea was to communicate with clarity, to dramatize your point. I think what the computer does is obfuscate the point, make it more difficult, more layered, instead of bringing out the thing that clarifies it. The computer adds. For us, it was always to subtract."

■ "MORE IS BETTER"

Experimental design and lack of reference points to long-held design standards resulted in a "more is better" approach in the late 1990s. Carol E. Holstead, a magazine professor at the William Allen White School of Journalism at the University of Kansas who studies contemporary magazine design, argues that the historical perspective of "less is more" has been sacrificed for flashy newsstand cover graphics featuring a plethora of cover lines (as many as 10) and spot colors (as many as 6) on top of the main cover. Inside pages aren't much better, she notes, with departments and features using four or five spot colors per page, irregularly cutout photos, decorative borders, numerous type weights and styles, and rakish title angles.[12]

That approach has spilled over into the 21st century, with the result that no one design style dominates. "Anything goes now, so there is no trend. The trend is no trend," says Roger Black, who started out as an art director for *Rolling Stone, New York,* and *Newsweek,* but is now known as the quintessential magazine redesigner whose classic, elegant approach has been applied to *Popular Mechanics, Reader's Digest, The New Republic,* and others.[13] "I've designed more magazines than you'll ever read," Black has been known to say.

Discussing magazine design, Black observes, "There hasn't been a big, blockbuster home run in years. When *Rolling Stone* came out in 1967, it had an enormous impact. Every college student in the country copied it. All the big wins over the last several years have been Oprah and Martha, where you can latch on to some giant celebrity thing."

Black says celebrity journalism has had an impact on design. He points out that so many magazines have the same celebrities, the same language, and the same cover lines that they all are starting to look alike. "If you go to the typical grocery store, at the checkout racks, they are all blowing out at you with bright colors and white T's and suggestions that are pretty much the same from magazine to magazine," Black says.

■ RELATIONSHIP WITH THE READER

Readers know when an article's title misrepresents or overhypes a story, and they recognize graphics that are superficially startling. Today's readers may still read words the same way as those in 1741, but they also read images and typography—and therefore, design. It takes discipline to maintain a visual identity that resonates with readers without boring them. Fortunately, there's plenty of room in the magazine industry for designs that are spare, simple, and classic as well as designs that are pyrotechnic, confrontational, and avant-garde—from magazines as disparate as *Martha Stewart Living, Real Simple, Harper's Bazaar, Details, Rolling Stone, Vibe, I.D. Magazine,* and *Flaunt.* After all, the reader can choose whether she wants to be soothed by uncluttered, color-coordinated pages of still-life fruits, deceptively simple room arrangements, and perfectly posed fashions or challenged by the unconventional perspective of

cutting-edge layouts, street-smart attitudes, and foldout articles that shatter the way she was taught to read.

Flaunt, with its nonformatted style, challenges the reader to interact with the magazine and spend some time figuring it out. That's a long way from the safe, comfortable embrace of a picture-perfect spread in *Martha Stewart Living.* But whether the design is that of a *Flaunt* or a *Martha Stewart Living,* the relationship with the reader is paramount. Despite the design extremes found in magazines today, art directors and editors take into consideration how the publication is used, when and where it is read, what the reader wants, how it is held, and how quickly it is read when they design each spread in each issue.

Consequently, the best magazine design operates on a continuum, taking into account that a magazine offers a series or sequence of impressions through its content and its images. Jan White sums up the complex relationship between the reader and the magazine:

> The best presentation is so natural and obvious that the readers are aware only of the wonders of the information they are reading. If they are tempted to notice the design then that design has interposed itself and is therefore a failure—no matter how exciting or pretty. The medium is not the message. The message is the message.[14]

design elements
· ·

The impact of visual literacy, where people read images, typography, and design as much as they do a story's words, has led designers to consider one of two broad approaches: ordered versus diversified. Ordered designs stress unity from page to page, with relatively few frills or complications. Ordered magazines have tightly organized pages with consistent typography and page margins, but that doesn't mean they are dull or unattractive. The order results in a crisp, clean, and attractive format that appeals to many readers. Magazines using this approach include *Scientific American, The New Yorker, The New Republic, National Review,* and *The History Channel Magazine.*

Diversified designs still use basic design principles, but with a lot more variety and liveliness. Although some diversified approaches may seem like a three-ring circus, there usually is order within the appearance of chaos. Designers taking a diversified approach use varying typefaces and are willing to change page margins to suit their needs. Examples of magazines taking a diversified approach are *Rolling Stone, Esquire, Outside,* and *More.*

Both approaches take into consideration such design elements as eye movement, grid, typography, color, and the basic design principles of unity, balance, proportion, sequence, and contrast. And both approaches revolve around the two-page spread, which is the primary unit of design in magazines because readers almost always view two pages at a time when reading.

■ EYE MOVEMENT

In general, people in the Western world read from left to right and top to bottom. Research shows that magazine readers also read from big to little, from heavy to light, and from color to noncolor. Consequently, a large, colorful focal point, such as a full-color photograph or even a spot color drawing, can pull a reader into a story.

Another eye path involves intentional or unintentional lines of direction, such as eyes in a photograph, raised capital letters in the middle of text, subtitles or subheads between paragraphs, or bulleted paragraphs. When a reader initially scans a page, his eyes tend to follow a "Z" formation. Because readers automatically gravitate toward the upper left quadrant of a page as a starting point, this is where most designers place an article's title.

However, some designers choose to ignore traditional eye movement as part of their lack of conformity. Articles may start at the end and work back to the top of the left-hand page, or begin in the middle of the right-hand page, an approach often followed by designer David Carson. Although his layouts may be hard to read, Carson points out that he

First issues of magazines in mint condition are almost as valuable a commodity as a stock certificate. The 1953 issue of *Playboy* with the nude of Marilyn Monroe sold for more than $3,000 on eBay in 2004, making it one of the priciest magazine collectibles to come on the market. The 1953 premiere issue of *TV Guide* with a photograph of just-born Desi Arnaz Jr., with his famous mom, Lucille Ball, shown in the upper right corner, would also go for a big bucks. It's estimated to sell for more than $3,000 if you can find one in mint condition.

doesn't forget about the subject matter and the audience in his design interpretation. "The starting point is about trying to interpret something about the article. The design and layout was, and is, influenced almost entirely by the content."[15]

■ THE GRID

The grid establishes margins, number of columns per page, widths of columns, cutline and photo placement, title placement, and most important, the use and placement of white space, or air, in a layout. Essentially, a grid provides structure and discipline for each page, as well as an ongoing format to follow from issue to issue. A well-designed grid system can produce a sense of continuity and balance while still allowing for contrast, variety, flexibility, and the use of sidebars, or short accompanying pieces, to support main articles. However, a poorly designed grid, or one that is not used effectively, can result in monotonous, rigid, and crowded layouts.

Will Hopkins, a partner in the New York design firm of Hopkins/Baumann, explains why the majority of art directors use grids: "Think of the grid as a container into which you pour content. It's difficult to carry water without a bucket, and it's difficult to carry content without a grid. It's a structural and visual aid that should be flexible, and not a straitjacket."[16]

The editorial staff benefits from a grid because it creates a design standard, allowing everyone to speak the same language in terms of column widths, photo sizes, and space requirements. The reader benefits from pages that are logical, organized, readable, and visually appealing. There are three grid possibilities, but because most magazines customize their grids depending on their page size, determining an exact system is difficult.

traditional

A traditional grid has standard margins and divides space into a two- or three-column format for a page size of about 8.5 inches wide by 11 inches deep (keep in mind that few magazines are exactly that size). There are no horizontal lines on a traditional grid, and the space inside the margins becomes the type page. In a traditional grid, margins often are progressive, with the most white space at the bottom of the page and the least in the gutter area separating the two pages. Photos fill one, two, or three columns of space; bleeds are possible, but not frequent on editorial pages.

A traditional grid may designate a three-column format for departments and two columns for features, or allow for either two- or three-column features. All design elements end at the same place from page to page, which provides a strong unifying factor and creates an orderly relationship of typography, photography, and illustration. Some traditional grids resemble book designs because of the emphasis on verticality and the tendency to treat each page as a separate entity rather than as a two-page unit. The traditional grid results in formal layouts.

nontraditional

The nontraditional grid starts off with the traditional vertical two- or three-column format, but it also uses horizontal lines for a modular approach to design. Because there are numerous horizontal units to consider, column width can expand or contract as needed, type can be wrapped around photos or set in varying widths, photos can cut across columns, and page margins can be changed. The nontraditional grid offers more options for the use of sidebar material than the traditional grid.

Unity and continuity are still emphasized in a nontraditional grid, although there are more design possibilities. The ability to manipulate white space is the strongest aspect of the nontraditional grid. With more emphasis on the horizontal flow of the pages, a sense of sequencing or movement can be developed. The majority of magazines—consumer, trade, and organization—use a nontraditional grid.

12-part grid

Developed in Germany by Willy Fleckhaus and brought to the United States by Will Hopkins in 1968 when he was art director at *Look*, this grid starts with 12 equal parts per page, which allows for a great deal of flexibility while still having precise margins and columns. The 12-part grid can operate with two, three, four, or six columns per page, and encourages the use of sidebars, thumbnail photos, and skinny design elements as well as large scale visuals, contrasting shapes, and dramatic bleeds. The 12-unit grid controls overcrowding of material and positions white space in powerful and surprising ways.

no grid

David Carson eschews grids of any form. His hyperkinetic page layouts take a lot more time to create, he says, because "it's not just this horrible grid where things are dropped in, which I think represents a certain amount of laziness. It's very work-intensive to do a magazine in which every page is completely different."[17]

■ TYPOGRAPHY

Typography is the primary visual component in the communication of words on a printed page. Whether a single typeface or series of typefaces are used for body copy, titles, and cutlines, a message is conveyed to readers about a magazine's character. Some art directors think of typography as an art form that allows for the musical expression of words.

Designers can choose among thousands of typeface possibilities, each with its own tone of voice. Type can shout, whisper, stammer, bawl, growl, or converse in a gently modulated pitch. In deciding which typefaces to use, several factors must be considered: legibility, suitability, font, size, line length, and spacing of letters and lines.

The advent of computers has made it difficult to identify or classify typefaces by design attribute or even by name. More than 10,000 typefaces are available, and computers allow for the modification of existing ones as well as the creation of new ones every day. While this unprecedented variety of available typefaces has had its greatest effect on advertising and promotional material, the fact remains that all sorts of typographic idiosyncrasies can be catered to in magazine page design—and are.

"It's very easy to get carried away with special effects. Take type. You can stretch it or bend it,

Flipping Through Folios

The placement of folio lines (page numbers, name of magazine, and date of issue) can be a unifying characteristic as well as a creative design element. Folios don't have to fall at the bottom left- and right-hand corners, although readers tend to expect that location, and most magazines place them there. The choice of typeface for folios is a stylistic decision, as are choosing whether to include the issue date and name of the magazine, and in what order.

Time puts numbers on the outside bottom corners and centers the name and date on editorial pages. *Esquire, Newsweek,* and *The New Yorker* locate the number, magazine name, and date on both pages for a mirror-image look. *AARP: The Magazine* puts the page number, name, and issue date on the bottom left-hand

page; the magazine's website and page number are on the opposite page. *The Advocate* also includes its website as part of its folio on the bottom of each page. *Utne* centers the page number, name, and date as one continuous line at the bottom of each editorial page. *The New Republic* places the page, date, and name as mirrored images in the upper-left and -right corners, with the page number in red and in a larger point size.

Unfortunately, magazines in general aren't good about placing page numbers on every page. A bleed page or a page with an advertisement generally does not receive a number, so a reader hunting for a story "continued on page so-and-so" has a difficult time finding it. Women's fashion magazines are notorious for having so

many ads at the front of the magazine that it's hard to find the start of the first department, much less the first feature page, because folios are so far back.

National Geographic begins page numbers in the center editorial well section; departments at the front and the back of the magazine don't even have page numbers. In the December 2005 issue, there were 51 actual pages before the first feature, "Hope in Hell," began with page 2 as its designated number on the table of contents and the folio.

Readers shouldn't have to flip back and forth trying to find a page number. After all, page numbers are supposed to help establish the proper sequence of material and should be there to let readers find and follow-up on every article.

---

vary its color, give it a shadow or a color outline, make it semi-transparent—all with a few clicks of the mouse," says design consultant David Herbick, who currently works with business-to-business and organization magazines such as *Regulation* and whose résumé includes stints at *Newsweek, Business Week, PC Magazine,* and *Civilization.*[18]

legibility

The ability of a typeface to jump off the page at a quick glance and into the reader's consciousness is its legibility. The term legibility describes how easily type can be read and comprehended. Yet even the most legible typefaces can become unrecog-

nizable through the poor arrangement of typography on a page. Serif and sans serif are two main categories of type to consider for body copy.

Serif If there is a large amount of text to digest, the type must be easy to read, which is why most magazine feature articles are set in a serif typeface. Serif typefaces have delicate vertical and horizontal lines, or "feet," at the end of letter strokes. The serifs serve as a guideline for the eye; if you cover the bottom half of a line of serif type, you still can discern the words because of the clues provided by the thick and thin finishing strokes. Most books, daily newspapers, and the majority of magazines use serif typefaces for their body copy. Typical serif typefaces include Times Roman, Bodoni,

Baskerville, Palatino, Garamond, and Century Schoolbook. Such typefaces connote stability, tradition, and formality.

Sans Serif Typefaces such as Arial, Helvetica, Gill Sans, and Verdana are sans serif—and geometric in appearance. As their name implies, they lack serifs. Sans serif typefaces work best when used in short copy blocks, such as sidebars, lists, photo cutlines, and titles. They suggest a modern, contemporary, and upbeat attitude.

The choice of typeface makes a difference in how fast people read. Reading speed is boosted an additional 7–10 words a minute when a serif type like Times **is used rather than a sans serif type such as** Arial.

suitability

The effectiveness of type in enhancing the message is its suitability; choosing a suitable type tends to be intuitive rather than grounded in research. Typefaces can create moods and motifs as a result of different characteristics involved in the shape and weight of the letterform. Some typefaces are said to be masculine, while others are feminine; some are powerful, while others are delicate. In reality, the psychological considerations of typefaces depend on individual interpretation by the art director—with the reader ideally in agreement. Certainly, the tone or shape of a typeface should match the mood of an article.

Cursive and script typefaces, such as Mistral and Bickham Script, look like hand lettering or ornate handwriting, while Old English seems to have come straight out of the King James Bible. Decorative or novelty typefaces, with names and shapes that reflect their attention-getting appeal—Chiller, Pistol Shot, Algerian, and Stencil—find usage as titles that reinforce an article's message. In general, cursive, script, and decorative typefaces are too difficult to read as blocks of body copy, although they can be effective when used for titles.

font and style

The name of an individual typeface is its font. Style refers to the various individual options within the font. A type font can have numerous style variations, such as italic, bold, extra bold, bold italic, extra bold italic condensed, extra condensed, and ultra condensed (the possibilities boggle the

mind), which affect the look, shape, and the weight of the letters. However, all of the various styles in a font have the same design. One way to have a bit of variety with strong consistency is to use a font that has several style variations: Bodoni Regular for body copy, Bodoni Bold for titles, Bodoni Bold Condensed for subtitles or subheads between paragraphs, and Bodoni Italic for cutlines. Because almost every typeface has several styles, it's estimated that there are upwards of 100,000 type possibilities available.

The use of computers in design has led to some changes in type terminology. At one time, family was the name of a particular typeface, and font referred to the various individual styles within the family. However, for most designers, font has come to mean a typeface in every size and every style. Consequently, when some art directors talk about changing the size or style of type, they don't think of it as changing the font; depending on the computer design software program being used, each variation may be listed as a font. For example, in some computer programs, Bodoni Bold is designated as a specific font and is different from the effect achieved by selecting Bodoni and bolding the words.

In general, copy that is set in uppercase and lowercase type is easier to read than all caps. Researchers say people don't like to read large blocks of italic type because it slows their reading speed. Italic tends to be used for emphasis or contrast. Bold, because it also slows readers, likewise tends to be used for emphasis, primarily to punch up titles for features and departments. The most popular weight and style choices for large masses of body text are the medium weight, regular width, and regular (or upright) version of a serif typeface, such as Times Roman, Palatino, Baskerville, or Garamond.

size

Points and picas are the two units of measurement in design. The point is the unit of measurement that indicates size of type. One point equals ¹⁄₇₂ of an inch, for 72 points in one inch. Picas are used to indicate width and depth of columns, photos, and page space. There are 12 points in one pica; 6 picas equal one inch.

$$1 \text{ point} = \frac{1}{72} \text{ of an inch}$$
$$72 \text{ points} = 1 \text{ inch}$$
$$12 \text{ points} = 1 \text{ pica}$$
$$1 \text{ pica} = \frac{1}{6} \text{ of an inch}$$
$$6 \text{ picas} = 1 \text{ inch}$$

Type size and point size are not interchangeable. This is because point size historically refers to the measurement of type as if it were cast in metal (although it isn't anymore). The actual height, or type size, of individual letters can vary significantly among typefaces that have the same point size. This size factor is the type's x-height, or measurement of a lowercase x. This affects how large the type looks on the page. For example, 12-point Times Roman is actually smaller—takes up less space on the page—than 12-point Palatino. Ten-point Baskerville has a smaller x-height than 10-point Times Roman, which is smaller than the x-height of 10-point Helvetica. This has an impact on readers because type that is too large slows down readability as well as comprehension of text. Type that is too small impedes word recognition and reduces visibility.

Most art directors opt for body type that is either 9, 10, or 11 points in size, assuming an audience that is not very young or very elderly. Both of those age groups prefer larger type sizes. Display type refers to type that is larger than 14 points and used for titles and subtitles.

line length

The number of letters on a line is the line measure or line length. The width of columns is a factor here, but art directors have to remember that lines that are too short are tiring to read because they create a jittery feeling. Lines that are too long also are tiring because readers' eyes may find it awkward to return to the following line. "Doubling" can occur after reading a very long line: When the eyes swing back to the left margin, they lose track of where they are and begin to read the same line again. This is not only irritating, but it also can result in a reader giving up on the entire article.

JANUARY 2000: David Carson's distinctive design of *Ray Gun*, which ceased publication in 2000, challenged the way people read magazines.

Because eyes take in several words, usually three or four at a time, a rule of thumb for line length has been identified as being about 40 characters. That would take up about 13–15 picas of space, depending on the size of the type (assuming 9, 10, or 11 points). This translates to a three-column format of about 15 picas each, on a page size of about 8.5 inches, which is used by many magazines. Magazines generally don't set large blocks of body copy more than the width of two columns, or about 30 picas wide.

Another factor in line length is whether copy is set justified, where all lines are set flush at both the left and right edges of the column (as found in books), or is set ragged right, where lines are flush on the left side, but have varied lengths on the right side. Justified type creates a formal, traditional look, while ragged right seems more casual and contemporary. However, numerous studies reveal that it really doesn't matter whether justified or unjustified lines are used. Both are equally readable, so which to use becomes an artistic decision rather than a functional one.

spacing of letters and lines

The amount of space between letters affects readability, as does the amount of space between lines. Computers have made kerning—the reduction or enlargement of space between letters—a simple operation. Tracking, on the other hand, involves adjustments to the amount of space between words, making them tighter or looser overall. Excessive spacing may look decorative, but it may not be readable. Tracking or kerning that is too tight can distort letter forms; some art directors call this "traumatizing the type."

Leading (pronounced "ledding") is the amount of space between lines of type. In the days of hot metal type, leading was done by inserting a thin strip of metal (called a lead) between lines. Today's computers automatically build in that space beneath the type lines. This is somewhat like double- or triple-spacing your copy when you type a paper or article. One rule of thumb is that there should be at least one point of leading between lines: Using a 10-point typeface for body copy would call for 1 point of leading, resulting in 11 points of space in each line. This creates an unconscious river of white that provides stability for the eyes. Again, computers have made a difference here, allowing for more or less leading. Too much or too little line space slows reading, and excessive line spacing results in a loss of reading function.

The relationship of typography to layout is critical. Art directors use type to draw a reader in and get her to read a story she might have ignored if she hadn't been attracted by a catchy title or subtitle. Typography helps pull a page together.

A 2005 Roper survey asked more than 1,000 American adults, "If your picture could appear on the cover of any magazine, which one would you choose?" The overwhelming response across all demographics was *Time*.

■ COLOR

Black on white is the most legible choice for large blocks of printed information. Black type on a white background is standard, and the use of any color other than black for type is risky. It once was a "never" to run body type in anything but black, with a short and very occasional use of reverse type—white type on black background—being acceptable. But many art directors today are willing to take risks, using such combinations as maroon type on pale blue or orange type on green for shock, surprise, or just sheer serendipity.

Color provides identification, creates associations, and attracts attention. The use of color adds visual excitement to pages, and readers say they prefer a page with full color to one with just black and white.

identification

The red border around *Time*'s cover and the yellow one around *National Geographic*'s are examples of how color provides editorial identification. *Time* first used a red border around the January 3, 1927, cover featuring a black-and-white head-and-shoulders drawing of Leopold Charles Maurice Stennett Amery, who was Great Britain's secretary of state for the colonies. Yellow has belonged to *National Geographic* since February 1910, although the earliest covers had a much paler hue than today's, as well as a border design with acorns, oak and laurel leaves, and four globes representing the four corners of the world.

Since November 25, 1985, *Newsweek*'s name has been set in white type against a red block, with a thin red border just inside the cover's edges; several different colors for the name were used during the 1960s and 1970s. While most magazines use color in the logo, or title, that color tends to vary from issue to issue depending on the dominant colors in the cover photograph or illustration.

association

Color has basic associations: Red is active and hot, while blue is peaceful and cool. Researchers have found that looking at red raises breathing rate, blood pressure, and number of eye blinks, while blue lowers all three.[19] Red has the connotation of passion ("red hot mama"), vitality, anger, and love, while blue connotes serenity, loyalty ("true blue"), reserve, and gloom ("blue funk").

Yellow is cheerful and optimistic ("sunny"), but also can mean caution and cowardice. Large blocks of bright yellow are hard on adult eyes, although yellow is a good color choice in children's magazines. Green has a tranquilizing and earthy effect and is often associated with spring. But green, too, has some negative associations: envy, mold, seasickness, and the skin of monsters and witches (the Wicked Witch of the West in *The Wizard of Oz*). Orange is almost always associated with Halloween and autumn, while purple belongs to royalty. Some art directors consider these associations when using colors in page layouts, although others ignore them.

attention

Color makes a page look special, and browsers often become readers after being hooked into a story through the use of color. Full-color photographs, in particular, attract attention because they suggest immediacy and drama. A single spot color can make a word in a title, a portion of line art, a chart, or a sidebar pop out at a browser and say "read me."

Remembering that the natural reading pattern is to start in the left corner, move to the right, and then down, some designers automatically place the biggest and brightest use of color slightly above and to the right of the geometric center of a spread. This creates a focal point or center of interest to which eyes are drawn when browsing. Similarly, because the bottom right corner of a spread is seen as "the end" by readers, most designers tend to avoid placing bright color there. They don't want to take the reader away from the article before she even starts reading it.

Jan White says the use of color should be disciplined and meaningful, with shades and tints representing certain kinds of information to help readers interpret and grade material. "Using lots of color isn't useful," he says. "It is just gaudy. Readers don't want gaudiness; they want guidance."[20]

■ DESIGN PRINCIPLES

Because the magazine's mission and audience must be considered when making design decisions, some art directors can ignore basic design principles and still produce a creatively designed magazine. Most, however, follow five established design principles, to one degree or another, because they believe that creativity is a matter of discipline, of knowing the rules and knowing when to modify or break them. These principles are unity, balance, proportion, sequence, and contrast.

unity

Unity is uppermost in an art director's thoughts when designing a magazine. Readers come to each issue expecting similarity and continuity in the format; where they want change is in the topics and issues that are covered. Using a grid can provide unity; it also is cost- and time-effective because the art director is merely modifying the wheel each time, not totally reinventing it.

Consistency in typeface also provides unity: Just having the same type for the body copy of both features and departments goes a long way toward providing a unified product even when titles may have wildly varied typefaces. Certainly the most controlled use of typeface consistency involves using a single font that has a variety of style possibilities throughout the magazine. With a controlled and unified design approach, even the cover logo and department headings use the same typeface; this results in a unification of the outside and inside pages.

Column rules and borders offer both unity and variety. Options beyond the standard line include Oxford rules (consisting of a thick and a thin line), Scotch rules (a thick line with a thin line on either side), and dotted rules. Equally abundant are the border possibilities, although Roger Black points out, "If you don't watch out, ornaments will make a layout look canned, like clip art."[21]

Unity is possible even when trying to provide variety through typography. One route is to have one typeface for department titles and body copy and another typeface for all the features. A third typeface could be used for all the photo cutlines and a fourth for sidebars. There would still be consistency because the use of type would be predetermined by where the material is placed. This diversified approach to unity takes attention to detail because too many typefaces can hurt readability and cause confusion. Some art directors try to match type with the mood of the article, so that each story has a different typeface.

David Carson made his own typography rules when creating layouts for such magazines as *Ray Gun* and *blue*, saying his work "is a very subjective, intuitive, and self-indulgent approach to design."[22] Carson's primary concern is expressing the tone of an article. "When the tone of the type and layout match the attitude of the article, you get the most powerful form of communication," he says. "I think it's a disservice to a writer to just flow his article into three columns of type because you've found that command on QuarkXPress. A secretary can do that. If a story is not presented in a compelling way, people bypass it."[23]

Unity also comes into play when determining how much white space to use around photos, whether to frame photos with rules (using the same size and same kind each time), and whether to have justified or ragged margins throughout the magazine. A dingbat, or small design device at the end of each article, provides unification, while clearly indicating the end of each piece. Another repetitive device can be starting all features with an initial cap, or large initial letter, or always making the first sentence in bold. These design devices draw the reader's eye to the start of the text. Color, also, can provide a connection, whether it's to pull together a particular spread, or to make departments stand out from features.

balance

The principle of balance in magazine layout has to do with whether the various elements on a page look natural and contained. Some readers notice if a page with several large photos appears top-heavy or bottom-heavy; their preference is for pleasing (if not orderly) boundaries that bring all elements together. Other readers like the juxtaposition of unequal shapes and see a dramatically exciting layout effect. Again, the use of basic design principles, successfully or not at all, is relative to the needs and demands of a magazine's audience.

Balance can be either formal or informal, with most magazines gravitating toward the asymmetrical approach of informal layouts. Formal balance requires placing elements of equal weight above and below the optical center of a layout in a mirror-image effect; what's on the left page is repeated on the right-hand one. Informal balance is intuitive and involves a dynamic relationship rather than a static one. Informal balance takes the teeter-totter effect into account: A 90-pound child can achieve horizontal board balance with a 45-pound child if the heavier child sits closer to the center of the teeter-totter.

The effective use of balance is subtle. For example, using the mathematical center as a focal point makes a layout appear off-kilter because readers visually perceive the optical center as being about one third of the way down from the top of a page. When the principle of balance is ignored—if photos or type appear to fall off the page—readers may become frustrated and stop reading. More serious, they may lose confidence in the magazine's mission.

proportion

Proportion has to do with the shapes of things, and is derived from the golden rectangle principle dating back to early Greece. The proportion of the golden rectangle is about 3:5, and historically it has been considered more interesting than the 1:1 ratio of the square.

A magazine's two-page spread starts out as a horizontal shape. Art directors generally try to maintain that shape through the use of generous white space around copy blocks, type wrapped around photos, and the way photos are grouped together or isolated. However, because the golden rectangle is a standard, some art directors gravitate toward the square to distinguish their magazines. While conventional theory states that a horizontal long shot showing a person's entire body as he strides across a room has more vitality than a square mug shot of his head and shoulders, that convention makes no sense if the mug shot is by a photographer noted for dramatically close-up face shots, such as Annie Leibovitz.

sequence

Most readers have a sequence of expectations when they read: title first, followed by a subtitle, byline, and the start of the article. That doesn't mean that layouts have to be rigidly hierarchical, but it does suggest that readers prefer a pattern that can be creatively modified. The logical arrangement of material is usually more readable than a complex one that ignores eye movement.

AUGUST 7, 1932: Mehemed Fehmy Agha's peers used one word to describe his design of *Vogue*: "elegance."

The editorial placement of features also offers an element of surprise through pacing and the unusual juxtaposition of content and form. Art directors see the magazine spread as a large, open canvas on which to work; that's why opening feature pages do not carry advertising.

integration of words and pictures

After all design decisions have been determined, the visual impact of a magazine depends on the integration of words and pictures. Decisions have to be made on the illustrative use of images—the photos, artwork, and infographics (charts, diagrams, graphs) to complement the words in the articles. Readout material has to be written to achieve a synergistic relationship of titles to stories, subtitles and pull-quotes to body copy, and cutlines to photos. How to approach special materials such as the table of contents and the last page of editorial copy also come into play here.

While there are some readers who read every issue from cover to cover, most are selective. In today's busy world, readers tend to leaf through a magazine, scanning the pages before honing in on a particular article to read in its entirety. Although magazine editors would like to have every reader read every article in every issue, the more realistic goal is to signal the text in such a way that those who might find it useful or interesting will read it.

Departments usually are highly sequenced, with standing titles for each topic and boilerplate formats involving similar images, shapes, or color that are repeated from issue to issue. Sequencing even involves the words of a title. There's a basic rhythm to writing titles that are on target. Words are read as groups of phrases with automatic pauses between certain words; readers expect a natural reading sequence to the material. Consequently, both readability and design considerations affects decisions on how to divide a long title into more than one line.

■ ILLUSTRATIVE IMAGES

Art directors and editors have to determine what is the best illustrative material for the words of each article: artwork, photographs, or infographic charts and diagrams. Historically, magazines offered a true rendition of what was happening at the time the illustration was drawn or the photo was shot. However, the choice of which image or angle to use always has been deliberate in order to evoke specific responses on the part of readers.

contrast

When contrast is used effectively, readers quickly realize what the most important elements are in a story. Contrast also helps readers remember those elements. Usually the title or the photo in an article is played "big" with an ample amount of white space. Contrast can be achieved through variations in typography, color, photograph sizes, irregularly shaped images, and the interplay of horizontal elements against vertical elements.

artwork

Drawings dominated the magazines of the 18th and early 19th century. Illustrators added a

Iconic Photos and 1,000 Words

When is a picture worth 1,000 words? When it becomes part of the collective historical memory of millions of people. Although photographs provide additional significance to the words on magazine pages, sometimes we remember only the photo because of its impact. An iconic photo is one that packs an abiding emotional wallop and that we remember, even if we hadn't seen or read the original story.

"No object is more equated with memory than the camera image, in particular the photograph," says Marita Sturken, a professor in the Department of Culture and Communication at New York University. "Memory appears to reside within the photographic image, to tell its story in response to our gaze."[1]

The Emmett Till photo that appeared in the September 15, 1955, issue of *Jet* magazine is one such image. The horrible picture of Till's mutilated body—the face is grotesque, battered beyond recognition—is an image that stays with people.

Till, who supposedly whistled at a white woman while visiting his uncle in Money, Mississippi, in August 1955, was kidnapped and brutally murdered—his face literally beaten into a pulp. Till's body was shipped back to Chicago in a locked casket. His mother insisted on opening the casket—and leaving it open for the funeral so all could see what had been done to her son. Two white men accused of the crime were found not guilty a month later by an all-white male jury in Mississippi. The following year they admitted their involvement in a *Look* magazine article.

The *Jet* photos of Emmett Till in his casket galvanized African Americans into supporting the burgeoning civil rights movement. Rosa Parks supposedly was thinking about Till when she refused to give up her seat on a Montgomery, Alabama, bus. Gwendolyn Brooks and Langston Hughes wrote poems and James Baldwin wrote a play based on the incident. NAACP leader Julian Bond and boxer Muhammed Ali, who were about the same age as Till, couldn't get the shocking images out of their minds.

Obviously, those photos of Emmett Till in *Jet* were worth more than 1,000 words. They made a difference in how a group of people viewed a particular incident and were affected by it. Soon, other magazines published the shocking *Jet* photo of Till in his coffin and told his story to readers across the country.

According to activist and comedian Dick Gregory, until *Jet* went out on a limb and reported on Till's murder, "White racists knew they could do anything to black folks and it would never be reported in the white press. But with *Jet* around, that changed. The number of lynchings declined after the Emmett Till pictures were published."[2]

In 2004, the Justice Department announced the reopening of the Till investigation. The two men, now deceased, who were acquitted on charges of murdering Till suggested the body wasn't his, so there was no forensic evidence to prove otherwise. An autopsy was never conducted, but evidence uncovered by a documentary filmmaker suggested that several men who participated in the murder are still alive.

The ongoing federal investigation is due in large part to that iconic photo first published in *Jet*. That photo offered an objective reality with built-in credibility and authority. Ultimately, iconic photos are a documentation of the way things are; after a while, words may no longer be necessary. ■

1. Marita Sturken, *Tangled Memories: The Vietnam War, the AIDS Epidemic, and the Politics of Remembering*. Berkeley: University of California Press, 1997: 19.

2. Herbert G. McCann, "Founder's Mission Keeps Jet Flying High," *San Antonio Express-News* (January 19, 2002): 1D.

silhouette of a famous person, a satirical cartoon, or a detailed landscape etching as the visual component to masses of gray type. From the start, few readers demanded absolute accuracy in a drawing of a place, person, or thing. Consequently, artwork tended to be interpretive and suggestive, although there was an early tradition of the illustrator as reporter, particularly in the works of Frederic Remington and Winslow Homer.

Illustrators at the turn of the 20th century were highly paid and admired, with Charles Dana Gibson receiving $100,000 for 100 pen-and-ink illustrations drawn between 1903 and 1907. Other famous illustrators were Maxfield Parrish, J. C. Leyendecker, Sarah Stilwell-Weber, and N. C. Wyeth. These artists broke away from realistically illustrating an article to presenting images that also were appealing in their own right. They offered fantasy, drama, excitement, and warmth, making magazines more accessible and popular than books because they were more visual.

The magazine illustrator who united realism and appeal and whose work still resonates with Middle America was Norman Rockwell. He is forever linked with the more than 300 covers he contributed to the *Saturday Evening Post*, from his first one on May 20, 1916, to his last on December 14, 1963.

Commissioned artwork still appears in today's magazines, but certainly not as frequently as it did before the camera lens came to dominate layouts. That's because working with an imaginative illustrator involves not just visual flair but editorial effectiveness. A custom-made illustration has to fit the content of the article—and if it doesn't, it's bad art even if it's graphically superb. For profiles, caricatures tend to be an accessible form of commissioned artwork. *Time's* illustrated—as opposed to photographed—cover portraits reveal a wide range of design styles and media over the years. Many of *Time's* early cover drawings were done in charcoal, although later portraits were rendered in oil, watercolor, or tempura.

A lot of art directors turn to old engravings in the public domain when they want to illustrate a historical piece or provide an interesting visual juxtaposition between the old and new. Line engravings more than 75 years old generally can be reproduced free, and because of the techniques used (cut from wood or etched from metal), they can be reduced or enlarged without becoming muddy.

Numerous artwork possibilities also can be found in clip book services and computer software art programs which offer ready-made illustrations for just about any topic. Unfortunately, the use of clip art can be cheesy and embarrassing unless a good deal of creative change is applied to the original piece.

The New Yorker and *Playboy* are primary users of cartoons now, although cartoons were wonderfully serendipitous layout fillers during the 1930s, 1940s, and 1950s in magazines ranging from *Redbook* to *Collier's*. Today, *Reader's Digest* tends to use only a few cartoons per issue, relying more on short, anecdotal material for laughs. *Esquire*, once known for its risqué cartoons, no longer uses them.

The decline of artwork as magazines' primary illustrative option didn't occur with the development of the photographic halftone at the turn of the 20th century. Rather, illustrations remained a visual star until after World War II, when a changing societal mood led Americans to demand realistic facts over lifelike fantasy. Only photography could offer the raw visual power desired by many readers.

photography

Photos confer additional power to words on the page because most readers accept photographic images as an objective reflection of reality with built-in credibility and authority. In 1859, when he was 50 years old, author Oliver Wendell Holmes identified photography as "the most remarkable achievement" of his time because "it allowed human beings to separate an experience or a texture or an emotion or a likeness from a particular time and place and still remain real, visible, and permanent." It quickly became an axiom that a photo does not lie, although Holmes cannily observed that this new technology "marked the beginning of a time when the image would become more important than the object itself and would in fact make the object disposable."[24]

Yet even if the photo didn't lie, liberties in providing a true rendition occurred as early as the Civil War. When woodcuts depicting Alexander Gardner's battlefield photos were made prior to printing, bodies were added for dramatic effect. But for the most part, early photos provided a window on reality that readers appreciated in modest doses at the turn of the 20th century.

During the 1920s and 1930s, editors reserved the most layout space to fashion photography, where the alteration of reality was acceptable. The great fashion photography of the 1950s, 1960s, and 1970s, with boldly posed and arranged bodies and spaces, made the visual image the predominant message. While photography remains a prime component in women's fashion magazines, shelter magazines are the ones now pulling out all the stops in their use of both surreal and super-real images that pack a visual wallop. A perfect world is created through enhanced computer and camera technology and saturated color coding.

National Geographic's early use of photography gave the new form aesthetic dignity by linking it to the geographical and social documentation of reality. Photography in *National Geographic* was semi-scientific rather than titillating, even if there were bare-breasted native women shown working in fields as early as 1903. Certainly, *National Geographic*'s booklike size was a factor in its academic as opposed to sensational ambiance. It was up to the oversized *Life* magazine, in its grandiose mission statement in 1936, to provide interpretation and commentary to dramatic photographs by articulating a new photojournalistic way of documenting reality:

To see life; to see the world; to eyewitness great events; to watch the faces of the poor and the gestures of the proud; to see strange things—machines, armies, multitudes, shadows in the jungle and on the moon; to see man's work —his paintings, towers and discoveries; to see thousands of miles away, things hidden behind walls and within rooms, things dangerous to come to; the women that men love and many children; to see and take pleasure in seeing, to see and be amazed; to see and be instructed.[25]

Enthusiastic magazine readers quickly realized *Life* was offering something new in the world of photography, bringing concise visual information into the home long before television. *Life* set the photojournalistic standard for many years, a standard which would be approached, but never surpassed, by news magazines during the Vietnam War.

The shift to a celebrity or personality photographic approach occurred in 1974 when *People* became the newest picture magazine. Although Richard Stolley, *People*'s first managing editor, was a *Life* editor for many years, he soon found himself using a different set of photo rules for his page images. Because *People* focused on celebrities and ordinary people who have been thrust into extraordinary situations, *Life*'s documentary photojournalistic approach wasn't appropriate. Instead, *People*'s photographers stage a lot of offbeat shots, to get outrageous or exuberantly posed celebrity pictures that seldom have the candor or the conscience found in photojournalism.

But sometimes that exuberance comes at a price. With more and more celebrities appearing on magazine covers and inside editorial pages, star treatment

Research in Brief

Life's Photojournalism Essay Formula

From the start, *Life* magazine offered readers something different from the traditional news photo that was a result of a photographer simply reacting to an event as it happened. The late journalism professor Caroline Dow said *Life* distinguished itself by providing readers with a system of visual reporting that anticipated and planned the coverage of events.[1] Many scholars believe *Life* essentially invented photojournalism through the use of a planned, formulaic approach.

Although "*Life* had been

1. Caroline Dow, "*Life* 's Photojournalism Essay Formula" (paper presented at the annual meeting of the Association for Education in Journalism and Mass Communication, Houston, Texas, August 1979).

Life's Photojournalism Essay Formula (continued)

envisioned as a showpiece of previously published photographs gathered on a pick-up basis," Dow said the weekly magazine quickly used up the available stock of photos and news. So the magazine began generating its own stories and photographers. The result was the "mind-guided camera," a photo formula that grew out of *Time* magazine's use of group reporting and a "round-up" news format while also incorporating photographer Roy Stryker's documentary approach. Stryker believed that photographers should be provided extensive background before they went out on a shoot so they would understand the people they were recording.

A key aspect of the "mind-guided camera" approach was having a shooting script. The script was designed to help the photographer understand the types of photos needed, their purpose, and the mood of the topic. More photos would be shot to go along with the story than actually would be used since no amount of previsualization could predict what would occur on site.

No longer were photos an adjunct to print. "*Life* elevated the photograph to an equal partnership with words," Dow said.

Dow analyzed the "*Life* process," pointing out that "the essence of the *Life* method was that a photographic feature had to be defined in words

first. Then the idea was researched. When the idea or experience was clear to everyone, a script of possible scenes would be prepared and approved." Following approval by an editor, a photographer would be assigned and a reporter selected who would work together as a team.

"The specific *Life* scripting formula has not been published. Perhaps it was not considered necessary to record it because it was so well understood by those who practiced it," said Dow. She determined the formula by researching how Robert L. Drew, *Life*'s first Detroit bureau chief, organized his photography workshops from 1949 to 1951. Dow took oral histories from participants in the Detroit Workshop and combined them with documentary research to discern what was involved in a *Life*'s photojournalism essay.

Dow's research revealed a list of eight types of photos that had to be part of the rolls of film shot by the photographer after the concept or story idea had been researched to see if it had news and/or social value. These eight photos of the scripting formula included the following:

1. An introductory or "overall" shot, usually a wide angle, often an aerial.
2. A middle distance or "moving in" shot, such as a sign, a street, or a building.

3. A close-up, usually hands, face, or detail.
4. A sequence or how-to shot.
5. A portrait, usually environmental.
6. An interaction shot of persons conversing or action portrayed.
7. The signature picture—the decisive moment, the one picture that conveyed the essence of the story.
8. The clincher or "good-bye" shot, signifying the end of the story.

"By thinking about the picture story in these terms," Dow said, "a photographer would prepare himself to see a story." Prethinking, or previsualizing a story, encouraged a photographer to shoot different views and angles of the same scene. The event was more likely to be covered in greater depth because the photographer, having thought through the obvious pictures, was prepared to see the unusual or unique picture as well as to recognize the signature shot when it happened, even though it might not be what was planned.

This formula helped define *Life*'s design personality as well as its editorial value. The relationship of the photos to the page and to the copy resulted in a distinctive narrative design that made *Life* a success with readers and advertisers from the start. ■

has become a design consideration. Some stars are demanding approval of the layout and photographs as a condition of publication. *Rolling Stone* gave Madonna photo approval and copyright to the photographs used for a 30th anniversary cover story about women in rock on November 13, 1997, but refused to give her layout approval. For photo shoots, publicists of top celebrities may specify makeup, clothing, food preferences for snacks, and even the lenses used by the photographer.[26]

Another photo trend is to run them big: *Life* and *Look* initially led the way here, with *Sports Illustrated* and *Rolling Stone* continuing the tradition. Of course, the corollary to larger photos is fewer ones, which means the selection and cropping process become very crucial. Large, tightly cropped head shots can make even a mundane photo vibrant, although small, one-column mug shots (head-on, static head-and-shoulder photos) still get published, as do boring group shots, awkward grip-and-grin award photos, and, the ultimate in blandness, pictures of individuals sitting at their desks (pretending to be on the phone does not negate the cliché). The best photographers, such as Annie Leibovitz and the late Richard Avedon, provide the large vistas of environmental portraits which combine fashion, place, and personality into one dramatic shot.

Magazines that can't afford Leibovitz turn to stock photo houses such as Getty Images, Corbis, Black Star, or Comstock. These picture agencies offer editors photographic variety and clarity at a reasonable cost. Historical collections at the Library of Congress provide a wealth of photo possibilities, although care must be taken when using historical shots to document them and make sure that no misinterpretations occur.

Following September 11, 2001, *The New Yorker* published some of the most provocative illustrated covers in its history, resisting any inclination to use photos. One cover showed Osama bin Laden and a henchman riding Segway scooters in the mountains of Afghanistan while another featured a turbaned driver of an American flag-bedecked taxi. The so-called "New Yorkistan" cover, which ran December 10, was a whimsical renaming of New York neighborhoods and boroughs à la Afghanistan—with such areas as "Botoxia," "Fuhgeddaboutditstan," and "Perturbia." It sold thousands of copies in poster form, with signed versions selling out within 3 days.

The choice of which photo or photos to run is both emotional and intellectual. Art directors frequently go beyond the limitations of the original photo through creative cropping to enhance or refine the message already present. Photo cropping is an important editorial tool because strong verticals or horizontals can be created, or the focus of the frame shifted to suggest a new meaning. In deciding how close to crop a scene, it's important to know the photo's purpose: Is it a documentary shot for an investigative article or a fashion shot showing elaborate evening wear? Is the intent to show reality or fantasy?

Photo retouching, which is usually done digitally today, is another editorial tool with a lot of power. When used to eliminate a sign behind a model's head in a fashion photo, or to remove an extraneous foot that could not be cropped out for a cover, retouching may be appropriate. Again, the content, intent, and goal of both the article and the photo must be considered before any changes are made in an image.

Unfortunately, computer digital manipulation has changed the boundaries of photo cropping and retouching, and destroyed the belief that photos don't lie. Some magazine editors use the term photo illustration to distinguish a picture that has been staged, retouched, or manipulated in some way from the news photo resulting from photojournalism. One of the earliest instances of photo illustration via electronic retouching occurred in February 1982 when *National Geographic* moved a Great Pyramid of Giza to fit the vertical shape of its cover. Since then, digital imaging technology has been used on covers featuring O. J. Simpson *(Time)*, Cher *(Ladies' Home Journal)*, Bobbi McCaughey *(Newsweek)*, and Princess Caroline of Monaco *(Harper's Bazaar)*.

infographics

Complex statistical data can be explained and compared through the use of charts, diagrams, and graphs—or infographics. Pie charts are the easiest explanatory visuals to use, with bar charts not far behind. Schematic diagrams can show how things work, while line graphs often reveal trends over time. Colorful maps pinpoint the location of exotic cities. Infographics can make relationships that would be boring if spelled out in words become clear and comprehensive through a few visuals.

"The job of infographics is to analyze and explain the numbers of the event, not to mirror what it 'looks' like," says Nigel Holmes, who was the graphics director of *Time* magazine for 16 years and whose work has appeared in *Esquire, The New Yorker,* and *Rolling Stone.*[27] Holmes, whose specialty is infographics, says the information value of the material must be kept uppermost when using charts and graphs in magazine layouts. For example, a chart to illustrate a story about improved mathematical test scores should not only show this year's scores, but also scores from previous years so readers can visualize the relationship of the data. Pitfalls can occur with the use of infographics. Cramming too many figures into a graph is as bad as not giving enough information. Every infographic device needs a title to tell what it's about, a scale line to tell what measurement is being used, and the source of the information.

Holmes offers several rules for the successful use of infographics in magazine layouts. First and foremost, he says, is to keep it simple. "Make it a little self-contained story," is Holmes's second rule. Third, he suggests using small images that are easy to understand and that simplify the complicated. Finally, he restricts the use of color in the infographic. The result, he argues, is visual information that is likely to be read because the reader has been provided with "little jewels that pack a punch."[28]

■ READOUT SYNERGY

Titles, subtitles, subheads, pull-quotes, and cutlines are the readout materials that should convert a scanner into a reader. A test of good design is how well the editorial copy meshes with the typographic format of readout tools. Good illustrations—photographs and artwork—are not enough to turn browsers into readers. Today's magazine audiences are bombarded with images and sounds; short attention spans must be factored into page design because readers will not stay with a magazine article that consists only of 9-point body type. The use of sidebars to support main articles is one way to deal editorially with reader hyperactivity.

Readouts are the ultimate readership design devices. Time-consuming and sometimes difficult to write, readout material virtually shoves words at people to get them intrigued enough to start reading the article. The creation of exciting and precise readout matter—particularly the title and subtitle—forces editors to confront what an article is all about in concise yet interesting words.

titles

Editors agree that the title is the most important typographic design tool in getting a magazine subscriber or browser to read a particular article. Many good stories are never read because the titles and subtitles (the information immediately following the main title before the start of the article) fail to interest the reader. Consequently, a lot of titles and subtitles feature "sell" language, essentially advertising words—best, most, newest—that help sell the story to the reader. The title should either entice readers to read the story or provide enough information to tell them they aren't interested in the topic. Titles can be as short as a single word or as long as several complete sentences taking up to five lines at the top of the spread.

An editor at a monthly magazine will write between 400 to 500 titles during a year—and they will begin to sound alike. It becomes a challenge to write a title that is descriptive, inviting, and accurate. "The thing that we try to work for in titles is, first of all, distinctive words and phrases," said Don L. Berg, former executive editor of *Medical Economics.* "We may have written 17 other stories in the same particular field in the course of a year. We look for something that is evocative and distinctive in the particular story. Beyond that we look for words that are stoppers or grabbers—the ones that arrest the reader."[29]

Take a *Medical Economics* story that was given the title of "My Million Dollar Malpractice Ordeal." That was rejected, Berg said, because "we decided that anybody can have an ordeal. It's not very specific and there is nothing there evocative or grabbing that's going to get you into the story. There's no grabbing word except 'malpractice.'" So the title was changed to "My Million Dollar Malpractice Lesson: Trust Nobody." That title was not only provocative, but also gave a reasonable expectation of what the article would contain.

subtitles

Most titles are supported by a subtitle, which provides additional clues as to the nature of the article—service, profile, investigative reporting—and pizzazz to intrigue the reader. The subtitle is where the modifying or qualifying information goes. For the "My Million Dollar Malpractice Lesson: Trust Nobody" title, a subtitle might have the qualification, "Perhaps you can trust your own attorney."

Subtitles either summarize the article in a straightforward way or tease readers through an intriguing phrase or play on words. The best subtitles build on the title and draw readers into the first paragraph of the article. The subtitle usually appears after the title, but not always. When a subtitle appears above the title, it's called a kicker. *Reader's Digest* placed this kicker above the title "Banks love you for all the fees they can charge you. Here's how to cut your costs." The title, in large capital letters, was "IS YOUR BANK RIPPING YOU OFF?"

subheads

Subheads help break up large blocks of text by providing organizational cues between paragraphs. When written in a clever as opposed to perfunctory tone, they also attract attention. The subheads in "Is Your Bank Ripping You Off?" were intriguing: "The ATM Junkie," "The Merger Orphan," "The New Saver," "The Workaholic," and "The Cyber-Banker."

Subheads can be large or small in type size; they don't have to fall at a natural pause in the story, but they should be consistent in tone. Subheads don't even have to have their own line—they can start on the first line of the paragraph in type that's larger, bolder, in color, or all three.

pull-quotes

Pull-quotes are another way to break up large blocks of text by taking an interesting or important sentence or two from the story and setting it off graphically within the body copy. Sometimes the pull-quote is an actual quote from an individual in the article; when that happens, quote marks are used around the words and attribution is included.

Roger Black especially likes pull-quotes. He notes, "Skillfully extracted from the piece, these devices allow a reader to get an idea of what a story is about before taking the cold bath of actually reading it. In a magazine you can't expect everyone to read everything, and a pull-quote will help people get something out of an article they only glance at."[30]

cutlines

Some people read the cutlines, or captions, of photos before they read anything else. Unfortunately, many editors wait until the last minute to write them, so the result can be unclear or cryptically short. Because the photographer usually is not around to aid in identification, cutline writing can result in unintentional bloopers. In 1981, *National Review* found a hilarious cutline correction in *Community Life* and reprinted it as a filler: "Mai Thai Finn is one of the students in the program and was in the center of the photo. We incorrectly listed her as one of the items on the menu."[31]

A mislabeled photo cutline in the February 22, 1993, issue of *Time* created an international outcry. Accompanying an article by Lance Morrow titled "Unspeakable" about rape as a weapon in war was a black-and-white photo of a young girl who apparently was a victim of rape; the cutline underneath read "Traditions of atrocity: A Jewish girl raped by Ukrainians in Lvov, Poland, 1945." Ukrainians in the United States and Canada were angered by the cutline, which they felt was a blanket indictment of Ukrainians as rapists over time, due to the phrasing of the sentence. Plus, although Ukrainians were singled out in the photo cutline, they were not mentioned in the article at all.

After receiving more than 750 letters, *Time* ran an apology in the April 19 issue in which it admitted that the photo was taken in 1941, not 1945, and that the city of Lvov was not a part of Poland at that time but was a Ukrainian city. Most damning was the admission that "despite our best efforts, we have not been able to pin down exactly what situation the photograph portrayed. But there is enough confusion about it for us to regret that our caption, in addition to misdating the picture, may well have conveyed a false impression."

The Pithy Promises of Pull-Quotes

Pull-quotes operate as advertising points in articles by highlighting key points or pithy statements and grabbing a reader's interest. John Brady, former editor-in-chief at *Writer's Digest* and *Boston Magazine*, and now a partner in the design firm of Brady and Paul Communications, offers seven tips for selling stories via pull-quotes:[1]

1. Write pull-quotes upfront, when editing a story, not later when the layout is being designed. Brady estimates that if an article takes four pages of space, five or six pull-quotes will be needed.

2. Put pull-quotes ahead of their actual location on the page. "The goal is to draw readers into your pages and to sell them on what's ahead," says Brady, "not to make them feel like they are watching a re-run."

3. Use only one pull-quote per page.

4. Write no more than 20 words, ending up with no more than four lines. Brady says that if an excerpt is going to run more than 20 words, condense it and be careful about not changing the meaning. "No ellipses or brackets are necessary to indicate the editorial tightening, unless it's a direct quote," Brady says.

5. Don't put quote marks around the pull-quote material unless it's a direct quote.

6. Place pull-quotes on the top half of a layout page. "Pull-quotes near—or worse, at—the bottom of a page can resemble afterthoughts or fillers," Brady observes.

7. Don't use a pull-quote that gives away the article's ending. Brady notes, "As editorial marketing devices, pull-quotes are intended to keep the reader in the story right to the last paragraph."

1. John Brady, "The Power of Pull Quotes," *Folio:* (November 1, 2005), http://foliomag.com/index.php?id=396&backPID+392&tt_news+1348.

Cutlines should not be omitted, however, because of the risk of photo misinterpretation. At many magazines there's a law: Every photo needs a cutline. Cutlines should do more than describe what is obviously in a photograph. Cutlines can point out something that may be overlooked by readers ("standing behind so-and-so is") or supply information that is missing ("John Jones painted the watercolor held by"). Some editors even use the cutline as an opportunity to include information that has been omitted from the original article. More frequently, though, the cutline reinforces the tone and thrust of the article by supplying material not elaborated on in the text. This gives the cutline a vital and synergistic role in overall layout design. Cutline styles vary from magazine to magazine, but there are at least eight used by editors today: identification, information, quotation, teaser, mood, intensifications, redirection, and contradiction.

Identification Cutlines must provide identification, but they don't have to be boring. Magazines such as *Outside, Entertainment Weekly,* and *People* make an effort to stay away from the obvious when providing identification by including an interesting tidbit along with the necessary name, title, or place. But there are still numerous magazines that use label cutlines, simply providing a name or a location without any context or even a complete sentence.

Information The best information cutlines are found in *National Geographic.* Captions here are so complete that some readers never get around to reading the entire article. Information cutlines expand on the identification approach by offering details about a landscape, an interior, or an individual. They are frequently used in travel and shelter magazines. This cutline style, which provides context to a photo, tends to be the longest, sometimes up to 100 words.

Quotation A quotation cutline frequently is used for a head-and-shoulders photo of an individual and involves using a controversial or illuminating quote from the main story. Usually, the cutline begins with the quote, which makes it more of an attention-getter than starting with the name. *Playboy*'s interviews always use quote cutlines under the subject's photo; the magazine's most famous cutline ran under a photo of a pensive Jimmy Carter, who admitted in November 1976, "I'm human and I'm tempted. I've looked on a lot of women with lust. I've committed adultery in my heart many times. This is something that God recognizes I will do, and God forgives me for it."

Teaser Some teaser cutlines begin with a question, while others parody a quotation or put a spin on a cliché. But more frequently, the teaser cutline features the most intriguing detail from the story and is likely to drive the reader into the text to find the answer or get additional details.

Mood Mood cutlines allow editors to remind readers of a story's ambiance and point of view. Some mood cutlines become mini-editorials, suggesting how a photo should be viewed or evaluated. Mood cutlines can even highlight the less obvious artistic values of a photograph. *Life* effectively used mood cutlines for many years.

Intensification Sometimes a mood cutline goes beyond the photo's image to provide intensification of the scene. David D. Perlmutter, a professor at the Manship School of Mass Communication at Louisiana State University, studied photos and cutlines of China in *Time* and *Newsweek* from 1949 through 1989 and discovered that intensification occurred when the information in the photo "was embellished through affective language. For example, a picture of a policeman hitting a protester was captioned, 'A policeman mercilessly beats a helpless hunger striker.'"[32]

Redirection Perlmutter says redirection occurs when the photo and the cutline seem unconnected because "an action referred to was absent from the pictures." He says portrait shots often have seemingly unrelated cutlines, and gives an example of a photo of Nationalist Leader Chiang Kai-Shek posing in front of his flag. The cutline: "Can he stop a Communist peace?"

Contradiction A cutline that contradicts definitely goes beyond the photo frame by totally changing its visual meaning. As a contradiction example, Perlmutter refers to a photo of a smiling Chiang waving to a saluting crowd with this cutline, "Chiang's days were numbered as the Communists roll on to victory."

Perlmutter argues that the editorial slant of a magazine can strongly affect how cutlines are written, and be an important indicator of a publication's ideology, perhaps even more so than the image. "No lens is wide enough to reveal all of any reality, but the caption can enhance or distort the engagement between the photographer and subject, and between publication and public," Perlmutter says.

Who writes the titles, subtitles, subheads, pull-quotes, and cutlines? At a very small magazine, the writer may be asked to supply that material. At many magazines, the editor who conceived, assigned, and edited the particular article is responsible for all the readout material. Sometimes, the copy editor completes this part of the editorial circle, although the final word on titles usually belongs to the editor. Readout material tends to be written and placed in the layout last so the editor can take advantage of having selected the photos and determined how much copy is going to be used.

All readouts have to match the tone of each article and reflect the magazine's editorial philosophy. Editors at *Harper's* and *The Atlantic Monthly* strive to be clever without being facetious or cute in their readout material. There's a fine line between a clever play on words and being obscure.

■ SPECIAL MATERIAL

The table of contents and the last editorial page in the magazine require special consideration in the merging of words and pictures. Unfortunately, these pages can look haphazard and unappealing if enough attention isn't paid to their role in the magazine's editorial and design package.

table of contents

While newsstand sales success usually is judged on the basis of cover content, the table of contents may pack the real wallop. Most browsers move quickly from the cover to the table of contents, where they pause for as long as a minute before making a financial commitment to the magazine. The cover may be the door-opener, but the table of contents is the marketing page that must be well designed to motivate purchase and reading.

The structure of an editorial formula is most obvious in the table of contents, or TOC. From issue to issue, year to year, the TOC of a successful publication demonstrates its continuity. Technically, the TOC tells what's inside and where things can be found. Of all the pages inside a magazine, the TOC has a clearly defined function as well as emotional and informational value. Consequently, it requires clarity in presentation and vision in structurally highlighting special articles.

last editorial page

For some readers, the last editorial page, opposite the inside back cover, is their first impression of the magazine, so it, too, needs special attention. Probably the best known closing page was *Life*'s "Parting Shots," usually with one large photo and a short amount of copy ending each issue. Magazines as varied as *National Geographic, AARP: The Magazine,* and *Time* all use their last single editorial page effectively: respectively with a "flashback" photo "from our archives," with a caricature of the latest celebrity to reach "The Big 5-Oh" and thumbnail photos of those who also reached 50, 60, 70, or 80 during the month, and with a thoughtful essay.

Puzzles are used by some magazines as a way of having a final interactive moment with readers. The last page of *The New Yorker* is a cartoon caption contest, while *The History Channel Magazine* does a "History Alive" crossword puzzle that tests readers on what they remembered from the previous issue. For years, *Town and Country* has closed its magazine with a horoscope page, while *Forbes* offers "Thoughts on the Business of Life" through a dozen or so inspirational quotes from an eclectic range of commentators: Abigail Adams recently shared space with Adlai Stevenson and Ernest Hemingway.

Many magazines use "The Last Word," "Rear View," or the even more mundane "The End" as the title for the last editorial page in the magazine, but others try for a moniker that reflects the character of the magazine. *Condé Nast Traveler*'s "Room with a View" shows the exact vistas seen from the window or balcony of a specific hotel room.

Using the last page for a strong editorial focus gives readers who flip from the back of the magazine forward a full editorial page to start with rather than jumped articles and fractional adver-tising. It adds to the illusion of having a magazine filled with information, from front to back; a very high page number listed in the TOC further reinforces the jam-packed image. Plus, those readers who start with the first page and read sequentially through the magazine are rewarded with a final page that bangs rather than whimpers.

Advertisers benefit also, because a strong last page tells them the editors place value on the entire magazine, not just the front half. It also indicates that the magazine is read from cover to cover, so there are no "bad" pages.

covers

The cover is the most important editorial and design page in a magazine. The cover, as the magazine's face, creates that all-important first impression. It also provides both continuity through format recognition and change through intriguing cover lines from issue to issue. Editors, art directors, publishers, and circulation directors spend hours trying to select the perfect cover for each issue—one that sells out at the newsstands and creates a media buzz.

"The business of editorial demands that we pay as much attention to our covers as we do to our content," says David Pecker, chair and CEO of American Media, Inc., whose magazines include *Star, Shape, Men's Fitness,* and *Country Weekly*. "Remember the old adage, 'You can't tell a book by its cover'? Well, you can't sell a magazine anymore without a good one."[33] Pecker argues that because 80 percent of consumer magazines' newsstand sales are determined by what is shown on the cover, a cover that sells can mean the difference between a magazine's life or death.

A 1986 panel made up of legendary design consultant John Peter, circulation consultant Ron Scott, and Hearst Magazines consultant John Mack Carter, who had been editor-in-chief at both *Ladies' Home Journal* and *Good Housekeeping,* offered a list of cover mandates that still hold true today:

- Photos sell better than artwork.
- Sex sells better than politics.
- Timeliness is a critical sales factor.
- Solutions sell better than problems.
- Subtlety and irony don't sell.
- Bylines don't sell.
- Puns don't work well in sell lines.[34]

Table of Contents: Location, Location, Location

There are five yardsticks—location, length, logic, linkage, and look—to use when measuring the design impact of a table of contents, or TOC. Of these, location is the most important (as in the real estate mantra of "location, location, location").

For 75 years, *Reader's Digest* used the TOC as its bland but useful cover, with all the yardstick components in a single place. As part of a major design overhaul unveiled with the May 1998 issue, the magazine switched to a full-page photo on the cover with a few cover lines, and located its now colorful, detailed two-page TOC inside.

A right-hand side, front-of-the-magazine location is the best spot for the TOC, says design consultant John Brady. He calls it "an unfortunate marketing blunder" to put the TOC on the left, reserving all front right pages for advertisers. "A left-hand table of contents is consumer unfriendly. Subliminally, these magazines are saying to their readers: Our advertisers are more important than you," Brady says.[1]

However, many art directors disagree, arguing there's no evidence that a right-hand page is a better position for the contents page. There are myriad successful and popular magazines with left-hand contents pages: *Ebony, Ladies' Home Journal, Texas Music, Condé Nast Traveler,* and *More.*

Brady says starting with a right-hand page and jumping to a second TOC page conveys "a jam-packed, value-added feeling to the reader." *Seventeen*'s right-hand to left-hand jump has just that feeling, as do the TOCs for *Outside, Esquire, Texas Monthly, Sports Illustrated, Entertainment Weekly, Forbes, Redbook, Utne,* and *Wired.* Some magazines with just a single right-hand TOC are *Newsweek, Texas Highways, New Republic,* and *American Journalism Review. Shop Etc.* also has a single TOC, but it's not traditional. No article titles or pages are listed. Instead, the reader is told, for example, that fashion starts on page 25, home on page 77, and beauty on page 121.

The conventional wisdom is to never use less than one full page for the TOC; no extraneous material such as a masthead or letter from the editor should compete for the reader's attention. During the 1920s and 1930s, *The New Yorker*'s TOC seemed to be an afterthought, a mere dollop of copy in the middle of entertainment listings, with page numbers only for such standing departments as books, cinema, theatre, and art. The first "real" TOC, with titles of articles and bylines, appeared in the March 22, 1969, issue. Even now, *The New Yorker*'s left-hand TOC still doesn't occupy a full page of space and shares the page with a one third-size advertisement.

A few magazines, such as *Archaeology Odyssey,* have colorful two-page spreads. *Texas Parks and Wildlife* gives the TOC three pages: Feature titles are placed on a dramatic two-page bleed photograph, while departments get the next page.

Lack of logic in the TOC is a big turn-off for readers. TOC design nightmares have unidentified photos, no page numbers, haphazardly placed artwork, and punning titles that have no relationship to the content of the article.

Closely related to logic is cover linkage. Readers should be able to find all stories mentioned on the cover quickly and efficiently without having to wade through cute or remote connections. Brady urges art directors to organize the copy either chronologically by page number or editorially by features, departments, columns, and miscellany. More important, article titles on the TOC

1. John Brady, "Perusing the Table of Contents," in *The Handbook of Magazine Publishing,* 4th ed., compiled by the editors of Folio: (Stamford, Conn.: Cowles Business Media, 1996), 197.

Of course, most editors can cite wildly successful cover exceptions to this conventional wisdom, or offer their own cover formula. Richard Stolley, who is now senior editorial advisor at Time, Inc., is recognized as a cover guru by his peers. He recalls that when he was at *People*, the cover mantra went: "Young is better than old. Pretty is better than ugly. Rich is better than poor. TV is better than music. Music is better than movies. Movies are better than sports. Anything is better than politics. And nothing is better than the celebrity dead."[35]

Speaking of the need for a cover with a persona who grabs the newsstand browser, Stolley says, "The face had to be recognizable to 80 percent of the American people. There had to be a reason for the person on the cover. There had to be something happening in the person's life the week it was out there. And then there was this X factor. There had to be something about that person that you wanted to know."

The quest for a recognizable X-face has led to more and more celebrities appearing on magazine covers. But not just any celebrity will do. Stolley points out that Mary Tyler Moore was never a successful cover subject, even when she was at the pinnacle of her television success. "There was nothing left of interest about her that people did not already know," he says. "They loved her, but that wasn't enough for *People*'s cover."

Of course, there is more to designing a cover than just slapping a celebrity's face on the page, just as there are many magazines that stay away from recognizable faces. Deciding what to put on the cover, and the type of cover to use, generally are determined by the magazine's editorial mission. No matter what is on the cover, it has to be backed up by solid editorial material. Regardless of how exciting the cover is, it doesn't guarantee a return customer or a satisfied reader. Only content can do that.

■ LOGO

The design of the magazine's logo, or title, is critical because it is the most important word on the cover. The typeface used for the logo helps set the tone and the mood of the entire magazine; the design has to visually match what the word or words of the title say. It also has to provide instant recognition of a magazine. Because the logo also appears in circulation promotion, in advertising, on stationery and websites, it becomes an important identification symbol of the magazine. The magazine title is like a corporate logo or trademark; it represents a product that has both recognition and value as a brand in the marketplace.

Naming a magazine with an identifying color that became part of the design was an early cover option for *The Yellow Book, The Blue Book, The Golden Book,* and *The Red Book* (which later adopted the more familiar spelling and name of *Redbook*). Many consumer magazines have a one-word title—short, catchy, and to the point: *Time, Vibe, Esquire, Playboy, Ebony, Latina, Elle,* and *Wired*. Two-word titles also abound among consumer magazines: *Rolling Stone, TV Guide, Real Simple, Cooking Light, Reader's Digest,* and *Popular Mechanics*. A one- or two-word logo can take advantage of specially designed typefaces that can be set in a type size large enough to be clearly seen and recognized at a distance of 8–10 feet away. Establishing a high contrast between the logo and the background also makes a cover pop out when it's on a rack with hundreds of other magazines, and all that might be seen is the top one third of the cover.

A distinctive, appropriate logo is one that will hold up over time. Consequently, most logos tend to be derived or modified from classic serif or sans serif typefaces rather than decorative or novelty ones. There are good arguments to be made for never changing a logo, although periodic and gradual refinements usually make sense to keep it up to date. *Time*'s logo has been modified over the years—it's generally become heavier and bolder—but the logo's recognition value essentially is the same as it was in 1923.

■ COVER TYPES

There are five recognizable cover types: poster; one theme, one image; multi-theme, one image; multi-theme and multi-image; and all-typographic. Regardless of which cover type is used, a cover has to be uniform from issue to issue in size, paper stock, logo, and placement of date and price. These items provide consistency for the magazine, while the cover images and cover lines provide change from issue to issue.

poster

A poster cover is one that has only a drawing or a photograph along with the name of the magazine, date, and possibly the price. There are no cover lines or themes announced, and the image generally is not covered by the logo. Also referred to as art covers, poster covers were dominant during much of the early part of the 20th century as artwork. Indeed, magazine covers were treated as miniposters to be framed from 1890 to about 1930. While poster covers for *Ladies' Home Journal, Good Housekeeping,* and *Redbook* were commercially inspired, Steven Heller and Louise Fili, writing in *Cover Story: The Art of American Magazine Covers, 1900–1950,* state that many of them "transcended their ephemeral natures and become documents of their times—represented a high-level artistic endeavor."[36] These covers sold because they were aesthetically appealing.

Most poster covers between 1890 and 1940 didn't even relate to a story inside the magazine. Rather, the poster cover depicted a season or conveyed a general mood. Poster covers are rarely used now by consumer magazines. *The New Yorker* stands out in its use of a poster cover with no cover lines,

at least in the version mailed to subscribers; a plain flap with cover lines overlays almost two thirds of the image on newsstand copies.

JAMA: The Journal of the American Medical Association has used original art for its poster cover for more than 40 years. The works of fine art range from American Primitive and German Expressionist paintings to photographs of elaborately decorated porcelain eggs and ornate silver tea sets. Senior contributing editor Dr. M. Therese Southgate, who discusses the covers in each issue, says, "Contrary to what some readers may believe, most of the works of fine art that appear on the covers of *The Journal of the American Association* are not intended to reflect the content of the particular issue. When one or another seems to do so it is usually because of some accident of timing or interpretation by especially astute or creative readers."[37]

Only occasionally—a mere handful out of some 1,900 works of art that have been reproduced through the years—has *JAMA* intentionally used a cover related to content, usually for an issue dedicated to a single topic. Southgate calls these "signature covers," or "covers that through repetition call attention to and identify on sight the special topic of that issue. In the past these 'dedicated' issues have concerned such perennial medical concerns as nuclear war, gun violence, tobacco, health care for the underserved." For example, Vincent Van Gogh's "Skull with Cigarette" was used for the March 28, 1966, and February 28, 1986, issues, which both were devoted to tobacco concerns. *JAMA* traditionally omits a cover image on the theme issue devoted to HIV/AIDS "because neither images nor words can express the worldwide devastation caused by HIV/AIDS over the past quarter of a century," Southgate says.

one theme, one image

In the one theme, one image cover approach, there's a photograph or drawing with a two- or three-word identification of the subject or a short descriptive phrase. The depicted cover image is featured in a major inside story. From 1936 through most of 1949, *Life*'s covers featured one theme and one image. A few *Life* covers during 1949 had a second story titled in the upper right-hand corner, and the practice become more prevalent during the 1950s. Once a second title is added to a single image cover, it becomes a multi-theme, one image format.

The majority of *Time*'s covers tend to be one theme, one image in format, although a slash was used sporadically in the upper-left or -right corner during the 1940s to highlight a second story of importance, such as a current affairs test that was popular with readers. The use of an occasional flapped right corner with a small thumbnail photo and title didn't occur until 1977. In recent years, *Time* has added one or two cover lines above the logo or run them diagonally across the upper right corner. At least half of *Time*'s covers in a given year will be one theme, one image.

Physics Today, the flagship publication of the American Institute of Physics, dramatically uses the one theme, one image cover approach in every issue, framing the single image with white space and placing a single title in the right-hand corner beneath the image: for example, lightning streaking across the sky for a special issue, "Special Focus: Benjamin Franklin Turns 300"; a colorful 1885 painting of ice skaters with the title "Why Is Ice Slippery" for a feature on research about the dynamics of ice surfaces; and an enlarged microscope view of organic polymers and molecules for "The Growth of Organic Electronics."

multi-theme, one image

The majority of magazines use a multi-theme, one image cover. From *Smithsonian* to *Tikkun* to *Vogue*, this is the prevailing approach today. Most designers believe that the image grabs the reader's attention, but the multi-theme aspect of cover lines is what clinches the sale.

How many cover lines are enough? The number of cover lines is at an all-time high these days, but six seems to be the average number. However, Michael Lafavore, founding editor of *Men's Health,* points out that for many editors, "the perfect number of sell lines is as many as will fit and are still large enough to read."[38]

Research has shown that a reader will buy a magazine for a single cover line. "The most effective buzzwords are rather well known: save, win, free. In a word, I would say the formula is, promises, promises," says Susan Kane, editor-in-chief of *Baby Talk.* The range of stories that a cover hypes is also important. "I would say 85 percent of your cover has to appeal to 100 percent of your audience. So this cover line I have here: 'Single Moms—Surviving and Thriving.' Very narrow.

The only reason I can run that is that everything else is a 100 percent."[39]

Another approach to using cover lines effectively is to think like a politician who has a certain number of constituents. A magazine editor wants to let each constituent reader know that there's something important for her in each issue.

Lafavore says:

A good cover line is worth a thousand pictures. At the newsstand post-mortems I attend, much more time is spent discussing the pros and cons of the cover photo than the quality of the sell lines. That's getting it backwards. A fabulous cover photo might catch a shopper's eye, but the lines are what close the deal. Unless you work at *Playboy, Maxim* or its kin, or at one of the decorating books, give most of the credit (or blame) for sales to your cover lines.

Designer Mary Kay Baumann of Hopkins/Baumann says where editors place cover lines ultimately depends on where the magazine is displayed most. If it's at the checkout counter, where magazines are displayed in individual racks, the entire cover space can be used for cover lines. Cover lines may be placed along the left-hand side of the cover because many newsstands shelve magazines horizontally and fan the covers so they overlap along the left edge. At some newsstands, however, stacking may occur vertically, so a few editors also consider the skyline area above the logo as an important design space, and cover lines may be placed there for increased interest.

"Newsstand magazine buyers are fringe buyers, so you need to do something to catch their eye," Baumann says. "The cover must have a package concept with a strong identity formed by the logo and the cover lines. The logo and the cover lines must lead to fast recognition."

Abe Peck, chair of the magazine program at Northwestern University's Medill School of Journalism, says cover lines offer some reassurance about the content of the magazine. "The average person at the newsstand spends a second or a second-and-a-half looking at the covers. Cover lines have always been a device, like when magazines use numbers and list '525 Ways to Beautify Your House.'"[40]

Commenting on the trend toward using numbers in cover lines, Lafavore says, "The perfect number in a sell line is an odd one. Numbers on covers get attention. I can't prove this empirically, but I'm convinced that odd numbers are more interesting than even ones. . . . In any case, don't overdo it. A couple of numbers on a cover are enough."

Another trend in recent years is the practice of asking a question. Peck says, "You're trying to engage readers by getting them to think about the question. With something as divided or unclear as the war or the economy, it's an open question."

Cover lines are just as important for specialized business-to-business magazines with controlled circulations. The magazine competes with all the other mail a busy executive receives each day. Effective cover lines can mean the difference between reading an issue immediately or tossing it aside for a later—or never—read.

multi-theme and multi-image

The second most popular cover format is multi-theme and multi-image. Here, there is more than one photograph, or more likely, a collage of cropped photos or cutouts, along with numerous cover lines. Celebrity-driven magazines such as *In Touch Weekly, Life and Style, Star, TV Guide,* and *People* are the most notable users of this cover approach, along with magazines as varied as *Consumer Reports, PC Magazine,* and *Metal Edge.*

all-typographic

The all-type cover is the exception to the rule of using a strong visual illustration. All-typographic means just that: not a single photo or drawing on the cover, just words. *Rolling Stone, New York,* and *Esquire* all have had big sellers with all-type covers, which usually tout a special topic, such as *Rolling Stone*'s November 17, 1994, "The Future of Rock: Generation Next" and *Esquire*'s October 1993 "60 Things Every Man Should Know," the 60th anniversary collector's edition.

Time's editors grappled with the concept of an all-type cover for a year before running its first one, on the April 8, 1966, issue, asking "Is God Dead?" That cover generated 3,500 protest letters. It would be 17 years before *Time* would use another all-type cover. This time the editors decided to run the first paragraph of the "Death Penalty" story on the cover of the January 24, 1983, issue:

The chair is bolted to the floor near the back of a 12-ft. by 18-ft. room. You sit on a seat of cracked rubber secured by rows of copper tacks. Your ankles are strapped into half-moon-shaped foot cuffs lined with canvas. A 2-in.-wide greasy leather belt with 28 buckle holes and worn grooves where it has been pulled very tight many times is secured around your waist just above the hips. A cool metal cone encircles your head. You are now only moments away from death.

A whimsical approach to an all-type cover is also possible. *Print*'s May/June 1998 cover is a 300-word essay about the various ideas the art director thought about for the cover. Starting with the words "This is my best idea yet," and sounding as if the art director is in his office thinking out loud, the reader is treated to possibilities ranging from blowing up the logo to cover the entire page, to making the cover all one color, just black on white. Each new idea is "my best idea yet." The essay, which takes up the entire cover except for the logo, is set in about 24-point Helvetica. Of course, it ends, "This is my best idea yet."

Magazines that use all-type covers all of the time tend to take a serious approach to their topics. *Commentary* and *Foreign Affairs* list several articles and their authors on the covers, but they do not include page numbers. Each has a regular TOC page inside. Most academic journals use their covers either as a TOC or as a short listing of some of the articles inside; *New England Journal of Medicine* and *Harvard Business Review* are two examples.

Following the September 11 terrorist attack on the World Trade Center, a number of magazines used an all-type cover. *Editor and Publisher*'s all-black cover on September 17, 2001, simply stated "September 11, 2001" in white type; *ESPN: The Magazine* followed an all-type approach for its October 1, 2001, issue, but started with the text of its lead story:

These were the days when heroism and villainy were redefined. This was the week when sports went dark, when its spotlight swung around to the firefighters who ran up the stairs, the police and EMS crews who braved the showers of destruction, the laborers who sifted through the debris of a cataclysm to find evidence of someone's life. The clichéd descriptions we so freely bestow on our athletes—words like courageous, tireless, inspirational—have taken on deeper meanings. . . .

MAY/JUNE 2006: *Print* **magazine often uses compelling typography to make a graphic point**.

What makes a good cover? Cover lines should be clever and not too long. "Cute kills," observes Lafavore. "Save the clever word play for the headlines inside. Newsstand shoppers will probably spend only a moment or two looking at your cover. They need to be able to understand the sell instantly and without much thought."[41]

Issues with several cover lines tend to sell better than those with just one. However, the cover shouldn't be crowded with so many cover lines that it looks cluttered or junky. "Too many typefaces spoil the cover," says Lafavore. "When you mix typefaces, or use script or small type sizes, you ask the viewer to do just a little more work to read the lines. That little bit may be too much, sending the potential buyer's attention elsewhere. And at the newsstand, there is always someplace else for their eye to go."

Like the logo, cover lines should be easy to read from a distance and should contrast with the background color. When there's a single image on the cover, editors have found that a photograph of a woman's face tends to sell better than a man's on newsstands; whatever gender, though, the person on the cover should be making eye contact with the reader. A crisp photo with an innovative use of color generally sells better than an illustration, and a realistic illustration usually grabs more readers than does an abstract one.

Although cover design is more of an art than a science, studying previous covers and how they sold on the newsstand can provide insight. That's why cover decisions aren't solely left up to editors. "The goal is to get the magazine purchased and not just admired," says Marie Clapper, president of Clapper Communications, which publishes *The Cross Stitcher* and *Crafts 'n Things*.[42] She urges editors, art directors, circulation directors, and publishers to sit down together and discuss covers.

An easy way to do this is to look at every cover for the past year—or more—and write down each issue's newsstand sell-through numbers. Note which backgrounds have sold best and which colors. Did covers with cover line numbers sell better than those without? Are photos selling better than illustrations? The results may be surprising.

redesigns

Magazine experts say publications should redesign themselves every 5 or 6 years, both as part of their evolutionary process and in order to stay current. Sometimes a full face lift and major body overhaul occurs, but more frequently a magazine has little nips and tucks, such as updating the TOC, tweaking the logo, adding more color, or changing to a different paper stock. While a redesign tends to be aimed at attracting new readers, editors have to be careful that old, loyal readers aren't alienated. As for the advertisers, media buyers agree publication touch-ups are really an appeal to new advertisers, who, of course, are concerned with readers' reactions.

A redesign can be introduced from one issue to the next, or it can evolve over several issues. A redesign will not help an ailing or unfocused magazine or one that's in trouble with declining subscription renewals, low newsstand sales, and evaporating advertisers. Several major changes over a few years may signal the last gasps of a magazine on the verge of folding. *Saturday Evening Post* went through two major redesigns (including a new logo) in 1961 and 1968, yet wasn't able to keep up with shifting audience needs, societal expectations, and economic downturns. The

Creation of Cultural Images Through Covers

"Your cover defines you in popular perception," says former *People* managing editor and former *Time* editor James Gaines.[1] Because of this, people remember cover images, and we refer to magazines by what or who is on the cover. Consequently, the choice of who or what to feature on the cover is not only an editorial one, but also can be viewed as a social indicator of where any individual or group in society is today in terms of importance and value.

The very existence of *People*'s "50 Most Beautiful People" list symbolizes one significant segment of American culture. Through the images on the cover, *People* emphasizes the cosmetic, celebrates physical looks over substance, and presents the country with a definition of contemporary beauty: thin, sexy, and young. But can we blame *People*? We go to the movies, watch the television shows, and buy the CDs that make these people celebrities. We are, after all, a celebrity culture.

Time magazine's top two best-selling covers of all time deal with an issue of significant national importance: the September 11, 2001, terrorist at-

tack on the World Trade Center. The September 14, 2001, and September 24, 2001, issues sold, respectively, more than 3.3 million and 2 million copies on the newsstands. But that was an anomaly in terms of *Time*'s typical newsstand sales of covers focusing on national and international news. Covers about nuclear safety, the U.S. economy, Bosnia, Somalia, Israel, and Russia sold around 100,000 copies.[2]

The next two top newsstand sellers for *Time* focused on celebrities. The July 26, 1999, cover about the death of John F. Kennedy Jr. and the September 15, 1997, issue commemorating the late Princess Diana of Wales sold 1.3 million and 1.1 million copies, respectively. Compare that to covers focusing on more significant national and international issues.

Norman Pearlstine, who was editor-in-chief of Time, Inc., for 10 years, from 1995 to 2005, and who now is senior advisor at Time Warner, Inc., admits that readers are less interested in international news and even hard national news. "There's always been a balance between educating your reader and serving your reader, but we're not getting a lot of demand for

international coverage these days in broad consumer publications. You obviously balance telling them what you think they ought to read with giving them what they want to read, and that balance has clearly shifted away from international news in the last decade."[3]

But Ray Cave, former managing editor of *Time*, points out that it's a cop-out simply to say people aren't interested in substantive international and national news. "The general public has never been interested in it. But we delivered it, like it or not. By so doing, we piqued public interest in the very matters that must, to some degree, interest the citizens of a democracy."[4]

Increasingly, magazines are stressing the bond that readers feel with movie stars. Entertainment reporter and media critic Nancy Jay says, "Where models once dominated the covers of magazines, now you see Hollywood actresses and actors, television and music entertainers, sports figures. If you put 20 models in a row and 20 movie stars in a row, readers will more closely identify with the movie stars. They have more variety and they have more personality. Readers think they know them.

1. Jill L. Sherer, "Celebrities Sell Magazines—Sometimes," *Advertising Age* (May 24, 1989): 84.

2. "Misses," *Time* (March 9, 1998): 177.

3. Neil Hickey, "Money Lust," *Columbia Journalism Review* (July/August 1998): 32.

4. Ibid., 33.

Creation of Cultural Images Through Covers (continued)

If I say Jennifer Aniston, you think—yes, I know her, I know what she likes, and what she's thinking. I know what her life is like. You can't say that about a typical model."[5]

Jay observes that the hot cover topic since the 1990s has been the celebrity—with Brad Pitt and Jennifer Aniston being the hottest and most covered celebrity couple of all time: "They had the breakup of the century and they continue to dominate magazine covers even though they are divorced. There's still a fascination about Brad and Jen and Angelina, and it's really due to magazines like *In Touch Weekly, Life and Style, US Weekly, People,* and *Star.*"

US Weekly's highest selling newsstand issue ever was the February 7, 2005, one, headlined "How Jen Found Out." It sold 1.25 million copies.

Celebrity covers with smiling stars in predictable poses are safe choices for magazine editors. "I don't know if it's a timidity, a reflection of the culture overall, or driven by a combination of marketing-driven covers and a cult of celebrity," says *Time* art director Arthur Hochstein. "There's a lot of ingredients in the goulash that have produced covers that seem less risk-taking."[6]

Jann Wenner, chairman of Wenner Media and editor-in-chief of *Rolling Stone* agrees

that newsstand sales are critical aspects in the decision of what to put on the cover. "It's usually related to the culture, and the culture today is demanding much quicker, faster, poppier, sexier, hotter, disposable stuff," he says. "Every now and then, there's an opportunity to do something, and we do it."

With the February 9, 2006, issue, *Rolling Stone* took the opportunity to push the envelope in terms of a risk-taking cover, and it even had a celebrity: Rapper Kanye West wearing a crown of thorns and posing as Jesus Christ. ■

5. Nancy Jay, Entertainment USA Radio, January 19, 2006.

6. Lisa Granatstein, "Timid Times," *Media Week* (January 5, 2004), http://www.mediaweek.com/mediaweek/headlines/article_display.jsp?vnu _content_id=206115.

magazine folded in 1969, but has since been revived in a nostalgia format.

Fortune has had at least 20 redesigns since 1930. *Time,* on the other hand, had minor modifications, but for all practical purposes remained the same for 69 years until a radical redesign in 1992. Nevertheless, it's still unmistakably *Time. The New Yorker* still runs its first cover, with the monocled, high-hatted, aristocratic Eustace Tilley, once a year—and it fits right in with all the other covers. Most consumer magazines do an in-house tweak, or rejuvenation, of their designs every few years, a process that's so subtle that few readers or advertisers notice the change. But it seems to make the magazines a little brighter and a little more contemporary.

Rob Sugar, president of AURAS Design, a full-service design studio in Silver Spring, Maryland, that has designed or redesigned more than 80 publications, says there are good and bad reasons

for a magazine redesign.[43] Some of the bad reasons have nothing to do with creating a better looking magazine:

- *Marking territory:* A new editor, publisher, or art director may want "to alter the look to inaugurate a new administration." Sugar says this is self-serving and usually adds nothing to the magazine, particularly if the changes are cosmetic and ungrounded.
- *Anniversary coming up:* Some editors will use an anniversary as an impetus for a makeover. "It's never a good idea to change the look just for the sake of novelty," Sugar says.
- *Not trendy enough:* Someone will say the magazine doesn't seem cutting-edge. Sugar points out that trendiness "is actually a copy of someone else's idiosyncratic and successful look" and may be inappropriate for any other magazine.

Editors agree that good reasons for a redesign revolve around knowing the magazine's editorial mission, audience, and advertisers. The best reasons to redesign include the following:

- Fine-tuning the design to reflect *changing editorial content*. Even if the magazine's mission remains the same, departments and features may need to be updated and made visually interesting.
- Showing prospective and current *advertisers* the magazine is always improving. Theme issues, new columns, or special advertising sections may demand changes in layout and design.
- *Boosting readership* within a certain demographic group or expanding a current base of readers. "If a magazine changes its mission to include new readers, redesign is the best outward signal that a potential audience member's opinions have been re-evaluated," Sugar says.
- Needing a *full relaunch* because shrinking newsstand sales and dwindling renewals show readers are dissatisfied. Other signs pointing to the need for a complete makeover include advertisers who say they aren't getting the response they want from the readers and competition that is outperforming the magazine.

Some magazines have a signature design style that's like the perfect outfit for an exclusive charity ball, from the diamond earrings down to the silver heels and beaded clutch. Others look organized, classic, and disciplined, as if they're wearing a tailored suit with necktie knotted just so and shiny wingtips. Some magazines opt for flamboyant colors and a retro appearance, mixing a trendy whizbang dress with a vintage kimono and Dr. Martens boots. Still others have a casual look that is as comfortable as wearing sweats and sneakers on a Sunday afternoon at home.

Designer Rhonda Rubinstein, who has been art director at *Esquire, Details,* and *Smart,* says design turns content into an experience. She describes the relationship that has developed between design and editorial:

> It's a kind of temporal, emotional connection that is the essence of today's magazine. The best magazines are creating this complete experience. In these highly competitive times, seductive covers, provocative images or compelling writing alone cannot make the magazine and garner impressive doorstop-size awards. It's the total product with a consistent voice and imagery. It's all about look and feel. The cover, the page-flipping and the skim-reading all lead to a particular world with its ideals and attitude.[44]

notes

1. Jan White, "Self Test: Do You Design for Your Readers?" in *The Handbook of Magazine Publishing*, 4th ed., compiled by the editors of *Folio:* (Stamford, Conn.: Cowles Business Media, 1996), 324.
2. Tim Bogardus, "Define Your Redesign," in *The Handbook of Magazine Publishing*, 4th ed., compiled by the editors of *Folio:* (Stamford, Conn.: Cowles Business Media, 1996), 335.
3. Jan V. White, "Editors Don't Know Design? Nonsense!" *Folio:* (April 1983): 66.
4. Rhonda Rubinstein, "Branding in Print," *U & lc* (Fall 1997): 102.
5. "Note on *Fortune,*" *Fortune* (February 1930): 180–81.
6. William Owen, *Modern Magazine Design* (Dubuque, Iowa: Wm. C. Brown, 1992), 50.
7. Ibid., 56.
8. "*Harper's Bazaar* at 100," *Print* (September/October 1967): 47.
9. Jim Nelson Black, "Magazine Design: The Evolution," *Folio:* (November 1983): 80.
10. Owen, 111.
11. Carol E. Holstead, "What's Old Is New: The Need for Historical Inspiration in Contemporary Magazine Design," *American Periodicals,* vol. 7 (1997): 74.
12. Ibid., 79–81.
13. Greg Lindsay, "Design Spotlight: Roger Black," Mediabistro.com (February 2, 2005), http://www.mediabistro.com/articles/cache/a3724.asp?pntvs+1&.
14. Jan White, "Self Test: Do You Design for Your Readers?" in *The Handbook of Magazine Publishing*, 4th ed., compiled by the editors of *Folio:* (Stamford, Conn.: Cowles Business Media, 1996), 324.
15. Paul Chapman, "David Carson Interview: Inspiration from Anywhere Any Time," *First Point Magazine* issue 2 (Fall 2005), http://www.firstpointmagaizne.com/davidcarson.html.
16. Will Hopkins, "Design Basics: Magazine" (Stanford Professional Publishing Course, Stanford University, Palo Alto, Calif., July 25, 1997).
17. Michael Kaplan, "Carsonogenic," *Folio:* (March 1, 1995): 51.
18. Stephen G. Smith, "From the Editor: A Farewell to Hot

Wax and X-Acto Knives," *Civilization* (May/June 1996): 6.

19. Robert Bohle, "Readers Tell Us About Color," *Journal of the Society of Newspaper Design,* no. 21 (1985): 9.

20. Jan V. White, "Using Color to Carry the Message," *Folio:* (April 1991): 89.

21. Roger Black, "Pulling out the Stops," *U & lc* (Summer 1997): 17.

22. Chapman.

23. Kaplan, 84.

24. Elizabeth Thoman, "Rise of the Image Culture: Re-Imagining the American Dream," *Media and Values* (Winter 1992): 7.

25. Loudon Wainwright, *The Great American Magazine: An Inside Story of* Life (New York: Alfred A. Knopf, 1986), 33.

26. Robin Pogrebin, "Magazines Bowing to Demands for Star Treatment," *New York Times* (May 18, 1998): A1.

27. Nigel Holmes, "Why Function Always Trumps Format," Nigel Holmes/Explanations Graphics, http://www.nigelholmes.com/media/snd05.htm.

28. Nigel Holmes, "Visual Information" (Stanford Professional Publishing Course, Stanford University, Palo Alto, Calif., July 25, 1997).

29. John Peter, "Stop! Read This Article," *Magazine Publishing Management,* compiled by the editors of *Folio:* (New Canaan, CT: Folio Magazine Publishing, 1976), 201.

30. Roger Black, 17.

31. Roy Paul Nelson, "Tracing the Circuitous Route of Publication Design," *IABC Communication World* (May-June 1990): 50–51.

32. David D. Perlmutter, "A Picture's Worth 8,500,000 People: American News Pictures as Symbols of China," *Visual Communication Quarterly* (Spring 1997): 5.

33. "Pay as Much Attention to the Cover as the Contents," *Folio:* (February 1, 1998): 9.

34. "What Makes a Cover Sell?" *Folio: (* September 1986): 51.

35. Judy Kessler, *Inside* People: *The Stories Behind the Stories* (New York: Villard Books, 1994): 11.

36. Steven Heller and Louise Fili, *Cover Story: The Art of American Magazine Covers, 1900–1950* (San Francisco: Chronicle Books, 1996): 11.

37. M. Therese Southgate, "The Cover," *JAMA: The Journal of the American Medical Association* (July 1, 1998): 5.

38. Michael Lafavore, "Newsstand Covers That Work," *The Circulator* (May 25, 2005).

39. Joe Hagan, "Cover Creation," *Folio:* (February 2002): 30.

40. Jon Friedman, "Magazines Have Questionable Covers," CMS Market Watch (June 18, 2004), http://www.marketwatch.com/news/print_story.asp?print=1&guid=[AF38D366-OE27-9Fi.

41. Lafavore.

42. Ray Schultz, "Circulators Encourage Design by Committee," *Circulation Management* (March 24, 2004), http://circman.com/ar/marketing_circulators_encourage_design/index.htm.

43. Rob Sugar, "Looks Can Kill," *Folio:* (November 1, 1997): 64.

44. Rubinstein, 102.

for additional reading

Abramson, Howard S. National Geographic: *Behind America's Lens on the World.* New York: Crown Publishers, 1987.

Blackwell, Lewis, and David Carson. *The End of Print: The Grafik Design of David Carson,* rev. ed. San Francisco: Chronicle Books, 2000.

Bryan, C. D. B. *The National Geographic Society: 100 Years of Adventure and Discovery.* New York: Harry N. Abrams, 1987.

Carlebach, Michael L. *American Photojournalism Comes of Age.* Washington, D.C.: Smithsonian Institution Press, 1997.

Carson, David. *Trek: David Carson, Recent Werk.* Corte Madera, Calif.: Gingko Press, 2004.

Cohn, Jan. *Covers of the* Saturday Evening Post: *Seventy Years of Outstanding Illustration from America's Favorite Magazine.* New York: Viking Studio Books, 1995.

Davis, Laurel R. *The Swimsuit Issue and Sport: Hegemonic Masculinity in* Sports Illustrated. Ithaca: State University of New York Press, 1997.

Duperray, Stephane, and Raphaele Vidaling. *Front Page: Covers of the Twentieth Century.* Weidenfield and Nicolson (Ukiah, Calif.: Orion Publishing Group Ltd.), 2003.

Heller, Steven, and Louise Fili. *Cover Story: The Art of American Magazine Covers, 1900–1950.* San Francisco: Chronicle Books, 1996.

Henkel, David K. *Collectible Magazines: Identification and Price Guide.* New York: Avon Books, 1993.

Holmes, Nigel. *Designer's Guide to Creating Charts and Diagrams.* New York: Watson-Guptill Publications, 1991.

———. *Wordless Diagrams.* New York: Bloomsbury USA, 2005.

Kessler, Judy. *Inside* People: *The Stories Behind the Stories.* New York: Villard Books, 1994.

King, Stacey. *Magazine Design That Works: Secrets for Successful Magazine Design.* Gloucester, Mass.: Rockport Publishers, 2001.

Kozol, Wendy. Life*'s America: Family and National in Postwar Journalism.* Philadelphia: Temple University Press, 1994.

Moser, Horst. *Surprise Me: Editorial Design.* New York: Mark Batty Publisher, 2003.

Owen, William. *Modern Magazine Design.* Dubuque, Iowa: Wm. C. Brown Publishers, 1992.

Rolling Stone: *The Complete Covers, 1967–1997.* New York: Harry N. Abrams, 1998.

White, Jan V. *Editing by Design: For Designers, Art Directors, and Editors. The Classic Guide to Winning Readers,* completely rev. ed. New York: Allworth Press, 2003.

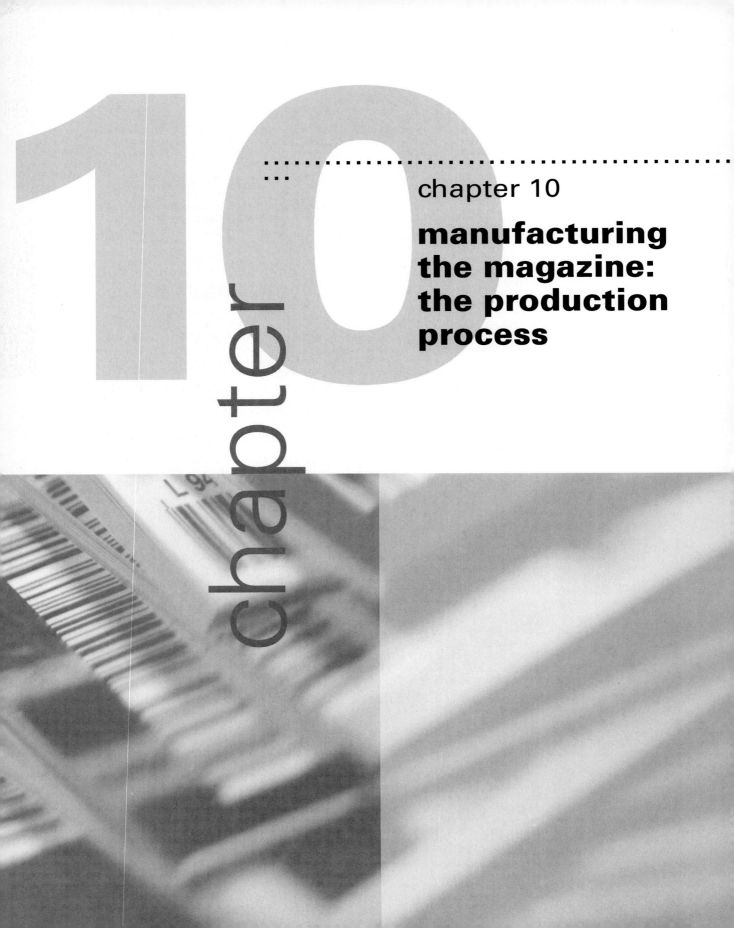

10

chapter

chapter 10

manufacturing the magazine: the production process

On the third floor of an office building next to the Raccoon River in Des Moines, Iowa, the Meredith Publishing production staff pores over planning sheets for *More* magazine, puzzling about where to place an adverting insert so that it doesn't cut into the magazine's editorial content. The decision includes the publisher, editor-in-chief, art director, and advertising director—all of whom are in Manhattan—and the production staff in Iowa, so electronic files are sent from one city to another as PDFs. The decision on placement is a collaborative effort, but the production staff actually makes the placement. ▌ In an office building a few blocks from the Potomac River in Washington, D.C., the staff of *FP*, or *Foreign Policy* magazine, the publication of the Carnegie Endowment for International Peace, is going through much the same process, but with a smaller staff: Decisions there are made by the design director, the managing editor, and the associate publisher. ▌ All types and sizes of magazines must go through the same basic manufacturing stage, called the production process, for the creation of the printed and bound publication. At the same time that the editorial, design, and advertising staffs are planning the magazine's content, the production staff is planning the most efficient and precise method of making that content into a tangible product. On a small magazine, all the work is done by a handful of people, sometimes only one or two. In a large publishing house, an entire floor of the building may be reserved for the production staff. Once the magazine closes—that is, reaches its final deadline for content—the production staff kicks into high gear.

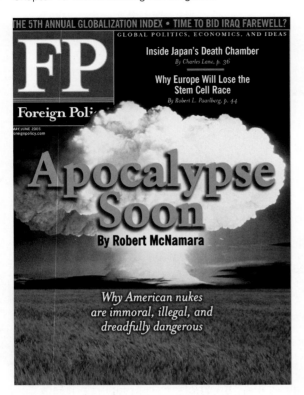

MAY/JUNE 2005: *FP*, or *Foreign Policy*, uses a gloss cover stock and a velvet interior sheet.

the production process

The production process includes placing all content, choosing paper and color, preparing art for reproduction, and overseeing printing, binding, and distribution. It's a high-tech operation that depends on human skill as well as on an array of machines ranging in size from desktop computers to printing presses the size of a house. Many production staffers fall into their jobs accidentally and end up loving the work for its mix of creativity and scientific problem solving.

The production of *More* provides a clear overview of the process. At the planning stage, the production staff organizes the placement of articles and advertising in the magazine. They follow the magazine's established editorial formula as well as directions from the editor and art director in determining the flow of articles; they place advertising according to the ad contract, making sure advertising and editorial mesh logically and serve the reader with a clear and consistent message.

Once placement has been established, the staff takes the computer-designed pages from the art director and formats all art and type in preparation for production. They send the finished pages on disk, plus all art, to a production company in Tennessee that converts the pages to print-ready files and sends them to a printing plant in Illinois, where they are printed, bound, and addressed. The plant transports the finished magazine by truck to newsstands and subscribers. Postal workers have an office in the plant, so they can determine postage and inspect the magazines to make sure they meet postal regulations.

On *FP*, the process is the same but most of the production work falls on the design director. The managing editor and design director also use the magazine's established formula as their guide in placement of elements, being sure that they represent the goals and mission statement of the institute. The magazine's small staff does all page de-

MAY 2006: The production staff of *More* magazine is at Meredith Publishing headquarters in Des Moines, Iowa, even though the editorial staff is in Manhattan. The magazine is printed in Tennessee. The staffs collaborate using PDFs and other computer-generated files.

sign, scanning, and placement of elements, instead of sending any files out to a production bureau. Files are then sent to the printing plant, which prints and binds the magazine. The printer sends the finished product to a mailing house, which mails copies to subscribers around the world.

production planning

The production planning process for each issue requires deciding on the placement of pages in the magazine, or doing a break-of-the-book (see Figure 10.1). Each issue builds on decisions about paper, special coatings, color, art, and printing process, which are made when the magazine is launched or redesigned. These decisions usually stay in place for years, unless budget changes require a modification of size or paper. In recent years, digital manipulation has become a significant ethical concern. The whole process has one goal: creating a quality product that serves the reader.

■ BREAK-OF-THE-BOOK

The determination of which article or advertisement goes on what page is called the break-of-the-book, also called the ladder or map. As explained in chapter 5, a well-planned magazine has such a consistent formula that the placement of elements from one issue to another is a natural process. At large publishing houses, the break-of-the-book is done by a production manager, following an outline from the editor and art director. At smaller magazines, it's done directly by the editor and art director. No matter who creates it, the editor, art director, and publisher all must approve the break-of-the-book.

For each issue, the staff starts with a blank worksheet—usually a tiny thumbnail showing all pages of the magazine—and begins to fill it with specific content. The break-of-the-book is a fluid document that changes often. An article that had been planned for four pages suddenly becomes a major story and is expanded by three pages. That means a six-page photo spread is cut to three pages. Then two pages of ads come in at the last

Advertisers Know Their Place

In addition to specific ad placement requests, production staffers have to keep their eyes open for ad-related problem areas. For example:

- Most consumer magazines make sure at least six pages separate two car ads.
- Coupons must back up to editorial or to another part of the same advertiser's message. No coupons can be placed behind another ad. In that way, when a consumer cuts out a coupon, part of the magazine's editorial con-

tent is sliced out, not part of another ad.

- Magazines must "make good"—that is, run the ad for free—on ads that are placed contrary to the ad contract.
- Advertising inserts—preprinted groups of pages—should not break up an article, but should come between articles or departments. Because they are preprinted, these inserts are numbered differently from the rest of the magazine.

- Regional advertising pages cannot be numbered as part of the magazine. U.S. postal regulations require that only those pages that are part of every edition of the magazine can be sequentially numbered. Pages in regional editions, then, typically bear a letter as well as a number, with the letter being the production staff's code for that particular edition. At *Good Housekeeping,* NC1 refers to the first page of the North Central edition. ▫

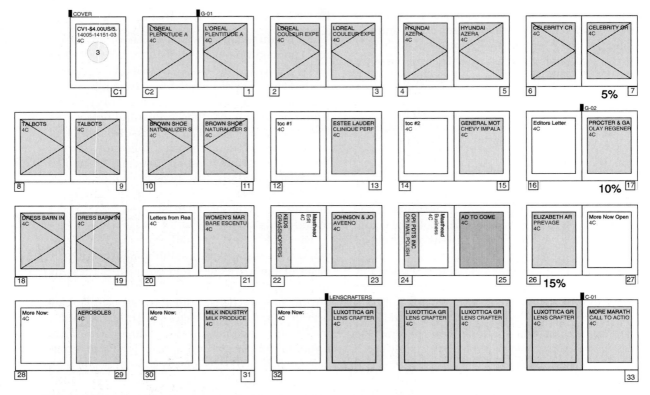

FIGURE 10.1 *More* **Magazine's Break-of-the-Book. The production staff of** *More* **magazine creates a digital break-of-the-book, or map, to determine placement of articles and ads. The first 33 pages of the 188-page March 2006 issue shows the first and second covers—C1 and C2—plus placement of inserts, shown with black bars at the top of a page. (Lenscrafters is inserted between pages 32 and 33.) Because some advertisers request placement at the front of the book, production staffers indicate where the first 5 percent, 10 percent, and 15 percent ads are placed.**

minute, forcing the staff to postpone one entire feature until the next issue.

editorial needs

The staff plans the magazine's editorial content months, often years, in advance. Editors and art directors make assignments according to the editorial formula; magazine editors often assign more articles than needed to make sure they have a back-up in case one falls through. They also generally have a file of extra articles—an article "bank"—to use if they need to add pages in the happy event that ad sales go beyond expectations.

Each editorial element has a predetermined spot in the magazine, so while the editor is making sure the article reads appropriately and the art director is overseeing design, the production staff is already assigning space to that article. Depart-ments may fall on the same page from issue to issue, or they may fall within a general range. In some magazines, a particular department is the same length in every issue; in others, the length varies according to the amount of material available, the importance the editors want to place on that department, or the design effect the art director is planning. Features are placed within the feature well, with lengths and pacing determined by the editor and art director.

advertising placement

Advertisers who buy specific placement in the magazine must be given that placement; they have a contract. The ad staff strives to sell specific pages—the covers, especially—and not to oversell other areas. That is, they try not to sell eight full-page ads to food advertisers who want to be in a food section that normally has only two editorial

Adding Pages: How Many Before It Pays Off?

In an ideal world, ad sales would be finalized far enough in advance to give editorial, design, and production staffs the time to prepare the right amount of editorial to keep the magazine's advertising-editorial ratio consistent. Too often, however, ads come in late and the staff is left scrambling to fill extra pages. Worse yet, ads may be pulled out late, leaving the magazine with a gap.

Magazine staffs know at what point it makes sense to add pages when extra ads come in and at what point it makes sense to simply take the ad and cut an editorial page or two. For example, a magazine with a 40:60 advertising-editorial ratio plans 60 pages of editorial for every 40 pages of advertising. If, at the last minute, two extra pages of ads come in, the magazine staff usually cuts two department pages or replaces a six-page feature with a four-page one, if possible. The six-pager can then be placed in a subsequent issue. Partial-page ads are less problematic, because magazines traditionally plan "advertising and editorial" (A and E) pages, which have partial-page ads and small articles all on one page. An additional ad might mean simply losing one of the articles, which can then be placed in a later issue.

Six or seven pages of extra ads, however, may require a whole new signature, which will consist of the ads, plus extra editorial pages with content from the magazine's editorial "bank," which is its store of articles of varying sizes that can be put in at any time to fill space. The magazine staff goes to this bank again when ads are lost at the last minute. ■

pages. Should these problems occur, the staff tries to accommodate advertisers; they may decide to reevaluate the formula and add more food pages on a regular basis, or they may encourage the ad staff to sell food advertisers on placements throughout the magazine.

Some magazines limit the number of partial-page ads. In many cases, the production manager places fractional ads next to the masthead or at the back of the book. Where there is a deviation from this norm, the editor makes the call.

The production manager places ads first, to assure all contracts are honored. The typical ad placement requests are the following:

- The second, third, or fourth covers, also known as the inside front, inside back, and back covers.
- Next to a specific department. Occasionally magazine ad sales staffs will sell ads next to features, but this can be tricky if the feature falls through; it also can look like that advertiser is getting preferential treatment.

- Front-of-the-book (FOB): before the table of contents or in the departments at the beginning of the magazine.
- Back-of-the-book (BOB): in the departments or columns at the end of the magazine.
- Run-of-the-book (ROB): anywhere in the magazine.

■ PAPER STOCK

On a regularly published magazine, the art director or production manager may not even know exactly what type of paper is used because it has been standardized for so long. The initial decision about paper—also called stock—is based on precise magazine needs and budgetary restrictions.

It's an important decision. Readers often have a visceral reaction to paper. They eye it, touch it, rub it between their fingers, and hold it up to the light. Even the least sophisticated reader notices paper quality. *Rolling Stone* started as a newsprint

MARCH 2006: *Traditional Home* **uses a heavier cover sheet for newsstand buyers than for subscribers.**

for the main editorial well and uncoated for certain departments. *Wood*, for example, is printed on a coated stock except for the project patterns, which are printed on uncoated.

Coated stocks can have a high gloss, a dull finish, a matte finish, or they can be coated-uncoated hybrids. Coated stocks are further defined according to grades of quality.

High Gloss A high gloss paper is lustrous and shiny; this is the result of coating as well as the amount of calendering. A gloss sheet is highly reflective and is a good choice for photos because it can make printed images sparkle. It may be less appealing when reproducing type, however, because it can cause too much glare. *FP* uses a gloss cover.

Dull Coat A dull sheet, often called velvet stock, is slightly less coated and less calendered; it may hold the ink well, but it is less reflective, which means colors are less brilliant but the sheet also has less glare. It can be a good choice for magazines with both photographic appeal and large amounts of

publication but ultimately moved to coated stock as the magazine matured and appealed to more upscale readers and advertisers; it now uses paper that has a mix of uncoated and coated qualities. Farm Bureau's *Family Ties* moved from a high gloss to a matte coated stock when readers complained about paper glare.

Paper is evaluated on its finish, grade, and weight.

finish

Paper can be coated or uncoated, which refers to the outer layer of finish applied to one or both sides. This coating is then polished to various levels of sheen on a machine called a calender, which smoothes the paper by compression.

Coated paper generally tends to hold ink better than uncoated, resulting in sharper, brighter images; its surface also allows more even reflection of light. Uncoated papers, such as newsprint, generally allow both ink and light to soak in, resulting in dull final images. Some magazines use coated inks

MARCH/APRIL 2005: Farm Bureau's *Family Ties* **uses a matte stock, rather than gloss, to improve readability.**

type, such as *FP*, which uses a velvet stock for interior pages.

Matte Coat A matte sheet has even less coating and polish, so it has the least gloss and the least reflectivity. It can be a good choice for magazines that want the understated effect of newsprint with the printing quality of a coated stock. *Country Home* moved to a matte stock to cut costs and ended up finding the new paper enhanced the look of the magazine.

Super Calendered Called "super cal" sheets by printers, these papers have less coating and finish than coated stocks, but more than uncoated. They are increasingly the choice of large circulation magazines such as *Rolling Stone* and *Family Circle.*

Many magazines print on coated stocks because of the quality of printing they provide. Yet some uncoated stocks are of extremely high quality and appeal, with the matching high price tag. These uncoated stocks usually offer an artistic appeal that is more appropriate for advertising brochures and public relations materials than magazines, however.

If all other elements are equal, gloss-coated papers are the most expensive, followed by dull, then matte, then super cal. Often, the cost of paper simply has to do with the kind the printer has in stock. When the printer can buy in huge quantities, his costs go down, and he passes the reduction on to customers.

grade

Top-grade papers have high brightness, whiteness, smoothness, and opacity.

Brightness Paper with high brightness reflects light, resulting in photos that look clean and brilliant.

Whiteness Paper with high whiteness evenly reflects all colors in the spectrum; it does not reflect any one color more than another.

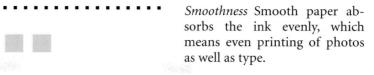

A magazine may choose paper based on the "plop factor," or the sound the magazine makes when dropped. A wimpy magazine makes a tiny "plop," while a magazine with presence makes a strong, sturdy "PLOP." A magazine can improve its plop factor by increasing pages or paper weight.

Smoothness Smooth paper absorbs the ink evenly, which means even printing of photos as well as type.

Opacity A highly opaque sheet lets little light shine through; it has little show-through of images from one side through to the other side.

Coated paper is offered in six grades: premium, and grades number 1, 2, 3, 4, and 5. The quality of the sheet lowers as the grade number gets higher. Brightness, whiteness, smoothness, and opacity are reduced gradually from grade to grade. Even the lowest quality grade—number 5—still offers viable printing, however. Many large circulation magazines, in fact, are produced on numbers 4 and 5.

Premium, Number 1, and Number 2 These papers are generally used for annual reports; they are usually too expensive for magazines. Some corporate communications magazines, however, which are printed in small quantities, can afford a number 1 or number 2 sheet. Farm Bureau's *Family Ties* uses number 2 paper.

Number 3 This paper still has a high-end look. Most consumer magazines printed by R.R. Donnelley, one of the country's largest printing companies, use this sheet for covers, including *Traditional Home* and *More.*

Numbers 4 and 5 These grades are affordable while still offering good quality. They may leave fibers—small black spots that printers call hickeys—on the printed product, however. *Rolling Stone* and *Elle* use number 4 paper. *Midwest Living, Parents,* and *Fitness* use number 5.

weight

Paper weight is determined by the weight in pounds of a ream—500 sheets—of paper cut to a standard size. That is, 500 sheets of a 40-pound paper weighs 40 pounds. Today's magazines are published on anything from 32-pound to 150-pound paper.

Paper is available either in cover or text weights. Cover weight papers are heavier than text papers. A 60-pound cover sheet is noticeably thicker than a 60-pound text sheet. A common choice for consumer magazines is 40-pound text stock with an 80-pound cover. *FP* uses a 50-pound interior and 100-pound cover stock. *Country Home*, which uses paper manufactured in Finland under the metric system, has a 43.9-pound text stock and a 119-pound cover.

Some magazines use a heavier cover stock for the newsstand than for subscription sales to cut postage costs. *Traditional Home* has a 146-pound cover sheet for newsstand buyers and a 124-pound cover for subscribers. *Better Homes and Gardens, Ladies' Home Journal,* and *Family Circle* have 100-pound newsstand covers and 60-pound subscription covers.

■ SPECIAL COATINGS

Special processes that add to the impact of paper include coatings that can reduce smears and add gloss.

uv

UV coating is added to the printed product, which is dried using ultraviolet (UV) lights; it adds gloss to the page and is often used for magazine covers. Some publishers coat only the front cover, not the back; some coat newsstand copies only, others do both newsstand and subscription. This coating is applied after the magazine is printed.

aqueous

An aqueous coating is water-based, so it is more environmentally friendly than UV coating; this finish comes directly from the ink jet of a printing press, so it is applied at the same time the magazine is printed.

varnish

Varnish is a slick coating printed atop a finished sheet. It is used to prevent ink from running, or for special effects, usually on covers. Occasionally an uncoated or matte sheet is highlighted with varnish, which acts almost like a subtle ink. Varnish is applied after the magazine is printed. *More* magazine uses a dull varnish, which gives the magazine an understated finish.

■ COLOR

Color may be process or spot color. Large circulation magazines typically use only process color because they print on full-color presses; adding spot color is an extra expense. Increasingly, though, even smaller publications have the option of color throughout because of improvements in printing presses.

process color

Full-color photographs in the printing world are referred to as four-color photos because they must be separated into the four process colors—magenta (red), cyan (blue), yellow, and black—for printing. Each color is screened at a unique angle, so that, when printed, each of the four colors falls onto the page dot-by-dot, next to one another, rather than on top of one another. This screening can be done in-house or by outside experts.

Color Separations Color photos that have been digitized and separated into the four process colors are called color separations. Process colors are referred to as CMYK—cyan, magenta, yellow, and black.

Much magazine photography is now digital, which means photographs are press-ready from the start and can be separated, color-corrected, and manipulated on the computer screen. Nondigital photographs must be scanned—or separated into process colors. The magazine staff can create its own separations, using a digital scanner and photo manipulating software, thus saving the cost of hiring outside experts. The savings may come at the expense of quality, however, because of the limitations of the equipment and because magazine staffers may not have the time and training necessary to create high-quality separations.

A prepress house, also called a production house, creates color separations and turns nondigital photographs into digital images. While they

Garbage In, Garbage Out

Not even the best printing plant can be expected to save a grainy photograph or a fuzzy illustration. Quality reproduction of art in magazines is largely determined by the type and condition of the original. When planning art, consider the following:

- Pencil drawings may be difficult to reproduce. Because they have gray tones, they are treated like continuous tones, and therefore have to be screened. However, the original itself has a natural dot pattern from the texture of the lead. That means the drawing is essentially screened twice. The printed product may lack definition and detail.

- Slide film reproduces better than prints. Printers call slides "transparencies," for obvious reasons. Transparencies produce clearer images because they are first-generation art, whereas prints are second-generation, being created from negatives. First-generation images are, by nature, more precise.

- 35mm film can be used for magazine photographs, but the images it produces have to be enlarged to such a degree—sometimes up to 2,000 percent—that they get grainy. Professional photographers avoid this problem by using large-scale cameras that produce transparency images up to 8 inches by 10 inches.

- Using already published art is dangerous, not only because of copyright issues, but because of quality problems. A printed image has already been screened; to use it again, it would have to be screened once more. This double screening could create a moiré pattern on the photo, or a wavy, shadowy pattern imprinted in the image. ■

may be more expensive than in-house scanning, prepress houses offer color-correction capabilities that may provide much higher quality reproduction.

Low-resolution Scans The art used in most photo-heavy magazines takes up so much memory that production managers don't want to store it in their computers, so the art staff uses low-resolution (low-res) scans for placement only (FPO) when creating their pages. Low-res scans have fewer dots per inch (DPI) than high-res scans, so they take up less memory. The production staff then gives the page with low-res scans to a printer or prepress house, which replaces them with the high-resolution (high-res) scans necessary for quality printing. Automatic Picture Replacement (APR) software can instantly replace low-res scans with high-res scans, retaining the exact cropping, sizing, and placement on the page.

Photo Blocks Often, pages are sent to a printer or production house with no scanned art at all, but with blank blocks left open for photographs and other page elements requiring special processing; these are scanned by the printer, then spliced into the rest of the page to create a final page. This is the process of choice for small magazines that don't create enough pages for in-house imaging to be cost effective.

Spot color is added to the page for special effect, usually for type or color blocks. Spot colors are standardized and given PMS (Pantone Matching System) numbers. PMS 122 is yellow-gold; PMS 512 is purple. Art directors select PMS colors the way interior designers choose paint—by looking at a swatch book, in this case a PMS book. PMS colors are included on most desktop computer software.

If spot color is used on a page that will be printed by the four-color process, the printer

Too Hot to Print

Magazine photos can hit readers' hot buttons, often for good reason. Both women and men wear skimpy clothing and ads use explicit sex to sell products. In most cases, however, staffs have more latitude with news photos than with feature or advertising photos. Most readers will forgive an explicit news photo if it does a good job of explaining an issue. However, readers may say even some news photos go too far, being unnecessarily graphic.

In some notable instances, the photo can't even get past the employees of the printing plant. *Editor and Publisher*'s printer refused to print an October 11, 1997, issue containing a story about a banned sex tabloid because of employee complaints: The article was illustrated with tabloid covers featuring topless women. The magazine tried to find another printer. After three tries, the publisher found a plant willing to print the image, but it was too late. The magazine was past deadline.

The magazine compensated by running a blank rectangle where the image would have been; inside the rectangle, the magazine added an explanation of why the image was missing. Publisher Chris Phillips addressed the issue in his letter to readers, asking if it is more important for printers to "placate their employees" than to "refuse to censor material protected by the First Amendment"?[1]

Teri Schrettenbrunner, spokeswoman for *Editor and Publisher*'s printer, Cadmus Journal Services, said the issue was simple: "We have an obligation to ensure that our employees can come to work and feel comfortable. We also have a reputation that we're proud of for standing by our ethical standards."[2]

The now-defunct *Might* also lost a printer in 1996 over a cover story about AIDS that offended some employees. And *Pop Smear* magazine, with a "Porn Reviews" column that's billed as the "most intelligent review of porn today" was turned down by 20 printers in 1996 before it was accepted by Kingston Press of Sussex, Wisconsin, recommended by *Hustler*. ■

1. Steve Wilson, "When Printers Just Say No," *Folio:* (December 1, 1997): 15.
2. Ibid., 15.

---

usually tries to create a match color, or match a PMS color, by using a combination of process colors, in much the same way a hardware store mixes paints. These matched colors add very little, if anything, to printing costs.

Adding spot color to a black-and-white page requires an additional press run and increases printing costs. Printing only in black is considered printing in one color. Printing in black and red is printing in two colors. When a printer gives a bid for a two-color job, that usually means black and one spot color. A three-color job usually means black and two spot colors.

special inks

Metallic and neon inks always require a separate run on the press, even with a full-color job, because they cannot be created using process colors. Many high-end cosmetics advertisers use special inks and, therefore, require special pricing for their ads because of the additional costs of these inks. Almay uses a signature silver in its promotional materials, which usually requires a different run on a separate press from the rest of the magazine. Production managers have to be especially careful to consider the extra costs of these ads, and include those costs in their contract with Almay.

■ ART

Artwork can be simple line drawings or photographs and may be printed in color, black and white, or with a second color.

line art

Art created with no gray tones is line art. This includes most cartoons, maps, and pen-and-ink drawings. When placed on the page in the correct size, line art is reproduced as part of the page and requires no extra preparation. Line art can be reproduced with any color ink.

continuous tones

Any black-and-white art that includes gray tones is considered a continuous tone. This includes photographs, paintings, and water colors. Continuous tones must be screened for printing, which turns them into a series of dots. Screened black-and-white continuous tones are called halftones; they are the one-color equivalents of color separations. Printers never speak of photographs, calling them halftones instead. The screening process to create halftones adds preparation time and, therefore, adds to the cost of the printing job.

The quality of halftones is determined by the fineness of the screen that is used to create them. In most cases, the finer the screen, the better the reproduction, although occasionally a too-fine screen can cause ink smears. Screens traditionally have been measured by lines per inch, with most magazines using at least a 133-line screen. For best reproduction, photographs should be scanned at twice the final screen resolution, which means a photograph to be reproduced with a 150-line screen would be scanned at 300 dots per inch (DPI).

Some publishers spend more on postage than they do on paper, and a rate hike in 2006 meant an estimated additional $180 million expenses a year for the industry. Banding together is one way to reduce the cost of delivering magazines to subscribers. Large printing firms, such as R.R. Donnelley and Quad Graphics, combine the magazines they print for several different publishers, sort them by zip code, bundle them together, and put them all on the same truck for delivery.

duotones

Black-and-white photographs can be printed with additional spot colors to create duotones, or halftones that are printed twice, once usually in black, and once in a second color. Duotones are screened in the same way separations are, with one color screened at one angle, another at a second angle, so the two patterns of dots fall onto the page cleanly and clearly and create two distinct colors that work together. Duotones retain the same level of gray tones as the original, so that if the original has large expanses of white, so does the duotone. A duotone can also be printed with two runs of black—that is, black is both the first and second color—to add punch to a black-and white photograph.

With a two- or three-color publication, duotone colors are selected from the PMS chart. With a full-color publication, duotones can get tricky. Many duotones arrive at the magazine already screened into two colors. If their screen angle does not match the screen angle of the rest of the separations, they can create a moiré pattern when printed. Production managers have to look at duotones carefully to ensure that they can be printed without additional preparation and cost.

duotints

When spot color is added as a block over the halftone, this creates a duotint. Duotints have an even coverage of the second color over the entire halftone. If the original has large expanses of white, the duotone will cover that white with a second color.

screens

Color blocks can be added behind type, creating the same effect duotints create with photography. When the color is applied full strength, it is called 100 percent color. If it is applied at less than full strength, it is called a screen, referring to the screen through which the printer

The $450,000 Word Choice

In 1997, an insert placed in *Woman's Day* carried the small word "catalog" at the front. As an insert, it would have been considered by postal authorities as part of the publication, and the magazine could then be mailed periodical class for 23 cents, based on its weight.

Catalogs, however, must be mailed third class. Because the insert was called a catalog, the entire magazine had to be mailed third class, for an additional 32 cents a copy, or a total of $450,000 extra postage.

It's critical for the production staff to see inserts before they are bound. Product samples—the CDs used in some computer magazines—may have to be mailed third class. Perfume strips, however, are not considered samples, so they can be included as regular advertising content. ▪

---

diffuses the color. Screens are measured by percentages of full color, so that a 50 percent screen has half the coverage of 100 percent color. On a one-color page, with the color usually being black, a screen can add interest with little extra cost. On a multiple-color page, a variety of screens can add almost as much life as full-color art. Duotints can also be screened.

The wise designer plans screens carefully. A vibrant red turns into a timid pink when screened. Hunter green turns pastel lime.

the printing process

Everything comes together in the printing process, in which printing presses transfer ink onto paper, creating the final images the reader will see. In their early history, magazines were printed in-house, often by the editor using a slow handheld press. Almost all magazines are now printed at printing plants devoted entirely to printing, binding, and mailing the finished product. Magazines are produced either on sheets or continuous rolls of paper using either offset or rotogravure printing presses.

■ SHEET-FED

Small magazines—those under 10,000 circulation—are usually produced on sheet-fed presses. These presses take one sheet of paper at a time.

These are oversized sheets on which multiple pages are printed. A typical sheet of cover stock measures 20 inches × 26 inches, and a typical sheet of text paper measures 25 inches × 38 inches, although individual paper producers may offer additional and varied sizes. Papers produced in Europe have to be converted from metric dimensions and, therefore, come in at odd sizes. Sheet-fed presses usually require at least a 50-pound sheet because thinner paper might get jammed in the press.

■ WEB

Magazines above 10,000 circulation can be printed on web presses, which use a continuous roll of paper. Web presses are much faster than sheet-fed presses, and can print on thin paper with accuracy. Web paper usually comes in 22.75-inch or 21.5-inch widths.

■ OFFSET

The majority of magazines today are printed on offset presses, which work well for small or large runs. The process gets its name from a rubber plate onto which the image is transferred—or offset—from the metal image plate; the paper comes into direct contact with the offset plate. Offset presses may be either sheet-fed or web. Large presses—those that run from 16 pages to 32 pages at once—print both sides of the sheet at the same time.

ROTOGRAVURE

Magazines with circulations above 1 million may be printed on rotogravure, or gravure, presses, which move with high speed and precision. Gravure presses use highly fluid ink, which can give better printing quality than offset presses, creating a finished product with excellent correlation to the original. Gravure also allows magazines to use less expensive paper without a loss of printing quality. A magazine that uses a 40-pound sheet for offset printing can drop to a 34-pound when using gravure. Moreover, because in gravure printing the image plate is mounted on a cylinder that makes direct contact with the paper, the impression is more exact than in offset.

Historically, gravure has been an expensive choice because of high preparation costs and because the image plates must be etched, or recessed.

Engraving the plates and creating the proper viscosity of ink is time consuming because of its precision and complexity. Also, gravure presses print with great speed, so it's essential that they be perfectly aligned before printing starts because stops and starts are costly. With recent changes in technology, however, printers have been reducing preparation costs, so lower circulation magazines are increasingly using gravure. Most European magazines, even those with circulations as small as 200,000, are printed on gravure.

Gravure presses are always web presses. They print only one side of a sheet at a time and generally run four-color only.

BINDING

The binding process turns a bunch of pages into a publication. Magazines may be stapled in the middle or bound like a book. The type of binding affects the way pages are organized within the magazine.

Research in Brief

When Desktop Publishing Was New

Imagine making rule lines by pressing printed tape evenly and precisely onto the page. Or creating headline type by rubbing one letter at a time onto a layout sheet. Or making type wraps by carefully measuring the number of characters to appear in each line and sending those calculations to a typesetter—a person who spent all day at a huge typesetting machine.

That was the mid-to-late 1980s. By the early 1990s, the picture had changed and graphic designers no longer had to learn drafting skills; instead, they had to learn to use the computer. The movement from hand tools to computer tools was swift and complete. Little is left of those precomputer artifacts. What was commonplace at the beginning of the 1980s was almost obsolete

a decade later. Art directors who have seen it both ways aren't so sure of the benefits of computerized design.

In the midst of the change from hand to computer—1991—Patsy Guenzel Watkins of the University of Arkansas studied the impact of computers on graphic design,[1] surveying art directors at more than 100 consumer, trade, and organization magazines.[2]

1. Patsy Guenzel Watkins, "Assessing the Impact of Microcomputers on Magazine Design" (paper presented to the Magazine Division of the Association for Education in Journalism and Mass Communication, Boston, Mass., August 1991).

2. Watkins grouped the magazines according to circulation: Group 1, circulation of half a million or more; Group 2, circulation of 100,000–499,000; Group 3, circulation of 50,000–99,999; Group 4, circulation of 20,000–49,999; and Group 5, circulation of circulations below 20,000.

(continued)

Research in Brief

When Desktop Publishing Was New (continued)

The art directors said they had moved into the new technology to save money and time, and to gain more control over the finished product. Interestingly, some said it was difficult to assess the amount of time saved because their jobs had changed with the new technology, and they were now responsible for other tasks. Many said a major impact of desktop publishing was an increased workload for designers.

The position of typesetter had been virtually eliminated by 1991, Watkins said. In addition, computers had blurred the distinctions between design and production jobs. It was less clear where the designer left off and the production manager took over. More and more designers were doing tasks that had been the domain of the production staff.

The art directors in the survey agreed that desktop technology had speeded up the production process and allowed them to experiment with different designs and ideas. "In fact, there is some sense that design skills are sharpened in this rapid evaluation of design alternatives," Watkins noted.

For all its heralded power, however, the computer has significant limitations, the art directors said. Losing the typesetter meant losing the expertise of an individual whose life revolved around type. Also, some designs were easier to create by hand. Lisa Bowser, art director of *Kansas City Live*, showed Watkins one page that took nearly 10 hours of computer time to produce; it was a complex five-color design with five overlays. That page, Bowser said, could have been done much faster by hand.

Travis Daub, design director of *FP*, entered the magazine field in the late 1990s and says production has changed dramatically since then:

Our first major change was to move from film to direct-to-plate in 1999. The second major change has been a transition to an all PDF workflow, which started in early 2004. This has resulted in saved time and money on both occasions. The next shift we're making is toward online proofing. Instead of waiting for the printer to send back physical proofs (or bluelines), we download PDFs of our proofs, print them on our own in-house printer and use that as our blueline stage. And we now produce a digital edition through Zinio, which is important to many of our international readers, who would rather not wait for their magazine to come in the mail. *FP* is a much different magazine today than it was when I started. In 1998, *Foreign Policy* published 4 to 8 black-and-white photos or illustrations in each issue. Today we use 100 or more. In 1998 we had 5 to 7 advertisements in each issue. Today we have 25 to 30. ■

---

saddle-stitch

Magazines that are saddle-stitched are stapled in the middle. All pages are placed within one another. Saddle-stitched magazines can have self-covers, which are covers that are made from the same paper stock as the rest of the magazine. *Playboy* was saddle-stitched for years to allow the reader to easily pull out the centerfold. The magazine is now perfect-bound, with the centerfold printed as a gatefold, or a foldout sheet.

perfect-bound

Perfect-bound magazines have a booklike binding; they require separate covers. Pages are stacked on top of one another, the edge is glued, and a cover attached. Cover lines, volume, and issue numbers are often printed on the spine. Magazines should be at least ⅛-inch thick to use perfect binding to allow enough surface area for the glue to work.

Perfect binding makes it easier to add inserts because they can simply be placed between two stacks of pages. However, perfect binding is usually more expensive than saddle-stitch, especially for small magazines.

Because of its perfect binding, *National Geographic* stacks easily on a shelf, and specific issues are easy to spot by reading the spine. Mike Mettler, then editor-in-chief of *Car Stereo Review*, began printing a message on the spine to his readers in 1997, one letter at a time: T-H-E M-O-B-I-L-E E-L-E-C-T-R-O-N-I-C-S A-U-T-H-O-R-I-T-Y, which was the magazine's motto. *Guitar Player* began spelling its name, also one letter at a time, on the spine in 1991. Conveniently, the name of the monthly magazine is 12 characters long.

■ SIGNATURES

Magazine pages are printed in multiples of four, with as many as 128 pages printed at one time. The sheets of multiple pages are called signatures or forms. Sheet-fed presses typically print signatures of 4, 8, 16, 32, 48, or 64 pages. Web presses typically print forms of 28, 56, 64, 96, or 128.

Both sides of the sheet are counted in the signature: A 16-page signature has 8 pages on each side. An 8-page signature has 4 pages on each side.

A typical 224-page *Better Homes and Gardens* is printed at R.R. Donnelley Printing on four 56-page signatures, using the gravure method. An additional gravure run would require at least 28 additional pages for efficiency. The production staff increases its options by printing part of the magazine on offset presses. That means print runs of 8 pages become a possibility. In fact, the regional editions of the magazine are printed offset on a regular basis.

Magazines that use limited color should use that color efficiently by placing it on the same signature. Most national magazines print the entire publication in full-color; smaller magazines don't always have that luxury. Signatures are folded, then stacked in preparation for binding. The type of binding has significant implications for placement of color.

Signatures and Color Placement

If a 64-page magazine can afford only 8 pages of color, it has several options. It can:

■ Use four 16-page signatures, with one side of one signature printed in color.
■ Use three 16-page and two 8-page signatures, with one entire 8-page signature in color.
■ Use three 16-page and two 8-page signatures, with one side of each of the 8-page signatures in color.
■ Use three 16-page signatures, one 8-page signature, and two 4-page signatures, with color on both sides of the 4-page signatures.

Smaller signatures allow the color to be placed throughout the magazine; however, they take more binding time, which will cost extra.

Binding affects the placement of color. Consider the same example of the 64-page magazine with 8 color pages:

■ If the magazine is saddle-stitched, it will have half of the pages of color at the front of the book, half at the back of the book. Every color page in the front will have a corresponding color page in the back. If the color is all in the middle signature, the magazine cannot have a color table of contents.
■ If the magazine is perfect bound, the color signature or signatures can be placed anywhere in the stack. If the color is all in one signature, it will be blocked together sequentially.

■ IMPOSITION

The way pages are printed on the signature is called the imposition. Pages are not printed sequentially; pages that follow one another in the magazine may not even be on the same signature. Imposition is determined by the binding method as well as the number of pages; it affects the placement of color. For example, a saddle-stitched magazine will have the pages from the front of the book on the same signature as the pages from the back of the book, with the first and last pages printed next to one another. Even-numbered pages are always on the left, odd-numbered on the right. Page 1, then, is a right-hand page. Figure 10.2 demonstrates the imposition for a 32-page saddle-stitched magazine printed in two 16-page signatures. Figure 10.3 demonstrates the imposition for the same magazine if it is perfect-bound.

■ IMAGE TRANSFERS

Images on the camera-ready pages are transferred directly to printing plates or cylinders. The production staff checks a variety of proofs for printing accuracy and color clarity.

camera-ready pages

These pages, almost always created on the computer, contain all finished art and type; they look essentially like the finished product, except for some final touches such as color and, occasionally, art. The computer files used to create these pages are electronically transferred to plates or cylinders.

plates or cylinders

The final step before printing is the creation of printing plates for the offset process or cylinders

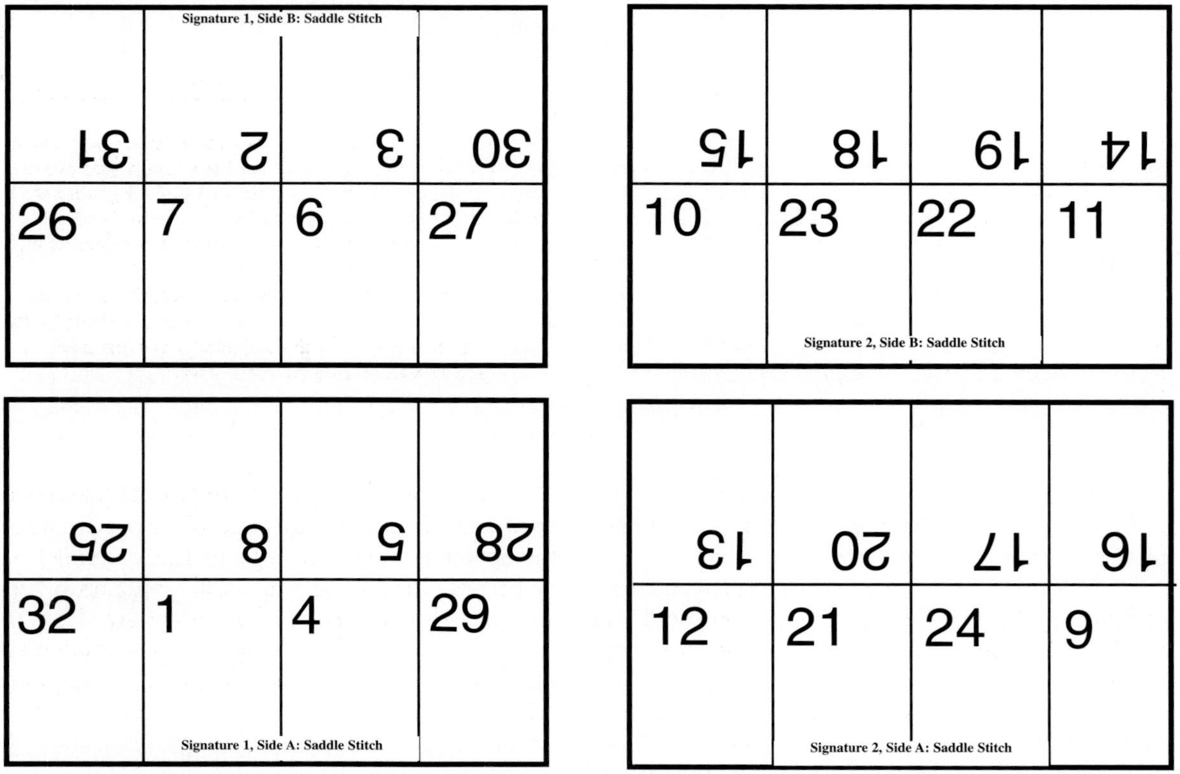

FIGURE 10.2 Signatures and Imposition: Saddle Stitch. A saddle-stitched publication places one signature within another, which means that the first and last page of the magazine are on the same signature. In this example, a 32-page saddle-stitched magazine is produced using two 16-page signatures; each signature has 8 pages on one side. Signature 1 contains the outer 16 pages of the magazine, or pages 1–8 and pages 25–32. Signature 2 contains the inside 16 pages, or 9–24. Signature 2 fits inside signature 1. Additional signatures would be placed inside signature 2.

A saddle-stitched magazine contains only one "natural" spread, that is, a spread in which the pages are actually printed side-by-side. In this case, the natural spread falls on pages 16 and 17, at the exact middle of the magazine.

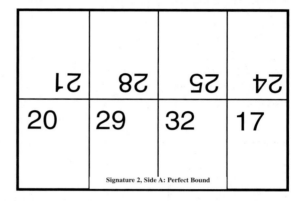

FIGURE 10.3 Signatures and Imposition: Perfect Bound. In a perfect-bound publication, signatures are placed on top of one another, which means that the first pages of a magazine are all on the same signature, and the last pages are on a different signature. In this example, a 32-page perfect-bound magazine is produced using two 16-page signatures; each signature has 8 pages on one side. Signature 1 contains the first 16 pages of the magazine, or pages 1–16. Signature 2 contains the last 16 pages, or pages 17–32. Signature 2 is placed after signature 1. Additional signatures would be placed after signature 2.

Each signature of a perfect-bound magazine contains one "natural" spread, that is, a spread in which the pages are actually printed side-by-side. A perfect-bound magazine, then, has as many natural spreads as it has signatures. In this case, the natural spread in signature 1 falls on pages 8 and 9, at the middle of the signature; the natural spread in signature 2 falls on pages 24 and 25. A perfect-bound magazine requires a separate cover.

for the gravure process. These metal plates or cylinders contain all the images to be printed. One plate or cylinder is required for every color used.

In the offset process, the metal plates have been chemically treated to repel water and accept ink. During printing, the plates are lubricated with water and then inked. All nonprinting surfaces soak up the water, and all printing surfaces accept the ink. The inked image is offset onto the rubber plate, paper is fed through the press, and the ink is then transferred to the page.

A gravure cylinder has tiny wells etched into its surface. The depth of each well determines the amount of ink to be used in a particular spot. The flow of the fluid ink is controlled by razor-thin wipers to ensure precise printing.

In the past, plates or cylinders were processed from film. Computer-to-plate (CTP) technology has eliminated the film stage. In 1993, *Family Circle* became the first magazine to create an image on a gravure cylinder without film. A year later, in 1994, *Scientific American* was the first to do so with web offset. Now it is commonplace throughout the industry

proofs

The production staff may ask for page proofs and color proofs from the printer; these come in a wide variety of forms, but with two general formats: bluelines and contract proofs.

Request for Printing Estimate

Printing costs can vary significantly depending upon paper, color, binding, art, special effects, and the printing company. The following form offers a format to use when asking a printer for a cost estimate. Large publishing houses have such a form standardized; correspondence with the printer is handled by the production staff. On smaller magazines, the editor or art director deals directly with the printer. Multiple requests for bids are usually submitted, with the printer offering the best quality at the most reasonable price being the one chosen for the job. Often, placement and use of color in the magazine changes, requiring another estimate.

Company Name: _____
Address: _____
City, State, Zip: _____
Phone/Fax: ( )_____ ( )_____
Attn.: _____

Description:

Trim Size:
Quantity:
Number of Pages:

Color:

      Cover: ____ pages process color
                        ____ pages PMS; Number of PMS colors: ____
                        ____ pages one color
      Interior: ____ pages process color
                        ____ pages PMS; Number of PMS colors: ____
                        ____ pages one color

Number of separations ____ (9×12); ____ (8×10); ____ (5×7); ____ (3×4); ____ (2×3)

Number of halftones:

Paper type:

Binding: ____ Perfect
                        ____ Saddlestitch

Proofs needed: ____ Blueline
                        ____ Contract proof

____ Camera-ready art provided
____ Disk provided
____ Material submitted electronically

Deliver to:

Blueline This shows all type and art, and is produced on light-sensitive paper in blue ink. It offers an accurate proof of the position and registration of color as well of the accuracy of binding. For magazines that use only black and white or spot colors, a blueline is the only proof they need. Most changes after this stage are expensive.

Contract Proof This shows the accuracy of color reproduction; it gets its name from the fact that it is actually a contract between the magazine and the printer that the final printed color will match the contract proof. Magazines that are mostly in color will receive an integral or composite proof—a proof of the entire piece. Magazines with limited color will get scatter or random proofs, which show only the sections to be reproduced in color.

Traditionally, art directors and editors have done press checks on the color of especially critical pages. This once meant a middle-of-the-night visit to the printing plant. Now, larger printing houses have video monitors directly on the press, allowing for remote press proofing. A printing plant in Tennessee can send the image to a production manager in New York, and all proofing can be done digitally. This often still happens in the middle of the night, though.

Advertising Proof Most advertising is delivered to magazines digitally, but publishers still often require a print proof of the ad from the client before going to press. This print proof becomes the magazine's contract with the advertiser and is the standard against which all printing of the ad is judged. If the advertiser does not provide a print, the publisher usually adds a disclaimer to the contract, saying the ad will be printed to match the ad's digital file. The contract may add that the ad will be printed in a "pleasing" color.

Standard Deviations

What's the typical size of an American magazine? Conventional wisdom holds that the average is 8.5 inches by 11 inches. As paper costs rise, however, many magazines have been reducing their page sizes, especially those printed on web presses. The digest size has become a popular for cost and marketing reasons.

A reduction in page size can be a huge budget saver. *Woman's Day* saved $500,000 a year in postage and paper by trimming ⅛ inch off its width. In the 1970s, the magazine measured the standard 8.5 inches by 11 inches. Through the years it has dwindled to 7.87 inches by 10.5 inches.

Pushing the standard dimensions too far can be costly. On many web presses, going longer than a 10.5-inch or 10.75-inch length requires a "long cut" of paper—a nonstandard roll—which can add as much as 7 percent to the cost of production. The expense can be worth it, though. *Traditional Home* measures 8.375 inches by 10.875 inches, with the longer page size being justified by the magazine's high-end audience and competition. *FP,* or *Foreign Policy,* is 8.125 inches by 10.75 inches; the magazine's staff cut ⅛ inch from the previous trim size, which had required a "long cut."

By contrast, the digest size can reduce printing costs by as much as 50 percent because it takes half the paper and half the press space, meaning 16 pages can be printed on the same cylinder or plate that will fit only 8 pages of a standard size. Added bonuses of the digest are that it can fit in existing small displays at the checkout counter that were created for crossword puzzles and smaller magazines, and it can be marketed for its handiness to readers who might want to throw it in a backpack, computer bag, or even a large pocket. The most famous magazine of this size, *Reader's Digest,* measures 5.25 inches by 7.25 inches. ■

The UPC Bar: Check It Out

All magazines sold through retail store checkout counters must have a Universal Grocery Product Council (UPC) bar. In 1975, *Family Circle* became the first magazine to use the UPC bar. At that time, UPC bars revealed only the title of the publication. Other information such as issue date and cost would come later. Now the UPC code is so universal that readers barely notice it when they scan a magazine's cover lines.

Production managers and art directors, however, pay close attention to this addition to the cover. For the store's register to read the bar correctly, it must be printed following rigid specifications, which include:

- Bars must always be 100 percent black, and black only.
- The maximum tint behind the bars must be
    yellow alone, up to 100 percent;
    magenta alone, up to 100 percent;
    cyan alone up to 10 percent;
    black alone up to 10 percent;
    combined values of yellow and magenta, up to 160 percent together; or cyan and black, up to 10 percent together.
- The preferred location is the left side of the front cover, although right is acceptable.
- Actual issue number should be on
    top for vertical bars;
    left for horizontal bars.
- Adequate quiet zone around bars (specified for vertical bar position):
    Left and right: minimum space (other than background tint) to be ⁵⁄₆₄ inches.
- No space is necessary between top and bottom of bars and surrounding image.

Each issue of a magazine has a different code, which allows magazine staffs, as well as retail outlets, to track sales of individual issues. When magazines run split covers—one cover for a specific region, for example, and another cover for a different region—tracking gets complicated. The magazine must use the same code for both covers, which means circulation managers can only tell which cover sells best by placing specific covers in specific stores and tracking sales through those stores. When the same covers are sold in the same stores, it's difficult to measure precise effects of different images. ▫

digital manipulation

A darker complexion for the O. J. Simpson mug shot on the June 27, 1994, cover of *Time*, straighter and whiter teeth for septuplet parent Bobbi McCaughey on the December 2, 1997, cover of *Newsweek*—these two examples of photo manipulation via digital computer techniques created an uproar in media circles. What are the ethical ramifications of digital manipulation? After all, it's impossible to tell when a digitized photograph has been manipulated—except by comparing it to the chemical original, or the real person or scene.

Time and *Newsweek* both used the same Los Angeles Police Department's booking shot of O. J. Simpson as the cover for their respective June 27 issues. *Newsweek*'s credit line read "Photo by Los Angeles Police Department." *Time*'s credit line read "Photo-Illustration for *Time* by Matt Mahurin. *Time*'s version had been altered, leaving Simpson with darker skin and heavier facial stubble; *Time* also reduced the size of the numbers and letters across Simpson's chest. Would the typical reader recognize that "photo-illustration" meant the original image had been altered? Was that enough of a disclaimer?

Apparently not. Side by side on the newsstands, readers could see the difference between *Newsweek*'s straight news cover and *Time*'s alteration. The president of the National Press Photographers Association called the *Time* cover "an abomination to the impact of the original truthful looking photo." Journalists charged that *Time* "had darkened Simpson's face in a racist and legally prejudicial attempt to make him look more sinister and guilty, to portray him as 'some kind of animal,' as the NAACP's Benjamin Chavis put it." One week later, *Time*'s managing editor, James R. Gaines, publicly apologized for the unintended effects of the Simpson photo manipulation. Gaines said the photo was not meant to be racist; rather, the digital manipulation was intended to shape the mug shot's "cold specificity" into "an icon of tragedy" to go with "the simple, nonjudgmental headline 'An American Tragedy.'"[1]

In 1997 *Newsweek* and *Time* both ran cover shots of McCaughey and her husband, arguably the most famous parents in America following the birth of their seven babies. Once again, two images were side by side on the newsstands and readers and media critics immediately noticed the differences in the photos. *Time*'s cover showed Bobbi with teeth that were not straight and not white. *Newsweek*'s cover had a different dental bite: small, white, and even teeth.

"The photo we decided to use had a considerable shadow over her mouth," Richard M. Smith, *Newsweek*'s president and editor-in-chief said. "The editors decided to lighten and improve the picture. In the process of doing that, the technical people went too far. The mistake was in guessing what was in the shadow and changing it." He said the *Newsweek* picture was not altered "to harm Mrs. McCaughey or deceive the reader," adding that the mistake was not similar to what *Time* did with the Simpson photo.[2]

But isn't digital manipulation still misleading, whether it's a small portion of the photo or the entire image? "There is never an instance where it is morally justifiable to alter a news photo," Tom Bentkowski, director of design for *Life*, said in 1989. "There is a grave responsibility to the reader. We should put out magazines that readers should never have to question. I think there is zero tolerance for making photos that never existed."[3]

What about removing indistinguishable blobs or background telephone wires, or touching up varying sky tones or removing a just popped-up pimple on the president's face? Most magazine editors say they won't change a news photo that is supposed to depict reality, but they agree that feature photos are more prone to manipulation. It's the difference between the unposed reality of photojournalism and the entertainment value and aesthetic sensibilities of the final page layout.

Shiela Reaves, a journalism professor at the University of Wisconsin in Madison, called magazine art directors and photo editors "ethical relativists" for

U.S. News and World Report **was the first magazine to send an entire issue of electronically composed pages, including photos, by satellite to its printers. Previously, magazines had to airmail photographs separately. The pages were scanned to create digital information, which was then transmitted; this allowed the magazine to cut its production time by 1 day. It also enabled editors to proof final pages of the September 5, 1977, issue with all graphics and text in place.**

The hologram on the cover of *National Geographic*'s **November 1987 centennial issue cost about 28 cents each, nearly five times the cost of a normal cover. The hologram featured a double laser image of the earth, one whole and one shattered, with the question, "As we begin our second century, can man save this fragile earth?" The front cover hologram filled the entire page, wrapping over the binding. On the back cover was a holographic ad for McDonalds.** *Venture*, **a travel magazine published in the 1970s, regularly featured holograms on the cover.**

indicating that there is a photo hierarchy "that allows feature photos and cover illustrations to be taken less seriously than news photos." She asked, "Do readers really understand an implicit hierarchy; news photographs are not touched, feature photographs may be retouched, and illustrations are usually retouched? Would readers agree with the underlying premises, or would they believe they are being deceived?"[4]

When celebrities are used on covers, do readers understand that changes have been made to create a cultural symbol rather than depict a regular, flesh-and-blood individual? Do readers agree that if an image is designated a "photo-illustration," then anything can and probably will be done to alter it to create the right look? Does the public perceive the difference between a satirical photo composition, such as the October 1990 *Texas Monthly* cover of Texas gubernatorial candidates Clayton Williams and Ann Richards apparently dancing together (done via computer transplants), and a celebrity feature cover, such as Tori Spelling's digital makeover in the August 1994 issue of *Details* which removed blemishes, increased her cleavage, decreased her waist, and lengthened her legs? Do we want to run the risk of readers losing faith with the graphic images that accompany magazine editorial copy?

Tom Wheeler and Tim Gleason, two journalism professors at the University of Oregon, suggest that the term "photofiction" should be applied "to any photo that has been manipulated enough during processing to change readers' perceptions of its meaning—whether material elements in the photo are altered, added, removed within the frame or re-arranged, and regardless of the method employed."[5] This would make it clear when photos have been altered and throw out such nuances as "news" versus "features" and "scenic" versus "portrait," or "photo" versus "photo-illustration." By eliminating such distinctions, the credibility of legitimate documentary photography would be protected.

Digital photography is here to stay. It's up to magazine editors and art directors to adopt strict standards for applying the technology so that readers are not mislead and photo credibility is not eroded.

the quality product

When one of the authors of this book edited a small Catholic magazine, she avoided looking at the printed product until somebody else on staff checked it over and gave it an A-OK. She worked with a tiny staff and often served as editor, designer, and production manager. By the time the magazine was printed, she had seen it in so many forms she no longer could read it clearly. No matter how carefully she had edited the magazine, however, she was terrified she might have missed something outrageous, such as a headline that used "bizarre" instead of "bazaar" or "pubic" instead of "public."

She clearly remembers the newly printed magazines arriving at the office one day when an archbishop was visiting. She watched as he opened the box, pulled the magazine out, smelled it, felt the paper, looked at the cover, turned the magazine over to see the back, then opened it up and began reading, all the while leaning up against the office refrigerator. He was so engrossed he didn't even notice her watching him. She left him to his reading, satisfied that she had done her job.

The archbishop had no idea how many mistakes the editor had caught before the magazine's final printing. The delicate pencil drawing on page 14 he was admiring had to be screened four times before it reproduced well. At one point, the printer had cropped one photograph wrong, cutting out what she wanted enlarged and enlarging what she wanted highlighted. Instead of a bucolic scene of cows, farm, silo, and barn, the page had only the

Smithsonian **magazine is largely a subscription publication, selling only 8,403 single copies despite overall circulation of more than 2 million. To beef up newsstand traffic, the magazine featured split covers in July 2005. Newsstand readers got a cover on "Inside Syria," illustrated with a news photo of Syrian political protestors, while subscribers got a more staid travel-based cover on "Mali's Elephant Highway," with colorful artwork of two pachyderms. Costs for the two runs were minimal because the magazine already has to print two versions—one with a UPC bar and one without.**

picture of the top of a silo and a lot of sky. She caught the mistake on the blueline.

What's more, the archbishop didn't care about the editor's production problems. He wanted his magazine to be of top quality and he wanted it on time. How it got that way was the editor's problem, not his.

Production is a process built on technology. Whoever is in charge of a magazine's production must know far more about printing technology than the great majority of people who roam the earth. As technology changes, the magazine staff has to change with it. And computer-generated change happens regularly and often.

But no matter how complicated the technology becomes, the bottom line on a magazine remains the readers. Jan White, award-winning designer for national magazines such as *Time*, says the reader is oblivious to the intricacies of printing. White observes:

Let's remember the fundamental truth: It is not the technology that matters, but the message. No matter how the message is produced or transmitted, it is its content that makes it useful and worthy. Recipients of communication couldn't care less about how or where the piece was produced. All they want is information, and they want it fast, to the point, easy to understand, easy to absorb, easy to use. To them, its technological provenance is immaterial.[6]

notes

1. James R. Gaines, "To Our Readers," *Time* (July 4, 1994): 4.
2. Kenneth N. Gilpin, "Doctoring of Photos, Round 2," *New York Times* (November 26, 1997): A14.
3. Shiela Reaves, "Digital Alteration of Photographs in Consumer Magazines," *Journal of Media Ethics,* vol. 6, no. 3 (1991): 176.
4. Ibid., 181.
5. Tom Wheeler and Tim Gleason, "Digital Photography and the Ethics of Photofiction: Four Tests for Assessing the Reader's Qualified Expectation of Reality" (paper presented to the annual meeting of the Association for Education in Journalism and Mass Communication, Atlanta, Ga., August 1994).
6. Jan V. White, *Graphic Design for the Electronic Age* (New York: Watson-Guptill Publications, 1988), ix.

for additional reading

Fishel, Catharine. *The Power of Paper in Graphic Design.* Gloucester, Mass.: Rockport Publishers, 2002.

International Paper Staff. *Pocket Pal,* 19th ed. Stamford, Conn.: International Paper, 2005.

Johansson, Kaj, Peter Lundberg, and Robert Ryberg. *A Guide to Graphic Print Production.* Indianapolis, Ind.: Wiley Publishing, 2002.

Kenly, Eric, and M.S. and Mark Beach. *Getting It Printed*, 4th ed. Cincinnati, Ohio: How Design Books, 2005.

chapter 11

**magazine
legalities:
understanding
the law**

chapter

Editors don't need to be lawyers. Many of the legal issues involved in publishing a magazine can be handled adequately and safely by editors because many legal decisions are also common sense editorial decisions. At the same time, though, publishers and editors need to understand enough about the specifics of the law to know when they need to call in their lawyer to help. Those decisions—whether to go it alone because good editing is also good law, or to seek outside help because an editor knows she is in risky territory—require editors to pick up a working knowledge of the basics of the law of publishing. These basics include an understanding of laws and key decisions related to censorship prior to publication as well as punishment for publication or distribution following publication. Because of guarantees under the Bill of Rights, most restrictions on content are imposed following publication and arise in the form of torts—civil litigation that is resolved through payment to the injured party. These torts include libel, invasions of privacy, and intentional infliction of emotional distress. In addition, those working for magazines must also be familiar with the legal aspects of third-party liability, copyright, and obscenity.

THE PROGRESSIVE

November 1979 $1.50

The H-bomb secret

How we got it— why we're telling it

NOVEMBER 1979: Although the federal government got a prior restraint order to stop *The Progressive* from publishing its article about the technology of hydrogen bombs, the piece eventually ran because other magazines printed similar articles about the H-bomb; the injunction against *The Progressive* became moot and the government dropped its case.

access to information

Information is at the foundation of good magazine journalism, and government at all levels is a trove of information. But while the First Amendment guarantees the right of magazines to publish information they have, it does not guarantee their right to access to information.

Generally, court decisions have recognized journalists' constitutional rights of access to information are no greater than the rights of the general public. Whether it is government documents, public meetings, or crime scenes, magazine writers can expect to be treated as any other person seeking access. Chief Justice Warren Burger summarized the law this way: "There is an undoubted right to gather news from any source by means within the law, . . . but that affords no basis for the claim that the First Amendment compels others—private persons or governments—to supply information."[1] Trespass laws; restrictions on access to government property such as military bases, jails,[2] and prisons; and police orders blocking admission to the scenes of accidents or disasters[3] all apply to journalists just as they apply to ordinary citizens. For example, in *Wilson v. Layne*, the Supreme Court of the United States found that media representatives had no right to enter the home of a man being served an arrest warrant, even though they were accompanying police on what is commonly known as a "ride along."[4]

■ FAIR ACCESS

A corollary to the principle that journalists have no greater right of access, however, can work to a magazine reporter's advantage; that is, the First Amendment requires that journalists be treated fairly in decisions granting or denying access. For example, *Sports Illustrated* assigned reporter Melissa Ludtke to cover the 1977 World Series between the New York Yankees and the Los Angeles Dodgers, but she was denied access to the Yankee clubhouse to interview players after a game because of a rule in the major leagues at the time that female reporters would not be allowed into locker rooms for postgame interviews. She and *Sports Illustrated* sued Bowie Kuhn, the commissioner of major league baseball, and a federal court ruled she must be given access.[5]

In another case, however, a denial of access was permitted under the First Amendment. *The Nation*'s White House correspondent was denied a press pass that was essential for covering the White House. The Secret Service, however, refused to give a reason for its decision, insisting that its policy was never to explain why it denied press pass requests. A federal appellate court ruled the First Amendment dictated that the Secret Service must at least give an explanation for the denial and give the applicant, Robert Sherrill, a chance to respond to the decision. The Secret Service complied, explaining that Sherrill's previous conviction for physically assaulting the press secretary of the governor of Florida motivated its decision. His application was still denied.[6]

A special First Amendment right of access is found only in the court system, where the U.S. Supreme Court has ruled broadly that the First

Amendment does guarantee journalists access to nearly all stages of criminal prosecutions—trials,[7] jury selection,[8] and pretrial hearings.[9]

PROTECTING SOURCES

Many states have provisions that protect journalists during the news gathering process. Currently, 49 states and the District of Columbia have laws that protect journalists from revealing confidential sources. These laws, referred to as "shield laws," protect journalists from liability when gathering information of a sensitive nature, including information that could be used in prosecuting criminals. Currently, this protection is not granted to journalists who are served a subpoena to appear before federal grand juries, though legislation is pending in Congress that would create a federal shield law, protecting confidential sources in all federal cases.

The debate over whether journalists have a constitutional right to protect confidential sources came to the forefront in 2005 when Judith Miller of *The New York Times* and Matthew Cooper of *Time* magazine were called to testify before a federal grand jury investigating the leak of top secret information about Valerie Plame, a former CIA agent. While Matthew Cooper was immediately released by his source to testify before the grand jury, Judith Miller was not released and refused to reveal her source. The courts, in turn, found no constitutional protection for journalists to protect anonymous news sources, and held Miller in contempt of court. She served 3 months in jail before agreeing to name her source.

The protection of confidential sources also became an issue during a high-profile libel case in 2005. In *Price v. Time, Inc.*,[10] Mike Price, the former head football coach for the University of Al-

In his September/October 1998 premiere issue of *Gear*, a magazine for young men, editor and publisher Bob Guccione Jr. gushed, "The exciting thing about starting this magazine is that we have no idea where we're going." He—and his fact checkers—also had no idea where "King of the Wild Frontier" Davy Crockett was born. It wasn't in Crockett, Texas, as stated in an article about then-Texas Governor George W. Bush and his political aspirations. Pioneer scout Crockett was "born on a mountain top in Tennessee."

abama, sued *Sports Illustrated* for libel. Price contended that an article published by *Sports Illustrated*, about his drunken adventures at a strip club followed by sexual encounters with two women at a hotel, was false and defamatory. As part of the discovery process, Price asked the court to make the *Sports Illustrated* reporter reveal the names of four confidential sources in the story. The reporter argued that Alabama's state shield law protected him from having to disclose the names. The Eleventh Circuit Court of Appeals ruled that the Alabama shield law, as written, protected newspaper, television, and radio journalists but not magazine reporters. The court also ruled, however, that a qualified First Amendment privilege protected the journalist's sources in this case. (See the libel defense section for additional discussion regarding privilege.)

Magazine writers, like all journalists, are not protected from publishing material they have gathered illegally—for example, intercepted from a cell phone conversation, stolen from a private business, or taken without permission from a government office. They are, however, allowed to publish material without chance of repercussion if a third party illegally gathered the materials, then turned them over to the journalist for publication. In two cases involving the nationally syndicated columnist Drew Pearson,[11] the Second Circuit Court of Appeals ruled that even though Pearson had received information obtained illegally from U.S. Senate staffers and employees of the think tank Liberty Lobby, he could not be held liable for intrusion or trespass and was permitted to reprint the material.

It is important to note that individuals illegally obtaining information, whether citizens or journalists, can and have been prosecuted for the act of gathering news. In 1988, a civilian analyst working for the U.S. Navy Intelligence Support Center received a 2-year jail sentence for selling classified photos of a Soviet aircraft carrier to the British magazine *Jane's Defence Weekly*.[12]

■ FREEDOM OF INFORMATION ACT

Because the First Amendment generally does not guarantee journalists access to government information, Congress and the state legislatures have responded with freedom of information statutes to designate many government records as being open to the public. The federal Freedom of Information Act (FOIA) was passed by Congress in 1966 to establish a basic assumption that federal records are open to the public, and that a closure of records must be justifiable under the law. It applies only to the executive branch of the federal government and covers paper and computer records held by federal agencies.

The exemptions in the law that allow some records to remain closed are typical of freedom of information laws at all levels. In the federal law, the exemptions are as follows:

1. *National Security*—Information that could damage the national interest if released can be withheld.
2. *Agency Rules and Practices*—Records of little or no public concern do not have to be released when they deal solely with internal personnel rules and practices, such as parking, filing procedures, sick leave, or use of the cafeteria. The point is to spare agencies from maintaining such records in a condition suitable for public inspection.
3. *Statutory Exemptions*—The so-called catch-all exemption allows Congress to declare in other laws that information is exempted from the FOIA.
4. *Confidential Business Information*—Trade secrets and confidential commercial information required by law to be submitted to the government can be withheld to prevent industrial espionage.
5. *Agency Memos*—The "executive privilege" exemption protects working drafts of documents from being released. That way, government executives have the benefit of frank and open comments and recommendations from staff members that otherwise might be watered down if the drafts were read by the public before a final decision was made.
6. *Personnel, Medical, and Similar Files*—Government records about individuals can be withheld from the public if releasing them would create an invasion of personal privacy.
7. *Law Enforcement Investigations*—Information compiled for law enforcement purposes can be kept closed if releasing it would compromise an ongoing investigation. Examples of such records include the identity of confidential informants, protected law enforcement techniques or practices, and information that must be kept secret to protect a defendant's right to a fair trial.
8. *Banking Reports*—Like trade secrets, information that federally regulated financial institutions must file by law is exempted.
9. *Oil, Gas, and Water Well Information*—Geological data about wells are exempted to prevent land speculators from easily getting information that was expensive for drilling and extraction companies to develop.

The most common way to use the FOIA to get a document is to write a letter to the Freedom of Information (FOI) officer at the agency that possesses it. The letter should emphasize that the request is being made under the FOIA and should describe the document in as much detail as possible. It also helps to state forthrightly that the request is being made for journalistic purposes so a quick response is important. Federal agencies are required under the law to acknowledge requests within 10 days, although it usually takes much longer for them to produce the documents.

Good samples of FOIA request letters can be found from organizations that support freedom of information causes, such as the Reporters Committee for Freedom of the Press in Arlington, Virginia, and the Society of Professional Journalists Project Sunshine in Greencastle, Indiana. Most states also have local FOI organizations that can lend a hand with FOIA requests or problems. Today, most federal government departments and agencies allow citizens to make FOIA requests through forms provided on agency websites.

In 1996, Congress passed EFOIA (Electronic Freedom of Information Act) amendments that mandated federal government departments and agencies to provide aides to locate records they hold and provide access to commonly requested documents via electronic (online) reading rooms.[13] These reading rooms provide magazine journalists with millions of documents that can be used as the foundation for important news stories on topics from education to low-income housing to the environment.

State open records laws and their exemptions are comparable to the federal law in their structure and content, though they can differ widely from state to state. There is no substitute for reading the law in a particular state to be familiar with the exemptions it allows. In every state, it is as important to know what records are exempted under the law as to know what is covered. Many state statues have exemptions comparable to the federal exemptions. Law enforcement information and personal privacy in medical or personnel records are

the most common exceptions, but state laws tend to allow many other exemptions as well, with the number of exemptions to state open records laws often running to more than 20.

■ SUNSHINE LAWS

State open meetings laws are also important access tools for magazine journalists covering public affairs. All 50 states have laws, often called sunshine laws, requiring that meetings of public bodies such as city councils or state boards be open to the public. Strong state sunshine laws explicitly state

Freedom of Information Act After September 11, 2001

Since the passage of the Patriot Act shortly after the September 11, 2001, terrorist attacks on the World Trade Center and the Pentagon, federal government departments and agencies have been more likely to restrict access to information. The Patriot Act of 2001 allows broad restrictions to information that could be used for the purposes of terrorism.

On October 12, 2001, U.S. Attorney General John Ashcroft sent a memo to federal agencies suggesting they should be more restrictive in access to federal government information. While the previous FOIA directive encouraged the dissemination of information, the post-September 11 memo en-

couraged restriction. Decisions, the memo stated, should be "made only after full and deliberate consideration of the institutional, commercial, and personal privacy interests that could be implicated by disclosure of the information."[1] In addition, the new FOIA memorandum informed agencies that the Department of Justice would back up any FOI decision that had a "sound legal basis," rather than the earlier, more stringent standard of "foreseeable harm." As early as October 20, 2001, the *Houston Chronicle* reported that the National Imagery and Mapping Agency "stopped selling large scale digital maps to the public through its websites."[2]

As a result of the Patriot Act, administrators at federal government departments and agencies have reclassified documents as "secret" or "top secret," making them exempt from FOIA requests, and removed information previously available from public databases and websites. For example, OMB Watch, a nonprofit public interest organization in Washington, D.C., reported in 2005 that the Department of Defense has "discontinued access to the hundreds of documents in its Defense Technical Information Center (DTIC) library," and the Office of Environmental Safety and Health at the Department of Energy, "is not allowing users to search its website."[3] ■

1. http://www.usdoj.gov/oip/foiapost/2001foiapost19.htm.

2. Freemantle, Tony, "Curbing Our Right to Know: Environmentalists Decry Removal of Useful Information from Web in the Wake of Terrorist Attacks," *Houston Chronicle* (October 20, 2001): A1.

3. http://www.ombwatch.org/article/articleview/213/1/1.

which groups are covered by the law, require public notice before a meeting is held, and prohibit public officials from conducting business at informal or social gatherings. They typically allow for meetings to be closed when a body is discussing real estate transactions, lawsuits, or personnel issues, but the strong statutes require that the final vote on all decisions be taken in open session. Help with open meeting complaints can usually be found from state attorneys general's offices and from state FOI organizations.

■ ACCESS TO INFORMATION DURING WARTIME

The U.S. government has regularly restricted information during times of war, including access to material about troop movements, military construction projects, and strategy plans. In recent years, magazine journalists have also challenged regulations governing access to soldiers during wartime.

During the Persian Gulf War, *The Nation,* along with several small magazines and newspapers claimed in court they had been denied access to government-established press pools, and therefore, denied firsthand access to the war.[14] The federal district court in this case ruled that, because the restrictions (and the war) had ended before they heard arguments, no decision could be made. *The Nation's* legal point was moot.

Larry Flynt, publisher of *Hustler* magazine, also took the federal government to court to gain access to soldiers during the war in Afghanistan. Flynt argued that *Hustler's* journalists had a constitutional right of access to troops in that country. The United States District Court for the District of Columbia disagreed in 2004 when they ruled against Flynt, noting that "there is no constitutionally based right for the media to embed with U.S. military forces in combat."[15]

In 1996, the United States District Court for the District of Columbia ruled that the government has the right to restrict access to Dover Air Force Base in Delaware where casualties of war enter the country.[16] Even in the face of such rulings, citizens and journalists continue to seek access to government information during wartime. In October 2004, a suit was filed under the FOIA in federal district court requesting copies of photographs and video of the flag-draped coffins of soldiers killed in Afghanistan and Iraq that were being transferred at the Dover base.[17]

prior restraints

A basic principle under the First Amendment is a ban on prior restraints, meaning a government representative—a police chief, a judge, or any other censor—cannot review material before publication or have wide discretion in deciding what should not be published. Thus the origin of the phrase: Prior restraint is a restraint prior to publication.

The injustice of such a system seems obvious to journalists, writers, and editors. Prior restraint keeps an idea, a fact, or an opinion from ever getting into the hands of readers. It flies in the face of the First Amendment ideal of a public free to inform themselves and then to make decisions based on the information they have. Because the free flow of information was always seen as important to civic, political, and commercial life in the United States, American law has always favored punishment after publication for articles that were libelous, invasive of someone's privacy, or in some other way deserving of liability.

The United States Supreme Court first ruled the prior restraint of media content unconstitutional in the 1931 case *Near v. Minnesota.*[18] In this case, Jay M. Near, the publisher of a small, controversial weekly newspaper in Minneapolis, Minnesota, published a series of scandalous articles using ethnic slurs, defaming city leaders, and calling into question whether police and those running other city services were corrupt. Instead of suing Near for libel, the city leaders demanded the newspaper be enjoined, immediately halting its publication. State courts agreed the newspaper could legally be enjoined, basing their decisions on a state law that allowed for any publication that was "obscene, lewd, lascivious, malicious, scandalous, or defamatory" to be ruled a "public nuisance" and shut down.[19] Near challenged this ordinance, saying it was an unconstitutional infringement on his free press rights. The Supreme Court agreed, ruling that the Minnesota state ordinance was designed not just to punish publications acting improperly, but to prevent them from publishing altogether. This was an unconstitutional prior restraint on a free press.

In 1963, the U.S. Supreme Court reinforced this belief, noting that a prior restraint challenged in court faces "a heavy presumption against its constitutional validity."[20] So the threat of prior restraint is rare, but it is not unheard of these days. Examples from three areas where magazine editors and publishers have run into problems—national security, the administration of justice, and unequal taxation—help illustrate the dangers of prior restraints and the general rule that gag orders against magazines are not usually upheld by appellate courts.

■ NATIONAL SECURITY

For national security reasons, *The Progressive*, a leftist political magazine, was ordered in 1979 not to publish an article about the technology of hydrogen bombs. Editors had titled the piece "The H-Bomb Secret: How We Got It; Why We're Telling It" and said they were publishing the article to spark a national debate about nuclear arms policy.

Before publication, though, the editors sent a copy to the federal Department of Energy for help in fact-checking the technical information about atomic physics. Without returning the article, Energy Department officials contacted the Justice Department, which sought an injunction from the federal court in Madison, Wisconsin, where the magazine was published, claiming that the article contained information classified as secret under the Atomic Energy Act.

The Progressive's editors argued in court that the article was based on information taken from public records that the writer, a freelancer, had compiled after many of hours of research in libraries and at national research laboratories. But the judge, applying a test taken from a 1971 Supreme Court case (in which the high court had denied the government's request for a prior restraint)[21] ruled that the publication must be blocked because it presented "grave, direct, immediate and irreparable harm to the United States."[22] The judge conceded that the article was not a "how-to" piece about hydrogen bombs, but he said the article's synthesis of all the available information could make it easier for a medium-sized country or a terrorist organization to develop nuclear weapons.

The case was never decided by an appellate court because in the months after the judge issued the injunction, other writers, incensed by what they considered the heavy-handedness of this prior restraint, prepared similar articles. Newspapers and magazines eager to flout the court's injunction published them. These publications undermined the federal government's argument that the publication of the H-bomb story would cause grave danger, and made the injunction against *The Progressive* moot. The government, subsequently, dropped the case, and *The Progressive* ran "The H-Bomb Secret" in its November 1979 issue.

■ ADMINISTRATION OF JUSTICE

Another case in 1996 illustrates the prior restraint risk when a magazine disrupts the smooth administration of justice. Through a combination of good reporting and good luck, *Business Week* acquired documents from a high-profile civil fraud case between two large corporations in 1995. Unknown to *Business Week*, though, the documents, which were fairly standard filings in a court case, had been sealed by order of a judge to protect the interests of the two corporations. In other words, the papers were not available for public viewing at the courthouse.

After obtaining the papers, *Business Week* called each side in the lawsuit for comments, but the lawyers for the corporations promptly ran to a judge seeking a restraining order. Just 3 hours before *Business Week*'s weekly deadline, the district judge faxed a restraining order to the magazine's offices forbidding publication of the article. On appeal, the federal circuit court quickly struck down the prior restraint order, but also took advantage of the case to lay out some important principles about prior restraints.[23]

First, the court emphasized that judges must not drag their feet when considering prior restraints. With a magazine blocked from publishing an article by court order, there is no time for a deliberate judicial process of holding hearings and gathering evidence. The court said all other matters should be cleared from the docket so the prior restraint can be considered on an emergency basis.

Second, the appeals court said the judge should not have issued the restraining order without giving the magazine's lawyers a chance to argue their position. The order against *Business Week* was issued after the judge had talked only to the corporations' lawyers.

Government Censorship and *The Masses*

The 1917 Espionage Act, which allowed the United States postmaster general to declare unmailable any publications that interfered with the war effort led to the death of *The Masses,* a socialist magazine produced by an editorial cooperative. The Espionage Act primarily was directed at the left-wing socialist press, which tended to advocate pacifism or noninterventionalism during World War I. Administered by the Post Office Department, the act made it a crime to oppose the government and the war; any opposition to conscription or censorship could be construed as obstruction:

> Whoever, when the United States is at war, shall willfully make or convey false reports or false statements with intent to interfere with the operation or success of the military or naval forces of the United States or to promote the success of its enemies and whoever, when the United States is at war, shall willfully cause or attempt to cause insubordination, disloyalty, mutiny, or refusal of duty, in the military or naval forces or the United States, or shall willfully

obstruct recruiting or enlistment service of the United States, to the injury of the service or of the United States shall be punished by a fine of not more than $10,000 or imprisonment for not more than 20 years, or both.[1]

The Espionage Act essentially voided the First Amendment and the right to disagree with the U.S. government.

The Masses was radical and irreverent for its time. It was critical of war, racism, sexism, and religion, and it supported free love, birth control, and divorce. Understandably, there were no advertisers. Many libraries refused to subscribe to it or even give it shelf space. Contributors to *The Masses* included John Reed, Amy Lowell, Sherwood Anderson, Bertrand Russell, Max Eastman, Walter Lippmann, Carl Sandburg, Pablo Picasso, and Upton Sinclair. Although editors and writers worked without pay, contributors had full control over their work, a luxury they didn't enjoy at other magazines.

When the August 1917 issue was barred from the mails by the postmaster general, the magazine's editors found few newsstands or bookstores will-

ing to carry *The Masses.* They feared that they, too, could be shut down and found guilty of trading with the enemy.

The Masses stopped publishing in December 1917, and five editors went on trial for personally violating the Espionage Act. They were charged with conspiracy against the government and with unlawfully and willfully obstructing the recruitment and enlistment of the soldiers in the armed forces. Articles in *The Masses* supporting conscientious objectors, editorials calling on President Woodrow Wilson to repeal conscription, and anti-war cartoons (one showed a skeleton measuring a military recruit) were the government's exhibits at the trial.

Fortunately, content was decided collectively at monthly meetings where editors and visitors voted on what would be in the next month's issue. This haphazard editorial approach made it difficult for the government to prove a conspiracy to disrupt the war effort existed on the part of the magazine. The trial resulted in two hung juries before the case was dropped.

Was the outcome a victory for free speech? It was a small start. Although the constitu-

---

1. Kirk Heinze, "Left-wing Tragedy or Comic Opera? A New Look at the Demise of *The Masses*" (paper presented at the annual meeting of the Association for Education in Journalism and Mass Communication, Boston, Mass., August 1980).

And finally, the appeals court emphasized the difference between a restraining order in a run-of-the-mill court case and one issued against a magazine forbidding publication. Ordinary restraining orders are issued by courts when there is a threat of irreparable injury that the court wants to prevent. But in the case of a prior restraint, the risk arising from the publication must be even more grave than a threat of irreparable injury. The court said: "Publication must threaten an interest more fundamental than the First Amendment itself."[24]

The *Business Week* case reiterates the "heavy presumption" courts have against prior restraints and stands for the proposition that while prior restraints issued by judges against magazines are rare, prior restraints upheld by appellate courts are rarer still. The *Business Week* example also shows the hurdles built into the law to keep prior restraints rare.

■ UNEQUAL TAXATION

The courts have also been quick to erect a barrier between governmental taxation and media businesses when that taxation is targeted and may cause the prior restraint of some kinds of content while giving freedom to others. For example, the

The April 11, 1938, issue of *Life* was banned in more than 50 locations, including Boston, Chicago, Brooklyn, Memphis, Savannah, New Orleans, all of Pennsylvania, and Canada. The controversy was over the publication of photos from an educational film titled *The Birth of a Baby*. All charges of obscenity and/or decency eventually were dismissed. A Gallup poll later showed that 76 percent of the American public approved of the story.

Supreme Court ruled in 1987 that generally applicable tax law must be enforced fairly against all magazines or the law violates the First Amendment. In that case, the monthly *Arkansas Times* challenged a law that required general interest magazines to pay a state sales tax while religious, sports, professional, and trade magazines paid no sales tax at all.

The Supreme Court sided with the magazine, ruling that the tax scheme unfairly singled out some publications while letting others off. The Court said the First Amendment did not prevent states from taxing magazines, but it did require that taxes on magazines be applied in a neutral way, without considering their editorial content. The Court said the First Amendment prohibits government from burdening one kind of editorial viewpoint or content with a tax while favoring another with a tax break.[25]

The Court reaffirmed this principle in the 1989 case *Texas Monthly, Inc. v. Bullock*.[26] This case revolved around a Texas state law that exempted religious publications from the state's general sales tax. *Texas Monthly*, a general interest magazine, challenged the law in court, arguing that this exemption violated the First Amendment by unfairly discriminating against secular content as well as promoting religious practices. The Supreme Court agreed and struck down the law as unconstitutional.

While the Supreme Court has consistently ruled that taxation cannot be targeted to suppress a certain kind of content, it has allowed taxation by medium. For example, it is constitutional to make cable television providers pay a tax, while other media are exempt as long as the taxation does not "present the danger of suppressing particular ideas."[27] In 1995, the Pennsylvania Supreme Court applied this concept to magazines when they ruled that a law establishing a general sales tax for magazines but not newspapers was constitutional.[28]

magazine distribution and sales

As in prior restraint cases, the courts have consistently ruled that hindering the distribution of media content after it has been created is also unconstitutional. In 1938, the United States Supreme Court heard the first case involving the distribution of literature. In *Lovell v. City of Griffin*,[29] Alma Lovell, a Jehovah's Witness, argued that a city ordinance "prohibiting the distribution, without a permit, of circulars, handbooks, advertising, or literature of any kind"[30] was an unconstitutional infringement on her First Amendment rights. While Mrs. Lovell based her arguments on the freedom of religion clauses, explaining that distributing her biblical pamphlets was a form of preaching that did not require a permit from the city manager, the Supreme Court of the United States ruled in her favor on much broader grounds. Chief Justice Charles Evans Hughes, quoting from an earlier court decision, explained: "Liberty of circulating is as essential to that freedom as liberty of publishing; indeed, without the circulation, the publication would be of little value."[31]

The Supreme Court has ruled, however, that it is constitutional to implement a city ordinance that targets the selling of all products, including magazine subscriptions. In 1948, Jack Breard was arrested in Alexandria, Louisiana, for selling magazines door-to-door. He was later convicted under a law that prohibited all such soliciting in the town. In his defense, Breard asserted that the law violated his constitutional rights because as a magazine subscription salesman he was protected by the First Amendment's guarantee of a free press.

The case went all the way to the United States Supreme Court, where the justices ruled against Breard's interpretation of the First Amendment. The court declared that when a general law such as this one is applied to magazines, it does not violate the First Amendment because the effect of the law falls evenly on the magazine subscription seller and the vacuum cleaner seller alike.[32]

In 2004, the Tenth Circuit Court of Appeals extended this restriction on solicitation to phone calls made to private homes. A year earlier, the Federal Trade Commission (FTC) and Federal Communication Commission (FCC) created a Do-Not-Call registry that barred those engaged in commercial speech—selling things—from calling the homes of those properly registered on the Do-Not-Call list. Nonprofit organizations and political candidates were exempted from the rules.

Following the implementation of the new program, several telemarketing firms brought suit against the FTC, which oversees the registry. These businesses claimed their First Amendment rights to freedom of speech, and the rights of potential consumers to listen, had been violated by the new agency regulations. The Tenth Circuit Court of Appeals disagreed, stating that the Do-Not-Call registry was constitutional as created. Residents could choose to "opt-in" to the program or listen to the commercial speech offered by the telemarketers. The rules, therefore, did not "restrict any speech directed at a willing listener."[33] In addition, this rule, like the ordinance in *Breard v. Alexandria*, was consistent with other limits placed on commercial transactions by the courts.

libel

One of the biggest legal problems facing magazines today is libel. Attorneys' fees can be astronomical because cases can last more than a decade, and the threat of losing a multimillion dollar judgment creates a "chilling effect" on the way a magazine exercises its right to publish. It is so serious that some editors have decided that it is easier and cheaper not to run controversial pieces than to raise the specter of a libel suit: It's good business to avoid the risk—even though it might be bad journalism.

Libel means publishing a false statement about a person that hurts the person's reputation in the community. Of course, responsible writers and editors never intend to run a false statement in their magazines, but potential libels crop up in every issue. Every article, photo, cutline, title, and illustration that runs in a magazine should be evaluated for their libel risks, no matter how routine they are.

To win a libel suit, a plaintiff must prove: publication (the statement was published), identification (the statement was of or concerning the plaintiff), defamation (the statement lowered the reputation of the plaintiff), falsity (the statement was not true), and fault (the publisher was at fault).

■ PUBLICATION

To be libelous, a statement must be communicated to someone other than the writer and the person it is written about. That is easy to prove when the article is published in a magazine. A statement doesn't have to be published to a large audience to meet the requirement of libel law, however. An e-mail from a writer to an editor could be the basis of a libel suit if the e-mail includes defamatory statements about another person. The e-mail would be "published" for the purposes of the law the minute it went from the writer's hands into the editor's hands because it went to a third person.

Magazines are also responsible for libelous statements they "republish," such as libelous quotations included in an article. A magazine is responsible even if the writer is simply repeating verbatim the words of a source. If a source says, for example, that investigators are sure Jones committed fraudulent stock dealings, the source has defamed Jones. But the writer commits a new libel by including the direct quotation in an article about the investigation. The potential of legal action arising from the republication of a libel is increasing as more and more magazines acquire content from syndicated services.

■ IDENTIFICATION

Damage to reputation is a personal offense. For a statement to be libelous, it must be made about a specific individual or, as the courts ask, Was the libel "of or concerning the plaintiff"? People are most obviously identified by their names, although courts have ruled that individuals can also be identified by their nicknames or job titles. Many libel cases arise from the misidentification of individuals. To avoid confusion about the identity of people, editors like to use middle initials, ages, job descriptions, titles, and other specific information in articles. Fact-checking to make sure all these small facts are scrupulously correct is an important part of preventing libel by misidentifying a person.

Research in Brief

Fact-checking Is More Than a "Fetish of Facticity"

In 1891, a boy rode the New York City rails going through both Grand Central and Penn Stations, according to the short story "The Boy on the Train" by Arthur Robinson. Wrong, said a *New Yorker* fact checker. Why? Because neither station existed in 1891. Ever vigilant, the fact checker hunted down 19th-century railroad schedules to correct those and other details. Presented with the facts, the writer made the necessary changes to his story before it

(continued)

Fact-checking Is More Than a "Fetish of Facticity" (continued)

ran in the April 11, 1988, issue of *The New Yorker*.[1] Of course, fact checkers at *The New Yorker* also verify the obvious, such as the latest population figures for Sweden or the number of homeless people in Manhattan who stayed overnight in shelters during Thanksgiving.

Fact checkers are the gatekeepers of truth at magazines, with responsibility for verifying every name, number, and quote in a story before it is published. Should they fail in their job, a magazine will suffer the consequences of diminished respect from readers who expect accuracy and fairness in articles and from advertisers who want to be associated with a reputable product. Fact checkers offer some legal protection against lawsuits due to the paper trail that grows from every verified fact, but it's not an absolute one.

Editors who have dozens of fact checkers on staff—*Time, Newsweek, The New Yorker, Reader's Digest, Rolling Stone,* and *National Geographic,* among others—believe a magazine's credibility is enhanced by the existence of such a department. There may be as many as one fact checker for every three writers or correspondents, and more than $1 million a year may be budgeted for fact checker salaries alone at a large weekly magazine, says sociologist Susan P. Shapiro, who studied fact-checking at three large weekly magazines—two general news magazines and one specialized sports publication—in 1990.[2]

Magazines that can't afford to have a slew of fact checkers on board because of budgetary restraints still care about accuracy. Editors there, however, will involve the entire editorial staff in the verification process, from editor-in-chief down to editorial assistant. Small magazines tend to trust the writers to get it right. A copy editor still checks for inconsistencies and misspelled words in the article, but without the extensive double and even triple checking of material that occurs in some fact-checking departments, where nothing is taken for granted.

Some trade magazines use professional peer review as a fact-checking mechanism, and a few even run routine accuracy checks with sources after the article has been published. Others have lawyers read each article before it goes to press. At most consumer and trade magazines, however, legal review occurs only if a fact checker or editor requests it because of concerns about libel, privacy, or potentially sensitive assertions.

Shapiro's report about the "long, tedious, ambitious, very expensive, and labor-intensive operation that saps the energy of scores of young journalists every week" reveals that fact checkers do more than verify straightforward assertions such as a person's name or title and unambiguous facts such as an individual's birthplace or age or the number of floors in a building. Contrary to popular thought, they are not obsessed with mindless nit-picking nor do they have a "fetish of facticity." Rather, they also "contribute valuable intelligence to questions of subjective fact, the kinds of questions that editors often agonize over and that can put a publication's reputation at risk." Shapiro writes:

> They painfully struggled over more subtle questions: Is the evidence credible? Does it support the conclusions drawn? Is the datum or quotation presented in the appropriate context? Is a word being misused or does a vague turn of phrase permit an inaccurate interpretation? Does a sequence of verified facts lead to a false conclusion? Is an assertion fair and balanced? Does the story show all sides of the controversy?

Shapiro shadowed fact checkers from morning until late at night—spending 16-hour

1. "Check the Facts: Fact Checking at *The New Yorker*," the *New Yorker* Education Program (1988).

2. Susan P. Shapiro, "Caution! This Paper Has Not Been Fact Checked! A Study of Fact Checking in American Magazines" (New York: Gannett Center for Media Studies, 1990).

Research in Brief

Fact-checking Is More Than a "Fetish of Facticity" (continued)

days—as she read, observed, and listened to their formal and informal interactions with writers, editors, and the computer screen. After spending more than 5 weeks studying fact checkers, Shapiro argues that their "ritualistic methodological routines" make it possible for magazines "to move through an extraordinary empirical morass on deadline."

Shapiro estimates that fact checkers pause—stop and evaluate an item—three times per column inch: "Half the words ultimately printed in an average story generate a pause." She says the fact checkers she studied investigated every item for accuracy.

About 16 percent of the pauses are clearly objective matters such as names, titles, and other proper nouns and their spelling (even if the reference is to the president of the United States, it is checked); 35 percent of the pauses are over relatively objective questions such as number, place, or date, which are slightly more difficult to verify; 24 percent are for less objective questions such as descriptions of people or events that may have fewer

authoritative sources for verification or which are comparative statements; and finally, 25 percent of the pauses are for subjective questions, the gray area that includes statements of feelings, future predictions, loaded adjectives, analogies, and qualifications that "lack a firm evidentiary basis." Shapiro says fact checkers spend more effort evaluating those subjective concerns than they do on routine objective ones.

What is the result of all this fact checking? Shapiro reports that the items generating more than half of the pauses (56 percent) are judged accurate, proper, or acceptable. That's to be expected since so many pauses are for clearly objective or relatively objective matters. But more significant, she says, is that more than one-third of the items causing pauses (32 percent) are found to be wrong (statements for which it is generally obvious how they ought to be corrected) or improper (the choice of remedies is problematic).

Fact checkers, writers, and editors (who have the final say on disagreements between the fact checker and the writer)

have four basic options when they find a problem: leave it as it is, change it, cut it, or kill the story. The last option seldom occurs, Shapiro says, and even cuts are limited. "Editorial surgeons are more apt to repair the damaged organ than to excise it," she points out. Consequently, most stories are changed by the addition of information for clarification or a change in wording.

Shapiro concludes that "other news media could benefit from magazine-like fact checking" to decrease the number of inaccurate accounts. She says the argument that fact-checking is a luxury for weekly or monthly publications doesn't hold up: She found that "most magazine stories are written, edited, and checked in the last 48 hours before publication, often requiring fact checkers to work the equivalent of a full-time job in two days' time." Finally, she adds, fact-checking not only ensures accuracy, but it is an important part of the editorial process because it's clear that fact checkers see both the forest and the trees. ■

People also can be identified by their photographs, so using a generic file photo to illustrate a story can be risky if the story contains any statement that might be construed as applying to a person who can be clearly identified in the picture. For example, using a file photo of a man under arrest to illustrate an article about the effects of plea bargaining on the courts could be libelous if the pictured man was never charged with a crime. The implication of a story about plea bargaining is that the man in the photo entered a guilty plea as part of a bargain for a reduced sentence.

As a rule, members of a large group of people, such as "all the students at the university" or "all the patients treated by Dr. Kilroy," cannot claim they were libeled unless they have been personally identified. For example, several businessmen in Butte, Montana, sued *Time* over a story in the September 22, 1975, issue that said arson was common in the city. The businessmen owned two buildings that had burned accidentally; the *Time* article said the local economy was so depressed that owners had taken to burning buildings to collect the insurance. The owners were not identified in any way in the article, and the Montana Supreme Court ruled there were too many people who owned burned buildings in Butte for the plaintiffs to assert that the article referred to them.[34] There is no hard-and-fast number for the group identification rule, but usually in groups of more than 25 people, individuals would have a hard time convincing a court they were identified if an article refers only to the group as a whole.

In the final analysis, whether a person is identified or not boils down to a simple proposition: Do the people who know the plaintiff understand the statement, whether a story or photo, to refer to the plaintiff?

■ DEFAMATION

A story damages a reputation if the false statement in it exposes the person to hatred, ridicule, or scorn among the members of the community. That can happen in any number of ways, such as false reports that a person was charged with a crime, carries the AIDS virus, is an alcoholic, or filed for bankruptcy. False accusations that a person is insane or mentally ill have traditionally been found by courts to be libelous.

Former senator and presidential candidate Barry Goldwater sued *Fact* magazine over an arti-

Photographer Annie Leibovitz sued Paramount Pictures for copyright infringement after they used her *Vanity Fair* cover of a nude and pregnant Demi Moore in an ad for the movie *Naked Gun 33-1/3: The Final Insult.* The advertisement, which appeared in *Sports Illustrated* and other magazines in 1994, featured actor Leslie Nielsen in the same proudly pregnant pose as Leibovitz's controversial 1991 photo. The judge ruled that because the ad was a parody, it fell under fair use protection and was not copyright infringement because it was commentary and clearly a satire.

cle during the 1964 presidential campaign that said Goldwater was paranoid, anti-Semitic, sadistic, and uncertain about his sexuality. The jury found the statements, which Goldwater proved false, to be damaging to his reputation.[35]

Similarly, a false statement that a person is sexually promiscuous is libelous, as an action against *TV Guide* illustrates. When author and TV personality Pat Montandon agreed to appear on a talk show, the talk show's producers submitted a blurb to *TV Guide*: "From Party Girl to Call Girl? How far can the 'party-girl' go until she becomes a 'call-girl' is discussed with TV personality Pat Montandon, author, 'How to Be a Party Girl,' and a masked anonymous prostitute!" *TV Guide* edited the item in its September 14, 1968, issue in such a way as to make Montandon sound like the only guest on a program about call girls: "From Party Girl to Call Girl. Scheduled guest: TV Personality Pat Montandon and author of 'How to Be a Party Girl.'" Testimony at the trial showed that average readers would conclude that Montandon had gone from being someone who liked to have fun at parties to being a prostitute. The jury awarded her more than $250,000, and an appeals court upheld the verdict.[36]

In 2003, *Sports Illustrated* ran a feature story on Mike Price, the University of Alabama's head football coach. The story alleged that Price accompanied members of his team to a topless bar in Pensacola, Florida, then brought two women back to his hotel room for sex. *Sports Illustrated* reported that Price and his female companion "started screaming 'Roll Tide,' and he was yelling back, 'It's rolling baby, it's rolling.'"[37]

Price was subsequently fired by the University of Alabama for inappropriate behavior. Price sued *Sports Illustrated*'s parent company Time, Inc., for $20 million in damages for defamation, claiming that while he did attend the strip club, he never engaged in sex with the women in his hotel room. The case was settled out of court in 2005.

But not every statement that makes someone angry is libelous, even though the plaintiff may feel it impugns his reputation in his profession. When *Newsweek* criticized Professor Stanley Kaplan's criminal law class at Stanford Law School as "the easiest five credits" at Stanford University, the professor sued. The *Newsweek* article reported that some students listened to the lectures over the radio while sunning by the pool and that two students took the exam while wearing top hats and sipping champagne. In 1985, the Ninth U.S. Circuit Court of Appeals ruled that the statements did not damage the professor's reputation for integrity or his ability as a teacher.[38]

■ FALSITY

Like the requirement of fault discussed in detail in the next section, the requirement of falsity in a libel case is dependent on the status of the plaintiff—is she a public or private figure? If the plaintiff is a public figure, she must prove the statement is false. If the plaintiff is a private figure, then she must only prove falsity when the matter addressed is of legitimate public concern. In all other cases involving private person plaintiffs, the media defendant must prove truth.

How does a plaintiff prove truth or falsity in a libel case? First, he or she must show the false statement is at the heart of the libel. For example, an article could contain many false statements, none of which are libelous or has a bearing on the libel that lowers the reputation of the plaintiff.

Carol Burnett's successful libel lawsuit against *National Enquirer* for falsely reporting that she was drunk and quarreled with former Secretary of State Henry Kissinger in a Washington, D.C., restaurant resulted in a $1.6 million award in 1981 to the comedian. Burnett proved the article was published with the knowledge that it was false or with reckless disregard for the truth. Although the appeals court slashed the size of the award, Burnett eventually settled for an undisclosed sum in 1984, which she used to establish the Carol Burnett Fund for Responsible Journalism to foster research, teaching, and public discussion of journalism ethics at the University of Hawaii in Honolulu.

Second, the court is looking for substantial truth, not exact statistical fact. In a case involving the *American Medical News*, a doctor sued the publication for libel when it reported he was being sued for stock fraud. In fact, the doctor was being sued for making deceptive statements related to stock trading. The court, in the case, said the comments were not perfectly accurate, but were substantially true.[39]

■ FAULT

Some confusion about libel comes from a series of U.S. Supreme Court decisions in the 1960s and 1970s to make the law of libel conform with the free press guarantees of the First Amendment. In the first of those cases, *New York Times v. Sullivan* in 1964,[40] the Supreme Court introduced the principle that, in addition to showing reputational damage, identification, and publication, libel plaintiffs who are public officials must show the defamation was published with actual malice, that is, with the publisher knowing it was false or with a reckless disregard for the truth. The actual malice rule, the Supreme Court reasoned, would require plaintiffs to prove that the publisher's decision to print the libelous statement was so outrageous that the publisher did not deserve First Amendment protection.

Before *New York Times v. Sullivan*, a publisher could lose a libel suit just because the defamatory statement got into print, whether by an innocent mistake or malicious intent, whether the damage to the plaintiff's reputation was great or slight. In the *Sullivan* case, the court recognized that there will be errors that creep into print as part of robust public debate, but some of them, while serious enough to injure a potential libel plaintiff, are not so serious that the First Amendment should allow the publication to lose a libel suit.

Following *Sullivan*, the Court extended the actual malice rule to "public figures," those persons who by their prominence affect public debate about public issues. Then, in 1974, the Supreme Court took advantage of the case of *Gertz v. Robert Welch, Inc.*,[41] to distinguish the treatment of public officials and public figures as opposed to private figures in libel law. In that case, Elmer Gertz, a prominent lawyer in Chicago, sued *American Opinion* over an article that described him as a key player in a worldwide communist conspiracy to undermine the authority of American police. After a Chicago police officer killed a young child and was convicted of murder in the case, Gertz represented the child's family in a civil lawsuit against the officer. The article in *American Opinion*, the monthly magazine of the John Birch Society, described Gertz as a communist and said he had a long criminal record. Both accusations were false, and both fell into those categories of aspersions that courts have traditionally found to be libelous. So Gertz sued.

In *Gertz*, the Court pointed out that the actual malice rule was originally applied to public officials because they have such influence on the outcome of public issues. Then it was extended to public figures for the same reason. In *Gertz v. Robert Welch, Inc.*, the Court said that public-figure libel plaintiffs have voluntarily thrust themselves into the center of a public debate with the objective of influencing its final outcome. Such people are not public figures all the time, but they can be public figures if they sue for libel over an article about their public issue. These limited-purpose public figures must also prove actual malice to sue for libel.

But Gertz himself, the Court ruled, was not a public figure for purposes of the *American Opinion* article. He only had taken on a client—an everyday activity for a lawyer. He had not inserted himself into the debate about police authority and social order that *American Opinion* had written about. So requiring Gertz to bear the heavy burden of proving actual malice on the part of the magazine struck the Court as too harsh. Private figures like Gertz, the justices reasoned, should not have to endure harsh public criticism in order to protect the First Amendment ideal of public discussion.

Nevertheless, it seemed to the Supreme Court that Gertz's suit could have a chilling effect on *American Opinion*, just as Sullivan's suit had on *The New York Times* if he had to prove only defamation, identification, and publication. So it didn't seem reasonable to let Gertz go forward with his libel action without showing some level of fault on the part of the magazine. To solve the conflict, the Court struck a compromise by ruling that private figures like Gertz, those people who have not made themselves part of the public discussion about a public issue, must show only that the defamatory statement was published negligently.

public officials

Public officials for purposes of libel are fairly easy to identify, thanks to the several public official libel cases American courts have heard through the years. The clearest test for defining a public official came out of the 1966 case of *Rosenblatt v. Baer*, where the U.S. Supreme Court said public officials are government employees "who have, or appear to the public to have, substantial responsibility for or control over the conduct of governmental affairs."[42] Elected officials and officials who control the use of public funds will almost always be considered public officials. But court decisions throughout the United States have applied the Supreme Court's test to find that public officials include school superintendents, county medical examiners, financial aid directors at public universities, and law enforcement officers and agents.

public figures

Public figures can be a little more slippery to define. The *Gertz* case made clear, though, that public figures come in two categories: all-purpose public figures and limited-purpose public figures.

All-purpose public figures are those whose influence over public issues is both broad and ongoing. For example, in the first case to extend the actual malice rule to public figures, the U.S. Supreme Court ruled in *Curtis Publishing Co. v. Butts* in 1967 that a high-profile football athletic director at the University of Georgia must prove actual malice on the part of the *Saturday Evening Post* to win his libel action against the magazine. Athletic Director Wally Butts, who was not paid with public funds, was sufficiently prominent to be a newsworthy figure in all regards.

All-purpose public figures are rare, though courts around the country have found that celebrities as diverse as comedian and television personality Johnny Carson, political pundit William F. Buckley, and actor Carol Burnett are all-purpose public figures. General Colin Powell and the Reverend Jesse Jackson, for example, might be safe bets to be all-purpose public figures, as would others of comparable renown.

Notoriety and celebrity do not necessarily make a person a public figure, however. For example, in 1976, the U.S. Supreme Court found that Mary Alice Firestone, a high-profile Palm Beach socialite, was not a public figure in her libel suit against *Time*. *Time* ran a "Milestones" piece stating inaccurately that Mrs. Firestone's husband, Russell Firestone, heir to the Firestone tire fortune, had been granted a divorce on grounds of cruelty and adultery. In reality, the court had not given a reason for granting the divorce, even though evidence of adultery and cruelty was presented at trial. So Mrs. Firestone sued for libel.

The Supreme Court ruled that for purposes of her divorce Mrs. Firestone was not a public figure even though she was a prominent member of Palm Beach high society. Although she held news conferences during the divorce trial and subscribed to a news clipping service to keep track of her mentions in the media, the Supreme Court said she was just like all other people forced into court to dissolve her marriage. She otherwise held no position of special prominence in public affairs, the Court said.[43]

Similarly, a person's standing as a public figure can fade as his prominence fades. In a case against *Reader's Digest*, the Supreme Court held in 1979 that a man who received substantial news coverage in 1958 for refusing to testify before a grand jury was not a public figure for purposes of a *Reader's Digest* book published 16 years later. Ilya Wolston refused to testify during an investigation of Soviet spy activities, but did not voluntarily thrust himself into the spotlight. After the controversy, he returned to his anonymous station in life until he was brought into the public eye again by *Reader's Digest* in its 1975 book, *KGB: The Secret Work of Soviet Agents*.[44]

Limited-purpose public figures, the Supreme Court explained in the *Gertz* case, are those people who voluntarily insert themselves into an existing public issue in hopes of influencing its outcome. They might otherwise be considered anonymous citizens, although as a practical matter many of the limited-purpose public figures identified by courts in libel cases have been well known. The key factors have been that a public controversy existed and the plaintiff had voluntarily entered the controversy in hopes of affecting its resolution.

Elmer Gertz was a good example of a person being widely known in certain circles, but for purposes of his libel action he was not a public figure. The Supreme Court acknowledged that Gertz was a prominent attorney who had represented controversial clients in Chicago. He also had served without pay on a city board, and he had published articles on local affairs. But because Gertz had not tried to influence public opinion about the police officer's murder trial that *American Opinion* wrote about, he was a private figure in his libel action, the Court ruled.

actual malice

Editors publish a libelous statement with actual malice, the Supreme Court said, when they knowingly publish an out-and-out lie or when they publish an article even though they have a serious doubt about its truth or accuracy. In the *Butts* case, the *Saturday Evening Post* was found to have published its article "Story of a College Football Fix," in the March 23, 1963, issue, with actual malice when it said Athletic Director Wally Butts of the University of Georgia intentionally lost a football game against the University of Alabama in exchange for a huge payoff. The Court chastised the magazine because it made no effort to verify the article, even though the freelancer said he uncovered the conspiracy only after he was inexplicably tapped into a telephone conversation between Butts and the Alabama coach. To make matters worse, the writer had a police record for fraud, yet the magazine showed no skepticism toward his work. Working with a longer deadline, the Court noted, a magazine is also in a much better position to verify facts than a wire service, which has deadlines around the clock.[45]

In Senator Goldwater's case against *Fact*,[46] a federal appeals court found the magazine had published its accusations about Goldwater with actual malice when evidence during the trial showed the publisher and managing editor agreed

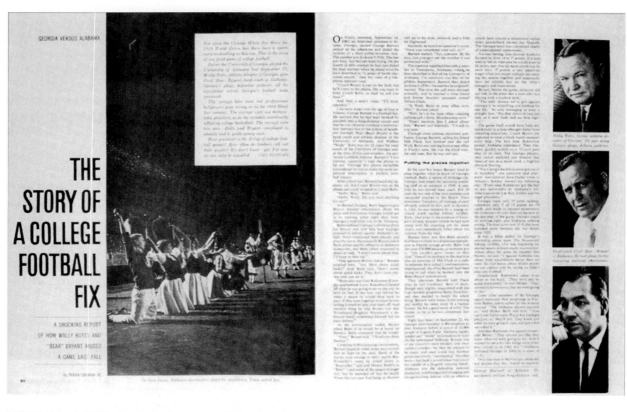

MARCH 23, 1963: The Supreme Court ruled that *The Saturday Evening Post* had published a libelous statement in "The Story of a College Football Fix" when it said Athletic Director Wally Butts of the University of Georgia intentionally lost a football game against the University of Alabama in exchange for a huge payoff.

to attack Goldwater as mentally unstable long before they started researching the articles. Their accusations were not based on their consultations with mental health professionals, and they altered psychiatrists' answers to questionnaires to make them look more critical of Goldwater than they really were.

However, in a case important for magazine writers and editors, the Supreme Court ruled in 1991 that altering direct quotations was not evidence of actual malice. Psychoanalyst Jeffrey Masson sued *New Yorker* writer Janet Malcolm, alleging that she defamed him by changing and rearranging his own words to make them sound more damaging than they were originally in the interviews. The quotations in Malcolm's article, which ran as a two-part profile in the December 5 and December 12, 1983, issues of *The New Yorker*, had Masson calling himself an "intellectual gigolo" and "the greatest analyst who ever lived." He said she exaggerated his words in a way that made him look irresponsible, vain, unscholarly, and dishonest.

The Supreme Court did not find the alterations to be libelous, though. It said all writers alter quotations to some degree, whether it is to insert punctuation, correct grammatical mistakes, or clean up sloppy diction. Words within quotation marks are often incomplete or inexact, so only those alterations that create defamatory meaning where none existed would constitute actual malice. Malcolm maintained that the quotations were accurate.[47]

negligence

The Supreme Court has said that libel plaintiffs who are ordinary citizens—not public officials or public figures—should be able to win a libel suit more easily than public officials or public figures. Because they haven't voluntarily entered public life, they can't be expected to endure the same kind of criticism public officials and public figures must endure. Private figures must show, however, that a libelous story was published with negligence. That means that a private-figure libel plaintiff must prove that the writers and editors who published the story did not prepare the piece with the level of professional care and behavior usually used for that kind of story.

One academic study of negligence in libel found three ways courts have found journalists to be negligent:

1. They fail to contact the person who is being defamed, unless there was a thorough investigation otherwise.
2. They fail to verify information through the best sources available.
3. There is an unresolved disagreement between the source and the writer over what the source told the journalist.[48]

Actual malice and negligence have been topics of debate and discussion by media professionals, attorneys, and legal scholars. But for editors worried about meeting a production deadline, they can be demystified to a simple rule: In preparing and editing all stories, insist on fairness and accuracy, without exception and without failure.

■ LIBEL DEFENSES

The law recognizes several defenses to charge of libel. These defenses do not guarantee that a magazine won't be sued for libel. The mire of a libel suit can be long and dirty before it gives the defendant the chance to present defenses to a judge and jury. In many cases, too, these defenses may give a magazine only partial protection from losing a libel suit by serving only to reduce the damages the magazine must pay. Nevertheless, understanding the defenses to a libel claim should help editors think through a libel problem.

truth

Truth is the first defense to a libel suit. If a published statement is true, by definition it is not libelous, even though it may damage a person's reputation. For an editor to rely on the truth defense, however, it is essential that each statement be provable in court, and that is how editors should think about every statement of fact in an article: Is there solid evidence to back up what the writer is saying? At the same time, though, errors in in-

significant facts, that is, facts that don't change the gist of the story if they're wrong, will not sabotage a truth defense.

fair comment and criticism

A second defense to a libel charge is that the statement was published as a fair comment or criticism. The law of libel allows public expression of opinions about public events and issues because it is in society's best interest to encourage open debate and discussion on public matters. Many articles and opinion columns operate under this protection. A bill to be introduced in Congress, a recently published book, or a controversial candidate for governor all can be commented on because each in its way was presented to the public for viewing and discussion.

The key technicality for claiming that a libelous opinion is justified by the fair comment and criticism rule is that the article, column, or review must outline all pertinent facts before the opinion is stated. In other words, each article or column should contain within it the answer to the question: "How did the writer come to hold this opinion?" It's not enough for a restaurant reviewer to opine that a new restaurant serves bad food and has lousy service. The reviewer must also explain why: Was the food cold? Were the rolls stale? Were the water glasses left unfilled? Was the calamari burned? If an editor can't find the facts underlying the opinion in the review, then the column needs to be rewritten.

Of course, because libel is meant to punish false statements, it should go without saying that the factual statements underlying the opinion must be true and accurate. Simply stated, however, the key to the fair comment and criticism defense is that every reader should be able to understand why the writer reached the opinion being offered.

privilege

The courts have recognized through the years that there are times when it is in society's best interest to excuse an admittedly libelous statement and let it go unpunished. Such libelous statements are said to be "privileged." Privileged statements generally are those taken from a government meeting or document and reported in an accurate and balanced article. Privileged libelous statements might be found in testimony given under oath during a court proceeding in which a witness accuses another person of a crime. They might be accusations made at a legislative hearing alleging corruption in the state's low-income housing agency. To rely on the privilege defense, editors must make sure several conditions are met:

- The libelous statement must be taken from an official meeting or document. In some states, the privilege also applies to nongovernment meetings that are open to the public to discuss an issue of public concern.
- The article must be balanced. That is, people libeled in the public meeting or document must be given a chance to respond in the article, even if they were not at the meeting to offer a public rebuttal.
- The article must be a fair and accurate report of what happened at the meeting. The writer cannot sensationalize or distort the libelous comment or the role it played in the meeting as a whole.
- Some states also require that a magazine publish the statement without any malice toward the person defamed to make sure that the magazine and its editors are truly motivated by their duties to inform the public about public business rather than by a desire to get even or bring down the defamed person.

statute of limitations

A state's deadline for filing a lawsuit, called a statute of limitations, is a sure-fire defense, because if a plaintiff lets the time lapse, a court will refuse to hear the case. In most jurisdictions, the statute of limitations is 1 or 2 years. Most states start clocking the statute of limitations on the first publication of the libelous statement, so a later publication, distribution, or display of a libelous article cannot be used to calculate the plaintiff's deadline for filing.

A libel action against *Hustler* in 1984 illustrates a quirky aspect of statutes of limitations for magazines with national distribution. Kathy Keeton, associate publisher of *Penthouse,* sued *Hustler* for a series of articles and cartoons, including a cartoon that charged that *Penthouse* publisher Bob Guccione infected her with a sexually transmitted disease. Keeton, a resident of New York, did not file her suit in time to sue *Hustler* in its home state of

Ohio, so she filed in New Hampshire, which had a longer statute of limitations. On appeal, the U.S. Supreme Court permitted the case to go forward, ruling that *Hustler*'s circulation of 10,000 to 15,000 issues in New Hampshire was enough to permit the libel action to go forward in New Hampshire courts.[49]

invasions of privacy
....

The right to privacy is the right of people to be left alone or to control the way they are portrayed to others. As a legal action, the right to privacy takes many forms, each of them significantly different from libel. Like libel, however, the law of privacy sets a minimum standard of acceptable behavior for magazines. And as in libel, writers and editors can prevent most legal problems by acting ethically or responsibly in gathering, writing, and packaging their articles.

The right to privacy consists of four different legal offenses:

- Publishing embarrassing private facts.
- Intrusion into an individual's sphere of privacy.
- Publishing offensive information that portrays an individual them in a false light.
- Appropriating a person's name or likeness for commercial gain.

■ EMBARRASSING PRIVATE FACTS

An article can be a legal invasion of privacy when it contains information that would be highly offensive to a reasonable person and is not legitimately newsworthy. Unlike libel, private facts are true. For example, in 1942 *Time* was found to have published private facts about Dorothy Barber when it ran an article in its March 13, 1939, issue about her medical condition—a strange eating disorder that allowed her to eat constantly without ever gaining weight. *Time* also published a photo of her taken against her wishes as she lay in her hospital room.[50] A court found the article and photo, published under the headline "The Starving Glutton," were both highly offensive to a reasonable person and not of legitimate public concern.

Barber's win in court, however, was not representative of the outcome in most private facts

One Way to Prevent Libel Suits: Be Polite

One way to prevent a libel suit is to be polite and respectful when a person calls with a complaint about a story. A study by the University of Iowa Libel Research Project found that before libel plaintiffs filed a lawsuit, all they really wanted was some satisfaction. Most of them simply wanted the publishers to admit their mistakes and apologize for the hurt they caused. When the plaintiffs didn't get that, they called their lawyers.[1] The lesson from the Iowa study is significant: When editors or writers get complaints alleging a libelous inaccuracy, they should take it seriously. The study recommends following these guidelines to keep a complaint from becoming a libel action.

- *Don't insult the caller; don't talk condescendingly; and don't hang up.* That may sound simple, but complaining phone calls have not always been warmly received by journalists.
- *Don't let writers handle complaints about their own stories, and don't let editors or designers handle complaints about their own titles or page designs.* Writers, page editors, and designers have too much invested in their work to be expected to talk dispassionately with an angry caller. Have the next editor up the chain of command—one not directly involved in the article—take the call.
- *If it is a problem that cannot be resolved in one conversation or if there is a question that should be investigated, tell callers an editor will phone them back—then make sure one does.* Don't leave an angry caller waiting more than 1 day.
- *If, after some investigation, supervising editors find there was an error in an article, writers and editors need to support them when they tell the caller that the magazine is sorry.* The management should get the right information—verifying it as carefully as an editor would verify a writer's story—and promptly prepare an accurate and carefully worded correction, admitting the error and taking responsibility for it. Hidden mistakes might be exposed later before an unsympathetic jury.
- *If an internal investigation proves the story was accurate, don't cram it down the complainer's throat.* Calmly explain the facts, the supporting evidence, and the reliability of the sources. Standing behind a writer's story doesn't mean adding insult to the injury the caller already feels.
- *If it's appropriate, the editor or managing editor may offer an angry caller a chance to write a brief rebuttal piece.* The editor can explain, of course, that the rebuttal will have to be edited to comply with style rules and libel laws and to fit the allowed space.
- *If a caller mentions the word "lawsuit" or "lawyer," immediately pass the call on to the top editor.* Those editors get paid to handle the really hot items. ■

1. Randall P. Bezanson, Gilbert Cranberg, and John Soloski, *Libel Law and the Press: Myth and Reality* (New York: Free Press), 1987.

cases. In fact, few plaintiffs win private facts cases, although those most likely to prevail sue over a revelation about their health or hospitalization.

An important defense in private facts cases is the simple fact that the information is "newsworthy." Courts have defined "newsworthy" broadly, often leaving it up to editors to decide whether a fact is newsworthy or not. For example, a federal court in California ruled for *Sports Illustrated* in 1976 in a private facts case filed by Michael Virgil, one of the most well-known surfers along the California coast. The *Sports Illustrated* article said

Virgil ate insects, dived head first down stairs to impress women, and extinguished cigarettes in his mouth. It also said he intentionally hurt himself to collect unemployment payments so he would have free time for surfing. The court ruled that the disclosures of Virgil's bizarre behavior were based on more than morbid fascination or voyeurism; they were a journalistic attempt to explain to readers Virgil's aggressive and daring surfing style.[51]

An old case against *The New Yorker* also illustrates that once people are newsworthy, they remain newsworthy for purposes of a private facts lawsuit. On August 14, 1937, *The New Yorker* ran a piece about William James Sidis. Twenty-seven years earlier, Sidis had been a child prodigy who lectured in the Harvard University math department when he was 11 years old. *The New Yorker* article described Sidis as being reclusive and eccentric, living in a disorderly apartment surrounded by his collection of streetcar transfers. When Sidis sued, a federal appeals court ruled he was still newsworthy.[52]

The American Society of Journalists and Authors keeps freelance writers informed about the latest contract information relating to magazines, newspapers, and electronic publishing. The website, "ASJA Contracts Watch," is a free service and can be accessed at http://www.asja.org/cw/cw.php.

■ INTRUSION

Invasion of privacy by intrusion might be compared to trespassing. The difference is that trespass is a criminal violation and intrusion is a civil cause of action, but both involve entering a place not open to the public. The classic case illustrating intrusion involved a *Life* reporter and photographer who were invited into the home of a "healer" under the pretense that they wanted medical care. As the healer examined the woman for breast cancer, the photographer used a small camera to record the session. After their article ran in the November 1, 1963, issue, "Dr." Dietemann sued for intrusion. In 1971, the federal appeals court found for Dietemann, ruling that his den, where he received his patients, was a private place in which he could determine who would control who saw or heard him practicing his brand of medicine.[53] The court said: "The First Amendment has never been construed to accord newsmen immunity from torts or crimes committed during the course of news gathering. The First Amendment is not a license to trespass, to steal, or to intrude by electronic means into the precincts of another's home or office."[54]

Unlike private residences, places of commercial business have generally been considered open to the public, and thus, not the basis for successful intrusion suits. In a 1995 hidden camera case, undercover reporters for the television news program *Prime Time Live* videotaped a segment at an eye clinic where doctors were suspected of performing unnecessary cataract surgeries. The owners of the clinic sued for intrusion, but the courts found no violation, ruling that there was no expectation of privacy in a business that solicits customers onto its premises.[55]

Technology is making it easier for writers and photographers to "intrude" on people by tape-recording conversations or shooting pictures from far away. As a general rule, people in public places can be photographed or tape-recorded without concern for intrusion. A person who can be seen by the public must accept the risk that actions or words may be captured in some form and passed along through publication.

But photographers, some of whom are notorious for their antics to get a good photo, can cross the legal line if they hound or harass their subjects. Some states, like California, have recently passed laws that allow large damage awards to plaintiffs hounded by overzealous paparazzi, but aggressive news gathering and confrontational interviewing alone are not considered intrusion in most states.

■ FALSE LIGHT

Invading privacy by placing a person in a false light often stems from publishing offensive statements or photos out of context. Stories that embellish the facts or leave out important facts run the risk of putting people in a false light. In one false light case, for example, *Life* published an article in February 28, 1955, about the link between an actual crime and the Broadway play, *The Desperate Hours*, it inspired. A family was held hostage in their home by escaped convicts for many hours. While the experience was difficult, the convicts actually treated the family well and released them unharmed. But *Life*'s article presented photos and a description of the play, saying the Hill family had been "besieged" in their home but that they rose to heroic heights to defend themselves. The Hills sued, saying they were not intimidated by the convicts, nor did they fight off the intruders as the *Life* piece portrayed. Lower courts supported the Hills' false light claim, but the U.S. Supreme Court reversed the decision for other reasons in 1967. The Court did not find for *Life* because the Hills were wrong in their false light claim; rather, the Supreme Court said false light claims must be proven with the same actual malice required by *New York Times v. Sullivan.*[56]

In a false light case against *Penthouse*, a federal appeals court ruled in 1982 that a former Miss Wyoming of 1978 could not sue because of the magazine's 1979 fictional story about a Miss Wyoming who twirled batons during the talent portion of the beauty contest and who levitated her coach as she performed a sexual act with him on national television. The court said the real Miss Wyoming, who had also twirled batons as her talent in the contest, was not put in a false light because readers would recognize the story as pure fantasy.[57]

False light cases often arise from the use of stock or generic photos with fresh editorial content. For example, *Boston Magazine* ran an article titled "The Mating Habits of the Suburban High School Teenager." Along with the article, the magazine editors included a photo of five students at a high school prom. The caption stated the photo was taken as part of a project on teen sexuality. One young woman in the photo sued for false light privacy, arguing that the combination of the article, caption, and her photo made her falsely appear to be promiscuous.

The court ruled that if the woman did not in fact behave in a sexually promiscuous manner, this article did indeed place her in a false light.[58] However, the case was dismissed due to the fact that the magazine also ran a disclaimer saying the individuals pictured were unrelated to the people or events described in the article. In this case, the disclaimer saved *Boston Magazine* from a potentially expensive lawsuit. Better editorial judgment, however, would have kept this case out of the courts altogether.

■ APPROPRIATION

The privacy offense of appropriation is usually a greater problem for advertisers than it is for magazine editors. Appropriation is the unauthorized use of a person's name, picture, or voice to endorse a commercial product or service. Appropriation cases most often arise from celebrities who have value in their names or likenesses that can be exploited by others for commercial gain. Celebrity magazines that make their profit from photographing and interviewing those in the limelight, however, cannot be sued under this tort as long as the articles or photos used are broadly defined as newsworthy.

Courts have also said magazines can use newsworthy photos on their covers and in their advertising for upcoming issues without fear of litigation. For example, *New York* won an appropriation action brought by a man who participated in the city's famous St. Patrick's Day parade. A freelance photographer took a picture of the man, and *New York* ran the photo on its cover. In 1971, the New York Court of Appeals said the picture was newsworthy because the parade is of broad public interest to New Yorkers.[59]

In a well-known case involving magazine promotions, *Holiday* successfully resisted an appropriation claim by actress Shirley Booth. The magazine had run a photo of Booth at a Caribbean resort as part of a travel story. It later republished the photo as part of its advertising for the magazine. Booth sued, but a New York court ruled in 1962 that the later use of the photo to promote the magazine was not appropriation as long as its purpose was to illustrate the content and quality of the magazine.[60]

intentional infliction of emotional distress

In the 1980s, plaintiffs who wanted to sue magazines over what they published changed strategies because libel and privacy became more complex and harder to prove. One alternative was to sue for "intentional infliction of emotional distress," meaning the plaintiff alleged that the magazine's conduct was so outrageous that it was outside any bounds of decency and that it was intolerable in civilized society. Many of these cases were brought against television news organizations, but two cases against *Hustler* illustrate how intentional infliction of emotional distress works. They also stand for another important principle: Few if any magazines have ever lost a case for intentional infliction of emotional distress.

In the 1986 case of *Ault v. Hustler*,[61] an antipornography activist, Peggy Ault, sued *Hustler* after being named the magazine's "Asshole of the Month." She sued *Hustler* for libel, invasion of privacy, and intentional infliction of emotional distress. The federal district court in Oregon, where she brought the suit, dismissed the claim, saying intentional infliction of emotional distress was just an attempt to sue *Hustler* for the libel twice by using another name for the offense. Some humiliation is sure to accompany the damage to reputation that is the basis of libel, but the humiliation and emotional distress cannot be separated from the libel to be the foundation of a different cause of action, the court ruled.

The U.S. Supreme Court resolved a similar case against *Hustler* in 1988 when the Reverend Jerry Falwell sued over a parody meant to portray him as a hypocrite.[62] *Hustler* ran a piece in the November 1983 issue patterned after a popular ad campaign of the time in which celebrities described the "first time" they tasted Campari Liqueur. The Campari ads always played on the sexual connotation of the "first time" theme.

Under the headline "Jerry Falwell Talks About His First Time," *Hustler* ran the televangelist's picture and a made-up interview in which he described his first sexual experience as a drunken encounter with his mother in an outhouse. The interview also said Falwell always got drunk before he preached a sermon. At the bottom of the page was a tiny footnote: "Ad parody—not to be taken seriously." It was typical *Hustler* fare: cheap, raunchy, and exaggerated to the point of being incredible. It wasn't libelous, because it was such an unbelievable insult; it wasn't an invasion of privacy because it was so obviously false that it was not revealing a private fact or putting Falwell in a false light before the public. But the parody certainly was outrageous, so it made a good foundation for an action for Falwell's suit based on intentional infliction of emotional distress.

The high court readily agreed with Falwell that the parody was repugnant. But the Supreme Court also pointed out that the ad parody contained important political opinions that deserved constitutional protection. Obviously, it was not meant to describe actual events in Falwell's life, but it was intended to criticize his political ideas, which he actively promoted through the 1980s, especially his attacks on pornography and lax sexual mores.

Poisonous or Precious: Parodies Pay Off

The editors at *Reader's Digest* weren't upset when *Mad* magazine published its parody, "Reader's Disgust," with a table of contents that promised a two-page condensation of the *Encyclopedia Britannica*.

"It really began to dawn on us that we weren't just any magazine," wrote the editors in the 75th anniversary issue of *Reader's Digest*. "Reach a certain level of acceptance and you're in for a lot of ribbing. Ac-

tually, we enjoy the jokes—whether it's a parody from *National Lampoon*, or that episode of 'The Simpsons' where Homer gets so head-over-heels smitten with the 'Reading Digest.'"[1]

1. The Editors, "How a Little Magazine Went Around the World," *Reader's Digest* (75th Anniversary Issue, 1997): 20.

Poisonous or Precious: Parodies Pay Off (continued)

If imitation is the sincerest form of flattery, then parodies are the most amusing. Three magazines have tickled funny bones over the years with their comical and satirical material: *Harvard Lampoon*, *National Lampoon*, and *Mad*.

Harvard Lampoon produced the earliest magazine parodies, which were locally distributed as undergraduate humor publications on the Harvard University campus and on Cambridge, Massachusetts, newsstands. Before *Harvard Lampoon* became a national phenomenon, spoofs were published of the *Saturday Evening Post* in 1912, *Popular Mechanics* in 1920, *Town and Country* in 1923, and *Vogue* in 1938, among others. The 1939 parody of *The New Yorker* was the first time the *Lampoon* successfully imitated an entire magazine format, including advertising layouts. Other parodies followed, of *Newsweek* in 1956 and the *Saturday Review* in 1960. But these were not nationally distributed. Finally, in 1961, *Harvard Lampoon* went national when *Mademoiselle*'s editors requested its own parody; the entire July issue was turned over to *Lampoon*'s editors. The issue "set some kind of circulation record of this usually doldrum month in the publishing business," and *Mademoiselle*'s editors asked for a repeat performance in 1962.[2]

By 1966, *Harvard Lampoon* was producing nationally distributed magazines under its own auspices, along with an annual parody. The entire run of 450,000 *Playboy* parodies sold out within 3 weeks in 1966. A 1968 *Time* parody, with the cover line "Does Sex Sell Magazines?" and hilarious letters to the editor from Jacqueline Kennedy Onassis and Timothy Leary (just about anything is possible in a parody), had more than half a million readers. However, the hottest seller so far is *Harvard Lampoon*'s 1973 takeoff on *Cosmopolitan*, complete with a nude centerfold of Henry Kissinger; that parody sold 1.2 million copies.[3]

Harvard Lampoon's outrageous parodies are clearly identified as such on the covers, which have an amazing technical resemblance to the original magazine. Everything is made to look like the real publication—layout, typography, artwork, content, and even sentence structure. There are real ads as well as bogus ones, and fake interviews with real people as well as real stories about fake people throughout the magazine parody, too.

Harvard Lampoon's most recent parody, in 2005, was of *Premiere* magazine and the movie industry's fascination with sequels. Who wouldn't want to see *Fight Club 2* or *Groundhog Minute*? The

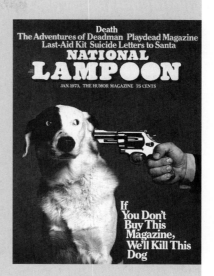

JANUARY 1973: *National Lampoon*, a model of parody, was one of the best-read magazines on college campuses in the 1970s. In 1998, the magazine shut down to focus on its website and television network.

somber black cover featuring Tom Hanks, headlined "Remembering Tom Hanks," was also a dead-on spoof of *Premiere*'s homages to recently deceased movie stars. (No, Tom Hanks really wasn't dead, though more than one newsstand browser stopped to see if Forrest Gump had died before noticing the slender corner flap stating "A *Harvard Lampoon* Parody.")

Not to be confused with the "Ivy League" title, National Lampoon, Inc., published 247 issues of *National Lampoon*

2. Martin Kaplan, ed. *The* Harvard Lampoon *Centennial Celebration, 1876–1973* (Boston: Little, Brown and Company, 1973): 24.

3. Lambeth Hochwald, "Ha-Ha's in La-La Land," *Folio:* (January 15, 1995): 43.

(continued)

Poisonous or Precious: Parodies Pay Off (continued)

between 1970 and 1998 before shutting down the satirical magazine to concentrate on its website and television network. At its height in the 1970s, *National Lampoon* was one the most widely read magazines on college campuses, with more than 1 million subscribers—a fact that contributed to the enormous success of the 1978 film *National Lampoon's Animal House.*[4] Often shortened to *Animal House,* that movie made a star out of John Belushi and sparked a nationwide craze for toga parties.

Mad's parodies tend to be cover treatments only. Its March 1987 takeoff on *Time*'s "Man of the Year" cover used the same typeface and red border, but with *Mad*'s name for the logo. The "Head of the Year" was television superstar Alfred E. Headroom (Alfred E. Neuman with slicked back blond hair and sunglasses), for an additional jibe at the TV show *Max Headroom.*

Jim Downey and Tom Connor have produced two popular parodies of *Martha Stewart Living,* titled *Is Martha Stuart Living?* (in 1994) and *Martha Stuart's Better Than You at Entertaining* (in 1996). These best-selling spoofs were so realistic in their mimicking of the *Martha Stewart Living* formula that an article on how to make water from scratch seemed downright reasonable and one on building and decorating a coffin both possible and plausible.

Downey and Connor also did a send-up of *Wired* under the title *re>Wired* in 1996. With the same fluorescent colors and digitally enhanced image manipulation found in the original, the parody trumpeted "How to Pick Up NetChicks" by Bill Gates IV on the cover.

In recent years, parodies of magazines have gone online. Hundreds of websites featuring parodies of print magazines are accessed by thousands of individuals each day. For example, modernhumorist.com features

an online parody of *O: The Oprah Magazine,* titled *J: The Jerry Magazine,* based on the sensationalist features of Jerry Springer's talk show. The parody includes a mock-up of the cover and table of contents. Feature stories include "Nourish Your Senses: Pull someone's hair. Harder" and "Find Your Voice: Articulate your feelings without the bleeps."[5]

How have magazine editors and publishers reacted to these precious parodies? Martha Stewart, who poked fun at her image in an American Express television ad by advising viewers to recycle their old cards as swimming pool tiles, called the parodies "the highest form of flattery."[6] *Playboy* publisher Hugh Hefner, however, had the last word with his telegram to *Harvard Lampoon:* "*Playboy* is delighted with its treatment at the hands of the venerable *Harvard Lampoon.* In fact, if a better parody of *Playboy* is ever created—we reserve the right to do it ourselves."[7] ■

4. Jake Tapper, "National Lampoon Grows Up by Dumbing Down," *New York Times* (July 3, 2005), http://www.nytimes.com/2005/07/03/arts/03tapp.html?th=&emc=th&pagewanted=print.

5. http://www.modernhumorist.com/mh/0004/jerry/index.cfm.

6. Doreen Carvajal, "What Is a Book Publisher to Do When a Parody Hits Home?" *New York Times* (February 12, 1996): C1.

7. Kaplan, 32.

The Supreme Court said *Hustler*'s ad parody, as tasteless as it was, was akin to the blistering humor of American political cartoons dating back to colonial days. The *Hustler* ad, like Thomas Nast's famous cartoons chastising the Tweed Ring in New York, was using outrageous language to skewer a prominent political figure. Punishing a publisher for running an outrageous cartoon or comment runs the risk of punishing the publisher just because the words or images shock the audience, the Court said. If the First Amendment protects anything, the justices said, it must protect unpopular opinions and statements from the people who would silence them because they disagree with them.

The Court's solution to the First Amendment problem presented by Falwell's suit for intentional infliction of emotional distress was to apply the *New York Times v. Sullivan* rule for actual malice. After *Hustler v. Falwell*, public figures and public officials cannot win a suit for intentional infliction of emotional distress unless they also show that the publication was made with the publisher's knowledge that it was false or with reckless disregard for truth of the matter.

third-party liability

Occasionally, plaintiffs have sued magazines over advertising and editorial content they claim caused people to do something harmful. These cases are called third-party liability cases because the magazine didn't actually do the harm itself, but it is blamed for being a key player in causing the injury. These cases fall into two categories: incitement cases and negligence cases.

■ INCITEMENT

An example of an incitement case is *Herceg v. Hustler*,[63] in which a woman sued the magazine over an August 1981 article about "autoerotic asphyxia," a dangerous practice of masturbating while "hanging" oneself. Supposedly it enhances orgasm by cutting off the oxygen supply to the brain at the moment of orgasm. Diane Herceg asserted in the lawsuit that her 14-year-old son died when he tried the practice after reading the *Hustler* article. In short, she claimed the article incited her son to try the life-threatening practice, so the magazine was responsible for his death.

The federal district court jury decided in Herceg's favor, but a federal appellate court reversed. While it is true the boy might never have tried autoerotic asphyxia if he had not read the *Hustler* article, that still does not follow the very narrow rules laid out in earlier Supreme Court cases for punishing speech because it "incites" action. Under the First Amendment, statements can be punished for incitement only if they are aimed at provoking or causing "imminent lawless action." In the *Hustler* case, the court of appeals said a speaker in front of an angry crowd can be punished for whipping the crowd into a riot, but the

editor of a magazine meant to be read in the solitude of one's home cannot be sued for incitement. The article, which even included a warning against trying autoerotic asphyxia, was not *advocating* any action, the court said, and it was not discussing an illegal practice or act. Therefore, there was no "incitement" and there was no "imminent lawless action." The boy might have found out about autoerotic asphyxia from the article, but the decision to try it was his own, as painful as that may have been for his mother to understand.

■ NEGLIGENCE

The legal principles drawn from the negligence cases against magazines are not so clear-cut, although it is safe to say that magazines cannot be successfully sued for negligence over most standard editorial or advertising content. In one case that illustrates the point, a young woman in California bought Playtex tampons after seeing them advertised in *Seventeen*. After using one, she became violently ill with toxic shock syndrome. She later sued *Seventeen*, claiming the magazine was negligent in running the ad. The California court ruled against her in 1987.[64]

In a similar case, the New Jersey court ruled in 1974 that *Popular Mechanics* was not negligent in running an advertisement for fireworks, even when the fireworks injured a child who was watching them being blown up.[65] In both these cases, the courts said it would simply be too onerous a task to require magazines to investigate the safety and suitability of every product they advertise.

endorsement

When a magazine endorses a product, however, it takes on extra responsibility—and courts can find more easily that it breached its duty to its readers. In *Hanberry v. Hearst Corporation* in 1969,[66] *Good Housekeeping* was held liable for injuries a reader suffered when she slipped and fell while wearing new shoes that bore the magazine's "Consumer's Guaranty Seal." The seal carried the promise, "If the product or performance is defective, *Good Housekeeping* guarantees replacement or refund to consumer." The seal is *Good Housekeeping*'s strategy for making the magazine a better vehicle for advertisers because readers could be confident about a product's quality. That endorsement of the shoes made the difference between liability in this case and no liability in the fireworks and the toxic shock cases.

advertising

Two cases involving classified ads in *Soldier of Fortune* are more complicated because federal appeals courts decided similar cases differently. Both cases arose out of classified ads for "personal services" in a magazine that focuses on military, paramilitary, and mercenary subjects. In both cases, a murder victim's survivors sued *Soldier of Fortune,* alleging that the magazine negligently contributed to the murders by publishing the ad that brought together the murderer and the person who contracted for the murder.

In *Eimann v. Soldier of Fortune,*[67] the mother and son of the murder victim sued the magazine, saying the victim's husband contracted for her murder after reading this ad that ran in the September, October, and November 1984 issues: "EX-MARINES—67-69 'Nam Vets, Ex-DI, weapons specialist—jungle warfare, pilot, M.E., high risk assignments, U.S. or overseas." The man who placed the ad was convicted of murdering the woman at her husband's behest, but he testified at *Soldier of Fortune*'s negligence trial that he and a partner originally ran the ad trying to recruit other Vietnam veterans for work as bodyguards and security agents for business executives. He testified that "Ex-DI" meant ex-drill instructor, "M.E." meant multiengine planes, and "high risk assignments" was intended to refer to work as a bodyguard or security specialist.

Eimann presented evidence at the trial that as many as nine *Soldier of Fortune* classified ads had been tied to criminal activity over the previous 2 years, and in some of those cases, police investigators had contacted the magazine's employees for help in identifying the people who placed the ads. She argued that with such a history the magazine should have known its ads were dangerous, so it should be held responsible for negligently contributing to her daughter's murder. The trial court in Houston agreed with her and awarded her $9.4 million.

The Fifth U.S. Circuit Court of Appeals, which sits in New Orleans and hears cases from Louisiana, Mississippi, and Texas, overturned the District Court's judgment in 1989, ruling that the wording of the ad was too ambiguous for the magazine to foresee it could lead to murder. "Given the pervasiveness of advertising in our society and the important role it plays, we decline to impose on publishers the obligation to reject all ambiguous advertisements for products or services that might pose a threat of harm," the judges wrote in their opinion. "The burden on a publisher to avoid liability from suits of this type is too great: he must reject *all* such advertisements."

Three years later, in 1992, the Eleventh U.S. Circuit Court of Appeals in Atlanta decided *Braun v. Soldier of Fortune*[68] with similar facts but a different result—it upheld a $4 million judgment against the magazine. In the *Braun* case, Michael and Ian Braun, the sons of the murder victim, sued *Soldier of Fortune,* alleging that their father's business partner found a hit man through a classified ad in the magazine. The ad, placed by a man named Michael Savage, said: "GUN FOR HIRE: 37-year-old professional mercenary desires jobs. Vietnam Veteran. Discreet and very private. Body guard, courier, and other special skills. All jobs considered."

While on its face, the ad in the *Braun* case appears very similar to the ad in the *Eimann* case, the Eleventh Circuit Court of Appeals emphasized the

In 2003, the *Maxim* magazine staff thought they were just being funny when they depicted a man in a muscle T-shirt stomping and hitting an image of Mahatma Gandhi, just 2 months after the magazine launched its first Asian edition. The article was intended to show that fighting can be a fitness regimen. Several thousand readers were not amused by the piece. Editor-in-chief Keith Blanchard formally apologized, saying "We chose Gandhi as the subject of our workout cartoon specifically because he is the least likely target of aggression imaginable."

differences in the wording to support its ruling that *Soldier of Fortune* negligently contributed to the death in this second case. While the ad in the *Eimann* case was ambiguous, as the Fifth U.S. Circuit Court pointed out, the Eleventh U.S. Circuit Court said Savage's ad was explicit enough for any publisher to foresee that it could lead to illegal and harmful activities. The warning signs the court singled out in the ad itself were the phrases "gun for hire" and "professional mercenary," the emphasis on privacy and discretion, the reference to "other special skills" after mentioning legitimate jobs of bodyguard and courier, and the open-ended lure that "all jobs" would be considered. "The ad's combination of sinister terms makes it apparent that there was a substantial danger of harm to the public," the court wrote. A reasonable publisher, then, would understand that Savage's ad presented a clearly identifiable threat to public safety, the court said. Because the magazine had not recognized such a threat, it negligently contributed to the elder Braun's death.

After Eimann and Braun, it won't be easy for magazine editors and publishers to know precisely when an ad crosses the line—there is not a bright line dividing acceptable ads from unacceptable ads. The principle, however, is helpful: Ambiguously worded ads from which physical harm results are not likely to support a ruling of negligence against the magazine. But an ad whose message, intent, or implication is more obvious could support a court's finding that the magazine negligently contributed to the harm.

The risk, of course, is that magazine editors and publishers may tend to overcompensate or self-censor in order to avoid even the hint of negligence. In the discussion of libel and privacy, that tendency was called "the chilling effect." But magazines are not just business enterprises; they also are vehicles for public information and the exchange of ideas and opinions. To uphold that objective, editors and publishers will need to balance their legal concerns against their journalistic principles in making decisions about which ads to run and which ads to reject.

copyright

Copyright may be the legal issue that magazine editors and writers confront most frequently—not

in the context of a courtroom battle, but in making sure, day in and day out, that their magazines have full rights to the articles, photos, and other content they publish. They also need to ensure that their rights to the content of their own magazines are respected by other publishers.

The purpose of copyright is to protect the intellectual and creative work of authors, artists, composers, performers, photographers, illustrators, playwrights, choreographers, architects, and other "creators." Protecting their work means others cannot claim it as their own, so credit is given where it is due. Also, copyright protection encourages people to pursue creative efforts by guaranteeing them control over how their work will be used. With creative people thus protected, the law reasons, all society stands to benefit. Copyright lasts for the life of the author plus 70 years.[69]

The federal copyright statute says that copyright protects "original works of authorship fixed in any tangible medium of expression, now known or later developed, from which they can be perceived, reproduced, or otherwise communicated."[70] In that mélange of legalese are hidden the basic components of copyright that editors and writers need to know.

■ ORIGINAL WORKS

"Original works" means that the creation must have a minimum level of intellectual effort. The alphabetized listing of names in a phone book is not original enough to merit copyright protection, the U.S. Supreme Court ruled in 1991.[71]

Lists, nevertheless, can be problematic. In 1980, a court ruled that *Newsweek* did not violate author Lawrence Suid's copyright of his book *Guts and Glory—Great American War Movies* by arranging quotations about John Wayne in the same order Suid arranged them in his book and taking the same excerpts from John Wayne's letters that Suid quoted in his book. Suid was not claiming a copyright to the quotations themselves, which came from sources he interviewed for the book, or in the letters. Copyright law would never have supported such a claim because the letters and the quotations were created by someone else, and those creators would hold those copyrights. But Suid was claiming that his very act of selecting particular quotations and excerpts and arranging them in a particular order in the book amounted to original, creative work that was stolen by *Newsweek*. The Washington, D.C., federal court disagreed, ruling in *Newsweek*'s favor that the magazine could draw on Suid's research, even citing the same sources he used in his book, without using or compromising the originality of his work.[72] His original work lay in the way he wrote the book, not in the way he chose or used his sources' words.

Generally, almost any freelance article that reflects the writer's creative effort to present research would have enough originality under the law to qualify for copyright protection. The use of type, illustrations, graphics, and photos that go into a magazine's page design for an article is also "original work" and thus deserving of copyright protection.

It's important to understand that "originality" applies to an article itself, not to the facts discussed in the article. If a magazine publishes an article about winter care for gardens just a month after a competing magazine does, it is not necessarily a copyright infringement. Facts, knowledge, and information about taking care of a garden plot in winter cannot be copyrighted; copyright protects the particular presentation of those facts—the wording of the article, a particular illustration, photo, or graphic, even the unique design of the whole package—but not the idea of an article about that topic.

■ TANGIBLE MEDIUM

The copyright statute's phrase "fixed in a tangible medium" is the key for knowing when copyright protection begins for a work. An original work is fixed in a tangible medium as soon as it is written

The Name Game

The title of a magazine is one of its most valuable, though intangible, assets. Titles of magazines are trademarked, not copyrighted. While copyright protects original artistic or literary works, a trademark protects the product's identifying name, slogan, design, or symbol. The U.S. Patent and Trademark Office handles trademarks, although a product does not have to be registered to be legally valid. It can achieve trademark status through common law, which recognizes usage over time. But whenever there is potential for confusion over two product names, lawyers get involved.

Selecting the right name for a magazine can be a time-consuming process. According to accounts about the November 1936 start-up of *Life* magazine, *Dime* was the first of the many possible titles considered. Others on the list included *Show-Book of the World, Rehearsal, Album, Eye, Candid, Go, News Focus, Spectator, Nuze-Vuze, Picture, Promenade, See, Quest, Snap, Scan, Vista, Flash, World, Witness,* and *Wide Awake. Life* was suggested as a name early on, but the title belonged to a 54-year-old humor magazine with a dwindling circulation.

Although more than 200 possible names were bandied

APRIL 2006: In 2002, the court ruled that *Entrepreneur* magazine did not own the exclusive rights to the word "entrepreneur" in the marketplace.

The Name Game (continued)

about, *Life* kept rising to the top. Finally, less than 1 month before the premiere of Henry Luce's new picture magazine, Time, Inc., acquired the name and assets of the old *Life* for $92,000. The humor magazine's staff members were given Time, Inc., jobs as part of the deal.[1]

Today's start-ups are a bit more complicated when it comes to naming a magazine. With so many brand extensions and franchises crowding the market, a name check requires extensive computer database searches and legal research through trademark registers. Two situations illustrate the problems that can occur in the magazine name game.

When Steven Brill, founder of *The American Lawyer*, announced in 1997 that he was starting a media watchdog magazine called *Content,* he immediately hit a brick wall. An arts quarterly titled *Contents*, based in Savannah, Georgia, had been publishing since 1993. Known in film and fashion circles for its elegant photo layouts—made more impressive by its oversized format—*Contents* had a national circulation of 50,000. Brill's lawyers contacted *Contents* founder and creative director Joseph Alfieris to reach an amicable settlement; Brill gave

Alfieris a six-figure sum in exchange for not suing.[2] Brill further distanced his magazine from *Contents* by titling it *Brill's Content* when the premiere issue hit the newsstands in August 1998. *Brill's Content* folded in October 2001, while the last issue of *Contents* hit the newsstands in January 2003.

Polo Ralph Lauren, the product line of designer Ralph Lauren, went to court in 1998 to get an injunction against the use of the name Polo by the U.S. Polo Association's official magazine, *Polo,* which had covered the sport since 1974. The problem was that the magazine had been revamped in late 1997 from a narrow sporting publication to an upscale lifestyle magazine that also covered polo. The changes, according to Polo Ralph Lauren, would cause people to view it as a product of the luxury designer, and that was an infringement on the company's name.

In August 1999, Polo Ralph Lauren won its trademark infringement case against the U.S. Polo Association, which was given 90 days from the date of the decision to change the name of the magazine. The judge said the "new, glossy format and altered editorial and advertising direction evidences

an intent to trade on the reputation and goodwill established by Polo Ralph Lauren over the last 30 years."[3]

With the advent of print magazines creating parallel websites, selecting names for new magazines has become even more difficult. Now, a start-up magazine must not only be concerned with other publications that have similar names, but also with other websites that have similar domain names. In 2002, *Entrepreneur* magazine, which held the trademark to that name as well as to two domain names, entrepreneur.com and entrepreneurmag.com, sued EntrepreneurPR, a public relations firm that published *Entrepreneur Illustrated* magazine, for trademark infringement. The publishers of *Entrepreneur* magazine claimed EntrepreneurPR could not use the word "entrepreneur" in its business or magazine titles without violating their trademark. The court ruled that only the name of the magazine, *Entrepreneur Illustrated,* violated the trademark by causing confusion in the magazine marketplace. The court was clear, however, that *Entrepreneur* magazine did not own the right to the exclusive use of the word "entrepreneur" in the marketplace.[4]

1. Loudon Wainwright, *The Great American Magazine: An Inside History of* Life (New York: Alfred A. Knopf, 1986).
2. Karen Hudes, "New Titles Play the Name Game," *Folio:* (January 1, 1998): 15.
3. "Magazine Loses Rights to *Polo* Name," *Dallas Morning News* (August 5, 1999): 10D.
4. *Entrepreneur Media, Inc. v. Smith*, 279 F.3d 1135 (2002).

on a piece of paper, drawn on a sketch pad, recorded on an audio- or videotape, saved on a disc or into the memory of a computer, or posted onto an Internet website.

The familiar copyright symbol, ©, does not have to be displayed for a work to be copyrighted. As the statute says, the author's or creator's right is recognized by the law as soon as the work is "fixed in a tangible medium." Nevertheless, giving proper notice of the copyright and registering the copyright with the federal government are important for editors. Copyright registration informs readers that they should have the magazine's permission before making copies of the work, and registration gives copyright holders greater rights if they have to sue a copier for infringement.

A proper copyright notice includes the word "copyright" or the abbreviation "copr.," the circled C, ©, the year of publication, and the name of the copyright owner. For an article, proper notice might read "Copyright © 2006 Desmond Jones." For an entire issue of a magazine, it might read "Copyright © 2006 Meredith Corp." for *Better Homes and Gardens* or another publication owned by Meredith. For an issue of *Sports Illustrated for Kids* published in 2006, proper notice would be "Copyright © 2006 Time Inc." because Time, Inc., is the parent company for *Sports Illustrated for Kids.* Proper notice for *NBA Inside Stuff*, a specialty magazine published by Time, Inc., was "Copyright © 1998 NBA Properties Inc." because even though Time, Inc., published the magazine, it did so under contract with the NBA, and the NBA kept all rights. Unfortunately, the magazine folded as a result of the 1998 NBA strike.

■ OWNERSHIP

The matter of resolving who owns the copyright is important. The statute grants rights to the copy to the "author." But the author for purposes of the law is not always the writer who prepared the copy, as the *NBA Inside Stuff* copyright notice implied. To be sure, freelance writers and photographers own the copyright to their original works, and because of that they can sign over publication rights to a magazine to publish the work.

Work prepared under contract, though, is what the copyright statute calls a "work for hire." A writer employed by Time, Inc., to prepare articles for *Sports Illustrated for Kids* does not own the copyright to her articles; they would be works for hire written under the terms of her employment contract, so Time, Inc., would hold the copyright. A freelance writer who accepts a specific assignment from a magazine and signs a work for hire agreement with the editor does not retain the copyright to the article. Editors should use explicit, written, work-for-hire agreements with all freelancers, and freelancers should require them of all editors they work for, because it is in everyone's best interest to have the question of authorship answered clearly before the work begins.

The Internet and CD-ROM technology have created new controversies over copyright ownership and works for hire. Freelance writers who sold rights to an article for publication in a magazine have been in conflict with magazines that want to reuse the articles in electronic databases or in CD-ROM anthologies. The Supreme Court recently ruled that freelance writers do retain subsidiary rights over articles that appear in electronic databases. Freelance writers for *Sports Illustrated,* along with those from other magazines and newspapers, brought suit against the publications where their articles originally appeared after those publications sold their contents to LexisNexis and University Microforms electronic databases. The Court in this case ruled that because individual articles could be reviewed in a format different from the original, this was not simply a reproduction of the original work, and therefore, violated the freelancers' copyright.[73]

In a similar case involving freelance photographers for *National Geographic*, the Second U.S. Circuit Court of Appeals ruled that the copyrighted work of freelance photographers that appeared in a 30-disc CD-ROM compilation of 108 years of the magazine did not comprise a copyright violation because the material could not be individually accessed and appeared in exactly the same visual format as the original.[74]

The legalities of copyright and new technology will continue to develop, but in the meantime, writers and the editors who buy their works should negotiate carefully and clearly to make sure all are in agreement on the terms for reuse of freelance articles.

■ FAIR USE

Magazine editors must expect that their copyrighted works will be used by readers, just as editors will use the copyrighted works of others in their magazines. The law protects the fair use of copyrighted materials as a way of ensuring that the creative work can be distributed widely for society's benefit. But for the use of a copyrighted work to be fair, the copyright statute says the new work must be original itself, not relying on the creativity of the original but rather transforming the original by making it a portion of a new creative work.

To be fair use, a new work also should take just a limited portion of the copyrighted work. For example, a magazine's review of a new book of poetry can quote a small passage to illustrate the reviewer's point that the poems are articulate and insightful (or wooden and hackneyed, as the case may be). But the review cannot quote several entire poems because that would eliminate the market for the book. A reader would not buy the poet's book if he could buy the magazine and read all the articles, plus get most of the poems from the new book. The poet's publisher, as the copyright owner, has lost all control over the original work, so the magazine's use of the poems is unfair.

APRIL 7, 1979: The courts declared that *The Nation*'s publication of 300 words from President Gerald Ford's autobiography about why he pardoned Richard Nixon was not a fair use of copyrighted material.

Fair use allows a writer to quote a copyrighted work as a source in an article, and it permits editors to use copyrighted works as sources in reviews or commentaries. It also permits readers to photocopy an entire article if their only purpose is to keep it for their personal use, such as filing away the article about winter care of garden plots for future use every winter.

Fair use does not allow editors to publish without permission significant portions of an article that belonged to a freelancer or that was published by another magazine. It would not allow a subscriber to make several copies of the main articles from a magazine to pass out to friends who just want to avoid buying the magazine themselves.[75] And it will not allow advertisers to copy a favorable review from a magazine for use in advertisements. For example, in 1987, a federal court ruled that a manufacturing company violated the copyright of *Consumer Reports* by quoting from a favorable review of a vacuum cleaner.[76] Similarly, a federal court ruled in 1952 that the Vogue School of Fashion Modeling in New York was not fairly using the cover of *Vogue* magazine when the school duplicated it for an advertisement.[77]

The fine line between fair use and infringement was illustrated by the U.S. Supreme Court in a 1985 case between *The Nation* and Harper and Row, the book publishing company.[78] In that case, *The Nation* ran a short excerpt from President Gerald Ford's book *A Time to Heal*, which Ford had written under a contract with Harper and Row. Shortly before the book was to be published, Harper and Row signed a deal with *Time* for $25,000, under which *Time* would have exclusive first publication rights for an excerpt in which Ford explained his decision to pardon President Richard Nixon of crimes growing out of the Watergate political scandal.

Just before *Time*'s exclusive was to run, *The Nation* obtained a copy of the unpublished manuscript from a secret source. *The Nation* rushed to put together an article, including about 300 words taken directly from the Ford manuscript, under the title "The Ford Memoirs—Behind the Nixon Pardon." After *The Nation* article ran in the April 13, 1979, issue, *Time* canceled its contract with Harper and Row, and the publishing house sued *The Nation* for copyright infringement. The federal district court sided with Harper and Row, but the court of appeals ruled for *The Nation*, saying the newsworthiness of the article made the publication a fair use of the Ford manuscript. The Supreme Court ruled that *The Nation*'s use of the excerpt was not a fair use under the copyright statute.

In evaluating whether *The Nation*'s use of the manuscript was fair or not, the Supreme Court followed the four considerations laid out by the copyright statute for determining fair use of a copyrighted work:

1. The purpose and character of the use,
2. the nature of the copyrighted work,
3. the amount and significance of the copyrighted work used, and
4. the effect that the use has on the market for the copyrighted work.

Regarding the purpose and character of the use, the Court noted that news reporting is specifically listed in the copyright statute as a fair use. But *The Nation*'s purpose was to beat *Time* and Harper and Row to the first publication of the Ford memoirs, thus undermining the copyright owner's right to control the manuscript's first publication. That made *The Nation*'s article more commercial than news, the Court reasoned. So for the first consideration, *The Nation*'s use tended toward not being fair.

Considering the nature of the copyrighted work, the Court focused on the fact that the manuscript was yet unpublished. The copyright statute grants wider protection to copyright owners of unpublished work to ensure they have control over when and in what form it is first published. At the same time, however, there is greater claim to fair use of factual or historical works, such as the Ford manuscript, than for works of fiction. So while this was a close call, the evidence tended to go against a finding of fair use.

The matter of amount and significance of the portion used raises questions of both quantity and quality. While the Court acknowledged that the amount was minimal—300 words from a whole book—the significance was substantial. Ford's account of pardoning Nixon was the most important part of the whole work from Harper and Row's and *Time*'s perspectives. So, in balancing amount and significance, this, too, was a close call, but the Court found it also weighing against fair use.

Finally, on the factor the statute calls the most important issue for evaluating fair use, the effect on the potential market for the work, the Court found it an easy call. "Rarely will a case of copyright infringement present such clear-cut evidence of actual damage," the Court said.[79] *Time*'s canceled contract proved the harm to Harper and Row by *The Nation*'s publication, so the final consideration clearly weighed against declaring *The Nation* article a fair use of the copyrighted memoir.

obscenity

Sex and sexuality are common topics for magazines of all kinds. From the cover of *Cosmopolitan* to the *Sports Illustrated* swimsuit issue to the titillation and teasing of some teen publications, an undercurrent of sex permeates many magazines. The law of obscenity in no way affects such magazine content.

As a legal concept, obscenity refers to a narrow category of hard-core pornography that is beyond the scope of First Amendment protection because it is so sexually explicit that it does not contribute to the exchange of ideas and information that the First Amendment protects. Obscenity does not include the material published in the most commonly circulated sex magazines, such as *Playboy*, *Penthouse*, *Hustler*, and the like.

Unlike most of the other legal issues discussed in this chapter, obscenity is usually a criminal matter. In other words, publishers, producers, and distributors of obscene materials are prosecuted for violating criminal laws. For that reason, defining obscenity—what materials will be subject to criminal prosecution—has been an important First Amendment challenge for the U.S. Supreme Court. If obscenity is not defined clearly and carefully by the court, police and prosecutors might take constitutionally protected publications and ideas out of circulation.

The Supreme Court's test for obscenity has three prongs:

1. Applying a contemporary community standard, the average person would find that the work as a whole appeals to a prurient interest in sex.
2. The pornography must depict in a "patently offensive" way some sexual conduct that is specifically defined by an applicable state statute.

3. The work as a whole must lack any serious literary, artistic, political, or scientific value.

All three of the factors must be present to find a work to be obscene.[80]

Such a test does not cover written descriptions of sex or sexual topics, photos or drawings of mere nudity, or the come-hither pandering of mainstream magazine advertising. Four-letter words in an article cannot come under the label of obscenity. So, for most editors and writers working in the mainstream of American magazine journalism, the law of obscenity will not cramp their style, even if they are developing or publishing sexually oriented content in their magazines.

The Constitution does permit the regulation of nonobscene, sexually explicit magazines in some ways, the Supreme Court has ruled. For example, cities can have zoning laws that restrict the locations of businesses that sell pornographic magazines, either to confine them to one part of town, to diffuse them throughout town so they are not concentrated, or to keep them from locating close to schools, churches, parks, or residences.[81] Cities and states can also require that pornographic magazines displayed in stores appear behind an opaque cover or inside a sealed wrapper.[82] Such laws protect minors and unwilling consumers from being exposed to pornography, but they do not unconstitutionally deprive adults of access to the magazines or restrict the free expression rights of publishers. Similarly, the Supreme Court has upheld a federal law that prohibited the sale of sexually explicit magazines on military bases. Postal regulations also prohibit mailing nonobscene sexual materials to the homes of people who do not want to receive them.

American magazines operate in a legal atmosphere meant to guarantee tremendous freedom, because freedom is assumed to inspire greater creativity and more open social discussion. Generally speaking, legal limitations on the editorial or advertising content of magazines violate the free press and free speech clauses of the First Amendment. But that broad freedom brings tremendous responsibility for editors and publishers. Editors and publishers must make careful ethical decisions about editorial and advertising content because not everything protected by the First Amendment is responsible journalism. Editors also must recognize where the fuzzy line lies between ethics and law, so they know when they are crossing over into a zone where they risk legal punishment for a misstep.

There's no point in becoming paranoid about all the legal risks and ethical responsibilities involved in publishing a magazine. With just a bit of his tongue in cheek, Edward L. Smith, who practices publishing law in New York City, pointed out, "To eliminate totally the legal risks associated with accuracy and factuality, a magazine would be limited to writing about dead people or printing nothing."[83]

notes

1. *Houchins v. KQED, Inc.*, 438 U.S. 1 (1978), in which the Supreme Court upheld restrictions that denied a television station access to an area in a county jail in California where an inmate had committed suicide.
2. See for example, *Pell v. Procunier*, 417 U.S. 817 (1974), *Saxbe v. Washington Post*, 417 U.S. 843 (1974), and *Houchins v. KQED*, 438 U.S. 1 (1978).
3. See for example, *State v. Lashinsky*, 404 A.2d 1121 (1979).
4. 526 U.S. 603 (1999).
5. *Ludtke v. Kuhn*, 461 F.Supp. 86 (S.D.N.Y. 1978).
6. *Sherrill v. Knight*, 569 F.2d 124 (D.C. Cir. 1978).
7. *Richmond Newspapers, Inc. v. Virginia*, 448 U.S. 555 (1980).
8. *Press-Enterprise Co. v. Riverside County Superior Court* (Press-Enterprise I), 464 U.S. 501 (1984).
9. *Press-Enterprise Co. v. Riverside County Superior Court* (Press-Enterprise II), 478 U.S. 1 (1986).
10. *Price v. Time, Inc.*, 416 F.3d 1327 (2005).
11. *Liberty Lobby v. Pearson*, 390 F.2d 489 (1968); *Pearson v. Dodd*, 410 F.2d 701 (1969).
12. *United States v. Morison*, 844 F.2d 1057 (1988).
13. For links to all federal department and agency online reading rooms, see http://www.usdoj.gov/04foia/04_2.html.
14. *Nation Magazine v. U.S. Department of Defense*, 762 F.Supp. 1558 (1991).
15. *Flynt v. Rumsfeld*, 355 F.3d 697 (2004): 706.
16. *JB Pictures, Inc. v. Defense Department*, 86 F.3d 236 (1996).
17. http://www.delawareonline.com/newsjournal/local/2004/10/05udprofessorsues.html.
18. 283 U.S. 697 (1931).
19. *Near v. Minnesota*, 283 U.S. 697 (1931): 702.
20. *Bantam Books, Inc. v. Sullivan*, 372 U.S. 58 (1963).

21. *New York Times v. United States* (The Pentagon Papers case), 403 U.S. 713 (1971).
22. *United States v. Progressive, Inc.*, 467 F.Supp. 990 (W.D. Wis. 1979) dismissed, 610 F.2d, 819 (7th Cir. 1979).
23. *Procter & Gamble Company v. Bankers Trust Company*, 78 F.3d 219 (6th Cir. 1996).
24. 78 F.3d, at 227.
25. 481 U.S. 221 (1987).
26. 109 S.Ct. 890 (1989).
27. *Leathers v. Medlock*, 111 S.Ct. 1438 (1991): 449–450.
28. *Magazine Publishers of America v. Pennsylvania*, 654 A.2d 519 (1995).
29. 303 U.S. 444 (1938).
30. *Lovell v. City of Griffin*, 303 U.S. 444 (1938): 444.
31. *Ex parte Jackson*, 96 U.S. 727 (1878): 733 as quoted in *Lovell v. City of Griffin*, 303 U.S. 444 (1938): 452.
32. *Breard v. Alexandria*, 341 U.S. 622 (1951), at 645.
33. *Mainstream Marketing v. FTC*, 358 F.3d 1228 (2004): 1246.
34. *Granger v. Time, Inc.*, 568 P.2d 535 (1977).
35. *Goldwater v. Ginzburg*, 414 F.2d 324 (2d Cir. 1969).
36. *Montandon v. Triangle Publications, Inc.*, 45 Cal. App. 3d 938 (1975).
37. Yeager, Don, "Bad Behavior: How He Met His Destiny at a Strip Club," *Sports Illustrated* (May 12, 2003): 38–44.
38. *Kaplan v. Newsweek, Inc.*, 776 F.2d 1053 (9th Cir. 1985).
39. *Schwartz v. American College of Emergency Physicians*, 215 F.3d 1140 (2000).
40. 376 U.S. 254 (1964). After the Sullivan case, the Court decided several cases to clarify, expand, and adapt the basic principle introduced in Sullivan. These included *Garrison v. Louisiana*, 379 U.S. 64 (1964); *Rosenblatt v. Baer*, 383 U.S. 75 (1966); *Curtis Publishing Co. v. Butts*, 388 U.S. 130 (1967); *St. Amant v. Thompson*, 390 U.S. 727 (1968); *Rosenbloom v. Metromedia*, 403 U.S. 29 (1971); *Monitor Patriot v. Roy*, 401 U.S. 265 (1971); *Ocala Star-Banner Co. v. Damron*, 401 U.S. 295 (1971); and *Gertz v. Robert Welch*, 418 U.S. 323 (1974).
41. 418 U.S. 323 (1974).
42. 383 U.S. 75 (1966).
43. *Time Inc. v. Firestone*, 424 U.S. 448 (1976).
44. *Wolston v. Reader's Digest Ass'n*, 443 U.S. 157 (1979).
45. *Curtis Publishing Co. v. Butts*, 388 U.S. 130 (1967).
46. *Goldwater v. Ginzburg*, 414 F.2d 324 (2d Cir. 1969).
47. *Masson v. New Yorker Magazine, Inc.*, 501 U.S. 496 (1991).
48. H. Wat Hopkins, "Negligence Ten Years After *Gertz v. Welch*," *Journalism Monographs,* 93 (August 1985): 19.
49. *Keeton v. Hustler*, 465 U.S. 770 (1984).
50. *Barber v. Time Inc.*, 159 S.W.2d 291 (Mo. 1942).
51. *Virgil v. Sports Illustrated, Inc.*, 424 F.Sup. 1286 (S.D. Cal. 1976).
52. *Sidis v. F-R Publishing Corp.*, 113 F.2d 806 (1940).
53. *Dietemann v. Time Inc.*, 449 F.2d 245 (9th Cir. 1971).
54. 449 F.2d, at 249.
55. *Desnick v. Capital Cities/ABC, Inc.* 44 F.3d 1345 (1995).
56. *Time Inc. v. Hill*, 385 U.S. 374 (1967).
57. *Pring v. Penthouse Int'l, Ltd.*, 695 F.2d 438 (10th Cir. 1982).
58. *Stanton v. Metro Corp.*, 357 F.Supp. 2d 369 (2005).
59. Murray v. *New York Magazine*, 267 N.E.2d 256 (N.Y. 1971).
60. *Booth v. Curtis Publishing Co.*, 223 N.Y.S.2d 737 (N.Y. 1962).
61. 13 Media L. Rptr. 1657 (D. Or. 1986).
62. *Hustler Magazine, Inc. v. Falwell*, 485 U.S. 46 (1988).
63. 814 F.2d 1017 (5th Cir. 1987).
64. *Walters v. Seventeen Magazine*, 241 Cal.Rptr. 101 (Cal.App. 4 Dist. 1987).
65. *Yuhas v. Mudge*, 322 A.2d 824 (N.J. App. 1974).
66. 81 Cal.Rptr. 519 (Cal.App. 4 Dist. 1969).
67. 880 F.2d 830 (5th Cir. 1989).
68. 968 F.2d 1110 (11th Cir. 1992).
69. "Legislation Extending Copyright Terms, Limiting Music Licensing Signed into Law," *United States Law Week,* vol. 67, no. 18 (November 17, 1998): 2278.
70. 17 U.S.C.A. §102 (West 1996).
71. *Feist Publications, Inc. v. Tel. Serv. Co.*, 499 U.S. 340 (1991).
72. *Suid v. Newsweek Magazine*, 503 F.Supp. 146 (1980).
73. *New York Times v. Tasini*, 121 S.Ct. 2381 (2001).
74. *Faulkner v. National Geographic*, 409 F.3d 26 (2005).
75. See *American Geophysical Union, Inc. v. Texaco, Inc.*, 60 F.3d 913 (2d Cir. 1994) in which a federal appeals court ruled that it was not fair use for Texaco to copy and distribute articles from scientific journals to its scientists for their research files to avoid buying a subscription to each journal for each researcher.
76. *Consumers Union of United States, Inc. v. New Regina Corp.*, 664 F.Supp. 753 (S.D.N.Y. 1987).
77. *Condé Nast Publications, Inc. v. Vogue School of Fashion Modeling, Inc.*, 105 F.Supp. 325 (S.D.N.Y. 1952).
78. *Harper & Row, Publishers, Inc. v. Nation Enterprises, Inc.*, 471 U.S. 539 (1985).
79. 471 U.S., at 567.
80. *Miller v. California*, 413 U.S. 15 (1973).
81. *City of Renton v. Playtime Theaters, Inc.*, 475 U.S. 41.
82. *M.S. News Co. v. Casado*, 721 F.2d 1281 (10th Cir. 1983); *Upper Midwest Booksellers Ass'n v. City of Minneapolis*, 780 F.2d 1389 (8th Cir. 1985).
83. Abbe Wichman, "Who's Responsible for Fact Checking?" *Folio:* (November 1989): 171.

for additional reading

Abrams, Floyd. *Speaking Freely: Trials of the First Amendment.* New York: Viking Adult, 2005.
Adler, Renata. *Reckless Disregard.* New York: Alfred A. Knopf, 1986.
Fishman, Stephen. *The Copyright Handbook: How to Protect and Use Written Works*, 8th ed. Berkeley, Calif.: 2004.
Friendly, Fred. *Minnesota Rag.* New York: Random House, 1981.

Goldstein, Paul. *Copyright's Highway.* New York: Hill and Wang, 1994.

Lewis, Anthony. *Make No Law.* New York: Random House, 1991.

Mason, Peter. *Magazine Law: A Practical Guide.* Oxford: Routledge, 1998.

Merrill, John C. *The Dialectic in Journalism: Toward a Responsible Use of Press Freedom.* Baton Rouge: Louisiana State University Press, 1989.

Powe, Lucas A. *The Fourth Estate and the Constitution: Freedom of the Press in America.* Berkeley: University of California Press, 1991.

Smolla, Rodney A. *Jerry Falwell v. Larry Flynt: The First Amendment on Trial.* New York: St. Martin's Press, 1988.

_____. *Suing the Press.* New York: Oxford University Press, 1986.

moral frameworks: codes of ethics

You've been invited to Spain—all expenses paid. The glitch: The trip is sponsored by a Spanish hotel chain that hopes to see your byline next to an article on Barcelona in the spring. Is it ethical to take them up on their offer? They haven't directly specified what they expect, but you will be staying at a suite in their expensive hotel. What about special seats at the NBA game offered by the advertiser whose products you review? Would the advertiser's generosity in inviting you to watch Shaquille O'Neal up-close and personal really compromise your objectivity? Or, what do you tell your boss when she offers to pay you a little extra on the side to design an advertising insert to match your magazine's pages? ■ How about the huge dilemmas magazines faced after September 11, 2001: Do we show people falling to their deaths, which is part of the story, or do we cut those out of the magazine in deference to the families of the victims? ■ These are all ethical issues that deal with the journalist's responsibility to her magazine and to society at large. Ethical problems are not as easy to resolve as legal ones. The law is usually unambiguous, while ethics is a gray area dealing with matters of conscience and responsibility.

Today's magazines face a set of ethical challenges unique to this time in history. Magazine staff members must wade through ethical waters full of freebies, conflicts of interest, advertising pressure, and the invasive effects of visual images. The ways in which professionals respond to these challenges will determine the legitimacy and credibility of the magazine in the 21st century.

Ethics professors Philip Patterson of Oklahoma Christian University and Lee Wilkins of the University of Missouri pose two questions related to professional ethics in all fields:

■ What duties do I have, and to whom do I owe them?
■ What values are reflected by the duties I've assumed?[1]

Ethics relate to what we should do, rather than to what others want us to do or what has always been done. Patterson and Wilkins distinguish between morals and ethics, noting that ethics is a "rational process founded on certain agreed-on principles," while morals are in "the realm of religion." The Ten Commandments and the Buddhist Eightfold Path are moral frameworks. "Ethics begins when elements within a moral system conflict," Patterson and Wilkins write. "Ethics is less about the conflict between right and wrong than it is about the conflict between equally compelling (or equally unattractive) values and the choices that must be made between them."[2]

The trip to Spain, the NBA tickets from an advertiser, the assignment to design a page that looks like an ad, and the use of images of death are all ethical questions that can be clarified by considering the moral framework in which you are making the decision, analyzing the other options available, and being honest about the effects of your actions.

Ethics scholars and philosophers help provide frameworks through which we can critique our actions. Professional codes of ethics offer straightforward direction on specific problems the industry faces.

hodges's essential questions

Louis W. Hodges, visiting distinguished professor of applied ethics and Knight professor of ethics in journalism, emeritus, at Washington and Lee University, suggests journalists ask seven essential questions when faced with an ethical dilemma:

1. What are the moral issues at stake in this case?
2. Who are the stakeholders?
3. What are the morally relevant facts?
4. What possible courses of action are available?
5. What are the predictable effects of each action?
6. Which set of possible outcomes is relatively better?
7. Will it pass the test of publicity?[3]

Hodges says these questions are not necessarily in order, but they should be addressed at some point when charting an ethical course. He clarifies that journalists have only a handful of fundamental moral principles, such as "keep confidences," "respect privacy," or "be truthful," and that ethical questions are subsets of these principles.

Hodges notes that the fourth of his essential questions—What possible courses of action are available?—is the point at which "many journalists and many human beings in other walks of life end up not doing their jobs well." By looking at the possible options, journalists can make a fairly easy and simple determination of whether there are other courses to follow and what they might be. If no other options exist—or if they offer additional problems—that changes the dynamics of the decision. "We need to find out what's possible to do," Hodges says, "because we never have the moral obligation to do the impossible."

Answering Hodges's questions regarding the free trip to Spain demonstrates how his framework can help determine whether taking the trip is ethical or not. Accepting the trip is in itself not a moral issue, but an example of an underlying moral standard of conflict of interest. The stakeholders are you, the hotel, the magazine itself, your readers, and potential advertisers; all could be affected by an article that reduces the magazine's credibility.

The morally relevant facts are that it will be difficult to be objective when you get first-class service that does not truly reflect the experience others might have. There are plenty of other possible courses of action: You could decide not to go or pay your own way. Or you could go and let your news judgment be your guide in whether or not the story is worth writing or printing. This latter can be a slippery slope, although it is the one many journalists take, especially freelancers who travel on their own dime. Determining which facts to use and which to ignore becomes difficult when you have enjoyed the hospitality of a host whose repayment is implicit rather than explicit: Treat me as well in your magazine as I treated you at my hotel. What do you do if, during your entire stay at the pricey hotel, you could not sleep because of the thin walls and the noisy street? Will you include those negatives in your piece? And will you also write about the charming hotel a block away that was quieter, cheaper, and more appealing?

The effects of your actions might be loss of credibility for you and the magazine once your stakeholders discover who paid for your jaunt. The best possible outcome is an article that is as solid and fair as it would be if the hotel were not involved. Finally, if the hotel's tactics are publicized within the industry—and your magazine is involved—how will that information affect you or the magazine?

The bottom line is that the cost of a free trip might be higher than if you had paid your own way. When faced with this type of freebie, use Hodges's framework and discuss this issue with others on the magazine to assure that you have considered all options and effects.

bok's model

Philosopher Sissela Bok offers a similar model consisting of three points:

- First, consult your own conscience about the rightness of an action. How do you feel about the action?
- Second, seek expert advice for alternatives to the act creating the ethical problem. Is there another way to achieve the same goal that will not raise ethical issues?
- Third, if possible, conduct a public discussion with the parties involved in the dispute. The goal of this conversation is to discover: How will others respond to the proposed act?[4]

Like Hodges, Bok suggests shedding the light of public discussion on the issue. If your actions might likely cause others to question your ethics or the credibility of your magazine, then you are likely on shaky ground and it is time to rethink your options.

Determining whether to accept the NBA tickets using Bok's model helps clarify the legitimacy of your actions. What does your conscience tell you about taking the tickets? Is there a little, niggling worry there? Do you wonder what your ethics professor might say about taking the tickets? If so, your conscience is sending you some warning signals.

What goal are you trying to achieve here? Appeasing an advertiser? How about doing that by creating a magazine readers can trust? Or will you have opened a door that the advertiser will expect to walk through on a regular basis? Is there a legitimate goal in there somewhere?

And if that advertiser got special mention in an article you wrote—or showed up in a prominent photograph—what will other advertisers say? Won't they expect the same treatment—perhaps without the benefit of the tickets? How will readers react? Will you and your magazine be believable if you can be bought so easily? Will readers trust any products you feature in your magazine once they realize advertisers are helping make your decisions?

The difference between the NBA tickets and the trip to Spain is that an advertiser has more clout and can affect your magazine's bottom line, so you might face pressure from within the magazine to make the advertiser happy. Again, discuss this openly, and take the stance that the advertiser is best served by a good magazine. Some magazines have specific standards related to gifts from advertisers.

Advertisers can pose multiple risks related to conflicts of interest. *InStyle* editors once received Rolex watches from an advertiser not related to Rolex and immediately returned them because they constituted a significant amount of money the advertiser had paid to a third party to buy the watches. If the expense is in-house, as it is with manufacturers, the issue is less troublesome, says *InStyle* managing editor Charla Lawhon. If a purse designer sends the magazine a purse, the magazine may use it as one of the purses the staff considers—usually one of several hundred for an article on six or eight styles—but the decision on which purse to feature comes from good old-fashioned editorial judgment: What serves the reader best? "We have to always remember what got us here—service that truly solves a problem," Lawhon says.[5]

codes of ethics

Proactive magazine staffs think about potential problems ahead of time and implement strategies to avoid and resolve conflicts. Codes of ethics have traditionally provided staffs with a well-defined response to ethical questions. The American Society of Magazine Editors (ASME), the American Business Media (ABM), and the Society of Professional Journalists (SPJ) offer ethical guides for consumer and business magazines. All are reprinted as appendixes to this chapter.

ASME's code specifically deals with advertising-editing conflicts and directly addresses the issue of designing advertising inserts to match a magazine's pages:

> Advertisements should look different enough from editorial pages that readers can tell the difference. To avoid confusion, any ad that looks enough like an editorial story or feature that it could be mistaken for one should be slugged "Advertisement" or "Promotion" at the top of each page in type as prominent as the magazine's normal body type.

The ABM code, because it is for business-to-business magazines, suggests that journalists not invest in companies they cover in their magazine because this can pose significant conflicts of interest. The code also deals with gifts, relationships with companies and associations the journalist covers, travel, and relationships with advertisers. Like the ASME code, it is clear on the separation of advertising and editorial:

> Editors have an obligation to readers to make clear which content has been paid for, which is sponsored, and which is independent editorial material. All paid content that may be confused with independent editorial material must be labeled as advertiser-sponsored.

In 2004, the ABM added a section on electronic media ethics, covering Web-related advertising-editorial responsibilities, such as including advertisers' links on the magazine's site and labeling online advertorials.

SPJ's code emphasizes the journalist's responsibility to society, dealing with issues such as accuracy and fairness, staged events, stereotyping, and compassion for those involved in the news. It provides the clearest means of critiquing coverage of September 11, advising writers, editors, and designers to "minimize harm" by showing "compassion for those who may be affected adversely by news coverage" and being "sensitive when seeking or using interviews or photographs of those affected by tragedy or grief."

But weren't those chilling photographs of people falling to their deaths from the World Trade Center an essential part of the story? *Time* and *Newsweek* chose not to put those images on their covers because they had plenty of other strong images that did not violate the victims' right to privacy: the second airplane heading into the towers, close-ups of firefighters, the buildings in a cloud of smoke and fire. Some magazines chose, however, to use the images in interior pages, causing the type of public outcry Hodges and Bok list as a warning sign in their moral frameworks.

One image, by Associated Press photographer Richard Drew, titled "A Person Falls Headfirst," is especially disturbing, as it focuses on one man, his figure clearly silhouetted against the vertical lines of one of the towers. Critics charged that the image should be suppressed out of respect; others argued that doing so meant the entire story of the attacks was not told.

Francis G. Couvares, E. Dwight Salmon professor of history and American studies at Amherst College, says both positions are weak. Couvares puts the issue into contemporary perspective in relation to photographs of soldiers killed in Iraq, which were largely kept from the public. Couvares believes such decisions keep readers from understanding the context of the story, protecting the public from important but "unwelcome truth":

> One argument for censorship was humanitarian, protective of persons: The victim's loved ones would suffer horribly if they were forced to see, over and again, the sight of a father or son or wife or grandchild flailing desperately against the inevitable. The other argument was communal, protective of something far more elusive—culture, values, common decency.
>
> Both arguments are suspect. It is not coincidental that they are echoed today in the rationales offered by government (and media) officials who

suppress images of war. Battlefield carnage—which, in this era of asymmetrical warfare mostly means their dead—is never shown and almost never mentioned on television or in the newspapers. And images of the stream of returning coffins—which means our dead—have been suppressed with perfect efficiency. To protect the families, says the Pentagon. To protect our culture from coarsening before the pornography of violence, say the moralists and pundits.[6]

Bob Steele, the Nelson Poynter scholar for journalism values at the Poynter Institute, says images can be suppressed if they serve no real value, which he believes was the case with the photographs of *Wall Street Journal* reporter Daniel Pearl's death in June 2002:

I just don't believe there is any journalistic imperative to show these terrible images of Daniel Pearl's death to the general public. I don't believe we learn anything substantive or new. Granted, we may get a vivid reminder of just how barbaric Pearl's killers are. But that doesn't carry enough weight in the ethical decision-making equation compared to the profound negative consequences.

Journalists have ethical obligations beyond seeking and reporting the truth about substantive issues and events. Journalists and their news organizations have a moral obligation and professional duty to show respect for human beings and compassion for those who are very vulnerable. The primary principle for journalists is to seek the truth and report it as fully as possible. But journalists must balance that principle with another principle that I call "minimizing harm."[7]

Following a solid ethical code is difficult. Journalists who challenge business assumptions can be called troublemakers. Often, though, the key to a successful challenge is in its presentation. Rather than implying that the boss or the publishing company is unethical when they suggest an act the journalist finds inappropriate, the best approach is dialogue. Talk the issue over with your editor or publisher. Ask your own essential questions.

Victor Navasky, publisher and editorial director of *The Nation*, says ethics gets short shrift in the everyday life of magazines because staffs are so busy doing their work they often don't have time to think about its implication. "I don't think ethics, as such, is on the mind of editors. They are too busy trying to get the magazine out. But it comes up every minute of the day," Navasky says.[8]

The ASME, ABM, and SPJ codes all strive to define a standard of behavior based on professional integrity. The SPJ code, which was initially adopted in 1926, is the oldest of the three. It provides a statement of principles in its "Preamble" that journalists might copy and hang on their office walls for guidance:

Members of the Society of Professional Journalists believe that public enlightenment is the forerunner of justice and the foundation of democracy. The duty of the journalist is to further those ends by seeking truth and providing a fair and comprehensive account of events and issues. Conscientious journalists from all media and specialties strive to serve the public with thoroughness and honesty. Professional integrity is the cornerstone of a journalist's credibility.

notes

....

1. Philip Patterson and Lee Wilkins, *Media Ethics: Issues and Cases* (New York: McGraw-Hill. 2005), 3.
2. Ibid.,3.
3. Personal discussion, January 20, 2006. Hodges has spoken and written regularly about his moral framework in publications such as *Journal of Mass Media Ethics* and the *Journal of Communication*.
4. Patterson and Wilkins, 4.
5. Personal discussion at Drake University, January 25, 2006.
6. Francis G. Couvares, "The Pain of War," *Amherst Magazine*, http://www.amherst.edu/magazine/issues/05winter/war/drew.html.
7. Bob Steele, "Pearl Photo: Too Harmful," www.poynter.org, http://www.poynter.org/column.asp?id=36&aid=839.
8. Michael Robert Evans, *The Layers of Magazine Editing* (New York: Columbia University Press, 2004), 83.

for additional reading

Christians, Clifford G., Kim B. Rotzoll, Mark B. Fackler, Kathy Brittain McKee, and Robert H. Woods Jr. *Media Ethics: Cases and Moral Reasoning*. Boston: Allyn and Bacon, 2005.

Cohen, Elliot D., and Deni Elliott. *Journalism Ethics: A Reference Handbook (Contemporary Ethical Issues)*. Santa Barbara, Calif.: Abc-Clio, 1998.

Evans, Michael Robert. *The Layers of Magazine Editing*. New York: Columbia University Press, 2004.

Fink, Conrad. *Media Ethics*. Boston: Allyn and Bacon, 1995.

Patterson, Philip, and Lee Wilkins. *Media Ethics: Issues and Cases*. New York: McGraw-Hill, 2005.

Sanders, Karen. *Ethics and Journalism*. London: Sage Publications, 2003.

appendix 12.1

American Society of Magazine Editors (ASME) Guidelines for Editors and Publishers, Thirteenth Edition

For magazines to be trusted by consumers and to endure as brands, readers must be assured of their editorial integrity. With that core conviction in mind—and the overwhelming support of its members—the American Society of Magazine Editors for over two decades has issued guidelines to make sure that the difference between advertising and editorial content is transparent to readers and that there is no advertiser influence or pressure on editorial independence. In this latest edition, we have aimed to make the guidelines easier to understand and to distill them into ten basic statements of principle and practice. ASME will continue to advise editors and publishers about how to interpret the guidelines. Repeated and willful violations will result in public sanction and disqualification from the National Magazine Awards.

Design

Advertisements should look different enough from editorial pages that readers can tell the difference. To avoid confusion, any ad that looks enough like an editorial story or feature that it could be mistaken for one should be slugged "Advertisement" or "Promotion" at the top of each page in type as prominent as the magazine's normal body type.

Covers

The front cover and spine are editorial space. Companies and products should appear on covers only in an editorial context and not in a way that suggests advertisement. (This includes use of cover "stickers.")

Adjacencies

Advertisements should not be placed or sold for placement immediately before or after editorial pages that discuss, show or promote the advertised products.

Logos

Advertiser logos should not appear on editorial pages except in a journalistic context. A magazine's logo should appear on advertising pages only in connection with advertisements for the magazine and its promotions or when an advertised product is touting editorial awards that it has won.

Sponsorship

Sponsorship language (i.e., "sponsored by," "presented by," etc.) should not appear in connection with regularly occurring editorial features. Such language may be used in connection with editorial extras (special issues, inserts, onserts and

American Society of Magazine Editors (ASME) (continued)

contests) as long as the editorial content does not endorse the sponsor's products and any page announcing the sponsorship is clearly an ad or is labeled "Advertisement" or "Promotion" in a type size as prominent as the magazine's normal body type. Single-advertiser issues that don't include sponsorship language do not have to be labelled, but should include an editor's or publisher's note disclosing the special arrangement to readers. Advertisers may sponsor "out of book" events such as awards shows and conferences, and that sponsorship may be acknowledged without labeling on either advertising or editorial pages.

Advertising Sections

Editorial-looking sections or pages that are not produced by a magazine's editors are not editorial content. They should be labeled "Advertisement," "Special Advertising Section" or "Promotion" at the top of every page in type as prominent as the magazine's normal body type.

Product Placement/ Integration

Advertisers should not pay to place their products in editorial pages nor should they demand place-

ment in return for advertising. Editorial pages may display and credit products and tell readers where to buy them, as long as those pages are solely under editorial control.

Editorial Staffing and Titles

A magazine's editorial staff members should not be involved in producing advertising in that magazine. Advertising and marketing staff should not use titles that imply editorial involvement (e.g., merchandising editor).

Editorial Review

In order for a publication's chief editor to be able to monitor compliance with these guidelines, every effort must be made to show all advertising pages, sections and their placement to the editor far enough in advance to allow for necessary changes.

Advertising Review

While editors or publishers at their discretion may share the general topic matter of upcoming editorial content with advertisers, specific stories, layouts or tables of contents should not be submitted for advertiser review. ■

Source: American Society of Magazine Editors: http://www.magazine.org/editorial/guidelines/index.cfm

appendix 12.2

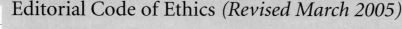

American Business Media (ABM):
Editorial Code of Ethics *(Revised March 2005)*

Business-to-business editors have earned the highest level of trust among their readers. Many surveys have shown that executives and managers believe business-to-business publications

provide the most accurate and credible information available.

That trust is both a high compliment and a challenge for those who plan, write and edit

(continued)

American Business Media (ADM) (continued)

publications. It sets a high standard they must maintain. American Business Media has always held its editors to such high standards. Indeed, the annual Jesse H. Neal Awards, named for the Association's first president, were established in the mid-1950s to encourage editorial excellence and have become the highest honors granted for business-to-business journalism. ABM's Code of Publishing Practice, a part of ABM's Constitution and By-Laws, has been in place for more than 33 years, and requires that ABM member companies maintain strict standards of journalistic ethics.

The Editorial Committee works with its members to maintain editorial quality at member publications. As part of that mission, the Editorial Committee regularly reviews and updates this Editorial Code of Ethics and Guide to Preferred Practices, which has been approved by the American Business Media Executive Committee. This revision has two parts. The first part is a code of ethics primarily for print editions of publications, and the second covers online versions.

I General editorial code of ethics

Editors, reporters and writers employed by American Business Media publications adhere to the highest standards of journalistic practice. In doing so, they pledge to:

a. Maintain honesty, integrity, accuracy, thoroughness and fairness in the reporting and editing of articles, headlines, and graphics.

b. Avoid all conflicts of interest as well as any appearances of such conflicts.

c. Maintain an appropriate professional distance from the direct preparation of special advertising sections or other advertisements.

d. Show the distinction between news stories and editorials, columns and other opinion pieces.

e. Accept as their primary responsibility the selection of editorial content based on readers' needs and interests.

II American Business Media Guide to Preferred Practices

II-1 Conflicts of Interest

a. Editors should not invest in companies and/or industries they personally cover (this does not preclude investments in mutual funds, pensions or 401(k) plans that hold shares in a manner not directly controlled by the editor). Their spouses and other immediate family members should also avoid personal investments that might reflect unfavorably upon the editor. Investing on the basis of "insider information" is, of course, a violation of securities laws.

b. If a conflict arises in an investment held by an editor before his/her employment, or because of a merger or acquisition, he/she should immediately bring the conflict to the attention of his/her editorial management.

II-2 Gifts

a. Editors should not accept any gifts or favors, except those of nominal value, from companies or associations they cover, their public relations representatives or any other person or organization related to companies they cover. The editor's supervisor should determine what is of "nominal value."

b. Editors may accept occasional meals and refreshments in the course of business dealings.

II-3 Outside Activities

a. Editors should not accept freelance work from companies, associations or any other entity they cover.

b. Because editors are expected to speak as authorities within their markets, they may accept invitations to appear on television, radio and other electronic media and may accept payment upon approval of editorial management.

c. Editors should not accept payment of any kind for making speeches, judging contests or making appearances at functions held by companies or associations they cover.

American Business Media (ADM) (continued)

d. Reimbursement of reasonable expenses incurred in connection with such speeches may be accepted.

e. Editors may also accept speaker gifts of nominal value for participating in such events.

II-4 Travel

a. Editors should not accept payment of travel and hotel expenses incurred in the course of performing editorial duties from any source other than their employers.

b. In cases of group press affairs, presentations and other events involving representatives from several publications, editors should reimburse information sources for these expenses.

II-5 Relationship with Advertisers

a. Selection of editorial topics, treatment of issues, interpretation and other editorial decisions must not be determined by advertisers, advertising agencies or the advertising departments of publications.

b. Editors must never permit advertisers to review articles prior to publication.

c. Advertisers and potential advertisers must never receive favorable editorial treatment because of their economic value to the publication. Similarly, non-advertisers should not receive unfavorable editorial treatment or be excluded from articles because they do not advertise. This provision applies not only to stories and articles but to all products of the editorial group, including lists, rankings, product or company of the year awards and other such special features and events.

d. Editors must have the right to review, prior to publication, all sponsored content and other advertiser-supplied content.

II-6 Separation of Advertising and Editorial

a. Editors must make a clear distinction between editorial and advertising. Editors have an obligation to readers to make clear which content has been paid for, which is sponsored and which is independent editorial material. All paid content that may be confused with independent editorial material must be labeled as advertiser-sponsored.

b. With respect to special advertising supplements or advertorials: The words advertising, advertisement, special advertising supplement or similar labeling must appear horizontally at or near the center of the top of every page of such sections containing text, in type at least equal in size and weight to the publication's standard body typeface [adapted from American Society of Magazine Editors Editorial Guidelines, Nov. 2004].

c. The layout, design, typeface and style of special advertising sections or custom publishing products must be distinctly different from those of the publication [adapted from ASME, Nov. 2004].

d. Special advertising sections must not be slugged in the publication's cover (including stickers) nor included in the table of contents. In general, the publication's name or logo may not appear as any part of the headlines or text of such sections, except in connection with the magazine's own products or services [adapted from ASME, Nov. 2004].

e. Editorial staff members and freelancers used by editorial should not participate in the preparation of custom publishing or advertising sections, except that the chief editor may review contents of such sections before they appear.

III Editorial Code of Ethics and Guide to Preferred Practices for Electronic Media
November 2004

Credibility is the key to the success of digital media offerings, just as it is for print publications; users must trust the advice and information presented. In order to build and maintain that trust, the distinction between independent editorial content and paid promotional information must remain clear. American Business Media believes it is possible to keep that clear distinction while still taking advantage of linking and other technologies that make digital media

American Business Media (ADM) (continued)

the unique and robust experience it has come to be for the user.

With that goal in mind, ABM recommends the following standards, adapted from those of the American Society of Magazine Editors for the express needs of business media:

a. The publication's Web site should display the publication's name and logo prominently, in order to clarify who controls the content of the site. All editorial content must be under the sole control of the editorial staff.

b. All online pages must clearly distinguish between editorial and advertising or sponsored content. Non-editorial must be clearly labeled. The publication's name or logo should not be used in any way that suggests editorial endorsement of an advertiser. The site's sponsorship policies must be clearly noted, either in text accompanying the article or on a disclosure page to clarify that the sponsor had no input regarding the content.

c. Hypertext links that appear within the editorial content of a site, including those within graphics, must be solely at the discretion of the editors. Links within editorial should never be paid for by advertisers.

d. Special advertising or "advertorial" features should conform to the same guidelines in section II that apply to print.

e. Special advertising sections or features must be displayed in such a way that users will not confuse them with editorial content.

f. To protect the brand, editors/producers should not permit their content to be used on an advertiser's site without an explanation of the relationship (e.g. "Reprinted with permission").

g. Advertisers or e-commerce partners must not receive preferential treatment in search engines, price comparisons, and other applications presented under the content provider's brand unless this is clearly disclosed. An editorial site should not vouch for others' tools that it may offer.

h. A Web site should respect the privacy of its users. If a site intends to collect information about its visitors—whether the data will be disseminated to third parties or not—it must offer users a chance to decline if they choose, through an "opt-out" option. As part of its privacy policy, the site should explain its use of cookies and other data collection methods and tell what it intends to do with the information it gleans. Potential benefits to the user—broader site access, better personalization features, etc.—should be presented as well.

i. Advertisements should not be intentionally placed next to editorial coverage of the specific product advertised. This does not preclude ads on search results pages, topic index pages, channel pages and the like, as long as selection criteria for those pages are not weighted in favor of advertisers and are free of other commercial consideration. ■

appendix 12.3

Society of Professional Journalists Code of Ethics

Preamble

Members of the Society of Professional Journalists believe that public enlightenment is the forerunner of justice and the foundation of democracy. The duty of the journalist is to further those ends by seeking truth and providing a fair and comprehensive account of events and issues. Conscientious journalists from all media and specialties strive to serve the public with thoroughness and honesty. Professional integrity is the cornerstone of a journalist's credibility. Members of the Society share a dedication to ethical behavior and adopt this code to declare the Society's principles and standards of practice.

Seek Truth and Report It

Journalists should be honest, fair and courageous in gathering, reporting and interpreting information.

Journalists should:

- Test the accuracy of information from all sources and exercise care to avoid inadvertent error. Deliberate distortion is never permissible.
- Diligently seek out subjects of news stories to give them the opportunity to respond to allegations of wrongdoing.
- Identify sources whenever feasible. The public is entitled to as much information as possible on sources' reliability.
- Always question sources' motives before promising anonymity. Clarify conditions attached to any promise made in exchange for information. Keep promises.
- Make certain that headlines, news teases and promotional material, photos, video, audio, graphics, sound bites and quotations do not misrepresent. They should not oversimplify or highlight incidents out of context.
- Never distort the content of news photos or video. Image enhancement for technical clarity

is always permissible. Label montages and photo illustrations.
- Avoid misleading re-enactments or staged news events. If re-enactment is necessary to tell a story, label it.
- Avoid undercover or other surreptitious methods of gathering information except when traditional open methods will not yield information vital to the public. Use of such methods should be explained as part of the story.
- Never plagiarize.
- Tell the story of the diversity and magnitude of the human experience boldly, even when it is unpopular to do so.
- Examine their own cultural values and avoid imposing those values on others.
- Avoid stereotyping by race, gender, age, religion, ethnicity, geography, sexual orientation, disability, physical appearance or social status.
- Support the open exchange of views, even views they find repugnant.
- Give voice to the voiceless; official and unofficial sources of information can be equally valid.
- Distinguish between advocacy and news reporting. Analysis and commentary should be labeled and not misrepresent fact or context.
- Distinguish news from advertising and shun hybrids that blur the lines between the two.
- Recognize a special obligation to ensure that the public's business is conducted in the open and that government records are open to inspection.

Minimize Harm

Ethical journalists treat sources, subjects and colleagues as human beings deserving of respect.

Journalists should:

- Show compassion for those who may be affected adversely by news coverage. Use

Society of Professional Journalists Code of Ethics (continued)

special sensitivity when dealing with children and inexperienced sources or subjects.

■ Be sensitive when seeking or using interviews or photographs of those affected by tragedy or grief.

■ Recognize that gathering and reporting information may cause harm or discomfort. Pursuit of the news is not a license for arrogance.

■ Recognize that private people have a greater right to control information about themselves than do public officials and others who seek power, influence or attention. Only an overriding public need can justify intrusion into anyone's privacy.

■ Show good taste. Avoid pandering to lurid curiosity.

■ Be cautious about identifying juvenile suspects or victims of sex crimes.

■ Be judicious about naming criminal suspects before the formal filing of charges.

■ Balance a criminal suspect's fair trial rights with the public's right to be informed.

Act Independently

Journalists should be free of obligation to any interest other than the public's right to know.

Journalists should:

■ Avoid conflicts of interest, real or perceived.

■ Remain free of associations and activities that may compromise integrity or damage credibility.

■ Refuse gifts, favors, fees, free travel and special treatment, and shun secondary employ-

ment, political involvement, public office and service in community organizations if they compromise journalistic integrity.

■ Disclose unavoidable conflicts.

■ Be vigilant and courageous about holding those with power accountable.

■ Deny favored treatment to advertisers and special interests and resist their pressure to influence news coverage.

■ Be wary of sources offering information for favors or money; avoid bidding for news.

Be Accountable

Journalists are accountable to their readers, listeners, viewers and each other.

Journalists should:

■ Clarify and explain news coverage and invite dialogue with the public over journalistic conduct.

■ Encourage the public to voice grievances against the news media.

■ Admit mistakes and correct them promptly.

■ Expose unethical practices of journalists and the news media.

■ Abide by the same high standards to which they hold others.

The SPJ Code of Ethics is voluntarily embraced by thousands of writers, editors and other news professionals. The present version of the code was adopted by the 1996 SPJ National Convention, after months of study and debate among the Society's members.

Source: Society of Professional Journalists: http://www.spj.org/ethics_code.asp

Bold page numbers indicate photographs.

AARP: The Magazine
　advertising in, 118
　appearance of, 265
　articles in, 7
　audience for, 118
　circulation of, 16, 22
　classification of, 16
　folio lines, 265
　last editorial page in, 281
　in MPA's future cover
　　campaign, 18
　purpose of, 137
AAUW Outlook, 183
ABA Journal, 17, 121
Abbey, Edward, 245
Aberlich, Michael, 48
Ability, 108
Abolition, 70, 96
Abrahamson, David, 41–42
Accent, 150
Adams, Abigail, 281
Adams, John, 61, 95
Adams, John Quincy, 68, 229
Addams, Charles, 4
Addison, Joseph, 58
Administration/operating costs,
　167, 168–69, 186–88
Advance Publications
　Condé Nast Publications, 37,
　　196, 209, 210
　Fairchild, 209
　The New Yorker and, 198,
　　208–10
　ownership of, 208–10
Adventure, 36
Advertising. *See also* Sponsorship
　2004 statistics on, 27
　ABM on, 358, 362–63
　advertorials. *See* Advertorials
　ancillary products and, 31–34
　appropriation, 339
　articles and, 17, 46–50, 141,
　　296–97, 360–61, 363
　ASME on, 48, 358, 360–61
　in association magazines, 16
　audience and, 44–45, 48–49,
　　51, 150
　audits and, 184
　autonomy and, 47–50, 140,
　　215, 356–58
　awards and, 231
　background on, 37–39
　broadcast vs. print, 41–42
　censorship and, 47
　circulation and, 34, 39, 178–79
　in city magazines, 10
　classified, 4, 24n1, 77, 344–45
　in consumer magazines, 15,
　　36, 67

controlled circulation and,
　15
copyright and, 349
on covers, 44, 50–51, 297
CPMs, 34, 35, 178–79, 186
in custom magazines, 18–19,
　212
demographics and, 7, 28–30
departments and, 296–97
design of, 254, 361–63
digital vs. print, 85
direct mail. *See* Direct mail
　marketing
discounts for, 179, 186
distribution of, 83
editorial formula and, 143–44
editorial philosophy and,
　46–51, 136, 140–41, 151,
　213
to editorial ratio, 39, 144, 178,
　181, 186
effectiveness of, 31
in 18th century, 37, 68
ethnicity and, 67
expenses from, 167, 168,
　186–88
by "experiential marketing,"
　111
fiction and, 247
first American, 37
Good Housekeeping's Seal of
　Approval, 32–33
halo effect and, 28
hard offers, 174
historical images of, 49
to homosexual market, 107
identity and, 140, 143
ink for, 302
inserts, 141, 295
integrated media in, 20–21
intrusiveness of, 51
last editorial page and, 281
local vs. national, 8–10
media kits, 170, 207
men and, 67, 238
in 19th century, 37
online, 28, 51, 171–72, 211,
　358, 364
outserts, 143
photographs in, 302
placement of, 31, 46, 49–50,
　148–50, 258, 271,
　295–97, 360–61
price per issue and, 39
proofs, 311
pseudoworld of, 113–16
psychographics and, 7, 28–29
publication frequency and,
　36–37, 177

in public relations magazines,
　18
race and, 67, 122, 238
rates for, 28, 34–35, 39, 42,
　177–79, 186
redesign and, 287, 290
refusal of, 17, 33, 39, 215
revenue from, 166–67, 179
for rural vs. urban readers, 67
in scholarly journals, 17
September 11 terrorist attacks
　and, 102, 103
soft offers, 174
in special issues, 236–37
spending on, 2004 annual, 36
success/failure and, 135, 158
swapping of, 157, 172
table of contents and, 282
in test issues, 175, 178
third-party liability, 343–45
in trade magazines, 31, 37, 51,
　67
trust in, 28
value of, 141
voice and, 143
women and, 44–45, 48–49, 67,
　113, 238
Advertising Age, 115, 237
Advertising Sales Director, 187,
　207
Advertising Sales Representative,
　207
Advertising staff
　chief, 187, 207
　duties of, 192
　editors and, 46–47, 200
　publication frequency and, 192
　salaries for, 168, 187
Advertorials
　ABM on, 358, 363, 364
　ASME on, 141
　Neal Award and, 244
　on websites, 364
Advocacy, 94, 95
Advocate, The
　appearance of, 265
　articles in, 138, 246
　audience for, 107–8
　cover of, **107**
　essays in, 246
　establishment of, 107
　folio lines, 265
　"Notes from a Blond," 246
　role of, 13, 107
Adweek, 43, 182, 237, 261
Affinity Research VISTA Print
　Tracking Services, 31
Afghanistan, U.S. military in,
　322

African Americans
　advertising and, 67, 122, 238
　buying power forecasts for, 30
　civil rights movement, 97–98
　content and, 67, 97–98, 238
　"counter-memory" of, 75
　on covers, **90**, 238
　HIV/AIDS and, 139
　lynching of, 272
　photographs of, **90**, 272,
　　312–13
　population of, 122
　reading habits of, 30
　titles for, 30, 98–99, 123–24
　in trade magazines, 238
Agenda setting theory, 91
Agha, Mehemed Fehmy, 80,
　253–54, 256–57
AIDS. *See* HIV/AIDS
Alcott, Louisa May, 3, 72
Alden, Cynthia May Westover, 203
Alden, Henry Mills, 246
Alfieris, Joseph, 347
Ali, Mohammed, 233–34, 272
Allen, Christopher C., 111
Allure, 209
Almay, 302
Altria Group, 36, 215
A. Magazine, 30, 125
American Angus Association, 230
American Antiquarian Society
　Library, 77
American Artist, 176
American Association of Retired
　Persons (AARP). *See AARP:
　The Magazine*
American Association of
　University Women (AAUW),
　183
American Baby, 209, 211
American Banker, 56, 65, 121
American Business Media (ABM)
　on advertising, 358, 362–63
　advertising studies for, 31
　ethical guide from, 358,
　　361–64
　members of, 21
　Neal Award, 109, 243–44, 362
　on trade magazines, 15
American Business Press, 208
American Dream Homes, 209
American Express, 147
American Fruit Grower, 56
*American Geophysical Union, Inc. v.
　Texaco, Inc.*, 352n75
American Hunter, 15
American Indian Report, 125
"Americanization of Paris, The,"
　258

American Journalism Review, 282
American Journal of Nursing, 56
American Lawyer, The, 347
American Legacy, 75, 124
American Machinist, 56, 65
American Magazine
   appearance of, 77
   articles in, 58–59
   Distribution and Distribution
     of, 81
   press used for, 84
   price per issue, 60
   publication of, 56, 73
American Mechanics Magazine, 65,
   73
American Media, 217
American Medical News, 331
American Museum, 73, 81
American Nurseryman, 56
American Opinion, 332–33
American Patchwork and Quilting,
   15
American Photo, 21
American Railroad Journal, The,
   12, 73
American Rifleman, 13, 56
American School Board Journal, 56
American Society of Association
   Executives (ASAE), 16, 21
American Society of Journalists
   and Authors, 338
American Society of Magazine
   Editors (ASME)
   on advertising, 48, 358, 360–61
   on advertorials, 141
   on cover art, 50–51, 360
   ethical guide from, 358,
     360–61
   NMA, 50, 98, 241–43
   on sponsorship, 50
American Spectator, The, 13, 138
Americans with Disabilities Act,
   108
America's Pharmacist, 56
Amery, Leopold, 268
Ancillary products
   advertising and, 31–34
   circulation and, 72
   editors and, 34, 200, 217–18
   exclusivity of, 114
   in inserts, 141, 305
   on Internet, 34
   September 11 terrorist attacks
     and, 176
   for subscriptions, 72, 175, 176
Anderman, Richard, 29
Anderson, Bob, 134
Anderson, Sherwood, 324
Angell, Roger, 199
Angus Journal, 230, **230**
Animal House, 341
Aniston, Jennifer, 289
Anthony, Susan B., 216
Apartment Life, 119. *See also*
   Metropolitan Home
Aphra, 100
Apkarian, Carol, 51
Appearance
   American vs. European, 257
   appeal of, 67
   approaches to, 262
   audience and, 262
   balance in, 270
   color, 80, 268–69, 300–304,
     307
   computers and, 261
   contrast, 271

of covers, 281–87
of departments, 264, 269, 271
editorial philosophy and,
   139–40, 254–56, 290
in 18th century, 67–68, 77–78,
   271–73
eye movement and, 263, 267,
   270
factors affecting, 254
of feature articles, 227, 254–56,
   269
folio lines, 265
gestalt in, 258
grids and, 263–64, 269
identity and, 254–56
illustrations. *See* Illustrations
in 19th century, 78, 273
optical center, 270
postal rates and, 43
proportion in, 270
readout materials, 255, 277–80
redesign of, 287–90
signatures, 307–9
of table of contents, 280–81
trends in, 60–61, 262
in 20th century, 78–80, 256–62
in 21st century, 262
typography. *See* Typography
unity in, 269–70
Apple Computers, 85, 261
Appropriation, 339
APR, 301
Aqueous coating, 300
Arbarbanel, Stephanie, 237
Archaeology Odyssey, 282
Archery Business, 27
Architectural Digest, 6, 111, 180,
   209
Arena, 248
Arizona Highways, 8
Arkansas Times, 325
Arnaz, Desi, Jr., 263
Arnold, David, 119
Art covers, 284
Art Director
   desktop publishing and, 305–6
   duties of, 201–2, 218, 258
   editors and, 254
   freelance designers and, 205,
     218
   for online magazines, 211
   photographers and, 204–5
   production director and,
     201–2
Arthritis Today, 140
Arthur Frommer's Budget Travel,
   121, 230
Articles
   advertising and, 17, 46–50,
     141, 296–97, 360–61,
     363
   banking of, 296, 297
   design of, 254
   essays, 224, 242, 244–46, 281
   feature. *See* Feature articles
   inserts and, 295
   Neal Award for, 243–44
   news. *See* News articles
   placement of, 148–50, 271,
     295–97
   titles for, 255
   underwriting of, 50
Artwork
   camera-ready, 308
   cartoons. *See* Cartoons
   computer-generated, 273
   on covers, 42, **97**, 98, 273, 281,

   284, 287
   in 18th century, 77–78, 271–73
   in 19th century, 78, 273
   planning for, 301
   printing of, 303–4
   in proofs, 311
   women in, 78, 112, 273
Ashcroft, John, 321
Ashley, Rhett, 235
Asian Americans, 30, 122, 124–25
Asian Week, 30, 125
Asiaweek, 103
As Nature Made Him, 237
Assistant Editor, 204
Assistant Publisher, 207
Associate Editor, 204, 205
Association Management, 16
Association Meetings, 16
Association Publishing, 22
Astor, John Jacob, 232
Atlanta, 10, 11
Atlanta Homes and Lifestyles, 11
Atlantic Monthly, The
   advertising in, 30
   articles in, 12, 65, 76, 229, 248
   audience for, 30
   circulation of, 30
   classification of, 15
   contributors to, 69
   cover of, **177**
   cutlines in, 280
   establishment of, 55, 56
   headquarters of, 66
   letters to the editor, 248
   needs met by, 6
   NMAs for, 243
   publication frequency, 177
   Reader's Digest and, 74
   reader's profile by, 36
   serialized novels in, 246
   short stories in, 247
   structure of, 150
   Sunset and, 227
   on Watergate, 100
   "Why Americans Hate the
     Media," 248
   women journalists and, 239
Atwood, Margaret, 69
Audience
   advertising and, 44–45, 48–49,
     51, 150
   appearance and, 262
   baby boomers, 118–21
   class of, 57, 60–62, 83
   for covers, 42
   data retention by, 30
   demographics of, 7, 28–30,
     118–21
   editors and, 150, 223, 249
   education level of, 29, 64, 66
   ethnicity of, 67, 173
   external, 18
   Generation X. *See*
     Generation X
   Generation Y. *See*
     Generation Y
   income of, 28–30, 60, 67, 179
   for inserts, 141
   internal, 18
   leisure activities of, 117
   letters from. *See* Letters to the
     Editor
   literacy rate, 59–60, 64
   local vs. national, 8–10
   loyalty of, 223
   men. *See* Men
   psychographics of, 7, 28–29

   race of, 67, 98
   reading habits of, 30
   research director and, 208
   women. *See* Women
Audit Bureau of Circulation
   (ABC), 22, 38, 176, 179
Audrey, 30, 91, 125
Audubon, 109, 160
August Home Publishing, 142,
   169, 210, 211
Ault, Peggy, 340
Ault v. Hustler, 340
AURAS Design, 289
Automatic Picture Replacement
   (APR), 301
Automotive Industries, 56
AutoWeek, 29
Autry, James, 224
Avedon, Richard, 276
*Aviation Week and Space
   Technology*
   agenda setting in, 92
   cold war and, 92
   ownership of, 208, 209
   Persian Gulf War coverage, 92
   Vietnam War coverage, 100

Baby boomers, 118–21
Baby Talk, 228
Baker, Ray Stannard, 93
Baking and Snack, 237
Baking Management, 15
Balance, 270
Baldwin, James, 272
Ball, Lucille, 263
Baltimore, 10
Banner, 255
Barber, Dorothy, 336–37
Bard, Rick, 134
Bark, 136
Barney, Mary, 216
Barrett, William, 77–78
Barron's, 116, 144
Baseline, 244
Bass Guitar Magazine, 121
Bathroom reading, 29
"Battered Child Syndrome, The,"
   92
Baumann, Mary Kay, 285
Beauregard, Pierre, 235
Beauty Myth, The, 113
Bell, Alexander Graham, 156
Ben Casey, M.D., 92
Benchley, Robert, 197
Benchmark studies, 110
Bentkowski, Tom, 313
Berg, Don L., 277
Bernt, Joseph P., 238
Best of Flair, The, 153
Better Homes and Gardens
   advertising in, 37
   ancillary products of, 34
   articles in, 224, 227
   circulation of, 15, 22
   copyright, 348
   cover of, **20**, 300
   editorial organization chart,
     194
   editorial philosophy for, 137
   illustrations in, 113
   interactive media from, 20, 23
   Mother Earth News and, 159
   online chat rooms for, 7, 111
   ownership of, 208, 209
   printing of, 307
   publisher of, 37
   purpose of, 137

redesign of, 7
regional data in, 307
Better Homes and Gardens New Cook Book, 34
Better Homes and Gardens Plan Ideas, 112
Bikini, 150
Binding, 305–9
bin Laden, Osama, 104, 276
Biographies, 232
Birds and Blooms, 142
Birth of a Baby, 325
Bitch, 136
Black, Cathleen
　on ancillary products, 34, 200
　career of, 44, 217
　on *CosmoGirl*, 126
　on editorial responsibilities, 34, 200
　Financial Times on, 217
　on women journalists, 217
Black, Roger, 261, 269, 278
Black Elegance, 124
Black Enterprise
　advertising in, 122, 124
　audience for, 7, 120
　Hispanic titles and, 123
Black Issues Book Review, 30, 124
Black Perspective in Music, 123
Black Politician, 123
Black Sports, 123
Black Tennis, 123
Blanchard, Keith, 344
Blender, 36
Bloomer, Amelia, 216
blue, 256, 270
Blue Book, The, 283
Bluelines, 306, 311
Blyth, Myrna, 216
Bok, Edward, 67, 72, 203, 225–26
Bok, Sissela, 357
Bok's ethics model, 357
Bon Appetit, 172
Bond, Julian, 272
Bonfire of the Vanities, The, 247
Boorstin, Daniel, 116
Booth, Shirley, 339
Boston Magazine, 339
Boughner, Genevieve Jackson, 203
Bourke-White, Margaret, 4, 80
Bowhunting World, 27, **28**
Bowser, Lisa, 306
Boyer, Paul, 173
"Boy on the Train, The," 327–28
Brack, Reginald K., Jr., 249
Bradford, Andrew
　American Magazine. See American Magazine.
　on content, 58–59
　Franklin and, 56
Bradley, Mike, 157
Brady, John, 279, 282–83
Brady, Mathew, 4, 78
Branding
　definition of, 20
　factors affecting, 34
　logo and, 283
　media kits and, 170
Brand Marketing, 209
Branham, Leigh, 201, 218
Braun, Ian and Michael, 344
Braun v. Soldier of Fortune, 344–45
Break-of-the-book
　for advertising, 31, 46, 49–50, 148–50, 258, 271, 295–97, 360–61
　for departments, 148, 296

for feature articles, 148–50, 271, 295–97
Breakout, 255
Breard, Jack, 326
Breard v. Alexandria, 326
Breslin, Jimmy, 11, 240
Brett, Richard, 37
Brew Your Own, 136
Bride's, 103
Bride's Guide, 103
Brideshead Revisited, 247
Brides Noir, 124
Bridges of Madison County, The, 102
Bright Lights, Big City, 210
Brightness of paper, 299
Brill, Steven, 347
Brill's Content, 103, 347
Brinkley, Christie, 118
Bristol-Myers, 215
Broadcasting and Cable, 51
Brodovitch, Alexey, 4, 80, 253–54, 256–57
Bronze Thrills, 123
Brooks, Gwendolyn, 272
Brown, Helen Gurley, 76, 115, 249
Brown, Tina, 197, 198–200, 247
Browner, Michael, 46
Buck, Pearl, 99
Buckley, Christopher, 69
Buckley, William F., Jr., 69, 333
Budgets, 166–69, 176, 180, 207
Builder, 208, 209
Building Design and Construction, 237
Bunyan, John, 93
Burger, Warren, 318
Burnett, Carol, 331, 333
Business 2.0 magazine, 209
Business Insurance, 121
Business Manager, 207
Business plans
　budget, 166–69
　definition of, 169
　executive summary of profitability, 184–89
　marketing plan, 170–84
　outline for, 169–70
Business Publication Audit of Circulation (BPA) International, 38
Business-to-business magazines. *See* Trade magazines
Business Week
　advertising in, 37
　articles in, 138
　audience for, 120
　illustrations in, 113
　ownership of, 208, 209
　prior restraint case, 323–25
　publication frequency, 177
　staff for, 103
Bust, 136
Butts, Wally, 332–33, **334**
Byatt, A. S., 69
Bylines, 255
Byron, Christopher, 135
Byron, George, 68

Cable News Network (CNN), 213
Cable television
　advertising on, 28
　ancillary products on, 34
　marketing and, 172
　vs. network, 6
　taxation of, 326
Cadmus Journal Services, 302

Cairns, William B., 66
Calendering, 298
Callout, 255
Camera-ready pages, 308
Campbell, Adam, 228
Campbell's, 140
"Can This Marriage Be Saved?," 226
Capote, Truman, 240, 247
Captions, 255, 278–80
Carbine, Patricia, 44, 150, 216
Card Player, 121
Carey, Mathew, 68
Cargo, 15, **48**
Caribbean Travel and Life, 121
Carnation, 48
Carol Burnett Fund for Responsible Journalism, 331
Caroline of Monaco, 276
Carr, Caleb, 247
Carson, David, 256, 263, 264, 270
Carson, Johnny, 333
Carson, Rachel, 91–92
Car Stereo Review, 307
Carter, Betsy, 49
Carter, Graydon, 102–4, 239
Carter, Jimmy, 115, 235
Carter, John Mack, 100, 281
Cartoons
　anti-war, 324
　in *Esquire*, 273
　in *Harper's Weekly*, 78
　in *Hustler*, 336
　intentional infliction of emotional distress suit against, 342
　libel suit against, 336
　in *Maxim*, 344
　in *The New Yorker*, 4, 102, 197–99, 233, 273, 281
　in *Playboy*, 273
　production of, 303
　in *Reader's Digest*, 273
Castro, Fidel, 235
Catalina, 122
Catholic Rural Life, 13
Cave, Edward, **57**, 58
Cave, Ray, 249, 288
Ceffalio, Debra, 151–52
Celebrities
　appropriation cases, 339
　content and, 276
　on covers, 101–4, 283, 288–89, 312–14
　libel suits by, 333
　memorials to, 43, 75, 123, 236, 288
　as pseudoevents, 116–17
　sales and, 288
　September 11 terrorist attacks and, 101–4
Censorship
　by advertisers, 47
　ethics and, 358–59
　by government representatives, 322–25
　by printers, 302
Century, The
　articles in, 65, 76, 229
　autobiographical profiles in, 235
　circulation of, 235
　departments in, 146–47
　publication of, 73
　Scribner's and, 86n36
Chaillé-Long, C., 232
Challenger explosion, 92

Chambermaid's Delights, 70
Charisma, 209, 210
Chavis, Benjamin, 313
Cheever, John, 69
Cher, 276
Chiang Kai-Shek, 280
Chicago, 10, 11
Chief Executive Officers (CEOs), 188, 193–95, 218
Children's magazines
　advertising in, 142
　ancillary products and, 34, 72
　audience for, 126
　circulation of, 72, 82
　demographics of, 126
　failure of, 72, 125
　publication frequency, 176
　Spanish-language versions of, 141, 146
　types of, 16
Cho, Margaret, 125
Choice, The, 247
Christian Century, The, 56, 99–100
Christian Examiner, 66
Christianity Today, 99–100
Christian Retailing, 209, 210
Christy, Howard Chandler, 113
Chronicle, 212
Chrysalis, 100
Chrysler, 47–48, 50. *See also* DaimlerChrysler
Cigar Aficionado, 121, 183
CIO, 231, 244
Circulation
　advertising and, 34, 39, 178–79
　ancillary products and, 72
　assistant publisher and, 207
　controlled, 15, 182–84
　definition of, 22
　distribution costs and, 80–83
　economy and, 22, 60, 180–81
　local vs. national, 8–10
　marketing director and, 206
　marketing for, 170–76
　price per issue and, 39
　vs. readership, 13
　revenue from, 166–67
　September 11 terrorist attacks and, 8
　sponsored agencies for, 176
　subscriptions and, 22
　trends in, 60–61
　web presses and, 304
Circulation department, 167, 168, 192, 205–6
Circulation fulfillment houses, 181, 206
City and Regional Magazine Association (CRMA), 11
City magazines, 10–12, 19
City View, 19
Civil rights movement, coverage of, 97–98, 272
Civil War, coverage of
　in *The Century*, 235
　Gardner photographs, 273
　in *Harper's Weekly*, 4, 78, 96
Clairol, 215
Clapper, Marie, 287
Classical Guitar, 121
Classified advertising, 4, 24n1, 77, 344–45
Clay, Cassius, 233. *See also* Ali, Mohammed
Clayton, Larry, 176
Cleland, T. M., 256–57

Clinkscales, Keith, 165, 175, 188, 189
Clinton, Patrick, 235
Close, Glenn, 235
Coated paper, 298–99
Code, 124
Coin World, 121, 177
Colapinto, John, 237
Cold War, coverage of, 96, 100
Coleridge, Samuel Taylor, 68
Colgate-Palmolive, 47
Collier's
  articles in, 93
  cover of, **42**
  Doyle and, 89
  failure of, 41, 241
  illustrations in, 78, 79, 112
  letters to the editor, 248
  photographs in, 79, 80
  publication of, 73
  Spanish-American War coverage, 79
  on women journalists, 203
Collins, Wilkie, 71, 246
Colors
  definition of, 300
  of UPC bar codes, 312
Color separations, 300–301
Colson, Bill, 47
Columbia Journalism Review, 239
Columbian Magazine, The, 73, 81
Columns
  articles in, 147
  "Can This Marriage Be Saved?," 226
  definition of, 146
  formats for, 245–46
  Neal Award for, 243
  NMAs for, 242
Commentary, 109, 286
Commentary NMA, 242
Communications Data Services (CDS), 181
Communication World, 183
Communities
  attributes of, 106
  building of, 107–11
Community Life, 278
Computer-to-plate (CTP), 85, 309
Comyn, Oliver, 50
Condé Nast Publications, 37, **196**, 209, 210
Condé Nast Traveler
  advertising in, 28
  articles in, 229
  circulation of, 121
  last editorial page in, 281
  table of contents in, 282
Connor, Tom, 342
Consumer Bulletin, 91
Consumer magazines. *See also specific titles*
  advertising in, 15, 36, 67
  advertorials in, 141, 244, 358, 363
  agenda setting in, 91–92
  association magazines and, 16
  community building by, 107–8
  description of, 15
  editorial philosophy of, 42, 133, 135, 137, 274
  editorials in, 246
  in 18th century, 56–62, 64, 68
  essays in, 244–45
  fact checking for, 327–29
  fiction in, 246–47
  health-based, 119

homosexual press vs. mainstream, 107
investigative reports in, 237–41
for leisure activities, 121
in 19th century, 64–66, 68–72, 235
NMAs for, 241–43
outserts in, 143
ownership of, 208–10
paper for, 297–300
on personal finance, 120
scholarly journals and, 17
scientific and technical data in, 238–39
service articles in, 224–28
on shelter, 119–20
Spanish-language versions of, 122
taxation of, 325–26
titles for, 136
in 20th century, 74–76
types of, 15
Consumer Reports, 49, 142, 286, 349
Consumers Digest, 49
Content
  advertising. *See* Advertising
  analysis of, 238–39
  approaches to, 4–5
  articles. *See* Articles
  changes to, 14
  consistency in, 13–14, 143, 269, 281
  departments. *See* Departments
  design of, 254
  editorial formula and, 143–44
  editorial philosophy and, 135–40, 143–44
  in 18th century, 61–64, 67–68
  fiction, 224, 235, 242–43, 246–47
  gestalt in, 258
  men and, 238
  MPA on, 12
  in 19th century, 65, 68–72
  planning for, 47–49
  purpose and, 138
  race and, 67, 97–98, 238
  September 11 terrorist attacks and, 102–4
  sequence of, 270–71
  structure of, 150
  tips for improving, 228
  trends in, 60–61
  in 20th century, 72–76
  women and, 112–13, 238
Contents, 347
Continuous tone art, 303
Contract proofs, 311
Contributing Editor, 205
Controlled circulation, 15, 182–84
Controlled Circulation Audit, 38
Cooking Light, 6, 110–11, 283
Cooper, Art, 85
Cooper, Matthew, 319
Copy Editor, 204
Copyright
  advertising and, 349
  in 18th century, 68
  fair use and, 348–50, 352n75
  of illustrations, 301, 348
  "original works," 345–46
  ownership of, 348
  purpose of, 345
  symbol, 348
  "tangible medium," 346–48
  vs. trademarks, 346

Corporate communications magazines. *See* Public relations magazines
Corporate Meetings, 16
Cory, Jim, 109
CosmoGirl
  audience for, 150–53
  editors, 206
  establishment of, 126
  illustrations in, 127
  role of, 126
  Sassy and, 153
  Seventeen and, 172
  tone of, 153
Cosmopolitan
  advertising in, 17
  anniversary issues of, 236
  articles in, 76, 89, 93, 115
  bathroom reading of, 29
  circulation of, 115–16
  editors, 206
  establishment of, 55, 56
  illustrations in, 78, 113
  international editions of, 8, 150, 259–60
  It and, 76
  letters to the editor, 248
  Marie Claire and, 172
  Maxim and, 116
  ownership of, 209
  parody of, 341
  publisher of, 37, 210
  September 11 terrorist attacks coverage, 101
  sexual revolution and, 76, 114
  Spanish-language version of, 122
  structure of, 150
  "The Treason of the Senate," 76
Cost per thousand readers (CPM), 34, 35, 178–79, 186
Cottage Living, 209
Council of Literary Magazines and Presses, 247
"Counter-memory," 75
Counter-Spy, 99
Country, 142, 174
Country Discoveries, 142
Country Gardens, **118**, 120
Country Home
  cover of, 300
  focus groups for, 110
  interactive media from, 23
  letters to the editor, 110
  ownership of, 209
  paper for, 299, 300
  redesign of, 7
  sales of, 156
Country Living, 209
Country Woman, 142, 143, 174
Coupons, 295
Cousins, Norman, 223, 249
Couvares, Francis G., 358–59
Cover Girl cosmetics, 152
Cover lines, 255, 281, 284–87
Covers
  ABM on, 363
  advertising on, 44, 50–51, 297
  appearance of, 281–87
  artwork on, 42, **97**, 98, 273, 281, 284, 287
  ASME on, 50–51, 360
  audience for, 42
  binding and, 306
  cultural standards and, 288–89

design of, 4, 70, 148, 261, 281–83
editorial philosophy and, 283
in 18th century, 77
"false," 51
future, MPA's campaign, 18
holograms on, 313
for Jevsek publications, 259–60
logo on. *See* Logo
men on, 140, 287
newsstand vs. subscription, **298**, 300
paper for, 298–300
photography on, 281, 284, 287
props for, 51
as pseudoevents, 116
race and, **90**, 238
September 11 terrorist attacks and, 102–4, 276, 286
size of, 39
special coatings for, 300
of special issues, 284
table of contents and, 282, 286
titles for, 255
types of, 284–87
UPC bar codes on, 312, 314
women on, **90**, 287, 302
Cowboys and Indians, 177
Cowles, Fleur, 141, 153–56
Cowles, Gardner "Mike," 98, 153–56
Crafting Traditions, 142
Crane, Stephen, 240
Creative Director, 201, 204–5
Critical essays, 245
Crockett, Davy, 319
Cronin, Mary M., 94
Crystal, Graef, 213
CSO, 244
Cuisine at Home, **142**, 142, 210
Culpepper, Mary Kay, 111
Cultural influences, 104–27
Current Literature, 203
Curtis, Cyrus, 66–67
Curtis, Gregory, 95, 247
Curtis, Louisa Knapp, 225
Curtis Publishing Co. v. Butts, 332–33, **334**
Curve, 107, 108
Custom Home, 209
Custom magazines
  advertising in, 18–19, 212
  community building by, 109
  creation of, 212–13
  description of, 18–19
  growth rate of, 18
  ownership of, 210, 212
Custom Publishing Council, 18, 21
Cutlines, 255, 278–80

DaimlerChrysler, 36, 212, 214
Dali, Salvadore, 4, 70
Databases, 348
Dateline, 5
Daub, Travis, 211, 306
David, Baird, 183
Davis, Cullen, 239
Davis, Miles, 233
Davis, Richard Harding, 240
Dean, John, 182
Dean, Maureen, 100
"Death by Exercise," 228
"Death Penalty," 286
DeCarlo, Tessa, 228
Deck, 255
Defense Technical Information Library, 321

Delaware Today, 11
Delineator, 74
Del Monte, 48
Demographics, 7, 28–30, 171
Dennie, Joseph, 68
Departments
    advertising and, 296–97
    appearance of, 264, 269, 271
    articles in, 147, 245
    inserts and, 295
    Neal Award for, 243
    NMAs for, 242
    placement of, 148, 296
    role of, 146
    tip boxes for, 227
Deputy Editor/Director, 214
Der Spiegel, 9
Design. *See* Appearance
Design Editor, 211
Design Industries Foundation for
    AIDS (DIFFA), 94–95
Design NMA, 242
Des Moines University, 212
Desperate Hours, The, 339
Details
    appearance of, 4
    articles in, 148
    audience for, 148, 150
    cover of, 314
    Instinct and, 108
    ownership of, 209
De Vita, Carol J., 122
Diamond, Edwin, 91, 182
Diana of Wales, 75, 236, 288
Dickens, Charles, 71, 246
Dickinson, Emily, 69
Didion, Joan, 240
Dietemann, "Dr.," 338
DIFFA, 94–95
Digital Home, 209
Dillard, Annie, 69, 245
Dingbats, 255, 270
Direct mail marketing, 171, 174,
    183, 186
Dirt Rider, 126
Disabled, publications for, 108
Disclaimers, 339
Disney, Dorothy Cameron, 226
Disney Adventures, 126
Display type, 255
Distribution
    of advertising, 83
    blending, 303
    circulation and, 80–83
    factors affecting, 80
    history of, 80–83
    legal issues with, 326, 351
    mailing houses for, 295
    of marketing materials, 175
    outlets for, 83, 99, 156, 183
    of pornography, 351
    process for, 294
    production director and, 207
    rural free distribution system,
        83
    trends in, 60–61
Distribution department
    duties of, 192
    expenses from, 167, 168, 182,
        183, 186–88
Diversified designs, 262–63
Dr. Kildare, 92
Dodge, 212
Dog magazines, 121
Dole, 48
Domino, 15, 49, 120
Dots per inch (DPI), 301, 303

Douglass, Frederick, 69
Dow, Caroline, 274–75
Downey, Jim, 342
Doyle, Arthur Conan, 89
DPI, 301, 303
Dragnet, 92
Dreiser, Theodore, 240
Drew, Richard, 358
Drew, Robert L., 275
Drop head, 255
Druggist, The, 39
Druggists' Circular, 39
Dry tests, 175
DuBois, Larry, 235
Dull sheets, 298–99
Duotints, 303, 304
Duotones, 303
Durkee, Cutler, 234
Dynamic Logic, 51

Eastman, Max, 324
Ebony
    advertising in, 122, 124
    anniversary issues of, 236
    articles in, 75, 89
    circulation of, 30
    establishment of, 99
    goal of, 99
    Hispanic titles and, 123
    logo for, 283
    September 11 terrorist attacks
        coverage, 104
    table of contents, 282
EBSCO Consumer Magazine
    Services, 176
Echelon, 108
Economist, The, **8**, 8, 50–51
Edison, Thomas, 89, 173
Editor and Publisher
    advertising in, 51
    cover of, 286
    Neal Award for, 244
    photographs in, 302
    on professional
        responsibilities, 94
    September 11 terrorist attacks
        coverage, 286
Editorial Assistant, 205
Editorial costs per page, 169
Editorial Director
    duties of, 195–200
    for interactive media, 211
    production director and, 207
    research director and, 208
    salaries for, 187
Editorial formulas, 143–44, 217,
    294
Editorial philosophy
    advertising and, 46–51, 136,
        140–41, 151, 213
    appearance and, 139–40,
        254–56, 290
    of city magazines, 12
    of consumer magazines, 42,
        133, 135, 137, 274
    content and, 135–40, 143–44
    covers and, 283
    cutlines and, 280
    identity and, 223
    for organization magazines,
        136, 250
Editorials
    health campaigns in, 21
    on last page, 280, 281
    Neal Award for, 243, 246
    role of, 246
Editorial Televisa, 122

Editorial-to-ad ratio, 39, 144, 178,
    181, 186
Editors
    advertising staff and, 46–47,
        200
    ancillary products and, 34,
        200, 217–18
    art directors and, 254
    assistant, 204
    associate, 204, 205
    audience and, 150, 223, 249
    autonomy of, 47–50, 106, 140,
        213, 215, 356–58
    chief. *See* Editorial Director
    computer skills of, 218
    contributing, 205
    copy, 204
    deputy, 214
    in 18th century, 68
    entertainment, 214
    executive, 201
    expenses from, 167–69,
        186–88
    integrated marketing, 214
    managing, 200–205
    in 19th century, 70
    online, 204, 211, 218
    philosophy of. *See* Editorial
        philosophy
    photo, 205
    publication frequency and, 192
    quality product and, 314–15
    research by, 207
    roles of, 12, 165, 192, 249
    salaries for, 187
    senior, 202–5
    trust in, 18, 24
Education Week, 91
Ehrlich, Gretel, 245
Eimann v. Soldier of Fortune, 344
Eisenstaedt, Alfred, 80, 97, 236
El Andar, 122
Electrical World, 47
Electronic Freedom of
    Information Act (EFOIA),
    320–21
Electronic Gaming Monthly, 126
Eliot, George, 71
Elle, 8, 37, 283, 299
Elle Decor, 21
Elle Girl, 7, 127
Ellington, Duke, 98
E-mail, libelous, 327
Emerge, 138
Endless Vacations, 20, **21**
Endmark, 255
Endres, Kathleen, 93
English Home, 174
Entertainment Editor, 214
Entertainment Tonight, 144
Entertainment Weekly
    appeal of, 31
    bathroom reading of, 29
    cutlines in, 279
    editorial duties at, 214
    Entertainment Tonight and,
        144
    in integrated media, 20
    memorials in, 236
    needs met by, 6
    NMAs for, 237
    ownership of, 209, 213
    profiles in, 237
    publisher of, 36
    reviews in, 245
    special issues of, 236
    table of contents, 282

Ticketron and, 176
    title, 137
Entrepreneur, 120, 145–46, **346**,
    347
Entrepreneur Illustrated, 347
Erdrich, Louise, 69
Erie Canal, 81–82
Erté, 70
Espionage Act, 324–25
ESPN: The Magazine, 23, 37, 90,
    286
Esquire
    advertising in, 50
    "The Americanization of
        Paris," 258
    anniversary issues of, 286
    appearance of, 257, 258, 261,
        263, 265
    articles in, 148, 229, 258
    audience for, 8, 114, 179
    cartoons in, 273
    on Communist witch hunts,
        96–97
    cover of, **117**, 286
    folio lines, 265
    illustrations in, 113
    launching of, 180–81
    logo for, 283
    in MPA's future cover
        campaign, 18
    new journalism in, 241
    NMAs for, 231, 243
    ownership of, 209
    Playboy and, 114
    price per issue, 179, 182
    profiles in, 233
    pseudoevents, 116–17
    publisher of, 37, 210
    semiotics in, 111–12
    short stories in, 247
    sponsorship of, 50
    table of contents, 282
    title, 136
Essays
    articles in, 244–45
    on last page, 281
    length of, 245
    NMAs for, 242
    objectivity of, 224
    types of, 245–46
Essence
    advertising in, 122, 124
    circulation of, 30
    Hispanic titles and, 123
    needs met by, 6
Estylo, 122
Ethics, 356–66
Ettlinger, Catherine, 152
European Americans, 67, 98,
    238
Everybody's magazine, 248
Excerpts, 247
Executive Editor, 201
Executive summary of
    profitability, 184–89
Expedia, 103
Expenses, 167–69, 186–89
Extreme Makeover: Home Edition,
    120
Eye movement, 263, 267, 270
E-Zines, 19

Fact, 330, 333–34
Fact checking, 205, 327–29
Fadiman, Clifton, 232
Fairchild, 209
Fairfax Limited, 45

Fairness and Accuracy in
Reporting (FAIR), 213
False light cases, 338–39
Faludi, Susan, 62
Falwell, Jerry, 340–43
Family Circle
articles in, 227, 237
circulation of, 22
classification of, 112
cover of, 300
CTP and, 309
in MPA's future cover
campaign, 18
NMAs for, 237
ownership of, 209
paper for, 299
Schwarz's story on Miller in,
244
"Toxic Nightmare on Main
Street," 237
UPC bar code on, 312
Family Fun, 28
Family Handyman, The, 120
Family Life, 103
Family Money, 103
Family PC, 103
Family Ties, 18, 298, **298**, 299
Farm and Ranch Living, 142
Farmer's Wife, The, 111
Farm Journal, The, 111, 157
Farm Wife News, 142–43
Faulkner, William, 69, 246
FBL Financial Group
*Family Ties. See Family Ties
Keeping in Touch. See Keeping
in Touch*
Fears, Lillie, 124
Feature articles
appearance of, 227, 254–56,
269
approach to, 5
audience for, 150–53
description of, 147–48
essays as, 245
grids for, 264
investigative reports, 224,
237–41
length of, 76, 147–48
Neal Award for, 243–44
pacing between, 148
placement of, 148–50, 271,
295–97
planning for, 296
profiles, 224, 232–37
purpose and, 138
reporting in, 224
service, 224–31
sidebars for, 263–64, 266, 277
sponsorship and, 50
television and, 147
tip boxes for, 227
writing modes used in, 224
Feature Writing NMA, 242
Felker, Clay
on design, 258–60
on education, 66
Ms. and, 44
on new journalism, 241
New York magazine and, 11, 12
Felt, W. Mark, 89
Feminism, 13, 62, 100–101, 236
Ferber, Sam, 12, 24
FHM, 184
Fiction, 224, 235, 242–43, 246–47
Field, Marshall, 99
Field and Stream, 9, 31, 56
Fili, Louise, 284

Filipinas, 125
Financial Times, 217
Fine Gardening, 120
Fine Homebuilding, 120
Fine Woodworking, 121
Fiori, Pamela, 224–25
Firestone, Mary Alice, 333
Firestone, Russell, 333
First Amendment rights
for access to information,
318–19
for distribution, 326
Espionage Act and, 324–25
FOIA and, 320
incitement and, 343
intentional infliction of
emotional distress and,
340–43
invasion of privacy and, 338
libel and, 331–35
obscenity and, 302, 350–51
parody and, 340–43
prior restraints and, 322–25
for sales, 326
source protection and, 319
taxes and, 325–26
Fisher, Harrison, 78
Fishman, Jim, 118
Fit, 119
Fitness, 119, 209, 211, 299
Fitzgerald, F. Scott, 246
Flag, 255
Flagg, James Montgomery, 78
Flair, 153–56, **154**, 161
Flaunt, **155**, 155, 262
Fleckhaus, Willy, 264
Fleischmann, Raoul, 208
Fleming, Ian, 115
Flynt, Larry, 322
Fly Rod and Reel, 235
Focus groups, 7, 110, 208
FOIA, 320–22
Folio lines, 265
Folio: magazine, 34, 187
Fong, Amy Lai, 110
Fonseca, Nicholas, 214
Font, 266
Food and Wine, 15
Food Technology, 183
Foot-Joy, 47
Forbes
audience for, 120
last editorial page in, 281
letters to the editor, 248
table of contents, 282
title, 137
Ford, Gerald, 349–50
Ford Motor Company, 36, 47
Foreign Affairs, 239, 286
Foreign Policy
advertising in, 306
cover of, **294**, 300
design editor for, 211
digital edition of, 306
illustrations in, 306
paper for, 298–300
production planning for,
293–95
size of, 311
Formal balance, 270
Forman, Allan, 203
Formats, broadcast vs. print, 5, 13
For Me, 21
For placement only (FPO), 301
Fortune
advertising in, 47, 102
appearance of, 256–57

audience for, 120
cover of, **256**
launching of, 181
ownership of, 209, 213
paper for, 257
photographs in, 257
publication frequency, 177
redesign of, 289
September 11 terrorist attacks
coverage, 101, 102
"Forty-winks Reducing Plan, The,"
257
Foster, Jodie, 118
Fox, Michael J., 210
FPO, 301
Franchise, 31–33
Frank Leslie's Illustrated Weekly, 73,
80, 216
Frank Leslie's Popular Monthly, 203
Franklin, Benjamin
articles by, 68
Bradford, and, 56
*General Magazine. See General
Magazine
Physics Today* special issue on,
285
as postmaster, 81
Frederick, Christine, 225
Freedman, Robert, 228–29
Freedom of Information Act
(FOIA), 320–22
Freelance writers, 205, 218, 338,
348
Free urban magazines, 19
"Frivolous Demagogue, The," 97
Frost, Robert, 69
Fry, John, 192, 201
Fuller, Bonnie, 217

Gaines, James, 288, 313
Galaxy, The, 246
Gambling magazines, 121
Game Informer, 126
Games, 138
Gandhi, Mahatma, 114, 344
Garden Design, 135, 136–37, 138
Garden Gate, 142, 210
Gardner, Alexander, 273
Garfield, James A., 216
Gatefolds, 51, 306
Gaviria, Ruth, 123
Gay Parent, 108
Gay Press Report, 107
Gear, 319
Gellar, Sarah Michelle, 115
General Excellence NMA, 241
General Excellence Online NMA,
243
General Foods, 42
General interest titles, 15
General Magazine
advertising in, 37
appearance of, 77
articles in, 68
cover of, **57**
distribution of, 81
press used for, 84
price per issue, 60
publication of, 56, 73
General Mills, 48
General Motors, 36
Generation X
appearance and, 227
columns geared toward, 147
inserts and, 141
Internet subscriptions for, 172
media and, 150

price per issue and, 180
spending power of, 118
thought patterns of, 227
year of birth, 118
Generation Y
appearance and, 227
columns geared toward, 147
inserts and, 141
Internet subscriptions for, 172
spending power of, 118
thought patterns of, 227
titles for, 150–53
year of birth, 118
*Gentleman and Lady's Town and
Country Magazine, The*
appearance of, 77–78
articles in, 229
audience for, 64
cover of, **65**
essays in, 244
publication of, 73
publishers of, 77
Gentleman of Color, 123
Gentleman's Magazine, The, **57**, 58
George, 103
German Life, 125
Gertz, Elmer, 332–33
Gertz v. Robert Welch, Inc., 332–33
Gibbs, Wolcott, 232
Gibson, Charles Dana, 78, 112, 273
Gibson, Mel, 235
Gill, Brendan, 197
Gillespie, Marcia Ann, 240
Gingrich, Arnold, 153–54, 156, 179
Girlfriends, 107
Giuliani, Rudy, 104
Glamour
advertising in, 35, 177
agenda setting in, 91
articles in, 89, 228
circulation of, 35, 115
cover of, **90**
CPMs, 34, 35
editorial duties at, 214
on HMOs, 228
illustrations in, 113
integrated media for, 21
"Is Managed Care Good for
Women's Health?," 228
"Making Managed Care Work
for You," 228
Men's Health and, 138
needs met by, 6
NMAs for, 228
ownership of, 209
publication frequency, 177
publisher of, 37, 210
title, 137
Glamour en Español, 30
"Glamour of Delinquency, The,"
245
Glaser, Milton, 11, 260–61
Glaxo-Wellcome, 50
Gleason, Tim, 314
Godey, Louis A., 64, 78
Godey's Lady's Book
articles in, 64–65, 216, 225
circulation of, 82
Hale and, 64–65, 216
illustrations in, 78, 216
Ladies Magazine and, 216
publication of, 73
Golden Book, The, 283
Golden rectangle principle, 270
Goldstein, Lew, 141
Goldwater, Barry, 330, 333–34
Golf for Women, 5

Golf Illustrated, 5
Good, Brian, 228
Goodby Silverstein, 47
Good Housekeeping
    advertising in, 32–33, 37, 140,
        200, 295, 343–44
    articles in, 33, 93–94, 227
    circulation of, 22
    cover of, 284
    covers of, 113
    establishment of, 56
    ownership of, 209
    publisher of, 210
    Reader's Digest and, 74
    regional data in, 295
    Spanish-language version of,
        122
    staff for, 103
    Testing Institute, 32, 93
    third-party liability case
        against, 343–44
    trust in, 31
    website certification by, 32–33
Goodman, Ellen, 101
Good Old Days, 75
Good Things, 34. *See also Martha
    Stewart Living*
Gordimer, Nadine, 69
Gospodarski Vestnik, 9
Gottlieb, Agnes Hooper, 202–3
Gottlieb, Robert, 197, 198
Gourmet, 8, 36, 37, 111
GQ
    audience for, 114
    cover of, 104
    illustrations in, 113
    needs met by, 6
    ownership of, 209
    publisher of, 37, 210
    reader's profile by, 36
Graham, Anne, 136, 246
Graham's
    contributors to, 68
    on culture, 127
    illustrations in, 78
    payments to writers, 70
    publication of, 73
Granger, David, 231
Grant, Ulysses S., 235
Graves, Michael, 95
Gravure presses, 305, 307–9
Gray, Zane, 227
Greenwich, 11
Gregory, Dick, 272
Grids, 263–64, 269
Gross receipts, 167, 186
Grosvenor, Gilbert Hovey, 34, 79,
    156, 250
Grow, Gerald, 234
"Growth of Organic Electronics,"
    285
Guccione, Bob, 336
Guccione, Bob, Jr., 319
Guideposts, 50
Guitarist, 121
Guitar Player, 121, 307
Gulf War (2003–2006), coverage
    of, 4, 37, 358–59
Gurganus, Allan, 140
Gutenberg, Johannes, 84
Guts and Glory, 345–46

Hachette Filipacchi, 18, 19, 21,
    37
Hadden, Briton, 72, 136, 208
Haegele, Patricia, 32
Hale, Edward Everett, 246

Hale, Sarah Josepha, 64–65, 66,
    216
Haley, Alex, 233–34
Half-tones, 78–79, 303
Hamilton, Alexander, 68
Hampton's, 93
Hanberry v. Hearst Corporation,
    343–44
Hancock, John, 68
Hanks, Tom, 341
Hanley Wood, 208, 209
Hardware Age, 108–9
Hardy, Thomas, 71
Harper, Fletcher, 96
Harper's
    advertising in, 38, 39, 140, 149
    appearance of, 140
    articles in, 65, 76, 138, 149,
        161, 236
    audience for, 30
    circulation of, 30, 135
    cover of, **134**, 149
    cutlines in, 280
    editorial philosophy of, 133,
        135
    establishment of, 55, 56
    illustrations in, 149
    interactive media from, 96
    letters to the editor, 248
    new journalism in, 241
    "The Prisoner of Sex," 236
    purpose of, 137–38
    short stories in, 246, 247
    structure of, 150
    title, 137
    on Watergate, 100
    women journalists and, 239
Harper's Bazaar
    appearance of, 4, 80, 253–54,
        257, 258
    articles in, 254, 258
    cover of, 70, 276
    establishment of, 56
    international editions of, 8
    memorials in, 236
    ownership of, 209
    photographs in, 80, 257, 276
    profiles in, 235
    publisher of, 37
    Spanish-language version of,
        122
    special issues of, 236
    "The Wonders of Water," 258
Harper's Monthly, 55, 82
Harper's Weekly
    cartoons in, 78
    Civil War coverage in, 4, 78, 96
    establishment of, 55
    Gilded Age coverage in, 96
    illustrations in, 4, 55
    letters to the editor, 248
    publication of, 73
    Reconstruction period
        coverage in, 96
Harrington, John, 184
Harris Interactive, 31
Harte, Bret, 227, 246
Hartford Steam Boiler Inspection
    and Insurance Company, 71
Harvard Business Review, 286
Harvard Lampoon, 341, 342
Haubegger, Christy, 122–23
Hawthorne, Nathaniel, 68
H. B. Smith Machine Company, 71
Headline, 255
Health, 6, 116, 119, 239
Healthy Kids En Español, 141, 146

Hearing Health, 108
Hearst, William Randolph, 210
Hearst Corporation
    advertising by, 37, 172
    ancillary products of, 34
    custom division of, 18
    group publisher in, 195
    ownership of, 209, 210
Heart and Soul, 124, 165
Hefner, Christine, 114, 217
Hefner, Hugh, 114, 235, 342
Held, John, Jr., 113
Heller, Steven, 284
Hemingway, Ernest
    in *Atlantic Monthly*, 69
    Old Man and the Sea, 247
    profile of, 232–33
    in "Thoughts on the Business
        of Life," 281
    travel articles by, 229
Hemispheres, 19, 136
Herbick, David, 264–65
Herceg, Diane, 90, 343
Herceg v. Hustler, 90, 343
Hersey, John, 102, 236
Hershey, Lenore, 100
Hewlett-Packard, 47
Hickeys, 299
High Fidelity, 134
High gloss paper, 298
Highlights for Children, 126, 142,
    176
High Times, 99
Hillenbrand, Lauren, 245
Hill family, 339
"Hiroshima," 102, 236
Hispanic, 122
Hispanic Americans, 30, 122–23
Hispanic Business, 30, 122, 123
History Channel Magazine, The,
    170, **171**, 262, 281
"History of the Standard Oil
    Company, The," 93
HIV/AIDS
    African Americans and, 139
    DIFFA, 94–95
    JAMA special issues on, 284
    Metropolitan Home on, 94–95
    Poz, 139
    printing of stories on, 302
    Rolling Stone on, 137
Hochstein, Arthur, 289
Hockney, David, 95
Hodges, Louis W., 356
Hodges' essential ethics questions,
    356–57
Holiday, 217, 339
Hollstein, Milton, 135
Holmes, Nigel, 277
Holmes, Oliver Wendell, 273, 325
Holstead, Carol E., 261
Home, 21, 120
Home Improvement Market, 109
Home Journal, 85n1. *See also Town
    and Country*
Homer, Winslow, 4, 78, 273
Homosexual press, 107–8. *See also
    specific titles*
Honey, 124, 165
Honolulu, 10
Hopkins, Will, 263, 264
Hormel, 48
Horn, Alvin, 98
Horticulture, 120
Houchins v. KQED, 351n1
House Beautiful, 74, 120
House organs, 18

House UnAmerican Activities
    Committee, 96
Houston, Whitney, 124
Houston Chronicle, 321
Howe, Julia Ward, 69
Howells, William Dean, 246
Hoyt, Eleanor, 203
hr: Watches Magazines, 121
Huey, John, 200–201
Hughes, Charles Evans, 326
Hughes, Langston, 272
Hume, Janice, 75
Humpty Dumpty, 126
Hunt, Paul, 123
Husni, Samir, 121
Hustler
    articles in, 90, 343
    intentional infliction of
        emotional distress suits
        against, 340–43
    invasion of privacy suit
        against, 340
    libel suit against, 336, 340
    obscenity in, 350
    "Orgasm of Death," 90, 343
    parody by, 340–43
    printer, 302
    third-party liability case
        against, 90, 343
    war, access to, 322

Identity
    advertising and, 140, 143
    appearance and, 254–56
    building of, 106
    in business plan, 170
    editorial philosophy and, 223
    voice and, 143
IEEE Spectrum, 231
"If I Were a Negro," 99
Illustrations
    artwork. *See* Artwork
    camera-ready, 308
    choice of, 271
    copyright of, 301, 348
    cutlines and, 255
    in 18th century, 77–78, 271–73
    eye movement and, 263
    FPO, 301
    infographics, 271, 277
    men in, 113, 238
    in 19th century, 78, 273
    photographs. *See* Photography
    planning for, 301
    production of, 300–304
    in proofs, 311
    scanning of, 301
    trends in, 60–61
    women in, 78–79, 112–13, 238
Imposition, 308–9
Imprint publication, 18
Inc., 120
Incentives, 16
In Cold Blood, 197, 247
Income. *See* Revenue
Independent, The, 248
Individual Investor, 103
Industry Standard, 103
Industry Week, 120
In-flight magazines, 19
InFlight Programs, 176
Informal balance, 270
Initial caps, 255, 270
Ink, printer's, 84, 298–99, 302, 305
inMotion, 108
Inserts
    advertising, 141, 295

ancillary products in, 141, 305
articles and, 295
ASME on, 358
audience for, 141
binding and, 306–7
catalogs, 304
departments and, 295
marketing, 171, 172
packaging of, 305
paper for, 141
pay-up rate for, 172
placement of, 172
postal rates and, 304
Instant Digital Fulfillment, 172
Instinct, 108
Institute of Electrical and
    Electronics Engineers
    (IEEE), 231
Institute of Food, 183
Institutional Investor, 121
Institutional profiles, 235
In Style, 20, 37, 209, 357
Insurance Meetings, 16
Integrated Marketing Editor, 214
Integrated media, 20–21
Intentional infliction of emotional
    distress, 339–43
Interactive media, 20, 23, 24, 211
Interior design magazines, 121
Internal audiences, 18
Internal Auditor, 230
International Association of
    Business Communicators,
    183
Internet
    advertising on, 28, 51, 171–72,
        211, 358, 364
    ancillary products on, 34
    business practices on, 24
    chat rooms, 7, 111
    integrated media, 20–21
    interactive media, 20, 23, 24,
        211
    pay-up rate, 172
    websites. *See* Websites
Interviews, 233, 334, 338
"Into Thin Air," 108
In Touch, 29, 286
Invasion of privacy, 320, 336–39,
    340
Investigative reports, 91, 224,
    237–41. *See also* Muckraking
Iowa Natural Heritage, 17
Iraq
    Gulf War (2003–2006), 4, 37,
        358–59
    Persian Gulf War, 92, 151, 322
Irish America Magazine, 125
Irving, Washington, 68
"Is God Dead?," 286
Islands, 121
"Is Managed Care Good for
    Women's Health?," 228
It, 76
Italian American, 125

Jack and Jill, 126
Jackson, Andrew, 64
Jackson, Jesse, 99, 333
James, Henry, 246
Jane, 108, 153, 209
Jane's Defence Weekly, 320
Janowitz, Tama, 235
Janus Head, 19
Jay, John, 61, 68
Jay, Nancy, 288–89
Jeep, 19, 212, 214

Jeffers, Dennis, 230
Jeffries, Karla, 169, 177
Jesse H. Neal National Business
    Journalism Award. *See* Neal
    Award
Jet
    advertising in, 122, 124
    Hispanic titles and, 123
    illustrations in, 272
    impact of, 99
Jevsek, Bostjan, 259
Jewish Voice Today, 177
Johnson, John H., 98–99
Johnson, Lyndon B. (LBJ), 99, 100
Johnson, Samuel, 58
Johnson, Willard, 98
Johnson and Johnson, 36, 50
Johnston, Joseph, 235
Jolie, Angelina, 289
Jones, Quincy, 175, 234
Jordan, Michael, 236
Jost, Rick, 214
Journalist, The, 203
*Journal of the American Medical
    Association (JAMA)*, 56, 92,
    284
Journey Group, 18
Justified margins, 267

Kable News Company, 181
Kael, Pauline, 245
Kalins, Dorothy, 94–95, 135–36,
    138
Kane, Susan, 285
Kansas City Live, 306
Kaplan, Stanley, 331
Keeping in Touch, 18
Keeton, Kathy, 336
Keillor, Garrison, 69
Kempe, C. Henry, 92
Kennedy, John F. (JFK), 42, 43
Kennedy, John F., Jr., 75, 288
Kennedy, Robert, 70
Kenyon Review, 247
Kerning, 268
Keynes, John Maynard, 69
*KGB: The Secret Work of Soviet
    Agents*, 333
Khomeini, Ayatollah, 248
Kickers, 278
Killing Time, 247
Kim, Dong, 47
Kimmel, Jimmy, 115
King, 124
King, Martin Luther, Jr., 69, 97,
    233, 235
Kingston Press, 302
Kipling, Rudyard, 72
Kiplinger's Personal Finance, 120,
    137, 176
Kissinger, Henry, 331, 341
Kitch, Carolyn, 74–75, 112–13,
    173–74
Kitchen Corners, 70
Kitchen Klatter, 157
Klapper, Joseph, 90
Knebel, Fletcher, 97
Knickerbocker, 68
Knowlton, Archa, 42
Kobak, James, 134
Konigsberg, Ruth Davis, 239
KoreAm Journal, 125
Kosner, Edward, 117
Kraft, 48, 102, 215
Krakauer, Jon, 108
Krause, David, 212
Krier, Bill, 14, 229

Kuhn, Bowie, 318
Kurns, David, 211
Kutcher, Ashton, 4

Lacy, Stephen M., 34
Ladder. *See* Break-of-the-book
Ladies' Home Journal
    advertising in, 67
    articles in, 72, 93–94, 225–27
    audience for, 65–67
    "Can This Marriage Be
        Saved?," 226
    circulation of, 22, 40, 66
    cover of, 79, **226**, 276, 284,
        300
    establishment of, 56
    interactive media from, 20, 23,
        248
    letters to the editor, 225–26,
        248
    ownership of, 208, 209
    photographs in, 276
    publisher of, 37
    Reader's Digest and, 74
    table of contents, 282
    Vietnam War coverage in, 100
    on women journalists, 203
Ladies Magazine, 63, 73, 216
Ladies' Repository, 65
Ladybug, 126
Lady's Emporium, 216
Lafavore, Mike, 136, 138, 285–86,
    287
Lamonica, Mary Cronin, 94
Lane, Gertrude Battles, 216
Lang, Dale, 45
Lange, Jessica, 118
Lapham, Lewis, 135, 140–41, 149,
    161
Larter, Ali, 116–17, **117**
Lasser, Wendy, 247
Last Tango in Paris, 248
Latina
    agenda setting in, 91
    ancillary products of, 175
    audience for, 30, 122–23
    logo for, 283
    marketing of, 175
    sell-through rate of, 184
    September 11 terrorist attacks
        coverage, 104
    test mailing of, 175
Latina Style, 122
Lau, Sam, 125
Lauren, Ralph, 347
Laurence, Leslie, 228
Lauters, Amy Mattson, 111
Lawhon, Charla, 357
Layout, formal vs. informal, 270
Lazare, Lewis, 50
Leading, 268
Lear, Frances, 216
Least Heat Moon, William, 69
Legal issues
    on access to information,
        318–19
    administration of justice,
        323–25
    appropriation, 339
    censorship, 47, 302, 322–25,
        358–59
    copyright. *See* Copyright
    with distribution, 326
    EFOIA, 320–21
    Espionage Act, 324–25
    false light cases, 338–39
    FOIA, 320–22

on gathering information,
    319–20
Good Housekeeping's Seal of
    Approval, 32–33, 343–44
intentional infliction of
    emotional distress,
    339–43
invasion of privacy, 320,
    336–39, 340
libel, 319, 326–36, 337, 340
national security, 323
obscenity, 302, 350–51
overview, 317
parody, 330, 340–43
Patriot Act, 321
prior restraints, 322–25
privileged statements, 335–36
with sales, 326
source protection, 319–20
statute of limitations, 336
sunshine laws, 321–22
taxes, 325–26
third-party liability, 90, 343–45
torts. *See* Torts
for war correspondents, 322
Leibovitz, Annie
    covers by, 4, 104, 270
    parody of, 330
    portraits by, 276
Leisure Interests NMA, 242
LemMon, Jean, 216
Lennon, John, 4, 75
Leonard, John, 197
Lependorf, Jeffrey, 247
Lesbian Tide, 100
Leslie, Miriam, 216
Letters to Ms., 111
Letters to the Editor
    on civil rights articles, 98
    community building by, 106,
        110, 111
    role of, 248–49
    service articles and, 225
Levine, Ellen
    on advertising, 140, 200
    on awards, 231
    on content, 228
    on editorial responsibilities,
        165
Levi's, 152
LexisNexis, 348
L'Express, 9
Lexus, 29
Leyendecker, J. C., 273
Libel, 319, 326–36, 337, 340
Liberator, The, 70, 73, 96
Liberman, Alexander, 257, 258
Liberty, 41, 42
Liberty Lobby, 319
Lichtenstein, Roy, 70
Life
    advertising in, 39, 43
    anniversary issues of, 236
    appearance of, 39, 42, 43, 80
    articles in, 4, 42–43, 80, 229
    Birth of a Baby, 325
    on child abuse, 92
    circulation of, 40–41, 43, 44
    civil rights movement coverage
        in, 97
    "core plots" of, 74
    cover of, **4**, 284
    cutlines in, 280
    editorial philosophy of, 42,
        274
    establishment of, 80
    false light case, 339

invasion of privacy suit
  against, 338
letters to the editor, 248
memorials in, 43, 236
new journalism and, 241
Old Man and the Sea, 247
"Parting Shots," 281
photographs in, 41–43, 274–76
premiere issue, **40**, 41
price per issue, 39, 41, 43
publication of, 41–44
serialized novels in, 247
special issues of, 236–37
title, 346–47
TV and, 41, 43
Life and Style, 286
Lift device, 171
Lilith, 100
Line art, 303
Line length, 267
Lingua Franca, 103
Lippmann, Walter, 113, 324
Lipstein, Owen, 159–60
Li, ___, 62–63

Logo
  ABM on, 363, 364
  ASME on, 360
  branding and, 283
  definition of, 255
  design of, 283–87
  on website, 364

___, 69

advertising in, 39
appearance of, 39, 264
articles in, 80
circulation of, 40–41
civil rights movement coverage
  in, 97–98
establishment of, 80
failure of, 41
fulfillment department, 181
illustrations in, **97**, 98
new journalism and, 241
NMAs for, 98
photographs in, 276
price per issue, 39
on Till murder, 272
Lopez, Jennifer, 115
L'Oreal, 36
Lorimer, George Horace, 67
"Los Angeles: A Race Relations
  Success Story," 98
Los Angeles Magazine, 5
Los Angeles Times, 5
Lovell, Alma, 326
Lovell v. City of Griffin, 326
Lowell, Amy, 324
Luce, Clare Booth, 41
Luce, Henry
  editorial philosophy, 42
  Life and, 41–42
  on newspapers, 72
  Time and, 72, 136, 200, 208
Lucky
  articles in, 170
  classification of, 15
  cover of, **172**
  Domino and, 120

media kits for, 170
ownership of, 209
Ludtke, Melissa, 318

MacArthur, Bob, 34
MacWorld, 121, 182
Mad, 50, 137, 138, 340–42
Mademoiselle, 103, 210, 257–58,
  341
MAD Kids, 126
Madonna, 235, 276
Magalogs, 15, 49. *See also specific
  titles*
Magapapers, 19
Magazine-Made America, 41–42
Magazine Publishers of America
  (MPA)
  on content, 12
  on coverage, 6–7
  future cover campaign, 18
  on market profile booklets, 30
  members of, 21
  publication statistics from, 21
Magazines
  2004 statistics on, 179
  2005 statistics on, 21
  buying vs. starting, 180
  community attributes of, 106
  definition of, 3, 14
  depth of, 5
  earnings from, 8
  18th century statistics on,
    56–57
  emerging technologies and,
    23–24
  factors affecting, 57–59,
    134–35
  first American, 37, 56
  geographic target of, 8–10
  job titles, 195
  launching of, 156, 180
  life cycle of, 157–61
  vs. newsletters, 17
  19th century statistics on, 65,
    70–71, 82
  ownership of, 208–15
  permanence of, 13
  purpose of, 137–38
  reading of, 254–56
  roles of, 12–13, 74–75
  specialization in, 5–6
  staff functions, 192–208,
    215–18
  terminology used by, 255
  timeliness of, 5
  trends in, 60–61
  turnover at, 201
  types of, 15–19
  voice of, 143
Magazine Section NMA, 242
Magazines for Libraries list, 21
Mahurin, Matt, 312
Mailer, Norman, 236, 240, 241
Makhazin, 3
Making an Issue of Child Abuse, 92
"Making Managed Care Work for
  You," 228
Malcolm, Janet, 334
Malcolm X, 235
Mamm, 137, 139
Management, 16
Managing Editor, 200–205
Map. *See* Break-of-the-book
Marie Claire
  advertising in, 35
  circulation of, 35
  Cosmopolitan and, 172

cover of, 104
CPMs, 34–36
origin of, 8
ownership of, 209
Marine Corps Marathon, 119
Marketing Director, 206, 207
Marketing plans, 170–84
Marquez, Gabriel Garcia, 69
Martha Stewart Living
  ancillary products of, 31, 34
  appearance of, 262
  brand awareness, 119
  parody of, 342
  publication of, 101
  stock in, 182
Martin, Peter, 233
Mary-Kate and Ashley magazine,
  101
Mas, 123
Massage, 236
Masses, The, 324–25
Masson, Jeffrey, 334
Matte coat, 299
Mattera, Marianne Dekker, 244
Maxim
  American debut of, 114
  ancillary products of, 31
  articles in, 114
  audience for, 114–15
  cartoons in, 344
  circulation of, 115
  Cosmopolitan and, 116
  cover of, 114–15
  CPM for, 179
  illustrations in, 89, 114–16
  origin of, 8
  sell-through rate of, 184
Maybelline, 152
McAvoy, Thomas, 80
McCall's
  ancillary products of, 33–34
  appearance of, 257
  articles in, 93, 227, 257
  audience for, 65–66
  circulation of, 40
  classification of, 112
  failure of, 33
  "The Forty-winks Reducing
    Plan," 257
  publication of, 73
  Rosie and, 33, 101
  "Why Mommy Can't Read,"
    257
McCarthy, Joseph, 96–97
McCaughey, Bobbi, 276, 312, 313
McClellan, George, 235
McClure's
  articles in, 93, 94
  cover of, **93**
  departments in, 146–47
  letters to the editor, 248
  photographs in, 79
  publication of, 73
  Reader's Digest and, 74
  writer's fees, 176
McCreary, Lew, 231
McCullers, Carson, 254
McDonald's, 141, 144–46, 313
McGraw, James, 47
McGraw-Hill, 208, 209
McInerney, Jay, 210
McPhee, John, 245
Mead, Margaret, 254
Mechanic, 71
Media Choices, 28
Media Industry Newsletter, The, 23
Media kits, 170, 207, 231

Mediamark Research, Inc. (MRI),
  29, 38
*Medical Device and Diagnostic
  Industry*, 137
Medical Economics, 277–78
Medical Meetings, 16
Meeting Professional, The, 16
Men
  advertising and, 67, 238
  content and, 60–61, 238
  on covers, 140, 287
  18th century magazines for,
    56–64
  in illustrations, 113, 238
  in labor force, 238
  letters to the editor, 111
  literacy rate, 59–60, 64
  19th century magazines for,
    64–66, 245
  Sports Illustrated swimsuit
    issue and, 261
  in trade magazines, 238
Men's Fitness, 113, 119
Men's Health
  appearance of, 140
  articles in, 138, 144, 228
  baby boomers and, 119
  circulation of, 138
  cover of, **138**, 140
  "Death by Exercise," 228
  excerpts in, 247
  international editions of, 8,
    138, 150, 259–60
  "malegrams" department, 147
  NMAs for, 228
  "100 Ways to Live Forever,"
    228
  "A Tale of Three Hearts," 228
  title, 136
  Understanding Men's Passages,
    247
  voice of, 143
Men's Journal
  advertising in, 34
  baby boomers and, 119
  illustrations in, 113
  ownership of, 209
  publisher of, 210
  special issues of, 34
Mercedes, 19
*Merchants' and Manufacturers'
  Journal*, 141
Meredith, E. T., **191**, 224
Meredith Corporation
  advertising by, 37
  ancillary products of, 34
  custom division of, 18, 19
  editorial cost per page, 169
  founding of, **191**
  interactive media from, 20, 23
  media holdings of, 208
  organization chart, 193
  ownership of, 209
  reader's profile by, 110
  Spanish-language titles from,
    123
Mergenthaler Linotype machine,
  84
Merry's Museum, 3, 73
Metal Edge, 286
Metropolitan Home, 37, 94–95,
  119, 135
Mettler, Mike, 307
Meyer, John, 169, 211
MH-18 magazine, 103, 126. *See
  also Men's Health*
Midwest Living, 8, 23, 209, 299

Might, 302
Military History, 177
Miller, Arthur, 96
Miller, Judith, 319
Miller, Kathy, 244
Ministries Today, 209, 210
Minnesota Bride, 10
Mirabella, Grace, 216
Mirror of Liberty, 123
Miss Black America, 123
Mitchell, Martha, 100
Mladina, 259
Mode, 103
Modern Baking, 138
Modern Bride, 103, 209
Modern Plastics Worldwide, 8
Mollenhoff, Clark, 97
Mondrian, Piet, 258
Money
    agenda setting in, 91
    audience for, 120
    bathroom reading of, 29
    pseudoevents, 116
    purpose of, 137
    title, 136
Monowell structure, 150
Monroe, Marilyn, 236, 257, 263
Montandon, Pat, 330
Monthly Review, The, 58
Moore, Ann S., 217
Moore, Demi, 4, 198, 330
Moore, Mary Tyler, 283
Moore, Peter, 228
Moral Fragments and Moral
    Community, 106
More
    appearance of, 263
    audience for, 118
    cover of, 101, 104, **294**, 300
    paper for, 299
    production process for,
        293–94, 296
    table of contents, 282
Morgan, Robin, 44–46, 216
Morgan, Thomas, 134
Morris, Jan, 230
Morrongiello, Christine, 238–39
Morrow, Lance, 278
Morthanos, John, 83
Mother Earth News, The
    advertising in, 158–60
    appearance of, 158
    articles in, 138, 158–61
    audience for, 150, 153, 157–61
    bathroom reading of, 29
    circulation of, 159, 161
    cover of, **156**, 158, 160
    launching of, 157, 158
    letters to the editor, 111,
        158–60
    pass-along readership of, 13
    philosophy of, 158, 161
    Rolling Stone and, 157
Mother Jones, 99
Motorhome Life, 158
Motor Trend, 31
Mott, Frank Luther, 71, 124
Mountain Bike, 116
Movies
    ads for, parody of cover, 330
    children's magazines and, 72
    "dear diary" column from, 235
    fact checker character in, 210
    reviews of, 245
Ms.
    advertising in, 44–46, 48, 142,
        179, 215

audience for, 150
cover of, 240
development of, 44, 150
feminism and, 13, 100
letters to the editor, 111
price per issue, 180, 182
title, 136
Muckraking, 92–93, 94, 248. *See*
    also Investigative reports
Muhler, Liz, 18, 212
Muir, John, 69
Multiwell structure, 150
Munsey, Frank, 38–39
Munsey's, 38–39, 73, 79, 248
Murphy, Cullen, 23–24
Murray, Judith Sargent, 244
Muse, 126
Mutuality, 106
Myers, Elissa Matulis, 16

Nabisco, 48
Naked Gun, 330
Nameplate, 255
Narang, Priya, 116
Nast, Condé, 141, **196**
Nast, Thomas, 78, 342
Nation, The
    access to information for, 318
    articles in, 12
    bathroom reading of, 29
    copyright case, 349–50
    cover of, **349**
    establishment of, 56
    focus of, 91
    letters to the editor, 248
    Persian Gulf War coverage in,
        322
    publication frequency, 177
    A Time to Heal, 349–50
    Vietnam War coverage in, 99
    on Watergate, 100
    on women journalists, 203
National Audubon Society, 109
National Directory of Magazines,
    21
National Enquirer, 331
National Fire Protection Agency
    (NFPA), 215
National Fisherman, 177
National Geographic
    ancillary products of, 31, 34
    anniversary issues of, 236, 313
    appearance of, 265
    articles in, 229–30
    binding of, 307
    The Bridges of Madison County
        and, 102
    circulation of, 16, 22
    classification of, 16, 17
    copyright case, 348
    cover of, 268, 276, 313
    cutlines in, 279
    editorial philosophy of, 250
    establishment of, 56
    folio lines, 265
    last editorial page in, 281
    photographers for, 102, 204
    photographs in, 79–80, 89,
        274, 276, 348
    purpose of, 137
    reader's profile by, 36
    retention of, 13
    structure of, 150
National Geographic Adventure, 16
National Geographic International,
    16
National Geographic Kids, 16, 126

National Geographic Traveler, 16,
    121
National Imagery and Mapping
    Agency, 321
National Lampoon, 340–42, **341**
National League of Families of
    American Prisoners and
    Missing in Southeast Asia,
    100
National Magazine, The, 216
National Magazine Awards
    (NMA), 50, 98, 241–43
National Origins Act, 173
National Press, 85n1. *See also Town*
    and Country
National Review
    appearance of, 262
    cutlines in, 278
    focus of, 91
    on Watergate, 100
    women journalists and, 239
National Rifle Association (NRA).
    See American Rifleman
National Wildlife, 109
National Wildlife Federation, 126
National Youth Ministries of
    Assemblies of God, 12–13
Nation's Business, The, 74
Naugle, Wendy, 214
Navasky, Victor, 359
NBA Inside Stuff, 348
Neal Award, 109, 243–44, 362
Near, Jay M., 322
Near v. Minnesota, 322
Negro Digest, 98–99
Neighborhood Salon Association,
    109
Nelly, 124
Nelson, Barbara, 92
Nelson, Jack A., 108
Nelson, Willie, 160
Neopets Youth Study, 28
Nest, 150
Net revenue, 167, 186
New England Journal of Medicine,
    17, 56, 286
New England Magazine of
    Knowledge and Pleasure, 68
New Hampshire Weddings, 10
Newhouse, Donald, 208, 210
Newhouse, S. I., Jr., 208, 210
New Journalism, 240–41
New Man, 209, 210
New Republic, The
    appearance of, 262, 265
    folio lines, 265
    letters to the editor, 248
    marketing of, 175
    table of contents, 282
    Vietnam War coverage in, 99
    women journalists and, 239
News articles
    approach to, 5
    ethics and, 358–59, 365–66
    fair use and, 350
    Neal Award for, 243–44
    photographs for, 312–14
    sources for, 319–20
    surveys for, 228
Newsletters, 17
Newspapers
    articles in, 6
    data retention by readers of, 30
    distribution of, 81–82
    Neal Award for, 244
    Sunday supplements, 19
    taxation of, 326

terminology used by, 255
Time and, 72
Newsweek
    advertising in, 9, 37, 50
    appearance of, 265
    articles in, 138, 223
    on child abuse, 92
    copyright case, 345–46
    "core plots" of, 74
    cover of, **224**, 268, 276, 312–13
    cutlines in, 280
    depth of, 144
    excerpts in, 247
    on *Flair*, 154
    folio lines, 265
    identity of, 106, 223
    international editions of, 8
    letters to the editor, 248
    libel suit against, 331
    memorials in, 236
    "My Turn" column, 147
    needs met by, 5–6
    nonfiction excerpts in, 247
    parody of, 341
    photographers for, 204
    photographs in, 276, 312–13
    price per issue, 182
    publication frequency, 177
    purpose of, 137
    reader's profile by, 36
    September 11 terrorist attacks
        coverage, 9, 101–2, 237,
        358
    special issues of, 74–75, 102,
        236–37
    staff for, 204
    table of contents, 282
    on Watergate, 100
New Woman, 112
New York
    appearance of, 10, 11, 258–62
    appropriation case against, 339
    articles in, 11, 241
    cover of, **11**, 286
    Felker on, 12
    Ms. and, 44
    new journalism in, 241
    "Radical Chic: That Party at
        Lenny's," 11
New Yorker, The
    advertising in, 47–48, 50, 160
    appearance of, 262, 265
    archives, digital, 233
    articles in, 72, 76, 89, 91–92,
        102, 148, 160, 197,
        197–99, 236, 245,
        327–28
    audience for, 10
    bathroom reading of, 29
    "Boy on the Train, The,"
        327–28
    cartoons in, 4, 102, 197–99,
        233, 273, 281
    In Cold Blood, 197, 247
    cover of, 102, **232**, 276, 284,
        289
    editorial directors of, 197–99
    essays in, 245–46
    fiction in, 247
    Flair and, 154
    folio lines, 265
    "The Glamour of
        Delinquency," 245
    "Hiroshima," 102, 236
    illustrations in, 276
    invasion of privacy suit
        against, 338

last editorial page in, 281
launching of, 160
letters to the editor, 198
libel suit against, 334
memorials in, 75
NMAs for, 243
ownership of, 198, 208–10
parody of, 341
profiles in, 232–33
prospectus of, 76
publication frequency, 14, 177
publisher of, 37, 210
September 11 terrorist attacks
coverage, 101–2, 276
short stories in, 247
"Silent Spring," 91–92, 197
special issues of, 102, 236
table of contents, 282
The Threepenny Review and,
247
women journalists and, 239
New-York Magazine, 61–62, 73
New-York Mirror, 68, 70, 73, 78
New York Times, The
on child abuse, 92
New York Times v. Sullivan,
331–32, 339, 343,
352n40
Plame investigation, 319
on publisher's challenges, 103
Sunday supplement, 19
on *Women's Home Companion*,
216
New York Times Magazine, The, 19,
239
New York Times v. Sullivan,
331–32, 339, 343, 352n40
New York Yankees, 236
Next, 9
NFPA, 215
Nickelodeon, 126
Nick Jr. Magazine, 126
Nielsen, Leslie, 330
Nixon, Richard M., 100, 182, 349
Nontraditional grids, 264
Nord, David Paul, 61–62
North American Review, 19, 66, 68,
232
"Notes from a Blond," 246

O at Home, 120
*O: Oprah Magazine. See Oprah
Magazine, The*
Oates, Joyce Carol, 100
Obama, Barack, 99
Obscenity, 302, 350–51
O'Callaghan, Kristin, 228
Octavo sheets, 82
O'Donnell, Rosie, 101
Offset presses, 304–5, 307, 309
Ogden Publishers, 161
Oklahoma City bombing, 102
Old-House Journal, 120
Old Man and the Sea, 247
Olsen, Ashley and Mary-Kate, 101
On Course, 12
"100 Ways to Live Forever," 228
Online chat rooms, 7, 111
Online Editor, 204, 211, 218
Ono, Yoko, 4
Opacity of paper, 299
Operation Desert Storm. *See*
Persian Gulf War, coverage
of
Oppenheim, Ellen, 231
Oprah Magazine, The
appearance of, 262

cover of, 101
parody of, 342
September 11 terrorist attacks
and, 104
TV show and, 157
Ordered designs, 262
Organization magazines. *See also
specific titles*
advertising in, 210
articles in, 7
categories of, 16
circulation of, **4**, 16, 22
community building by, 108,
109
description of, 16
editorial philosophy for, 136,
250
editorials in, 246
fiction in, 247
for leisure activities, 121
online versions of, 183
ownership of, 210–12
profiles in, 235–37
sale of, 182–83
service articles in, 230
taxation of, 325–26
"Orgasm of Death," 90, 343
Osborne, Stephen, 157
*Oscar Night: 75 Years of Hollywood
Parties*, 34
Out, 107, 149
Outdoor Life, 56
Outside
advertising in, 49, 178, 179
appearance of, 263
articles in, 108
circulation of, 178
CPM for, 178
cutlines in, 279
"Into Thin Air," 108
pseudoworld of, 116
table of contents, 282
Owen, William, 256–57
Oxford rules, 269

Packaging
advertising on, 51
of inserts, 305
of outserts, 143
of pornography, 351
Pages From the Past, 74–75
Paine, Thomas, 68, 95
Palaestra, 108
Panel quote, 255
Panorama, 9
Pantone Matching System (PMS)
numbers, 301–2
Paper
choice of, 140, 257, 297–300
cost of, 299
in 18th century, 77, 84
finish of, 298–99
grade of, 299
for gravure presses, 305
for inserts, 141
in marketing, 175
in 19th century, 84
octavo sheets, 82
for offset presses, 304–5
"plop factor" of, 299
ream of, 299
for sheet-fed presses, 304
size of, 311
special coatings for, 300
in 20th century, 84
for web presses, 304, 311
weight of, 299–300

Parade, 19
Paradise of the Pacific, 10
Parenti, Michael, 116
Parenting, 28
Parents, 37, 89, 211, 299
Parker, Dorothy, 197
Parks, Rosa, 272
Parody, 330, 340–43
Parrish, Maxfield, 79, 273
Pass-along readership, 13
Passport, 108
Patagonia, 49
Patriot Act, 321
Patterson, Philip, 356
PC Magazine, 15, **16**, 121, 286
PC Tools, 177
PC World, 15, 121
Pearl, Daniel, 359
Pearlstine, Norman, 288
Pearson, Drew, 319
Peck, Abe, 10, 285–86
Pecker, David, 281
Peer review, 17
Pennsylvania Magazine, 95–96
PentaCom, 47
Penthouse, 114, 339, 350
People
advertising in, 37, 49, 102
anniversary issues of, 236
articles in, 104
bathroom reading of, 29
cover of, **234**, 283, 286
cutlines in, 279
"50 Most Beautiful People"
list, 288
illustrations in, 113
inserts in, 141
interviews in, 233
launching of, 156
memorials in, 75, 123, 236
needs met by, 6
Oklahoma City bombing
coverage in, 102
ownership of, 208, 209, 213
personality sketches in, 233
philosophy of, 234
photographs in, 274
"Picks and Pans" department,
147
profiles in, 233, 234
profit from, 181
pseudoevents, 116
publisher of, 36
September 11 terrorist attacks
coverage, 101, 102
special issues of, 236
People en Español, 30, 123
People for the Ethical Treatment of
Animals (PETA), 200
Perfect binding, 306–9
Perlmutter, David D., 280
Persian Gulf War, coverage of, 92,
151, 322
Personal essays, 245–46
Personality sketches, 233
Personal Service NMA, 241–42
Peschke, Don, 142, 143, 150,
210
Petek, Lidija, 260
Peter, John, 281
Peterson, Laci and Scott, 4
Peterson, Theodore, 12
Peterson's Magazine
articles in, 225
audience for, 65
circulation of, 82
headquarters of, 66

illustrations in, 78
publication of, 73
Pfizer, 36, 50
*Pharmaceutical & Medical
Packaging News*, **136**, 157,
179
Phenomenistic approach, 90
Philadelphia, 10
Phillips, Chris, 302
Phillips, David Graham, 76
Phoenix, 10
Photo Editor, 205
Photofiction, 314
Photography
ad/editorial separation and, 47
in ads, 302
balance in, 270
blocks, 301
celebrity approval of, 276
color, 80, 300–304
copyright to, 348
on covers, 281, 284, 287
cutlines and, 255, 278–80
digital, 274, 276, 300, 312–14
editing of, 276, 312–14
ethics and, 358–59
eye movement and, 263
fashion, 274
feature vs. news, 302
film for, 301
iconic, 272
invasion of privacy and, 338
libel and, 329
in *Life*, 41–43, 274–75
moiré patterns on, 301, 303
in *National Geographic*, 79–80,
89, 274, 276, 348
in 19th century, 78–79, 273
NMAs for, 242
objectivity of, 273
paper for, 298–99
planning for, 301
printing of, 78–79, 300–303
proportion in, 270
of September 11 terrorist
attacks, 102, 104, 358
shooting scripts for, 275
staff for, 204–5
stock pictures for, 276, 339
in trade magazines, 238
trends in, 60–61
in 20th century, 79–80, 84
unity in, 270
Photo Portfolio/Photo Essay
NMA, 242
Physical Culture, 74–76
Physics Today, 285
Pica, 266–67
Picasso, Pablo, 324
Pilgrim's Progress, 93
Pillsbury, 48
Pitt, Brad, 289
"Plague Years, The," 137
Plame, Valerie, 319
Plath, Sylvia, 69
Playboy
agenda setting in, 91
ancillary products of, 114
anniversary issues of, 236
appearance of, 261
articles in, 115
audience for, 114
back issues of, 263
bathroom reading of, 29
binding of, 306
cartoons in, 273
circulation of, 115

cultural standards and, 106,
114
cutlines in, 280
Esquire and, 114
illustrations in, 89
international editions of,
259–60
interviews in, 233, 235, 280
logo for, 283
obscenity in, 350
parody of, 341, 342
Playmates, 4, 91, 114
short stories in, 247
Plurality, 106
PMS numbers, 301–2
PN/Paraplegia News, 108
Poe, Edgar Allan, 68, 70, 127
Points, 266–67
Political influences, 90–104
*Politicks and Other Human
Interests*, 134
Polo, 347
Pope, Alexander, 7
Pop Smear, 302
Popular Mechanics
advertising in, 343
appearance of, 262
bathroom reading of, 29
establishment of, 56
logo for, 283
Mother Earth News and,
157–58
ownership of, 209
parody of, 341
Reader's Digest and, 74
Spanish-language version of,
122
third-party liability case
against, 343
Popular Mechanics for Kids, 34
Popular Photography and Imaging,
21
Popular Science, 56
Pornography, 350–51
Porter, Katherine Anne, 100
Porter, Rufus, 70
Port Folio, 68, 73, 78, 229
Postal rates
appearance and, 43
blending and, 303
inserts and, 304
setting of, 81–83
weight and, 43, 82
Postcards, 171
Poster covers, 284
Powell, Colin, 333
Poz, **139**, 139
Poz Focus, 139
Practical Horseman, 5
Pratt, Jane, 151–52, 153
Premiere
integrated media in, 20–21
parody of, 341
profiles in, 235
publisher of, 37
reviews in, 245
Prepress houses, 300–301
President, Corporate, 195
Prevention, 29, 119, 239
Price, magazine
advertising and, 39
circulation and, 39
Generation X and, 180
sales and, 179–80, 182, 183
trends in, 60–61
Price, Mike, 319, 330–31
Price v. Time, Inc., 319, 330–31

Prime Time Live, 338
Primo, 125
Print, 6, 183, 286, **287**
Printers, censorship by, 302
Printing
coatings and, 300
of color photographs, 80,
300–304
digital vs. hand tools, 305–6
ink for, 84, 298–99, 302, 305
on offset presses, 304–5, 307,
309
proofs, 309–11
request form for, 310
on rotogravure presses, 305,
307–9
screens, 303
on sheet-fed presses, 304, 307
on signatures, 308
of UPC bar codes, 312, 314
on web presses. *See* Web
presses
"Prisoner of Sex, The," 236
Private ownership, 208–10
Privileged statements, 335–36
Prize Fighter's Joys, 70
Process color, 300–301
Procter and Gamble, 36, 215
Production
binding, 305–9
break-of-the-book. *See* Break-
of-the-book
in 18th century, 77, 84
format and, 43
of illustrations, 300–304
in 19th century, 78, 84
paper. *See* Paper
for permanence, 13
planning stage, 294, 295
printing. *See* Printing
process for, 294–95
publication frequency and, 177
signatures, 307–9
trends in, 60–61
in 20th century, 78–79, 84
Production department
desktop publishing and, 305–6
duties of, 192
expenses from, 167, 168,
186–88
Production Director, 201–2, 207,
211
Products
ancillary. *See* Ancillary
products
vs. brands, 31
Profile Writing NMA, 242
Profit, operating
1998 vs. 2004 statistics, 217–18
2004 statistics on, 167, 169
buying vs. starting and, 180
definition of, 169
modeling of, 188–89
Progressive, The, 99, 248, **318**, 323
Progressive Farmer, 56
Proofs, 309–11
Proportion, 270
Pseudoevents, 116–17, 358, 365
Pseudoworld, 113–16
Psychographics, 7, 28–29
Psychology Today, 89, 104
Publication
centers for, 66, 110
frequency of, 14, 36–37,
176–77
loans for, 156
seasonality of, 14

Public Interest NMA, 242
Public ownership, 208
Public Relations Director, 207
Public relations magazines
articles in, 211–12
audience for, 18
community building by, 109
description of, 17–18
editors for, 211–12
in 19th century, 71
ownership of, 210–12
Public Relations Society of
America (PRSA), 18, 22
Public relations techniques, 178
Publisher, 195–96, 206–8
Publishers' Clearinghouse, 176
Publishers Information Bureau
(PIB), 38, 43
Publishers Weekly, 56
Pull-quotes, 255, 278, 279
Pulse of the Twin Cities, 19
Pure Food and Drug Act, 94

Quad Graphics, 303
Quarterly reviews, 247
Queen Anne's Act, 81
Question and answer articles,
233–34
Quick Fiction, 247
Quill, 12, 17
Quinn, Lisa, 160

"Radical Chic: That Party at
Lenny's," **11**, 11
Radio
advertising on, 28, 51
children's magazines and, 72
magazine complements to, 157
Ragan Communications Media
Relations Report, 114
Ragged right margins, 267
Ramparts, 99
Ranger Rick, 126
Rassmussen, Larry, 106
Rate dealing, 39
Ray Gun, 256, **267**, 270
Reader discussion groups, 109
Readers. *See* Audience
Reader's Digest
advertising in, 50
appearance of, 262
articles in, 72, 73–76, 173–74
bathroom reading of, 29
cartoons in, 273
circulation of, 15, 22, 40
classification of, 15
cover of, **174**
cultural standards and, 106,
173–74
international editions of, 174
launching of, 173
libel suit against, 333
parody of, 340
purpose of, 137
size of, 311
Spanish-language version of,
122
subtitles, 278
table of contents, 282
voice of, 173–74
writer's fees, 229
"Real Little Rock Story, The," 98
Real Simple, 37, 209, 283
Realtor, **225**
Reaves, Shiela, 313–14
Redbook
advertising in, 33

appearance of, 261
articles in, 227
cover of, 284
establishment of, 56
goals of, 77
illustrations in, 113
logo for, 283
ownership of, 209
publisher of, 210
table of contents, 282
title origin, 77
Redford, Robert, 235
Reed, Barbara Straus, 238–39
Reed, John, 240, 324
"Reel to Real," 102
Reiman, Roy, 142, 172–74
Remington, Frederic, 273
Reminisce, 75, 142, 174
Remnick, David, 102, 197, 199, 233
Replacement Contractor, 208, 209
Reporters Committee for Freedom
of the Press, 320
Reporting NMA, 242
Research Director, 207–8
Residential Architect, 209
Revenue, 166–68, 184–89
Revere, Paul, 77, 95
Reviews, scorecard, 245
Reviews and Criticism NMA, 242
Revlon, 44
Reynolds, Rodney J., 124
Richards, Ann, 314
Ridgeway, Rick, 49
"Right to Work, The," 93
Riis, Jacob A., 240
Ringe, Alexandra, 140
Riordan, Robert, 182
RN, 6
Road and Track, 37
Robb Report, 120, 121
Robert Traver Fly-fishing Fiction
Award, 235
Robinson, Arthur, 327–28
Robinson, Kathie, 215
Rockefeller, John D., 93, 232
Rock Products, 237
Rockwell, Norman, 42, **97**, 98, 273
Rolling Stone
advertising in, 157, 177
appearance of, 254, 263
articles in, 137, 237
audience for, 118, 150, 153
cover of, 4, **192**, 286, **289**
CPM for, 179
excerpts in, 247
inserts in, 141
logo for, 283
memorials in, 75
Mother Earth News and, 157
new journalism in, 241
NMAs for, 237, 254
ownership of, 209
paper for, 297, 299
photographs in, 276
"The Plague Years," 137
publisher of, 210
purpose of, 137
serialized novels in, 247
staff for, 103
title, 137
"The True Story of John/Joan,"
237
Roome, Hugh, 127
Roosevelt, Eleanor, 99
Roosevelt, Theodore, 69, 72, 93
Rosenblatt, Alfred, 231
Rosenblatt v. Baer, 332

Rosie, 33, 101
Ross, Harold, 76, 197, 208, 232
Ross, Lillian, 232–33
Rosso, 19
Rotogravure presses, 305, 307–9
Round Table, The, 70
Rovere, Richard H., 97
Royal American Magazine, The, 73, 77, 95
R. R. Donnelley, 299, 303
Rubenstein, Atoosa, 51, 127, 153, 206
Rubinstein, Rhonda, 256, 290
Runner's World, 134
Rural free distribution system, 83
Russell, Bertrand, 324
Ruth, Babe, 232

Saddle-stitching, 306–8
St. Nicholas, **67,** 72, 73, 125
Sales
    cable vs. network, 172
    circulation fulfillment houses, 181
    direct mail marketing, 171, 174, 186
    economy and, 22, 60, 180–81
    expenses from, 168, 186–88
    free issues and, 172–74
    hard vs. soft offers, 174
    incentives for, 171, 176, 181, 186
    from insert cards, 172
    legal issues with, 326
    list kits, 167, 171
    online, 84, 171–72
    price per issue and, 179–80, 182, 183
    renewals, 176
    revenue from, 167, 184–89
    sell-through rates, 184
    September 11 terrorist attacks and, 102, 237, 288
    single-copy vs. subscriptions, 83, 182, 183–84
    through sponsored agencies, 176
    test issues, 175–76, 178
    UPC bar code tracking of, 312
Sales and Marketing Management, 237–40
Salisbury, Harrison, 50
Salmon, E. Dwight, 358
San Antonio Magazine, 12
Sandburg, Carl, 324
San Diego Home/Garden Lifestyles, 11
Sanger, Margaret, 216
Saralegui, Alvaro, 47
Sasso, Richard, 84–85
Sassy, 89, 151–53, 206
Saturday Evening Post
    advertising in, 39, 67
    appearance of, 39, 78
    articles in, 68, 233, 332–33, **334**
    audience for, 67
    on child abuse, 92
    circulation of, 39, 40
    cover of, 42, 273
    establishment of, 56
    failure of, 41, 241, 287–89
    headquarters of, 66
    "I Call On" series, 233
    illustrations in, 78
    libel suit against, 332–33, **334**
    parody of, 341

price per issue, 39, 179
    redesign of, 287–89
    short stories in, 246
    on "Silent Spring," 91
    "Story of a College Football Fix," 332–33, **334**
Saturday Press, 72
Saturday Review, 341
Saudi Aramco World, 137
Saveur, 28, 135, 150
Savoy, 124, 165
Schlesinger, Arthur, Jr., 12, 69
Scholarly journals, 17
Scholastic, Inc., 126
Schrettenbrunner, Teri, 302
Schuler, Lou, 228
Schwarz, Ted, 245
Science News, 239
Scientific American
    appearance of, 262
    articles in, 70–71
    cover of, **64**
    CTP and, 85, 309
    Edison and, 89
    establishment of, 56, 85n1
    production of, 84–85
    Reader's Digest and, 74
Scotch rules, 269
Scott, Byron T., 224
Scott, Ron, 281
Scott, Walter, 68, 78
Screens, 303–4
Scribner's
    advertising in, 39
    articles in, 65, 76
    audience for, 39
    departments in, 146–47
    publication of, 73, 86n36
    Reader's Digest and, 74
Sea Kayaker, 83
Seelig, Jill, 120
Seinfeld, 237
Selena, 123
Self
    appeal of, 31
    baby boomers and, 119
    illustrations in, 113
    needs met by, 6
    ownership of, 209
Selicciones, 123
Sell lines, 255
Sell-through rates, 184
Semiotics
    on content, 111–12
    definition of, 111
Senior Editor, 202–5
September 11 terrorist attacks
    advertising and, 102, 103
    ancillary products and, 176
    circulation and, 8
    content and, 102–4
    covers and, 102–4, 276, 286
    direct mail marketing and, 186
    ethics and, 358
    FOIA and, 321
    foreign response to, 9
    narrative template from, 75
    photos of, 102, 104, 358
    sales and, 102, 237, 288
Serialized novels, 246
Service articles, 224–31, 243
Settje, David E., 99
"Seven sisters" magazines, 227
Seventeen
    advertising in, 51, 343
    articles in, 89
    audience for, 126

bathroom reading of, 29
CosmoGirl and, 172
    covers of, 51, **127**
    editors, 206
    illustrations in, 127
    ownership of, 209
    Sassy and, 152
    Schwarz's story on Miller in, 244
    special issues of, 236
    table of contents, 282
    third-party liability case against, 343
"Sex, Lies and Advertising," 48
Sex and the Single Girl, 115
Shakur, Tupac, 124
"Shame of the Cities," 93
Shape, 113, 116, 119
Shapiro, Susan P., 328–29
Shaw, David, 10
Shawn, William, 197–98
Sheehy, Gail, 11, 247
Sheet-fed presses, 304, 307
Shepley, Pete, 27
Sherman, William Tecumseh, 235
Sherrill, Martha, 116–17
Sherrill, Robert, 318
"Shield laws," 319
Shop Etc., 282
Shop-Notes, 142, 210
Short stories, 246
Show, 257, 258
Shuttleworth, Jane, 157–58
Shuttleworth, John, 157–59
Sidebars, 227, 263–64, 266
Sidis, William James, 338
Siempre Mujer, **122,** 123
Sierra, 16, 56, 109, 137
Signatures, 307–9
"Silent Spring," 91–92, 197
Silvers, Rob, 236
Simmons Market Research Bureau, 38
Simpson, O. J., 276, 312–13
Sinatra, Frank, 75
Sinclair, Upton, 324
Single-topic Issue Neal Award, 244
Single-topic Issue NMA, 242
60 Minutes, 5
Sketches, 233
Slug, 255
Small Market Meetings, 16
Smart Computing, 137
SmartMoney, 34, 120
Smith, Edward L., 351
Smith, Jessie Willcox, 113
Smith, Margaret Chase, 100
Smith, Richard M., 313
Smithsonian
    classification of, 16
    cover of, 285, 314
    on *Jeopardy,* 13
    sale of, 182
    single-copy vs. subscriptions, 314
Smooth, 124
Smoothness of paper, 299
Snow, Carmel, 80
Snowboarder, 121
Soap Opera Digest, 6
Social utility of information, 6
Society and association magazines, 16–17. *See also* Organization magazines
Society of National Association Publications (SNAP), 21–22
Society of Professional Journalists

ethical guide from, 358, 365–66
    FOIA letters from, 320
    Quill, 12, 17
    statement of principles, 359
Soldier of Fortune, 4, 24n1, 344–45
Sonneschein, Rosa, 216
Soria, Sandra, 110
Sound and Vision, 21, 134
Source, The, 183
South-Carolina Price-Current, The, 62, 73
Southern Literary Messenger, 73, 96
Southern Living, 8, 209
Southern Lumberman, 136
Southern Pacific Railroad, 227
Southgate, M. Therese, 284
Spanish-American War, 79
Spears, Britney, 115
Special interest titles, 15
Special Issue Neal Award, 244
Specialized business magazines. *See* Trade magazines
Spectator, 58
Spelling, Tori, 314
Spin, 36
Spock, Benjamin, 69
Sponsored circulation agencies, 176
Sponsored publications. *See* Custom magazines
Sponsorship, 50, 141, 360–61
Sport, 29
Sporting News, The, 5, 56
Sports Afield, 29, 56
Sports Illustrated
    access to information for, 318
    advertising in, 37, 47, 177
    anniversary issues of, 236
    articles in, 5, 148
    audience for, 261
    bathroom reading of, 29
    digital vs. print, 23
    invasion of privacy suit against, 337–38
    libel suit against, 319, 330–31
    ownership of, 208, 209, 213
    photographs in, 276
    Price v. Time, Inc., 319, 330–31
    profiles in, 233
    profit from, 181
    publication frequency, 177
    publisher of, 36
    semiotics in, 111
    special issues of, 236
    table of contents, 282
    Ticketron and, 176
    women journalists for, 318
Sports Illustrated for Kids, 126, 348
Sports Illustrated on Campus, 23
Spot color, 301–3
Springer, Jerry, 342
Stackpole, Peter, 80
Staff Writer, 204
Standard Periodical Directory, 21
Standard Rate and Data Service (SRDS), 21, 38, 71
Stanton, Edwin, 96
Stanton, Elizabeth Cady, 216
Star, 217, 286
Starcom USA, 18
Stars and Stripes newspaper, 197
Start-Up Publication Neal Award, 244
"Starving Glutton, The," 336–37
Steele, Bob, 359
Steele, Richard, 58

Steffens, Lincoln, 92–93, 240
Stein, Gertrude, 69
Steinbeck, John, 69, 96
Steinberg, Saul, 199
Steinem, Gloria
    investigative reports by, 240
    Ms. and, 44, 48, 150
    New York magazine and, 11
    roles of, 216
    "Sex, Lies and Advertising," 48
Stereo Review, 134
Stern, 9
Stevenson, Adlai, 281
Stevenson, Robert Louis, 72
Stewart, Martha, 182, 217, 342
Stilwell-Weber, Sarah, 273
Stock. *See* Paper
Stockholders, 188, 208, 210, 362
Stolley, Richard B., 234, 274, 283
Stone, Sharon, 235
Stone Soup, 126
Storch, Otto, 257
"Story of a College Football Fix,"
    332–33, **334**
Stouffers, 48
Stowe, Harriet Beecher, 69
Straight Arrow Publishing, 212
Strang, Stephen, 210
Strang Communications, 209, 210
Strategic Fulfillment Group, 181
Stryker, Roy, 275
Student Lawyer, 136
Student Press Review, 206
Study circles, 109
Study of Media and Markets, 38
Sturken, Marita, 272
Subheads, 255, 278
Subtitles, 255, 277–78
Success, 76, 244
Successful Farming
    cover of, **191**
    launching of, **191**
    ownership of, 208, 209
    publisher of, 37
    regional data in, 9
    special editions of, 9
Successful Meetings, 16
Success in Home Care, 229
Suede, 124
Sugar, Rob, 289
Suid, Lawrence, 345–46
Sullivan, Sean, 33
Sumner, David, 241
Sunday supplements, 19
Sunjata, Daniel, 49
Sunset
    articles in, 227, 229
    The Atlantic Monthly and, 227
    cover of, 15
    establishment of, 56, 227
    ownership of, 209
Sunshine laws, 321–22
Super calendered paper, 299
Supernatural, 141
Supreme Court
    on access to information,
        318–19
    on copyright, 345
    on distribution, 326
    on fair use, 349–50
    on false light cases, 339
    on incitement, 343
    on intentional infliction of
        emotional distress,
        340–43
    on libel, 331–35
    on obscenity, 350–51

on parody, 340–43
on prior restraint, 322–23
on sales, 326
on subsidiary rights, 348
on taxation, 325–26
Sweepstakes, 176
Sweet, Kimberly, 229
Swet Information Services, 181
Swisshelm, Jane Grey, 216

Table of contents, 280–83, 286, 363
Tabloids
    approach of, 4
    libel suit against, 331
    Neal Award for, 244
    photographs in, 302
Taft, William Howard, 79
"Tale of Three Hearts, A," 228
Talese, Gay, 240
Talk magazine, 199
Tan, Amy, 69
Tarbell, Ida M., 92–93, 94, 176
Taste of Home, A, 7, 142
Tatler, 58
Tattler's Teapots, 70
Taxes, 325–26
Teddy Bear and Friends, 121
Teddy Bear Review, 121
Teen, 126, 152
Teen People, 126, 127, 150
Teen Vogue, 127, 150
Telephone sales calls, 326
Televisa, 123
Television
    advertising on. *See* Television
        advertising
    ancillary products on, 34
    articles and, 147, 161
    attention span and, 260
    broadcast magazines on, 5
    cable. *See* Cable television
    data retention by watchers of,
        30
    ephemeral nature of, 13
    Houchins v. KQED, 351n1
    insert ads for programs on,
        141
    as leisure time activity, 117
    Life and, 41
    magazine complements to,
        120, 121, 157, **166**
    network vs. cable, 6
    new journalism and, 241
    Prime Time Live hidden
        camera case, 338
    program profiles, 237
    Smithsonian 35th anniversary
        and, 13
    timeliness of, 43
Television advertising
    credibility of, 28
    effectiveness of, 31
    intrusiveness of, 51
    vs. print, 41
    as public relations technique,
        178
    timeliness of, 43
Tennyson, Alfred, 72
Test issues, 175–76, 178
Texaco, 352n75
Texas Golfer, 5
Texas Highways, 282
Texas Monthly
    circulation of, 11
    classification of, 8
    cover of, 314
    publication frequency, 177

table of contents, 282
Texas Monthly, Inc. v. Bullock,
    325–26
Texas Music, 282
Texas Parks and Wildlife, 171, 282
Thackeray, William, 246
"That's Entertainment?," 240
Theatre Magazine, 74
Theroux, Paul, 230
Third-party liability, 90, 343–45
This Old House (magazine), 83,
    120
This Old House (TV show), 120
Thom, Mary, 111
Thomas, Dylan, 69
Thomas, Isaiah, 68, 95
Thompson, Bradbury, 257–58
Thompson, Dorothy, 203
Thompson, Hunter S., 240
Thoreau, Henry David, 69
Thornton, Brian, 248–49
Threepenny Review, The, 247
Thurber, James, 69, 197
Tiberis, Elizabeth, 216
Ticketron, 176
Tiegs, Cheryl, 118
Tikkun, 109, 285
Till, Emmett, 272
Time
    advertising in, 9, 37, 50
    ancillary products of, 175
    anniversary issues of, 236
    appearance of, 265
    articles in, 72–73, 138, 248,
        278, 286, 336–37
    bathroom reading of, 29
    brand awareness, 119
    on child abuse, 92
    circulation of, 22
    "core plots" of, 74
    cover of, 70, **196**, 268, 276, 285,
        286, 312–13
    cutlines in, 278, 280
    "Death Penalty," 286
    depth of, 144
    excerpts in, 247
    first editorial, 100
    on *Flair*, 154
    folio lines, 265
    format for, 275
    on Gulf War (2003–2006), 4
    identity of, 106
    illustrations in, 113, 273
    international editions of, 8
    invasion of privacy suit
        against, 336–37
    "Is God Dead?," 286
    last editorial page in, 281
    letters to the editor, 248
    libel suits against, 330, 333
    linguistics, 104
    logo for, 283–84
    "Man of the Year," 104, 248
    marketing of, 175
    memorials in, 236, 288
    needs met by, 6
    ownership of, 208, 209, 213
    parody of, 341, 342
    photographs in, 275, 276,
        312–13
    Plame investigation, 319
    price per issue, 182
    Price v. Time, Inc., 319, 330–31
    publication frequency, 177
    publisher of, 36, 73
    purpose of, 137
    redesign of, 289

on *Sassy*, 151
September 11 terrorist attacks
    coverage, 101–2, 237,
    288, 358
serialized novels in, 247
on "Silent Spring," 91
special issues of, 74–75, 101–2,
    236–37
staff for, 103, 204
"The Starving Glutton,"
    336–37
subscriptions to, 81
A Time to Heal, 349–50
title, 136
"Unspeakable," 278
on Watergate, 100
on *Women's Home Companion*,
    216
Time for Kids, 126
Time to Heal, A, 349–50
Time Warner
    advertising by, 36–37
    conflicts of interest, 213
    executive compensation
        packages, 213
    media holdings of, 208, 213
    ownership of, 209
    titles of, **196**
Tip boxes, 227
Titleist, 47
Titles
    appearance of, 277–78
    choice of, 136–37
    definition of, 255
    division of, 271
    legal issues with, 346–47
Tobacco Reporter, 56, 65
Today's Christian Woman, 244
Toll, Roger, 123
Tools of the Trade, 208, 209
Torts
    appropriation, 339
    definition of, 317
    false light cases, 338–39
    intentional infliction of
        emotional distress,
        339–43
    invasion of privacy, 320,
        336–39, 340
    libel, 319, 326–36, 337, 340
Tory, 95
Town and Country
    anniversary issues of, 236
    establishment of, 56, 85n1
    last editorial page in, 281
    ownership of, 209
    parody of, 341
    photographs in, 80
    serialized novels in, 247
"Toxic Nightmare on Main Street,"
    237
Toyota, 36
Tracking, 268
Trade magazines. *See also specific
    titles*
    ad/editorial separation in, 47
    advertising in, 31, 37, 51, 67
    agenda setting in, 92
    ancillary products and, 34
    articles in, 235–40
    community building by, 108–9
    covers of, 51, 286
    description of, 15–16
    editorials in, 246
    in 18th century, 62–64
    fact checking for, 328
    fiction in, 247

health-based, 119
on leisure activities, 121
Neal Award for, 243–44
in 19th century, 65, 70–71
outserts in, 143
ownership of, 208–10
on personal finance, 120–21
research director for, 208
sale of, 182
seminars and shows by, 34
service articles in, 228–30
on shelter, 120
Spanish-language versions of, 123
special issues of, 237
taxation of, 325–26
titles for, 136
women journalists and, 217
Trademarks, 37, 283, 346–47
Trading Spaces, 120
Traditional grids, 264
Traditional Home
cover of, **298**, 300
interactive media from, 23
ownership of, 209
paper for, 299
sales of, 156
size of, 311
Transparencies, 301
Travel and Leisure, 6, 121, 217, 230
Travelocity, 103
"Treason of the Senate, The," 76
Tricycle: The Buddhist Review, 6, 13
True Story, 29
"True Story of John/Joan, The," 237
Truman, James, 150
TV-Cable Week, 135
TV Guide
advertising in, 37
audience for, 180
back issues of, 263
brand awareness, 119
circulation of, 22
cover of, **23**, 286
format of, 19
libel suit against, 330
logo for, 283
memorials in, 236
price per issue, 180
special issues of, 236
Twain, Mark
in *Atlantic Monthly*, 69
autobiographical profile of, 235
children's stories by, 72
in humor magazines, 72
investigative reports by, 240
travel articles by, 229
12-part grid, 264
20/20, 5
Typography
consistency in, 269–70
in 18th century, 77
factors affecting, 264
font and style of, 266
justified margins, 267
legibility of, 265–66
line length, 267
for logo, 283–84
in 19th century, 78
ragged right margins, 267
reading speed and, 266–68
size of, 266–67
spacing, 268
suitability of, 266
voice of, 264–65

Uihlein, Wally, 47
Ulrich's Periodicals Directory, 21
Uncoated paper, 298
Understanding Men's Passages, 247
United States Magazine, 73, 96
United States Postal Service, 83
Unity, 269–70
University Microforms, 348
Univision, 123
Updike, John, 69, 115
Urban magazines, free, 19
Urban Profile, 165, 166
USAA Magazine, 109
Uses and gratifications theory, 5–6
U.S. News and World Report
"core plots" of, 74
cover of, 51, **101**
letters to the editor, 248
memorials in, 75
printing of, 313
pseudoevents, 116
September 11 terrorist attacks
coverage, 101–2, 237
special issues of, 236–37
staff for, 103
on Watergate, 100
US Weekly
bathroom reading of, 29
inserts in, 141
ownership of, 209
profiles in, 235
publication frequency, 177
publisher of, 210
sales of, 289
Utne
appearance of, 265
articles in, 89
as community builder, 105–6
cover of, **105**
folio lines, 265
launching of, 160
online chat rooms for, 111
salons, 109–10
table of contents, 282
title, 137
voice of, 143
Utne, Eric, 254
UV coating, 300

Van Gogh, Vincent, 284
Vanguard Media, 165
Vanity Fair
advertising in, 43
ancillary products of, 34
appearance of, 80, 113, 256–58
Brown and, 198
covers of, 4, 104, 198–99
Felt and, 89
illustrations in, 113
ownership of, 209
photographs in, 80, 257
profiles in, 233, 235
publisher of, 37, 210
September 11 terrorist attacks
coverage, 101, 104
sharing of, 13
women journalists and, 239
Varick, Richard, 61
Varnish, 300
Vassar Quarterly, 236
Velvet stock, 298–99
Venture, 313
Verne, Jules, 72
Vibe
appearance of, 254

audience for, 124, 150
cover of, **166**
CPM for, 179
Jones letter for, 175
launching of, 165
logo for, 283
marketing of, 175
NMAs for, 254
Vibe Vixen, 124
Vida Cristiana, 209, 210
Video, 134
Vietnam War, coverage of, 99–100
Vilanch, Bruce, 246
Virgil, Michael, 337–38
Vision, 19
Vocations for Social Change, 157
Vogue
appearance of, 80, 253–54, 256–58
copyright case, 349
cover of, 4, 70, **196**, **271**, 285
establishment of, 56
ownership of, 209
parody of, 341
photographs in, 80, 257
profiles in, 235
publisher of, 210
Vonnegut, Kurt, 115

W, 4, 209
Wainwright, Loudon, 98
Walgreen World, 18, 212
Wallace, Carol, 104
Wallace, DeWitt and Lila, 73, 173
Walljasper, Jay, 105–6, 143
Wal-Mart, 83, 183
Ward, Douglas B., 67
Ward, Sela, 118
Ware, Chris, 199
Warhol, Andy, 257
Washington, George, 61, 68
Washingtonian, The, 204
Watergate, 89, 100, 182, 349
Watkins, Patsy Guenzel, 305–6
Waugh, Evelyn, 247
Wayne, John, 345
Web presses
circulation and, 304
CTP and, 85, 309
gravure, 305, 307–9
paper for, 304, 311
vs. sheet-fed presses, 304
signatures and, 307
Websites
ABM on, 363–64
advertising on, 51, 358, 364
domain name of, 347
editorial monitoring of, 7
ethics, 358
Good Housekeeping's
certification of, 32–33
links to/from, 364
media kits on, 170
Neal Award for, 244
NMAs for, 243
parody, 342
Patriot Act and, 321
reference material on, 14
user privacy, 364
Webster, Noah, 56, 68
Weeden, Job, 77–78
Weiss, Jennifer, 239
Welles, Orson, 99
Wells, Ida B., 216
Welty, Eudora, 254
Wenner, Jann, 137, 157, **192**, 289
Wenner Media, 192, 209, 210, 212

West, Kanye, 124, **192**, 289
Wharton, Edith, 69
Wheeler, Tom, 314
Whigs, 95
Whitaker, Mark, 51
White, Brenda, 18
White, E. B., 50, 69, 197, 199
White, Jan, 254, 262, 269, 315
White, Katharine Angell, 197
White, Trumbull, 77
Whiteness of paper, 299
Whitman, Walt, 69
Whitney, Ruth, 216
Whittier, John Greenleaf, 68
"Why Americans Hate the Media," 248
"Why Is Ice Slippery," 285
"Why Mommy Can't Read," 257
Wiggin, Kate Douglas, 69
Wiley, Harvey, 32
Wilkins, Lee, 356
Williams, Clayton, 314
Willis, Nathaniel Parker, 70
Wills, Garry, 69
Wilson, Woodrow, 69
Wilson Quarterly, 17, 177
Wilson v. Layne, 318
Winfrey, Oprah, 101, 178, 217
Wintour, Anna, 199, 200
Wired
appearance of, 140
articles in, 140
audience for, 150
circulation of, 23
logo for, 283
online chat rooms for, 111
ownership of, 209
paper for, 140
parody of, 342
price per issue, 180
table of contents, 282
Wolf, Henry, 257, 258, 261
Wolf, Naomi, 113
Wolfe, Tom, 11, 240, 247
Wollstonecraft, Mary, 63
Wolston, Ilya, 333
Woman's Day
advertising in, 37
articles in, 112, 227
circulation of, 22
price per issue, 182
size of, 311
Woman's Home Companion
articles in, 93
audience for, 65–66
circulation of, 40
failure of, 41
publication of, 73
Women
advertising and, 44–45, 48–49, 67, 113, 238
in artwork, 78, 112, 273
content and, 112–13, 238
on covers, **90**, 287, 302
18th century magazines and, 62–64, 244
feminism, 13, 62, 100–101, 236
in illustrations, 78–79, 112–13, 238
journalists, 202–3, 216, 217, 239, 318
letters to the editor, 111
literacy rate, 59, 64
19th century magazines and, 64–65, 72, 216, 244
in *Reader's Digest*, 173
sphere of influence, 93

in sports magazines, 47, 261
subscriptions for, 61
in trade magazines, 238
war correspondents, 216
Women in Journalism, 203
Women's Health, 144
Women's Home Companion, 216
Women's rights movement, 62, 236
"Wonders of Water, The," 258
Wood
    articles in, 13–14, 138, 229
    cover of, **14**
    interactive media from, 23
    marketing of, 176
    ownership of, 209
    paper for, 298
Woodrow Wilson International
    Center for Scholars, 17
Woods, Bruce, 160

Woodsmith
    advertising in, 142
    audience for, 150
    cover of, **205**
    launching of, 142
    publisher of, 210
    renewal rate for, 142
    voice of, 143
Woodward, Bob, 247
Woolf, Virginia, 254
Wordsworth, William, 68
Word Ways: The Journal of
    Recreational Linguistics, 17
Workbench, 142, 210
WorkBoat, 31, 179, 182, **183**
"Work for hire," 348
Working Mother, 45
Working Woman, 45, 103, 112
World Coin News, 121

World's Work, 248
World Traveler, 19
World Vision, 18
World War I, articles on, 216,
    324–25
World War II, articles on, 4, 102,
    236
Worth, 120, 144
Wright, Rosalie Muller, 227
Writers
    fact checkers and, 205
    freelance, 205, 218, 338, 348
    objectivity of, 105, 224, 241,
        273
    staff, 204
Wyeth, N. C., 273

Xerox, 50
x-height, 267

Yankee, 11
Yankelovich Partners, 31
Yellow Book, The, 283
Yolk, 30, 125
You, 134
"You *Can* Breastfeed," 228
Young Dancer, 126
Young Miss, 126–27, 152
Youth's Companion
    ancillary products of, 72
    circulation of, 72, 82
    establishment of, 72
    failure of, 72, 125
    headquarters of, 66
    publication of, 73

'Zines, 19
Zinsser, William, 69